The Development of the Modern Tram

by Brian Patton

Published by Adam Gordon

CONTENTS

FOREWORD   5

CHAPTER 1
THE PIONEERS   7
Pay as you Enter Cars 7
Nearside Cars 9
The Peter Witt Car 9
The Low Floor Car 11
One Person Operation – the Birney Safety Car 12
Summary..14

CHAPTER 2
BOGIE CARS 1927-1940   15
Italy...15
Netherlands..20
Denmark...20
Belgium..20
Germany...21
USSR and Eastern Europe 23
Norway and Sweden..23
France..24
Australia...24
North America...25
Great Britain...26

CHAPTER 3
CENTRAL ENTRANCE TRAMS   29
French Designs 29
City Cars in Europe 1920-1960.......................................30
British Single Deck Cars 32
Designs in Various Countries for Suburban Operation......35
The Australian Drop-Centre Car 37
Double-Deckers 38

CHAPTER 4
THE PCC BOGIE CAR   41
North America..41
Cars with PCC Characteristics 46
Europe..47
Great Britain...51
Australia...52
Japan 52

CHAPTER 5
STANDARDISED TWO-AXLE CARS   53
Predecessors 53
The Proposed German Standard Tram (ESW) 55
The KSW 55
The Aufbau and Verbandstyp Trams 56
The Werdau Cars in the DDR 57
Gotha Cars..58
The Reko trams of the DDR 59
Other German Designs 60
Polish N Class Cars 61
Austrian Designs 61
Romania 62
USSR 62
Rebuildings in Other Countries.......................................62
New Designs in Other Countries 63

CHAPTER 6
THREE-AXLE CARS   65

CHAPTER 7
GERMAN BOGIE GROSSRAUMWAGEN   71

Chapter 8
BOGIE CARS FROM 1940   79
Scandinavia..79
Sweden 79
Göteborg 79
Stockholm 80
Malmö 81
Norrköping 81
Norway 81
Trondheim City System 81
Trondheim Gråkalbanen 82
Oslo 82
Bergen 82
Finland 82
Helsinki 82
Turku 83
Denmark 83
Copenhagen 83
Summary 83
Derived Design 84
Switzerland 85
The "Standard" Bogie Trams 85
Standard Trailers 87
Bogie Cars of Tram 2000 Design 88
Other designs 89
Exports 89
Rotterdam 89
Toronto...89
Italy..90
France 91
Belgium 91
Tatra Bogie Trams 93
Types T1 and T2...93
Types T3 and T4...94
Types T5, T6 and T7 97
Other Bogie Cars in Eastern Europe 99
Bulgaria 99
Romania 99
Kroatia and Serbia 100
USSR and Successor States 100
Hungary..102
Poland..103
Argentina..104
Great Britain 104
Single-deckers...104
Double-deckers..105
China and Vietnam..106
Spain and Portugal 106
Japan 107
Home Models 107
Exports 109
Philadelphia 109
Egypt 109
Single-deckers..109
Double-deckers.......................................110
Australia 110

CHAPTER 9
ARTICULATED CARS   111

Six-Axle Designs 111
  Prototypes 111
  Post-war German Six-axle Trams 113
    Single-ended designs 113
    Double-ended designs 118
  Designs in Other Countries 120
    Italy 120
    Switzerland 121
    Belgium 123
    France 123
    Sweden 124
    Austria 125
    Tatra Trams of Class K2 125
    Other Designs in Eastern Europe 126
    USSR and Successor States 127
    PCC Ccars (including eight-axle) 127
    Canada 128
    Japan (including eight-axle cars) 129
    Australia 129
    China 130
Eight- and Ten-axle Cars 130
  The First Steps 130
  German Multi-section Designs 130
    Single-ended Designs 130
    Double-ended Designs 133
  Designs in Other Countries 135
    Tatra KT8 135
    Italy 135
    Netherlands 136
    Romania 136
    Kroatia 136
    Bulgaria 136
    Hungary 136
    USSR and Successor States 137
    Switzerland 137
Four-axle Cars with Suspended Articulation 138
  GT4 Cars of the Maschienenfabriek Esselinghn....138
  Hansa Cars..139
  Tatra KT4D cars 140
  Bremen Stadtbahn Cars 142
Four-axle Cars with Suspended Centre Sections 142
  Sweden, The Netherlands, Italy 143
  Hungary 143
  Poland 144
  Soviet Union 144
  Switzerland 144
  Spain 144
  Germany 144
  France 147
  Austria, Wien 147
  Belgium 147
Six-axle Trams with Suspended Centre Section 148
Eight-axle Trams with Suspended Centre Section...........148
Three-section Trailers..149
Three-section, Six-axle Trams 149
Nachlaufer Trams 150
  Germany 150
  Austria 151
  Italy..151
  Netherlands 152
  Russia..152
Three- and Five-axle Trams 152

CHAPTER 10
STADTBAHN CARS   153

Pioneers 153
Frankfurt (M) Stadtbahn Cars 156
  Prototypes 156

  U2/3/4 Classes...156
  Export Models 157
    Canada 157
    USA 157
    Mexico 158
    Salzburg..159
  Frankfurt (M) Class P8 159
Düwag Stadtbahn B and M/N Designs and
Derived Designs 159
  Stadtbahn B 159
  Stadtbahn M and N..161
  Duisburg Class GT8NC 162
  Designs for Karlsruhe.......................................162
  Tyne and Wear Metrocars 163
  Tunis 164
  Bursa 164
  Stadtbahn T 164
Hannover Cars 164
  Prototypes 164
  GT8 Cars 164
  2000 Class 164
  The Docklands Light Railway Cars 166
Other German Designs 167
  Würzburg 167
  The CitySprinter 167
  Bombardier Cars 167
  The Dresden Cargo Trams 168
Stuttgart DT8 168
  Prototypes 168
  Production cars classes S-DT8.4 – S-DT8.9 168
  Class S-DT8.10/11 168
  Rack Tramway Bogie Cars...............................168
Sweden 169
  Istanbul Stadtbahn 169
  Baltimore 169
  Philadelphia 170
Norwegian Designs 170
  Oslo 170
Switzerland 170
  SIG designs 170
  Vevey designs 171
Italian Cars 171
  Cleveland 171
  Torino..171
  Greater Manchester Metrolink 171
  Genova and Rome 172
  San Francisco 172
  Los Angeles 172
Japanese Designs 173
  Home systems 173
Exports...173
  Boston 173
  Los Angeles 173
  Buffalo 174
  Tuen Mun..174
  Dallas 174
  Phoenix 174
Belgian Designs 174
  Manila 174
  Rio de Janeiro 175
  Amsterdam Sneltram Cars................................175
  Portland (OR) 176
  Proposed Métro Léger for Brussels..................176
Australian Cars for Tuen Mun 176
Designs in North and South America 177
  Boeing Vertol cars 177
  UTDC Cars 178
  Tatra Cars...178
China..178
CAF Spain..178

CHAPTER 11
LOW FLOOR CARS 179

The Pioneers 179
   Switzerland..179
   Italy..180
   France 181
   Germany...181
   Belgium 183
   Netherlands – Amsterdam 183
Products of Various Manufacturers 183
   Bombardier...183
      AEG Design GT4/6/8M/N Trams 183
      Eurotram..184
      Variobahn...185
      Cobra 185
      Incentro..185
      GT8N Trams, second series 186
      Brussels Cars....................................186
      Köln K4000 design – Flexity Swift..............186
      Cityrunner – Flexity Outlook 187
      Other designs for German systems –
      Flexity Classic...................................187
      Dresden Designs 188
   Düwag and Siemens 189
      Düwag Low Floor Trams 189
      Leipzig Cars.......................................190
      Combino 190
      Leoliner 192
      Wien ULF Trams 192
      Sheffield Cars 193
      Trams for De Lijn, Flanders 194
      Iberian Designs.................................194
      Avanto Stadtbahn cars 194
LHB (latterly in conjunction with Alstom) 195
GEC Alsthom/Alstom Transport.....................195
   French Standard Tram TSF2 195
   Citadis 196
Alstom Ferrorroviaria (formerly Fiat) 199
   Torino...199
   Rome ....`199
Socimi 199
ANSALDO/BREDA (including vehicles supplied by
Firema) 200
      Lille 200
      West Midlands...................................200
      Boston...200
      Oslo 200
      Sirio Trams 201
Vevey..201
Japanese Designs...201
   Home Market 201
   Exports 202
CAF 202
Tatra, Skoda and Other Designs in Eastern Europe........202
Stadler...203
Trailer Cars 203
      LHB Design – Darmstadt Class SB9 203
      Trailers for Rostock and Leipzig 203
      Czech Republic.................................203

ALTERNATIVE FORMS OF PLACE NAMES

Many of the places referred to in the text have alternative forms of their name, sometimes for historical reasons, sometimes because they are located in a bi- or tri-lingual country. Generally the name used in the text is that of the form most commonly used locally at the time referred to or to-day, apart from one or two cities such as Brussels and Rome, where the English form is well established and it might have seemed pedantic to use a local name in an English text. The following list gives the versions used in other languages. In addition it should be noted that Volgograd was formerly Stalingrad, Lugansk was Voroshilovgrad and Sankt Petersburg, Leningrad. In a few cases, captions give street names which are no longer current and in these cases, the present form is given in brackets.

Aachen (Ger)	Aken (Ned)	Aix-la-Chapelle (Fr)
Antwerp (Eng)	Antwerpen (Fl)	Anvers (Fr)
Athenai (Greek)	Athens (Eng)	
Basel (Ger)	Bâle (Fr)	
Batavia (Ned)	Djakarta (Indon.)	
Beograd (Serb)	Belgrade (Eng)	
Bern (Ger)	Berne (Fr)	
Bilbao (Sp)	Bilbo (Basque)	
Brasov (Rom)	Kronstadt (Ger)	
Bratislava (Slovak)	Pressburg (Ger)	Poszony (Hung)
Brno (Cz)	Brünn (Ger)	
Brussels (Eng)	Brussel (Fl)	Bruxelles (Fr)
Bucuresti (Rom)	Bukarest (Ger)	Bucarest (Eng)
Bydgoszcz (Pol)	Bromberg (Ger)	
Chorzow (Pol)	Königshütte (Ger)	
Cluj (Rom)	Klausenburg (Ger)	
Copenhagen (Eng)	København (Dan)	Kopenhagen (Ger)
Dalian (Cantonese)	Darien (Eng)	
Den Haag (Ned)	The Hague (Eng)	La Haye (Fr)
Dublin (Eng)	Baile Atha Cliath (Irish)	
Elblag (Pol)	Elbing (Ger)	
El Qahira (Arabic)	Cairo (Eng)	Le Caire (Fr)
Firenze (It)	Florence (Eng)	Florenz (Ger)
Gdansk (Pol)	Danzig (Ger)	
Genève (Fr)	Genf (Ger)	Geneva (Eng)
Gent (Fl)	Gand (Fr)	
Gorzòw (Pol)	Landsberg (Ger)	
Göteborg (Sw)	Gothenburg (Eng)	
Helsinki (Finland)	Helsingfors (Sw)	
Isai (Rom)	Jassy (Ger)	
Iskandariyah (Arabic)	Alexandria (Eng)	
Köln (Ger)	Cologne (Fr and Eng)	
Leuven (Fl)	Louvain (Fr)	
Liberec (Cz)	Reichenberg (Ger)	
Liège (Fr)	Luik (Fl)	Lüttich (Ger)
Luzern (Ger)	Lucerne (Fr and Eng)	
Lvov (Pol)	Lviv (Ukr)	Lemberg (Ger)
Kaliningrad (Russ)	Königsberg (Ger)	
Katowice (Pol)	Kattowitz (Ger)	
Kraków (Pol)	Krakau (Ger)	Cracovie (Fr)
Łodz (Pol)	Lodsch (Ger)	
Masr-el-Gedifa (Arabic)	Heliopolis (Eng and Fr)	
Milano (It)	Milan (Eng)	Mailand (Ger)
Moskva (Russ)	Moscow (Eng)	Moscou (Fr)
Most (Cz)	Brüx (Ger)	
Mumbai (Hindi)	Bombay (Eng)	
Napoli (It)	Naples (Eng)	Neapel (Ger)
Neuchâtel (Fr)	Neuenburg (Ger)	
Oberbozen (Ger)	Soprebolzano (It)	
Olomouc (Cz)	Olmutz (Ger)	
Oradea (Rom)	Grosswardein (Ger)	
Ostrava (Cz)	Mährische Ostrau (Ger)	
Plzen (Cz)	Pilsen (Ger)	
Poznan (Pol)	Posen (Ger)	
Praha (Cz)	Prag (Ger)	Prague (Eng)
Sibiu (Rom)	Hermannstadt (Ger)	
Szczecin (Pol)	Stettin (Ger)	
Szeged (Hung)	Szegedin (Ger)	
Tallinn (Estonia)	Reval (Ger)	
Timisora (Rom)	Temesvar (Hung)	Temeschburg (Ger)
Torino (It)	Turin (Eng)	
Tòrun (Pol)	Thorn (Ger)	
Turku (Finnish)	Åbö (Swed)	
Usti nad Labem (Cz)	Aussig an der Elbe (Ger)	
Warsaw (Eng)	Warsawa (Pol)	Warschau (Ger)
Wroclaw (Pol)	Breslau (Ger)	
Zagreb (Kr)	Agram (Ger)	

INTRODUCTION

The inspiration for this book came from another book, *Moderne Trams,* published over thirty years ago. I have referred to this so often that the binding on my copy is now coming apart at the seams and I can only hope that its author, Dr Frits van de Graagt, believes that imitation is the sincerest form of flattery! A great deal has happened in the field of tramways and light rail in the intervening period and it seemed that the time was ripe for a new study of the topic. In the present volume, I have attempted to widen the scope of the study to include trams which have been designed and built outwith Europe. The aim is to show why, how and when the modern tram evolved. It is not in any sense a technical work, but aims rather to look at the factors which made engineers and operators design trams in the way they did.

The book is arranged by tram types and from chapters 1 to 9, designs are classified by country of origin, rather than by operator, so that, for example, the original Rotterdam articulated trams are described under the heading on Swiss designs. However, in chapters 10 and 11, designs are arranged by manufacturer; changes in the market for new cars since 1990 mean that the geographical arrangement would no longer be appropriate

In the early days of electric operation, entry and, usually, exit were by a platform at the rear, since that had been the accepted position in horse car days. It was soon realised that this need not be so with electric cars, but in many countries conservatism had already set in and generations of conductors and even the occasional liebe kleine Schaffnerin* were to spend much energy – often fruitlessly – shouting to passengers "pass right down the car" "Ik beet U door te lopen, als't U blieft", "Avanti, Signore, per favore" or "Bleiben Sie bitte nicht in der Mitte, gehen Sie bitte nach vorn". However, engineers soon began to experiment to avoid the bottleneck of the rear platform and in tracing the story of development of tramcar design, it is at once apparent that in the early years this was almost completely a process in the USA and Canada. Although Germany (and to a lesser extent France and Italy) contributed much in the technical field, their operational practices remained generally conservative and saw little sign of development until the mid-1920s, when the Italians took the lead. The diffusion throughout Europe of the ideas which they adopted and the influence of the North American PCC car, which was being developed at the same time, form much of the story of the first part of this book. One of the recurring themes, which has continued to the present day, is the desire for standardisation on the part of car builders, engineers and, to an extent, politicians and the equally strong pressure from operators to provide trams tailor-made for the requirements of each individual system. The Second World War perforce brought a good deal of standardisation, led by Germany, and some of this was carried over into Eastern Europe where, combined with the adoption of the PCC car, it allowed a handful of designs to serve almost all systems. In the west, the return of peace-time conditions from about 1950 onwards brought back a certain amount of variety, although here again the pre-eminence of the Düwag factory in Germany and the adoption of the PCC elsewhere did bring about a measure of standardisation. The low floor revolution at first threw all such ideas out of the official window and only in recent years has the emergence of a few large manufacturers brought about again a degree of standardisation, although the debate continues and the recent entry to the market of other firms such as CAF in Spain shows that the question is still open.

I have also tried to show the part played in the story by individual engineers, managers and, to a lesser extent, politicians. Again the pre-eminence of the USA in the early years is soon apparent, with Germany and Italy playing a major role at a later date and France coming very strongly into the story from 1975 onwards. Unfortunately there is little to record from Britain or Ireland and the efforts of the few innovative managers that there were, such as C.J. Spencer in London, William M. Murphy in Dublin and E.R.L. Fitzpayne in Glasgow, were generally set at nought by political changes and politicians. Only in Blackpool was the partnership of Walter Luff and far-sighted local councillors able to carry through a real revolution in tramcar design and operation, drawing on the skills and ideas then apparent in the staff of the English Electric concern. Elsewhere some operators did build cars, such as the Glasgow Coronations, which were attractive and comfortable, fully comparable with any competing motorbus or trolleybus but, in operational terms, were totally traditional. In any event, the success of one system was not enough to change established practices, especially when it took place against a background of political apathy, physical run-down and abandonment.

When *Moderne Trams* appeared in 1973, it seemed as though the future lay with the Stadtbahn design in its various forms and that conventional street tramways had only a limited life. For some years, the first part of this statement was certainly accurate, but the oil crisis occurred in the same year and it was not long before the process of wholesale abandonments came to an end, that of Hamburg in 1978 being the last to affect a major city. In 1975 it was made clear that official thinking in France had begun to change, as it did, with rather less publicity, in Eastern Europe. During the early 1980s developments – still along Stadtbahn lines – came apace in North America and were under way in France, pointing the way to a much more secure future for street tramways. Although Nantes was the first new tramway in that country, it was really the opening of the Grenoble system in September 1987 which changed public and official opinion about trams, not only in France but throughout Europe and even beyond. The technical developments which had led to the first practical application of low floor technology were soon to be backed up by political changes, with the fall of communism in Eastern Europe and the introduction of the single market in Western Europe. Together these completely altered the parameters of vehicle design and supply and the changes begun in 1990 continue today. In 1973 no one could have dreamed that, thirty-three years on, there would be over 100 new systems in operation worldwide, with many others in the pipeline.

For someone writing from Britain, it is sad that history seems to be repeating itself and that so few of the new systems are located in this country. Thanks to the policies of the present British government, development seems to have come to a total standstill in England, with only some extensions in Manchester having any expectation of becoming a reality, and then not in full form. Fortunately the support of the Scottish government for the planned system in Edinburgh and the enthusiastic commitment of the Irish government to extend the successful Luas system in Dublin suggest that the modern tram has some chance to show its capabilities in these islands.

Where possible, I have tried to use photographs which show tramcars in service, with passengers. Trams are, after all, about people and the practice which J.H. Price once castigated of using only views of vehicles standing at sunlit suburban termini certainly does not put the tram into perspective. However, it was not always possible to find views which met the bill in every respect and the result has had to be a compromise, to show vehicle design as well as operational conditions. I hope that readers will nonetheless enjoy the illustrations.

Place names are given in the form which was current at the time under discussion. Thus the Polish city on the Baltic is referred to as Danzig pre-1945 and as Gdansk since then. A table lists the different forms of place names in the various languages.

Brief technical details are given for many types and a word of explanation of the system adopted may be useful. All measurements are given in metric form. For passengers, standing capacity has been calculated at four persons per square metre and where a higher figure, denoting crush loading, is given, this is denoted by *. In the case of double-deckers, seating capacity is shown in the form of upper over lower deck, e.g. 50/30.

Bibliographies are given at the end of each section, but some books have been used as works of reference throughout and details are given here. Firstly and most importantly the original edition of *Moderne Trams* has been consulted in every case where its information was appropriate. Much use has been made of the excellent annual Netherlands publication *Trams,* which has now been running since 1979 and is an invaluable source of information. It will also be noticed that the magazines *"Modern Tramway"* and *"Tramways and Urban Transit"* have been used in almost every chapter and it should be mentioned that these are one and the same journal; it was

(*This refers to a song popular in Germany about 1942, when women conductors were still a novelty and attracted much interest from male passengers, though often they were neither liebe (dear) nor kleine (little)!)

renamed *"Light Rail and Modern Tramway"* in January 1992 and *"Tramways and Urban Transit"* in January 1998, but the numbering scheme was continued and is consecutive from January 1938 to the present date. Other books which have been used as general sources of reference are:

Trams in Western Europe and Trams in Eastern Europe. Michael Taplin and Michael Russell. Capital Transport, Harrow, 2002 and 2003.
Trams in Britain and Ireland. Various authors. Capital Transport, Harrow, 2002.
The Definitive Guide to Trams in the British Isles. D. Voice, Adam Gordon, Chetwode, 2001.
By Bus and Tram in the Czech Republic. Martin Harák. Rapid Transit Publications, Ilford, 2004.
Strassenbahnatlas 2004 Rumänien. Blickpunkt Strassenbahn, Berlin, 2004.
Strassenbahnatlas 2005 Deutschland. Blickpunkt Strassenbahn, Berlin, 2005.
Strassenbahnatlas Österreich Ungarn Jugoslawien. Blickpunkt Strassenbahn and Light Rail Transit Association, Berlin and London, 1988.
Tramways and Light Railways of Switzerland and Austria. Light Rail Transit Association, Milton Keynes, 1984.
Veteran and Vintage Transit. Andrew D. Young. Archway Publishing, St Louis, 1997. (N. American preserved trams and transit museums).
List of preserved Italian tramcars provided by Marco Montanarini.
Taschenbuch Deutsche Strassenbahn-Triebwagen 2. M. Pabst. W. Keller & Co, Stuttgart, 1982.
Taschenbuch Deutsche Strassenbahn-Beiwagen. M. Pabst. W. Keller & Co, Stuttgart, 1983.

The information in this book is correct to 31 December 2005, except for chapters 9 to 11, which have been updated to June 2006. With a work of this type, there will inevitably be some errors – some no doubt due to the author's carelessness, but some due also to the availability of conflicting information, even for quite modern designs. In all such cases, I have chosen the information which has seemed most logical for the design concerned.

Acknowledgements

It would have been impossible to have compiled a book of this scope without the help of a great many people in many different countries and to all those who have given their time to answer queries and provide illustrations I am most grateful.

Michael Aze, Vancouver, Hugh Ballment, Victoria, Marcelo Benoit, Montevideo, Alan Brotchie, Aberdour, Roy Budmiger, Norway, Michel Byrne, Edinburgh, Bradley Clarke, Boston, Mme C. Coquelard, RATP, Paris, Pam Eaton, London, A. George and Mrs J. Lawson, West Yorkshire Library Service, Ray de Groote, Chicago, Alastair G. Gunn, Edinburgh, Stig Hammarson, Göteborg, Herrn Hansel and Lösch, Dresdner Verkehrsbetriebe, Mike Harrison, Houston, Tom Hart, Beith, Peter Haseldine, Buckhurst Hill, Essex, Aaron Isaacs, Minneapolis, Martin Jenkins, Walton-on-Thames, Roger Jones, Horsham, Dr Karsten Kietz, Leipziger Verkehrsbetriebe, Carlos Mendes, Santos, Marco Montanarini, Bologna, Bill Parkinson, Melbourne, Noel Reed, Hornsby NSW, Mal Rowe, Melbourne, Sam Rushton, Hednesford, Mike Russell, Reading, Jim Schantz, Boston, Alexander Shanin, Moscow, Greg Travers, Melbourne, Vincent Walsh, Bradford, Peter Waller, Ian Allan Ltd, Surrey, Peter Williams, Burgess Hill, Julian Wolinsky, Los Angeles, Trustees of the Seashore Trolley Museum, Kennebunkport, Maine, Staff of the Mitchell Library, Glasgow, Archive staff of ATM, Milan, Staff of Konstal, Chorzow in 1994.

I must also express thanks to those who have allowed me access to their collections. The London Area of the Light Rail Transit Association has most generously permitted me to use some historic material from the collections of the late Frank Hunt and Jack Wyse and to the committee members and to Roger Jones, who spent much time identifying particular subjects, I am most grateful. David Young of St Louis has kindly allowed reproduction of illustrations which first appeared many years ago in the catalogue of Evda Slides and Dr Iain D. Frew has likewise agreed to use of material from the Electrail slide collection of the Electric Railway Society. The committee of the Tramway and Light Railway Society kindly allowed access to the collection of the late Father Benedict Sankey and I am grateful to them and in particular to Peter Williams who spent much time looking for Italian subjects. The gratitude is tinged with regret that Father Benedict, with whom I discussed the project when in its initial stage, did not live to see it completed. Lars Richter of Hamburg has provided views of some of the rarer subjects from his extensive collection and the committee of the Leeds Transport Historical Society has kindly agreed to the use of material from their archives.

Again I have to extend thanks to Dr Michel Byrne of the University of Glasgow for checking doubtful points of French texts (as well as taking his first steps into tramway photography) and to Dr Noel O'Regan of the University of Edinburgh for help with Italian material and also for making valiant and time-consuming efforts to track down photographs of trams in Rome.

It would not have been possible for me to have written the sections dealing with China, Japan and Egypt without the unstinting help of Mike Russell, who, apart from providing photographs, read and corrected the text to ensure that, as far as possible, it did not contain the errors which it otherwise might have done, since I have no personal knowledge of those countries.

Finally I owe a great debt to Judith and Trevor Preece, who between them have patiently made a book out of a jigsaw of a great deal of text and over 800 photos.

Brian Patton

Foulden, Berwickshire, Scotland
16 August 2006

ISBN: 978-1-874422-64-8

A catalogue entry for this book is available from the British Library.

Publication no.68.

Published 2006 by Adam Gordon, Kintradwell Farmhouse, Brora, Sutherland KW9 6LU.
Tel: 01408 622660

Printed by Launton Digital Press Ltd Oxfordshire

Production and Design:
Trevor Preece: trevor@epic.gb.com

CHAPTER 1
THE PIONEERS

In the early days of electric traction, the design of most trams was based very closely on that of horse drawn vehicles, whether double- or single-deck. In some cases, the first electric trams were actually ex-horse cars. To the basic design was added a heavy motor slung under the floor, an equally heavy controller mounted on each platform and some form of current collector on the roof. Such cars weighed about 3.5 tonnes and carried at most 26 passengers, 12 of these seated. Usually there was a single motor of about 7kW. Not surprisingly, car bodies built to withstand the strains imposed by the pulling power of two horses did not cope well with the added weight. In a few cases, bogie single-deckers showed some links with steam or cable tram design, but the end result was much the same.

Many studies were undertaken to develop a car body more suited to the demands of electric operation and in the 1890s a variety of types of tram appeared. By 1900 most builders in North America had abandoned body designs based on horse cars and turned instead to those derived from main line railway carriages. These were still made of wood but were mounted on a steel underframe of great strength. Meanwhile, technology continued to develop at a rapid rate and in consequence obsolescence was equally rapid, although many operators countered this by rebuilding. In the USA, the Thomson-Houston Company led the way, as illustrated by a line which it equipped in Washington City in the autumn of 1888. General Electric developed greatly improved controllers with series-parallel operation, with the K series, of which the first appeared in 1893. Westinghouse produced lighter and more efficient motors such as the W3, designed by B.G. Lamme and first made available in 1891. The effect of these changes in practice may be studied by considering the cars of the Manx Electric Railway which are still in service to-day. The first cars of 1893 had plate frame bogies, two 16kW motors and a control system which has been described as "frankly experimental". Current collection was originally by two upright bows, as was also the case in Hobart, where service began with double-deckers, in the same year. The cars of 1900/01 had air brakes, four 16kW motors, Brill 21E bogies and General Electric KT1 controllers. Current collection was by trolley pole. Although both classes have been much rebuilt, enough of their original condition survives to illustrate the rapidity of the pace of change at that time.

Most of the standard features of the classic tram had therefore been defined by the turn of the century, and the way was open for the mass production of vehicles and components for the expanding markets. Current collection was normally by spring-loaded trolley pole, very often now with a swivel head to allow contact to be maintained with the overhead if and where that was off-centre to the running rails. However, some systems, mainly those equipped by Siemens, used an early form of bow collector. Cars rode on trucks of a standard pattern. For single-truck cars this was often the Brill 21E truck, a design much used in both Britain and

North America and on cars built in both countries for export. Larger cars were mounted on bogies, of which the Brill 22E maximum traction bogie developed by that firm from 1893 onwards was the first successful design for use in urban service. Although the designation was not strictly in accordance with the laws of physics, since each bogie had only one pair of driving wheels, the type became extremely popular in North America and Britain and allowed the construction of large single-deck cars for city service in the former, and double-deckers in the latter. Other manufacturers copied the design. Driving wheels were generally of 84cm diameter and this necessitated a high floor level. The technical parameters thus set in the USA in the 1890s were to remain unchanged for the next forty years. There is little to distinguish cars built at the turn of the century from those built in 1926 for New Orleans and still, albeit rebuilt, in service to-day.

This rapid development of technology made it possible to build larger and larger trams, whether single- or double-deck, and by 1903 it was possible to accommodate 90-100 passengers in one vehicle. There was a corresponding increase in both weight and the power-weight ratio. Cars built for the Chicago Surface Lines from 1903 onwards weighed about 24.5 tonnes. While the first cars used by Frank Sprague in Richmond in 1888 had a ratio of 2.54kW/tonne, just twenty years later four-motor bogie cars in North America required a ration of 4.54-6kW/tonne. In Britain and Ireland the double-decker, with a ratio of 4.26kW/tonne for a bogie car, had become virtually standard despite the use of single-deckers in some early electrification schemes. The "room and kitchen" car preserved in Glasgow is a reminder that in the early days opinion on this point was not yet fixed. In North America the bogie single-decker soon reigned supreme in large cities, despite occasional experiments with double-deckers. Cities in Europe generally settled on small two-axle single-deckers and capacity was increased as necessary by the use of one or two trailers. This form of operation resulted in high wage costs, though it did lighten the load of individual conductors, and formations could be flexibly adapted to the needs of traffic at different times of day. With quite a few exceptions, systems in other continents tended to follow the practice of Europe or the USA, depending on which country actually controlled them. The double-decker found little favour

outwith the British Isles and southern Africa.

Unfortunately once the basic design had been established, stagnation set in both in Britain and Europe and it was only in North America that there were attempts to develop design to keep abreast of both technical possibilities and passenger demand, and also to reduce costs. Traction companies in the 1900s were under pressure to increase staff wages, while in most cases they were unable, by the terms of their franchises, to increase fares without agreement from local authorities. Generally this was not forthcoming. In 1909, Charles O. Birney, equipment engineer of the Stone and Webster Corporation, developed the first steel lightweight bogie car and this was placed in service in Dallas. This Corporation controlled 26 systems scattered throughout the USA, ranging from cities such as Dallas to small towns such as Beaumont, Texas and, with a total fleet of 1340 trams, offered a considerable market for car builders. Weighing only 19.3 tonnes, the steel car allowed a considerable saving in current costs over conventional wooden cars. Rather later, in 1926, the first all-aluminium car was placed in service by Cleveland Railways. This was a Peter Witt car, no.1376, constructed by the undertaking in its own workshops and weighing 13.6 tonnes, a reduction of about 7.5% on contemporary cars in other cities.

However, many of the improvements in design were driven by problems of fare collection. It seems to have become generally accepted that a single conductor could not efficiently service a vehicle load of more than 80 passengers. Operators began to worry about missed fares and platform accidents, with associated claims, and found that the economies of scale promised by the larger cars were whittled away by these difficulties. A conductor conscientious about fare collection might not always be able to get back to the platform at every stop, while one who made a point of doing so might miss fares. Much of the later history of tramcar design revolves around attempts to reconcile these two objectives. Only in very recent times, when payment of fares on board has largely been replaced by sales off the car, has it been possible to free vehicle design from the constraints imposed by these considerations.

The following sections examine the first significant attempts to resolve these difficulties and to design the first cars which could be considered "modern".

PAY AS YOU ENTER CARS

The first step towards the resolution of the above problems was taken in or soon after 1895 by A.B. DuPont, who was then manager of the Detroit system. He designed a car with a very large rear platform and a double-width entrance so allowing for quick boarding. Passengers alighting used either a single-width rear doorway or the front exit, thus separating the two flows. DuPont may also have used this design in Louisville and he took it to Saint Louis, where he became vice-

president in 1901. Such cars had to be single-ended and a considerable amount of track reconstruction was necessary to accommodate them. Fare collection continued to be by a roving conductor. Although an improvement on earlier designs, this system was certainly not ideal, from the angles of both platform safety and fare collection, and further refinement was necessary.

In 1905 a new type of bogie car appeared in Montréal when car 990 (later renumbered 900)

The preserved Montréal car at the Seashore museum and a close-up of the platform. (Author)

over 100 passengers. Two motors delivered at least 140kW. The extreme length of the rear platform, with corresponding overhang, ensured the survival of at least one Montréal car, which became a line marker after withdrawal from passenger service and is now, fully restored, in the collection of the Seashore Museum at Kennebunkport, Maine.

Helped by the flat fare system used in North America – at that date normally US$0.05 – the PAYE concept was extremely successful there and thousands of such cars were built between 1907 and 1917. Despite the advantages of the system, and setting aside half-hearted experiments in Gateshead, Leicester and Aberdeen, there was no real attempt to use it in Britain until Cardiff adopted it in the 1940s. The standard double-deckers were modified to suit, but the platform could not be enlarged and in any case the idea had to be abandoned when inflation brought about the end of the universal penny fare. Until many years later there was no interest at all in mainland Europe, where tiny motor cars pulling two trailers required a crew of four to carry the same number of passengers as could be carried in one PAYE car. The main limitation to further development was the size of the rear platform, which in turn governed overall length and a restriction on availability. Unfortunately it required only one passenger tendering a dollar note to bring the whole boarding process to a halt, with the result that a queue then formed in the carriageway rather than on the car's platform. There were also problems in cities where many passengers boarded at a single central terminus, such as Public Square in Cleveland, and at points where there was heavy interchange traffic. Further refinement of the design was required.

One operator which found itself saddled with a large (772) fleet of fairly new but now obsolete bogie trams was the Philadelphia Railway Company. The cost of rebuilding these for PAYE operation was quoted as US$760.72 per car, plus the US$100 licence fee and the undertaking therefore decided in 1909 to carry out its own form of rebuilding. The cars concerned were fitted with platform doors and the bulkhead which separated the platform from saloon was removed. The rebuilds were known as "Pay Within" cars and a subsidiary company was set up to issue licences for the design. But despite the change in layout and terminology, the PAYE Corporation regarded this as an infringement of its patents and threatened legal action. After discussion, the two companies amalgamated as the Prepayment Car Sales Company. Thereafter platforms were invariably enclosed with power-operated doors and folding steps and the conductor was given a seat. It should be mentioned that in North America, PAYE cars were sometimes called prepayment cars, although there were in fact no ticket sales off the car in the modern sense of "prepayment".

of the Montréal Street Railway was demonstrated to the public on 4 May. Exactly who "invented" this design is not now clear, but it was adopted by W.G. Ross and Duncan MacDonald, Managing Director and rolling stock engineer of the MSR respectively. The car had a very much enlarged rear platform, 2.3m long, which was divided into two sections by a rail and there was a post for the conductor against the rear bulkhead. In the rear bulkhead, there were two doors, one inward- and one outward-opening. Passengers boarded at the extreme rear of the platform, paid their fares as they filed past the conductor and moved on into the saloon. The rear platform was open but at the front there was a sliding door for an exit under control of the driver. When leaving the car, passengers did so either by using the right hand side of the rear platform (as viewed from the roadway) or by the front exit. This system was known as the "pay as you enter" system, or PAYE.

After a Montréal car was demonstrated south of the border in 1906, a first order for PAYE trams was placed in 1907 by the Chicago City Railways, who took 300 of the design, and thereafter the concept was adopted with enthusiasm by managers of many systems in North America. It was clear that receipts went up and accidents decreased with PAYE cars. In 1907-08, fatal accidents on the CCR fell by 40% compared to the previous year, while non-fatal accidents fell by

16%, platform accidents being almost completely eliminated. Receipts went up by anything between 6% and 15%. By 1910, over half of all city cars built were for PAYE operation. MacDonald left the MSR to patent the design and set up the Pay-as-you-Enter Car Corporation, with headquarters in New York City. This undertaking issued licences, at US$100 per tram, to operators who wished to adopt the system.

The system seemed to deliver the advantages which had been promised. However, adoption of PAYE operation required either substantial purchase of new cars or equally substantial rebuilding of older vehicles, and it was therefore confined to the larger and better-off systems. It was almost essential to use single-ended four-axle cars and this in turn required alterations to the track layout at termini and intermediate reversing points. As the system only worked properly with a large rear platform – a later Montréal car had a rear platform 2.9m long – car length had to be correspondingly increased and steel construction replaced wooden bodywork to achieve the necessary strength. In turn this removed the need for internal bulkheads and most PAYE cars were built on the open saloon or Grossraumwagen principle. The increased length also required easing of curves and clearances. Typically, as used in Montréal, PAYE cars were 13.5m long, 2.68m wide and accommodated just

Bibliography

Der Stadtverkehr 1/1981, 6/1981 and 9/1989.
The Colorful Streetcars we Rode. CERA Bulletin 125. Chicago, 1986.
Lightweight Street and Interurban Cars. D. Engel. Branford Electric Railway journal, vol.37. East Haven CT, 1998.
Strassenbahn Magazin no.47, February 1983.
Street Cars, Light Rail & Utility Cars of Saint Louis, 1899-2003. A.D. Young. Archway Publishing, Saint Louis, 2003.

NEARSIDE CARS

The next attempt to modify the PAYE design was made in Buffalo in 1911, with the building of the first "nearside" tram. The concept was developed by T.E. Mitten, general manager of that undertaking, in conjunction with R.T. Senter, the master mechanic. The conductor was stationed immediately behind the driver and the front platform was rearranged to hold up to 15 passengers. Passengers entered by the forward part of the front double door and left by the rear part. The name derived from the supposed advantage that the design afforded on systems where stops were located on the near side of intersections and passengers were obliged to walk across unpaved and often muddy roads to reach the rear platform of a car. Similar cars were built for the Chicago City Railway and for Philadelphia, with both of which systems Mitten was connected, and the latter city's order for 1,500 "nearsides" was probably the largest single order for one type of car ever to be placed by one city. A few were supplied to other operators, including a version for the British Columbia Electric in Vancouver, designed for operation in left hand traffic. The Chicago cars were 10.4m long and could seat 55 passengers.

In practice, there were problems with this design. The small rear door was initially intended for use in emergencies only and the front platform therefore became a bottleneck, as passengers were reluctant to "pass right down inside". Many of the cars in Philadelphia were later given a central exit to alleviate the problem. Operators also feared that the proximity of motorman and conductor would encourage "idle conversation" and some later moved the conductor's post further to the rear, at the expense of three seats. However, the design is important as it paved the way for the Peter Witt car, and also as a two-axle version built in 1912 for service in Lockport, NY, had some influence on the design of the Birney car.

Bibliography

The Near-Side Car. Mervin E. Borgnis. Winchester, Virginia, 1994.
Srassenbahn Magazin no.53, August 1984.
Du tramway au métro léger. Patrice Malterrre. Metram, Paris, n/d, c.1984.

Philadelphia 8501 turns into the loop at the City Hall, August 1956 (W.B. Thomas, Evda Slides)

Small Witt 2766 of class E running on the Belt Line tourist service in August 1973. (Author)

THE PETER WITT CAR

In the first decade of the twentieth century, one of the most progressive tramway systems in North America was that of Cleveland. Although operated by a private company, the Cleveland Railway Company, from 1 March 1910, the municipal authorities took a close interest in its working, particularly during the mayoralty of Thomas L. Johnson, who himself had experience of the transit industry. Unusually, he also campaigned for, and subsequently implemented a reduction in the flat fare from US$0.05 to US$0.03. While welcomed by passengers, this had the effect of increasing the workload of the conductors, since there is no coin of that denomination in the USA and most passengers continued to tender a "nickel" (five cent coin) and request change. During Johnson's administration, the city clerk was one Peter Witt, who on

New Year's Day 1912 was appointed by the new mayor, Newton Baker, to the post of street railway commissioner, responsible for liaison with the tramway company over all matters relating to operation and development. He received full co-operation from the general manager John Stanley, who shared many of his ideas.

Witt's first suggestion to the CRC was that it should obtain 100 lightweight trailer cars to increase both line capacity and also that of the loop termini in Public Square. The first of these was delivered by Kuhlman in November 1912. These had two single-width centre doors, one for entry and one for exit. Passengers boarded by the former and either immediately paid their fare to the conductor, who had a post between the doors, and passed on into the other half of the car or remained in the front half and paid as they

Toronto – large Witt 2992 at Glen Echo loop on the Yonge Street line in January 1954. (J. F. Bromley, Evda Slides)

passed to leave. Three hundred of these trailers were delivered by the end of 1913, to be followed by 201 central entrance motor cars, 17m long, in 1913-15. While popular with passengers, these were slow to load at busy stops, owing to the narrow single door and the change problem mentioned above.

When new rolling stock was under discussion, Witt, with help from Terence Scullion, rolling stock engineer, designed a car which combined the best features of his own city's centre entrance cars with those of Mitten's "nearsides". The result was a car in which passengers boarded at the front and passed directly into the saloon area; the conductor was given a seated position on the left, immediately forward of a pair of centre exit doors. The front part of the car had longitudinal seats, the rear section transverse. There was ample room in the front portion to hold all the passengers likely to board at even the busiest stop and fare collection and change giving could take place when the car was on the move. Having passed the conductor, short distance passengers could then alight, while those travelling further could move to find a seat in the rear saloon. There were no bottlenecks.

The first such car, numbered at first 33, soon renumbered to 330 and known unofficially as "Pete's Pet", entered service on 1 December 1914 and was brilliantly successful. Soon the CRC was ordering 130 more for use on cross-town lines which had many transfer points where they intersected lines radiating from the city centre.

These were followed by further batches until 1930, by which time there were 532 in service, plus 26 older cars rebuilt to this layout. Witt's official title for the type was the "Car Rider's Car" and this was carried on a small brass plate above one of the centre doors. However, they were almost universally referred to as "Peter Witts". Dimensions were 15.7m long and 2.5m wide. The design was patented on 25 April 1916 but Witt refused to take any royalties arising from this. The idea spread and similar cars were used in cities as diverse as Brooklyn, St Louis, Cincinnati and Louisville. Experience showed that, when 15 or more passengers boarded at one stop, the Peter Witt car was significantly faster to load than was a PAYE car, requiring a dwell time of 17 seconds for 20 passengers compared to 27.5 for the older type. Service speed could thus be proportionately increased without the need to run any additional cars.

Southern operators found that the design could be worked under the laws governing racial segregation if the door arrangements were reversed. Thus in Birmingham, all passengers boarded at the centre, while "whites" left at the same point and "colored" left by the front doors.

The greatest triumph of the Peter Witt car came some years after its first appearance when, in 1921, the newly formed Toronto Transportation Commission found itself with the task of having to replace, within a short space of time, almost half the fleet of antiquities it had inherited from the Toronto Railway Company. The energetic General Manager, H.H. Couzens, chose to do so by ordering 350 motor Peter Witt cars and 225 trailers, from three builders. Of the motor cars, 250 were intended for operation with trailers and were known as "large Witts", the balance being correspondingly known as "small Witts". The first ran on 2 October 1921 on the Broadview line and all were in service by 1923. Although trailer operation had

A more modern version of the design is shown by Baltimore's 6119 working on service 8 in June 1956. This Brill car was based on that firm's Master Unit design. (A.D. Young, Evda Slides)

been practised in Cleveland, it was not common with Peter Witt cars elsewhere, but it proved to be successful on the busiest lines, such as Yonge Street, in the Ontario capital; some 165 of the TTC trailers had three doors to speed boarding, a modification devised by the Assistant General Manager, D.W. Harvie. Corresponding alterations were made to the track layout to allow the larger cars to operate freely. The success of the new fleet, familiarly known as the Red Rockets, immediately placed the TTC in the forefront of transport operations in North America, a position it has retained ever since. Some of the cars were later converted for one-person operation and the last Witt ran in traffic on 24 April 1963. The last in service, 2766, is preserved in running order by the TTC and in the 1970s was, with others hired from museums, used on a tourist service known as the Belt Line Tour Tram. This service proved to be very popular but unfortunately it has not run in recent years. The car is still available for private hire and is often seen on the city's streets.

Apart from the Toronto cars, several other Peter Witts have been preserved, though sadly this total does not include any of the original Cleveland cars, despite their historical significance. However, an almost identical car from Rochester NY (1213) has been saved and is under restoration at the Seashore Museum. More recently, a Milan car was added to the heritage fleet in San Francisco and in 1999 eleven more were purchased from the same source to work on the revived Market Street F line alongside restored PCC cars.

Technical details
TTC "Large Witt"
Length 15.5m, width 2.6m, weight 22.67 tonnes, 4 x 32kW motors, 113 passengers, 55 seated.

Bibliography
Der Stadtverkehr 9/1989.
Headlights vol.59, nos.7-9, July-September 1997.
The Witt Car. TTC factsheet, April 1984.
Fifty Years of Progressive Transit – A History of the Toronto Transit Commission. J.F. Bromley and J. May. Electric Railroaders' Association, New York, 1973.
Strassenbahn Magazin no.53, August 1984.

An interior view of the car below. (Author)

A rather decrepit Peter Witt on an enthusiasts' tour was no.2028 in Akron, Ohio. (A.D. Young, Evda Slides)

THE LOW FLOOR CAR

Most trams built up to 1914 stood high off the ground – the floor level of the Mitten "nearside" cars was 99cm above rail level – and therefore commonly required three or four steps between road level and the floor of the saloon. While there was then no consideration given to the problems of passengers with any kind of disability or impediment such as a piece of heavy luggage, operators were aware that the high platform level slowed down the service, and that high steps were a source of platform accidents and thus of claims for compensation. About 1912 the problem was compounded by the fashion for the tight "hobble skirt" which had become all the rage; a lady wearing one had to raise her skirt to what was considered an indecent level to negotiate the steps. Although it is unlikely that many traction managers took much heed of this, perhaps they had noticed that the attention this drew could also slow up the boarding process!

Some trailers with low centre entrances were built in Germany in the years immediately before 1914, of which the most famous were the series of bogie cars built in 1914 by van der Zypen for the line Bonn-Bad Godesberg-Mehlem. But it was in the USA that the first attempt was made to introduce motor cars with a low entrance step level. The problems of boarding, alighting and platform accidents were noticed by Frank Hedley, an Englishman who had worked with Charles T. Yerkes in Chicago and who had advised the latter on some features of the design of underground trains for London. In 1903 he had become general superintendent of the Interborough Rapid Transit in New York City and later, when that company took over part of the Manhattan tram system as the New York Railways, he became President and General Manager of that network.

Working with rolling stock engineer J. Doyle, who also held that position on the IRT, he designed a totally new type of tram which was intended to avoid the problems. The first, no.5000, was built by Brill and entered service on 21 March 1912. This was a single-decker with smooth body contours and a centre entrance with a step height of only 25.4cm above rail level. To achieve this the maximum traction bogies were placed at the extreme ends of the car with their driving wheels outwards. The designers seem to have taken much of the inspiration for this layout from contemporary underground trains, with which both were of course familiar. They may also have been aware of the cars in use on Budapest's first underground line, the Földalatti, one of which had been shown at the Paris Exhibition of 1900. The cars were 12.09m long, seating was provided for 51 passengers and there was standing room for 38. Internal finish was to a high standard and the conductor had a post directly opposite the door. The car was deemed to be a success and orders were then placed for 175 others. The design was often referred to as the "stepless" car, though of course there was still one step up from street level. A few were also bought by operators in California, and British Columbia Electric bought one for city service in Vancouver, this being arranged for left hand traffic. Two further similar examples were bought by Perth and Brisbane. But the design did not really catch on and very soon the spread of one person operation

The New York double-decker, in its summer form, soon after entering service. (Author's collection)

sealed its fate. Some much smaller battery driven cars of the same type were built for use on lightly-trafficked cross town lines by the NYR and, later, by the Third Avenue Railway. There were in all 456 of these.

The concept was then tried on a double-decker and in the summer of 1912, a new tram appeared in New York City and a converted car appeared in Pittsburgh. The second car, also numbered 6000, was placed in service by New York Railways and was a version of the single-deck cars described above. Intended for use on the conduit lines only, it was probably the lowest double-deck tram ever built and had an overall height of only 3.65m. The bogies were displaced outwards to the ends of the car and this made it necessary to have the stairs at the ends of the saloons. This feature gave it a rather fearsome appearance and earned it the nickname of "The Broadway Battleship". Despite the very careful attention which had been given to the design, 6000 was a failure. It had one central doorway, only 3'10" wide and enclosed by power-operated sliding doors, interlocked with the controller, with a conductor's post in the vestibule. As the total capacity was about 174 passengers, acute congestion developed at busy stops and the car gained a reputation for causing delays in the service. It lasted until 1922 or 1925 (sources differ) and was then scrapped. A similar car was tried in Columbus, with an even shorter life, and a car of the same layout, but of full height, was built for Washington City in 1913 but was cut down to single-deck form three years later.

Pittsburgh Railways, under the innovative leadership of P.N. Jones, approached the question from a rather different angle. In the absence of any progress towards smaller and lighter motors, this undertaking had subsidised the development of a new motor by Westinghouse, the 328, a 25kW motor, weighing only 0.66 tonne, about 0.25 tonne lighter than any earlier designs. As it could be used with wheels of reduced diameter, a lower floor was now possible. In 1910 PR bought some central entrance trailers which had wheels of 56cm diameter and only one intermediate step between road level and the saloon floor. These showed a reduction in dwell times at stops and to maximise this, Jones went on to design a motor car with wheels of 61cm and a floor height of 90cm above rail level. This concept was then tried on a double-deck trailer, also numbered 6000, and in fact placed in

service just before the New York car. It was motorised later in the year. There were actually two doorways in the centre of the car and two staircases, and by using these it was possible to institute a form of passenger flow, the conductor being stationed facing the rear door and all passengers filing past him before taking a seat. The undertaking was sufficiently impressed by its success to order five new double-deckers from the St Louis Car Company for delivery in 1913. These trams (60001-6005) were built of steel and could carry 56/54 passengers, plus standees. Despite this, the tare weight was only 17.25 tonnes. The wheels were of only 61cm diameter and the height of the floor at the entrance was only 35cm above rail level, a figure exactly matched by most of to-day's low floor trams. Of conventional construction, they nonetheless had a low overall height. They were considered reasonably successful and lasted until 1924. Faster schedules were then being introduced and they were not sufficiently powerful to keep up with these. Nor could any of the trams described above have been operated as one-man cars.

Two cars to the New York design, but smaller, were built for Wien in 1915. The step height was only 190mm above rail level, a figure not reached on most of to-day's low floor trams. Although prone to derailment, they were generally considered successful, but war and post-war troubles prevented any further experiments of this kind. The two trams ran until 1938.

The Hedley car built for Perth has been preserved and can be seen at the Western Australia Tram Museum in that city.

Technical details

Western Australian Government Tramways Perth 63
Length 13.4m, width ? weight 17.27 tonnes 2 x 20.6kW motors, 66 passengers, 52 seated.

Bibliography

The Hedley-Doyle Stepless Streetcar. H. Elsener. NJ International Inc, Hicksville NY, 1997
Double-deck Trams beyond the British Isles. B. Patton. Adam Gordon, Brora, 2002.
Der Stadtverkehr 10/1987 (Pittsburgh).
Strassenbahn Magazin no.53, August 1984.
Destination Subiaco (Western Australia). J. Richardson ed. Traction Publications, Melbourne 1957.

ONE PERSON OPERATION
– THE BIRNEY SAFETY CAR

Even in the era of the horse tram, driver-only operation was not unknown, although it was not at any time widespread, either in Britain or North America. The system was sometimes used on lightly-trafficked lines and relied on a method by which the driver could either collect the fares or ensure that passengers paid these into a fare box. In a few cases, this type of operation was continued on electric lines, most commonly using cars which had been superannuated from front line service, but these were not particularly satisfactory and in the first decade of the 20th century engineers began to turn their attention to the development of a new design of car which could be operated by the driver only.

Unusually it was in the UK that the first such design appeared. This was the Raworth demi-car, which was first built in 1904 and was subsequently bought by a few systems, but the total number built was very small. It was in the USA that a design with real commercial potential was developed.

Just before Europe became involved in the First World War, the traction industry in North America received a shock from the first wave of competition from the internal combustion engine, not from the motor bus as such, but from "jitneys" – private cars or "flivvers" whose drivers carried fare paying passengers at fares below and speeds above those offered on street railways. While the phenomenon did not last long, opera-

tors began to think that the practice of running fairly large cars at extended intervals, each with a crew of two, would not in future be the best means of stimulating traffic. There was also the matter of wear and tear on the track from such cars, at a time when much of this was falling due for renewal, and the question of high current consumption.

One of the systems most interested in the development of a lightweight design for driver-only operation was the Illinois Traction System, which, apart from radial lines, also operated trams in 19 towns along these, eight of these having fewer than 25,000 inhabitants. To serve these, the motive power superintendent of the ITS, J.M. Bosenbury, developed in 1913 a two-axle version of the "nearside" car and adapted for driver-only operation. The main innovation of the ultra-light design was the use of compressed air not only for braking but also to operate various features which would allow safe operation by one person. A "dead man's pedal" ensured that the motors would be cut out and an emergency brake applied should the driver topple over unconscious. In later versions, the pedal was replaced by a hinged controller handle. The doors were interlocked with the controller to prevent the car starting while they were still open, and conversely opening of the doors while the car was in motion led to an immediate application of the emergency brake. These features were manufac-

tured by the Westinghouse Air Brake Company, which later set up a subsidiary, Safety Car Devices Company, to handle marketing and sales. The first car, built by the Saint Louis Car Company, went into service in Quincy, Illinois, in 1913 and proved to be totally successful.

This success was noticed by Charles O. Birney of the Stone and Webster Corporation. In co-operation with the American Car Company, he devised an alternative version of the one-person car. His main concerns were standardisation, economy and the safety of one-person operation. In the event, the Saint Louis Company's design proved to be just too light and it was the American Car Company's version which went on to become the standard lightweight one-person car, for which a great demand was soon to be expressed throughout North America. Strictly speaking, the cars should have been called "Bosenbury-Birneys", but Bosenbury had the handicap of a rather long name and it is as Birneys that they, and later some buses built on similar lines, were known. In any case, it was Stone and Webster who first showed faith in the concept by large-scale orders for the design and they had 250 such cars on order by 1917. To reassure passengers and other road users about the security of one-person operation, the cars were commonly referred to as "safety cars" by operators and some had this inscription painted on the dash.

Pacific Electric Birney 331 as preserved, seen in October 1987 at the Orange Empire museum at Perris, California. (Author)

As with other so-called standard trams, there was really no standard Birney, since the design had the merit of being easily adapted to meet the particular needs of individual operators. However, the typical Birney was 8.56m long, 2.35m wide and rode on a Brill 79E1 truck of wheelbase of 2.44m or 2.6m. Seating for 30 or 32 passengers was provided on rather spartan wooden seats and there was standing space for an equivalent number. Total unladen weight was around 7.5 tonnes, about half that of other contemporary designs. The possibility of weight reduction had been helped by the development in 1915 of the Westinghouse Electric Efficiency motor, ironically sometimes referred to as the "WEE motor", a 13kW motor which weighed only 0.75 tonne. However, interiors were rather basic, with unlined ceilings and little in the way of decorative trim. Most cars were double-ended, but a single-ended design could be specified. Despite the apparent complications of the safety features, the cars were easy to work and drivers, now re-named "operators", took to them with alacrity. Perhaps their greatest advantage was that they did live up to their name and proved to be safe vehicles, with good acceleration and braking and an interior layout which allowed the operator a good overview of the doorway. In Gary, Birneys were in the 1920s responsible for 25% of all car mileage but for only 5% of all accidents to passengers. The initial cost in 1916 was US$4,500 (about £900) but war-time inflation had increased this to US$7,000 by 1921.

Between 1916 and 1926, a total of almost 6,000 Birneys were built by ten manufacturers in the USA and Canada. The peak year of production was 1920, when 1,699 Birneys were produced. Traction companies were pleased by the reduction in running costs of around 40% and, where they were used to provide an increased frequency, passengers liked them too and receipts increased. They operated in 337 towns and cities in the USA, 21 in Canada and one in Newfoundland. Many were exported to Central and South America and eight went to Australia. These cars, along with those supplied to Invercargill and New Plymouth in New Zealand, and five which went to the South Manchurian Railways, were arranged for left hand running. The cars built for Halifax were built to this layout in 1920, but were soon converted to right hand operation. The only European Birneys were three supplied to Arnhem in 1921, which were ultimately converted to trailers. A very close copy of the design was later supplied to Coimbra in Portugal.

Then, just as quickly as it had arisen, demand for the lightweight cars waned and only 565 were sold in 1921. Some systems were already too far gone to be rescued by them and other operators in small towns refused to alter track layouts to allow a more frequent schedule. In many places, the innate tendency of the Birney to buck and bounce when running at speed was exaggerated by run-down trackwork. On the other hand, they were not really suited to main line service in large cities and, where they did succeed in stimulating traffic, as in Detroit, they had soon to be replaced by larger cars, in this case Peter Witts (whereupon the Birneys became "Half Witts"). As short-distance passengers tended to crowd around the doorway, this became an internal bottleneck and to minimise this problem, some later deliveries, such as those to Columbus and Nashville, had an additional rear exit. Their problems with any

Melbourne X2 class 676 awaiting its next turn of service on vintage tram duty at Camberwell depot on 16 March 1986. (Author)

The depot in Bendigo on 19 March 1986. On the left is ex-Adelaide 302, while on the right is Bendigo 30. (Author)

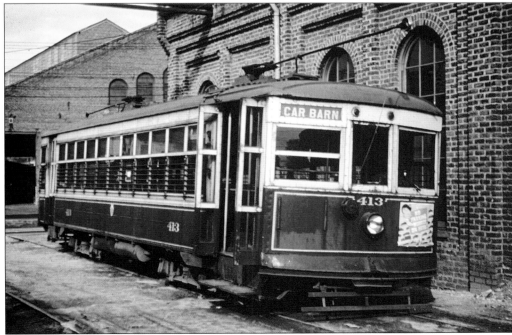

The bogie version, as typified by Richmond 413 at the depot on 14 November 1948. (A.D. Young, Evda Slides)

depth of snow did not endear them to northern operators, while in southern cities the practice of racial segregation led to waste of space in what was already a small car. The main problem was that "coloreds" had to use the same exit as "whites", this being contrary to established practice in the cities concerned. In 1927 Birney developed a bogie version of the design for Houston and a few other cities, such as Johnstown, later took delivery of similar cars. These went some way towards solving the problem of limited capacity and ran successfully for many years.

However, attempts by Birney and others to produce a modernised two-axle car in the late 1920s were failures. In 1928 he designed an improved model, of which one was built by the Saint Louis Car Co. and had individual steerable wheels. It was tried in Houston, but in service proved to behave like a car with normal fixed wheels and was also prone to derailment. Three similar cars were also built by the Twin Coach Co., using many components from the firm's motor buses, and these were tried in Oakland and Kansas City, with much the same result. The firm of Brill in the same year built two cars to a two-axle version of its "Master Unit" design, one of which ran briefly in Lynchburg, Virginia but was soon returned to the builders, owing to its habit of derailing. The other ran in New York until about 1942. However, the concept was successfully taken further in Melbourne, where the Melbourne and Metropolitan Tramways Board (MMTB) built ten cars of class X1 (459-468) in the period 1926-28 and went on to refine the concept in six cars of class X2 (674-679) of 1930. These were much more successful and, of the latter, 676 has been fully restored and painted in the chocolate and cream livery of the 1920s (which in fact it never carried in service) and is in regular use as a relief tourist tram. Car 467 of class X1 has also been preserved in running order by the Tramway Museum Society of Victoria.

Normal Birney service in North America ended on 30 June 1951 in Fort Collins, Colorado and the cars in Bendigo, Victoria, were probably the last to run in normal service anywhere when they finished in April 1972.

Historians have since derided the little cars as the Trabants of the tramway world. While they did have several shortcomings, it would be absurd to suggest that over 300 operators ordered a design which was basically unsound, and many ran for over twenty years. For example, Birneys latterly provided the entire service in Halifax, where they successfully coped with extremely heavy traffic during the war years, carrying over 32 million passengers in 1942. Although the concept of modular construction was not new, having already been practised by Brill with its convertible and semi-convertible cars, it was the Birney which first accustomed operators to the idea of a basic design based on standard components. But the main success of the Birney was to prove the practicability of safe one-person operation and in so doing paved the way for later operation of much larger cars in the USA and, ultimately, in Europe. It must therefore be regarded as the pioneer of what is now an almost universal concept in tramway operation.

Strangely, it is in Australia rather than in its native USA that the Birney car is now best known to the general public. Of the eight Birneys imported to the Commonwealth, seven and the truck of the eighth survive. Thanks to the efforts of the Bendigo Trust, the closure of 1972 was not to be the end of the line for the city's trams and five Birneys now form part of the fleet of cars which operates a tourist service. They have become famous as Bendigo's talking trams (they are fitted with recorded commentaries) and are now more familiar to both Australians and visitors than when they ran in commercial service. One (302) runs in the livery of the Municipal Tramways Trust of Adelaide and was in 1972 the subject of an attempted hi-jack to return it to its native city. However, the Bendigonians welded it to the track and it remained in Victoria! The episode brought a great deal of useful publicity in both states and harmony was later restored when the body of 27 (Adelaide 303), which had been sold off in 1958, was repurchased by the Trust, married once again with its truck and fully and finely rebuilt to be presented to the Saint Kilda tramway museum in Adelaide. Melbourne 217 of class X, one of two imported in 1923 and among the last Birneys built, is preserved in its native city.

In the USA, individual Birneys run on heritage lines in Dallas, Tucson Fort Smith and, fittingly, Fort Collins and a double-truck version may be seen on a similar line in Tampa. Several others are in museums and in 2005 three replicas were constructed by the firm of Gomaco for the heritage line in Charlotte, on which they will be used along with a restored car (85) from the city's original system.

Technical details
Melbourne 217
Length 8.53m, width 2.55m weight 8.5 tonnes, 2 x 19kW motors, 33 seated passengers.

Bibliography
Der Stadtverkehr. 3/1982.
The Birney car. Harold E. Cox. Forty Fort, Pennsylvania, 19xx.
Lightweight Street and Interurban Cars. op.cit.
Bendigo and its Vintage Talking Trams. S. MacKinnon. The Bendigo Trust, Bendigo, 1981.
Destination City – Melbourne's Electric Trams (5th ed). N. Cross, D. Budd and R. Willson. Transit Australia Publishing, Sydney, 2001.

SUMMARY

By the mid-1920s, therefore, all the above developments had combined in North America to allow passenger flow on almost all city cars, often combined with one-person operation, even of large cars.

Britain was still wedded to its double-deckers and Europe to its small two-axle single-deckers and trailers. But engineers in these countries were not unaware of what was happening in North America and it would not be long before some of these practices began to make their way into operation in Europe, once that continent had recovered from the chaos of the war and its economic aftermath.

The years between 1927 and 1929 were especially significant for developments in Europe, since the first trials with Peter Witt cars began in Milan in the former year and in Britain, Bradford placed a modern single-decker in service. In the latter year, Dresden introduced the revolutionary "Hechtwagen" bogie car, while Rotterdam, with its central entrance bogie cars, began a wholesale modernisation of its fleet and in London the first prototype Feltham cars appeared. In the Netherlands, Arnhem, no doubt drawing on its experience with Birney cars, placed in service the first bogie car in Europe to be designed for one-person operation. That same year saw the formation in the USA of the Electric Railway Presidents' Conference Committee, the progenitor of the PCC car. How these pioneers changed established practice and led to the development of the modern tram will be traced in the chapters which follow.

As mentioned, Coimbra operated what were Europe's neatest approach to the Birney car, apart from those which ran in Arnhem. Nos 14 and 15 were built by Brill in 1928 and ran on standard 79E 1X trucks, but were designed to be worked by a two-man crew and lacked the safety features of the standard Birney. On 24 April 1974 car 14 is on Avenida Navarro on line 3, while behind, at the city's railway station, Estácão Nova, a Sunbeam trolleybus loads up for line 5. (Author)

CHAPTER 2

BOGIE CARS 1927-1940

Although the bogie car had by 1914 become the standard for urban operation in North America, it had made little headway in Europe. A few large cities such as Berlin had a substantial number and in the-then UK, double deck bogie cars could be found in quantity in cities such as Manchester, London and Dublin. In Italy, Modena placed in service in 1920/1 the first bogie trams to run in urban service in that country. But most operators preferred the traditional two-axle car, operated with trailers on the continent and as double-deckers in Britain and Ireland. The scope for development of a modern design was thus limited and might have remained so had not the ATM of Milano decided that the time had come for a radical departure from traditional European tramway technology. The change of the rule of the road in Italy from left to right on 1 March 1925 and a complete reconstruction of the tramway network in November 1926, with through services replacing those previously terminating at Il Duomo, gave added impetus for radical change.

ITALY

To ascertain if bogie cars could be run on the urban system, two were borrowed from suburban Società Trazione Electrica Lombarda and operated successfully on line 20 in February 1927. The tramways were then authorised to buy two experimental bogie cars. The design was developed by the department's manager, G. d'Alio and G. Cuccoli, head of the department of research and development, both of whom favoured the US Peter Witt system. The two trams, 1501/2, were constructed by Carminati e Toselli, and were first tried on 29 November 1927 and placed in public service the next day. They were initially laid out in classic Peter Witt style, with passenger circulation from front to centre and a seated conductor, with a post just ahead of the single centre door. A total of 125 passengers could be carried, 33 seated. The fare structure was also changed with the introduction of these cars to what was virtually a flat fare. These trams were revolutionary and at a stroke, Milano had rendered obsolete not only its own fleet of two-axle cars, but also virtually every other tram in Europe.

Success with both public and operator was immediate and in June 1928 it was agreed to order no fewer than 500 trams and to rebuild termini to allow operation of single-ended cars. The new trams were built by six manufacturers, all however being almost identical. These were numbered 1503-2002 and individual batches were as follows:

Carminati e Toselli	(110)	1503-1612
Breda	(110)	1613-1722
Officine Mecchaniche di Emilia Reggio	(50)	1723-1772
Officine Mecchaniche (Milano)	(110)	1773-1882
Officine Elettroferroviarie Tallero	(110)	1883-1992
Officine Mecchaniche Lodigiane	(10)	1993-2002

A Ventotto in its prime! Car 1868 is in green livery and carries a trolley pole in April 1962. (Pam Eaton)

Electrical equipment was supplied by a consortium of Compagnia Generale di Electtricità di Milano (CGE) and Ansaldo and an improved version of the US K35 controller was fitted.

Delivery of the class was completed by June 1931. In September 1929 one car, number unknown, was tried on line 23 in Frankfurt (M) during the UITP congress. Although the public approved of it, the trial was really too short to be conclusive and the complicated Frankfurt fare structure militated against the Peter Witt system. Another, taken from the Breda series, was sold to Brussels in 1929. It was really too wide for the clearances of that system and, although it was mounted asymmetrically on its bogies, some curves on line 15 still had to be eased. From 1932 it ran regularly as 5001 (1) on the Tervuren line and it gave every satisfaction. In Brussels it was invariably known as "la voiture de Milan". The experience gained with it was used in the construction of the later 5000 class. In November 1935 it was sold on to Madrid, the first bogie car on that system and it thus paved the way for the later operation of PCC type cars (qv). In Madrid it was known as "Pepe" (Joey) and lasted until 1965. A

replacement for this car was built for Milano. In Milano the cars were not known as Peter Witts but as Ventotto, or '28 cars'. They cost 155,000 lire each, a relatively expensive figure for the time.

After the cars had been in service for some time, an additional single-width rear exit was fitted to reduce dwell time at stops. In October 1937 car 1881 was rebuilt to have a double-width rear entrance, with reversed passenger flow, and between 1938 and 1940 the entire class was similarly converted. This change also made it necessary to replace the transverse seating in the rear section with longitudinal seating. Cars 1748 and 1835 were fitted with m.u. equipment, but this experiment was not continued. Over 200

In May 1984 Peter Witts, now fitted with pantographs, still maintained the circular services 29/30 and there were always plenty at Piazza Repubblica, where the crews took a break. Car 1732 is on the right on line 30, with another one behind, while to the left car 1522 is on another service. (Author)

cars were damaged in air raids and for some time after the end of the war 24 ran as trailers, using the central door only and having their fleet numbers prefixed with 0. Ultimately all but one were rebuilt and returned to service as motor cars. In the early 1950s 94 trams were fitted with semi-automatic Brown Boveri controls and were also given rubber-insert wheels and electro-pneumatic brakes. All were converted for one-person operation after 1970 and at the same time fitted with a pantograph, though for a time most cars also retained their trolley poles.

It is impossible to overstate the importance of these cars in the development of the tram in Europe. Not only did many other Italian operators copy the design, but it was exported to other countries and was ultimately the inspiration for the Swiss and Scandinavian bogie trams and also for the German Grossraumwagen of the 1950s. In turn this led to the modern articulated tram. The Italian Peter Witt may be considered the father of all modern European trams. Its longevity has also been remarkable. Seventy-seven years after the two prototypes entered service, about 180 trams are still running, having outlasted many of their successors in Milan and elsewhere. Nor has their's been a decrepit old age, such as afflicted the standard cars in Glasgow, kept in service only because no one in authority could make up their mind how to replace them. The "Ventotto" trams have been retained because they are simply so efficient and easy to operate. They still run smartly and provide a quality of ride that far surpasses that of many modern designs. They would probably go on for ever, were it not for the high floor level and three entrance steps which make them relatively difficult for passengers with reduced mobility. As mentioned elsewhere, two were used to make up an experimental low floor car. Various others have been modified for sightseeing and promotional duties and cars 1723 and 1847 were repainted green in 1994/5 for use on tourist line 21. No.1699, known as "Tramito" was painted red and blue in 2001 and is used at week-ends as a children's tram, while no.1702, the Tram Bianco, has carried a white livery since 1984 and is used for ceremonial trips. Eleven have gone to San Francisco for use on line F along with the restored PCC cars (qv), while another (2001) is in San José and one is in Melbourne. In Milano, car 1502 was in 1977 recreated from car 1667, using also parts from others, and no.1908, formerly 1502 and the oldest still in existence, has also been set aside for preservation. Another two are preserved in Japan and it is thought that eight others survive at different locations in Italy. They have paid for themselves many times over and even now it would be premature to write their obituary.

Technical details (as built)
Length 13.5m, width 2.53m, weight 15 tonnes, 4 x 21kW motors, c.132 passengers, 42 seated.

Bibliography
Modern Tramway no.619, July 1989.
Un Tram che si chiama Milano. Guido Boreani. Calosci-Cortona, 1995
Histoire des Transports Publiques à Bruxelles. Tome 2 – L'Age d'Or. STIB Brussels, 1980.
In Tram – Storia e miti dei trasporti pubblici milano. C. Pirovano, editor. Milan, 1982
Tram e Tramvie a Milano. G. Cornolò and G. Severi. ATM Milano. N.d., c.1987.

The concept was also taken up in Rome at almost the same time. In 1927 what was then the ATAG (Azienda Tranvie e Autobus del Governatorato) placed in service the first of 27 bogie trams, built by Carminati e Toselli, with electrical equipment by GEC (2001-2053, odd numbers only). These formed class MRS, Moto Rimorchiata Saglio or Saglio motor and trailer, Saglio being the name of the engineer responsible for their introduction. These had front and rear doors only, with passenger flow from the rear, and a seated conductor.

ATAC 2029. (Father Benedict collection)

Only the front bogie was motored and the cars were prone to slipping, especially noticeable given the acceleration practised by drivers in Rome. They could carry 90 passengers, of whom 29 were seated, were 13m long and weighed 14.5 tonnes. A further batch of 70 (MRSII, 2065-2203) arrived in 1932, with four fewer seats and another 30 followed two years later. The class proved to be fast and smooth riding and had long

No.2233 was built to a slightly different design. It is taking a layover at Porta Maggiore in July 1993. (Author)

lives, the last in normal service being withdrawn in 2003, pioneer 2001 having attained the respectable age of 76. Latterly all were converted for one person operation and many were rebodied with rather angular bodywork. Four are still used on a tourist line which links sites of archaeological interest. Nos.2035 and 2137 have also escaped withdrawal, the former having been rebuilt as a mobile school classroom and the latter as a café car, while 2047 has become an official museum car. A further development of the design was attempted in 1937 with a split level car, 2P1, but this was not successful in service, being slow to load and unload and it was rebuilt as a single-decker in 1947 (2265). As such, it is still in existence. The other Roman tramway undertaking, STEFER, acquired twelve cars identical to the first series of the city tramways (301-312) but fitted with four motors, and in 1936 a further eight (321-328) which had electro-pneumatic equipment and were fitted for m.u. operation, although in the event this was not used. In 1964 this undertaking also bought four MRS cars from what had by then become ATAC.

Bibliography
Binari sulla Strada Interno a Roma. G. Angeleri, A. Curci, U. Bianchi. Edizione Abete, Rome, 1982

Bologna in 1934 bought from Stanga the first (201, class F) of 29 similar but double-ended cars. These had electro-pneumatic control, automatic acceleration and an attractive sloping windscreen. They ran on Brill 90E bogies and had four CGE 25kW motors. The first series (202-216) followed in 1935 while further deliveries (217-229, class F1) in 1938/9/40 brought the total to 29. There were some slight detail differences in the later series and they were mounted on Brill 84E bogies. Unfortunately plans to buy additional cars of this type remained unfulfilled and they remained a relatively small

group in the total fleet. Two (201 and 210) were fitted with PCC trucks in the post-war years, but the system was then run down and ultimately closed on 3 November 1963, bogie car 210 being the official last car. Four cars (201/10/18/28), were then sold to STEFER, where they were converted to single-ended layout and fitted with pantographs. They, with the operator's own cars, lasted until the system closed in 1972. No.218 was then returned to its home city and restored in time for the centenary of the tramways in 1977. It is now in the local transport museum collection.

Rebuilt car 2165 at Porta Maggiore in July 1993 (Author)

The bi-level car 2P1. (ATAC)

No.2265, rebuilt from 2P1, negotiates the complex track layout at Porta Maggiore in July 1993 (Author)

One of the STEFER bogie cars, probably 324 of the second series, seen on 20 September 1970. (Father Benedict collection)

An interior view of this car. (Father Benedict collection)

Technical details

Bologna 210 in STEFER condition
Length 13.46m, width 2.15m, 15.13 tonnes, 4 x 25kW motors, 99 passengers.

Bibliography

Storia dei Trasporti Urbani di Bologna. F. Formentin e P. Rossi. Calosci-Cortona, 2nd edition, 1998.

Torino waited until 1932 before acquiring any modern bogie trams. In that year it built two (2500/1) on Brown Boveri trucks, fitted out with passenger flow as in Milano. As they proved to be successful, 98 similar cars followed from Fiat (2502-2599) in 1933. A further seven (2100-2106), with a slightly altered doorway layout, were built in the workshops in 1933 and 70 (2111-2180) more came from Fiat and Savigliano in 1935. The latter manufacturer delivered 40 more trams in 1937/8 (2201-2240), making a total of 217 units. One car was destroyed in an air raid and, as detailed elsewhere, 116 were converted to articulated cars between 1958 and 1960. Of the remainder 30 were fitted with new bodies by Fiat and renumbered in the 35xx series.

After trials with a prototype based on the Milano cars in 1930, Napoli bought 50 bogie cars (951-1000) in 1933/4, arranged as the MRS class in Rome. A further 54 followed one year later. All these had two motors only. In 1960, 50 were modified with new streamlined front ends and 14 were soon afterwards converted to trailers, although four were later re-converted to motors. One was also fitted with a middle doorway. In the late 1970s the survivors were given new bodies and these are about to be replaced by new low floor cars, some in the meantime having acquired pantographs.

Several smaller systems also bought bogie cars at this time. Padova took nine from Stanga in 1931 and sold these on to Cagliari when the system closed in 1956. They lasted there until 1969. Bergamo bought four double-ended cars from Carminati e Toselli in 1934 and, surprisingly, a further four and three trailers in 1946/7. These were later sold to the Tranvie del Friuli and ran there until about 1960. Trieste had two batches of a total of 28 cars (401-428) from Stanga in 1933/4, with rear and front doors, of which car 427 is preserved in the local railway museum. In 1935 this system acquired a further five (101-105) for the line to Opicina, on part of which the trams are assisted by a cable. These were followed by an additional two in 1942 (106/7). All but one of these trams are still in service, now numbered in the 400 series. These trams have four 25kW motors and Brill BF3/1 bogies and, although double-ended, have doors – front, centre and rear – only on the left hand side, as seen when travelling in the uphill direction.

One of the ex-Bologna cars as running with STEFER in Rome. It is at the city terminus on 20 September 1970. As it is fitted with PCC bogies, it must be either 201 or 210. (Father Benedict collection)

Technical details

Torino 2500 after internal alterations in 1945
Length 13.79m, width 2.25m, weight 16.29 tonnes, 4 x 25kW motors, 121 passengers, 23 seated.

Bibliography

Strassenbahn Magazin nos.51/3, February/August 1984, (Turin), 128, June 2000 (Trieste).
Modern Tramway no.360, December 1967 (Trieste).

Genova in 1931 bought a total of 36 cars (765-800) from different manufacturers for its long coastal line 15. Although these did not have a seated conductor, they were of great technical interest since they used motors suspended from the body and cardan drive to the wheels, thus anticipating the later practice of the Belgian SNCV and the Maschinenfabriek Esselingen (qv). In 1934 30 trailers (821-850) were rebuilt to the same design, although these were single-ended. Messina (10 trams) and Pescara (1) had bogie trams with some modern features.

Bibliography

Modern Tramway no.317, May 1964 (Genova).

While these trams were still being built, Milano had already moved on to the second stage in the development of the modern bogie tram. In 1935 Breda delivered one prototype tram (5000) which was mainland Europe's first streamlined tram.

Torino 2804 passing 2531 in the city centre in October 1975. (Jim D. Schantz)

Napoli 966 in original condition at Borelli terminus in February 1975 (Author)

A rear view of modified car 972 in Napoli at Piazza Garibaldi in February 1975 (Author)

Napoli 970 – one of the rebuilt cars seen in May 1986. (Author)

A commercial card showing Trieste 103 on the cable line. (Father Benedict collection)

Streamlining was of course very much in vogue at the time, but in this case, its application was more than a publicity gimmick. This tram was designed by the engineer Renato Ferrari, who wanted to explore the potential for energy saving which might result from the adoption of an air smoothed body in conjunction with the use of lightweight metals in its construction. As this was also the time of the Italian war in Ethiopia, sanctions had been imposed by the League of Nations and Italian industry was devising new methods of construction, particularly in the aircraft industry, to circumvent these. The car was therefore constructed in a type of duraluminium, known as avional, already used in the construction of aircraft, and, for its size, had the very low weight of only 13.5 tonnes. Given the speed of city traffic, the streamlining was probably of less importance than its performance, but it certainly gave car 5000 an attractive and eye-catching appearance. There was a distinct pointed nose and neatly domed roof, rather like the front end of the Blackpool railcoaches and it would be interesting to know if Ferrari had seen these, or illustrations of them. Large side windows gave excellent visibility and Venetian blinds could be lowered to cut off the glare of the

Italian sun. Internally comfortable upholstered bucket seats were fitted, rather similar to those used in Britain by the LNER on the Tyneside electric stock of 1937, and lighting was provided from two continuous tubes in the centre of the roof. Passenger flow was from rear to middle and front doors. With a view to possible use on radial lines, the car was designed to be easily converted to double-ended configuration and the rear end was a mirror image of the front. Nothing quite like no.5000 had been seen before in any large European city. Sadly this fine tram had a short life, being destroyed in Via Messina depot during an air raid in August 1943.

A second prototype, 5001, followed in 1937. This car had a redesigned rear end, as the idea of suburban operation had been given up, and also had different bogies. It was rather heavier than 5000, but still weighed only 14.67 tonnes. Based on this, a production series of 60 trams (5002-5061) was delivered in 1938. These made use of heavier materials and weighed 16.5 tonnes. The air raid of 13 August 1943 already mentioned was a disaster for this class and no fewer than 41 were destroyed, including car 5001. Those which remained after the war ran until 1976 when they were all withdrawn, not having proved to be as durable as the 1500 class. Car 5003 was sold to the ATAN of Napoli and used there as a store and a canteen. It is not known if it still exists, but if it did, it would make an ideal candidate for preservation.

For use on the radial line to Milanino, the operator also bought 18 end entrance bogie cars in three batches between 1931 and 1942 (110-128). These were built by Breda, Tallero and Stanga and there were also matching trailers (301-334), from Tallero and Breda. These were worked by an itinerant conductor. None are now in service.

Technical details

5000 class production trams
Length 13.64m, width 2.4m, weight 16.5 tonnes, 4 x 23.7kW motors, 150 passengers, 27 seated.

Bibliography

Tram e Tramvie a Milano. Op.cit.
In Tram. Op.cit.

The first city to follow Milano's example and place streamlined cars in service was Trieste, which bought 20 (429-448) from Stanga in 1938. Originally they did not have a seated conductor, but in 1953 cars 429 and 434-440 were rebuilt for passenger flow. With the run-down of the Trieste system, eight were sold to STEFER in Rome, but not all were placed in service. The others were scrapped in 1970.

Genova ordered in 1939 a class of 99 double-ended streamlined trams (901-999), built by four different manufacturers (UITE, Piaggio, Bagnara and Ansaldo), after trials with a prototype built in the city's own workshops (900). In the

5003 in service at Piazza Razzaro on line 23 in August 1964. (Peter Haseldine).

The front end of car 5031 and a view of a Blackpool railcoach for comparison. The former is on Via Michele da Carcano on 3 October 1967, the latter at Gynn Square on 27 October 1963, just before the closure of the Dickson Road line. (Father Benedict collection (Author)

Suburban car 128 at Via Valtellina terminus in Milan in May 1984. (Author)

event, only 93 were actually delivered to Genova, the balance of six being diverted to fulfil an export order received by Breda for Beograd (qv). These cars had electro-pneumatic control, passenger flow from front to rear and doors at the ends only. The first fifty had semi-PCC control, while the remainder had an accelerator designed by Brown Boveri. Both of these systems had excellent acceleration and braking characteristics

Genova 931 on Via Quinto at Via Fabrizi in May 1963. (W. J. Wyse, courtesy London Area, Light Rail Transit Association)

Ex-Trieste 445 after transfer to STEFER in Rome. It is at Cinecitta on 23 September 1967. (Father Benedict collection)

Peiraeus 80 waits at the city terminus bound for Perama. (Father Benedict collection)

and gave a particularly smooth ride. This, however, came at the expense of complexity and in 1947 car 995 was fitted instead with a normal control system, being at the same time rebuilt to single-ended layout, with a central door. No other car was so treated. After the system closed, these trams remained intact in the depot for some years, in the hope that they could be sold for further service, but no buyers were forthcoming and they were ultimately scrapped. As part compensation for the lost cars, Breda supplied four articulated cars (qv) to Genova in 1942. Car 973, re-labelled "900", is preserved in one of the city's bus garages.

Technical details

Genova 901
Length 13.57m, width 2.25m, weight 16.2 tonnes, 4 x 25kW motors, 113 passengers, 17 seated.

Bibliography
Modern Tramway no.317, May 1964.
Strassenbahn Magazin June 2000.

Italian builders were active in the export market during this period and naturally offered trams similar to those being built for use at home. The first bogie cars to be sent abroad were twelve double-ended cars (71-82) built in 1938 by CGE of Milano for the EHE of Peiraeus, where they were used on a new standard gauge radial line to Perama. These had central entrances and front exits and were worked by a roving conductor. The cars normally worked in pairs, but m.u. equipment was not fitted. Instead each car had its own driver and they communicated with each other by signalling via the control system. They carried exactly 100 passengers, 24 seated. They were of rather more square appearance than cars built for use in Italy but were successful and had long careers, running until 1977. Two (82 and another) have been preserved and are now displayed, in somewhat vandalised condition, at two stations on the new tram line. This success was followed by an order for 60 double-ended cars for the IES metre gauge system in Athenai (101-160), divided between Breda and Fiat and delivered in 1940, just as both countries were being drawn into the war. These had the flat front of post-war Milano cars and at first were worked by an itinerant conductor, with front entry and central exit. In 1943 half the fleet was lost in a fire in Kallithea depot, but it was found possible to rebuild 15, which were then given doors and a fixed conductor's post at the rear. There were

seats for 30 passengers and total capacity was 98. The system was neglected after the war and by 1954 the bogie cars looked battered and bruised and were also rather noisy. However, they were noted as being exceptionally steady and also fast. These cars were scrapped when the last lines closed in 1960.

At the same time as the cars for Athenai were under construction, an order was received by Breda for 15 trams for Beograd and, as mentioned above, six of the Genova cars (which would have been 984-989), were diverted to meet this order. Jugo-slavia had not yet become involved in the war and perhaps Italy wished to remain on good terms with it. The cars were modified to the extent that heaters were fitted under the seats. They became Beograd 37-42 and in the 1950s were converted to single-ended layout. They ran successfully until 1978. The seventh car was not completed until 1943 and, as the Germans had by that time set up the puppet Salo republic in northern Italy, its fate was actually decided by the Ministry of Transport in Berlin. It was sent to Innsbruck in April 1944 and there, as car 60, it was for long the only modern car in the fleet. The IVB was in fact so pleased with the design that it decided to take the balance of the Beograd order as 61-68, there being at this time no chance of delivering these trams to their original destination. They were to have been completed as central entrance cars, but only two bogies ever reached Tirol and Beograd finally received the balance of the order in 1949/50 (qv). No.60 ran until 1977 and, after a spell in Klagenfurt, returned to its adopted city, where it is currently undergoing restoration in the local transport museum.

The Italian bogie trams built from 1927 onwards revolutionised tramway operation and for the first time brought standards of operation up to the level of efficiency attained in north America at an earlier date. At more or less the same time, possibly following the example of Blackpool, they brought an innovative style to tramcar building – no longer was the tram simply a box on wheels but an excellent example of industrial design. It was a great pity that politics prevented wider adoption of Italian ideas and later consigned so many of the home systems to a premature end. But through the Swiss standard car, some of these ideas did reach systems in other countries and played a part in the development of post-war standard trams elsewhere.

A somewhat battered car in Athenai. (Father Benedict collection)

Bibliography
Modern Tramway no.201, September 1954 (Athens and Peiraeus), no.360, December 1967 (Trieste).
Strassenbahn Magazin no.78, November 1990 (Athens and Peiraeus), no.181, November 2004 (Innsbruck 60).

Beograd 44 in the woods near Topcider, on 9 February 1972. (A.D. Young, Evda Slides)

Innsbruck 60 at Berg Isle on line 1 in 1956. (F. Hunt, courtesy London Area, Light Rail Transit Association)

A combination of the economic conditions of the 1930s and entrenched ideas prevented the widespread adoption of the standards pioneered in Italy. However, there were other developments.

NETHERLANDS

The replica Arnhem car at the depot in the open air museum, March 2004. (Author)

Arnhem in 1929 bought six bogie trams (70-75) of attractive and modern appearance, arranged for one-person operation. It may be assumed that they were based on the experience obtained with the city's Birney cars and they were pioneers in Europe in this respect. They could carry 69 passengers, 32 seated. Sadly all were destroyed in the air raid of August 1944 which put an end to the city's trams. However, the design has been reincarnated in a single car (76) built for service at the new open air museum near the city in 1998. It was constructed in the museum workshops and apart from a few modern features, the only difference from the originals lies in the gauge – Arnhem used 1067mm gauge whereas the museum line is built to standard gauge.

DENMARK

Copenhagen (KS) in 1930 built a prototype motor car (501) and trailer (1501) in its own workshops and followed these in the years up to 1940 with a series of 107 motor cars (502-608) and 82 trailers (1502-1583). The first entered service on 31 January 1930 and the matching trailer arrived in May. All the motor cars were built by KS, but 30 of the trailers were built by Scandia. External styling was by the city architect, Ib Lunding. As built the motor cars had end doorways while the trailers were central entrance. They were heavy cars and had excellent riding qualities. A further 10 came in 1941 for the suburban NESA lines and, when these closed, they were absorbed into the city fleet as 609-618. From 1950 to 1953 all were converted for single-ended operation and passenger flow with a seated conductor, the trailers receiving rear doors in the process and the motors a central

Car 509 in Nørrebro on line 5 in April 1971 (Author)

door. Two sets (529/1577 and 562/1581) were used on sightseeing duties in the early 1960s and for this duty they were painted light blue. Due to the sale of articulated cars to Alexandria, many remained in service until the end of the trams in 1972 and quite a number have been preserved. Two motor cars (587 and 617) and three trailers (1552, 1572 and 1582) belong to the Sporvei Historisk Selskab and cars 550 and 1575 have also gone to that collection, on closure of the KS city transport museum.

The design was copied, in two-axle form, by Åarhus, with cars 53-56 in 1943. These had a sadly brief life, being destroyed in June 1944 when resistance fighters blew up the depot.

Technical details
KS production series, as built
Length 12.3m, width 2.2m, weight 19 tonnes, 4 x 22kW motors, 59 passengers, 28 seated.

Bibliography
Modern Tramway no.355, July 1967.
Strassenbahn Magazin no.86, November 1992

BELGIUM

In view of the approaching world fair to be held in Brussels in 1935, the Tramways Bruxellois ordered 25 bogie cars (5001-5025) from Dyle en Bacalan. These were both comfortable and very fast, with 4 x 45kW motors, and as a result were noted for their frequent clashes with other traffic. They carried 90 passengers, 34 seated. As built

Brussels 5009 negotiating the Barrière de Saint-Gilles in November 1968 (Author)

they did not have platform doors or passenger flow, although the driver did have the luxury of a seat, but in 1950 they were given air doors and passenger flow from rear to front, with a fixed conductor's post just ahead of the rear door. As mentioned elsewhere, car 5018 was rebuilt to provide information prior to the ordering of the first PCC cars and at various later dates cars 5006 and 5020/1 and 5023 were all given new PCC style bodies, retaining their original equipment. Car 5001 was given a central door but retained its original body. Between 1967 and 1979 5018 was mounted on Düwag trucks and given Siemens electrical equipment while 5020 was given Westinghouse Durand trucks and Kiepe equipment, in both cases to test these features for possible use in cars using the new tram tunnels. They later reverted to their original equipment. As the class was not fitted with track brakes, it could not itself be used on tunnel services and was withdrawn in the 1980s. Nos. 5001 and 5008 are preserved in the transport museum at Woluwe, as is car 5018 in its rebuilt condition. No.5009 now helps the environment by transporting waste bins around the system.

Belgium also had the distinction of operating the largest bogie cars in Europe at that time. In 1932/3 the Railways Economiques de Liège-Seraing placed in service 21 double-ended cars (301-321) which were said to have been ordered originally for Egypt. These large and handsome cars had a good turn of speed, being capable of 70km/hr, although in service they were limited to 60km/hr, and they were noted for their smooth ride. They had rear, centre and front doors and the floor at the centre was lower than that in the saloons, making them in effect a version of the Australian drop centre car. Initially they carried two conductors but in 1958 they were rebuilt with a fixed conductor's post with passenger flow from the rear and at the same time the floor in the centre section was raised to give a level floor

Brussels 5020 as rebuilt approaching Place de Brouckère in November 1968 (Author)

throughout. They were withdrawn in 1968 when the system closed and only 321 was preserved. It has since been restored to running order.

The Belgian Vicinal radial lines around some of the main cities had been electrified since before the first world war, but electrification of many cross-country lines did not begin until after 1930 and in fact continued into the 1950s. The first bogie cars with any modern features entered service on the long coastal line from De Panne to Knokke in 1929. These had Pennsylvania bogies and a good turn of speed, provided by 4 x 47kW motors. A production series of ten for the Brussels network followed. Both series were equally well received. Subsequently 21 motor

Liège-Séraing 304 at the city terminus of line 2 in September 1965. (Alastair G. Gunn)

and 14 trailer cars were built for the coast line, these being 2.4m wide, while 72 motors and 48 trailers were built for various inland groups, 2.2m wide. All but three of the trailers were soon afterwards rebuilt into motor cars. These 152 cars had wooden bodies but from 1935 an improved version with riveted metal bodies was introduced and 185 cars were built to this design. These were followed into service by 63 cars with welded bodies, construction continuing into the war years. They were all comfortable and serviceable cars but until the post-war years showed few modern features, although the use of small wheels and modern electrical features allowed a relatively low floor throughout. Between 1953 and 1955 40 of the metal bodied cars were rebuilt at Eugies works with air doors, a seated conductor and passenger flow. Seven others had previously been converted to single-ended layout with air doors but did not have passenger flow. Between 1954 and 1959 193 standard bogie cars were rebuilt as S class trams (qv). The others lasted until scrapped in the 1970s. Many have been preserved, including a complete train on the coastal line, which sometimes runs in public service.

Technical details

Brussels 5000 class
Length 13.57m, width 2.19m, weight 16.82 tonnes, 4 x 50kW motors, 99 passengers, 30 seated.

Liège bogie car
Length 15.2m, width 2.33m, weight 21.5 tonnes, 4 x 45kW motors, 128 passengers, 33 seated.

Bibliography

Histoire des Transports Publiques à Bruxelles, Tome 2 – L'Age d'Or. J. Delmelle et al. STIB Brussels, 1980.
100 Years of the Belgian Vicinal, 1885-1985. W.J.K. Davies. Light Rail Transit Association, London, 1985.
Strassenbahn Magazin, no.131, 9/2000.
Modern Tramway nos.270/1, June/July 1960 (Liège).

Standard Vicinal car 9741 and two matching trailers parked beside the ramp to the new subway at Brussels Midi in September 1958. (Author)

The preserved train on the coast line, seen in Oostende depot yard in September 1985. (Author)

GERMANY

The first bogie car of modern design to take to the rails in Germany was the Dresden "Hechtwagen" (pike tram), so called from its tapered ends. The car had been designed by Professor Alfred Bockemühl, at that time chief engineer of the Dresdner Strassenbahn AG, in co-operation with the builders Christoph and Unmack in Niesky. Dresden was then considering the building of high speed lines which would run to outer suburbs and this design was intended to allow the tramways to compete on equal terms with the motorbus with regard to speed, passenger comfort, capacity and safety, and to provide improved conditions for the crew. However, the undertaking required very strict budget control over the project and insisted that the cost should not be greater than that of a conventional car. The first car was delivered on 23 December 1929, an excellent Christmas present for the people of Dresden and the two prototypes were demonstrated during a conference of the Verband des Deutscher Verkehrsverwaltungen (Union of German Transport Undertakings) in September 1930.

The design was that of a double-ended bogie car, whose floor height was only 70cm above rail level, considerably lower than that of most existing cars. There were no internal partitions and this was really the first "Grossraumwagen", although that designation was not used at the time. The driving position was closed off by a door when in use. The saloon provided comfortable accommodation for seated passengers and the sharply-tapered ends allowed the car to have unrestricted route availability. It also afforded the driver good protection in the event of a collision. But the most novel feature of the design was the push-button control system, linked to an underfloor master controller, which provided 16 steps for acceleration and ten for braking. This gave fast and smooth acceleration and also lessened driver fatigue. For the carefully-controlled expenditure of a few thousand Reichsmarks, Dresden had a car which could compare quite favourably with the PCC.

After trials with two prototypes (1701/2), which were a complete success, 31 cars (1703-1733) were acquired between 1931 and 1933. Cars 1715-1724 were built by LHB, the rest by Christoph and Unmack, though some were completed in the undertaking's own workshops. Regular service on lines 11 and 15 began on 20 October 1931. Eight trams were totally destroyed in the air raids of February and April 1945 and the survivors were then renumbered up to 1725. Two new cars to the original design were built by VEB Waggonbau Görlitz in 1954 and all the earlier cars were fitted with new bogies, also from Görlitz, between 1951 and 1955, the originals having begun to develop cracks, due to the over-

Hechtwagen 1705 at Weinböhla, on the occasion of the opening of the tramway to that village on 14 November 1931. Professor Bockemühl is standing nearest the car. (Dresdner Verkehrsbetriebe)

crowding of the war and immediate post-war years. These bogies were a modified version of those designed for the planned German standard tram, four sets of which had been delivered to Dresden and the fitting of them to the Hechtwagen required the floor height to be raised. As they were considered to be unsuitable for conversion to one person operation, the

Dresden car 1716 at Postplatz after a special tour in September 1992. (Author)

The driving position of a Hechtwagen. (Author)

Essen 2902 as a trailer at the rear of a set on line 8 in 1963. (F.W. Hunt collection, courtesy London Area, Light Rail Transit Association)

Ex-Düsseldorf 118 in service with Stern und Hafferl as 20.108, at Gmunden Traundorf station in June 1981. (Author)

Hechtwagen were all withdrawn in 1970/1. Nos. 1702 and 1716 have been preserved, the former in the city's transport museum, the latter by the undertaking in running order. This was a revolutionary design, which gave excellent service in difficult conditions and most cars ran over three million kilometres. But for the economic crisis and the arrival of Hitler, there would probably have been more.

Bogie cars with some modern features were also built for Essen, Düsseldorf, Halle and Hamburg. Only those for the first of these showed any great degree of innovation. They were developed as a result of co-operation between Dr Kreissig, director of the Uerdingen factory, and Dr W. Prasse, engineer of the Essen undertaking. The intention was to develop a bogie car using lightweight construction, which would thus achieve improved performance using existing types of equipment. The first two, delivered in 1933 (503/4) were very light, at 11.6 tonnes, but nonetheless could carry 84 passengers, 34 seated. They had monomotor bogies with cardan drive on to one axle and rubber insert wheels, which did not become standard until the 1950s. Riding qualities were excellent. Their length of 12.63m gave them the nickname of "Lange Essener". Twenty slightly shorter and heavier cars (511-530) came from Düwag between 1938 and 1940. In these the single motor drove both axles and the bogies had inside frames, as on PCC cars. Nine cars and prototype 503 were destroyed in the air raids of 1943/4 and the others were renumbered 501-512 after the war. Unfortunately the main series had been built with inferior materials and by 1950 this was showing in bowing of the body and frequent motor problems. Five were rebuilt as trailers but all had gone by 1971. The Düsseldorf cars (106-119) were more conventional and of metre gauge, though the bogies were constructed in such a way as to be easily converted to standard gauge. Five of the ten survivors were sold to Aachen in 1962, where they lasted until 1969. The other five went to the Stern und Hafferl undertaking in Austria and remained in service until the mid-1980s. However, most operators remained wedded to the traditional concept of vehicle design and further development was hindered by the onset of economic depression, which effectively ended the building of new trams for some years, then by the attitude of the NS government which, in common with views held elsewhere, regarded trams as being out of date. A design of a new bogie tram was prepared

for Berlin, and showed a car with attractive rounded ends, but it was not actually built and it may simply have been a propaganda exercise.

It was only when the manager of the Nürnberg undertaking pointed out forcefully – and rather bravely – that without his trams there would be no Nürnberg rallies, that official attitudes began to change. It was also realised that trams ran on home-produced fuel, a useful point in time of war, and that Germany was not keeping pace with other countries, in particular Norway and Sweden. NS thinking favoured centralisation, which would now work to the advantage of the tram, and in 1938 a working party of the Reichverkehrsgruppe Schienenbahnen (State Working Party on Tramways) was set up to plan a range of standard trams (Einheitsstrassenbahnwagen) for future construction. There would have been three types each of motor cars and trailers and some of the features of the "Hechtwagen" were adopted for the proposed bogie car. The trucks were almost exact copies and the body styling, with five windows per side and pointed ends, followed the Dresden example closely. Internal layout would have been of traditional design, with partitions separating platforms from the saloon, and fare collection would have been by an itinerant conductor. The car was intended mainly for operation on radial lines. None of the proposals showed much reference to developments elsewhere. However, due to the pressure of war, the Ministry of Transport on 8 July 1942 suspended all work on this and other designs in favour of the war time two-axle standard car, the KSW (Kriegsstrassenbahnwagen) (qv). Eight bogie cars built for Halle in 1940 (28-35), for use on the radial line to Merseburg, were the nearest approach to the planned design to enter service, but they were shorter and had a different window layout. There were also eight matching trailers (191-198) delivered in 1942, of which car 193 is preserved.

The influence of the Dresden Hechtwagen, in a more concrete form, was through Hamburg, where several types of bogie car were already in service, alongside a large fleet of two-axle cars. Between 1938 and 1941 three prototypes (3067/8/9) of what was intended to be class V4 entered service. They were not all identical as they were built by Westwaggon, Credé and Uerdingen respectively and the last, 3069, was a lightweight car of only 15.2 tonnes, but all shared the general outline of the Hechtwagen and the first two had the same semi-automatic push-

button control. Unfortunately all three were lost in the air raids of 1943.

Technical details

Dresden Hechtwagen
Length 14.475m, width 2.3m, weight, 21 tonnes, 4 x 55kW motors, 81 passengers, 36 seated.
Essen 511
Length 11.84m width 2.16m, weight 12.8 tonnes, 2 x 59kW motors, 68 passengers, 28 seated.
Hamburg 3069
Length 14.6m, width 2.2m, weight 15.2 tonnes, 4 x 42kW motors, 87 passengers, 36 seated.

Bibliography

50 Jahre Einheitsstrassenbahnwagen – Der Weg bis zum KSW. G. Bauer/B-L Schmidt. E.K.Verlag, Freiburg, 1994.
Der Stadtverkehr 11/12/1981 (Dresden Hechtwagen).
Der Grosse Hechtwagen. DVG reprint from house magazine, 1992.
Die Fahrzeuge der Dresdner Strassenbahn. M. Schatz. Verlagsbüro I Reintzsch, Leipzig, 1993.
Strassenbahn Magazin no.192, October 2005. (Essen cars), no.198, April 2006 (Hamburg).

Preserved trailer 193 in Halle in October 2002. (Author)

USSR AND EASTERN EUROPE

Leningrad car 4041 leads another of the class in 1966. (Pam Eaton)

Although there were a few bogie cars in the USSR built by the Kolomna factory from 1926 onwards, based on USA interurban design, the first modern bogie trams did not appear until 1933. Their construction followed on from a decision taken at the All-Union Communist Party Plenum on Housing and Development on 15 June 1931 to build a special factory for the production of bogie trams. This was duly constructed and was located on the outskirts of Leningrad. Before it was completed, a design team under the leadership of Dmitry Kondratev, prepared a two-car set of motor and trailer (4021/2), each being 15m long and 2.6m wide, built in the Leningrad tramway workshops. These were double-ended, but were found to be heavy and too cramped for city service. The next prototypes were single-ended Peter Witt style cars with two doors (4023/4), and with three doors (4025/6), which appeared in 1934. A poll revealed that neither passengers nor crews liked the Peter Witt system and production cars used the middle door as entrance and the two end doors for exit. Originally known as MA and MP (American motor and American trailer), the production vehicles were re-designated LM and LP (Leningrad motor/trailer) at the height of the cold war. Between 1934 and 1936 no fewer than 240 motors and an equal number of trailers were placed in service (4001-4480), the motor cars having odd and trailers even numbers. They had composite wood and metal bodies, 15m long and 2.6m wide. The wooden doors were air-operated and the conductor normally stood near the middle door, the front and rear doors being used as exits. Pennsylvania bogies gave a good ride, even on poor track. Many trams were destroyed during the siege of Leningrad, but the survivors ran until 1979 and cars 4275 and 4454 were saved and fully restored to running order in 1997.

Moscow was clearly not going to be outdone and in December 1935 four streamlined all-metal cars (1001-1004) were delivered by the SVARZ works in that city. The first two cars worked in multiple unit formation, having contactor control and regenerative braking, while 1004 was a trailer. In styling they resembled the Brill pre-PCC car for Chicago (7001) and it would be interesting to learn if this was deliberate! A production series of 60 cars (1006-1065, class M38) followed in 1938 from the Mystischstchi factory. These also had some resemblance to the PCC cars then being placed in service in the USA but copied the passenger flow of the Leningrad LP33 cars. Length was 14.5m, weight 22.5 tonnes and a total of 101 passengers could be carried, 49 seated. They ran until the early 1980s. Leningrad in 1936 had one set known as the "blue train" which had a PCC type accelerator and triple width central doors, but no further examples of this type were built. Nine broadly similar cars were built for Kiev, which had in 1934 equipped two traditional, though new, bogie cars with contactor control and regenerative braking and converted two two-axle cars to run as control trailers with these. In 1938 Kiev also had a three-car train with a bogie non-driving motor in the centre. But all the other systems in the USSR still had to make do with very conventional equipment and pre-war plans for a standard bogie car foundered on arguments about the length that this should be. No further progress had been made by the time war engulfed the country.

Apart from Jugo-Slavia, all other countries in the region remained faithful to the two-axle car for urban service during this period. Beograd acquired two batches of bogie cars in the late 1930s, one built by Skoda, to an attractive streamlined design, the other, with a boxy and old-fashioned outline, built in Jugo-slavia by Duro Dakovic. Neither class was technically advanced in any way. Of the second class, car 27 has been preserved.

Bibliography

Tramways and Urban Transit nos.657, September 1992 and 661, January 1993.

Beograd 3, in August 1969. (Author)

NORWAY AND SWEDEN

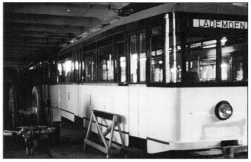

Trondheim 6, seen under overhaul in Voldsminde depot in May 1983. (Author)

The modern era of bogie trams in Scandinavia began in 1937, when Trondheim, Oslo and Göteborg all placed cars of this type in service. The Trondheim cars, nos.1-4, built by Skabo, were single-ended and of attractive contemporary design, but did not show many modern characteristics apart from air operated folding doors and a separate cab for the driver, who was given a seat. As the control equipment, by SSW, did not allow for series/parallel operation, they were heavy on current. Two further cars (5, 6) were delivered in 1942 but lacked motors as the Siemens factory in Berlin had just been bombed and it was not until 1948 that these cars could be put into service, having been fitted with BT-H motors. These proved to be unreliable and the two cars spent much time out of service. This probably ensured the survival of car 6, which was stored in Voldsminde depot on 10 October 1956 and so escaped destruction when all other modern bogie cars were burned in the fire which destroyed Dalsenget depot. The car has since been preserved in operating condition. Trucks, frames and motors from most of the others were used in the construction of replacement bogie cars in 1957.

Although the Oslo city operator, Oslo Sporvej (OS) had considered both the Dresden Hechtwagen and the PCC car in pre-war years, none were bought and the old two-axle cars soldiered on. The firm of Strømmen instead persuaded OS to experiment with a new design, suitable for both city and suburban service. Due to the form of the rear end, the class was known as "Guldfiskar" or "Goldfish" and these trams were unlike any seen elsewhere before or since. The design did, however, owe something to the PCC car and also to buses which had recently been built by Strømmen for Norwegian Railways.

Six prototypes were placed in service in 1937, using a variety of motors and control equipment. Some had Metropolitan-Vickers equipment and in service sounded exactly like a Glasgow Coronation car. Despite considerable teething troubles, the operator liked the design and two production batches, each of 20 cars, followed in 1938-40, class E1 for the city lines and class B1 for the suburban lines. The latter had been fitted for m.u operation. Class E1 was built by Skabo with AEG equipment, class B1 by Strømmen with M-V equipment. These were a good deal heavier than the prototypes, which had variously weighed 12.9 or 13.4 tonnes. Apart from the streamlined body form, the most revolutionary feature of the type was the lightweight frameless construction in aluminium. They were the first

Oslo "goldfish" car 159 on LRTA tour in May 1983 and a rear view (below). (Author)

single-ended cars in Oslo. Internally they were divided into two saloons, with seats for 48 passengers, mainly four abreast, while 52 standing passengers could be carried.

Three cars (164-166) were sent for service in Düsseldorf during the later years of the war. The Germans seem not to have noticed their width of 2.65m or their single-ended design and the Norwegians did not see any need to remind them of these features. In consequence they saw no service in their temporary home and all returned safely after the war. Having only a centre doorway for entry and exit and a small front exit door, the cars were not totally suitable for urban operation and two conductors had to be carried at peak periods. In the early 1950s, all were concentrated on the suburban lines, where they served until 1985. Unfortunately the class was responsible for the only serious accident in the history of OS. On the morning of 2 August 1958 a fire broke out in car 198, owing to an electrical fault, and spread so rapidly that four passengers died. The class was converted for one-person operation in 1970/1, when the prototypes were withdrawn. Ten have been converted for use as works cars or preserved, one as a static café in the city centre, and one, no.299 ex-188, was sold to Kochi in Japan, where the body was narrowed and the trucks converted to 1067mm gauge. A door was also fitted on the former offside, to allow left hand running.

The "Goldfish" were revolutionary cars, perhaps too much so, since they required very careful maintenance and the design was not copied anywhere else. They had the acceleration of a sports car, their riding qualities were superb, speeds on Oslo's reserved track suburban lines were high and they were incredibly quiet in operation.

Technical details
Oslo prototype 158
Length 15.4m, width 2.4m, weight 12.9 tonnes, 4 x 36.5kW motors, 100 passengers, 48 seated.
Trondheim 1-4

Length 12m, width 2.6m, weight 14.5 tonnes, 4 x 30kW motors, 90 passengers, 38 seated.

Bibliography
Modern Tramway no.301, January 1963 (Trondheim)
Oslo-Trikken – Storbysjel på skinner. H.A. Fristad. Glyndal Norsk Forlag, Oslo. 2nd edition, 1990
Die Strassen- und Vorortbahnen in Oslo. N.C. Aspenberg. Baneforlaget, 1994

Although GS in Göteborg had begun to develop bus services from 1925 onwards, they had no intention of neglecting the tram network and in 1935 a study visit was made to Dresden, where the members of the group were much impressed by the "Hechtwagen". Many of the electrical features of this design were then incorporated into a new bogie car, no.210, which was delivered by ASEA in 1937. This elegant car had a tapered front end, like the German cars, but the windscreen was sharply raked and the rear end was square. The car was single-ended but double-sided, to allow passengers to load from central islands on reserved track. The centre and rear doors were double-width, that at the rear being used for boarding and the central and front doors for alighting. It was scrapped in 1957.

Bibliography
Zeppelinare, Limpor och Mustanger. S. Hammarson. F Stenvalls Förlag, Malmö, 1979

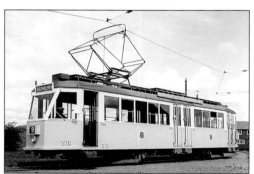

Car 210 when new. (GS, S. Hammarson collection)

FRANCE

The only modern bogie cars in France at this period was a series of 16 built for the radial Electrique-Lille-Roubaix-Tourcoing by Brissoneau et Lotz in 1937, to increase capacity on the boulevard lines. They were somewhat similar to the cars of the Vicinal but had an attractive rounded end design – they were double-ended – and rode smoothly on Pennsylvania bogies. They were numbered 200-215 and were the first modern bogie cars in France. They lasted until the 1970s and car 213 has been preserved in Paris by AMTUIR.

Car 213 in the St Mandé musuem. (Author)

AUSTRALIA

Melbourne car 469 on driver training duties at Thornbury depot in March 1986, with Z3 car 188 passing on the left. (Author)

In 1927 the MMTB in Melbourne built one car (469, class Y) which was a double-ended Peter Witt design, but lacked the post for a seated conductor. Contemporary reports issued by the operator suggested that it was built to test the practicability of one person operation, but, if so, this idea was not followed through and instead 469 spent its first years in service as a tourist car. From about 1936 it was transferred to all-night services and peak hour extras and was withdrawn from these in 1965. From 1972 it reappeared as a driving instruction car, in which capacity it is still sometimes used. However, in 1992 it was given a very thorough overhaul and most of its original features restored. In 1929 it was followed into service by four similar cars of class Y1 (610-613) which had a slightly different windscreen design. Their history is basically that of car 469 and they were withdrawn from normal service in 1965. All still exist and are used on driver training duties, except for 613 which had a similar overhaul to 469 in 1992 and is often used on tourist services. It was unfortunate that this design was not taken further, but given that these trams appeared just before the economic depression, it was inevitable that they would be looked on with suspicion by the trade unions as a Trojan horse for one person operation, and that the traditional design would be preferred.

Technical details
MMTB Y class 469
Length 13.87m, width 2.64m, weight 16.8 tonnes, 4 x 30kW motors, 53 seated passengers.

Bibliography
Destination City. Op.cit.

An interior view of Melbourne 469. (Author)

NORTH AMERICA

In North America, a few operators continued to prefer modern bogie cars to PCC cars even after development of the latter was well under way. Indianapolis Railways opted for state-of-the-art traditional cars and bought three batches of modified Brill Master Unit cars (101-190) between 1933 and 1935. These had pedal control and an interior that was fully up to PCC standards and may be considered the ultimate traditional bogie car in the US. However, it seemed that passengers preferred the new trolleybuses and the new cars could not save the system, which finally closed on 11 January 1953. United Railways and Electric Company of Baltimore took 150 similar cars and other operators bought the design in small numbers, a total of around 412 being built. Sixty of these were exported to Santiago, Chile and that operator later built or rebuilt 16 cars to the same design.

The Third Avenue Railway Company in New York City was caught between a rock, in the form of anti-tram mayor La Guardia, who would not allow any increase in the five cent fare, and the hard place of public demand for something better than its antiquated fleet. It went some way to solving the problem by constructing 334 cars in its own workshops between 1934 and 1940, after buying a prototype from Brill. Of the new trams, 75 (551-625) were double-ended Peter Witt cars for use on Broadway and were equipped for conduit operation only. The remainder were of front entrance, rear exit layout and equipped for both conduit and trolley working. All ran on Brill-type 77E trucks and incorporated many parts from scrapped cars. They were all of lightweight construction, though weight varied from batch to batch. The last few Broadway cars were built solely of aluminium and weighed 14.75 tonnes. One of these, no.555, remained unpainted, the aluminium simply being varnished over. While these were certainly an improvement on the cars they replaced and did incorporate some modern refinements, the lightweights could not approach the standard of the PCC car. The management was slightly defensive about these trams and the engineer wrote a letter to the technical press pointing out the advantages of re-using old parts and the reduction of costs thus brought. No other operator seemed to be convinced by this! Political manoeuvrings would have had them off the streets by 1942 but the war prolonged their service until 1946 in the city centre and 1952 in the suburbs. Many were sold for further service. Sao Paulo bought the 25 newest Broadway cars which ran until the late 1960s and one has been preserved. Of the rear exit cars, 20 were bought by Lima in Peru, 40 went to Bombay where they

New York Third Avenue car 674, as running at Crich. (Author)

Ex-New York car 4222 in service on line 11 in Wien in August 1968. (Author)

New York car in Bombay, as BEST 45. (Hugh Ballment)

Ottawa 1000 at the depot. (Lars F. Richter collection)

were narrowed and gave good service until the end of that system in 1964, while 42 were shipped to Vienna under the auspices of the Marshall Plan. In that city, where they were classed as Z and given numbers in the 42xx series, passenger flow was reversed to run from rear to front. Of these, one (679) is preserved in Vienna, one has been returned to the USA for preservation at the Branford Museum and car 674 is at the National Tramway Museum at Crich.

Although chronologically belonging to another chapter, the strange case of Ottawa can more logically be mentioned here. In 1947 that undertaking bought four totally conventional bogie cars (1000-1003) from the Ottawa Car Company, based on its last new cars of 1934 and using trucks acquired from New York. They were expensive, given the nature of the order and it was calculated that ten PCC cars could have been obtained for the same amount! They lasted until just before the system closed in 1959.

Technical details

Brill Master Unit – prototype 1928
Length 12.36m, width 2.52m, weight 13.55 tonnes, 4 x 25kW motors, 44 seated passengers.
Indianapolis cars
Length 12.4m, width 2.56m, weight 165.2 tonnes, 4 x 25kW motors, 55 seated passengers.
Third Avenue Railway Co. 685 (1939)
Length 12.96m, width 2.53m, weight 16.95 tonnes, 4 x 25kW motors, 44 seated passengers

In the US export field, the only non-PCC development in this period was the supply of at least 15 cars to Bogotá in 1938, almost the last export order for trams completed by Brill. They were single-ended cars of Peter Witt layout, but lacked platform doors at the front and ran on metre gauge. They were nicknamed "Lorencitas" after the wife of the-then president of Colombia. The tramways closed after a riot in 1951 and the cars disappeared.

Bibliography
Across New York by Trolley. F.A. Kramer. Quadrant Press, New York, 1975.
Latin America by Streetcar. Allen Morrison
Electric Car Builders' Images. Branford Electric Railway Journal, vol.38, 2004.

GREAT BRITAIN

It is sad to have to record that Britain played very little part in the development of modern trams from 1927 onwards. Municipal conservatism, the attachment to the double-decker, the reactionary thinking of the Metropolitan Police in London and the large dose of cold water thrown on tramways by the Royal Commission on Transport of 1930 all militated against development. Even where new designs were placed in service, such as the Glasgow Coronation cars and the many new cars in Liverpool in the 1930s, these were essentially traditional and, although very comfortable, showed no operational advance on the trams which had gone before them.

One of the main innovators in the 1920s was Christopher J. Spencer, tramways manager of the Underground group of companies in London. Along with other officers from the group, he took part in a study visit to the USA in the autumn of 1919 and, among other cities, visited Cleveland, whose system he greatly admired. He was also quite impressed by the Birney car and by coupled car operation as practised in Philadelphia. When reporting to senior staff after his return, he had a good many harsh things to say about British tramcar manufacturers and their continued attachment to designs of twenty years previously.

The first practical result of this visit was the conversion of a Metropolitan Electric Tramways single-decker for one man operation in 1920. This had doors interlocked with the control circuits, but seems not to have had the other safety features of the Birney car. It was tried on the line to Alexandra Palace but later went to the London United Tramways, where it was joined by three converted bogie cars, cut down to single-deck form. They worked successfully enough in the Hanwell area but were withdrawn and replaced by double-deckers in 1928, being scrapped in 1931.

The next innovation was an experiment in 1923 with passenger flow from rear to front on a conventional double-deck bogie car, no.315 of class H. To avoid the need for additional staircases, this car was fitted with a unique rotating staircase. In service this was turned through 180 degrees to allow passengers to leave by a front exit which had been cut in the side panels. The platforms were extended by 75cm to accommodate this feature. The need to turn stairs at termini caused delays and after a very short period, the stairs remained fixed in the normal position. By 1925 the car had been rebuilt to standard layout.

However, Spencer still hankered after a chance to put into practice the ideas which had so impressed him in Cleveland, and in December 1925 received permission to construct an experimental car laid out for passenger flow from rear to front. This he called a "circulating car". This tram was built by the MET at Hendon and the result was no.318, often known as "Bluebell" from its attractive light blue livery. For the first time in Britain a double-decker had been designed specifically for this form of working, as opposed to rather awkward conversions of existing designs. The body was of lightweight construction and the saloons, which had no internal bulkheads, had a light and airy appearance. The crews who worked it in service were carefully chosen and were kitted out in light blue uniforms to match the tram. Air brakes were fitted but these gave a good deal of trouble in service and, with a view to m.u. operation, contactor control was installed. No.318 entered service on 12 March 1927 and proved to have excellent acceleration. Unfortunately on 17 June 1927 it was involved in a crash when the air brake failed, and the driver was killed. It was then rebuilt with standard controllers and fitted with magnetic track brakes. The entrances and exits were enlarged at the same time. In 1929 a deep domed roof was fitted and the tram was withdrawn in 1936 and scrapped. As the board of the Underground group had decided that there should be a second experimental tram, a second car, no.319, known as "Poppy", was built by the London General Omnibus Company at Chiswick works. It was not laid out for passenger flow, although it had additional standing space on the enclosed platforms; it looked rather like two NS type motorbuses coupled back-to-back. After the accident to no.318, this tram was also given magnetic track brakes and was scrapped in 1935.

Experience gained with these two trams was then used in the construction of three experimental trams built by the subsidiary Union Construction Company, located at Feltham in Middlesex and which gave this class of tram the name by which it was always known. These were numbered 320 and 330 and were constructed to the pattern of no.318. However, they were

Feltham car 549 at Halton terminus in Leeds on 26 March 1958. (Author)

An enthusiastic crowd, representing a good cross-section of Bombay society, gathers round no.751 on a demonstration run at Fort terminus in 1931. (Author's collection)

designed to give room for an increased number of standees, had straight stairs and the second car was also originally given a post for the conductor on the nearside just ahead of the entrance doors. To allow this system to operate, the stairs were reversed and so rose towards the rear of the car. This car also had four motors. The trams entered service in May and November 1929 respectively and both proved to be successful and very popular with the travelling public, but the PAYE system on no.330 was abandoned after a very few trips, as the complex fare structure made it impractical. No.320 was scrapped in 1937 but no.330, by now 2167, was transferred to south London in 1938 and ran there until 1949.

The third experimental car was of central entrance design and is dealt with in the appropriate chapter.

There followed a production series of 100 cars, 54 for the MET and 46 for the London United Tramways, in December 1930. They followed the design of no.320, but the driver's cab was raised to allow easier operation of the controller from a seated position. Seats were provided for 42/22 passengers, but generous standing space in the vestibules for 20 passengers took the total capacity to 84, slightly more than a conventional LCC bogie tram. The front exit was fitted with an air-operated door, under control of the driver. The accommodation was to a very high standard and the trams proved popular with crews and passengers alike. The front exits fell out of use during the wartime blackout and were not reinstated after the war ended. The cars had been transferred to south London in 1937/8 and, on the post-war conversion of these routes in 1950-52,

91 were sold on to Leeds. Not all were commissioned in their new home, but those which were gave good service until 1959.

The Felthams and their two experimental predecessors represent the only large-scale trial in Britain of the feature of modern trams which were by 1939 taken for granted in other countries and, although they came too late for London, were successful and popular cars in both that city and in Yorkshire. They were fast and smooth riding and in the pre-war years showed that passenger flow could be made to work in British conditions. A simplification of the very complex London fare system would also have allowed operation with a seated conductor. But by 1934 the new London Passenger Transport Board had decided in favour of the trolleybus and by 1946 even that form of transport had been rejected in favour of small motorbuses, of traditional layout. The Felthams did not stand a chance of influencing future development.

The LCC seems to have thought of copying the front exit principle and a car classified E2 was designed with this feature. To accommodate it, the bulkheads were angled across the car. There were no other new features of the design and, perhaps fortunately, it was not actually built.

Technical details

Production Feltham design, without plough for conduit operation
Length 12.34m, width 2.18m, weight 18.5 tonnes, 2 x 45kW motors, 84 passengers, 64 seated.

Bibliography

The Metropolitan Electric Tramways. C. S. Smeeton. Light Rail Transit Association, Broxbourne, 1986.

Liverpool Corporation acquired one single-deck car from English Electric in 1928, no.757. This was designed for possible use in subways, with trailers, or in m.u. formation and was based closely on the Blackpool "pantograph" cars, built at the same time. In layout it was totally conventional, with platforms which were really too narrow for urban service, but it was fitted with monomotor bogies and so anticipated modern practice by many years. It remained a one-off and was scrapped in 1935.

Glasgow in 1926 acquired one high speed single-decker, no.1089, which was intended to test a design which could win back passengers lost to competing bus services. Technically this car was a success, being fast and comfortable with excellent acceleration, but its seating capacity of only 36 was too low for Glasgow conditions and its narrow platforms delayed it and following cars in service. It was only 9.6m long and to have been a success, it would have had to be longer and wider, but clearances would not have allowed this. Nonetheless, unlike many one-off experimental trams, "Wee Baldy" (a nickname derived from its cream, domed roof) led a charmed life and survived the Clydebank blitz of March 1941, at the expense of spending several days out in the street, cut off from the rest of the system. It really came into its own in 1951 when it was rebuilt as a standee car for shipyard services and it could then accommodate a total of 58 passengers. It thus survived until 1960 when a ridiculous change in regulations reduced its standing capacity to only five. However it continued to make odd appearances and came back

Car 1089 on a peak-hour working at Yoker on 13 April 1961, after its return to traffic (Author)

Johannesburg no.9 at the depot in post-war years. (Tony Spit, author's collection)

fitting a narrow doorway at the front. They lacked the safety interlocking of the Birney cars. In 1930/1 the three cars mentioned above were similarly converted, by the simple expedient of removing the rear platform and moving the stairs to the other side of the body. Finally one car which had been in an accident was rebuilt to this design. There was very little that was modern about the Hobart cars but they deserve a mention as pioneers of one-man operation by double-deckers.

In 1934 Johannesburg Municipal Transport acquired two all-metal double-deckers built by Metropolitan-Cammell, a bogie car (2) and a two-axle car (9). Both were very well-finished and had straight stairs and front exits, with air-operated doors. However, these features reduced the seating capacity to 60 and 48 respectively and this was a drawback on a system whose traffic patterns had always required cars with high seating capacity. Although both cars were licensed for 30 standees, the designs were not perpetuated and later deliveries reverted to conventional layout and a greater number of seats.

Bibliography

Double-deck Trams of the World. B. Patton. Adam Gordon, Brora, 2002

It would seem that attempts to build double-deckers with a layout suitable for passenger flow were almost all unsuccessful. Only the design of the Felthams and Bombay no.751 surmounted the basic problems, while the Johannesburg bogie car might have worked better on a system which had more short distance riders in the city centre. Single-deckers were better adapted to the development of new methods of operation.

into service in March 1961 following the loss of trams in the fire in Dalmarnock depot. Its luck thus held and it appeared in the final procession on 4 September 1962. To-day it is preserved in the city's transport museum, an excellent illustration of what might have been.

Technical details

Length 9.6m, width 2.18m, 4 x 18kW motors, 46 passengers, 36 seated.

Bibliography

Liverpool Transport vol.3, 1900-1930. J. B. Horne and T. B. Maund. Transport Publishing Company and Light Rail Transit Association, Glossop, 1982.

The Glasgow Tramcar. I. Stewart. Scottish Tramway Museum Society, Glasgow, 1983

Some other British operators in the 1920s fitted front exits to conventional double-deck cars, both bogie and two-axle but only Newcastle Corporation persisted with these for any length of time. These were two-axle cars and, as platform doors were not fitted, the upper decks tended to become wind tunnels and they were not popular with passengers. The neighbouring Gateshead and District Company had many long bogie front exit single-deckers and they worked well until final closure in 1951, but were always operated with an itinerant conductor. None of these designs could really be classed as modern.

In the then-British empire, Bombay operated double-deckers with front exits, although the extent to which passenger flow was enforced is debatable. From photographs it would seem that Bombay passengers boarded a tram by the doorway nearest to them, using both the nearside and offside of the car in the process. There were at least 58 cars, known as the LCC class and built, after a careful study of the LCC class E/E1 cars, from 1923 to 1933. Unlike the London cars, they had straight stairs, which led down directly to the exit. A further seven, with improvements such as air brakes, were built in 1934/5, with eight following during the Second World War and 29 after it. A very fine car (751) was bought from English Electric in 1931. This was to the same basic layout but had many up-to-date features and its conception seemed to owe a good deal to the Feltham design. Unlike these cars, however, this was given a high seating capacity (50/36) and, as passengers were not allowed to stand on the front platform, no separate cab was provided for the driver.

Hobart Municipal Tramways in 1925 acquired three new two-axle cars with straight stairs and front exits. This same operator also converted seven two-axle double-deckers for one-man operation in 1930 and 1932, by closing off the rear platform, altering the stairs and

An interior view of the tram. (B. T. Cooke, author's collection)

CHAPTER 3
CENTRAL ENTRANCE TRAMS

Of all the variations from the traditional rear entrance design, the central entrance tram is by far the oldest. It is not clear when the first such tram was put into service, but it was in the 1890s. At least two advantages were claimed for this layout. The main one was that the conductor could never be more than half a car's length away from the platform, making it much easier for him to return there at stops. The other was that it was easy to segregate passengers by class, as was common in France, or to keep the smokers away from the non-smokers, as in Glasgow's first electric cars, while still allowing the former a roof over their heads.

A two-axle central entrance car was in service in the USA in 1893, though this may not have been the first. Shortly after that date, Saint Louis found this a convenient way in which to combine the bodies of two former horse cars for electric service. In Britain, both Liverpool and Glasgow used the design for some of their first electric cars, Liverpool's manager apparently being influenced by what he had seen in Cleveland and what he had been told by the manager of Montréal Street Railways, namely that the UK would soon follow the example set in North America and switch to single-deck designs. Other cities also used the concept; Dresden had in 1897 a tram of such fearsome appearance that it was nicknamed "Grosser Kurfurst" after a contemporary battleship. In Paris the Tramways de Paris et Département de la Seine placed in service in 1899 three small two-axle cars of type PC with a central platform, the first of what was to become the most typical design of Parisian electric tram. Central entrance trams in cities such as Cleveland and the experimental double-deckers in New York, Pittsburgh, Columbus and Wien have been mentioned in Chapter 1. The Glasgow trams were prone to derail and were all out of passenger service within ten years, but the Liverpool cars fared rather better and lasted until the early 1920s. Three were rebuilt with an upper deck and in this condition could carry 114 passengers.

Liverpool then tried to adopt some of these concepts in a very advanced bogie tram (572) ordered from the UEC at Preston on 2 May 1912 and placed in service on 13 March 1913. This had a central platform divided into three sections, the outer ones for exit and the middle one for entry and two straight staircases, similarly designated, both of which led upwards from one of the saloons. The platform sections were separated by gates and barriers were used to close the platform when the car was in motion. These were interlocked with the starting signal, which could not be given until they were closed. When the car first entered service, there was no information about which part of the platform served which function and passengers were somewhat bemused until signs were applied to remedy this. Seating capacity was 51/32 and passengers in the lower saloon enjoyed the luxury of rattan-upholstered seats; no standing passengers were carried. UEC equal-wheel bogies were fitted, with air brakes, which were perhaps not suffi-

cient for the car's weight of 18 tons under all conditions, since it was confined to services in the flatter areas of the city. Sadly, this tram remained alone in the fleet; it was probably too advanced for its time and was unpopular with staff. It also came at the wrong time, since the years immediately after 1914 were not conducive to experiments and it was out of service by 1921, though not scrapped until later. The tram had certain features in common with the cars in Pittsburgh, but it is not clear if there was any exchange of information before the trams were built. For the time being, the future in Britain lay with the conventional double-decker.

In the USA, Cleveland continued to favour the central entrance layout and the first cars ordered after Peter Witt had become Street Railway Commissioner were 100 such trailer cars, built by the G. C. Kuhlman Car Company in 1912.

FRENCH DESIGNS

The first large scale use of the type in the modern sense was seen in Paris. In 1905, the Compagnie Générale des Omnibus (CGO) – despite its title the city's main tramway operator – placed in service the first of its 400 class cars, with platforms which were strictly speaking off-central, since the two saloons were not of equal length, due to the provision of first and second class. These were followed by the 500 class, of which 579 is preserved. In 1912 two of seven experimental cars were of central entrance layout and it was decided that this should be adopted as standard. Subsequently a total of 200 bogie cars of class B and 386 two-axle cars of class G were

These were soon followed by 200 more, then by 201 similar motor cars and other operators copied the layout. Genève acquired a batch of handsome cars in 1911 and these continued in service until the late 1950s. Some other European cities used central entrance motor trams and trailers in the 1920s and 1930s, the latter having generally a low step height and being fairly accessible. Brno had one motor car (150) in 1931 as had Stettin and Istanbul (Asiatic lines). Amsterdam had two-axle trailers of this type, known as "nougat blocks", while the NZH interurban operated some very fine trailers with double centre entrance layout. Frankfurt (M) also had some well-designed bogie trailers. In other continents, the design appeared in cities as diverse as Madras, Shanghai, Tunis, Cape Town, Colombo and Batavia, often in conjunction with a two-class fare system.

Paris. An L class car with an A trailer, operating as a "rame reversible" turns into the loop terminus at Porte Maillot on New Year's Day 1932. (RATP)

constructed, these being symmetrical in layout. There were also 325 one-class bogie trailers of class A. As there were only two steps from road level to the platform, the trams were much more accessible than those they replaced. The design worked well in practice and was copied by other operators in Paris as well as in many French provincial systems. In 1914 the CGO tried multiple unit operation with an intermediate trailer and also placed in service the first "rame reversible" (reversible two-car set) consisting of a G class motor car and an A class trailer fitted with a driving position.

One of the USA operators to adopt this layout was the Philadelphia and Western radial line and one of their cars has been preserved. No.62 is seen at the Seashore Trolley Musuem in August 1974. (Author)

The preserved Glasgow central entrance "room and kitchen" car 672, in the original transport museum in the former car works at Coplawhill, the place of its birth. (Author)

Liverpool car 572 in service in Whitechapel in July 1913. (H. G. Dibdin, courtesy Martin Jenkins)

Although the m.u. experiment was short-lived, owing to complaints of the congestion caused by such a long train in the city streets, the concept of a reversible motor/trailer set was adopted by the Société des Transports en Commun de la Région Parisienne (STCRP) which took over all the capital's tramways on 1 January 1921. For this operator 100 motor cars of an improved G class were placed in service in 1922, with 150 new trailers, many of which were fitted with a driving position. These were followed in 1923 by the first of class L, a two-axle design, of which

Detail of the central entrance of 572. (MPTE, courtesy Martin Jenkins)

NZH trailer B408 at Leiden station in September 1959. (Author)

475 (2001-2475) were ultimately built. This was an advanced design using some concepts already applied to automobile technology. There was no truck frame as such, the body resting directly on the axles, with a new system of suspension by resorts and screws, and the motors were hung from the body, connected to the axles by cardan drive. Braking was by drum brakes acting on the transmission shaft of each motor. All these innovations meant that the tram was considerably lighter than its predecessors – 12.8 tonnes. A new type of self-ventilated motor was used and altogether class L was a revolutionary tram. As these motor cars were normally reserved for first class passengers, each saloon was of the same length and they were truly central entrance trams. Unfortunately this class was not totally successful in service and the lightweight construction meant that the body soon began to show signs of bowing. Expensive modifications were also necessary to the suspension and the transmission. Rubber insert wheels were tried on one tram in 1932. To run with class L in reversible formation, 245 new bogie trailers were constructed. Despite its problems, class L, operating with a trailer as a "rame reversible" proved to be a flexible unit of operation and it was a great pity that politics intervened and prevented any further development of the concepts adopted by the STCRP. Many trailers were sold to provincial systems when Paris closed and two of these (1535 and 1630) have subsequently been preserved by AMTUIR.

But in 1929 the city council had already decided to replace all tramways within the city area within five years and the suburban lines later followed, the last tram running in 1938. There were no further developments in rolling stock but the STCRP deserves every credit for innovation on a scale not seen in many other European tramways in the 1920s.

In the provinces, Nice and Saint-Quentin bought cars of class G and Lyon acquired two batches of central entrance bogie motor trams, the second with an attractive sloping windscreen, and a series of matching trailers. All these lasted until the end of the system in 1957. One of the first batch is preserved in the local transport museum.

Technical details

STCRP class L and class A trailer
Length 10.65m, width 2m, weight 12.8 tonnes, 2 x 39kW motors, 49 passengers, 28 seated.
Length 12.36m, width 2m, weight 8 tonnes, 69 passengers, 24 seated.

CITY CARS IN EUROPE 1920-1960

Rotterdam war time car 305 leaving Centraal Station on 1 September 1959. (Author)

In 1929/30 the central entrance design suddenly came back into favour on mainland Europe, with RET Rotterdam leading the way with a series of 50 bogie motor cars (401-450) and 20 matching trailers (1001-1020). They were heavy cars, the motors weighing 19.5 tonnes and the trailers 13 tonnes, but they rode superbly and were fast and comfortable in service. This was the first, and for many years the only acquisition by any city in the Netherlands of a fleet of modern trams to replace old two-axle cars, and the newcomers became extremely popular with the public. The trailers were soon rebuilt into motor cars (451-470) and 100 additional motor trams were bought in 1931 (471-570) together with 20 new trailers (1001-1020). The trams of this design were variously constructed by Allan of Rotterdam, Talbot of Aachen and Werkspoor of Utrecht. This programme provided sufficient modern trams to maintain the base service on the entire network and a number of older cars were rebuilt for peak hour use. Within a couple of years, Rotterdam had transformed itself into one of the most modern tram systems in Europe. During the war 35 of these trams were requisitioned for service in Germany, being used in Dortmund and Bremen and six were destroyed there during air raids.

The design proved to be so successful that, using spare parts and the remains of two bombed cars, Allan managed to build six new trams during and just after the war (301-306). These trams were single-ended. By this time the manager had become so convinced of the superiority of the central entrance design that it was decided to adopt it for post-war construction and in 1948 Allan delivered two prototypes (571/2) to test different control systems. The first was given an electro-pneumatic system by Sécheron and the four 63kW motors had cardan drive as on the Swiss standard trams. The second car represented one of the few successes of the British tramcar industry in the post-war years, since it was an all-electric car with Metropolitan-Vickers electro-magnetic control and four Crompton-Parkinson motors, also with cardan drive. Both could carry 85 passengers, 29 of them seated and they were soon converted to single-ended layout and renumbered 100/1. In 1963 the bogies of car

Before the first metro line was opened, Rotterdam 521 and trailer climb to the Willemsbrug on line 2 on 21 September 1962. (Author)

BVG Berlin 3344 on the former U-bahn line at Nollendorfplatz in August 1983. (Author)

BVB works car 721 016 approaches the junction at Dimitroffstrasse (now Eberswalderstrasse) in June 1979. (Author)

Leipzig's preserved car 1043 at the museum in June 2004. (Author)

Zürich. Preserved "elephant" climbs to the Zoo terminus while working on line 6 in May 2003. (Author)

100 were given air suspension by Schindler, the first application of this technology to a motor tram in Europe, but sadly it was soon afterwards involved in so serious an accident that it had to be scrapped. The production series was based on car 572, with slightly greater capacity, and entered service in 1948-50 (102-135). There were also 36 double-ended trailers (1021-1056). The development of one-person operation spelled the end for all the central entrance trams in the 1970s, but they should be remembered as an innovative design which did much to ensure the continuation of tram service in the Netherlands.

Nos. 130, 507, 525 and 542 and trailers 1040 and 1050 are preserved in Amsterdam, while nos.526, 533 and 535 are at the Netherlands open air museum at Arnhem.

Also in 1929 Zürich placed in service 50 very heavy single-ended motor trams (301-350). Because of their weight and power they became known as "elephants" and were capable of hauling two loaded trailers on gradients of 6%. During the war years, this was sometimes increased to three! Again one-person operation meant the end of their use in passenger service, but three have been preserved, one (1346) as a party tram. Leipzig in 1930 bought 56 handsome double-ended trams with clerestory roofs (Type 29, 1001-1056), which normally worked on the longer lines to the outer suburbs, pulling central entrance trailers. Unlike their counterparts in the west, these were converted for one-person operation in the late 1960s, suitably equipped with various optical and acoustic warning devices. Between 1967 and 1970 a total of 14 of these trams was transferred to the Strausberger Eisenbahn, a suburban line to the east of Berlin, where three were rebuilt as trailers. They lasted there until the 1980s, the trams remaining in Leipzig being withdrawn in 1969-71. Car 1043 has been preserved. Ten rather similar cars were built in the same year for Danzig (300-309). When one-person operation arrived in Poland in the 1950s, they all became works cars. There were also ten cars built for the Verkehrsbetriebe Oberschleschien in Gleiwitz, (then a German operator), which after the war became part of the fleet of Katowice and lasted until the late 1960s.

Technical details
Zürich 301
Length 12.2m, width 2.17m, weight 25.5 tonnes, 4 x 80kW motors, 57 passengers, 25 seated.
Leipzig 1043, as preserved
Length 15m, width 2.2m, weight 21.5 tonnes, 4 x 45kW motors, 68 passengers, 36 seated

Rotterdam 401
Length 11.5m, width 2.3m, weight 19.5 tonnes, 4 x 40kW motors, 63 passengers, 24 seated.

In 1928 the BSZKRT of Budapest introduced class OP1 trams, which had two single-width central doorways. There appear to have been 51 (3200-37 and 3300-12) of these and, in keeping with the operator's established practice, they worked as coupled sets, each car having only one driving position and one motor. They were followed by 48 double-ended cars (3500-3547) of class RV and 75 trailers of the 5600 class, some of which later acquired one controller. They survived until the 1970s.

In 1926 the Berliner Strassenbahn followed the lead of Paris and introduced a small class of ten central entrance cars (6201-6210, class TEM26) intended to operate permanently coupled back to back as a single unit. These were two-axle cars with a single motor and cardan drive. They seem to have been unsuccessful in this form and in 1932 were rebuilt as single-ended units with two nose-suspended motors per car. From 1929 onwards a series of 300 two-axle motor trams followed (originally 3301-3600, later 3300-3355, 3401-3594 and 3801-3850, classes TM33, TM36 and TM34). They were built by four builders but all had AEG electrical equipment. These were intended for m.u, operation, with two 40kW motors and an advanced all-electric control system using an underfloor master controller. This was fed directly from the overhead line supply and any failure of this rendered the braking system inoperative. After a dozen serious accidents, the entire class was put into storage in February 1931. It proved to be impossible to modify this system and in 1933 56 (TM33) were modified to run on a double control system, in which the controller in the leading car handled all the power for the unit. In 1934 50 further trams were rebuilt (TM34) with single control only and could only be used in solo operation. Finally the remaining 194 cars were rebuilt with double control, to provide additional capacity for the traffic expected for the Olympic Games of 1936 (T36). These and class T34 were also given an additional door at the front end of the car, suggesting that the central entrance had been a bottleneck in city traffic. The saga of these trams was distinctly embarrassing for what had by then become the BVG, but it had nothing to do with the use of the central entrance design. These trams were the last to run in West Berlin in 1967 when on 2 October 1967 car 3566 headed the parade of trams from Spandau to Hakenfelde. They were used in the east until 1969 when most were either rebuilt as Reko cars (qv) or converted to works cars. Five (3566, 3802, 3493, 3344 and 3337) have been preserved in Berlin and restored to represent the

Genève 159 follows two-axle car 129 up the Rue de Mont Blanc on 16 July 1955. (Author)

type at different stages of its history. Another car (3434, which lasted until 1990 as a shunter, is at the Amsterdam museum and car 3412 is at the Seashore Museum in Maine. Between 1978 and 1990 car 3344 was used on a museum service on the-then disused section of the U-Bahn between Nollendorfplatz and Bülowstrasse, along which it trundled at a very sedate pace, only the series notches of the controller being used. With re-unification, the U-Bahn was reinstated and this operation came to an end. There were also 101 further central entrance trams of class T31U (3600-3700) which were constructed by the National Automobil Gesellschaft (NAG) in 1930 using electrical equipment from old cars; these were the first to provide a seat for the driver. They had a less chequered history than the trams which were built new.

Berlin also had 50 two-axle trailers of this layout (851-900, class BDM26) built by Orenstein and Koppel between 1926 and 1928. There was one step at the entrance and the floor was only 38cm above rail level, giving rise to the nickname of U-boote (submarines). These originally had no axles and single, steerable wheels, but this feature did not work well in practice and they were rebuilt in 1937 with conventional trucks and axles. These were the first trams in Europe which were designed specifically to improve accessibility and perhaps because of access, they spent the war years on goods traffic. There were also 50 conventional two-axle trailers (1501-1550).

All in all, the German capital certainly gave the central entrance design a fair trial.

Düsseldorf in 1928 tried a somewhat similar concept with two permanently-coupled cars (241/2), which worked in double traction, each car having one 34kW motor. The system did not work well and in 1932 both were converted to trailers. They had stylish all-metal bodies with a capacity for 48 passengers, 30 seated.

Technical details

BVG 3601
Length 11m, width 2.2m, weight 11.8 tonnes, 2 x 33.5kw motors, 54 passengers, 32 seated.

Rotterdam post-war car 124 at Centraal Station in November 1968. (Author)

Gdansk. Car 1371 in service as works car, seen at Nowy Port in September 1964. (S. Hilkenbach, Evda Slides)

BRITISH SINGLE DECK CARS

No.1 outside the works when new. (West Yorkshire Library Service)

Probably the first modern single deck car was that built by Bradford Corporation in its Thornbury works in 1926/7, to the design of the General Manager, R.H. Wilkinson, and first presented to the press and the public on 8 March of the latter year. It was numbered 1 and officially called "The Pullman Car". Bradford used a gauge of 1220mm, which precluded the operation of fully enclosed double-deckers on two-axle trucks. It was hoped that a single-deck car could offer a higher standard of comfort and allow passengers to enjoy the luxury of a totally-enclosed tram, while also having a speed to match that of the new buses. The car entered service in March 1927 on the Leeds Road services. Equal wheel bogies were fitted but to avoid the expense and complication of four motors, these were each fitted with a single English Electric motor, which drove the outer axle on each bogie through worm gear. The drive was then transmitted to the other axle by a coupling rod, as on a locomotive. Air brakes and air operated sliding doors were fitted and a safety interlock prevented the doors being opened while the cars were running. The doorway had a clear width of 1.22m, but unlike later central entrance cars, there were three steps to the level of the saloon floor, which was 91cm above rail level. Externally the car was finished in varnished mahogany with a deep domed ivory roof, and internally a high standard of comfort was indeed provided for passengers, with red leather seats, diffused lighting and green linoleum covering on the floor. The driver also had a red leather seat and the controls seem to have been designed to minimise driver fatigue. In service the tram proved to be speedy, easily reaching 56km/hr and on one memorable occasion achieving 88km/hr when descending the reserved track from Thornton. Few if any contemporary buses could match that! It also ran exceptionally smoothly over points and crossings. In service, however, the

bearings of the coupling rods wore out with distressing frequency, as they could not stand up to the strains transmitted, and the car then clanked embarrassingly when running. It was also prone to wheel flats. Unfortunately the financing of this fine car was allowed to run out of control and in the end it cost almost £4,000 instead of the £2,000 allocated. No doubt this was taken into account when it was decided that the future form of transport should be the trolleybus, which Mr Wilkinson preferred anyway. Car 1 was withdrawn in April 1931 and its body used as a holiday bungalow at Filey until about 1980, when it was burned out. It was a sad end to a promising experiment, but the involvement of English Electric perhaps ensured that some good would result.

Technical details

Length 11.62m, width 2.06m, weight (est) 9.65 tonnes, 2 x 46kW motors, 70 passengers, 34 seated.

The first direct involvement of that firm with this type of tram came in 1931, when a class of six single-ended bogie trams were built for the Calcutta Tramways Company (301-306, class J). This was not strictly a central entrance design, since it was designed to take two classes of passenger and the rear portion, for those travelling second class, was rather longer than the front portion, the entrance to the second class saloon being slightly forward of centre. Entry to the first

One of Blackpool's first series English Electric railcoaches on the turning circle at Pleasure Beach in June 1958. (Author)

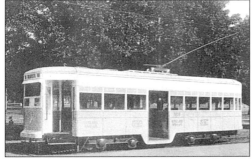

Calcutta J class 302 on Kidderpore Road when new. (English Electric, Author's collection)

Blackpool Brush car 287 leaving Starr Gate loop in February 1965. (Author)

A Marton Vambac awaits departure from Talbot Square in September 1957. (James Patton)

class saloon was by a doorway at the front, the partition enclosing the driving position being angled to accommodate this feature. Nevertheless, the main entrance was a narrower version (1.07m) of that used in class K articulated trams (qv) and this must have had some influence on the designs which followed. Class J proved inadequate for Calcutta's needs and in the 1960s all were rebuilt as class L articulated trams.

In the early 1930s the English Electric company was experiencing a decline in orders for its tramcars. At the same time, Walter Luff was appointed manager of the Blackpool undertaking, taking up his duties on 1 January 1933. Very shortly afterwards, the works manager of English Electric, W.L. Marshall, showed Luff a model of a proposed new design of bogie single-deck tram, with a central entrance. This so impressed Luff that he borrowed the model to show to his committee and their reaction was equally favourable, the result being an order for one tram, at a cost of £2000. English Electric set to work at once and the completed tram arrived in Blackpool on 19 June, just in time to have its première during the conference of the Municipal Tramways and Transport Association on 21 June. Free rides were offered from a siding at Gynn Square and a great deal of publicity for operator and manufacturer was gained. The tram was numbered 200 and painted in the new cream and green livery. It was then fitted with a pantograph but this was changed to a trolley pole by the time it entered public service on 23 June. Mr Luff's arguments for favouring the central entrance layout were ease of fare collection and supervision of the platform by the conductor, rapid loading and, rather strangely, ease of cleaning. He claimed that boarding and alighting accidents had been "considerably reduced". He did not mention accessibility, but clearly the new design was much easier of access than any other tram in Britain at that time. In service car 200 also proved to be fast, being able to cover the 12.8km from North Station to Fleetwood in 30 minutes, an average of 25.6km/hr.

Everything about this design was revolutionary. For the first time anywhere a tram had been constructed not merely as a box on wheels but as a vehicle whose attractive contemporary design would in itself be both an advertisement and an inducement to travel. The public showed their appreciation. Never before – and not often since – has a public service vehicle in Britain provided luxury of a comparable standard. Comfortable upholstered seats, heaters, extensive glazing, attractive lighting and even clocks in the saloons all showed the desire to attract the travelling public and in this respect the new tram was brilliantly successful. Within days, a batch of 24 almost identical cars (201-225) had been ordered

from English Electric and when these arrived in 1934, it was possible to run the Promenade-Fleetwood service entirely with what were now known as railcoaches. In December 1934 a further batch of 20 trams (264-283) arrived from the same builders, to be followed in 1937 by 20 further cars, this time built by Brush (284-303). There were also eleven open cars (226-236), officially known as "luxury toastracks" but generally called "boats". These proved also to be popular with passengers, except during a sudden downpour! Perhaps because of this, the last pre-war cars were twelve "sun saloons" (10-21) – semi-open cars with wooden seats, but also having folding roofs to deal with the showers. The first of these arrived only in August 1939 and they had very little chance to prove themselves in their original form.

Although these trams have been adequately discussed elsewhere, it is impossible to over-emphasise the contribution they made to British transport history. Not only did the holiday-makers love them, residents of the area also appreciated their comfort and the increased frequency which was a corollary of the operation of cars with a relatively low seating capacity (48). They encouraged the spread of urbanisation to the north of Norbreck and in the late 1930s a great deal of new housing was built along the line of the Fleetwood route. The trams were also important in that they demonstrated what a modern tram was like and what it could do, at a time when British tramway development was otherwise stagnant. Sadly even they could not ensure retention of other systems, but the reasons for this lay in municipal politics, apathy and the attitude of successive governments, not in the design of these trams.

Immediately after the end of the war in 1945 attention turned to the question of the inland Marton route, whose track had been due for renewal in 1939. The town council asked Mr Luff to prepare estimates for three options – relaying the track and buying new trams, replacing the trams with trolleybuses and replacing

In almost original condition, Coronation 313 is at Fleetwood Ferry terminus on 22 June 1958. (Author)

Trailer car 685 heads a two-car set to Fleetwood in Broadwater in August 1987. (Author)

Car 611 (ex-264) was in 1966 rebuilt with ends similar to those of the towing cars and given plastic "Darvic" panelling by ICI. This did not wear well in the salt-laden atmosphere and the car was withdrawn in 1974 to become OMO car 12. It is seen here at Manchester Square in July 1972. (Author)

Leeds 600 as preserved at Crich. (Author)

A Khartum car and trailer. (SEF photo, C. P. Mendes collection)

them with motorbuses. The costs were respectively £136,380, £87,360 and £56,940. He had also made it clear that the new trams would be of a type not hitherto used in Britain and which would offer a greatly improved standard of performance. The council decided to patch up the track while experiments with a tram of this kind were conducted.

In 1945 Crompton Parkinson Ltd had obtained from the USA certain patents used in the design of the PCC car (qv) and using these had begun to develop the system which came to be known as VAMBAC – Variable Automatic Braking and Acceleration Control. This used a joystick control, by which the driver could select the rate of acceleration and braking required; these would then take place automatically while the joystick remained in that position. If it were desired to vary them, all that was needed was to move the joystick. The system used motors permanently coupled in series-parallel pairs, fed by a resistance which had 94 steps instead of the usual eight. This gave an extremely smooth and flexible form of control. It was to be used in conjunction with trucks having rubber-insert wheels and inside frames, designed by Maley and Taunton Ltd (type HS44). Finally that firm also designed a new form of compressor, which would be almost silent in operation. A set of these trucks

was obtained and placed under car 303 and sound recordings made by the BBC on 26 April 1946, with a microphone only three feet from the wheels, showed that they were indeed almost silent in operation. Later in that year, the trucks were transferred to car 208, which was also fitted with the new form of control. Trials began in December 1946 and were so convincing that on 8 January 1947 the council decided to take the option of modernising the tram route rather than going for buses or trolleybuses. It says a great deal for the performance of the modernised 208 that hard-headed business men were prepared to follow this course of action, despite its cost, and it must be concluded that they had been convinced that the modernised Marton route would soon pay for itself in increased revenue. The increasing cost of new trams led to a decision to fit the new bogies and equipment to the 1939 "sun saloons", which were also fitted with new upholstered seats, fluorescent lighting and new floor covering. Technically the modernisation of the Marton route was a brilliant success and the trams, admired by the public, did everything that was asked of them. Unfortunately wage inflation meant that the service did not pay for itself and within a very few years it became totally uneconomic to run an urban service with trams which could carry only 53 passengers, with a two-person crew. By the mid-1950s, too, the streets along which the service ran were increasingly being used by motorists as a back door into Blackpool and, as many of these motorists were not familiar with trams, there were some accidents and many near-misses. The upshot was that the service was converted to motor buses in October 1962. Car 11 is preserved at the East Anglia Transport Museum and, after a full and very fine restoration, re-entered service there in 2005.

The next batch of central entrance cars delivered to Blackpool did not begin to arrive until 1952 and between June of that year and January 1954 25 large cars (304-328), built by C. Roberts & Co. of Horbury, Wakefield and also fitted with VAMBAC equipment went into service on the Promenade-Fleetwood route. Officially these were known as "Coronations" but to the staff they were "Spivs". While they were handsome vehicles and soon popular with passengers and crews, the maintenance staff had other views. Their purchase, which almost bankrupted the department, was really a case of buying the most advanced technology and trying to make the service fit that rather than buying the best technology for the service. Mr Luff's enthusiasm had run away with him. The equipment could not reach its full potential on the Promenade, partly because of pedestrians, partly because no one wanted to traverse that section at high speed and the bogies were not really suited to reserved track. In any case, the control equipment was susceptible to ingress of sand and dust particles, no one having realised that these would be common on a line running beside the sea. These led to short circuits and failures in traffic. They were very heavy (19 tons) and the four motors placed such a drain on the electrical distribution that substations had to be upgraded. From 1964 onwards, the VAMBAC equipment was removed from 13 cars and replaced by English Electric Z4 controllers from scrapped railcoaches. As soon as the loan charges which had covered their purchase were repaid in 1968, withdrawals began and all were out of normal service by 1975.

It was a sad end to what had promised so well, but they were quite simply an extravagant way of transporting 62 people. A tram of that size should have been carrying about a hundred passengers and indeed they could have taken more than they did, but Union regulations limited the number of standing passengers to six. What is now car 660 (ex 324) remains in occasional service and two others (304 and 327) have been preserved, the former having just been completely restored to its initial glory thanks largely to a television programme.

From 1954 the tramway was under the management of Joseph Franklin and, with a view to improved economy, he decided to investigate trailer operation. In 1957 a delegation visited Zürich to study this and as a result, two of the 1935 railcoaches (275/6) were in 1958 rebuilt as the "Progress Twin Car" to test the concept. The trials were considered successful and an order was placed with Metropolitan-Cammell for ten trailers, which entered service in 1960 as T1-T10. They were similar to the Coronations in design, and the trams which would pull them were rebuilt with new front and rear ends and given power operated doors. Although it seemed that at last a British tramway was adopting a successful continental practice, the trailers were not quite the success hoped for when they were first introduced. It had been intended to use them on a limited stop service, but this caused confusion among passengers and was soon discontinued and they were mixed in with single cars, often having to draw up twice at stops. From 1964 onwards, seven motors and trailers were rebuilt into semi-permanently coupled sets, the motors losing one driving cab and the trailers being fitted with a driving position and this increased their operational flexibility, as they could now use any crossover. The other three trailers were laid up and ultimately two were sold to GEC for experiments in automatic control

Since the 1960s many changes have been made to the Blackpool single-deck fleet. In 1968 car 618 (ex 271) was lengthened and given tapered ends, seating capacity now being 56. In 1969 Brush car 638 (ex 302) was rebuilt to test the practicability of one-person operation, being given a single width door behind the driving position. This was too narrow for normal use and the car did not run in service without a conductor, being ultimately re-converted to its original

Blackpool boat car 227, newly equipped with windscreens, passing Pleasure Beach on 22 June 1958. (Author)

Leeds 602 poses on the depot fan at Crich on 5 May 2005. (Author)

layout. However, the two rebuildings did convince the department that one-person operation was practicable. Details of further conversions are given in chapter 8.

The inspiration for the design of the Blackpool Coronations clearly lay in ten-motor and nine-trailer trams built in 1950/1 by the same builder, Charles Roberts and Company, for use in Khartum by the Sudan Light and Power Company. These were the last trams built in Britain for export to a part of what was still the empire. They were built under sub-contract to English Electric and the electrical equipment was supplied by that firm. Air brakes were fitted to both motors and trailers. They were for use on 1067mm gauge tracks. Overall length was 14.6m and width was 2.28m. Motor cars had a harim compartment seating nine, a first class section seating twelve and a second class section seating 21. Trailers were second class only and seated 46. Standing capacities were officially 30 and 32 respectively, but were often exceeded. An attractive blue and silver livery was used. This last outpost of tramway colonialism closed in 1967 and the cars were apparently simply dumped in the sand outside the city, where some lasted for many years.

When the Cunarder trams were being built in Glasgow in 1948, E.R.L. Fitzpayne, the system's innovative manager, proposed to build ten of the 100 cars on order as single-deckers for evaluation of this type in urban service. He stated that trams up to 45ft (13.68m) long could operate successfully on routes not using Renfield, Hope or West Nile Streets, and it would therefore seem that he was intending to use these cars on Argyle Street. In recommending single-deckers, he had been influenced by, among others, Walter Luff, who cited the successful Blackpool railcoaches as a precedent. Drawings show a car with a lower saloon like that of the double-deck Cunarders but with two single width sliding doors in the centre. The city's transport committee did not share his enthusiasm and rejected the proposal in April 1949.

However, shortly afterwards Glasgow's chief engineer, A.B. Findlay, became general manager in Leeds and there inherited plans for the construction of two experimental single-deckers, with a view to future subway operation. It was not surprising that these trams (601 and 602), when they emerged in May 1953, should display a strong resemblance to the abortive Glasgow design. Both cars were actually bodied by C. Roe and Company, builders of most of the city's buses, and were externally identical, having a double width central entrance, seats for 34 and standing room for 36. In equipment, however, they were totally different. The first car, 601, was fitted with conventional EMB lightweight trucks, rubber insert wheels and electro-pneumatic equipment by Metropolitan-Vickers, as fitted on the post-war Rotterdam cars. Car 602 was technically much more advanced, with lightweight motors mounted directly on to the bogies, VAMBAC equipment and rheostatic brakes, with solenoid brakes to bring the car to a complete standstill. At 16.5 tonnes, it was the lighter of the two, car 601 being one tonne heavier. Dimensions were the same in both cases. In service both cars performed well, but the public commented particularly on the completely smooth acceleration and deceleration of 602, which was also marginally quieter in operation. Although lacking the luxury of the Blackpool cars, the Leeds trams had attractive and spacious accommodation, but passengers did not take kindly to the low seating capacity. Externally both were painted purple and cream to mark the Coronation year. In 1954 a similar car (600), with conventional equipment, appeared, in the normal red and cream. This was a rebuild of a car originally built for Sunderland in 1931 and bought in 1944 by Leeds. It had four 48kW motors and may have been intended for experiments with trailer operation. Whatever their merits, the new cars had no real chance to prove themselves, since abandonment was decided on later in 1953, and for the rest of their brief active lives, they eked out their existence on the short back street Hunslet route, on which they could not show their capabilities. Both 600 and 602 are preserved in the National Tramway Museum at Crich.

While not strictly trams, the trains built for Southend's pier railway in 1949 had much in common with the design of the Blackpool cars. They were built by AC Cars Ltd and had electrical equipment by Crompton Parkinson, with two-axle trucks, having rubber insert wheels. They normally ran in seven-coach trains of four motor cars and three trailers and, at a time when one steamer might land a thousand passengers at a time, they proved to be excellent crowd movers. They were also less temperamental than the post-war Blackpool cars and gave good service until changing holiday patterns rendered a pier service of this kind unnecessary.

Technical details

First series Blackpool railcoaches
Length 12.95m, width 2.28m, 2x 42kW motors, 53 passengers, 48 seated

Blackpool Coronation cars
Length 15.24m, width 2.44m, weight 20 tonnes, 4 x 33kW motors, 61 passengers, 56 seated

Leeds 602
Length 12.62m, width 2.2m, weight 16.5 tonnes, 4 x kW motors, 70 passengers, 34 seated.

DESIGNS IN VARIOUS COUNTRIES FOR SUBURBAN OPERATION

While recognising the limitations of the central entrance car for urban service, some undertakings adopted this design for use on lines to suburban areas, on which it was important to maximise seating capacity and on which extended dwell time at stops was less of a drawback. The first system to adopt the design for such service was Barcelona, which in 1923 built a prototype in its own workshops (900) and followed this with an order for 50 (901-950), together with 14 similar trailers from La Brugeoise. These were built for metre gauge lines, but in 1947-50, 37 were rebuilt to standard gauge, fitted with power operated doors and a seat and desk for the conductor adjacent to the doors. Passengers were led to this point by a maze of handrails and they were the only European central entrance trams ever to have operated with this facility. The experiment was not totally successful but the trams survived until the last days of the system.

At almost the same time, the HTM of Den Haag was planning for the electrification of the steam tram lines to Delft and Leiden and for these acquired 30 large central entrance bogie cars (51-80) from four builders. There were also 20 matching trailers (101-120). These were really fast, regularly attaining 60km/hr in service, and extremely comfortable. The motor cars were given new equipment after the Second World War and lasted until 1965. In 1950 ten rather similar motor cars (81-90) and 20 trailers were bought from the Limburgse Tramweg Mij, which had replaced its trams by motorbuses.

In the late 1930s, Stockholm was developing rapidly with new

A four-car set of ex-Köln cars, headed by no.18, at Meidling on the Wien-Baden line in June 1981. (Author)

An ex-Köln coupled set working on the Linzer Lokalbahn in June 1981. (Author)

In Stockholm, car 42 on the Lidingö line 221 heads a motor-trailer-motor set at the outer terminus, June 1983. (Author)

suburbs being built at some distance from the centre and to serve these some lines were extended over long distances. To provide increased seating capacity, 110 bogie trailers (519-628, type B11), with seats for 74 passengers were built by ASEA and ASI between 1936 and 1941. They were followed in 1944 by 16 further trailers (630-645), of which some were control trailers, and then by 28 semi-streamlined motor trams (366-393) from ASEA and ASI and six (394-399) from Hägglund. By this time, the building of the T-Bana had already been decided on, but as an interim solution 18 further central entrance trailers and 37 motors were built, some of the latter using parts from older motor cars. By 1954 there were 71 such motors and no fewer than 144 trailers, providing rail service of a high standard of comfort to the suburban passengers. For the lines on Lidingö island, 18 similar motor trams and 12 control trailers were built between 1945 and 1952. Most of the central entrance material was withdrawn in the 1960s as the T-Bana expanded, but 16 motors and eight control trailers were retained for use on line 12 and most of the Lidingö material also survived. All these cars have since been overhauled and converted

for one-person operation and there are still 24 motors (301-324) and 13 control trailers (601-613) in service. For Sweden, this design also had the advantage that it was not necessary to convert the trams when the rule of the road changed in 1967!

Köln also had a number of long suburban lines and central entrance material was used on these from 1928 onwards. These trams were all scrapped in the mid-1960s, as the lines concerned were either closed or incorporated into the urban network. In 1958 DWM of Berlin built a series of 25 motor trams (1141-1165) and 21 control trailers (2141-2161), each with only one driving position, also for suburban use. These incorporated parts of older trams. They were moved on to peak hour duties on the urban network from 1965 and, as the operator did not think them suitable for conversion to one-person operation, scrapping began in 1968. However, nine motor trams and five trailers were bought at the last minute by the Wien-Baden Lokalbahn. The trailers were here adapted for one-person operation and the equipment gave excellent service until replaced in the 1980s by modern articulated cars. As they latterly used some of the tunnels opened in 1969, track brakes had to be fitted.

Köln and Bonn both also used an unusual tram type which is a variant on the central entrance design. This was a permanently close coupled motor/trailer set, each pair of which was single-ended and coupled back-to-back with its partner. Each unit had two doors, not quite in the centre but immediately on either side of it. Westwaggon built 14 of these sets in 1953-55 and followed these with three individual cars to the same layout. When the line on which they were used was incorporated into the city system, eight pairs were sold to Stern and Hafferl in Austria and used on the Linzer Lokalbahn, where some ran until 2005. Bonn bought three similar sets (30/1-34/5), known as "Silverpfeilen" (Silver Arrows) for its lines to Siegburg and Bad Honnef, from Talbot of Aachen in 1953/4. These were some of the most comfortable trams to run anywhere in Germany and one set originally had a buffet counter. Unfortunately the Bonn commuters did not take to this and it was removed in 1961, having been disused since 1957. These sets were replaced by Stadtbahn cars in the 1970s and none was preserved.

Milan first acquired central entrance cars for its radial line to Monza in 1941 and used most of these to replace double-deckers. The cars (130-139) were built by Stanga and had both a pantograph for use on the interurban section and two trolley poles for the city overhead. Twelve similar cars (501-512) were bought in 1953 for the Adda line, and these were later upgraded to Stadtbahn standards, when the line was re-equipped for pre-metro operation. As both this line and the Monza line were later converted to full

Barcelona 984 and trailer at Plaza Palacio in 1959. (Pam Eaton)

Den Haag cars at Turfmarkt on 5 September 1959. HTM 60 is on the left and ex-Limburg 90 is on the right. (Author)

metro standards, all the trams concerned were re-converted for on-street operation and transferred to the line to Llimbiate, on which they pull up to four trailers, an impressive sight in an urban setting.

Technical details
Bonn Silver Arrow cars, complete unit
Length 37.6m, width 2.35m, weight 48.15 tonnes, 4 x 63kW motors, 230 passengers, 96 seated.
Köln 1141
Length 14.02m, width 2.37m weight 18.5 tonnes, 2 x 74 kW motors, 107 passengers, 34 seated.

Milan 543 pulling no fewer than three trailers clears the intersection of Via Carlo Farini and Viale Stelvio, outward bound for Carate in March 1983. (Author)

Köln pre-war central entrance set headed by no.1115 on line B to Bernsberg. (F.W. Hunt, courtesy London Area, Light Rail Transit Association)

Stockholm 371 and trailer at Alvik on line 120 in May 1983. To afford cross-platform interchange with the T-Bana train at that station, left hand running was used and the set is here reverting to right hand running. (Author)

THE AUSTRALIAN DROP-CENTRE CAR

Ex-Melbourne W2 class 482, working on the heritage line in Seattle at Broad Street in October 1988. Technically it is no longer a drop-centre car, since the middle section has been built up to allow same-level boarding for passengers in wheelchairs. (Author)

Class SW7 1033 at Bourke street terminus in March 1986. (Author)

An interior view of an SW6 car, seen on 21 March 1986. (Author)

This was Australasia's main contribution to tramcar design and, although now thought of as typically Australian, the type actually originated in New Zealand. It was a variation on the central entrance layout and consisted of a bogie car with two end saloons and a central section, open at the sides, at a lower level. The open section, or "drop centre", was ideally suited to the Australian climate and also allowed easier access. From 1925, when the design was first introduced to Australia by Brisbane City Council, many hundred such cars were built, of which the most famous are probably Melbourne's W2 class, many of which are now in service on heritage lines in various countries. On later cars the central section was enclosed, giving what was in effect a car with dual central entrances. Sydney's R class of 1935 was of this type but, owing to complaints about the low seating capacity, the following class R1 had only a single doorway, making these virtually central entrance trams. Two of these were fitted briefly with resilient wheels, but otherwise they were totally conventional, although very comfortable in service. Brisbane's "four-motor" cars built from 1938 to 1963 were similar to the R class, but had sliding doors to the drop centre.

Only those built latterly for Melbourne had any modern features. The first signs of these came with class SW5,

which initially consisted of ten cars built in 1939/40 (840-849). These had power-operated sliding doors to enclose the drop centre and some other features of the prototype SW6 car, which had entered service in March 1939. Two conversions of class W5 cars followed in 1956 and, surprisingly, a further 83 in the period 1983-86. Class SW6 consisted of 120 basically similar cars built between 1939 and 1951. Outwardly identical were class W6 (970-979, 981-1000) but these were initially fitted with resilient wheels, later replaced by conventional wheels. In 1956 the motor buses which had replaced cable trams on the Bourke Street routes were themselves replaced by cars of class W7 (1001-1040) which had sound-proofed bodies and, originally, resilient wheels. Many of these various classes are still in service on Melbourne's city circle tram

service. Three trams similar to class SW6, but smaller, were built in 1942 for the local tram services of the Victorian Railways and, after these closed, they were bought by the MMTB, two only being placed in service as 52/3. They were withdrawn in 1977 and 1980. There were also six rebuilds of class W2 cars to class SW2, with sliding doors and it was once intended that the entire class should be so treated. Fortunately for the heritage movement, cost prevented this plan being put into effect!

With the arrival of the European-inspired classes Z1-Z3, it seemed that the idea of the drop centre had had its day. However, these new designs were, as stated elsewhere, not ideally suited for Melbourne conditions and in 1984 the first of class A1 appeared from the Comeng factory. With two doors in the centre these trams are essentially an updated version of the drop centre design, although the centre portion is no longer at a lower level than the rest of the tram. They also reverted to the traditional itinerant conductor, although all have now been converted to one person operation. Class A1 consists of cars 231-258 and class A2 of cars 259-300. Outwardly all are identical, the main difference being in the disc brakes of class A2. These also had pantographs from new, whereas A1 cars entered service with trolley poles. Both types have chopper control, regenerative braking and Düwag monomotor bogies. The trams have proved to be popular, in particular because of their excellent riding qualities.

Technical details
Class A1
Length 15m, width 2.67m, weight 22.2tonnes, 2 x 185kW motors, 42 seated passengers
Class W7
Length 14.17m, width 2.73m, weight 17.7 tonnes, 4 x 30 kW motors, 48 seated passengers.

Bibliography
Destination City. Op.cit.

Class A 231 outside Kew depot in March 1993, leaving on a short working inbound to Prahran. It has been repainted into the chocolate and cream livery of the Prahran and Malvern Tramways Trust, to commemorate the 75th anniversary of that depot. On the right, 232 waits to enter the depot. (Author)

DOUBLE-DECKERS

Early experiments with these have been detailed elsewhere.

It is quite certain that the New York car had an influence on later British designs. In 1919 a party of four senior staff members of the London Underground group made a study visit to the USA. One of the systems which they looked at was that of New York City and on the return of the group, a series of papers was presented to a meeting of senior staff held on 30 January 1920. That on vehicle design given by C.J. Spencer, general manager of the Metropolitan Electric Tramways, contained an illustration of NYR 6000. In 1922 the MET decided to build a car "with centre entrance and platform for fare collection". This proposal was also supported by the London Traffic Advisory Committee. The car would have had two staircases and separate entrance and exit doors, automatically controlled, and the conductor would have been stationed on the central platform. Unfortunately the project was then abandoned, possibly because of restrictions on the width of tramcars in London. However, a series of 23 double-deckers to a design very similar to that proposed for London was constructed in 1923 by La Brugeoise in Belgium for interurban use at Valparaiso, Chile, where the system had just passed from German to Spanish ownership. These trams (501-523) had two-step entrances and platform doors, but seem to have been worked by an itinerant conductor. They were double-ended and at certain stops the offside door was used in conjunction with a central loading island. They lasted in double-deck form until 1943 and seem to have been successful.

The abandoned plans for an MET car were revived in 1930, at a time when experiments with what became the Feltham cars were under way. However, this tram was not sponsored by the London Underground group but was the responsibility of the MET alone; it seems that C.J. Spencer still wanted to try in practice the concepts he had seen in the USA eleven years previously. Safety of operation was claimed to be the main advantage, but accessibility would also be improved. The result was MET 331, which entered service in December 1930. This car had a specially designed frame which allowed a low step height at the central entrance, and it was fitted with power operated sliding doors under joint control of the driver and conductor. These were interlinked with the controller to prevent the car starting before the doors were closed. As shown to the press, the car had a post for the conductor on the central platform, with a combined ticket machine and cash register, but this was removed before it went into service. Seating in the lower saloon was mostly longitudinal, rather like that of an underground train, and the internal fittings were to a very high standard. Total capacity was 42/28 plus (probably) 20 standees. In service car 331 was fast and had excellent riding qualities, but the practice of having an itinerant conductor, rather than pay-as-you-enter operation gave rise to delays at stops, as the conductor had always to return to the platform to close the doors. After some time, an additional conductor was provided at peak times, which undermined the economics of the tram. It was sold to Sunderland Corporation in 1937 as it could not be converted for conduit operation.

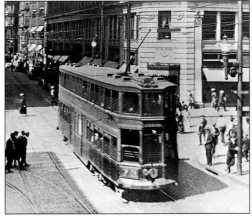
One of the Pittsburgh cars. (Author's collection)

A crowd awaits Blackpool 239 in Fleetwood town centre on 25 July 1967. (Author)

Blackpool 244 in Rigby Road depot in June 1958, still carrying its war-time paint scheme. (Author)

Blackpool 709 as rebuilt, seen in Talbot Square during the illuminations in October 2002. (Author)

"Princess Alice" in Fleetwood on Fleetwood Tram Sunday, 1987. (Author)

The door interlock was removed and, fitted with a pantograph, it ran there as no.100 until 1952, when it was purchased for preservation. Now fully restored, it is in service at the National Tramway Museum at Crich. It was a great pity that the London fare system defeated this particular attempt to run a thoroughly modern tram.

However, the car had shown that a central entrance double-decker was a practical proposition and, given the success of the new rail-coaches, it was not long before English Electric and Walter Luff were formulating plans for a double-deck version to run in Blackpool, that manufacturer having apparently acquired certain patents from London Transport. As it was necessary at this time to replace the elderly hand-braked "Dreadnought" open-top cars, a sample open-top version of the new design was ordered first and this tram (226, later 237) entered service in February 1934. Trap doors in the stair wells allowed it to function as a single-decker at times such as this. It created such a good impression that an order was immediately placed for twelve similar cars (238-249) and 14 fully-enclosed double-deckers (250-263). The cost of the enclosed cars was £3,500 each. These seated totals of 94 and 84 passengers respectively, the seats on the open upper decks being wooden. The double-deckers of both types proved to be just as popular as their single-deck counterparts. The open cars were fitted with roofs and (thinly-upholstered) seats on the upper deck in 1941/2, to allow them to be used to their full potential in war-time traffic. In the 1950s seating on the cars built enclosed was increased to 94. In Blackpool, the double-deckers have always been worked by a crew of three, partly because of the manually-operated platform doors, though off-season they sometimes run as single-deckers, with the upper deck out of use. Nineteen are still in service, having outlasted the "Coronations" which were intended to replace them. For the 1985 centenary, what was by then car 706 was re-converted to open-top form and named "Princess Alice". In 2000/1 two cars were totally rebuilt with new ends and fluorescent lighting.

Anticipating the success of these trams, English Electric began to offer the design to other operators. The first customer was Sunderland Corporation, which acquired a slightly shorter version of the Blackpool design in August 1934, numbered 99. This was followed in 1935 by an order from Darwen Corporation for two similar trams (23/4) for operation on 4'/1100mm gauge tracks. Their narrow width of 2.06m meant that only 2+1 seating could be fitted and the total seating capacity was only 56. In 1948 they were sold to the Llandudno and Colwyn Bay Electric Railway but here again their design was against them, as they could run in passenger service only at the two ends of the line and not on the exposed section in between. They were little used in later years and were scrapped in 1955/6. They represented the only attempt to run modern double-deckers on narrow gauge tracks and cannot be considered to have been successful in this. In 1937 the Bombay Electricity Supply and Transport undertaking, which had close links with English Electric, placed in service the first of 23 cars (117-139), generally known as "Pullmans". These had EE trucks and motors and differed from their British

MET 331 as running at Crich. (Author)

counterparts in having elliptical rather than domed roofs and stairs which rose from the left hand sides of the platforms in the direction of travel. The central entrance concept seems not to have worked well in India and after the war all were converted to conventional end platform layout, though the stairs remained in the original position.

In Sunderland, car 99 had shown an impressive reduction in platform accidents compared with all other cars in the fleet and it was decided to acquire other trams (and also buses) with this layout. However, as bogie trams were not suited for all routes in the city, the manager, Charles Hopkins, asked the firm of Maley and Taunton, working together with Brush, to design a two-axle truck with a cranked frame which would allow the fitting of a central entrance body. Two trams were then built in 1935/6 using this design of truck, one by Brush (55) and one by the Corporation (54) to the same design. Although the lower deck was somewhat cramped, the trams were comfortable and quite successful in service. Four similar cars from English Electric followed between 1936 and 1940, all being a shortened version of car 99. Having inspected the Sunderland cars in 1935, South Shields Corporation then ordered one of its own, from Brush. This became car 52 and when the system closed in 1946 it was sold to Sunderland, where it became no.48.

Finally in June 1939 Aberdeen Corporation ordered two central entrance bogie cars from English Electric, together with two end platform two-axle cars, to test which type would be most suitable for renewal of the fleet. The trams arrived in Aberdeen in July and August 1940, the bogie cars being numbered 139 and 140. They were extremely well finished cars and in their cream and green livery provided a welcome bright note in these troubled years. The central entrance type seemed to be best suited for future construction and, when war ended, an order for 20 similar cars (19-38) was placed. English Electric sub-contracted the building of the trams to R.Y. Pickering of Wishaw, Scotland and they were finally placed in service in 1948/9. Mounted on EMB lightweight trucks, they were fast and smooth riding, although expensive on current. Internally they set new standards of luxury, with concealed lighting, roof glazing and comfortable seating and became very popular with passengers, though not always with crews. Seating capacity was 44/32. They had a public address system to allow drivers to announce

stops, but this was later disconnected, after a driver had forgotten to switch off before giving his opinion of a passing motorist! Initially worked with two conductors, they were given power operated doors in 1954 to allow operation with a crew of two. Sadly abandonment was decided on after they had been in service for only five years and, attempts to sell them to Glasgow and Blackpool having failed, all were burned on closure of the system in May 1958. This episode marked one of the most tragic failures to persist with modern tramway equipment in Britain.

One of the might-have-beens of tramway history is the proposed Liverpool car of 1944. This was a double-decker on PCC bogies and using PCC equipment. It would have seated 34/28 and would have had an additional single-width exit door at the front. Dimensions would have been 10.87m by 2.26m. Owing to the change of policy adopted in 1945, this interesting project did not see the light of day.

Anecdotal evidence also suggests that the Dublin United Tramways in 1936 may have been planning a central entrance version of the successful "Luxury" bogie trams of 1931. A sudden change of management and the desire to dismantle a fine system with indecent haste ensured that the proposal, or pipe dream, would remain just that.

The central entrance tram, in both single- and double-deck form, was a design which was a considerable advance over conventional types, both in safety and in improved accessibility. It was also one of the very few modern designs which could be applied to double-deckers. It was the chosen means of modernising two important systems – Rotterdam and Blackpool – and without the latter, there would have been no modern trams in Britain to link early systems with those of the present day and to keep the concept alive when it was the only tram system left in these islands. In the immediate post-war years, it was seen by many as the design for the future and the proposed Liverpool car bore some similarity to a design proposed by what was then the Light Railway Transport League in the booklet *"Towards Ideal Transport"*. This envisaged the "Railspeed" car, a double-decker 12.3m long, accommodating 80 seated passengers (48/32). The same publication also anticipated Stadtbahn practice of the 1970s, with central entrance single-deck trams running in coupled pairs along the median strip of a motorway; unfortunately trolley poles detracted from the impression of modernity!

Yet somehow the design never seemed to reach its full potential. In Britain, the cars were really too small for economical operation, at least in the years after 1945. The design was also difficult to modify for one person operation, though, as experience in the DDR showed, this could be done successfully when necessary. Its success was to a large extent bound up with the fare system under

which it had to operate and a complicated system militated against this. Nonetheless, some of its features have passed down into modern tramcar technology and it certainly deserves a place in the history of the development of modern light rail vehicles.

Technical details

Aberdeen 19-38
Length 11.58m, width 2.18m, weight 20.3 tonnes, 4 x 28kW motors, 76 seated passengers.
Blackpool 250, as built
Length 42'3", width 7'6", 2 x 42kW motors, seating 44/40.

Bibliography

The Glasgow Tramcar. Ian Stewart. Scottish Tramway Museum Society, Glasgow 1983.
Liverpool Transport vol. 2. J.B. Horne and T.B. Maund. Transport Publishing Company,

A close-up of the platform of MET331, as seen at Crich in April 2004. (Author)

Aberdeen 33 at Bridge of Don on a wet day in April 1958. (Author)

Two of Valparaiso's double-deckers, 507 and 513, at a point where loading was from a central island and the cars ran "wrong line". (Author's collection)

Bombay 127 and trailer, in war time grey livery, at Flora Fountain in September 1944. (M.J. O'Connor, author's collection)

Glossop, and Light Rail Transit Association, London, 1982.

Blackpool's Century of Trams. S. Palmer. Blackpool Borough Council, Blackpool, 1985.

English Electric Tramcar Album. G. Lumb, Ian Allan Ltd, Surrey, 1998.

Blackpool Coronation Cars. Martin Wilson. Lancastrian Transport Publications, Cleveleys, n/d.

The Tramways of Sunderland. S.A. Staddon. Advertiser Press, Huddersfield, 1964.

The Metropolitan Electric Tramways, vol.2. C.S. Smeeton. Light Rail Transit Association, Broxbourne, 1986.

Double-Deck Trams of the World. B. Patton. Adam Gordon, Brora, 2002.

Destination City. Op.cit.

Modern Tramway, nos.137 and 150, May 1949 and June 1950 (Aberdeen), nos.156, December 1950 and 176, August 1952, (Khartum), no.186, June 1953, (Leeds), no.316, April 1964 (Bradford 1), no.334 October 1965 (Berlin), no.348, December 1966 (Budapest), no.363, March 1968 (Proposed Liverpool car).

Headlights vol.59, nos.7-9, July-September 1997 (Cleveland).

Les Tramways Parisiens. J. Robert. Paris, 1992.

Du Tram au Métro Léger. Op.cit.

Strassenbahn Magazin nos.72, May 1989 (Den Haag), 119, June/July 1999 (Berlin).

Die Rheinbahn – Stadtverkehr in und um Düsseldorf. A. Schild and D. Waltking. Alba Verlag, Düsseldorf, revised edition, 1985.

Bradford Corporation Tramways. J.S. King. Venture Publications, 1998.

125 Jahren Strassenbahn in Berlin. S. Hilkenbach and W. Kramer. Alba Verlag, Düsseldorf, 1990.

Towards Ideal Transport. C.R. Bizeray. Light Railway Transport League, London, (2nd ed.) 1947.

New Tramcars for Calcutta. English Electric Company Ltd, Preston, 1931.

The tramway of the future, as envisaged by Bryan de Gruneau in 1937 and subsequently used in publicity material by the Light Railway Transport League. (Author's collection)

LUXURY TRAMCAR DESIGN

Mr. W. Luff, Transport Manager, Blackpool Corporation, says:—"1933 season was exceptional for weather and unfortunately 1934 season was very unfavourable. In spite of this, revenue was actually increased by nearly £16,000, a big percentage of which can be ascribed to the popularity of the new rolling stock.

Another important feature which is of particular interest in connection with the efforts of the Ministry of Transport to reduce road accidents, is the fact that the new centre-entrance vehicles have considerably reduced accidents to passengers entering or leaving tramcars in Blackpool."

BLACKPOOL Double-deck Open-top Car Interior of Lower Saloon

BLACKPOOL

SUNDERLAND Double-deck Car Interior of Upper Saloon

SUNDERLAND

Mr. C. A. Hopkins, Transport Manager, Sunderland Corporation, says:—"By modernising our tramway rolling stock ... I am convinced that our traffic receipts have maintained a much higher level ... in spite of the unprecedented depression on the North-East Coast. The new central-entrance car ... at once established itself in high favour with the public."

BLACKPOOL

REVENUE · PASSENGER COMFORT · AND SPEED WITH SAFETY

One of the Blackpool open cars and Sunderland 99 as shown in English Electric publicity material. (English Electric, Author's collection)

CHAPTER 4

THE PCC BOGIE CAR

NORTH AMERICA

Although there had always been a certain amount of standardisation in car building in North America, particularly by Brill, these trams had usually been bought by smaller operators, most of whom went out of business in the 1920s. Competition from the private car began to have an effect on tramways, generally known locally as "street railways", at a much earlier date than in Europe and had been apparent from as early a date as 1915. The entry of the USA into the war slowed the process for a few years but by the mid-1920s it was once again in full swing. It became apparent that, if the tram were to survive, a radically new approach to its design and construction would be required and that it would also be necessary to introduce a degree of standardisation, rather than allowing the larger systems the luxury of individually specified vehicles. In 1917, under pressure of wartime needs, the American Electric Railway Association set up a committee (the War Board) to develop standard cars and under Birney's leadership, two were designed, a double-ended Peter Witt and an end-entrance car. Only a few of the latter were actually built. In 1921 the AERA went on to set up a committee on the unification of car design and in due course this produced a report with standard designs for both urban and radial cars. Opposition from individual undertakings led to these recommendations being ignored and the

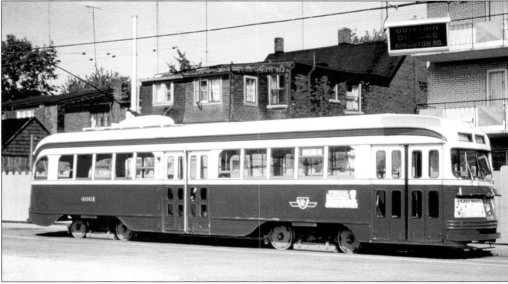

Toronto 4061 of the original batch at Dufferin Street in 1964. This shows the standard pre-war design. (J.F. Bromley, Evda Slides)

only concrete result was in the building of twelve lightweight cars for the Berkshire Street Railway in 1927. In the same year, Brill, still hoping to persuade operators of the merits of accepting a range of standard designs, began production of its "Master Unit" range of cars, which was intended to meet this criterion, while still offering a choice of body layouts and of electrical equipment (see Ch.2). Osgood Bradley in 1928 copied the idea and introduced its Electromobile, which looked very like the Brill car, but only 28 were built. A combination of the economic depression and the knowledge by 1931 that work on the PCC car was under way ensured that these designs would not see widespread use – Philadelphia Rapid Transit Company considered ordering 500 Master Units, but finally opted to wait for better times and a better product.

These and other efforts to persuade city operators of the value

Cleveland 4228 in Public Square is one of the cars with a monitor roof for improved ventilation. (Lars F. Richter collection)

of standardisation during the 1920s fell largely on ears which were not only deaf but positively hostile. Two men in particular saw that entrenched attitudes were holding back the entire industry. These were James H. ("Mac") McGraw, of the McGraw-Hill Publishing Company, and Charles Gordon, editor of the "Electric Railway Journal" produced by the former.

In the autumn of 1928, Gordon addressed the American Electric Railway Engineering Association and berated the industry for its failure to meet the requirements of modern conditions and lack of co-operation. As a result of this and other speeches and writings, the AERA's advisory council in October 1929 agreed that operators should take steps to "meet the acute situation presented by the need for development of the electric railway car (i.e. tram)" and to translate this into action the council asked Gordon and Thomas J. Conway Jr. to prepare a plan for the industry to follow. From this was born the Presidents' Conference Committee, which first met in Chicago in December 1929; the words "Electric Railway" were added in front of the title in 1931. Conway was chairman and Gordon secretary.

No-one had ever before taken a close and thorough look at the electric railway car or tram as an entity. It had simply grown in a welter of different designs. The Committee proposed a three year

The Brill Master Unit in the form used by the Philadelphia Red Arrow system. Car 84 approaches Drexel Hill inbound in October 1980. (Author)

The Clark PCC in service on the Coney Island line in Brooklyn on 30 July 1955. (A.D. Young, Evda Slides).

Baltimore Pullman-Standard 7407 on a tight curve at the city's tramway museum in September 1984. (Author)

M.u. operation on Queen Street, Toronto, on 2 August 1974. The leading car, 4677, is ex-Cleveland while the second, 4468, is one of those new to the TTC in the post-war period. (Author)

In the early 1970s. the TTC made an excellent job of rebuilding some PCC cars for further service. An unusual feature was the provision of water bumpers, as seen here on post-war car 4526, inbound on Mount Pleasant, against a background of autumn colours, October 1975. (Author)

Ex-Birmingham Pullman Standard car 4705 of the TTC, on Dundas Street at Yonge Street on a wet evening in June 1978. (Author)

America. Two Canadian members joined in 1933, when a change of government in the Dominion altered the question of tariffs between it and the USA. Some operators, such as Twin Cities Rapid Transit, declined to become members. All the major manufacturers were members, except for the Clark Equipment Company, which in the event would produce about 90% of all PCC trucks made. On 1 September 1930 Dr C.F. Hirshfeld became chief engineer. He had come from the electricity industry but had no previous experience in tramways. The committee considered that such experience might have been a handicap to the holder of the post and hindsight suggests that they might have been correct in this view.

Field studies were then instituted, based on a depot in Brooklyn which the Brooklyn and Queens Transit Corporation had made available, and these were backed up by a survey carried out by operators of 610 trams built between 1927 and 1930. The actual trams used in experiments were Peter Witts from Baltimore (6002) and Chicago (3322) (the latter was called a "sedan") and two cars loaned by the Brooklyn company. These were 5200, an experimental car built by the bus manufacturer Twin Coach Company and 6139, a Peter Witt. Theoretical tests on braking and acceleration were carried out at the University of Michigan. Both General Electric and Westinghouse supplied electrical equipment to the Committee's specifications and

in 1933 road tests of these began using Brooklyn car 5200. Given the thorough approach and bearing in mind that the USA was currently in the grip of an economic depression, the rate of progress was remarkable, but nevertheless there were some complaints about the time being taken and calls for the construction of an "interim" car. Hirshfeld rejected this, being what he called a "half baked pacifier" and the Committee backed him. However, by 5 February 1934, studies had advanced to the point at which a sample car could be ordered, from the Pullman-Standard Manufacturing Company. This arrived in September 1934 and was assigned to Brooklyn, as 5300. Both this car, car B, and 5200, car A, were then placed in normal revenue service in Brooklyn. While in service in early 1935, 5300 sustained an accident and as a result, the decision was made to abandon hydraulic brakes and instead use only dynamic and air brakes in production trams. Final design work went ahead and on 8 July 1935 the Brooklyn undertaking announced that it had placed an order for 99 cars from the St Louis Car Company and one from the Clark Equipment Company. After five and a half years of concentrated study, a great deal of hard work and the expenditure of $630,000, the Committee had reached its goal. The ERPCC's patent rights were then transferred to a new body, the Transit Research Corporation, which would license production. Again Conway was president and Gordon secretary. This body continued to undertake research and technically a PCC car is any one constructed using patents licensed by it.

The control equipment developed by General Electric and Westinghouse, using the guidelines laid down by the ERPCC, was the secret of the success of the PCC car. This used an accelerator placed under the car floor, fitted with contactors and able to provide 260 steps of acceleration and braking. This accelerator was driven by a master controller activated, in most cases, by a foot pedal operated by the driver. Initially separate master controllers were used for acceleration and braking but later both functions were combined in one. Clearly such equipment would give a much smoother ride than conventional controllers, albeit at the expense of a high consumption of current and the generation of a good deal of heat. This could be used to warm the interior, but went to waste in operations in hotter areas. It was in their rate of acceleration that PCC cars really scored over their predecessors – and contemporary private cars. The Brooklyn cars had an acceleration rate of 7.6km/hr/second, while the Indianapolis Brill cars could manage only

research programme, to be funded by subscriptions from invited operators and manufacturers and there were originally 25 backers. Although this represented only a fraction of the total number of operators, it included those owning 40% of the total number of trams in North

PCC trams also make useful works cars when their passenger-carrying days are over. In Toronto two ex-Cleveland cars were converted to rail grinders, as W30 and W31, and are seen here in September 1975. They were originally Cleveland 4206 and 4243 and became TTC 4631 and 4668. This pair has since been preserved by the TTC. (Author)

Although dating from post-war years, these cars built for Kansas City did not have standee windows, as the then-president of the undertaking did not like these. By the time this photograph was taken in San Francisco, at the terminus of line N. Judah, in September 1975, the car (1180) was with its third owner, having come via Toronto, whose livery it still wears. (Author)

One of the former Illinois Terminal cars (451) at an unusual stage in its history. It had been preserved when its own system closed, but later, as seen here, found itself re-activated on the Cleveland Shaker Heights line, when that system had a shortage of rolling stock in the 1970s. It was unusual in being double-ended but single-sided. May 1977. (A.D. Young, Evda Slides)

5.6km/hr/second. Air wheel brakes were initially standard, backed by magnetic track brakes and dynamic brakes. The use of these was determined by the position of the brake pedal. All-electric cars developed from 1940 onwards used a drum brake in place of the air brake. The cost of a typical PCC, as supplied to Baltimore in 1938, was US$16,000 or about £3,800 at contemporary rates of exchange.

Initially PCC cars were mounted on B2 trucks built by the Clark Equipment Company. These gave an excellent quality of ride on street track but were less satisfactory on open sleeper track and operators who had long radial lines, such as Pittsburgh, required something which would be equally at home on both. Wartime conditions prevented proper trials of a new design from the St Louis Car Co., but these were conducted in 1946 and resulted in the B3 truck, which was used under many post-war cars. An improved version of the B2 truck was also available and some operators still preferred it. Resilient wheels were standard.

Although Brooklyn had placed the first order, the first entry of a PCC car to service occurred in Pittsburgh. Pittsburgh Railway (PR) placed its first car (100) in free demonstration service on 12 September 1936 and two weeks later it entered normal revenue service on line 50. Service in Brooklyn began on 1 October, when Mayor La Guardia cut a ribbon in front of car 1009 to allow it to enter service on line 68 to Coney Island. These two cars were to be the predecessors of 4334 trams built for service in the USA, 594 built in Canada and one each built in the USA for Mexico and Belgium. This total of 4930 cars far outweighed that achieved by any other contemporary design. Cars built in Europe, Australia and Japan are not covered in this total. It should be noted also that 1009 PCC rapid transit cars were also constructed, mostly for Chicago.

In the years before the USA entered the second world war, most of the PCC cars delivered were to a very standard design, that of the first Pittsburgh car. Apart from the one car supplied to Brooklyn by Clark Equipment Company, only two manufacturers were involved – St Louis Car Co. and Pullman-Standard – and cars were available in single- or double-ended configuration. There was very little external difference between the products of the two manufacturers, but those built by Pullman could be distinguished by their slightly more upright windscreen. Orders were placed by Baltimore (200 cars), Boston (21), Brooklyn (100), Chicago (83), Cincinnati (28), Kansas City (24), Los Angeles (30), Pacific Electric (30, double-ended), Philadelphia (260), Pittsburgh (401), St Louis (200), San Diego (25) and Washington (239). The only export orders received at this period were from Toronto (250) and Vancouver (4) and there seems to have been no attempt to interest overseas buyers in the design. From 1942 to 1945 output was controlled by the War Production Board and under its auspices further orders were completed for Baltimore (75), Boston (225), Los Angeles (30), Pittsburgh (65) and Washington (190). A new customer was Johnstown, which, being a centre of steel production, was allowed to order 17 cars, but they were not received until after the end of the war. Export to Canada was severely rationed. Montréal had ordered 25 cars in 1942 but in fact received only 18, Toronto asked for 55 in 1942 but was given only 40 while Vancouver had 32. The Dominion government also ordered 30 cars

on its own account but these were not built and were cancelled after the end of the war.

Just before pre-war production came to an end, a series of cars for St Louis Public Service Company, the 1500 class (1500-1599), was built in 1940 incorporating all-electric equipment and a redesigned front end. In 1941 a further 100 cars (1600-1699) were built to the same design but incorporating standee windows, previously only seen in the Clark car in Brooklyn. In this class also, the earlier window spacing was reduced, to allow this to coincide with seat spacing. While this had the advantage of giving every passenger a window seat, it did give the cars concerned a more fussy appearance. Cars built during the war ("war babies") were to pre-war design but research continued and in 1945 it was agreed that these changes, together with a further altered windscreen arrangement, would become standard in post-war cars. Minor rearrangements internally increased the length of the car and also its weight. A further option offered in the post-war design was that of pressure ventilation, with equipment mounted in a clerestory in the roof. The last major change in design came in 1949, with double width side windows, set at a slightly lower level in the car body. This design was supplied only to Boston, where these were known as picture window cars.

The PCC had the great merit that it was a standard car whose basic design still allowed for variations to suit local conditions and several operators took full advantage of this facility. Thus almost all of Boston's cars had centre doors on the offside to allow for the platform layout at Park Street station on the subway section. These doors had to be offset from those on the right to allow space for the underfloor electrical equipment. The Pacific Electric cars had doors on both sides and in this case the central doors were exactly opposite each other, the matter of the equipment being solved by making the cars longer than normal. Chicago's first series had a triple width front entrance doorway and these cars also had hand controls, to comply with local regulations. Owing to restrictions in depot layout, Washington's cars were shorter than standard, the reduction in length being achieved by removing one window bay in the after part of the body. The Illinois Terminal cars were double-ended but with doors on one side only. Post-war cars for Kansas City did not have standee windows. In all, 2,095 cars showed some variation from standard designs. Washington's cars were all equipped for conduit operation.

In the early post-war years, sales of the PCC car boomed. New customers were found in Birmingham (48), Cleveland (50), Dallas, (25), Detroit (186), Illinois Terminal (a radial line based in St Louis) (8), Louisville (25), Minneapolis (141), San Francisco (35) and Shaker Heights (25). Most pre-war purchasers came back for more. Boston took the first 25 all-electric production cars and the 50 picture window cars in 1951. Chicago took no less than 600 new cars in 1947/8, Cincinnati (25), Kansas City (85), Los Angeles (40), Philadelphia (210), Pittsburgh (200), St Louis (100) and Washington (50). Toronto (250) bought more cars to take it to the top of the league of PCC operators. A prototype car was sold to Mexico City. But the success was short-lived and the cars delivered to San Francisco in 1952 were to be the last PCC cars built for use in North America.

A Pittsburgh car was taken to Buffalo in 1941

The best of British, and the best of US technology! San Francisco 1149 (ex-St. Louis) seems to be racing an elegant Rolls-Royce in Market Street in September 1975. (Author)

Former double-ended car 1006 in bound on Market Street, in San Francisco in September 1975 (Author). Marmon-Harrington trolleybus 741 is on the right. (Author)

Despite its sophisticated technology, the PCC car could stand up to a great deal of neglect, as witnessed here by Philadelphia 2733 on Woodland Avenue at 49th Street in October 1980. (Author)

Ex-Pacific Electric cars in service on the General Urquiza line in Buenos Aires. (Lars F. Richter collection)

The standee windows of St Louis 1600 class are clearly visible in this excellent night shot of car 1654. It is on Millbrook Street in September 1962. (A.D. Young, Evda Slides)

for static demonstration but, probably due to the war, no sales resulted. Oakland had plans to buy 20 cars in 1939 but decided not to proceed with the order. The idea was revived in 1944 but National City Lines bought the system and that was the end of the matter. Similarly, the Key System, which connected San Francisco and Oakland by the Bay Bridge, had drawn up a specification for two- and three-section articulated PCC cars and expected to order two of the latter type in 1947/8. The same take-over applied to that system and the plan was cancelled.

The reasons for the decline of the PCC car are complex and to an extent outwith the scope of a book such as this. They lie in the structure of the US transport industry at that time, its precarious financial situation and the policies of the Republican administration of 1952-60. Most systems were in the hands of private companies, many of which in the post-war years were acquired by National City Lines, a consortium in which oil and motor vehicle interests had a strong position. Even this group, however, was not anti-tram as such, but was concerned only to operate its lines at a profit and in a few places, such as St Louis, maintained the cars to a high standard and continued service on lines which were profitable, well into the 1950s. It was the unchecked growth of private motoring, aided by the Republican Federal Highway Act of 1955, which threatened all urban transport and this was soon to be coupled with the flight to the suburbs, often outwith city limits, which militated against continuing successful operation of car lines. Chicago, which had seemed to show such confidence in the tram, suddenly decided that the future lay with heavy rapid transit operation and most of its post-war cars were converted into rapid transit cars before they were ten years old. San Francisco, a municipal system, might have gone against the trend but by an ordinance of 1918, trams had to have a two-man crew, while trolleybuses could be operated by one man, and there was therefore an incentive to replace car lines by trolleybuses. By the time the offending ordinance was repealed in 1954, most of the conversions had taken place and the system was basically reduced to its present level. At a later stage, and in much reduced form, the development of subway services also caused a decline in Toronto's fleet, which was, nevertheless, one of the few examples where PCC cars lived out their natural life span. However, attitudes towards public transport and urban development in the Dominion were much closer to those in Europe than to those south of the border and these factors, coupled with superb maintenance of track and cars, created a totally different environment for the PCC and allowed it to maximise its potential. Had there been more PCCs in other Canadian cities, their story could have been the same, but in Montréal and Vancouver the number of such cars was just too small to have any real effect on future plans. As in Britain, there were also political influences at work. In New York, mayor La Guardia was against further purchases of PCC cars, despite the success of the first 100 in Brooklyn, where ridership on the lines served by PCCs had increased by 21.3 million passengers and revenues by 31%. These successes had no effect on the political mind, already set in anti-rail mode. Washington City then lacked any kind of democratic local government, being ruled directly by the US Congress, whose members

Boston, ex-Dallas, double-ended car 3333 looks rather the worse for wear at Mattapan station in August 1974. (Author)

Boston picture window car 3276 approaches North Eastern University in August 1974. (Author)

Car 1171, a post-war car of Cincinnati which used double trolleys. Apart from that feature, this represents the standard post-war car. It is at Vine Street car house in 1948. (A.D. Young, Evda Slides)

Boston 3268 at Mattapan in October 2000 shows the off-side centre doors and the monitor roof fitted to these war-time cars when forced ventilation was installed. This tram was one of those to be rehabilitated by MBTA staff, down to the finishing touch of wings around the headlamp. (Author)

Pittsburgh, rebuilt car 4012 in September 1986. (Jim D. Schantz)

saw to it that a new franchise let to DC Transit in 1956 required complete abandonment by 1963. In other places, such as Minneapolis, take-overs which were questionably legal saw the cars replaced by buses with indecent haste. Perhaps the most bizarre case was that of Louisville, which, impressed by a demonstrator from Pittsburgh in 1940, ordered 25 cars in 1945. These were all sold to Cleveland before delivery had been completed and without any of them actually entering service, in exchange for a number of buses and an undisclosed amount in cash. Even the finest of street rail vehicles was powerless against this combination of adverse factors. The PCC survived in the USA only where there were special infrastructure considerations, usually in the form of subways.

With the abandonments, a brisk trade grew up in second-hand PCC cars. Toronto was especially active in this field and acquired excellent bargains from Birmingham (48), Cincinnati (52), Cleveland (75) and Kansas City (30). As many of these were only five years old at the time of purchase, the TTC was able to use them for almost as long as the cars which it purchased new. Philadelphia acquired 50 cars of the 1600 class from St Louis, and Boston bought eight double-ended cars from Dallas. Using second-hand cars, both El Paso and Newark were able to join the ranks of PCC operators. The former bought 20 cars from San Diego for its international line into Mexico, while the latter took 30 cars from Minneapolis. Some of these were to remain in service, still in good condition, until 2001. An unusual venture began in 1962 when five cars were acquired from Washington to be used on a short line in Fort Worth, connecting a parking lot with a city centre department store via a subway. The cars were modified for high platform operation and air conditioned. Service began in 1963 and two additional cars were acquired later in that year. Despite the line, patronage of the department store declined, but in 1975 the Tandy Corporation, who had in the meantime taken it over, decided to refurbish the entire line and cars. New and very boxy bodies were constructed, using many parts of the originals, and eight cars were bought from Boston to ensure a supply of spare parts. Thus rejuvenated, the Fort Worth line ran until 1997. Minneapolis also sold 20 cars to Shaker Heights, which also bought 10 cars from St Louis in 1959. That city had already sold 50 cars to Philadelphia in 1954 and in 1957 it leased 66 surplus cars to San Francisco. In 1966 the latter city acquired the cars outright. By 1960 the home market was virtually saturated and further sales went overseas. At a much later date, cars continued to change owners, but now for different reasons.

Philadelphia acquired 30 cars from Toronto after a fire at Woodland depot in October 1975 had led to a serious shortage of serviceable vehicles. The cars concerned were ex-Kansas City and ex-Birmingham. By this time the tide had turned and, faced with the considerable growth in passenger numbers of 27% in three years, Shaker Heights in 1978 bought cars from both Toronto and Newark. The tide had also turned financially – whereas in the early 1960s cars in good condition were traded for little more than scrap value, these now cost about US$12,500 each. In San Francisco, construction work on the Market Street subway for both light and heavy rapid transit increased running times and made it essential to acquire some cars as a stop-gap;

Toronto further rebuilt a few cars in the 1980s, but 4600, seen here in the city centre, has already been assigned to the vintage trolley service! (Author)

One of the Pittsburgh cars which was less thoroughly modified, 4005, is seen at Library in October 1987. (Author)

Ex-TTC cars in service on the Ramleh line in Alexandria, led by 626 at Pl Zaghoul in January 1976. (HUS, A.D. Young, Evda Slides)

An interior shot of a car of the Newark subway line in October 2000. (Author)

eleven ex-Kansas City cars came from Toronto late in 1973.

The first sale to a foreign operator occurred in 1956 when one Baltimore car was sold to the Ferrocarril Norte in Costa Rica; it was regauged and converted to diesel power and was still in service in at least 1967. In 1959 the 30 large double-ended Pacific Electric cars were sold to the Ferrocarril Nacional General Urquiza of Argentina, for use on a radial line out of Buenos Aires. Twelve cars were rebuilt to run as intermediate cars in three-car sets and lost both their driving cabs, being given corridor connections at each end, while thirteen others lost one cab and were given one connection. As the vehicles had been stored for some years they were in poor condition and ran only from July 1960 to December 1962. The most avid purchaser of PCCs was, however, Mexico City. After a very unpleasant accident in 1953, in which there were 60 fatalities, new trams were required immediately and in September of that year 91 were bought from Minneapolis. Single width front and centre doors were fitted on the left hand side, to allow loading from centre islands. These were followed in 1956 by 183 from Detroit, at a bargain price $506,900 or $2,770 per car (just under £1,000 at contemporary rates of exchange). The reason for the bargain was that Kansas City was also trying to unload its surplus PCC cars to Latin America! The arrival of these allowed the entire system to be converted to PCC operation. From 1971 to 1976 175 cars were substantially rebuilt, with new seats, floor coverings and driver's consoles. However, with the development of the subway network, the end of the tramways was in sight and, although a three-section articulated car was built in 1986 using PCC parts, all had gone by 1990.

Other cars went overseas. In Bosnia-Herçegovina, Sarajevo was then building a completely new standard gauge tram system and to start it, 74 trams were acquired from Washington in 1960 and 1963 (1-74) and ran into the 1970s, still in Washington's green livery. As detailed elsewhere, some were converted to articulated form. Barcelona bought 101 PCC cars from the same source between 1961 and 1964, of which 97 were put into service (1601-1697) and, fitted with a conductor's post near the front door, these ran until the abandonment of all tram lines in 1971. One has been preserved. In Egypt, Alexandria bought 140 trams from Toronto from 1966 to 1968 and used these on both the city lines and on the Alexandria-Ramleh line, in the latter case in three-car sets. Cairo bought 134 cars from Los Angeles in 1965 and regauged these from 1067mm to metre gauge. Not all entered service, some being used as a supply of spare parts. They lasted until the late 1970s. Experience in Egypt (and some cities in the US!)

showed that, despite the delicate and sophisticated control system, the PCC could take a good deal of punishment in service and cope with minimal maintenance.

The last part of the story of the PCC in North America concerns the rebuildings which took place in a few cities, to supplement fleets of new light rail vehicles, and the entry of the PCC into heritage operation. In Boston, Philadelphia and San Francisco PCC cars were given very thorough overhauls, with, in the case of the last two, a new paint scheme. Pittsburgh went much further and in 1981 produced in its own workshops a virtually new tram. Car 4000 used some components

This car, 1059, on the San Francisco heritage F service in September 1996 wears Boston's traction orange colour scheme. While technically inaccurate for this type of car – it is actually ex-Philadelphia 2099 – it nevertheless makes a most attractive picture as it enters the turning loop at the outer end of the service. (Author)

The Chicago cars had a triple-width rear doorway, as seen on 4391 at the Illinois Railway museum at Union, in September 1996. (Author)

which had been salvaged from scrapped cars of the 1700 class, but an entirely new frame was constructed for the body, new fibreglass ends were manufactured and the side body panels were made from Alucobond, a plastic material with an aluminium covering. These panels could not be welded, but had to be riveted, making this only the second ever riveted PCC car, the Clark car for Brooklyn being the other. All interior fittings were new and the trolley pole was replaced by a pantograph. A new red and white colour scheme, set off by black window surrounds, completed a most handsome vehicle and there were suggestions that a fleet of up to 40 cars would be so treated. In the event, the costs proved to be too great and only four cars were produced. Others received a much less radical rebuilding, including the fitting of a pantograph, and for some years these were successfully used to supplement the new fleet of Stadtbahn cars. However, in the case of every city except Boston, the reprieve was short-lived and all cars were withdrawn by 1990. The cars in Newark ran until 2001 and to-day only in Boston do PCC cars still survive in commercial service, on the isolated Ashmont-Mattapan line, which officially forms part of the Red Line subway. This line will be closed for renovation throughout 2006 and while this is being done, the trolley poles on the cars will be replaced by pantographs.

But that was by no means the end of the story. The PCC has lasted long enough to acquire the status of "heritage" and as such has been used on several of the lines which have opened in recent years, as in Kenosha and Dallas. But the most interesting development has taken place in San Francisco where the last PCC car ran in normal service on 19 September 1982. Although the Muni-Metro subway under Market Street has been a success, there seemed to be still a niche for a tram line on the surface, to cater for short-distance riders and tourists. The undertaking therefore acquired a number of PCC cars from Philadelphia, which have been thoroughly renovated and made accessible for wheelchair passengers. They have been repainted in the colours of operators who have in the past run PCC cars and are maintained in excellent condition. Even although some of the liveries are technically not correct for the type of car employed, the cars look most attractive and the service (F – Market) has become very popular with the travelling public. Eighteen cars for a similar operation on line 15 in Philadelphia have been thoroughly reconstructed with new trucks, motors and suspension and IGBT control with regenerative braking. They now have wheelchair lifts and air conditioning, which, along with other equipment, is housed in a monitor on the roof. Repainted in the traditional green and cream livery, these presented a most attractive appearance when they re-entered service in September 2005. Eight ex-Newark cars have been given by New Jersey Transit for use on a heritage line in Bayonne. Toronto's 4000 and 4600 are preserved at the Halton County Radial Railway and many other PCC cars have been preserved elsewhere, almost all operators being represented in at least one collection. Even as the PCC car approaches its 70th birthday, the story is far from finished.

Technical details
Brooklyn and Queens Transit 1936
Length 14.14m, width 2.54m, weight 14.8 tonnes, 4 x 35kW motors.

CARS WITH PCC CHARACTERISTICS

San Francisco 1003 as preserved at the Western Railway Museum, Rio Vista junction, photographed in 1987. (Author)

Before production was under way, a few cars were built for Washington, generally along the lines which would be followed in the final PCC specification. Ten each were built by Brill (1001-1010) and the St Louis Car Co (1051-1060), and to the passenger their performance was probably indistinguishable from that of the later PCCs. The two classes were not identical, the St. Louis cars having ribbed body sides, as in experimental car B, and were the first production all-welded cars in the USA. These proved to be heavy on maintenance. Internally both types owed much to the Brill cars recently supplied to Indianapolis. Cost per car was almost the same in each batch and was approximately $36,200 or about £7,000 at contemporary rates of exchange. They introduced to the city a new and most attractive livery of turquoise blue lower panels and dove grey upper areas. These trams were withdrawn in 1959. No.1053 was preserved at the National Capital Trolley Museum but unfortunately was destroyed in a fire at the premises in September 2003.

Chicago in 1933 decided to buy two sample cars which would be "the best ... that can be produced at this time". One each came from Brill (7001) and Pullman (4001) and electrical manufacturers used these cars to test equipment which they were considering for the PCC. The Brill car looked rather like those which would be built for Washington some months later, being designed by Otto Kuhler, its inspiration being contemporary motor car design. The Pullman car was very light for its size, being constructed of aluminium throughout, and had some affinity with contemporary railway streamlined trains. Both lasted in service until 1947 and the body of the Pullman car is preserved, unrestored, at the Illinois Railway Museum.

The potentially greatest challenge to the PCC came from Brill. That manufacturer had originally been a member of the Committee, but had later withdrawn, for reasons best known to itself, and then became bitterly hostile to the whole concept, refusing to build cars to the PCC design. The success of the ten cars supplied to Washington perhaps persuaded it that an alter-

Philadelphia Suburban Brilliner 7, in SEPTA livery at Drexel Hill in October 1980. (Author)

native car would attract orders, which would fill the empty order book of 1937. The result was the Brilliner, the first of which was, with some financial help form the Pennsylvania Railroad, placed in service in Atlantic City in 1938. It was styled by Raymond Loewy, the noted industrial designer, and was a lighter car than the PCC, but offering most of the advantages and an equally smooth ride. The bolted truck used, the Brill 97-ER-1, caused fewer problems than early PCC trucks. But in all only 40 Brilliners were built, mostly going to Atlantic City (24) and the Philadelphia Suburban Transportation Company, a radial line out of Philadelphia (10). The few large city systems which took one or two as demonstrators did not come back for more and none were built after 1941. The PST cars, however, ran successfully until 1982 and one has been preserved.

Washington – Brill car 1009 at Friendship Heights loop on 13 September 1941. (Seashore Trolley Museum Library collection)

Chicago's Brill car after withdrawal. Vincennes yard, October 1956. (A.D. Young, Evda Slides)

No.1053, one of the city's St Louis cars, emerges from Lincoln Park car house, running on the conduit system, on 27 June 1959. (A.D. Young, Evda Slides)

In 1939 Brill supplied two sets of these trucks to the St Louis Car Co. which was currently building five PCC cars for San Francisco Municipal Railway (1001-1005). Due to the use of Brill trucks under two of the five, the TRC refused to allow them to be called PCC cars, although they did make an attempt to collect the royalties on the cars. The SFMR fought back and the matter was allowed to drop, although the cars were thenceforward referred to as "Magic Carpet" cars. They were withdrawn in 1959/60 and car 1003 has been preserved.

Post-war, the only PCC-type cars to be built were a series of 14 for the Philadelphia Suburban (11-24) which appeared in 1949. These were double-ended cars with end doors only and, while they looked identical to other PCCs, they were not classed as such, since they rode on Commonwealth equalised trucks, which gave an exceptionally smooth ride. They ran until the early 1980s and nos.14, 23 and 24 are preserved.

Technical details

Washington Brill cars

Length 13.27m, width 2.54m, weight 15.87 tonnes, 4 x 37kW motors, capacity not given.

Still wearing its Red Arrow livery, Philadelphia Suburban 20 is seen at Drexel Hill in October 1980. (Author)

EUROPE

HTM pioneer car 1001 at Scheveningen in 1955. (W.J. Wyse, courtesy London Area, Light Rail Transit Association and Electric Railway Society)

In 1943, while Belgium was still occupied by German forces, the director of rolling stock of the Tramways Bruxellois, R. Hanocq, began to consider new designs for post-war construction and to acquire information on both the most recent Swiss trams (qv) and the PCC car. At the same time, the electrical firm of ACEC, building on experiments with a car of the Brussels 5000 class, was investigating the possibilities of multi-notch control systems. In its own workshops the TB also constructed two bogies of modern design, based closely on those under the Brilliner cars. In 1944 both the new control system and these bogies were placed under car 5018, which made one trial run through the city. Although the bogies performed satisfactorily, the control system did not function well and the car was then laid up in the workshops. On 1 January 1946 the TB was provisionally replaced by the Transports Urbains de l'Agglomeration Bruxelloise (TUAB).

This new administration immediately resumed the studies undertaken during the war and in July 1946 a delegation visited Zürich to experience the new Swiss cars at first-hand. This group included Ijr de Vooght, chairman of the board of the TUAB. On 29 August 1946 the Belgian Electrorail group obtained the licence to build PCC cars for the three Benelux countries and, on a non-exclusive basis, for the Middle East, China and South-East Asia. A second study visit, to the USA, was undertaken in November 1946 but, tragically, the aircraft in which the participants were travelling crashed on landing and de Vooght and an engineer of ACEC lost their lives. Despite this setback, the tour went ahead. The conclusion reached was that the PCC car was superior with regard to bogies and electrical equipment, but that the bodywork of the Swiss car, with passenger flow from rear to front, would be more suitable for Belgian conditions. To test the concept in practice, car 5001 was rebuilt with a fixed post for the conductor and a new central door and placed in service on 5 April 1947. It was a resounding success.

The first appearance of a PCC car in Europe was on 25 January 1948 when a prototype built by the St Louis Car Company and imported from the USA was tried on the Brussels-Tervuren line,

HTM Den Haag 1016 demonstrating passenger flow in the city centre in September 1959. (Author)

HTM 1128 at Scheveningen Zeebad terminus in September 1959. (Author)

its width of 2.5m preventing its use elsewhere. It was painted green with beige trim. It was then fitted with metre gauge trucks and tried on the Brussels-Leuven line of the SNCV and later in the Liège area. While it was generally successful, its riding on sleeper track was bouncy, to say the least, and some passengers complained of mal-

HTM non-driving motor car 2117 at Holl. Spoor terminus of line 11 in August 1975. (Author)

HTM 1332 and a motorised trailer in service on line 11 in August 1975. (Author)

HTM works car H23 was formerly one of the 1300 class and is now a rail grinder. It is on line 11 in March 2003. (Author)

Gent nos.25 and 50 at St. Pieter's Station in August 1985. (Author)

Antwerp's no.2026 crosses an older car at Wilrijk in September 1962. (Author)

SNCV management had been impressed by the acceleration, noiseless operation and smooth riding of the PCC car on street track, as had both the TUAB and HTM of Den Haag in the Netherlands. The last of these was first off the mark and ordered two prototypes from the factory of La Brugeoise, with electrical equipment by ACEC of Charleroi. The first of the two trams (1001/2) went into service on 19 September 1949 on line 9 to Scheveningen, with the second following in December. They were shorter and narrower than the US standard, with dimensions of 14m x 2.2m, but the standee windows gave them an authentic transatlantic appearance. They had front and rear doors only, the seated conductor had a post at the rear and 80 passengers could be carried, 38 of them seated. They were successful in service and an order was then placed for a production series of 22 trams (1003-1024). These were slightly shorter again, at 13.5m, and had front and centre doors only. These were designed for one person operation and the two prototypes were converted to this layout in 1952. All received a major overhaul in 1970-72. The prototypes were rebuilt in 1975/6 and were then converted to the same door layout as the production series. In 1988/9 they spent some months on driver training duties in Amsterdam, to give drivers experience of pedal control which was about to be introduced in the new low floor cars. Car 1002 was scrapped in 1992 after an accident, but its sister survived until the end of PCC operation in the next year and has been preserved.

The HTM was so pleased with the performance of the PCC cars that it ordered a further series of 100 cars (1101-1200) from La Brugeoise, with delivery in 1957/8. These trams had a much more European appearance, with five large picture windows instead of eleven small ones and there were no standee windows. Less visually obvious was an alteration to the suspension, with secondary springs fitted to dampen the tendency to yaw when travelling at speed. The control system was also modified to allow the cars to coast. A single width exit door was fitted at the rear and this limited the seating capacity to 36. This class was fitted with Scharfenberg couplings and m.u. equipment and generally ran in coupled pairs. The last four trams of this order had Düwag trucks with tandem drive, in an effort to improve their riding qualities. This experiment was not successful and, as these bogies required the body to be set higher than on the other 96 cars, they were incompatible with these. In 1972 they were fitted with standard bogies. A further series of basically similar cars (1201-1240) followed in 1963. These had a width of 2.35m and could carry 101 passengers. To cope with route extensions, further batches of 40 driving motor trams (1301-1340) and 30 non-driving motors (2101-2130) were delivered in the years 1971-73. The latter seated 40 passengers and were fitted with simple controllers at front and rear for shunting only. The last five of the driving motors had thyristor control.

In Den Haag their success ensured the retention of the tram, which had been under threat of replacement by buses c1950 and they provided the entire service for a period of twenty years, giving the Dutch capital an excellent service of swift and silent trams, in keeping with the character of the city. They were appreciated by passengers and crews, although the 1000 class could be just too lively and cause feelings of tram-sickness, even for the drivers, and HTM occasionally received doctor's notes requesting that a driver should not be allocated to one of these cars. However, it has to be said that notes were also received asking that a driver should be assigned to PCC cars only! The 1200 class was probably the most popular owing to its excellent riding qualities. It may be questioned why the design was not further developed and unfortunately it has to be said that this was due much

de-tram. Its high current consumption, more than 60% above that of a comparable standard car, did not endear it to the SNCV's accountants. However, it was taken into the fleet as 10419 and from August 1948 ran for some time on the coast line, before being sent to Charleroi, where it languished in Jumet depot before an early withdrawal. It was scrapped in 1964.

Meanwhile the TUAB engineers were working on a second prototype and car 5018 was again taken into the workshops, stripped to the floor and fitted with a new body which clearly owed much to the Swiss bogie car. Despite the success with the trials of car 5001, this tram was not given a central door, but once again passenger flow from rear to front was installed. The latest type of ACEC controller was fitted and passengers were dazzled by the fluorescent lighting. The tram entered service on 7 August 1949 on line 40 and once again the trials gave brilliantly successful results.

Despite the mixed results of its trials, the

Vicinal 10339 in Charleroi in 1957. (F.W. Hunt, courtesy London Area, Light Rail Transit Association)

An ex-Vicinal car in service as Beograd 131 at Nemanjuna on 13 September 1975. (Roger N.H. Jones)

Antwerp. On the new line on the left bank of the Scheldt, no.7114 heads a two-car set inbound to the city via the cross-river tunnel, March 2004. (Author)

Hamburg's PCC car in service. (Lars F. Richter collection)

The rebuilding has not improved the appearance of the Gent cars, a good deal of equipment now being mounted on the roof, as seen on car 6211 at Kornmarkt in March 2004. (Author)

more to changing social habits rather than to any shortcomings in the PCC cars themselves. Because of staff shortages, it became more and more necessary to operate coupled sets, in which the rear car was unstaffed, and by 1980 a serious problem of vandalism had emerged. Despite a concerted campaign in local schools, the HTM was unable to stop this and it was recognised that the articulated car would in future provide a more secure environment. The PCCs had to go and the last ran in public service in 1993. However, apart from works cars, one survives as a party car (P1 ex 1302) and trucks and motors from many others are still running under the current articulated trams. Nos. 1024, 1227 and 1306 are preserved in Amsterdam and three (1165, 1210 and 1304) in Den Haag, where in 1999 they were briefly returned to traffic to cover a shortage of articulated cars.

In 1950 the SNCV ordered 24 PCC cars from La Brugeoise (10395-10418) and these went into service on the Brussels-Leuven line and in the Charleroi area. They were of standard US design, but narrower (2.32m), and had a conductor's desk immediately behind the entrance door on the nearside, which in service proved to be something of a bottleneck. On the Leuven line they soon experienced the same problems as had the prototype and all were then concentrated in Charleroi. They proved to be expensive to maintain and in 1960 all were sold to Beograd, where they ran until the early 1980s. Car 10409 has now returned to Belgium for preservation and is

in operation on the museum line at Thuin, near Charleroi.

The Brussels undertaking had meanwhile placed an order for 50 PCC cars (7001-7050) on 30 May 1950 and the first entered service with a press run to Tervuren on 28 November 1951. This tram was closely based on the design of 5018, as rebuilt, but was given an additional centre exit door. The trams were built by La Brugeoise, with ACEC motors, Westinghouse electrical equipment and rode on B3 trucks. Like the trams for Den Haag, these were all-electric cars and, after teething troubles had been corrected, proved to be very successful in service. A further series of 30 (7051-7080) followed in 1955/6 and in 1957 the undertaking bought 77 sets of trucks and equipment from Kansas City, on which La

Brugeoise built and equipped 75 new bodies (7081-7155). These trams differed from the earlier classes in that they had B2 trucks. Finally in 1970-71, to meet a shortage of rolling stock occasioned by delayed delivery of articulated cars, a further 16 (7156-7171) were built on B3 trucks acquired from Johnstown, when that system closed. The Brussels cars were built for passenger flow from rear to front, but in 1969-71 all were converted for one-person operation. By 1977 all cars had received pantographs in place of trolley poles, many having carried both forms of current collection for some years. Almost all received a major rebuilding from 1987 onwards and in this process, the driver's position became an enclosed cabin. Although many have now been withdrawn, all of the last batch received substantial overhauls from 1996 onwards and were still in service in 2004, along with some veterans such as 7003 and 7008. It is expected that about 23 will still be required after the current order for low floor trams has been completed. Four have been rebuilt into double-ended cars for driver training. Already nos.7047 and 7093 have been set aside for museum purposes and no doubt others will follow. In 2004 car 7037 was shipped to San Francisco for use on the Market Street line F, on which it now runs as Zurich 737. While there is no logic in this new

The two Stockholm PCC cars, with no.11 leading, on sightseeing duty. (W.J. Wyse, courtesy London Area, Light Rail Transit Association)

The terminus at Heysel Esplanade during the Brussels International Exposition of 1958. Car 7028 is nearest the camera and to its left is rebuilt car 5021. (Author)

A Brussels PCC in later days. No.7033 carries its 52 years lightly as it speeds past Woluwe depot (on the left) in March 2004. (Author)

identity, it does provide an interesting example of what might have been! Despite their high current consumption, these have been immensely successful cars, perhaps at their best when transporting the crowds to the 1958 International Exposition.

When the first batch was under construction, one further car was built for Hamburg (3060, class V8) and delivered in 1951. It was tried for some years, at first on line 8, then on a suburban shuttle service for some years. Passengers and staff appreciated its quietness and good riding qualities. However, its high current consumption – the lights on nearby cars dimmed when it accelerated from a stop – placed it at a severe disadvantage compared with the undertaking's own V6 class and its use was limited by the tight clearances of the Hamburg system. In January 1958 it was loaned to Copenhagen and ran there on line 7 from 24 February to 18 March, but again German cars were preferred for fleet replacement, and it then moved on to join its sister cars in Brussels, where, renumbered 7000, it entered service on 16 June 1958. The only

lasting result of this experiment was the design of doors on the class V7 bogie cars. It is now preserved in Denmark, at Skjoldenaesholm, restored to Hamburg livery. Hannover briefly showed some interest in the design, but as its introduction would have required expensive modifications to both track and electrical supply lines, the project was still-born. The US authorities which occupied the southern part of the new Federal Republic also tried to interest the various undertakings in their zone in the PCC, but without success; what was needed for speedy reconstruction were simple trams which would not require any alterations to the infrastructure and, by the time these immediate post-war problems had been solved, the US had lost interest in the PCC.

A further five cars were also constructed for Beograd in 1952 (112-116), this being the only export order received by Western Europe from a system in a communist country. These differed from the standard Belgian design in that they were mounted on B6 bogies for metre gauge. In the mid-1970s the trolley poles were replaced by

Three views of Brussels 7155 as displayed at the Transport Pavilion. Visitors could inspect it from below and also from inside and a section of the flooring has been replaced by a Perspex panel to allow a view of the accelerator. It was also possible to drive the car, although of course it did not actually move! (Author)

pantographs and the original livery of green and white was changed to red and white. They were withdrawn in 1984/5.

Antwerp soon followed the example of the capital and placed the first of its PCC cars in service on 18 October 1960 (2000-2060). These had the front end fitted to the cars for St-Étienne (qv) and, at 13.7m long, were slightly shorter than the Brussels cars. As they were built for metre gauge, they had B6 bogies with the frame outside the wheels. Forty further cars followed in 1966 (2061-2100), 25 more (2101-2125) in 1969-70 and a final 40 (2126-2165) in 1974/5. The Antwerp cars had, as built, passenger flow from front to rear with the conductor's desk a little way behind the front door. After prolonged negotiations with the unions, they were converted for one-person operation. They are fitted for m.u. operation and have very successfully operated in the tram tunnels which have been built in this city, including the long one under the river Scheldt, opened on 21 September 1990, by cars 2100 and 2165. Almost all are still in service, those from 2061 onwards having been substantially rebuilt with thyristor control between 1990 and 1999. A further 35 cars of the first batch have since been similarly treated, with a further five awaiting their turn, while the others are in course of withdrawal. Now under control of "De Lijn", the PCCs have been renumbered in the 7xxx series. Car 7000 has been preserved, in operational condition, in the city's transport museum in Groehnhoek. The PCC car made an excellent job of modernising what had by 1960 become an operational museum and, coupled with tunnel operation, has been a fine advertisement for light rail.

In 1958/9 30 single-ended cars (501-530) were constructed for Saint-Étienne by the Ateliers de Strasbourg under licence from La Brugeoise. Equipment and motors were supplied by Le Matériel Eléctrique SW, under licence from ACEC. The bogies were also of French manufacture, being made by CAF de la Loire. These trams were based closely on the Brussels trams, but were narrower having a width of only 2m and had a redesigned front end with a panoramic windscreen. The Strasbourg undertaking showed some interest in these trams but any possibility of a trial was refused by the local authority and Strasbourg had to wait another thirty years to sample a modern tram! They not only saved the Saint-Étienne system but succeeded so well in developing traffic on one of France's few remaining tramways that they soon had to be supplemented by articulated cars. All were substantially modernised between 1981 and 1983 and given a new livery of white with dark green bands. Many were withdrawn in 1993, after the arrival of low floor trams. Car 507 was briefly tried in Gent in 1994, not in passenger service, but that undertaking then decided to buy second-hand cars from Germany and it was scrapped, the bogies being kept as a reserve. The remainder ran for the last time on 10 July 1998. Car 502 has been preserved in its native city, while cars 503 and 510 are preserved in Lille and Paris respectively.

In 1969 Marseille bought 16 cars (01-16) from La Brugeoise to modernise its one short line. These were double-ended, since both ends of the line had stub terminals, and had three doors per side. In view of the short length of the tram line, they had seats for only 16 passengers. They were fitted for m.u. operation. Although Marseille has a gauge of 1430mm, the narrow width of the Saint-Étienne cars was repeated in this version. To avoid any accidents on the down gradient in the subway on the inner part of the line, an automatic control system limited the speed on inbound cars to 28km/hr. A further three cars (17-19) followed from BN in 1984, these being the last PCC trams to be built anywhere. Fleet numbers became TA01-16 and TB17-19. After modernisation of the first batch in 1983/4, all continued in service until 4 January 2004, when the line was closed for re-gauging and extension. Nos.TA11, 15 and 16 have been preserved locally and the bogies of the remainder were bought by HTM of Den Haag to provide a float of spares.

The last European city to convert to PCC operation was Gent, where the Marseille design was copied in double-ended configuration. The city had pursued a policy of bus substitution for its tramways in the 1960s but then reversed this after study visits were made to several modern systems both in Belgium and abroad. An idea of importing PCC cars from Pittsburgh having foundered on the question of gauge, the MIVG then ordered 30 cars from BN in 1969 (01-30). These were based closely on the design of those recently supplied to Marseille but with doors at front and rear only and a different accelerator. A further series of 16 (31-46) followed in the autumn of 1972 and a further eight (47-54) arrived in 1974, to complete the modernisation of the system. In 1998/9 cars 14 and 19 were rebuilt with thyristor control by Mittenwalder Gerätebau in Germany and almost all the others have been similarly treated since 2000. The trams are now owned by De Lijn and have been renumbered in the 62xx series. It is likely that most of the Gent PCC cars will remain in service for some years and it is planned to retain 6201 in its original condition for future preservation.

In 1951 Stockholm Spårvägar decided to experiment with PCC cars and ordered two from AB Svenska Järnvägskaderna, the PCC licence holder for Sweden, with electrical equipment from the St Louis Car Co. They were classed A28 and numbered 10 and 11. They entered service in 1952 and externally were a clear blend of US and Swedish styling. They were operated with a seated conductor and passenger flow from front to rear. They were fitted with m.u. equipment and generally ran coupled. After some time they were allocated to the sightseeing tour until the contraction of the system made this unworkable and car 10 was scrapped in 1964. The other has been preserved at Malmköping. They came too late to have much effect on the future of the city's tramways.

With a total of 443 bogie trams built to this

Beograd Brussels-type 116 has just left Novo Groblje terminus and is southbound on Ruzveltova in July 1975. (Peter Haseldine)

basic design, this must be counted as one of the most successful European trams of the post-war period.

Technical details

Brussels 7001
Length 13.95m, width 2.2m, weight 15 tonnes, 4 x 40kW motors, 100 passengers, 32 seated.
Den Haag 1100 class
Length 13.45m, width 2.2m, weight 17,700kg, 4 x 41kW motors, 93 passengers, 36 seated.
Stockholm 10
Length 13.9m, width 2.18m, weight 15 tonnes, 4 x 40kW motors, 100 passengers, 34 seated.

GREAT BRITAIN

Towards the end of the Second World War, there seemed to be a possibility that several of the 20 remaining tramways in Britain would be modernised in the post-war years and English Electric, in association with the Westinghouse Corporation of the USA, therefore made an attempt to interest operators in a production run of PCC cars. It is thought that discussions were held with Blackpool, Glasgow, Leeds, Liverpool and Sheffield Corporations. A drawing of the proposed car was produced, based on the double-ended cars constructed in pre-war years in the USA, but with reduced dimensions. This would have been for one person operation. A single-ended option would have been offered, as would have been two person operation, m.u. equipment and a control trailer. Unfortunately, the operators, as always, could not agree on a standard design and in any case, when Liverpool in October 1945 announced its plans to abandon trams, about half of the estimated demand evaporated. US business interests were also becoming nervous about what they perceived as the left-wing policies of the Attlee government. Britain's nearest approach to the PCC, the Vambac car, is dealt with in the chapter on central entrance trams. However, Glasgow did go as far as to construct a model of a car rather like this proposed design, but with more pointed ends and fitted with a bow collector and this still exists, a memorial to another failed opportunity.

Technical details

Proposed British PCC
Length 13.48m, width 2.28m, weight c16.5 tonnes, 4 x 33kW motors, passengers according to layout – 47-61 seated, 12-40 standing.

St. Etienne 403 in revised livery in September 1987. (Author)

Marseille 2001 on Bvd Chave inbound to Noailles in March 1983. (Author)

AUSTRALIA

In 1938 the Melbourne and Metropolitan Tramways Board had proposed to import complete a double-ended PCC car for evaluation. This proposal foundered, probably on grounds of cost, and instead it was decided to import a set of trucks, control equipment and motors and, using these, build a tram locally. The war hindered any progress on this scheme, but in 1947 the MMTB obtained the licence to build PCC cars not only for its own use but for the rest of Australia, New Zealand and Asia, excluding Japan and the USSR. It was not until 1949 that the B3 trucks and General Electric equipment arrived and were fitted to a new body, the result being car 980, which entered service in July 1950. In layout, this followed the traditional Melbourne drop centre plan, although, as the floor level in the middle of the car had to be raised to give clearance for the equipment, the centre was not "dropped" and there was a level floor throughout. An extra, recessed step gave access to the car. The control equipment was modified for hand rather than pedal operation and the top notch on the control system was locked out of service, to minimise the risk of accidents with other trams. For the first eleven years of its career, car 980 was confined to inter-suburban service 69 (Kew – St Kilda) and was not used in the central area, but from 1960 it ran on the Bourke Street services, in company with the MMTB's most modern trams of class W7. It was withdrawn in May 1971 and was then used to test some of the components for the class Z trams. It was finally withdrawn in November 1972 and its trucks and much of the equipment, but not the control system, were transferred to prototype car 1041. The body was sold to the Tramway Museum Society of Victoria in 1982 and has since been preserved on un-motored trucks. An excellent model also exists in the driver training school at Hawthorn depot. Car 1041 is a double-ended Peter Witt style tram, built to test the features which it was proposed to incorporate into class Z trams (qv). It has ACEC control equipment, built in Belgium. It entered service on 26 August 1973 and was tested throughout the system before settling down to work on Bourke Street services. However, it was taken out of service in April 1975 and stored until very recently, when it was moved into the new museum set up in Hawthorn depot.

It has to be questioned if the PCC had a fair trial in Melbourne. A single car running among over 600 conventional trams was unlikely to

Car 1041 pauses in the Royal Park while working an enthusiasts' tour. (Mal Rowe and B. Parkinson)

make much impact or have a real chance to show its paces. There were also problems with foreign exchange and the government of Victoria exerted some pressure on the MMTB to use a more conventional design of tram for its new building programme in the mid-1950s. But perhaps the basic Melbourne design had been so successful that there was no real need to experiment with anything else in any serious way. Similarly, reports in 1952 that Sydney was considering acquiring ten PCC cars seem to have been based on optimism rather than fact!

Technical details

980
Length 14.17m, width 2.77m, weight 17.4 tonnes, 4 x 41 kW motors, 48 seats.
1041
Length 16.16m, width 2.67m, weight 20.2 tonnes, 4 x 44 kW motors, 48 seats.

Bibliography
PCC The Car that fought back. S.P. Carlson and F. W. Schneider III. Interurban Press, Glendale CA, 1980.
PCC From Coast to Coast. S.P. Carlson and F. W. Schneider III. Interurban Press, Glendale CA, 1983.
An American Original – the PCC car. S. Kashin and H. Demorro. Interurban Press, Glendale CA, 1986
Fifty Years of Progressive Transit – a History of the Toronto Transit Commission. J.F. Bromley and J. May. Electric Railroaders' Association, New York, 1973.
Lightweight Street and Interurban Cars. Op.cit.
Harbingers of a New Era (Washington experimental cars). P.C. Kohler. National Capital Trolley Museum Journal, vol 11, no.1, Spring 1995.
Street Cars, Light Rail & Utility Cars of St Louis. A.D. Young. Op.cit.
Electric Car Builders' Images. Op.cit.
Der Stadtverkehr 1/1981.
Destination City. Op.cit.
Modern Tramway nos.172, April 1952 (Brussels),
181, January 1953 (Stockholm), 369,370 and 372, September, October and December 1970 (Technical description of PCC equipment), 437, May 1974 (Melbourne 1041).
PCC's (Den Haag). J Kres en P. Muré. Haags Openbaar Vervoer Museum, Den Haag, 1992.
50 Jaar/Ans PCC – deel/partie 1 and 2. HK (Luxembourg) SA, Lentzweiler, Luxembourg, 2000.
Strassenbahn Magazin, nos.60, May 1986 (Hamburg), 120/1, July and September 1999, 137, March 2001 (San Francisco heritage fleet).
100 Years of the Belgian Vicinal. W.J.K. Davies. Light Rail Transit Association, London 1985.
Instappen a.u.b! Honderd Jaar Buurtspoorwegen in Belgie. C. Henrard ed. De Nederlansche Boekhandel, Amsterdam and Antwerpen, 1985.
Liverpool Transport vol 4. J. B. Horne and T. B. Maund. Transport Publishing Company Ltd, Glossop, 1989 (Proposed UK design).
NB Articulated PCC cars are dealt with in the chapter on that type.

JAPAN

In 1952 Sumitomo Metal Industries acquired a licence to build PCC cars in Japan and in 1954 produced one car for Tokyo (5501), using its version of the B3 truck, the body being built by Naniwa Koki. As it was anticipated that the tram would at most run for only fifteen years, the body was somewhat austere. This tram along with other non-PCC cars of similar design ran only on service 1, and when that was withdrawn in 1967, it was taken out of service. It has since been preserved. Trucks using PCC components were supplied to Kobe, Osaka and Nagoya and PCC equipment was used to rebuild a single tram in Hanshin. None of these cars is now in service and it seems that the PCC car came to Japan at the wrong time, abandonment of most large systems having already been decided.

Melbourne 980 at the terminus at Bourke and Spencer Streets in February 1971. (G.J. Travers)

CHAPTER 5
STANDARDISED TWO-AXLE CARS

It may seem strange to consider a two-axle tram as in any way "modern", but some of the trams built for service in Germany in the 1930s had features which carried over into post-war designs and also began the process of standardisation which was to become prevalent in the post-war years. This was despite the economic depression of the early 1930s and the anti-tram attitude of the NS government, which did not alter until the approach of war. As in other countries, competition from the motorbus was growing and those undertakings which believed in the tram sought to maximise its inherent advantages over that form of transport.

PREDECESSORS

Improvement in the basic two-axle design began in Norway where Trondheim took delivery of five cars (35-39) in 1930 from Strømmen; these had automatic folding doors, a seat for the driver and a capacity of 80 passengers and could be considered the first modern two-axle trams. Originally double-ended, they were rebuilt to single-ended layout between 1949 and 1956 and in the latter year all but car 36 were lost in the depot fire of 10 October. By a most unkind twist of fate, that car was itself burned out when in service just two months later, but was rebuilt by the undertaking in its own workshops, to the basic design of the contemporary bogie cars, and returned to service as car 8. It is now preserved in the city.

The first year in which any real progress was made in the design of the two-axle tram in Germany was 1934. In that year, the small system of Nordhausen replaced its entire fleet by eight new cars (21-28) built by the Wismar factory. While there was nothing striking about these cars, they set new standards, which would

In pre-U-Bahn days, Nürnberg 907 has just left the stop at Lorenzkirche's city centre in August 1967. (Author)

Nordhausen 23, seen near the depot in June 1990. (Author)

Preserved Rheinbahn 267 in Düsseldorf in May 1981. (Author)

have considerable influence in the dimensions and layout of post-war trams. No.2 is preserved in running order in its home town. In the same year, Dresden placed in service a two-axle, single-ended version of the "Hechtwagen". This car had a modified version of the control system fitted to the bogie cars, with 140 notches for acceleration and 118 for braking, this being also designed by Prof. Bockemühl. This tram showed the possibilities of having a two-axle design with fairly large carrying capacity and much of the comfort of the bogie car. Series production, with a yet more refined control system, followed in 1936 (25 cars) and 1938/9 (22 cars). These were double-ended and the prototype was rebuilt to conform. There were ultimately 48 of these trams, numbered in the 18xx series and known as the "Kleinen Hechten" (Little Pikes). The control system gave considerable problems and most cars were laid up by 1943. Twenty-two were destroyed by bombing in 1945 and the remainder were ultimately given new control systems developed by the workshop staff, from 1952 onwards. The last was withdrawn in 1972 and car 1820 has been preserved in the city. Magdeburg also acquired 18 trams (61-78), of which 11 were destroyed in air raids and of which car 70 has also been preserved, rebuilt as a single-ended car.

In 1935/6 the Rheinbahn in Düsseldorf placed in service two cars, numbered 1935/6, in which motors of small size, located at the outer ends of the truck, allowed the floor height to be lowered and in consequence these trams were much more accessible than those of other contemporary design. They were built by Düwag and were known as "Niederflur" trams, though of course they were very different from modern trams of this type and should really be considered to be lower floor, rather than low floor trams. Despite being of all-steel construction, they were not heavy. On no.1936 electrically-operated sliding doors enclosed the roomy platforms and in both

cars there were seats for 22 in the saloon. This tram had Siemens equipment with a multi-notch controller and cardan drive. No.1935 had conventional equipment but with a semi-automatic control system, the motors being placed under the seating area. Its larger wheels necessitated an additional entrance step and, at 12.5 tonnes, it was the heavier of the two. These trams were subjected to extensive testing and, as they proved to be successful, a series of 47 further cars (250-296) was delivered between 1937 and 1941, followed by a further 15 (350-364) in 1943. There were also 40 trailers (300-339). They were equally successful and those which

Erfurt's preserved 92, surrounded by Combinos in Bahnhofstrasse in June 2004. (Author)

Praha 3008 two-axle Peter Witt cars, Pavlov Square, May 1966. (A.D. Young, Evda slides)

Magdeburg's "Kleiner Hecht" at the central workshops in September 1992. (Author)

On 6 July 1955 one of Dijon's cars leaves the terminus at Ville station. (Author)

Toulouse 79, as preserved in the former AMTUIR museum in Paris. (Author)

survived the war ran until the early 1970s. Cars 267 and 316 have been preserved. All were built by Düwag, who between 1939 and 1942 also provided similar cars to Braunschweig (2), Bremerhaven (2), Bielefeld (4), Ennepe (2), Mülheim (4), Neuss (3), Remscheid (6) and the Vestische Strassenbahn (11). Dimensions of production cars were as for the prototypes, but they were slightly heavier at 12.15 tonnes and had more powerful motors of 65 or 75kW. Following some pressure from the Transport Ministry, thirty almost identical trams were built by Düwag and MAN for Nürnberg (901-930) and by Wismar for Rostock (34-39). Nürnberg staff were rather sceptical about these imports from the north and, despite the needs of the war years, took their time about placing the fleet in service. Nos.901 and 910 have been preserved, the latter in running order. There were in all 126 motor trams and 44 trailers of this type. Erfurt had 36 trams (82-117) of a rather different design, not of lower floor layout, built between 1936 and 1944 by the Gotha factory to the design of Wilhelm Klockow. One of these (92) has been preserved and another is still active as Bad Schandau 8, having arrived there via the Lockwitztalbahn in Dresden. Hannover had

eleven very attractive semi-streamlined motor cars (221-231) and six matching trailers (1038 and 1042-46) built by Credé between 1938 and 1943. The motor trams had a controller mounted in a central position under the floor. The last of these cars to be built were constructed of inferior materials and those which survived the war had a relatively short life. None has been preserved.

Technical details
Rheinbahn no.1936
Length 10.4m, width 2.35m, weight 11.3 tonnes, 2 x 52 kW motors, 64 passengers, 22 seated.

In Czecho-Slovakia, the Smichov factory in 1930 delivered four central entrance cars to Praha, two of which (3001/2) were very soon rebuilt with a double-width front entrance and a post for a seated conductor by the centre door. They proved to be successful, but delivery of further new cars was hindered by the question of changing the rule of the road from left to right. Once this had been done, two successive batches of similar trams arrived, cars 3005-3043 in 1939 and 3044-3068 in 1942. A further 30, from what had now become the Tatra factory, came out in 1948. On these, an additional rear exit was fitted. Although internal space was somewhat restricted, these trams showed that it was possible to work the Peter Witt system on a two-axle tram. Unfortunately the control system fitted was completely worn out by the mid-1960s and with the success of the T3 bogie cars, it was not worth trying to repair these trams. All except 3063 and 3083 were scrapped, these two being preserved in the city's transport museum. Brno bought one similar car in 1931 (150) and Plzen bought a total of twelve between 1933 and 1942. These lasted rather better than the trams in the capital and were in service until the mid-1970s. Brno clearly liked the type and bought 30 motor trams (117-146) and 30 trailers (297-326) in 1950. These

were attractive semi-streamlined cars and had passenger flow from rear to front. They lasted in service until the late 1970s and one has been preserved.

Torino also had 50 two-axle Peter Witt cars in 1929/30 (2001-2050) but then switched to bogie cars for further construction, since it was found that the restricted dimensions of these cars militated against the smooth running of the Peter Witt system.

Technical details
Nürnberg 901 class as built
Length 11.05m, width 2.2m, weight 15.13 tonnes, 2 x 75 kW motors, 73 passengers, 20 seated.

In Paris the STCRP began to experiment with one-man cars from 1927, with a view to reducing expenses on lines of light traffic. These had a dead man pedal, release of which applied the brakes, opened the doors and cut off the traction current. In all 34 old two-axle cars were converted and in July 1931 there appeared the prototype (2476) of what was intended to be a class of such cars to be built new. This was in the event the last new first-generation tram to be built for Paris and it remained a one-off, being used on line 94, a short line in Malakoff, until that closed in 1934. All these trams were quite successful in service and, had they been given a proper chance, might have led the way to a more economical method of working certain lines.

However, certain features were used in the Satramo trams which were built in the 1930s for a few other systems such as Dijon and Bordeaux. The title of this organisation, which was formed by a group of manufacturers led by Alsthom, was an acronym of Société Anonyme des Tramways Modernes and in 1932 it launched a completely new type of tram on to the French market, the first going to Versailles. The car had no separate

Hannover 222 pulling a KSW trailer. (A.D. Young, Evda Slides)

Zaragoza 161 in 1972. (A.D. Young, Evda slides)

underframe, the body being mounted directly on to two axles, 3.4m apart. There were two high-speed motors of 14kW, coupled permanently in parallel, which drove the axles through cardan drive and both regenerative and air brakes were fitted. The trams had an attractive all-metal body of 10.3m length and could be operated as one- or two-man cars and had a fairly low floor height of only 68cm. Unfortunately, there were not enough of them to make any real impact on the decline of the tram in France. A late export order for trucks came from Zaragoza in 1943 (101 class); some of these cars were fitted with attractive central-entrance bodies by Cardas y Escoriaza, while others had end doorways. They worked with matching trailers as "rames reversibles". Six motor cars and two trailers have been preserved. They were followed in 1945 by a class of similar design (151-166), from the same builder, of which most were constructed using motors and trucks from older cars, although some may have been built new. Of these no.166 has been preserved.

The basic Satramo design was also used in articulated cars in Algiers. (qv).

Technical details

Dijon 1938 design
Length 8.85m, width 2.2m, weight 10.6 tonnes, 2 x35kW motors, 48 passengers, 18 seated.

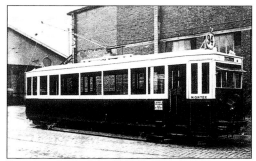

Prototype 2476 of the STCRP, 1931. (RATP)

THE PROPOSED GERMAN STANDARD TRAM (ESW)

In 1938 a transport exhibition was held in Düsseldorf and the new Niederflur cars served on a special line A from the city to the site of this. Officials from the Ministry of Transport were impressed, and the attitude of the NS government to tramways began to change from this time onwards. It was evident that the earlier practice of allowing individual undertakings to develop their own designs was not compatible with the government's policy of "Gleichschaltung" (standardisation) and would satisfy neither the current demand for transport nor the likely demands in time of war, which were outlined in the Wehrleistungsgesetz (Defence Capacity Law) of 13 July 1938. It was clearly necessary to develop a range of standard trams, which could be used on any system, and to this end the industry set up a working party, the Reichsverkehrsgruppe Schienenbahn (State Rail Working Group), under the direction of Paul Bayer, manager of the Nürnberg undertaking, which first met on 31 December 1938. The managers of the transport systems of Berlin, Dresden, Düsseldorf, Essen, Hamburg and Stuttgart were all members of this group, while, among the representatives of the car builders, there were two from Düwag and one each from MAN, Westwaggon and Christoph and Unmack. Given this membership, it was not surprising that the trams recently supplied to Düsseldorf and Nürnberg should have considerable influence on the planning for standard trams. An international transport exhibition was planned for 1940, in Köln, and it was hoped that the first standard trams could be on show there. In the event, this exhibition could not take place and the only tram built for it, Halle 500, was not to one of the proposed standard designs.

The group, however, continued its work and by 1941 had evolved designs for a range of standard trams, normally referred to as Einheits Strassenbahnwagen (ESW) or Standard Tram. It was estimated that annual production would be in the range of 2000 trams and that a total of 15,747 motor trams and 14,091 trailers would be produced in the next 15 years. All technical parameters would be standardised, but the choice of interior fittings and decoration would be left to the individual undertakings. There were designs for bogie, three-axle and two-axle motor trams and trailers, for both standard and metre gauge, but it was soon recognised that only the last two were likely to be produced in war time. Unfortunately very little of the great deal of detailed planning undertaken by the group actually had any result. The only trams built to any of the standard designs were 30 trailers built by the factory of Graaff, in Elze near Hannover for the BVG of Berlin, ten of which were still in the Hannover area in 1945 and remained there. Those which made it to Berlin were numbered 1601-1605 and 1616-1630. Ten cars (550-559) which were under construction for Bochum-Gelsenkirchen when the plans for the standard trams were fairly advanced, were constructed with many of their features incorporated, but were slightly shorter. The standard two-axle car would have been very like the cars built for Nürnberg, as detailed above, but would have had only three side windows. In June 1942 orders were given to halt all design work and the few contracts which had already been agreed were cancelled. It was a poor reward for all those who had worked so hard on the project, but, as will be seen, not all the effort was wasted, since some of the technology appeared in the standard cars built for DDR systems at a later date.

THE KSW

The reason for the change of policy mentioned above was the realisation that the need for new trams was greater than could be met by continuing to work on these projected designs, and on 8 July 1942 the Minister for Armaments and Munitions ordered the design of a much simpler and lighter car. It was expected that 300 each of motors and trailers would be required each year and that the first could be ready in the middle of 1943. The tram, initially referred to as the Kriegswagen and later and more generally as the Kriegsstrassenbahnwagen (KSW) (War Tram) would offer minimal comfort to passengers and crews but would technically comply with all safety requirements. There would be a pre-production run of 86 motor cars and 55 trailers for nine undertakings and this would be followed by two main programmes each delivering 810 motor trams and 1140 trailers. The Ministry of Armaments would have a considerable say in the delivery of the cars and these would be allocated to individual undertakings according to the needs of war production.

In the event, this plan proved to be somewhat optimistic. As conditions worsened, it became clear that the targets of 1943 could not be met but construction did begin in that year and the first tram was delivered to Berlin in the summer of 1944. This was done for propaganda purposes, but the BVG was not impressed by this relatively small car and dispatched it to the suburban Woltersdorf undertaking as soon as the official back was turned. There it remains to this day as car 7, now fully restored to operational condition and paired with matching trailer 22. As it became increasingly difficult to keep accurate records, and as some trams ended up in what became other countries in 1945, sources vary considerably as to how many cars were actually constructed before the war came to an end. It is clear that some did not reach their intended destination, as military traffic took priority in the last months of the war and in what became the British zone (BBZ) in 1945, trams were transferred between undertakings to fill the most urgent shortages. However, it seems certain that 18 undertakings received these trams, with the Berlin car being passed on as stated above. Of this total, two were in Austria (Wien and Graz) and three in what would soon be Poland (Kattowitz, Danzig and Posen). The second batch of five for the last of

The preserved pioneer KSW, 7, as restored at Woltersdorf, September 1992. At this date it carried the sand-brown paint scheme of 1944, but it has now been returned to cream livery. Preserved car 2 is on the right. (Author)

these were sent after the war had finished and were without electrical equipment, this not being installed until 1949/50. Of large German cities, only Frankfurt (M), München and Köln received substantial numbers of trams. Of the pre-production series, 67 motor cars and all trailers were actually built and only a few trailers of the first production batch. All that can be said with certainty is that about 100 each of motors and trailers had been built by May 1945.

However, production was soon resumed in the three western zones of occupation and two factories in particular were reasonably well placed to supply new trams, despite the prevailing difficulties. These were the Düsseldorf factory and Fuchs of Heidelberg. Production went ahead as soon as possible and continued until 1949, by which time a total of 246 motors and 414 trailers had been placed in service.

Despite all the problems surrounding its construction, the KSW tram proved to be a most successful design. It was, as planned, very basic, having seats for only 12 and two long platforms (2.96m) to accommodate the maximum number of standees. Although this gave a considerable overhang and a slight pitching motion when running at speed, its riding qualities were by no means bad. Mechanically and electrically, it was robust, and easily maintained in the difficult post-war years. Later, some undertakings modernised the trams in various ways. Improvements included power-operated doors (Stuttgart), improved ventilation (Köln) and

KSW 22 passing the national museums on the Ring in Wien in August 1968. (Author)

An interior view of Woltersdorf 7. (Author)

rebuilding to single-ended layout (München). Later still, as recorded elsewhere, some were rebuilt as articulated cars. Many remained in service until the mid-1970s, outliving by a long period contemporary "Austerity" buses in Britain, and, in addition to the Woltersdorf car mentioned above, others have been preserved in Augsburg (501), Frankfurt (M) (580 and trailer 1468), Heidelberg (59), Köln (1732) and München (721 and trailer 1509). Two (2 and 25) are preserved in Wien, the former fitted with a bow collector.

KSW 721, as rebuilt to single-ended layout, at Karlsplatz in München in August 1972. (Author)

Technical details

Length 10.4m, width 2.17m, weight 10.5 tonnes, 2 x 60kW motors, c.82 passengers, 12 seated.

THE AUFBAU AND VERBANDSTYP TRAMS

During the bombardments many trams had been damaged but not totally destroyed and quite a few undertakings were therefore left with many serviceable parts such as trucks and motors, which could be incorporated into a rebuilt vehicle. Also, as early as 1948, criticisms were being levelled at the spartan interior of the KSW and the public, at least in the western zones, began to look for something better in new trams. The result was a programme of rebuilding carried out from 1948 to 1950, mainly by Düwag and Westwaggon, to produce quickly and at minimal cost some very useful trams. Externally the design varied from one undertaking to another, depending on the parts incorporated, but Aufbau trams still had a good deal of the KSW about them. However, they had four instead of three side windows and two-section telescopic doors. Length was normally 10.45m but width and weight varied, the latter being between 12 and 13.5 tonnes. There were normally 22 seats and standing room for up to 60 passengers. Most cars had two 60kW motors and could easily cope with two loaded trailers. Most of the systems which used the type were concentrated in the-then British zone in the north-west. Some further construction was undertaken between 1951 and 1954 and in all, there were 358 two-axle motor cars and 248 matching trailers, delivered to 32 systems. With 65 motor trams and 42 trailers, Frankfurt (M) was by far the largest user of the type and the last to place Aufbau cars in service. Many were later updated in various ways and, as stated elsewhere, some were

converted into articulated cars. All have now been withdrawn but many survive as works cars. Several have been preserved, a fine example being Hannover 236. A few Aufbau cars were built on three-axle trucks and are dealt with in the chapter on this type of tram.

A similar process was carried out on a much smaller scale in the DDR, beginning in 1950. In that year the Lokomotiv and Waggonbau Werdau showed a car thus rebuilt at the first post-war Leipzig fair. This tram was for Dessau (31), which took five similar cars in the next year and other rebuilds were placed in service by Karl Marx Stadt (8 motors) and Magdeburg (5 motors and 12 trailers). Rebuildings continued until 1956, but, as the new standard tram began to appear in 1951, most operators preferred to wait for that and there were fewer Aufbau trams in the DDR than there were on western systems.

In the west, most of the available spare parts had been used by 1950, but the demand for such trams continued. Larger undertakings wished to continue to improve their services while awaiting the development of the standard bogie car and smaller systems in any case preferred a two-axle

An unusual duty still carried out by Aufbau cars is that of the Ebbelwei Express in Frankfurt. This provides an excellent sightseeing tour and included in the price is a glass of cider (apple wine). This view actually dates from June 1980. (Author)

car on grounds of cost or to fit the parameters of their track layout. By this time the Verband öffentliche Verkehrsbetriebe (VöV) (Union of Public Transport Undertakings) had begun to function and had drawn up a specification for a standard two-axle tram, based closely on the Aufbau concept. From 1950 to 1956, therefore, a wide variety of builders constructed 171 motor trams and 235 trailers to this specification, for 17 undertakings. Mannheim/Ludwigshafen, at that time a combined undertaking, was the main user, with a total of 60 trams. The first Verbandstyp cars were outwardly almost indistinguishable from the Aufbau cars, apart from the much lower side panels which almost covered the truck. However, from 1951, following the example of trams built by Credé for Kassel, many were given a new and very attractive sloping windscreen and most, but not all later deliveries were to this

design. Some had modern features, such as rubber insert wheels incorporated, and a series for Bochum-Gelsenkirchen even had a seated conductor and passenger flow. Some were later rebuilt into articulated cars and the basic design was used by Freiburg for the bodywork of its first three articulated cars. By the time the Verbandstyp cars appeared, the writing was already on the wall for some of the smaller systems which bought them, such as Regensburg and Flensburg, and they were not able to stave off closure. There was therefore a brisk trade in almost new, second hand cars. Most had rela-

tively short lives, the last to run being in Darmstadt, where they lasted until 1985. The systems using Verbandstyp trams were – Aachen, Berlin (W), Bochum, Bremerhaven, Darmstadt, Flensburg, Frankfurt (M), Freiburg, Heidelberg, Kassel, Lübeck, Mainz, Mannheim/ Ludwigshafen, Monheim, München, Offenbach and Regensburg. Darmstadt has preserved three cars (12 and trailers 184 and 197) as a party train named "Datterich"; one of the trailers even incorporates a small dance floor! Cars from Flensburg, Frankfurt (M) (104) and Lübeck have also been preserved.

Frankfurt (M) Aufbau car 121 at Hauptbahnhof in August 1968. (Author)

Verbandstyp 16 at Darmstadt Hauptbahnhof in June 1984. (Author)

Freiburg works car 405, formerly passenger car 66, shows the more usual body design of the Verbandstyp car, at Bertoldsbrünnen in June 1996. (Author)

THE WERDAU CARS IN THE DDR

In 1949 the government of the DDR asked the Görlitz factory to prepare plans for new standard trams for the country. It was intended to produce robust and economical trams, capable of running on metre and standard gauge, in both single- and double-ended versions. There would be both motor cars and trailers and two-axle, three-axle and bogie cars were envisaged. It is not surprising that the designers drew heavily on plans of ten years earlier for the standard trams which were not built, with some changes due to experience with the KSW cars. Only one bogie tram/trailer set was built (qv chapter 7) and only a single three-axle trailer appeared, but the two-axle design went on into series production. The newly-created Vereinigung Volkseigener Betriebe Lokomotive-und Waggonbau Werdau (LOWA) was entrusted with the construction of the cars; the choice of this particular manufacturer was somewhat surprising, since its predecessor, Schumann AG, had been concerned mainly with the building of bodies for buses and lorries, but other firms were busy with reparation work for the USSR. Considerable changes were made to the original Görlitz plans and the bodywork owed something to that of the buses previously constructed by the factory. Although the body design was quite different, the tram had much in common with contemporary design in the Federal Republic, due to the common parentage of many components.

Production began in 1950, under the leadership

of Werner Pestel and, despite problems of material shortages and the migration of one of the design team to West Berlin, the first set was shown at the Leipzig Fair of 1951. This was designed for use in that city and carried the numbers 1601 and 834, class ET50 and EB50. Although a two-axle car, this was a Grossraumwagen, with no internal partition between platforms and saloon. The tram appeared to fulfil all the requirements and provided quite a high standard of comfort compared to earlier designs, since upholstered seats were fitted and the driver had a separate cabin. Double sliding doors enclosed the platforms. The body sides were widest at waist rail level and this feature gave the cars a distinctive bulky, duck-line appearance. Motors and control equipment came from VEB Hennigsdorf. Until 1953 production was concentrated in the Werdau factory and was then moved to Gotha, the state planning commission having decided that Werdau should revert to building lorries. The Gotha factory continued with this design until 1956. The design found widespread acceptance, Erfurt being the only large undertaking of the DDR not to use it, while Berlin had trailers only. Leipzig was the only system to take single-ended cars new but later some other cities rebuilt their double-ended trams in this way. In all 148 motor cars and 318 trailers were built for home use in 23 and 21 cities respectively, and 96 and 97 were exported to the USSR, for service in Kaliningrad,

Gera 130 in the city centre in June 1979. It is Saturday afternoon and the streets are deserted – there was little incentive to go window-shopping in the DDR! (Author)

Leipzig 1601 on the turning loop at Möckern, while working a special service from the city centre in connection with an open day at the transport museum in June 2004. (Author)

Tallinn, Simferopol, Lvov and seven other cities. Warsaw received 16 trailers, of a slightly modified design, but did not use these and they went to Szczecin. Probably due to its rather basic construction, the design soon began to develop faults and some undertakings rebuilt cars in various ways. Under the computer numbering scheme in the DDR, the motor trams became class 212. None has run in passenger service since the late 1980s, but they are still to be found in some cities in the works fleet and several have been preserved and, as in Halle (505 and trailer 328) and Dresden (1538 and trailers 1361/2), fully restored to operational condition. Two each of motors and trailers are preserved in Berlin and one of the latter (1707) carries on the dash a contemporary quadri-lingual instruction forbidding overtaking on the left. The Leipzig prototype, along with trailer 803, frequently runs on museum services in the city.

Although numbers were limited, these trams showed the practicability of producing a standard design which would have widespread availability and they certainly helped DDR undertakings to begin to make good the losses of the war years.

Technical details
Single-ended version
Length 10.5m, width 2.2m, weight 11 tonnes, 2 x 60kW motors, about 80 passengers, 16 seated.

Dresden 212.104 of the single-ended version waddles up to Postplatz on line 4 to Weinböhla in June 1979. (Author)

Trailer 838 in service in Leipzig in 1971. (B. Barehem, author's collection)

GOTHA CARS

As soon as production of the standard tram had been moved to the VEB Waggonbau Gotha factory, the designers there set about producing an improved version. The head of the factory was now Dip-Ing Herms, a pupil of Klockow of Erfurt, and it was therefore no surprise that the new design should have much both of the pre-war design for that city and the planned standard car. The prototypes appeared in 1955 and displayed a new and more elegant form of front end and a three-window saloon, instead of the Werdau car's four side windows. It was also slightly longer. Internally the trams were very comfortable and particular attention was paid to the driver's cabs, these having a separate heating system, individual lighting and defrosting equipment for the windscreens. The truck and electrical equipment were basically that of the Werdau design. These trams went to Gotha (38-42) for use on the radial Thüringerwaldbahn and three were later converted to single-ended layout.

Dr Herms had intended that the new design should be for DDR systems only, but he then fell foul of the state planning commission, which considered the Werdau design adequate, and he was able to proceed with development of the new type only on the fiction that the new design was intended solely for export to the Soviet Union. The first drawings accordingly were labelled in Cyrillic script and designated ST 2 m SU (two-axle metre-gauge tram for the Soviet Union). His ruse was successful, but the trams were therefore built for metre, standard and Russian broad gauge (1524mm) and in single- and double-ended versions, though only Erfurt took the former. Internally they were similar to the Werdau cars, with comfortable upholstered seating. Platforms were enclosed by double sliding doors, electrically operated and fitted with both optical and acoustic warning devices – combined with the grinding of the doors themselves, these features made travel in these trams somewhat noisy. The front and rear ends were of a much improved design and the cars did not have the pronounced bulge at waist level of the earlier cars. The motor trams originally had a conductor's post(s), but these were removed in the late 1960s when one person operation became the norm in the DDR. The trailers were built for this type of operation and were originally used by season ticket holders only. The prototype motor/trailer set was delivered to Gotha in 1956 (43/83). To maintain the idea that the trams were destined for the USSR market, they carried the red marker lights on the bodysides which were characteristic of trams in that country! Production, to a slightly different design, began in 1957 and the cars are accordingly classed ET57 and EB57.

In 1962 an improved design was introduced

Preserved prototype car 38 in the depot at Gotha, June 1996. This shows the original blue livery, of which the Gotha citizens were quite fond. There was later a considerable public outcry – by DDR standards – when this was replaced by the universal cream. (Author)

The first production car, Gotha 43, is also preserved in that city and is seen here at Hauptbahnhof in July 1995. Car 56 on the right was built for use on the Thüringerwaldbahn in 1929. (Author)

(T2-62/B2-62), with an underfloor mounted controller, operated by a wheel in the driving position. This version was available in single-ended configuration only, which caused problems for some of the small undertakings which

Neatly modernised, car 28 is in Woltersdorf village in October 2002. (Author)

received these before they had had time or material to install turning circles at termini! A total of 725 motor trams and 706 trailers were exported to the Soviet Union, the main recipients being Lvov, Odessa, Tallinn, Kaliningrad and Volgograd, which between them took 275 motors and 279 trailers. The balance went to 17 other cities, some of these trams being fitted with typical Russian bow collectors for current collection. Production ceased in Gotha in 1967 but was briefly carried on by Tatra, as recorded elsewhere, and was equally briefly revived, for trailers only, by Gotha in 1969. In the DDR computer numbering scheme, the motor trams became classes 213 and 214 and the trailers 241 and 263. The total number of trams of this type built for DDR systems was at least 620 motor cars and 906 trailers, but the number of exports to the USSR could have increased these figures to 1046 and 1278 respectively. There was latterly much exchanging of these cars between undertakings in the DDR and they are still in service in Bad Schandau and Woltersdorf, the trams in Woltersdorf having been rather attractively modernised. Of those which were exported, some are still in service in at least Odessa. Several are preserved in Germany, as in Dresden (1587), Gotha (38, 43 and trailer 93) and Leipzig (1332 and trailer 483). Potsdam has a very fine three-car set of no.109 and two trailers, and incredibly this was returned to normal service in

March 2004 when the new Combino trams had to be abruptly withdrawn! Rather surprisingly, two motor cars and eight trailer cars were exported in December 1995 to Arad in Romania, where they have replaced much younger native cars. The operators clearly considered that a well-built and well-maintained German two-axle car of the 1960s was of more use than a cheaply built and badly maintained Romanian bogie car of more recent date!

Technical details
Single-ended version
Length 10.9m, width 2.2m, weight 13 tonnes, 2 x 60 kW motors, 82 passengers, 22 seated.

The single-ended design is shown by Leipzig 1326 in June 1980. (Author)

THE REKO TRAMS OF THE DDR

By the end of the 1950s the worst arrears of wartime neglect had been made up in the DDR, but there were still a large number of sound but out-of-date trams in service. This was especially true of Berlin and in 1959 the S-Bahn overhaul works in Schöneweide (Reichausbesserungswerke or RAW) began to rebuild trams of the 1920s and 1930s, fitting these with a new body based closely on the Gotha trams but having four side windows. These trams did not have a separate underframe, the body being mounted directly on the truck and, in consequence, their riding qualities were execrable. Most of the Berlin cars were single-ended, only a few being produced with two driving positions. A total of 297 motor trams and 391 trailers were thus rebuilt for Berlin. From 1971 similar rebuildings were undertaken for provincial systems but only 68 motor cars and 161 trailers were produced, for which the inhabitants of the provinces were no doubt duly thankful. In this case, there was a good deal of new material used in the "rebuildings" which were to an extent political, to allow continued construction of trams in the DDR. When the computer numbering system was introduced, the single-ended motor cars became class 217 and the double-ended cars class 223, while the trailers became classes 267 and 269 respectively. None is now in normal service but, despite the reputation of the class, a surprising number have been preserved, more than 20 in Germany itself. An operational set is at Strausberg (479 603/879 603). Berlin

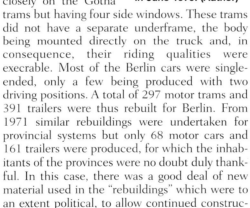
BVB Berlin 217 263 under the Hochbahn at Dimitrofstrasse (Eberswalderstrasse) in June 1979. (Author)

3006 is preserved at the National Tramway Museum at Crich, having been modified to accommodate passengers in wheelchairs, while car 4501 was acquired by the new Sheffield system as a works car. Three motor cars and three trailers have gone to Bergen for use on a proposed heritage line and 3018 is in Stockholm for the same purpose. The furthest travelled are two motor cars (3007/8) and a trailer (3717) which have gone to the South Pacific Electric Railway museum at Loftus, Sydney and are in use there as a shuttle set, the motor cars now having acquired trolley poles. Four others are in service on a heritage line in the Asiatic part of Istanbul.

Apart from conversion to works cars, Gotha cars have also survived in a variety of forms. In Plauen, car 78 has been rebuilt as a very popular mobile pub, the Bier-Elektrische. (Author)

Dresden 213.210 prepares to reverse at Postplatz in June 1979. (Author)

Leipzig trailer 927 at the rear of a set leaving Hauptbahnhof in 1972. (B. Bareham, author's collection)

Halberstadt 29 was one of the last of this type to remain in service and in June 1995 turns on to the main line at Dominikanerstrasse on the short branch to Friedhof. (Author)

OTHER GERMAN DESIGNS

A very few undertakings built new two-axle trams which were not derived from the KSW. Some, such as the 25 motors and 25 trailers built for Bremen by Bremer Dock, were very old-fashioned in concept; this series included both cars built using parts from damaged vehicles as well as completely new trams. Nürnberg had 26 new motor cars (101-126) and 80 trailers (1231-1310) built by MAN in 1952-54, to what was basically the design of 1940, but nonetheless they were more attractive than the Bremen cars and some remained in service until the end of the 1970s. Five motor cars and one trailer have been preserved. Hagen in 1954-57 bought from Düwag 27 motors (314-340) and 25 trailers (110-134) which were basically an improved Verbandstyp design, with automatic doors, better suspension and improved heating and ventilation.

Only two manufacturers developed a really modern design of two-axle tram. As detailed in the chapter on the Grossraumwagen, Düwag in 1956 built the first of a class of trailer which looked very like a scaled-down version of that car and Köln, evidently seeing a future for this type of tram, in 1956-58 bought from the same manufacturer 50 new motor trams (1601-1650) and no fewer than 80 trailers (2601-2680). Many incorporated parts of older cars and they were intended to be a quick solution to the pressing need to replace many of these. This concept proved to be short-term thinking.

Stuttgart also still had a place for the motor-trailer-trailer concept, which Professor Bockemühl saw as the most economic way to serve lines on which there was a marked differ-

Nürnberg post-war car 111 as preserved. (Author)

Kiel 236 at Hauptbahnhof. (Lars Richter collection)

Köln 1602 and trailer at Bahnnhof Sud in April 1957. (W.J. Wyse, courtesy London Area, Light Rail Transit Association)

ence between peak and off-peak traffic. They would also allow retirement of all wooden bodied cars in a short space of time. Between 1953 and 1957 the SSB bought 123 motor cars (701-823) and 146 trailers (1501-1646) were acquired, to a modern design, with many technical improvements. The motor cars were built by Maschinenfabriek Esslingen and the trailers by Fuchs. These were in fact the only such cars which could be claimed to be state-of-the-art of the 1950s, having rubber-insert wheels and excellent suspension. Reutlingen followed suit with three motor trams (56-58) and seven trailers (43-49), the last of which was, in 1964, the last two-axle tram built for service in the Federal Republic and in Western Europe. As stated elsewhere, none of these vehicles lasted long in their original form since the articulated trams had already begun to appear when they were built and the Köln and Stuttgart cars were soon rebuilt to this form, the latter with much more success. A few of the Stuttgart cars were sold in original condition to Mülheim for use as works cars. The Kiel undertaking, under the management of Dipl-Ing Gilbert, was the only one to develop in its own workshops a really modern two-axle design. Between 1953 and 1956 seven trams (230-234 and 236/7) were turned out, of a very advanced concept. They were built for one-man operation and had PCC-style pedal control. Older trucks

Stuttgart 806 at Hauptbahnhof in September 1969, with GT4 4500 on the right. (Author)

were re-used but rubber-insert wheels made for a very comfortable ride and passenger flow was from front to rear, with electrically-powered doors at both entrance and exit. They were successful in service, but unfortunately the undertaking's policy changed to one of abandonment and all were scrapped in October 1969. They could have served as a model for a design to work on lightly-used lines in other cities, but no one seemed to be interested. In Stuttgart motor cars 802 and 804 and trailers 1547 and 1605 are preserved, the first of these being in running order.

Technical details
Stuttgart 701
Length 11m, width 2.1m, weight 13.2 tonnes, 2x 81kW motors, 89 passengers, 22 seated.
Kiel 230
Length 11m, width 2.2m, weight 12.7 tonnes, 2 x 60kW motors, 77 passengers, 30 seated.
Köln 1601
Length 10.5m, width 2.35m, weight 13.2 tonnes, 2 x 65kW motors, 91 passengers, 22 seated.

Bibliography
Modern Tramway no.314, February 1964 (Gotha cars), no.366, June 1968 (Brno), no.467, November 1976 (Düwag low floor cars).

Strassenbahn Magazin, nos. 119, March 1999 (Aufbau cars), 124, February 2000 (Düsseldorf and Nürnberg pre-war cars), 147 and 148, January and February 2002 (Verbandstyp cars), 164-167, June-September 2003, (Gotha cars and other German designs), 189/190, July/August 2005 (Werdau cars).

Die Fahrzeuge der Dresdner Strassenbahn. Op.cit.

Fahrzeuge deutscher Strassen- und Stadtbahnen – Zwei- und Dreiachswagen ab 1945. D. Höltge. Zeunert, Gifhorn, n/d.

35 Jahre LOWA-Einheits Strassenbahnwagen. *Der Stadtverkehr* 9/1986.

Der Stadtverkehr 11/12/1977 (Nürnberg 901 class), 8/1982 (KSW in Posen).

Die Rheinbahn – stadtverkehr in und um Düsseldorf. A. Schild and D. Waltking. Alba Verlag, Düsseldorf, revised edition, 1985.

Die Nürnberg-Fürther Strassenbahn im Wandel der Zeiten. S. Scherer (ed). Freunde der Nürnberger-Fürther Strassenbahn e.V., Nürnberg, 1977.

Les Tramways Parisiens. J. Robert. 3rd edition, 1992.

100 Jahre Stuttgarter Strassenbahnen 1868-1968. Stuttgarter Strassenbahn, Stuttgart, 1968.

POLISH N CLASS CARS

Given that KSW trams were running in three cities which became Polish in 1945, it is not surprising that the design was chosen as the basis for future standard construction in that country. Plans were drawn up by the staff of the Poznan undertaking in 1948, this having been one of the cities to operate KSW cars, and the first were produced by the Konstal factory in Chorzow in the same year. This tram was classed N (normalne/standard) and 501 were produced between 1948 and 1956. An improved version, class N2, with greater seating capacity, better ventilation and double width doors was introduced in 1952 and built up to 1956, with a total of 287. Trailers were classes ND and ND2 (404 cars). Further improvements were made with classes N4 (425 cars) and N5 (320). The corresponding trailers were 4ND and 5ND and these totalled 541 cars. Some trailers were built at Sanok and Swidnice. Total production between 1948 and 1962 was therefore 1533 motor cars and 945 trailers. Class N cars had 16 seats and officially a total capacity of 95, but in the early post-war days at least, they carried far more than that figure, including external hangers-on, clinging tightly to any handhold they could grasp. Very often two loaded trailers would be found behind each motor car, but in such circumstances their braking capacity left a good deal to be desired. These were extremely robust trams, which for many years uncomplainingly put up with gross overcrowding. They ran on all Polish systems, almost all were double-ended cars and, apart from those in Krakow and Gdnask, all were painted red and cream. The latter city rebuilt

some of its N2 trams into single-ended cars and fitted new windscreens, giving them an appearance akin to the German Grossraumwagen. The last went into service in 1962 and in some cities they lasted into the mid-1990s, many having been improved with such facilities as multi-notch controllers, magnetic track brakes and automatic folding doors. In Poznan some were given tapered windscreens. All have now been withdrawn, apart from a couple of class N used on a suburban shuttle service in Katowice. Some are preserved and many are still to be seen as works trams. In its various incarnations, class N was successful, not only in that they transformed the chaotic tramway scenes of the post-war years into efficient, if still over-crowded systems, but also that, for the first time in Europe, they showed that one standard class of tram could meet almost all the needs of an entire nation's tramways. The German planners of the Einheitsstrassenbahn

Car 116 of Krakow shows the double-ended version of class N, as it shares a terminus with no.223. (A.D. Young, Evda Slides)

were vindicated at last – in Poland!

Technical details
Class N4
Length 10.4m, width 2.2m, weight 14 tonnes, 2 x 55kW motors, 112 passengers, 16 seated.

Bibliography
Modern Tramway no.384, December 1969 et seq.
Chorzowska Wytwórnia Konstrukcji Stalowych KONSTAL 1864-1989. Konstal, Chorzow, 1989

Elblag 015, rebuilt to single-ended layout, and trailer 155, June 1994. (Author)

An interior view of an N1 class car in Sczecin, in June 1996. (Author)

AUSTRIAN DESIGNS

The first post-war trams for Wien were based closely on the KSW, but with refinements. In 1950/51 the Simmering factory delivered fifty motor trams of class B (51-100) and 90 matching trailers of type b (1401-1490). They had steel bodies, electro-pneumatically operated sliding doors, a seat for the driver, transverse seats, and were among the most comfortable trams of this type. However, the hissing noise made by the doors when opening and closing soon gained the class the nickname of "Zischer" (whisperer). Car 51 and trailers 1401 and 1482 are preserved. Graz acquired 50 trams (201-250) of somewhat similar concept, built by Simmering-Graz-Pauker in 1949/50 but these had attractively streamlined ends. Unfortunately due to post-war shortages, they were built of wood and so fairly soon became an embarrassment to both the operator and the local authority. They were accompanied by trailers of rather more square appearance (401-450). Most of the trailers were converted for passenger-only operation in 1968, and the last of the class was withdrawn in October 1988. Two

Linz 8 in a busy scene at Hauptbahnhof in August 1968. (Author)

further motor trams (251/2) with steel bodies were built on reserve trucks and frames in 1961 and were the last two-axle motor trams constructed in Western Europe. They were rather longer than the first batch and had four side windows instead of three. They remained in service until 1993. Car 225 is preserved at the Summerlee Industrial Museum in Coatbridge, Scotland. Linz bought 15 motor trams in

Wien 72 pulling a Stadtbahn trailer in the street at Schönbrünn in August 1968. (Author)

Graz 217 inbound on line 5 at Grazerstrasse in June 1981. (Author)

1949/50 (1-15) from Simmering and twelve of a rather larger version (51-62) from Gräf und Stift – a firm more known for bus building – between 1955 and 1959. There were also 26 trailers (101-126) based much more closely on the KSW design.

All these Austrian trams were well built and reasonably comfortable for passengers and many lasted into the mid-1980s.

Bibliography

100 Jahre Grazer Tramway. Grazer Stadtwerke AG, 1978
Strassenbahnen in Österreich. W. Kaiser. GeraMond Verlag, München, 2004.

Graz 252 waits as a reserve car at Jacominiplatz in June 1981. (Author)

ROMANIA

From the mid-1950s to around 1970 a large number of two-axle standard trams were built in the workshops of the Bucuresti undertaking, in many cases using parts of older vehicles. These were for both the capital and provincial cities and were all single-ended. Motor trams had three side windows and trailers four. Some of the latter were constructed in the workshops of the Braila system. The trams had quite an attractive appearance but were very basic; the windows could not be opened and, as the roof ventilators were insufficient for the heat of a summer's day, normal practice was to remove the first side window behind the front door for the summer. This solved the ventilation problem, but was not helpful if a sudden shower arrived! Timisoara also had some two-axle cars built in its own workshops. These had five side windows and an attractive sloping windscreen, rather like that on Italian bogie trams. Some of the trailers were fitted with control apparatus to allow reversible operation, although doors were provided in one side only. Rather oddly for a communist country, Romania maintained a two-class fare structure at this time and trailers were second class. Itinerant conductors were used. As far as could be ascertained, there were 570 motor trams and about 1030 trailers of this type, none of which now remain in service.

5/44 Bucuresti 21 and a matching trailer, in April 1978. (Martin Jenkins)

USSR

Designs for standardised two-axle trams, in a larger and smaller variant, were prepared for the second All-Union Tramway Congress, held in 1925, and the first were built in 1926/7 for Leningrad and Tsarytsin (Volgograd). Experience soon showed that one size of car could meet all requirements and thousands of what was designated class KH were built throughout the 1930s. There was a matching trailer of class M, which had no separate truck. By 1937 the combination KH+M made up 80% of all tramway fleets in the USSR, but, though sturdy and generally reliable, by no stretch of the imagination could these be considered modern. During the period of industrialisation enforced by Stalin, they often worked with two trailers. In 1940 an improved version, with air doors was produced by the Ust-Katav plant, to which production of motor cars had by then been transferred. Kiev in 1932 built one experimental two-axle car (901) of considerable length, with radial arm suspension, but attention then turned to bogie cars and it remained the only one of its type. Just before war was declared in 1941, work was under way on a design for a two-axle car with some PCC features, but mounted on a conventional truck. Although no KSW trams had run in cities in the USSR, the concept may have inspired the development of the first post-war standard design, as the Council of Ministers decided to adopt a two-axle design for mass production, this being simpler to build and operate in the immediate post-war conditions. The first appeared in January 1948 and the class was built until 1961. This was class KTM1 built by the Kirov factory in Ust Katav, under its engineer Stroganov, and supplied to most provincial undertakings but not to Moscow or Leningrad. It was a single-ended car with an attractive semi-streamlined body design, 12.5m long and 2.5m wide and weighing 12.5 tonnes. Seats were provided for only 16 passengers. There was a matching trailer design, class KTP1. In 1960 an improved motor car appeared, class KTM2, with a trailer KTP2. These were designed by the engineer Tjurin. The motor car was slightly wider at 2.55m, weighed only 10.5 tonnes and could seat 22 passengers. These had multi-notch controllers and resilient wheels. Unfortunately, in an attempt to save on materials and also to reduce wear on the track, the KTM cars were lightly built and soon began to fail under pressure of the loads they had to carry. No more were built after 1968 and of a planned all-electric version (KTM3), only a prototype was built. The last KTM1 and 2 cars ran in 1986, in Zaporozhe and Odessa respectively.

Bibliography

Strassenbahn-Betriebe in Osteuropa II. H. Lehnhart und C. Jeanmaire. Verlag Eisenbahn, Villigen, Switzerland, 1977
Light Rail and Modern Tramway nos.681 and 683, January and March 1993.

Motor car 57 and trailer 58, classes KTM2 and KTP2, of Irkutsk at Rabochyee loop on ul. Bratskaya in September 1972. (J.F. Bromley, Evda Slides)

REBUILDINGS IN OTHER COUNTRIES

In the 1950s, Wien was chronically short of new trams but lacked the finance to remedy the situation. In 1956 Lohner built a series of 29 new bodies to be placed on (very) old trucks as class T2 (421-449). These had a seated conductor, passenger flow and Düwag folding doors, but were otherwise fairly basic and, having only 12 seats, were not popular with the public. They were followed in the next two years by 50 similar cars of class L3 (451-500), in which the seating capacity was increased to 16. The last 13 were built new. After a very serious fatal accident in 1960 the need to modernise the rolling stock with all-metal bodies and track brakes became even more pressing and it was decided to rebuild a further 160 cars with bodies in the style of the Grossraumwagen, but of course shorter. Simmering completed the first part of this order in 1960-62 as class L4 (501-610) but it was then decided to rebuild the remainder as articulated trams owing to the increasing shortage of personnel. Gräf und Stift built 200 trailers of the same design (class l3) and these were operated in three-car trains, to give a capacity of about 200 passengers. In later years these trailers were operated without conductors. While these trams worked reasonably well as an emergency solution, they were slow and in service could not keep up with class E articulated cars. Nonetheless they lasted quite a long time, the last running on 30 April 1990. T2 432 and L4 576 are both preserved in the local museum, along with trailer 1840.

In Belgium, the Liège-Séraing system rebuilt the nine trams of the 50-58 series, dating from

Preserved Oslo car 38 in the city's tram museum, Wagenhalle 8. (Author)

T2 class 402 on the Ring in Wien, August 1968. (Author)

Wien L4 class 537 heads down into the subway in August 1968. (Author)

Lisbon car 496 pauses in the Rua do Graça while working on line 11 in April 1972. (Author)

1926, in 1954/5. They were given all-metal bodies and were both widened and lengthened. However, as the old motors were retained, they were no faster and their riding qualities suffered from the increased length. In much the same way, Brussels rebuilt 101 old standard trams with new bodies in the style of the PCC cars of the 7000 class in 1960/1, although unlike the Liège cars, these were single-ended. They were numbered 9001-9100 and 4000 were laid out for passenger flow, but from 1966 were rebuilt for one-person operation. The increased overhang of the body emphasised the galloping motion of the Brill truck and they were not popular with passengers. As they lacked track brakes, they could not run in the new subways and were withdrawn in the mid-1970s. Car 9062 was preserved at the Summerlee industrial museum in Scotland but in 2004 was so badly damaged by vandals that it had to be scrapped. However, another (9079) is preserved in Brussels.

Rather earlier, in 1943/4, Barcelona had twelve two-axle (701-712) cars rebuilt by Maquitrans, in the style of the new bogie cars. They had passenger flow, with air doors and looked quite modern but they retained the old motors and were unable to keep pace with modern trams in service. All were withdrawn in 1962. Madrid followed suit after 1950 with an unknown number of cars which were rebuilt to resemble the semi-PCC bogie cars. The closure of many lines made them redundant in the mid-1960s.

From 1954 to 1962, 61 old cars in Lisbon were rebuilt with new bodies to the same style, with air doors and 101 matching trailers were built new, but lacking power doors. Whether these could really be classed as modern trams may be argued; some were underpowered, with two 20kW motors, and all were flimsily built. Significantly they had a much shorter life than the earlier classes, some of which are still in service, and the last ran in 1994. Car 741 has been retained for preservation, along with trailer 101. The same criticism may be made of the 28 post-war motor cars (350-373, 402-405), and two trailers (25/6) built for Porto, the latter two spending much of their lives motored as cars 400/1. The undertaking did build one car (500) in 1952 which had air doors, a seated conductor and passenger flow, and externally resembled recent Italian bogie cars. With two 50kW motors, it was also quite powerful in relation to its weight of 12 tonnes. It was intended to be the prototype of two classes of tram, bogie and two-axle, but no further were built and Porto had to wait until 2002 to see its next modern tram. Car 500 was withdrawn in the 1970s and has been preserved in the city's transport museum, as have car 373 and trailer 25.

The new three-axle cars were not enough to modernise the Amsterdam fleet, but as financial

Brussels 9080 and 9028 on line 93 in the Rue Royale in October 1969. (Author)

Amsterdam rebuild 406 inbound on Utrechtsestraat at Keizersgracht in September 1959. (Author)

problems prevented a repeat order, plans were drawn up in November 1948 to rebody 135 two-axle cars along similar lines. Fortunately for the ultimate future of the undertaking the plan was not carried out. However, in 1950, ex-Utrecht car 12 was rebodied and fitted for passenger flow with a seated conductor and folding doors. In this form it ran until 1956. In the following year one of the unsatisfactory "Bergamann" cars (393) was similarly treated but after an accident in 1952, it was withdrawn. Between 1952 and 1954 six other motor cars and four trailers were similarly rebuilt. Like these, they had passenger flow with a seated conductor and power doors. There were also 12 matching trailers (650-661). Unfortunately the only angle known to these cars in track geometry was the right angle and they were extremely uncomfortable. All were withdrawn in the 1970s but no.37 has been preserved in the city's transport museum.

Technical details
Brussels 9000 class
Length 10.63m, width 2.14m, weight 13.3 tonnes, 2 x 68Kw motors, 85 passengers, 18 seated.
(NB Various types of motor were fitted to this class).

NEW DESIGNS IN OTHER COUNTRIES

Few new trams were built anywhere during the Second World War, but, using parts from scrapped trams KS in Copenhagen managed to construct 109 two-axle cars – motor cars 447-490 and trailers 1001-1065 – which were built to a high standard and, despite their nickname of "Scrapvogn" (scrap cars), had quite a long career. They managed also to build one car to this design in 1945 for Aarhus. Very little attempt was made in the post-war years to develop a modern design of two-axle tram in other countries. However, in Sweden, a few undertakings were interested in a two-axle version of the Mustang bogie cars, which could be operated by one person on more lightly-trafficked lines. In 1948 ASEA delivered 15 trams of this type to Hälsingborg (41-55). This interesting type had a single, three-width front door, of which the two rearmost sections were used for entry while the front section functioned as the exit, passengers paying the operator immediately before leaving the tram. They could accommodate 64 passengers, 26 seated, and weighed only 12 tonnes. They ran until 1967, when the system closed with the change in the rule of the road, and two have been preserved. Two batches of similar trams were built for Norrköping, but the first had a separate exit right

at the rear and the second an exit in the middle (39-45 and 46-63). They were not rebuilt for right-hand running but cars 51 and 56 have been preserved, the former in Malmköping, the latter in its home city. Malmö acquired 22 similar cars between 1949 and 1954 (type H, numbers between 26 and 56), of which the bodies were built by Svenska Karosseri and the trucks were rebuilt from those of older trams, in the undertaking's own workshops. These were 11.5m long and could accommodate 76 passengers, 24 seated. There were also ten matching trailers from Hägglund (180-189), also mounted on old trucks. All these ran until September 1967 and three trailers have been preserved.

These classes were a successful attempt to develop a modern tram suitable for less busy services, but no other system copied the idea.

Lisbon in 1947 had bought ten new trams with the last Maley and Taunton swing link trucks to be supplied to any operator (736-745), adding a further three soon after (761-763). The bodies were lightly constructed and were later replaced by those of the earlier domed roof design. No.741 has been preserved.

In Croatia, a prototype modern two-axle car (100) was constructed in Zagreb in the undertak-

Zagreb 167 in the city centre in December 2004. (A.W. Brotchie)

Britain's leading tramway historian, the late J.H. Price, takes a break from depot visiting in Essen in May 1981, beside works car 618, formerly Aufbau passenger car 877 of 1948. (Author)

ing's own workshops in 1949, and this was followed first by three further cars with attractively streamlined bodywork (101-103), then by a series of 60 cars (104-163) built by the Duro Dakovic manufacturer between 1957 and 1966, as class TP101. These have German Kiepe/AEG control and can carry 80 passengers, of whom only 16 have a seat. In service they normally operate with a bogie trailer, on occasions with two and have proved a very successful design. Fifty-four are still in service, Zagreb being one of the few large cities still to operate two-axle cars in 2004. Osjek acquired twelve similar cars (31-42) and four double-ended cars, without the central door, were built for Dubrovnik (11-14), whose track gauge was only 76cm. In Serbia, Belgrade had ten cars identical to those in Zagreb

One of the cars in Brno, at an unknown location in May 1965. (W.J. Wyse collection, courtesy London Area, Light Rail Transit Association)

Copenhagen's war time car 488 (right) at Svanemollen depot in September 1966. (Evda Slides)

Norrköping no.63 at Norra Tull on 12 September 1966. (S. Hilkenbach, Evda Slides)

(61-70), none of which is now in service.

In Czecho-Slovakia, the Tatra factory turned out some very basic two-axle cars with few modern features in the immediate post-war years. Brno placed in service a series of 25 motor cars (117-141) and 30 trailers (1297-1326), built by Královopolská Strojírna in 1950/1, having attractive streamlined bodies, arranged for passenger flow from rear to front. The motor cars were 11.37m long and the trailers 11.6m, these carrying 60 and 70 passengers respectively. Five similar cars were built in 1953 by the undertaking itself (142-146) and were the last Czech non-Tatra trams. One has been preserved in the city.

However, at a very much later date, 1995/6, 45 of Lisbon's two-axle cars underwent a very substantial rebuilding to allow them to maintain, along with the Siemens low floor cars, the remaining tramway services for the foreseeable future. The cars chosen were the best of the standard cars (203-282) built between 1932 and 1937, which had already been converted for one-person operation, with power operated platform doors, in 1984. Car 270 was rebuilt as a prototype by AEG in the former MAN factory in Nürnberg in 1994 and, with a few modifications, the rest of the class followed in 1995/6. The existing bodies were thoroughly overhauled, new AEG welded trucks, new Skoda motors and new Kiepe control equipment, with 17 power and 15 braking notches to give more comfortable travel. There is provision to fit a pantograph in place of the trolley pole and this has now been done on most cars. Thus rejuvenated, the "Remodelados" (remodelled cars) should delight enthusiasts, residents and visitors to the Portuguese capital for many years to come.

Technical details
Lisbon "Remodelados"
Length 8.38m, width 2.38m, weight 10.73 tonnes, 2 x 50kW motors, 59 passengers, 20 seated.

No further two-axle cars were constructed new after the last trams for Zagreb in 1966 and it is most unlikely that any more will ever be built. But it was this type that paved the way to standardisation in Germany and for that alone it deserves a place in the history of the modern tram. The post-war cars in Sweden and the five built for Kiel, also showed the possibility of using such trams with one operator long before that concept became universal and, had the idea been adopted

Car 425 of the Tramways Electriques de Pays de Charleroi, seen in October 1968. (Author)

Antwerp was one of many systems which gave older cars power doors and passenger flow. Rebuilt two-axle car 262 is at Koningen Astrid Plein in September 1958.

elsewhere, some smaller systems might have survived. Sadly these designs evoked little interest elsewhere.

Bibliography
Die Strassen- und Vorortbahnen in Trondheim. N.C. Aspenberg. Baneforlaget, Oslo, 1994.

Modern Tramway nos.198, June 1954 (Liège rebuild). 301, January 1963 (Trondeheim), 355, July 1967 (Danish systems), 687, March 1995 (Lisbon).

The Tramways of Portugal (4th edition). B. R. King and J. H. Price. Light Rail Transit Association, London, 1995.

Strassenbahnen in Österreich, op.cit.

STIB factsheet.

MSS Torr och Nu. Op.cit.

Lisbon 740, seen in August 1970. (Author)

One of Lisbon's "Remodelados", no.568 on line 28 in September 1997. (A.G. Gunn)

CHAPTER 6
THREE-AXLE CARS

The search for a successful three-axle tram was almost as old as the electric tram itself and became a kind of holy grail which led countless engineers to expend a great deal of time and money on what was generally a fruitless quest. The three-axle concept, if brought to perfection, would, it was hoped, combine the riding qualities of the bogie car with the simplicity and low cost of the two-axle car. The vehicle which emerged from most studies in fact combined the riding qualities of the two-axle car with the cost and complexity of the bogie car, and usually added a few quirks of its own.

The first recorded trials of such a tram on an electric line took place in Boston in the autumn of 1889. The inventor of the truck used was one William Robinson, whose career had been in railway signalling and who had, for the previous five years, been actively developing a three-axle truck initially of course for horse trams. He seemed to have success with the new electric cars and a flow of orders came in during the early 1890s, one even being from Hamburg. Robinson also exhibited at the World Columbian Exposition in Chicago in 1893. But his success was short-lived. The trucks proved prone to derailment, at least after they had been running for some time, and most of the trams concerned were re-mounted on bogie or two-axle trucks from about 1898 onwards.

There were also experiments in other countries. MAN built some three-axle cars for several German undertakings and in Britain a truck designed by T.R. Barber was tried under London United bogie car 52 for some time from December 1909, and this truck or another was later tried under a sand car of the Metropolitan Electric Tramways. The only other recorded instance of the use of a Barber truck was under Dublin United car 286 in 1911-12.

Interest in the concept revived after the First World War and in 1927 a car built by the Versare Corporation was briefly tried in Grand Rapids, Michigan. This had a body constructed in Duralumin and used several components taken from the motor industry. It did not last long in service. Much more important for the future was the experience of the tramways in Gent, where most of the cars were mounted on two-axle radial trucks. In 1925 one car was given a third, centre axle. Unlike those in previous experiments, this was fixed and on curves the car body itself moved sideways, this feature allowing greater clearance. By 1932 the system had 105 three-axle cars (301-405) running and several had also been placed in service on the Vicinal, where they were less successful. The cars in Gent worked well and the last was not retired until 1974; five have been preserved. Complications inherent in the design militated against its adoption elsewhere.

In Switzerland Jacob Buchli was also investigating the three-axle concept. He had worked with both SLM in Winterthur and Brown Boveri and had become chairman of the former in 1932. After briefly experimenting with a design in which a central bogie with small wheels was used, Buchli then replaced this feature with a single central axle, fitted with wheels of reduced

diameter which still, however, carried some of the car's weight. This axle was not connected directly to the body and had a certain amount of play on curves. In these, it steered the outer axles by a system of rods and this arrangement gave good riding qualities. The motors were mounted parallel to the outer axles. Two trams with trucks of this type, in which the motors were suspended in a kind of cradle from the body, were delivered to Wien in 1929 (455/6 class P), but were not totally successful and were rebuilt as two-axle cars of class M in 1949. The next step was to replace the body-hung motors with motors mounted on the shafts between the axle assembly, and this was much more successful. Five trams (1-5) with this design of truck were then built by SLM for Winterthur in 1930/1 and performed well, lasting in service until the system closed in 1951. Possibly because of the onset of the Depression, no further orders were received.

The city system in Lille had also been experimenting and placed 18 three-axle cars (700-717) in service at more or less the same time. These reverted to body-mounted motors and may not have been too successful, since the trucks were rebuilt in 1950 to a novel design. In this, each of the central wheels was linked to one of the end axles in an arrangement which, viewed from above, looked like a right-angled triangle. This seems to have given an excellent ride, but maintenance costs were high. When withdrawn in 1962, two were preserved, one (701) by AMTUIR in Paris.

The real impetus to the use of the three-axle car in city service came from the undertaking of Saarbrücken, under the auspices of its Director, Adolphe von Lengerke, who seems to have been possessed of considerable technical ingenuity. He could see great potential in the Buchli truck but thought that the mounting of the motors was too complex and limited the application of the three-axle concept. In 1930 the undertaking bought ten trailers, of which five were mounted on Buchli trucks, this time, of course, without motors. Apart from the noise produced when running on rails mounted in asphalt paving, these worked very well. The noise problem was cured by allowing one of the centre wheels to rotate freely on its axle, thus foreshadowing a principle used in to-day's low floor

Gent car 355 and two others parked near St Pieter's station in September 1958. The logo of the Brussels World Fair can be seen on the front side panel. (Author)

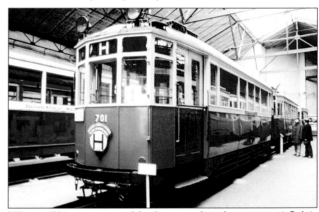

Lille car 701 as preserved in the now-closed museum at Saint-Mandé. (Author)

Saarbrücken 111. (Lars F. Richter collection)

Basel trailer 1342 behind one of the Birseckbahn articulated cars at Basel SBB station, September 1989. (Author)

cars. Having proved the success of the trailers, von Lengerke went on in 1932 to devise a motor tram along similar lines. This used a truck having conventional axle-hung motors and track brakes, but with alterations to the springing, with leaf springs attached both to the truck frame and to the axle boxes. SLM were persuaded to supply one truck to this design and it was fitted under car 50. This combination gave an excellent ride, even at high speed, without excessive maintenance costs, and it seemed that at last the goal of so many engineers had been reached and the three-axle concept was able to take its place as a contender for future standard trams in several countries of western Europe. Pleased with the success of the trial cars, Saarbrücken went on to rebuild four older two-axle cars in 1934/5 and to buy two new cars (111/2) from Credé in 1936. The trucks were actually manufactured to the Buchli design by Westwaggon of Köln, (though they may have been constructed in Heidelberg). That firm had gained the German licence for Buchli trucks in 1935. Two further cars (123/4) were built in 1952 using parts from war-damaged cars. At first these worked as a coupled set and were painted red, rather than the standard cream, to which they later reverted. Unfortunately the city council became anti-tram, in pursuit of the "autogerechte Stadt" (a city for the automobile) and the system was run down from 1953 onwards until final closure on 22 May 1965, none of these pioneering cars being preserved.

Technical details

Saarbrücken 123
Length 12.2m, width 2.08m, weight 16.75 tonnes, 2 x 60kW motors, 92 passengers, 28 seated.

The design was then applied to a number of cars built in the immediate pre-war period. Basel BVB adopted it with enthusiasm as far as trailers were concerned, buying 20 in 1933 (703-722), ten in 1943 (723-732), six in 1956-58 (1333-1338) and finally six (1339-1344) in the period 1960-64. Two conversions brought the total number up to 44. There were, however, only two three-axle motor cars (73 and 301), the latter a rebuild of an existing two-axle vehicle. A few of the later trailers are still in use on the suburban lines and two have been rebuilt as bicycle transports. The suburban Briseckbahn rebuilt seven of its older motor cars and 16 trailers with three-axle trucks between 1934 and 1950. Of these, motor car 4 has been preserved and fully restored to running order, while ten trailers have gone to Beograd. Two of the BVB trailers have been preserved and are run behind the preserved central-entrance bogie car of 1914. Bern, however, only ever had one three-axle trailer car (310) and this was scrapped in 1973.

In Zürich the radial Forchbahn line rebuilt one car (6) with a three-axle truck in 1934 and this had a long career, lasting until February 1983. Of rather greater importance for future development were two three-axle cars (31/2) with lightweight steel bodies built for the city system by SWS-Schlieren in 1939 on SLM trucks. With sharply tapered ends, automatic doors and passenger flow from rear to front, these cars were the forerunners of the Swiss standard car. The first had only front and rear doors, but the second had an additional centre door, and this was in 1946 retrofitted to the first car. A few changes were

Zürich 1032 at Klusplatz on line 8 in May 1955. (F.W. Hunt collection, courtesy London Area, Light Rail Transit Association)

made in the design of the truck, to provide a stronger frame and also make maintenance easier. As they used motors and control gear from old two-axle cars, they were underpowered for the more hilly routes and the transition from series to parallel running was

Köln 1825 awaits departure from Neumarkt on line K in April 1957. (W.J. Wyse, courtesy London Area, Light Rail Transit Association)

accompanied by an unpleasant jerk. Although fairly successful, their limited capacity and relatively low speed prevented their being adopted as a standard design and they were soon out-classed by the new bogie cars. They lasted in service until 1971 and car 32 has been preserved in the Swiss Transport Museum in Luzern.

In 1945 and 1948 Lausanne converted two older motor/trailer sets (28/9 and 111/2), which had originated on a radial line at Genève in 1913. The motor cars were quite long, at 10.1m, and were completely rebuilt and given more powerful motors of 90kW when fitted with the three-axle trucks. In this state they worked on both city and radial lines until abandonment in 1963, when the trailers were scrapped. The motor cars, however, were sold to the Bex-Villars-Bretaye line and ran there until 1978. No.28 has since been restored to its Lausanne condition for preservation on the Blonay-Chambay museum line.

A few light rail lines, such as the Bremgarten-Dietikon line, converted older stock, both motor and trailer, to three-axle configuration using Buchli trucks in the years up to 1940. In all just under 90 Buchli trucks were sold in this period, two-thirds of these being for use under trailers and almost half for rebuilding of older cars.

Technical details

Zürich 31
Length 11.87m width 2.2m, weight 15.3 tonnes, 2 x 62kW motors, 53 passengers, 20 seated.

Outwith Switzerland, success was at first limited. The Luxembourg city system bought five motor cars and three trailers in the pre-war period, of which motor car 26 of 1938 has been preserved in the local transport museum. Rather surprisingly interest also came from Spain, where Seville bought a sample car in 1936 and ultimately followed this by 13 others (301-314). These were sold to Vigo when the system closed and ran there until abandonment in 1968. In the Netherlands, the NZH converted one older central-entrance car and one trailer (A101 and B111) in 1935, but there were no others. The Limburgse Tramweg Maatschappij had greater success with the design, and converted twelve two-axle cars (2501-12) dating from the mid-1920s. When the system closed in 1950, they were sold to Saarlouis and ran there until 1961. But the breakthrough for the three-axle concept came only after Europe had become engulfed in the Second World War.

In the immediate pre-war period there were experiments in other German cities. Older cars were rebuilt in Braunschweig, Leipzig, Lübeck, Hagen and Erfurt and three new cars (24-26) were built by Fuchs in 1938 for Gera. None of these achieved any great success. However, three cars built for Stuttgart's rack tramway in 1935 and 1937 by Maschinenfabrik Esslingen proved to be rather better, despite the complication of combining rack mechanism with a three-axle truck, of the builder's own design. They lasted in

Preserved Lausanne 28 on the Blonay museum line in May 1984. (Author)

Sevilla 313 and trailer 78 negotiate Plaza General Franco in June 1957. (Ray DeGroote)

27 March 1946 it was decided to order 60 motor cars (491-550) and 50 trailers (951-999). The desired length of 12m was rather too long for a two-axle car, while it would have been difficult to adapt a bogie car to Amsterdam's particular track geometry, given the number of bridges and tight curves, and so the three-axle type was chosen. At that time, no other operator had experience of so large a fleet of such cars, and the GVBA was definitely breaking new ground with this order. Hindsight would later suggest that it would have been better to have opted for a more conventional design, given the condition of the system at that time. The trams were constructed in the Netherlands by Werkspoor under licence from SLM and clearly owed much to the two Zürich cars. Two prototypes arrived on 23 and 27 January 1948 and the production series arrived from 1949 to 1950. As built, they had passenger flow from rear to front, originally with three doors. In service it was found that the single-width front door was too narrow for passenger use and it was thereafter used by crews only. They were comfortably finished and for the first time passengers enjoyed the luxury of seats upholstered in red leather. They also rode well on track which, at that time, had not always been maintained to the highest standards.

Unfortunately there were problems, as was to be expected with pioneers. The Amsterdam network has many more curves than does that of Zürich, and the wheels on the middle axle were prone to develop flats and were extremely noisy. In turn this had a deleterious effect on the track. The two 45kW motors were really too weak to cope with trailer operation and soon became prone to overheating and breakdown. Breaking could also be a problem. The materials used in construction were inferior, due to post-war shortages, and a good deal of rebuilding had to be undertaken after the cars had been in service for a few years. Availability of the new cars between 1950 and 1954 sank to an embarrassingly low level and older cars had to be kept in service to cover for them. Together with the effect of some nasty accidents, it became questionable if the Amsterdam tram would survive. In 1954 the manager, W.B. Hofman, resigned. Under his successor, W. Ybema, the three-axle cars were speedily returned to full service, in an operation which amounted to a total rebuilding. It was said that by this time the wiring no longer hung from the side panels, but the panels hung from the wiring! A low volt battery was fitted to run the traffic indicators, the door mechanism and the optical signal lamps, while the wheels were also fitted with rubber-insert suspension, which cured many of the problems. The motor cars were also renumbered from 891-950. They were

service until 1982. Bremen bought two sample cars in 1937, one each from Westwaggon and Uerdingen, the latter having yet another design of three-axle truck, in which the middle axle carried 19% of the body weight, with a consequent reduction in tractive and braking power. The operator seemed pleased with the Westwaggon car and three more were bought in 1939/40. Only two of these cars survived the war and were fitted with track brakes in 1960, to comply with new regulations. Thereafter they had a tendency to derail and were scrapped in the 1960s.

The only system to order three-axle cars in quantity was Köln. Following trials with two rebuilt trailers (969-70), motorised in 1938 and mounted on Westwaggon's Buchli trucks, a series of 31 motor cars (501-531) and 15 trailers (1-15) was acquired from Westwaggon (motors) and Düwag (trailers), the first just as war broke out in 1939. The first 16 motors were single-ended but double-sided and had "niederflur" bodies, finished internally to an extremely high standard, a modern touch being the map of line 18 on which stops were indicated by small lights, illuminated by the driver as the car approached the stop concerned. The second batch of 15 and all the trailers were double-ended and less luxuriously furnished, not being delivered until 1941. These were all used on belt line 18. Only 22 motor cars and nine trailers survived the air raids and two motors were scrapped in the early post-

war years. All but one were converted to single-ended layout in 1958 and they survived until dates between 1963 and 1968. Motor 1824 and trailer 2825 are preserved in running order. Clearly these cars were a success, but otherwise the verdict on three-axle cars in Germany at the time of the Second World War was at best "not proven". It is therefore surprising that the concept figured largely in the plans for a new design of standard tram for city service, and that the BVG of Berlin designed a longer version, laid out for passenger flow with a seated conductor.

Technical details
Köln 1824
Length 11.15m, width 2.3m, weight 13 tonnes, 2 x 57kW motors, 65 passengers, 23 seated.

Just after the German occupation of the Netherlands had begun, the GVBA of Amsterdam requested from two Netherlands vehicle builders, Verheul and Werkspoor, tenders for the supply of 30 three-axle cars, laid out in the classic Peter Witt design, with front entrance and central exit. The design prepared by the first of these showed considerable resemblance to its buses, while that from Werkspoor was much more tram-like. Not surprisingly, the matter was not taken any further at that stage, but the idea was revived immediately after the war, and on

Amsterdam 535 and trailer on the Rokin in September 1959, outbound to what was then known as Rivierenlaan terminus. (Author)

completely outclassed by the new articulated cars from 1957 onwards, but continued to fulfil a useful function on peak-hour extras until the 1970s.

Mid-life overhauls began in 1963 and 46 cars were converted for one-person operation between 1967 and 1974. As these were at first available only to holders of season tickets, the earlier conversions were given a red band on the dash to distinguish them from other trams and this feature gave rise to the nickname of "bloed-neuzen" or bloody-nosed cars. At a later date, these and all later conversions were fitted with on-board ticket cancellers and were available to all with tickets. To bring them into line with the articulated cars, many were also fitted with a much larger box for the line number and colour code. To increase capacity and at the same time reduce personnel, a plan was devised by the technical staff in 1969 by which 48 three-axle motor cars would be converted to trailers and, with the existing trailers, would be used behind two-section articulated cars. On the nights of 29 and 30 October 1969 nocturnal trials were made with articulated car 580 and trailers 953 and 954, to test the practicability of this scheme, but it was abandoned when doubts were raised by Siemens about possible overheating of, and damage to, the motors of the articulated cars by haulage of relatively heavy trailers. Ten older trailers from 1929/30 would have been rebuilt to run with the remaining motor cars. Conductors remained on the trailers until the end, but 35 of these, which were used behind the one-man cars, were given a red waist band.

The last three-axle cars in normal service ran in May 1983, but until 1999 they continued to appear on odd workings. No.533, restored to the condition of about 1960, has been preserved by the RET group, while nos.891, 903 and 909 are preserved by other organisations as "bloed-neuzen" and sometimes still appear on the city tracks. Trailer 987 has been restored to partner no.533, while nos.958, 961 and 968 are preserved in later condition. No.902 is now preserved by the local tramway museum in Graz. Another trailer, no.999 became an open car, in which capacity it provided accommodation for a band on special occasions. It has now retired to the local tramway museum. One became a works car but has now been withdrawn.

Although they had some initial shortcomings, the Amsterdam three-axle cars ultimately gave good service over quite a long period, and proved convincingly that the concept could work successfully in intensive city service.

Technical details

Prototype motor car as built
Length 12m, width 2.2m, weight 15 tonnes, 2 x 45kW motors, 83 passengers, 25 seated.

Amsterdam 927 and trailer, as rebuilt for one-person operation at Centraal Station in April 1971. (Author)

Reference has already been made to the proposals in Germany for the development of a range of standard tram. For the busier urban services, a three-axle car, mounted on a truck which, from the description, was based closely on the Westwaggon/Buchli design, was envisaged. The car would have had the same length as the single truck version – 10.94m – but would have ridden on a truck with a wheelbase of 4.7m. No car was actually built to this design, but in 1942 a version was planned for Berlin, with an additional door behind the middle axle and a wheelbase of 6.2m. This would have had a seated conductor and passenger flow from rear to front. It is not certain that this design ever progressed beyond the drawing office.

The first post-war three-axle cars to appear were to the Aufbau design, with new trucks, whose length was identical to that of the proposed standard car. The bodies were, however, somewhat shorter, at 10.5m. A total of 47 motor cars and 15 trailers was produced for eight systems, all except Mainz being in the British zone in northern Germany. Only Oberhausen took any quantity, having 23 motor cars (301-323) and all 15 trailers (406-420). It later also bought eight other motors, when their original systems, Herne and Rheydt, closed. In service these trams proved to be a disappointment, and soon looked obsolete beside the new bogie and articulated cars bought by neighbouring systems. Two were rebuilt in 1962 by Westwaggon into an articulated car. However, largely because of the poor experience with these cars, the municipality decided on abandonment and the last tram (for the time being) ran on 13 October 1968. Seven motors and three trailers were then sold to the neighbouring Mülheim, but lasted there only for a further ten years. Individual cars are preserved in Mainz, Mülheim and Dortmund. In the summer of 1949 the VöV organisation published guidelines for future standard trams and among these was a three-axle car with a length of over 12m.

While these trams were entering service in the north, a much more significant development was taking place in Bavaria. München, which had a long history of using bogie cars, was faced with an urgent need to replace many elderly vehicles, as well as catching up with war damage. It would therefore have been a retrograde step to have introduced two-axle cars as a post-war standard,

München 837, working on line 7 to Milbertshofen, turns from Bayerstrasse to the loading point in front of the Hauptbahnhof in August 1967. (Author)

The bright and attractive interior of one of the trams in München. The ticket cancellers had then just been introduced, August 1967. (Author)

Drei Wagens von der Linie 8! A three-car set led by no.985 heads across Karlsplatz, when work on the S-Bahn tunnel was under way in July 1968. (Author)

but on the other hand, clearance problems ruled out a modern bogie car such as Hamburg's V6 class. A three-axle design could provide the same accommodation as the older bogie cars, at less cost, and meet all the requirements of the system. The manager, Dr Ulsamer, adopted the idea with enthusiasm and as early as 1946 three three-axle trucks were ordered from Westwaggon. When they arrived in 1948 they were tested under two old motor cars and one trailer. These tests seem to have shown that the three-axle concept would be ideal for the city's new cars, and four new motor cars (764-767) and two trailers (1601/2) were ordered as prototypes from the local firm of Rathgeber, based closely on the Westwaggon designs. The first entered service in May 1950 and in external appearance looked very like the abortive Berlin design of eight years earlier. Telescopic sliding doors were fitted. These cars had an unusual feature of two single-width centre doors, along with front and rear doors, the reason for the splitting of the central entrance being to allow clearance for the middle axle. The conductor sat at a desk between the doors and facing them, and both streams of boarding passengers had to converge at this point before separating to pass into the front or rear portion of the car. This layout proved to be unworkable in city traffic, and very soon the forward of the two centre doors was blocked off and the conductor's post transferred to a point on the nearside just ahead of the rear platform. Apart from this, however, the cars proved successful and were much liked by passengers. The original motors of 80kW seem to have been replaced by more powerful motors of 100kW at an early date.

In 1953 the first production series was placed in traffic. In these trams, the rear entrance layout was installed from new, with a double-width door, and the pantograph was moved from its central position to one at the front of the motor car. The windscreen was slightly raked to give a more pleasing outline and 100kW motors were fitted from new. With these few changes, successive orders placed up to 1964, plus the prototypes brought the total of what was a very successful design up to 286 motors (764-1049) and 246 trailers (1601-1846), plus eleven similar cars of each built for Augsburg by MAN (511-521 and 263-273). In the last 75 of München's motor cars, delivered between 1962 and 1965, the centre door was repositioned ahead of the middle axle and plug doors, and single-arm pantographs were fitted. The last 30 of these were fitted with GEMATIC electro-hydraulic control and two 112kW motors, and in service worked in motor-motor-trailer formation on line 8, the busiest of the system and immortalised in the music-hall song "Ein Wagen von der Linie Acht". These trams finally proved that the concept could offer a level of service almost equal to that provided by bogie cars. All were converted to one-person operation after 1967. Unfortunately by this time the trams were being displaced from their premier position by the new U-Bahn network. The last day of these trams in normal service was to have been 31 May 1997, but due to problems with the low floor replacements, some survived until at least November of that year. Forty-nine motor cars and 53 trailers were sent to Bucuresti between 1994 and 1998. Despite receiving many spare parts along with the trams, that undertaking found it difficult to maintain the three-axle trucks, and the cars concerned have since been rebuilt into bogie vehicles. Brasov received six each of motors and trailers in October 1997, as well as a snowplough, and seemed to have had fewer problems. Motor cars 2401, 2412, 2448 and 2615 and trailers 3390, 3404 and 3407 are preserved in their native city.

Technical details
M3 class
Length 13.25m, width 2.2m, weight 17.4 tonnes, 2 x 100kW motors, 111 passengers, 26 seated.

Only a few other operators put three-axle trams into service. The only other one to acquire cars laid out for passenger flow with a seated conductor was Wuppertal, which in 1954 bought four (3001-3004) from Westwaggon. These trams were longer than the München cars and at 14m

On an enthusiasts' tour in May 1981, Mülheim's 233 has attracted a curious young spectator. This ex-Oberhausen car has now been restored to the livery it carried there and has also been given its former number of 322. (Author)

Ex-München 2510 in Bucuresti in June 1995, still running on its three-axle truck, but since rebuilt as a bogie car. (Martin Jenkins, OnLine Transport Archive)

Bonn 334 leads a motor-trailer-motor set at Bonn in September 1972. (Jim D. Schantz)

Mainz 201. (Lars F. Richter collection)

equalled the length and capacity of a Grossraum bogie car. However, they proved to be difficult to maintain and, as more articulated cars were acquired, they saw less and less use and were scrapped in 1976/7. The other four operators were Neuss (29, 30), Mainz (101-105) and two radial lines, Opladen-Ohlligs (20-24) and Bonn-Bad Godesberg-Mehlem, which by 1959 had bought a total of 20 motor cars (15-34) and 11 trailers (51-61). All were built by Westwaggon and the Bonn cars were particularly comfortable, with luggage racks, two continuous rows of strip lighting and deeply-cushioned seats with armrests, all this being set off by polished mahogany woodwork with anodised, bronze aluminium trim. Apart from the first four, the motor cars had only one driving position, being intended for operation in motor-trailer-motor sets. They were very popular with the travelling public and ran until 1976. Two motor cars and one trailer have been preserved. This line also had two conversions from older trailer cars by Westwaggon in 1950 and of these, no.14 has survived as a party car. The Opladen cars introduced pedal control on the Zürich model to Germany and were sold to Bremerhaven when their own system closed in 1955. As nos.68-72,

they lasted there until 1977 and no.68, 70 and 71 have been preserved, as has one of the Mainz. The second of the Neuss cars was initially fitted with what was then, for Germany, a revolutionary form of pedal control, by Kiepe, but this proved unsatisfactory and was later replaced by a conventional controller. No.29 has been preserved.

Bochum in 1952 bought one truck and placed it under an older two-axle car (187). If this was done to allow a comparison with the new Grossraumwagen bogie car design, no details

Bex-Villars-Bretaye no.16 at Bex station in May 1984. (Author)

were actually published, but as no further three-axle trams were bought, it would seem that the verdict was in favour of the latter. Five three-axle trucks were acquired by the BVG (West) in Berlin in 1950 and were used under older cars dating from 1912. They were scrapped in 1959. At about the time that these arrived, the only three-axle car to be built for the DDR also arrived in Berlin. This was a trailer, intended as a prototype for a series of three-axle motors and trailers, and looked rather like a stretched version of the then-new Werdau two-axle cars. Its truck was of a novel design, which in some ways anticipated current technology, in that the end wheels were not linked by an axle but rotated independently at the end of fork-shaped connecting rods which linked them to the middle axle. In service this tram (256) proved prone to derailments and was soon shipped off to Potsdam, where it was scrapped in 1956.

The only post-1945 Swiss three-axle motor trams were two cars (15/6) built in 1948 by SWS for the local service of the Bex-Villars-Bretaye radial line. This service was ended on 15 December 2002 but they still perform relief duties on the upper end of the line. Eight trailers (51-58) were built for St Gallen in 1948, that undertaking's only post-war cars, and were sold to Basel when the system closed in 1959. There they became 1241-1248 and were scrapped in 1967.

All other operators except München seem to have come to the same conclusion as Berlin, and no further three-axle cars were bought by any other system after 1959. There was clearly no future for a design which had seemed so promising just ten years earlier. The München cars, attractive in their traditional Bavarian "weiss-blau" (white and blue) livery, ran well and gave excellent service until displaced by newer vehicles and extensions to the U-Bahn. They certainly proved that three-axle cars could handle the traffic of a large city, at less cost than bogie cars. But the Düwag monomotor bogie had made it possible to have a bogie car without the cost and complication of four motors and this consideration seems to have won the day. It was especially important on systems which included hilly routes, on which the lack of adhesion of the three-axle car might have been a drawback. And by 1956 the six-axle articulated car had begun to assume the place of the German standard tram, making both three-axle and bogie designs obsolete. The München cars were certainly a vindication of all those engineers who had for sixty years tried to put the concept into practice – but the vindication came just too late to have widespread application.

Bibliography

3-Axle Streetcars from Robinson to Rathgeber, volumes 1 and 2. Henry Elsner. NJ International Inc, Hicksville, NY, 1995.

Der Stadtverkehr 8/1991 (Amsterdam cars).

De Amsterdamse drie-assers. J. van Huijksloot. Uitgeverij Uquilair, 2003.

Van paardetram naar dubbelgelede. (Amsterdam) W. J. Leideritz. Uitgeverij de Alk, Alkmaar, 1979.

70 Jaar Elektrische Trams in Amsterdam. C. van Mechelen. Uitgevers Wijt, Rotterdam, 1970.

Strassenbahn Magazin no.136, February 2001 (Germany).

Fahrzeuge Deutscher Strassen-und Stadtbahnen. Op.cit.

An unidentified Wuppertal car. (Lars F. Richter collection)

GERMAN BOGIE GROSSRAUMWAGEN

While there had been bogie trams in use on certain German systems since the early days of electric traction, with fleets in Berlin and München, most operators remained faithful to the concept of the two-axle motor tram pulling one or two similar trailers until several years after the end of the second world war. A Peter Witt car from Milano (1502) ran in Frankfurt (M) in July 1929 during the congress of the UITP, the manager of that undertaking, Herr Kremer, being interested in the possibility of using bogie cars. While it was well received, its length of 13.47m and the track spacing confined it to three lines and the complicated fare system could not be worked efficiently by a single seated conductor. The trial was therefore without result. This and other contemporary designs have been described in chapter 2.

The Reichsverkehrsgruppe Schienenbahnen produced plans for a standard bogie car and matching trailer, intended for use on radial lines. This was originally conceived as a double-ended car, with some similarities to the cars bought by Düsseldorf for its metre gauge lines in 1935, but at the insistence of the Hamburg (HHA) manager, F. Lademann, an alternative single-ended version was also included in the range. Lademann was an exponent of this type of construction on grounds of cost and ease of operation at termini, but his ideas were not well received by the majority of his more conservative contemporaries. Using the remains of the body of one car of class V4, and the trucks of the lightweight car, the Hamburg HHA then built the prototype of class V5, a class first conceived in 1938. The twenty cars which had been ordered at that time also entered service in 1943, ten

Hamburg bogie car 2982 of class V5 at Billbrook. (Lars F. Richter collection)

Bremerhaven 77 was second-hand from Offenbach and is seen in the town centre in June 1980. (Author)

being lost almost immediately in air raids. While this class had a traditional square front end and conventional controllers, it was laid out as a "Grossraumwagen", that is a car without any internal partitions. It was also single-ended. Class V5 trams were 14.1m long and weighed 15.5 tonnes. The eleven survivors lasted in traffic until 1969. There were also 14 matching trailers, of which one has been preserved. The standard bogie car had not yet gone into production when, on 8 July 1942, the RVS was told to put its plans into cold storage for the duration of the war and concentrate on the two-axle KSW car. Eight motor and trailer sets (28-35 and 191-198) built by Ammendorf for Halle in 1940 were the nearest approach to the standard bogie car actually to go into service. They were used on the radial line to Merseburg until 1972.

There was a good deal interest in Germany in the concept of the PCC car and information about the standard bogie trams built in Sweden and Switzerland had reached the country during the war, but the pressing need to make up for war losses meant that only two-axle cars of the Aufbau and later Verbansstyp (qv) could be built in the immediate post-war years. The design of these followed guidelines drawn up by a working group of the Arbeitsgemeinschaft der Vereinigungen öffentlicher Verkehrsbetriebe (AVV) (later Verband öffentliche Verkehrsbetriebe (VöV)), which had been set up in February1948. This same organisation recommended that various designs of bogie car should be built to evaluate different layouts, but did not produce any specific plans.

However, the HHA, anxious to replace war losses with bogie cars and to modernise its fleet, had no wish to wait for the outcome of extended trials. In 1949 it built the prototype of class V6, which in dimensions followed exactly class V5. The conductor was given a fixed post by the rear doors and passenger flow, from rear to front, was

Hamburg V6 car 3616 near Damtor station in March 1971. (Author).

enforced. The internal finish was sombre, with much dark wood, and plywood seating was provided for 26 passengers. The angular external styling resembled that of the Swiss cars and appeared rather traditional, but had the advantage of ease of repair after accident damage. There was an underfloor controller and a separate driving cabin. With a matching trailer, 197 passengers could be processed by a crew of three. The car was an instant success and soon 103 motors and 100 trailers were ordered from Linke Hofmann Busch and the HHA's own workshops, to be delivered in the years 1950-52. Even while these were being delivered, the prototype of an improved version, class V7, was built. Externally the main difference was the fitting of folding in place of sliding doors and a rearrangement of seating allowed 112 passengers to be carried in the motor trams and 119 in the matching trailers.

During the lives of these trams, there was a good deal of renumbering of individual cars and all members of both classes were rebuilt for one-person operation in 1966-68. The V6 trailers were withdrawn in 1970/71, but the V7 trailers and all motor cars survived until the end of the

Essen 1516 in the centre of Mülheim on line 18 in August 1971. This was a joint service by the two undertakings. (Author)

One of the later deliveries to Hannover, showing the sloping windscreen favoured in that city. Car 476 is at Hauptbahnhof on an evening in October 1985. The panels on the lower part of the side were fitted to allow these cars to serve tunnel stations. (Author)

city's trams in 1979. They were steady-riding and comfortable trams and the end of the system had more to do with local politics than any shortcomings on their part. Ahead of all other designs, they proved the practicability in Germany of the "Grossraum" layout and the seated conductor. In 1952 the HHA published some details of the

The double-ended version of the standard Düwag car. This tram, 210, is seen at Bismarckplatz in Mainz in June 1985, having previously run in Aachen and, before that, Mönchen-Gladbach. (Author)

economies achieved by the new cars, as against the three-car trains of two-axle cars formerly used on line 3. While there had been a 10% increase in capacity offered, there had been a reduction in vehicle-kilometres, particularly for trailers, and there had been a reduction of 8% in drivers' hours and 23% in conductors' hours.

Alone of German undertakings, Hamburg ordered one PCC car (qv) for comparative trials.

Technical details
Class V6
Length 14.1m, width 2.2m, weight 16.55 tonnes, 4 x 50kW motors, 109 passengers, 31 seated.

Meanwhile some other operators, manufacturers, and the VöV continued to co-operate on the design of a standard Grossraum bogie car. It was an uphill struggle – an enquiry made of 72 undertakings in February 1948 showed that 35 still preferred two-axle cars, 12 preferred a three-axle car and 25 opted for a bogie car. But only six

Frankfurt (M) 229 and matching trailer at Hauptbahnhof in August 1968. (Author)

favoured a single-ended design! The real impetus for this concept lay in an address given in 1950 by Walter Prasse, the chair of the rail group of AVV, in which, drawing on a report he had written, he outlined the advantages of single-ended Grossraum bogie cars and trailers and also pointed out how far Germany was lagging behind developments elsewhere. These ideas were taken up by Theodor Held, director of the Düsseldorfer Waggonfabriek and like Prasse, a former member of the standardisation working group. In the autumn of 1950 this factory began the construction of prototypes for the Rheinbahn in the home city and for Hannover. In 1950 also the latter operator placed in service a rebuilt pre-war bogie car (711) which incorporated many features of the planned new design and which was very well received by the travelling public. Finally on 28 April 1951 the first Düwag motor and trailer set (301/1301) was placed in service in Hannover, to be followed a month later by a similar set for Düsseldorf (22/62) and a metre gauge version for Essen (513). There was also a double-ended interurban set for use on Hannover's line 11, consisting of two motor cars flanking a matching trailer (715, 1524, 716). This and the Düsseldorf set were shown at the transport exhibition "Schiene und Strasse" held in Essen in September 1951. A double-ended version of the urban design was first delivered to the Vestische Strassenbahn in 1952.

Technical details
Hannover 301
Length 14.1m, width 2.2m, weight 16.85 tonnes, 4 x 50kW motors, 96 passengers, 28 seated.

All these prototypes rode on bogies of conventional design, but in 1952 a second car for Düsseldorf (26) was delivered with an entirely new type of transmission, which was to revolutionise tram design in Germany and ensure the superiority of the bogie car over the then rival three-axle design. This was the Düwag tandem drive, by which one motor of 50kW drove both axles of each bogie. This gave a considerable saving in weight and cost over the conventional two motor design. A further advantage was the total synchronisation of wheels on both axles, which prevented slipping when accelerating, and acceleration was excellent, a tram/trailer set being able to reach 65km/hr in a very short space of time. There were some minor disadvantages in problems with suspension, and on single-ended cars it was necessary to turn the trucks periodically to equalise wheel profiles – but the monomotor bogie proved to be an outstanding success and was fitted to around 65% of all Grossraum bogie cars. A further new Düwag feature was the electrically-powered folding door, a design which proved far superior to any other

No.245 heads another car in multiple in Kiel in December 1972. (Michael J. Aze)

Rastatt bogie car 134 at Mühlburger Tor, Karlsruhe, in May 1984. (Author)

No.8, one of the handsome bogie cars in Ulm in August 1971. (Author)

One of the Herforder Kleinbahn's sets in very rural surroundings. (Lars F. Richter collection)

on the market and which was fitted almost universally, even on cars built by other manufacturers. Generally the cars were 14.10m long and 2.20m or 2.35m wide and could carry 28 seated and 68 standing passengers, with a weight of 17 tonnes. Both driver and conductor were seated.

Technical details
Rheinbahn 2101
Length 14.1m, width 2.35m, weight 17.6 tonnes, 2 x 108kW motors, 138 passengers*, 27 seated.

The double-ended version of the design was much less common and generally was supplied in small numbers to undertakings which had long rural lines. Many had end doors only.

Although the Grossraumwagen was, at about DM 165,000 or £13,750, not cheap, orders flowed in and between 1953 and 1960 this classic design was delivered to 15 undertakings. Most were in fact built before 1957 and only a series for Hannover, ten for Bonn, a dozen for Kiel, and in 1961 a pair of double-ended cars for the Kleinbahn Wesel-Rees, were built after that date. Cars built up to 1955 had four small windows between each set of doors, but in later batches this was reduced to three. With conductor operation, there were usually double-width doors at the rear and centre and a single-width door at the front, but when conversion to one-person operation was undertaken, this last was often rebuilt to double. Windscreens on earlier cars were either upright, as in Essen, or sloping as in Hannover, but those built after 1957 for Kiel and Bonn had PCC style windscreens, as on the new articulated cars. Internal finish tended to be rather old-fashioned, with much use of wood veneer and seats were normally of shaped plywood.

To the despair of the VöV, which had hoped that operators would standardise on a few types, there was considerable variation in the electrical and control equipment of these cars, but almost all had rubber-inset wheels by the Bochumer Verein or SAB and in service proved to be smooth riding and steady. Most cars were built with a capacity to pull one bogie trailer, but Krefeld bought six cars with only one motor, for use in multiple in peak periods and as solo cars at other times. M-u. operation was unsuccessful and after 1959 these cars always ran solo. Essen also tried this concept with three cars and built lightweight trailers for use with them. Düsseldorf also bought 15 one-motor cars in 1955/6 with a view to running a five-minute headway on the busy line 1. The cars were fast and gained the nickname of "pony cars" but in practice this led to irregularities in the service and when articulated cars were introduced, the bogie cars were in 1959/60 rebuilt as trailers. Kiel successfully used m.u.operation with two-motor cars. Hannover

bought 60 cars with only one truck motorised and used these in coupled sets with 56 motorised trailers, which did not have a driving position and were controlled from the leading car. A further variation was formed by the eight cars built for use on the Düsseldorf-Krefeld interurban line, which used bogies and axles supplied in 1940, for trams whose construction had been prevented by the outbreak of war.

Matching trailers, normally seating 30, were supplied to many operators and as these were also used behind articulated cars, they continued to be built well into the 1960s, with final batches built by Düwag being supplied to Kassel in 1970 and Braunschweig in 1974. These last had large windows, to match the "Mannheim" type of articulated cars then being bought. The first trailers to be built did not have a front door, as it would have been impossible for a crew member to supervise this, but the development of a system of safety contacts in the step treads solved this problem and front doors were fitted to all later batches. Latterly, of course, most trailers were operated without a conductor. The majority of trailers were single-ended, but a few double-ended examples were built for operators with interurban lines. Unusually, between 1957 and 1971 Krefeld built twelve trailers, of a rather square design, using parts from scrapped cars, two dating back to 1896. The first of these did not have a fixed post for the conductor, but the difficulty of dealing with 100 passengers by conventional methods of fare collection meant that these were provided from 1958 onwards. Some of those built for Hannover and Düsseldorf were fitted out as buffet cars. Braunschweig continued to favour trailers, and acquired six from LHB in 1977 (7771-7776), followed in 1981 and 1984 by 14

more from the same manufacturer, to a design resembling its new articulated cars. These trailers (8171-8182 and 8471/2) were the last conventional trailers to be built for any undertaking and will be the last to remain in service by a considerable margin, although at the time of writing, about 50 survive in Düsseldorf.

The Essen trailers mentioned above were 25 two-axle cars, built by Düwag in 1956, with bodies of matching outline to the bogie cars. To avoid overloading the motor cars, they were of lightweight construction, having no sub-frame and weighed only 6.3 tonnes. They had seats for 22 and could in total carry about 80 passengers. Unlike the motor cars, they were double-ended and initially they were often detached from their towing car at an intermediate point, where the heavier traffic had lessened, and attached to a car going in the opposite direction. However, their riding qualities were appalling and just a year after delivery, all were mounted on new frames,

Hansa bogie car 819 of 1954 negotiating track repairs in Bremen in June 1980. (Author)

No.12, one of the large END cars in service on that line in June 1977. (Jim D. Schantz)

Braunschweig 11 on Bohlweg in 1959. (A.D. Young, Evda Slides)

Köln 1367 on line 15 in 1962. (F.W. Hunt, courtesy London Area, Light Rail Transit Association)

Nürnberg 214 leaves the reserved track near Zoo terminus inbound to the city on line 11 in August 1967. (Author)

bringing distinct improvement for passengers. In 1966 22 were rebuilt for conductorless operation and these remained in service until the late 1970s. Krefeld and Neuss copied the idea, with eight and five trailers respectively, and the latter were sold to Duisburg when Düsseldorf took over the Neuss system. All survived in service until about 1980 and two are preserved in Krefeld. The Düsseldorf-Krefeld cars mentioned above were accompanied by four trailers, two of which were fitted out as buffet cars, complete with curtains and wall lights. These two did not have middle doors. When the buffet service came to a (fortunately temporary) end in 1962, they were rebuilt to conform with the other trailers.

Nürnberg trailer 1568 at Hauptbahnhof in June 1985. (Author)

In all a total of 336 single- and 68 double-ended motor trams and 419 and 47 bogie trailers respectively were built by Düwag and delivered to 24 undertakings. There were also the 38 two-axle trailers detailed above. The speed with which that firm had cornered the lion's share of the market might have been a deterrent to other manufacturers, but some operators preferred to patronise a factory in their own Land and in the event most of these did develop their own design of Grossraumwagen. A total of 224 single- and 33 double-ended trams were supplied to 13 under-takings in almost exactly the same period, though the last motor cars to be built, for the OEG at Mannheim, did not appear until 1963. There were also 182 and 80 trailers, to which should be added the Hamburg cars already mentioned. Many of the cars built by other manufacturers such as MAN incorporated Düwag trucks and/or doors. None of the other builders mounted a national challenge to Düwag and only Westwaggon, with 80 trams for Köln, and MAN with 69 motors and 110 trailers for Nürnberg (201-269 and 1501-1610) built more than a few cars. One of these trailers, 1521, was in 1975 converted to a motor car, to test three-phase equipment. A pantograph was mounted on the roof, the rear bogie was motorised and the equip-ment was located in a cupboard in the former post for the conductor. After tests, it was placed

in normal service working with motor car 208 and proved the practicability of three-phase equipment for trams and U-Bahn trains. On withdrawal in 1981, it was set aside for preserva-tion. Other builders were Fuchs (OEG), Talbot (Aachen), DWM (Berlin (W) and Braunschweig), Hansa (Bremen), LHB (Braunschweig and Bremen), Rastatt (Karlsruhe, OEG and Pforzheim), and MF Esslingen (Ulm, Kleinbahn Siegburg-Zündorf and END). Both Rastatt and Fuchs built quite a large number of trailers for the OEG. Credé built trailers only, for Dortmund, and DWM built 20 for Duisburg and Essen. Osnabrück bought three cars from Elze and Hansa which were basically conventional bogie cars without passenger flow and not included in the above total.

The trams for Köln had a width of 2.5m and could carry 125 passengers, but were not the largest Grossraum cars to be built. That honour went to two motor/trailer sets built by the Maschinenfabrik Esslingen for the Esslingen-Nellingen-Denkdendorf (END) radial line; these could carry 156 and 170 passengers respectively. These trams were sold to the Sud Tiroler Autobusdienst and still run on the Rittnerbahn line in Italy, but, being considered "too modern" (!) for what is essentially a tourist line, are normally used only for school services. The hand-some bogie cars supplied at the same time by

Braunschweig Mannheim-type trailer 7772 in the city centre, June 2000. (Author)

Braunschweig LHB-type trailer 8176. (Author)

Maschinenfabriek Esslingen to the system of Ulm were the most innovative Grossraum cars built by a manufacturer other than Düwag, having cardan drive and outward-opening plug doors. They were also the first trams in Germany to be designed for one-person operation, though they ran initially with conductors. The two handsome motor-trailer sets built by DWM for West Berlin might have been the first of a large fleet but almost as soon as they went into service, a political change of policy to one of tram replacement was instituted and they had no chance to prove themselves.

Technical details
Bochum 200, 1952
Length 14.1m, width 2.2m, weight 17 tonnes, 2x48kW motors, 102 passengers, 27 seated.
Nürnberg trailer 1501
Length 14.1m, width 2.34m, weight 12,600kg, 103 passengers, 29 seated.
Rheinbahn buffet trailer
Length 15.2m, width 2.2m, weight 15.65 tonnes, 54 seats, no standing passengers.

Although one of the double-ended cars built by Düwag for the Vestische Strassenbahn (341, still in service in Gmunden, Austria) ran in Helsinki during the Olympic Games of 1952, no export orders were ever received for the type. However, the Austrians were quick to follow the example of their neighbours and in 1953 a prototype set (101/1201) was supplied by SGP to Wien. Unfortunately the electrical installation in this car gave much trouble and it saw little service before being scrapped in 1969. The production series, class C1, was therefore built under licence from Düwag and consisted of 58 motor cars built by Lohner in the years 1955-59 (102-159). When withdrawn by Wien, 13 of these trams and an equal number of matching trailers were gifted to Sarajevo, to help rebuild that system after the Bosnian war. They were renumbered 400-412 and 4000-4012 and entered service without any great problems in 1997, but shortage of spare parts has meant that none are still running. Car 141 is preserved in Wien. Finally in 1967 a car intended for one-person operation (160, class C3) appeared. This had an advanced electronic "Gematic" control system, but, owing to the current success of the articulated design, no series order followed. Eight cars were also built for Innsbruck between 1960 and 1969, the last of these being the last Grossraumwagen to be built. There was also a single car (8) of unusual double-ended design for Gmunden, which had doors on one side only. Two others (9 and 10) were later acquired from the Vestische Strassenbahn and converted to the same layout.

Ex-Pforzheim trailers in use on the Bern-Worb line, in Bern in May 1984. (Author)

Aachen 1006 on the right passing articulated car 1107. 27 February 1972. (A.D. Young, Evda Slides)

However, it was in the use of Grossraum trailers that the Austrians excelled. In the late 1950s, the WSW were running many trailers which had long passed their scrapping date and, as trailers are cheaper to build and less complicated to maintain than motor cars, it was decided to build a large fleet as a quick way of modernising the system. Including the 58 trailers built to run with the class C bogie cars, no fewer than 499 trailers were built by Lohner and, latterly, by Rotax (classes c1-c5, numbers between 1001 and 1488, with gaps). This was by far the largest batch of Grossraum cars constructed for any single operator. These have run very successfully, at first behind ancient motor cars, latterly with modern articulated cars and only now are withdrawals beginning.

Not surprisingly, operators in the DDR were watching developments in the west and in 1951 the first attempt to build a Grossraum car was made. Managers of the larger systems such as Berlin, Dresden – which still hankered after a new bogie car – and Magdeburg viewed the limited capacity and low maximum speed of the two-axle cars with disfavour and their opinion was shared by Rudolf Stur, formerly of Nürnberg and now the foremost transport expert in the DDR. The Werdau factory supplied a bogie version of its current two-axle design as a motor/trailer set to what was then the BVG (Ost) in Berlin. This was placed in service on 30 November 1953 and hailed as "Der Wagen der Zukunft" (the car of the future). Unfortunately, despite the known constraints of Berlin's track spacing, the cars were 2.5m wide and their future was to be confined to shuttling between Grunau and Schmöckwitz on line 86 in the far south east of the city.

Wien trailer no.1344, class c4, on the Schottenring in June 2001. (Author)

Leipzig's Grossraumwagen set 1100/2100 on sightseeing duties at Volkerschlachtdenkmal on 11 June 1966. (A.D. Young, Evda Slides)

One of the Düsseldorf sets at Krefeld, Ostwall, with a Krefeld car on the left. (Leeds Transport Historical Society)

OEG 75 shares Edingen depot with articulated car 99 in June 1985. (Author)

Berlin (BVB) prototype 218.001 approaches Mahlsdorf S-Bahn station in August 1983. (Author)

Berlin BVB Gotha 218.042 and trailer in the rain in Köpenick S-Bahn station in September 1992. (Author)

Dresden 1742 approaching Postplatz, with the ruins of the Schloss in the background in 1971. (B. Bareham, author's collection)

Attempts to sell the set to Karl Marx Stadt failed and it was scrapped in 1969. The reduced floor height at the rear entrance was perhaps the only redeeming feature of these trams and anticipated the Schindler cars in Rotterdam by several years. Little more success attended the set built by Leipzig in its own workshops in 1955, using parts of old two-axle cars. This motor car turned the scales at no less than 25 tonnes and was distinctly sluggish in traffic. The set was sold in 1967 to the line at Schöneiche near Berlin but was scrapped in 1975. That enterprising undertaking also rebuilt five old motor cars and six trailers with new bodies between 1963 and 1966 and one of these (62) has been preserved.

Much more successful were the Grossraum cars built by the VEB Waggonfabriek Gotha between 1958 and 1965. In 1956 the VEB Waggonbau Ammendorf prepared a design of a Grossraum bogie car and built a mock-up of the front end. The car seems to have been intended for Halle, since it was shown as mounted on metre gauge bogies. However, the state planning commission did not agree with this and instead ordered that the prototype, and any series production, should be built by the VEB Waggonbau Gotha. The Ammendorf designers therefore passed on all the papers relating to this design to their counterparts in Gotha and a prototype tram/trailer set appeared in the summer of 1959. This was sent to Berlin and on 7 December began trial service, also on line 86 as Berlin 8002/3002. These cars were based directly on the Ammendorf designs, though of course for standard gauge, and the motor car had a sharply raked windscreen. The floor level sloped down towards the front and rear in both vehicles and the interior was airy and inviting, with light green panelling and seats covered in green artificial leather. From the passenger's point of view, these were more attractive cars than their counterparts in the west, to which they outwardly looked very similar. The cost of the prototype set was given as DM1.5m, (about £12,400), that currency then still being valid in the DDR. The control equipment was that of the Dresden Hechtwagen and cardan drive was fitted.

A certain amount of re-arrangement of the Gotha factory had to be undertaken before series production could begin, and the first production trailers did not enter service in Berlin until March 1961, motor cars following in 1962. Unlike the prototype, these had passenger flow from front to rear and to accommodate this, the single-width front door was replaced by one of double-width. The raked windscreen was replaced by one almost identical to that fitted on the two-axle cars. Production sets cost MDN 306,000, but it is almost impossible to translate this accurately into a western equivalent. Initially 32 motors and 88 trailers were supplied to Berlin (8003-334 and 3003-3090), 19 of each to Dresden (1731-1749 and 2001-2019) and 14 of each to Magdeburg (431-444 and 561-574). They were classed as T4-62 and B4-61. Leipzig was also interested in acquiring this type and many more were planned for Berlin. Export sales were also intended and it is thought that one car, painted red and ivory, did go to Moscow for exhibition, but returned to the DDR. However, despite the obvious success of the design, production came to an abrupt end in 1964, since the VEB Gotha was planning the introduction of other new designs and the factory capacity was required for these. As in the west, the bogie car had arrived too late. In 1968-70 all were concentrated in Berlin. They became class 218 under the computer numbering system and were used mainly in Köpenick. The reason for this move was that Tatra T4D cars could not operate in Berlin owing to the narrow track spacing and it was desirable to give the capital at least a small fleet of modern cars. All have now been withdrawn. They were fast and comfortable cars, and many Berliners would have liked to see them continue on inner city lines in preference to the grinding Reko two-axle cars. A set originally used in Dresden (1734 and trailer 2015) has returned to that city and has been fully restored to original condition. It entered museum service in 2003. In Berlin car 218.001 has also been preserved.

Technical details
BVB 8001
Length 14.59m, width 2.5m, weight 17.8 tonnes, 4 x 50kW motors, 96 passengers, 40 seated.
Gotha motor car, production series
Length 14.1m, width 2.2m, weight 18 tonnes, 4 x 55kW motors, 113 passengers, 25 seated.

The Grossraum trams were well received by the public in both Germanies. With their pleasant rounded form and chrome styling they seemed to typify the Federal Republic and its dawning economic miracle, and they certainly gave the lie to the idea that trams were necessarily out of date. In some cities they were nicknamed "Sambawagens" after a dance popular at the time. But they came too late to have any real impact on public transport and were the design which Germany should have had twenty years earlier. In an article on the trams in 1954, *Modern Tramway* probably got it right when it pointed out that, while the PCC car had been a remarkable technical advance, the

BVG (West) Berlin 7001 as part of the museum collection in Britz garage, August 1983. (Author).

Schöneiche 73 and trailer await passengers at Friedrichshagen in July 1973. (A.D. Young, Evda Slides)

Grossraumwgen was simply a "considerable advance", intended to bring about a reduction in costs of construction through standardisation. Series production began only in 1952 and by 1954 the first of Stuttgart's articulated cars was already pointing the way to the future. In correspondence in the technical press in 1954, Professor Bockemühl of Stuttgart repeatedly criticised the concept on the grounds of inflexibility and the need for a crew of three. In fact Stuttgart, along with Mannheim and Kassel, was one of the operators who had nothing to do with the design, preferring to go straight from two-axle cars to the articulated model. Generally the cost of the design put it out of reach of the smaller systems. Even when systems such as the Herforder Kleinbahn, which had four double-ended Düwag cars, did buy them, they were successful only in postponing the inevitable closure; of the 35 systems in the Federal Republic which bought Grossraumwagen, 17 ultimately closed, some very soon after placing the cars in service. The first scrapping took place in 1964 (Düren) and the first car to enter a museum did so in Berlin in 1967. Pforzheim bought one motor car and four matching trailers from Rastatt in 1957, for peak hour working on its line to Ittersbach. When closure came in 1968, no buyer was found for the motor car, which went into a local museum, at the ripe old age of 13, but the trailers went to the Bern-Worb line in Switzerland.

Those operators who intended to maintain their tramways were then faced with a dilemma of how best to use trams which were still almost new but already obsolete. As detailed elsewhere, several systems such as Bochum rebuilt their bogie cars into articulated units, some of which are still in service. Bielefeld simply de-motored its four cars in 1962 and ran them as trailers. Düsseldorf did the same with 29 of its fleet, though others continued in service in their original form for many years. There was also a brisk trade in second-hand cars, some of which turned up in unusual places, in unusual forms. Thus Offenbach's three cars were acquired by Bremerhaven in 1967, when Offenbach ceased to be a tramway operator in its own right. The six double-ended cars from Mönchen-Gladbach were sold to Aachen in 1968 and when that system closed, some went on to Mainz, which had not previously operated the type. The two cars from the DB-owned Ravensburg line went first to the RTM line in Rotterdam, where they were rebuilt into a diesel set and when the RTM

in turn closed, they were sold to the Zillertalbahn line in Austria.

More recently many have gone east, and trams from Nürnberg ran for ten years from 1993 in its twin city of Krakow while ten each of motors and trailers from the same source are in Braila in Romania. The same total of each type from Frankfurt (M) are now running in Bucuresti alongside ex-München three-axle cars rebuilt to bogie configuration, and one motor car and four trailers from Mülheim are running in Arad, one trailer having been fitted out as a café tram. Galati has five each of motors and trailers from Frankfurt (M).

Mainz was the last system to use double-ended cars, the last being withdrawn in 1987. The systems which latterly made most use of the single-ended version were Hannover, Frankfurt (M), Mülheim and Nürnberg, of which Mülheim was the last to keep the class in service, until 1996. The last motor cars to serve in Western Europe are to be found in Gmunden in Austria. At least 70 motor cars have been rebuilt to serve as works cars of different types and a large number have been preserved. A link with tramways in the British Isles was forged in 1976 when six cars were sold by Aachen to the Manx Electric Railway in the Isle of Man. The bogies and electrical equipment were used to refurbish the six cars of the Snaefell Mountain Railway, the

Well filled, Gmünden 8 leaves the town centre in June 1981. (Author)

WSW Wien C2 class car 141 at the terminus of line 46 at Ottakring Depot, in September 1987. At that time, these cars still carried a conductor, who can be seen just ahead of the rear door. (Author)

One of Wien's modern trailers, no.1469, near Gumpendorferstrasse Stadtbahn station in June 2001. (Author)

work being carried out by London Transport. Unfortunately it was not found possible to use the bodies, only one of which actually made it to the Isle of Man, where it became a tool shed. Whether the Snaefell cars can now be classed as Grossraumwagen is debatable!

Table 1
German Grossraumwagen Bogie Trams

Motor trams	single ended	double ended
Built by Düwag	336	68
Built by other manufacturers	419	33
Built by operator		1
Built in Austria	1	
Built in Austria under licence	65	
Built by VEB Gotha for DDR systems	66	
Other DDR cars/rebuilds	7	
Sub total	894	102
Total motor trams		996
Trailers built new		
Düwag	419	47
Others	392	76
Built in Austria under licence	499	
Gotha	122	
Other DDR cars	8	
Sub totals	1440	123
Total trailers		1563
Grand total		2559
Rebuilds of motor cars to trailers (included only once in above tables)		33

German systems using Grossraum bogie cars: Aachen, Berlin (BVG and BVB*), Bielefeld, Bochum-Gelsenkirchen, Braunschweig, Bremen, Bremerhaven, Dortmund, Dresden*, Düsseldorf, Duisburg, Essen, END, Frankfurt (M), Hagen, Hamburg, Hannover, Herforder Kleinbahn, Karlsruhe, Kiel, Köln, Krefeld, Magdeburg*, Mainz, Mönchen Gladbach, Mülheim, Neuss, Nürnberg, OEG, Offenbach,

Ex-Nürnberg 113 at Krakow Wiadukty on 11 June 1994. The car still wears its original livery but advertisements in Polish have been applied. (Author)

Pforzheim, Ravensburg-Weingarten (DB), Siegburg-Zündorf, Vestische Strassenbahn, Wesel-Rees, Wuppertal.
* DDR system

Almost all of these used trailers also, and in addition Darmstadt and Kassel used trailers only.

Ex-Frankfurt 241 and trailer in Bucuresti. (Martin Jenkins)

The front end and driving position of one of the Hannover cars, as modified for one person operation, in June 1986. (Author)

Bibliography

Modern Tramway nos.167, November 1951 (Hamburg), 168, December 1951, 177, September 1952 (Hamburg), 204, December 1954, 213, September 1955 (Rheinbahn buffet cars), 314, February 1964 (Gotha cars).

Strassenbahn Magazin nos.52, March 1984 (Hamburg V6/7 cars), 75, February 1990 (Bremen and Hannover), 101, March 1996, 129, July 2000 (lightweight trailers), 141/2, July and August 2001 (Grosraumwagen), 168, October 2003 (Gotha bogie cars), 193, November 2005 (Rheinbahn interurban cars).

Die Strassenbahn der Berliner Verkehrsbetriebe, 1949-1991. S. Hilkenbach and W. Kramer. Transpress, Stuttgart, 1997.

Die Nürnberg-Fürther Strassenbahn im Wandel der Zeiten. Op.cit.

Three generations of Düwag cars at Stadtmitte depot in Essen in May 1981. Grossraumwagen 1511 is on the left, articulated car 1606 is in the centre and a Stadtbahn M car is on the right. (Author)

Rheinbahn 5164 began life as motor car 2024 in 1954. In 1967 it was converted to a trailer, as 2034, and in 1979 it was re-motored as a track car. It is seen at the main workshops in May 1981. (Author)

BOGIE CARS FROM 1940

SCANDINAVIA
SWEDEN

GÖTEBORG

After trials with prototype 210, a production batch of 15 cars was ordered by Göteborgs Spårvägar (GS) from ASEA, but, although neutral, Sweden was affected by the outbreak of war and it was not until 15 June 1943 that these were ready, being placed in service on line 8. They took the numbers 211-225 and were eventually classed M22. Unlike the prototype, they had a bulbous front end and originally only front and rear doors, with passenger flow from rear to front. This led to bottlenecks within the car and a single centre doorway was incorporated when they were rebuilt in 1953. Dimensions were 13m x 2.50m, this width requiring some alterations to the infrastructure before the cars could run on certain lines. Electro-magnetic control was fitted, with four motors. These trams were very successful but, as it was not considered worth rebuilding them for right-hand traffic, they were withdrawn in 1967. Nos.211 and 224 have been preserved, the latter at Malmköping.

When peace had returned to Europe, GS ordered a further 58 basically similar trams from Hägglund. These were numbered 1-58, class M23 and had a centre doorway from new. In most respects, however, they followed the design which had by then been introduced to Stockholm. Two similar cars with foot pedal control were placed in service in 1952, as 59/60. Three further similar, but slightly longer cars, double-ended and having front and rear doors

Car 224. (Stig Hammarson)

As built for left hand running, a set consisting of motor 21 and trailer 438 of classes M23/S27 is seen at Stigberstorget on 11 May 1962. (Stig Hammarson)

Class M25 591, one of those which remained in left hand configuration, is part of a three-car set at Central Station in June 1983. (Author)

only, were delivered in 1953 to the radial Bomhusbanan at Gävle but unfortunately they were not able to prevent the closure of that line just two years later. They were then acquired by GS, converted to single-ended layout, fitted with a centre door on the left and placed in service as 61-63. From 1965 onwards, all these cars were given door openings, covered by wooden panels, on the offside and these were fitted with doors either just before or after the change to right hand traffic on 4 September 1967, the existing doorways then being covered in the same way. Many of the class became redundant in the late 1970s and seven were sold to Oslo, where they became nos.254-260. As their equipment was identical to that of the Oslo bogie cars, they fitted easily into their new home. All have now been withdrawn in both cities, but six cars were sold to Stockholm and, as 328-333, and for some years after its opening on 2 June 1991, provided the basic service on the heritage tram line 7. Cars 15 and 61 are preserved in Göteborg by the local museum group Ringlinien and are used on its services.

There were also 70 trailers built to work with this class of tram (401-470, class S27). These were likewise rebuilt for right-hand running and were withdrawn in the 1970s. Ten were sold

to Oslo, where they took the numbers 582-591.

The system expanded considerably in the late 1950s and no fewer than 125 new bogie cars of class M25 were bought between 1958 and 1963,

As rebuilt and now in museum operation, no.15 is seen at Brunnsparken in October 2003. (Author)

In 1983 some cars of class M23 were still maintained as a reserve fleet and 31, at Majorna depot, shows how the doorways were altered for right hand traffic. (Author)

Trailer 407 at Drottningtorget on 11 May 1967. (Stig Hammarson)

Class M28 704 picks up a crowd of shoppers at Kungsports Platsen in June 1983. (Author)

An interior view of car 15 as running in museum service in October 1983. (Author)

numbered 501-625. Unlike their predecessors, these were "all-electric", akin to PCC cars, with PCC trucks, and had front and centre doors only. Passenger circulation was reversed to run from front to rear, in classic Peter Witt style, and in slack periods they were worked as one-man cars. They were larger than most contemporary trams elsewhere in Europe and were the first trams in the world to be fitted with electronic transistor control, this having been developed in the city's university. They were prepared for the change in traffic in the same way as was the previous class, but 15 (579-593) remained in left hand layout. The reason for this was that they were to be used on a new express line, 8, which ran on the formation of a former light railway, with platforms on one side only and a stub terminal. They ran back-to-back with rebuilt cars until 1985. In 1991/2, 21 of these cars were hired by Oslo and were bought by that undertaking in 1994, when 17 more were acquired, three to serve as a source of spare parts. They took the numbers 266-299 and the last in Oslo was withdrawn in 2002. The last in Göteborg ran in 1994 but two cars (518 and 552) survive as driver training vehicles. Three (582, 606 and 621, of which the first is still in left hand layout) have been preserved by Ringlinien. In Oslo no.277 (ex-599) has also been preserved and no.602 is in a museum near Ornsköldsvik, where the Hägglund factory was situated.

In 1966/7, a further 70 trams of a basically similar design, but with a rear door, were delivered by ASJ as class M28 (701-770). These were already configured for right-hand traffic and initially operated back-to-back with a car of class M25. On the day of the change, all that was required was to turn the set around and it was ready for the new rule of the road. Class M29 (801-860) followed from Hägglund in 1970-72, by which date all the fleet were operated as one-person cars. These had air brakes and air-operated doors and the control system allowed operation of up to four-car trains. The Scharfenberg couplers were heated in winter, to allow for speedy formation of a train or uncoupling.

There were no corresponding trailers, as m.u. operation was now preferred.

Classes M28 and M29 were at the time of their introduction world leaders in design, putting Göteborg at the forefront of light rail development, and they have given years of excellent service. They are to be replaced by low-floor trams in the next few years.

Collectively all the bogie cars were known as "Mustangar" (Mustangs) and this name spread to other cities also.

Technical details
Class M23
Length 13.05m, width 2.5m, weight 14.5 tonnes, 4 x 50kW motors, 100 passengers, 31 seated.

M29 850 at Drottningtorget in June 1983. (Author)

S27 trailers
Length 13.1m, width 2.5m, weight 12 tonnes, 104 passengers, 38 seated.

Class M29
Length 14.16m, width 2.65m, weight 17 tonnes, 4 x 50kW motors, 116 passengers, 38 seated.

STOCKHOLM

In 1946 Stockholms Spårvägar (SS) took delivery of 70 single-ended motor trams (400-469), based on those already in use in Göteborg, but of a more attractive design, with a tapered front end. The cars, classed as A25, were built by General Motors Nordiska, with motors and equipment by ASEA. Owing to a local authority regulation that there had to be 50cm clear between passing cars of straight track, these trams were narrower than those at Göteborg. Doors were provided at the rear, centre and front of the car and that at the rear was of triple-width configuration. Passenger flow was from rear to front, with a seated conductor and the driver had a separate cab. There were four motors and electro-magnetic control equipment. Maximum speed was 60km/hr. There were comfortable leather upholstered seats for 34 passengers, arranged 2+1. This series was followed in 1947-50 by two further batches from Hägglund, classes A26 and A27 (470-500), which were constructed of lightweight materials and weighed only 13.5 tonnes, unlike the 16.5 tonnes of class A25. These trams were popular, being fast and almost silent in operation, but despite their purchase Stockholm saw no long-term future for the tram, concentrating instead on construction of the T-Bana. At the change of the rule of the road in 1967, all were withdrawn. Two have been preserved, car

Car 411 in the city centre in July 1962. (Lars F. Richter collection)

410 in the city and car 500 at Malmköping museum. Between 1950 and 1952 Hägglund delivered 70 matching trailers (939-999 and 1491-1499), which weighed only 10 tonnes. The last of these was later sold to Oslo and was scrapped, due to corrosion, in 1984. Of these, 992 has been preserved.

Technical details
Class A25
Length 14.2m, width 2.2m, weight 16.24 tonnes, 4x48kW motors, 104 passengers, 34 seated.

MALMÖ

In 1941 this undertaking rebuilt car 53 of 1914 vintage with passenger flow and a fixed post for the conductor and this was followed by eight similar conversions. Ten new cars identical to Stockholm class A25 (70-79) were delivered in 1946 by General Motors and Stockholm's car 416 was acquired in 1949, becoming no.80. In 1964 a further car (413) was acquired from the capital (81), but it was not used. Car 80 was in 1965 rebuilt for right hand traffic to assess the practicability of altering the entire fleet and this was duly done in time for the change in 1967. There were also nine matching trailers (190-198) built by Ecksjö Verken in 1959. When H-day came in 1967, these were simply turned around, given new couplings at the previous outer end and run in reverse! However, the system closed in 1972. Nos.71 and 196 have been preserved by the city's Technical Museum and in 1991 were loaned to the Djurgården line in Stockholm on condition that they were restored to running order. This was duly done and the cars have since been in service there, painted in Stockholm's blue livery but still carrying their original numbers. Car 74 is preserved in Denmark.

No.71 at the city centre terminus in April 1971. (Author)

NORRKÖPING

In 1959 this small undertaking of, by that date, only three lines, took delivery of 12 cars from Hägglund, nos.64-75. These had only two motors and, remarkably, were mounted on maximum traction bogies, the last application of this type on any tramway. Electromagnetic equipment was fitted. They were rather shorter than cars in other cities and carried only 80 passengers, with seats for 27. They were adapted for right hand traffic in the same manner as Göteborg's trams and renumbered 111-122 when rebuilt. They did not last very long in their new form and were withdrawn in the

Car 118 as seen at Malmköping in June 1983. (Author)

Car 131 at the railway station in June 1983. (Author)

1970s, but car 118 is preserved at Malmköping.

In time for the change to the rule of the road in 1967, 25 new bogie cars were bought from ASEA, numbered 131-155 of class M67. Eleven of these are still in service, having undergone fairly extensive rebuilding and have been renumbered 81-9.

Bibliography

Modern Tramway no.154, October 1950 (Stockholm), no.187, July 1953 (Gävle)

Zeppelinare, Limpor och Mustanger. Op.cit.

Die strassen-und Vorortbahnen in Oslo. N.C. Aspenberg. Baneforlaget, Oslo, 1994.

GS factsheets.

Malmö Stads Spårvägar Förr och Nu. MSS, Malmö, 1952.

NORWAY

TRONDHEIM CITY SYSTEM

In 1949, when conditions had returned to normality, 10 further bogie cars (40-49) were delivered by Strømmen. They were based closely on the pre-war cars but had slightly more rounded ends, were 12.6m long and weighed 15 tonnes. Originally these had no centre door, but this led to congestion within the car and an additional door was retrofitted. In 1955 they were followed by six further cars from the same builder (7-12), which had centre doors from new and

The width of 2.65m allowed these trams to offer comfortable 2+2 seating. Unusually, fare collection involved use of a farebox, as can be seen in this view from June 1983. (Author)

were slightly shorter, at 12.5m. All the post-war cars had normal series/parallel control. These allowed the retirement for the last two-axle cars, thus allowing Trondheim to become the first city in Europe to run its entire service with bogie cars. This happy state of affairs was not to last! In the fire mentioned above, the entire fleet of post-war bogie cars was annihilated and the old cars, which had fortunately been stored rather than being scrapped, had to be recalled to keep a service going. The ill-fated 7-12 had the shortest lives of any modern trams, being in service only from June 1955 to October 1956.

In 1957/8, 28 new motor trams, virtually identical to the 1955 design, but equipped for passenger flow with a seated conductor, were delivered by Strømmen as replacements. They were numbered 1-5 and 10-32. Only cars 26-32 were completely new, as all the others used parts from the cars which had been destroyed. All except no.2 were rebuilt for one-person operation with a farebox in 1968. Owing to falling traffic, the cars were withdrawn between 1975 and 1988. However, four (14, 19, 22

and 29) have been preserved and of these 22 and 29 are still used to supplement the fleet of articulated cars, while it is planned to rebuild 14 as a party car. There were also 15 trailers (50-64), but these were taken out of service by 1983.

For a relatively small city, affected by a major disaster in 1956, Trondheim showed great resource in developing a fleet of modern cars and persevering with these. It was an example not followed by larger cities such as Brisbane, which simply gave up on its tramways after a serious depot fire.

No.20 and trailer 56 in blue and cream livery on Kongensgate in April 1967. (Tom Hart)

TRONDHEIM GRÅKALBANEN

This radial line running through very attractive countryside to the south-west of the city had one modern motor/trailer set, delivered in 1955, numbered 7/55. These were built by Høka and the motor car was identical electrically to the cars

Preserved Gråkalbanen car 7 outside Voldsminde depot in June 1983. (Author)

in Oslo, but had only front and rear doors and was worked by an itinerant conductor. Although single-ended, there were doors on both sides of the body, as some stopping places had central platforms. The motor car was used as a works car from 1983 and both were withdrawn in 1988 and have been preserved.

Technical details

1958 city cars

Length 13.2m, width 2.6m, weight 15 tonnes, 4 x 43kW motors.

Bibliography

Die Strassen- und Vorortbahnen in Trondheim. N.C. Aspenberg. Banenforlaget, Oslo, 1994.
Strassenbahn Magazin no.155, September 2002.
Modern Tramway no.301, January 1963.
Trondheims glemte trikker. R. Kjenstad. Banforlaget, Oslo, 1997.

OSLO

Car 245 and trailer 565 near the National Theatre on 21 May 1976. (M.J. Russell).

One of the Bergen motor trams (qv below) was tried in Oslo, but did not find favour with OS and it was decided that the electrical equipment of future cars should come from Sweden. It was not until 1952 that the first of these cars, numbered 204-233, were delivered. The very square body was built by the Norwegian firm of Høka (Hønefoss Karossarifabrik) and was laid out for passenger flow. The motors and control equipment came from Hägglund in Sweden and were identical to those fitted in Swedish bogie cars of the period. A further series of 20 (234-253) followed in 1957/8. The cars proved to be extremely reliable and were popular with maintenance staff and passengers, giving good service until 1993. Between 1985 and 1991 eleven cars were rebuilt by OS in their own workshops, with new internal fittings, electronic control equipment and a new raked front end, which greatly improved their appearance. Multiple unit control was also fitted and it was intended that these rebuilds should have a life of fifteen years. They originally took the numbers 261-271, later 201-211, class S83. No.264 appeared in a new livery of red with blue doors, but such was the outcry from Oslo citizens, who are much attached to their "blå trikken" (blue trams), that no more were thus treated. The cost of further rebuilding to allow the trams to continue when the line voltage was increased from 600 to 750 precluded further cars being so treated. All have now been

withdrawn and no further modern cars were built in Norway. No.249 was sold to Stockholm in 1992 and has seen use on heritage line 7. Of the rebuilt cars, 203 has gone to the Danish museum at Skjoldenaesholm, 207 is preserved in the local museum in Oslo, 210 is in Stockholm and 201 is in Göteborg as a source of spare parts for the rebuilding of an M23 car.

There were also 30 matching trailers, twelve metres long, built in 1956 by Høka (551-562) and in 1957 by Strømmen. All were withdrawn in 1993.

Technical details

Series 204-253 as built.

Length 14.74m, width 2.5m, weight 16.9 tonnes, 4 x 45.6kW motors, 114 passengers, 41 seated.

Car 262 as rebuilt, on an enthusiasts' tour. (Lars F. Richter collection).

BERGEN

Bergen in 1947/8 bought ten modern bogie cars built by Strømmen (50-59). These had passenger flow and were 14m long, powered by four 28kW motors. They could accommodate 85 passengers, 23 seated. In service they pulled light, centre entrance trailers (131-139) built between 1936 and 1940. Unfortunately the use of modern cars did not prevent the closure of the system in 1965 and, as it proved impossible to sell them, all were scrapped.

Bibliography

Strassenbahn Magazin no.136, February 2001.
Modern Tramway nos.186, June 1953 (Oslo), 311, November 1963.
Die Strassenbahn- und Vorortbahnen in Oslo. Op.cit.
Oslo Trikken – Storbysjel på skinner. Op.cit.

No.52 at an unknown location in 1964. (Ray Oakley, author's collection)

FINLAND

HELSINKI

In 1952 trials took place with a double-ended German Grossraumwagen bogie car, Vestische Strassenbahn 341. The Finns were impressed and this operator HKL/HLT decided to order 30 cars of this type from the national firm of Karia. These entered service in 1954/5, numbered 301-330. Unlike the trial car, they were single-ended. A further series of 45 (331-375) followed in 1955/6 from Valmet and these were equipped for m.u. operation. Finally 30 further cars were delivered in 1959, the order being split equally between the two national firms, those from Karia being 1-15 and from Valmet 16-30. Passengers entered at the rear, where there was a conductor's post, and left by the centre or front doors. The electrical equipment was based very closely on Swedish practice. To take account of the climate in winter, a forced air ventilation and heating system was fitted. Unlike the bogie cars elsewhere in Scandinavia, they were heavy, weighing 19.5 tonnes and were rather ponderous in opera-

Car 318 is followed by a new articulated car in the city centre in June 1983. (Author)

tion. Conversion for one-person operation took place from 1980 onwards. Withdrawals began in 1984 but most cars of the last batch are still in service and car 15 has been converted to a "pub" tram, re-numbered 175 and painted in an all-over red livery to advertise the local brewery which sponsored its conversion. Of earlier cars, 320, 332, 337 and 339 are all preserved in running order by the operator. Three others, 313, 331 and 521 have been earmarked for the local museum but are not yet on display.

There were also 30 bogie trailers (501-530) built by Valmet in 1957. These saw little use after about 1970 and were withdrawn on the arrival of the second series of articulated trams in 1984. No.505 has been preserved. No further bogie cars were built, as the undertaking was in the 1960s more interested in a metro than in tramway development and when that was resumed, it was with German-inspired articulated trams.

Technical details
Series 1-30
Length 13.5m, width 2.3m, weight 20 tonnes, 4 x 54kW motors, 98 passengers, 29 seated.

Bibliography
Strassenbahn Magazin no.58, November 1985 and no.132, October 2000.

TURKU

This small tramway, operated by TKL/ALT, followed the example of the capital and in 1956 placed in service eight bogie cars built by Valmet (48-55). They were similar to those in Helsinki, but narrower, and were in fact based on the Swiss standard tram, from which they took the sharply tapered ends to take account of the track geometry. Doors were fitted at front and rear only. Their silence in operation earned for them the nickname of "Aavevanaut" ("Ghost trams"). Despite their popularity they were unable to prevent the abandonment of the system in 1972 and all were scrapped. One modern trailer was built by the undertaking on a Rastatt underframe (141) but otherwise the bogie cars ran with old two-axle trailers. No.141 was withdrawn in 1969 and donated to a playground.

DENMARK

COPENHAGEN

In 1949 KS placed in service a prototype modern bogie car, 701, mounted on Swedish trucks. There were rear, centre and front doors and a forced ventilation and heating system was fitted, for which purpose one of the resistances was mounted on the roof. As it was considered successful, six further cars followed in 1951/2. Of these, the last three had cardan drive. Although the cars ran well and were popular, the series was really too small to make much impression on what was then a large system, and when development was resumed, it was with German articulated cars. No.705 was used as a sightseeing car in 1960/1 and was then painted in an attractive colour scheme of two shades of blue. All were withdrawn in 1969, as the system began to contract. No.701 has been preserved in Skjoldenasholm museum.

Waiting for opening time! Pub tram 175 on the terminal loop at the waterfront in August 1998. (Author)

Car 335 leaves a pleasant piece of reserved track on line 1 in June 1983. (Author)

Car 7 of the last series in the city centre in June 1983. (Author)

No.50 on an enthusiasts' tour in August 1967. (F.W. Hunt, courtesy London Area, Light Rail Transit Association)

Bibliography
Modern Tramway no.328, April 1965.

No704 at Sundby depot in September 1966. (SH, A.D. Young, Evda Slides).

Technical details
Length 13.5m, width 2.3m, 93 passengers, 30 seated.

Bibliography
Modern Tramway no.140, August 1949.

SUMMARY

There can be no doubt that the Scandinavian bogie trams were well-designed vehicles, which gave – to those operators who did not indulge in premature scrapping – excellent service over a long period. They also provided much of the inspiration for the later development of the German Grossraumwagen bogie car. But they were expensive cars, since most operators preferred to incorporate their own ideas, and as a result there was little attempt at standardisation. The home market was small, with (in 1950) only 15 systems, of which three had no interest in large bogie trams, while Stockholm had already set its sights on becoming a metro city. Apart from the use of ASEA equipment in Melbourne's bogie cars, there was no export success to broaden the cost base.

The idea was excellent, the practice less sound. In the end, German ideas and technology were to take over.

Total number of bogie motor cars and trailers built:

SWEDEN	
Stockholm:	101 + 70
Malmö:	10 + 9
Göteborg:	331 + 70
Gävle:	3
Norrköping:	37
Total:	482 + 149
NORWAY	
Oslo:	50 + 30
Bergen:	10
Trondehim:	45 + 16
Total:	105 + 46
DENMARK	8
FINLAND	
Helsinki:	105 + 30
Turku:	8 + 1
Total:	113 + 31

Total: 708 motor cars, 226 trailers = 934 trams

DERIVED DESIGN

The concept and some of the technology were used in the construction of class Z in Melbourne in the 1970s. These cars which were unlike any built in Australia before or since, were in part Scandinavian inspiration and in part German and may best be considered under this heading.

The tram services of the Melbourne and Metropolitan Tramways Board had suffered a significant decline in patronage during the 1960s and at times it seemed that the future of the system was in doubt. However, in 1969 a new chairman, Francis R. Kirby, was appointed and it seems that he was able to persuade the government of Victoria that the trams should be retained and modernised with cars of a new design. The first step towards the realisation of this policy was the rebuilding of PCC car 960 as 1041 (qv) to gain experience of the proposed layout, and this was followed by the delivery of what was initially known as class Z.

There were in all three batches of this class and as later cars were delivered they were sub-divided into classes Z1, Z2 and Z3. The first hundred cars (1-100) formed class Z1 and the next 15 (101-115) Z2 – there is in fact very little difference between them. The first tram (1) entered service in May 1975 and delivery extended through to 1979. The bodies for the two classes were built by the Commonwealth Engineering Company (Pty) Ltd (Comeng) at Dandenong near Melbourne. They are double-ended and were originally laid out in classic Peter Witt lines, with a seated conductor having a post near the front entrance and, unusually, angled towards boarding passengers. Exit is by a centre door and the usual Melbourne style of fixed seating was installed. Trucks and electrical equipment were supplied by ASEA and assembled in Australia. To emphasise the new passenger flow system, the cars were initially painted a deep orange, known officially as Marigold, with gold roofs and cream window surrounds. In service these colours did not wear well, and following the advent of the MTA in 1983 the class was fairly rapidly repainted green. More seriously, deficiencies in the body layout soon became apparent and passengers tended to congregate around the conductor's post and the centre door, rather than heeding advice to "pass down the car". In complete contrast with the elderly cars of classes W and SW, class Z trams showed a pronounced

Class Z1 no.48 at the terminus of service 69 at Kew, Cotham Road, in March 1993. These cars had only just begun to work on this service and had not as yet acquired destination blinds, hence the slip board in the windscreen. (Author)

tendency to oscillate when running at speed, especially on track with concrete foundations. In 1977 car 5 was experimentally converted to ASEA thyristor control, with regenerative braking, and reclassified ZC. Although the new control system worked well, the car was prone to mechanical failure and was in 1983 reconverted to class Z1.

This experiment was in preparation for the introduction of the third batch of modern trams, class Z3, which were placed in service between 1979 and 1983. To eliminate congestion within the car, a single width rear exit was fitted. The bogies are of the standard Düwag tandem drive design, with runner suspension, and AEG/Siemens thyristor control is fitted. Another new livery appeared with class Z3, a deep yellow with gold roofs and cream window surrounds but this was equally unsuccessful, and all cars were repainted green by the MTA. More recently several class Z trams have been repainted in advertising or other special liveries, the first being 4, which was repainted for the bi-centenery in 1988.

While class Z3 was more successful than its immediate predecessors, it was still not ideal for Australian conditions and the next designs reverted to the traditional Melbourne layout. Two cars were withdrawn after fires, and three members of class Z1 were cannibalised for spares, and withdrawals of the earlier cars have now begun. The classes have now spread to all routes from their original home on Bourke Street services. All have now been converted for one-person operation with

removal of the conductor's post, increasing seating capacity to 52, and have also been fitted with pantographs.

The building of class Z was a courageous attempt to bring new ideas of design to Melbourne but in retrospect it would seem that these European concepts were not ideally suited to local needs, and the classes cannot be considered the most successful to have run in the city.

Technical details
Class Z3
Length 15.1m, width 2.67m weight 22.2 tonnes, 2 x 195 kW motors, 42 seated passengers.

Bibliography
Destination City. Op.cit.

A busy scene at East Preston in March 1986, just prior to the opening of the extension to La Trobe University and (later) Bundoora. Z1 64 is on the left and Z3 214 on the right still carries its original yellow livery. (Author)

An interior view of a Z1 or Z2 car. (Author)

SWITZERLAND

THE "STANDARD" BOGIE TRAMS

With the exception of the trams built for Toronto, all those described in this section were built for operation on metre gauge tracks.

By the mid-1930s, it was clear to the managers of the Städtische Strassenbahn Zürich that it would soon be necessary to renew much of the fleet which consisted largely of elderly, though modernised, two-axle cars. They were also aware of developments in Italy and the USA and in particular the entry into service of PCC cars. Their use of pedal control appealed especially to A-M Hug, one of the engineers. He was later strongly supported by D. Straub, who had been employed by TIBB in Italy but who returned to Switzerland in 1939. His proclaimed intention was to work for the development of a modern tram design which would be better than the PCC car and which would therefore give Swiss industry a leading place in this field.

On 9 September 1938 the city council agreed to the construction of one experimental car and the transport department then entered into correspondence with operators of modern trams, among them the ELRT of Lille and Chicago, Toronto and New York, the last three of these by then running PCC cars. In November a delegation visited Milan for three days, where they were greatly impressed by the lightweight trams of the 5000 class (qv). After this visit, it was decided that the new car should be laid out for passenger flow on the Peter Witt system. In 1939 it was agreed to build a second prototype. Correspondence with Oslo followed and, from the enthusiasm with which that operator reported on the advantages of electro-pneumatic control in the "Goldfish" cars (qv), it was decided to adopt this form of control in the first of the new cars.

In August 1939 BBC began work on the first car and preliminary sketches showed a distinct Italian influence. The first Swiss standard tram to enter service was Zürich 351 which was placed in service in 1940 and it was followed in November of that year by the second prototype, 401, which came from the factory of SWS Schlierern. The body design of both cars was based closely on the two three-axle cars which had entered service the year before (qv) but technically they were far more advanced and were to set the pattern for almost all bogie trams built thereafter for service in western Europe.

Car 351 had an attractive semi-streamlined body of lightweight metal construction, which could accommodate 100 passengers, 27 of them on shaped wooden seats arranged to face the direction of travel. To cope with Zürich's track geometry, the ends were sharply tapered, as in the "Hechtwagen". The driver had a separate cabin and the conductor a seat by the rear doors. The tram was single-ended and there were three sets of double-width doors, at the front, middle and rear of the car; that at the front was controlled by the driver, the others by the conductor. The folding doors were air operated, as was a folding lower step, which allowed for easy access. Electro-pneumatic control was fitted and the large number of notches made the car very responsive in braking and accelerating. Braking was rheostatic, but an air brake was used to bring the car to a complete halt and to hold it there. Four motors were mounted in conventional manner on the bogies, but a novelty was the provision of rubber-insert wheels, using Swedish SAB elements. It was intended that the car would in service pull a bogie trailer.

The second prototype, 401, had a much lighter body and rode on Brown Boveri "Simplex" bogies, which had already been fitted to a car built in 1937 for the Biel-Meinisberg radial line. (This car, which spent most of its active life in Locarno, is now preserved at the Blonay-Chamby museum line.) It was intended that car 401 would operate solo, or with one light two-axle trailer and great emphasis was placed on swift acceleration. To that end, pedal control was fitted, as on the PCC car. This was not ideal for emergency stops and, as motor traffic grew, it became something of a liability. Cardan drive was fitted, but in all other respects, this tram was identical to car 351.

Further orders were placed for both types of tram and by 1954 there were 65 heavy and 52 light motor trams in service. The former were, after renumbering in 1945, numbered 1351-1415 and the latter 1501-1552. They had long careers and the last lightweight car, 1549, ran in passenger service on 19 June 1987, while the heavyweight cars remained in service until 1998. In 1955 car 1415 and trailer 761 ran in St Gallen, but evidently did not persuade that operator of the value of modern trams and the system closed some years later.

Basel trailer 1470, seen in 1989, carried an advertising livery for Swiss Federal Railways. (Author)

By the time the same car was photographed again in May 2003 it had acquired a low floor centre section. (Author)

Zürich 1549 speeds along the right bank of the River Limmat towards Bellevue in March 1983. (Author)

With a two-axle trailer in tow, preserved car 1392 is at the Zoo terminus in Zürich in May 2003. (Author)

VBZ 1422 and trailer 777 approaching Central in May 2003. (Author)

VBZ snow plough SP 1925 at Escher-Wyss Platz depot in May 2003. (Author)

Bern trailer 330 at Ostring in May 2003. (Author)

Basel 415. (Author)

Neuchâtel 82 at Ste Blaise in 1956. (F.W. Hunt, courtesy London Area, Light Rail Transit Association)

Basel 251 at Schiffslände on 21 September 1969. (W.J. Wyse, courtesy London Area, Light Rail Transit Association)

Ex-Luzern motor, running in Genève as trailer 323, in the depot yard in May 1984. (Author)

Naturally other Swiss operators were interested in these developments and in 1943 car 403 spent some time in passenger service in Basel. In December of the same year, two cars were run in Bern, but at night only and not with passengers, while between September and November 1945 car 409 was tried in Luzern. In December 1944 the Verband Schweizerischer Transportanstalten (VST, Association of Swiss Transport Undertakings) drew up guidelines for future tram construction. It was hoped that this would lead to a degree of standardisation among operators, using the Zürich designs as a basis. There would be three types of motor car – lightweight and heavy single-ended cars and an intermediate type of double-ended car. There would also be two types of trailer for use with these. Luzern placed an order for ten lightweight cars which were delivered in 1947, as 101-110, but on closure of the system in 1961 they were sold to Genève where, after some time in service, they were in 1969 converted to trailer cars (321-330), as they were underpowered for the remaining line, 12.

Basel bought 52 heavyweight cars, with hand control, in the years 1949-51 (401-452) and a further four in 1958 (453-456). Bern acquired 20 trams, 101-120, in the same period and a further ten in 1960 (121-130). These last remained in service in 2003, but were due for early withdrawal when additional low-floor cars were delivered. In both cities, these trams were operated with trailers and had hand control. However, the trams built for Genève in 1950 (701-730) used pedal control, although they were also heavyweight and worked with trailers.

In the event only one operator, Neuchâtel, bought the double-ended version of the standard tram and then only with three cars (81-83). These had doors at the front and rear only.

Clearly there was a good deal of variety in the vehicles actually delivered and it may be questioned how standard the Swiss "standard" tram actually was!

In 1959/60, Schlieren built for Zürich 15 bogie cars to a modified design (1416-1430), intended to be compatible with the new articulated trams then entering service (qv). All three doors were incorporated in the straight portion of the car sides, to allow them to align exactly with the platforms at loading islands and so speed up boarding and alighting. In consequence, the front of the car had to be somewhat blunt, to accommodate clearance on curves, rather than the elegant tapering end of the classic Standard car. These are still in service, but may soon be replaced by Cobra low-floor trams. After a gap of some years, there was a further and final development of the type. In 1967 Basel bought 20 further cars (457-476) which differed in having air suspension and sliding ventilators in the windows. These are still in service.

Unfortunately the Second World War and the economic troubles which followed precluded any export orders for the design. The nearest approach was made following a visit by a delegation from Lyon in 1945, when an order for between 60 and 80 lightweight trams was considered. The bogies and electrical equipment would have been built in France under licence. The cost per car would have been about CHF220,000 or about £18,000 at current rates of exchange and financial problems intervened. Although work had started on four bodies, Lyon suddenly withdrew from the project and no further interest was shown in the purchase of modern trams. The bodies were utilised on the batch of cars then under construction for Zürich (415-418). Had the trams entered service, the history of French tramways between 1950 and 1985 might have been quite different! Car 1531 was shown at a transport conference in Aachen in 1950, at which the future German standard bogie car was being discussed. The local manufacturer, Talbot, had obtained a licence to build this type in Germany but, despite great interest, there were no orders from German undertakings. However, in 1948 the HTM of Den Haag bought 16 cars fitted with Oerlikon electro-pneumatic equipment of the type fitted to many standard cars. These were built by Werkspoor in the Netherlands and were comfortable cars, with accommodation for 76 passengers. They were fitted with four 56kW motors and were fast and smooth riding. Unfortunately there were constant problems with the electrical equipment, especially in the winter months, and, when placed on the express line 11, they often had to

Genève 725 in the pedestrianised central area in May 1984. (Author)

Luzern 109 approaching Kriens village centre. (Leeds Transport Historical Society)

be replaced by cars of the 801 class, which dated from 1927. In 1965 all were withdrawn, no.215 being preserved in the city. Nos.205 and 210 were sold to Rotterdam, where one was rebuilt into a track-cleaning car. This was probably the most disappointing design of the post-war period in Europe.

The only significant variation on the design came in 1952 when Basel bought three ultra-lightweight motor trams (601-603), based on a combination of the standard car and the low-floor cars tried in Rome in 1948. They had Simplex bogies, of which only the forward was motored and that at the rear had wheels of greatly reduced diameter to allow a floor height of only 43cm above rail level at the rear. The aim was to reduce boarding times and thus speed up the service, but solo motor cars could not cope with peak traffic, and at that time Switzerland had three peaks per day as many people went home for lunch. No further such cars were built and the three did not have long lives in service.

Most standard trams were scrapped when they reached the end of the road, but nine of the Zürich cars (1351-1359) were converted into snowploughs (1921-1929) and one of these, no.1922 was in 2002 further converted into a cargo tram. This performs a rather different function to the Dresden cargo trams, as, towing two container trailers, it makes a round of various termini each day to pick up large items such as electrical goods which residents may wish to dispose of. Of the lightweight cars, no.1501 was

The interior of one of the later motor cars for Bern – bright, slightly clinical, seen in May 2003. (Author)

in 1980 sold to the Bex-Villars-Bretaye line for use as a works car. Four motor cars and four trailers from Genève have gone to Sibiu in Romania. Basel sent redundant car 456 to Beograd, to help with the rehabilitation of that system. The most unusual fate to befall any cars of this type was that of 18 motor/trailer sets from Zürich, which in 1995 were sold to Pyonyang for CHF250,000 (£100,000) in total, to serve on a new tram line to convey visitors to the mausoleum of Kim Il Sung, the former leader. The motor cars were from the batch numbered between 1384 and 1415, the trailers between 723 and 763. As the city system is laid to standard gauge it must be assumed that the decision to construct this line to metre gauge was dictated by the availability of the Swiss cars. They were renumbered from 100 (motors) and 200 (trailers), smartly repainted in two shades of green with a silver roof and the line opened in July 1995. They were still operating in 2005, four or five being in service each day.

In Zürich motor car 1392 and trailer 732 have been beautifully restored to their original appearance and on certain summer Sundays may be sampled in action on line 6.

VBZ trailer 773 at Central in May 2003. (Author)

HTM 213 on line 3. (F.W. Hunt collection, courtesy London Area, Light Rail Transit Association)

STANDARD TRAILERS

The first trailers to run with the bogie trams did not appear until 1945, when Zürich placed a batch of 60 in service. These were of very light construction, weighing only 9 tonnes. They had end and centre doors only, as it would have been impossible for a seated conductor to have a clear view of a front exit. Further series entered service in 1958, 1962 and 1973, bringing the total to 91 cars. Basel took 15 of the same type in 1947 but Bern and Genève opted to have three doors in their orders of 1950/51. A system of contacts in the steps and time relays indicated to the conductor when it was safe to close the doors, this being the first use of devices which would later allow one-person operation of large trams. Deliveries to Zürich (31) and Basel (91 cars) from 1958 onwards were fitted with three doors and the last of these were similar in outline to the bogie cars of the 1416 class. Basel's trailers 1416-1435 of 1961/2 were the first trams anywhere to be fitted with air suspension, developed by the builders Schindler, to allow the floor height to remain constant no matter the degree of loading of the car. To work with its 14xx class of bogie cars, VBZ also bought 28 matching trailers (771-798). Some of the trailers in Basel have now been given a low floor centre section, with windows in the off-side to allow passengers seated in that section to see where they are. Others have been given advertising liveries and one, disguised as a pink piggy-bank, exhorts the citizens to save with the local savings bank.

The Swiss standard tram was an elegant but functional car, which was popular

Bern 625 at Hauptbahnhof in May 2003. (Author)

Bern 102 and trailer 323 at almost the same location in August 1972. (Author)

with passengers and staff and performed well for many years. It was, sadly, so expensive that the original hopes of export orders could not, in the post-war climate, be realised. Its influence on the design of German Grossraumwagen is clear and it thus forms a link between Italian designs of the 1930s, these German cars and the later articulated trams. However, it was the heavier version of the car, operated with a matching trailer, which had most success and the attempt to popularise a lightweight car which would run a frequent service either solo or with a light trailer, did not spread beyond Zürich and Luzern.

Technical details
Zürich lightweight car 1519
Length 13.5m, width 2.2m, weight 15 tonnes, 48kW motors, 93 passengers, 27 seated.

Zürich 1351
Length 13.95m, width 2.2m, weight 18 tonnes, 4 x 71hp motors, 100 passengers, 31 seated.
Basel 457
Length 13.75m, width 2.2m, weight 19.3 tonnes, 4 x 90hp motors, 96 passengers, 28 seated.
Zürich trailer 711
Length 13.7m, width 2.2m, weight 9.4 tonnes, 110 passengers, 33 seated.

BOGIE CARS OF TRAM 2000 DESIGN

When the articulated cars of Tram 2000 (qv) were being built for Zürich in 1976, three similar bogie motor car twin sets (21/22-25/26) were built by Schlieren for the radial Forchbahn line in that city and further deliveries of these in 1980/1 (27/28-31/32) took the number to six sets. Each car has only one driving position and in service they work permanently coupled back-to-back in pairs. To work with these, four bogie control trailers (201-204) were bought from Schlieren in 1981/2. As these have a single driving position and a pantograph, they can at first sight be mistaken for motor cars, but the pantograph is fitted only to supply current for lighting and other on-board systems. Eight single motor cars (51-58) followed from Schindler/SIG in 1994.

In 1981 Neuchâtel acquired four bogie motor cars (501-504) and four control trailers (551-554) of similar design to replace the ex-Genoa articulated trams on its line along the lakeside.

Neuchâtel 503 and 554 form an inbound set near Serrières in May 2003. (Author)

Forchbahn control trailer 202 at the rear of a set at Stadthofen loop in May 2003. (Author)

Zürich 2435 leaving Central in May 2003. (Author)

These were also built by Schlieren, with electrical equipment by BBC and in design are also based closely on Tram 2000. The motor cars are double-ended, but the trailers have a control position at one end only. These trams are quite unlike earlier Swiss bogie trams, with large windows, upholstered seating and good accessibility. Two further motor cars (505/6) were bought in 1988. The most recent series of non-driving bogie motors of type 2000 in Zürich have been mentioned in the section on articulated cars.

Rather surprisingly, Basel reverted to bogie cars in 1986, when it took delivery of 26 cars (477-502) built by Schindler, running on SIG bogies and having Siemens control equipment. The undertaking needed new trams urgently following the success of the "Environment" ticket introduced on 1 March 1984, which had swollen passenger numbers by 8% in that year and 10% in the following year. It was also intended to make use of some trailers which still had about ten years of useful life ahead of them, and this would not have been possible had articulated cars been bought. The undertaking was also aware that the low floor tram was on the horizon and did not want to spend any more than was strictly necessary on these trams. Hence the decision was taken to buy fairly conventional bogie cars. Nonetheless, the total cost of the order was CHF37 million (about £14.5 million). The design was based closely on the six-axle articulated trams supplied to the suburban BLT in 1977. Although they were certainly not low floor cars in the modern sense, a four step entrance, with the lowest step only 30cm above rail level, made them fairly accessible. To enable

One of the Forchbahn sets leaving the city terminus at Stadthofen, May 2003. No fleet number is visible, but according to the legend below the windscreen, it had run 2 million km by the time this view was taken in May 2003. (Author)

BVB Basel 498 heads a three-car set at Heuwaage in September 1989. The other motor car is 483. (Author)

all doors to be placed in the straight side of the car and at the same time to allow negotiation of all curves on the system, the ends of the tram had to be asymmetrical. These trams can work in multiple and also pull one trailer. They are probably the last conventional bogie trams to be placed in service in Western Europe.

Technical details
Neuchâtel motor cars
Length 17.48m, width 2.4m, weight 25.5 tonnes, 2 x 138kW motors, 107 passengers, 42 seated.
Basel 477
Length 13.3m, width 2.2m, weight 20 tonnes, 2 x 150kW motors, 98 passengers, 28 seated.

OTHER DESIGNS

At the time when the standard tram was being developed, Lausanne still operated quite a large tramway network, but it showed no interest in the type. Instead, in 1954 it acquired three double-ended cars (191-193), based closely on the design of those then entering service on many Swiss light rail lines, but fitted with trolley poles. These were used on the radial line to Moudon and when that closed on 5 March 1963, they were sold to the Trogenerbahn at St Gallen.

The Forchbahn was in the 1940s and '50s still very much a traditional light rail line and its post-war rolling stock had much more in common with that on other light rail systems than it had with city trams. This type is still exemplified by motor coaches 12-16 delivered between 1959 and 1966 and now in course of withdrawal, and by control trailers 102-108 of 1967/8. It should also be mentioned that several light rail lines, such as the Trogenerbahn at St Gallen and the Lausanne-Echallens-Bercher line have short sections of street running and have now come to perform some functions of an urban tramway, with the spread of the cities concerned. However, their rolling stock has always been of light rail design and for that reason is not covered in this book.

EXPORTS

ROTTERDAM

In 1956/7 15 trams (1-15) based on the Basel design of low floor cars were bought by RET. These had two steps, of very low height, at the rear door, rather than the single step of the Basel cars, and the floor height was 56cm above rail level. For their capacity, they were very light, but seem to have performed well enough. However, the articulated tram was the chosen type for the future.

TORONTO

The technology of the Swiss bogie tram found a surprisingly late application in North America. When in 1971 it decided to retain tramway operation, the Toronto Transit Commission (TTC) intended to replace its PCC cars with a version of the new US standard articulated car. Fortunately its staff had second thoughts about this and began to consider the development of a new Canadian design, along with rehabilitation of 173 PCC cars. The new design was to be progressed under the auspices of the Urban Transit Development Corporation, a crown corporation which had begun as the Ontario Transit Development Corporation and had then been taken over by the Dominion government. The main stumbling block was that the last purely Canadian tramcar design had appeared in 1922 and neither the know-how nor the technology was available locally. When finance had been agreed between the TTC, the provincial government and the metropolitan council of Toronto, the UTDC therefore agreed to provide 200 cars of the new design, to be known as the CLRV, Canadian Light Rail Vehicle. It turned to SIG of Neuhausen, with a contract for all design work and the manufacture of ten prototypes. This number was later reduced to six to allow production of two articulated cars (qv). The six were delivered in 1977

Lausanne 193 at Place du Tunnel in May 1955. (W.J. Wyse, courtesy London Area, Light Rail Transit Association)

Technical details
Lausanne 191
Length 16.5m, width 2.25m, weight 28 tonnes, 4 x 78kW motors, 100 passengers, 34 seated.

(4000-4005, class L1). They were fitted with m.u. equipment and standard gauge trucks and were tested in Switzerland on the Orbe-Charvoney light rail line near Lausanne and also in a climate chamber. They were then exported complete to Canada, where they arrived between 29 December 1977 and 13 July 1978, and were then regauged for use in Toronto, which has a gauge of 1495mm. Based on these, Hawker Siddeley Canada Ltd constructed the main batch of 190 cars (4010-4199 class L2) in its plant at Thunder Bay. These trams introduced a new livery of cherry red, white and black to Toronto. The first car entered revenue service on 30 September 1979 and the last in 1982. They gradually took over from the PCC cars and now maintain services on most lines with the exception of Queen Street. They are fitted with Garrett chopper control, rubber and steel primary suspension and airbag secondary suspension, giving a very supple balance. There is a good deal of the PCC car about them, in particular in

the doors, driving position and pedal control, but, although acceleration at 5.25km/hr/second is good, they are more ponderous in service. They also have a high floor level and are not easily accessible to those of reduced mobility. But they have allowed the continuation of conventional tramway operation in this Canadian stronghold and for this deserve credit.

Technical details
Rotterdam
Length 13.3m, width 2.3m, weight 12.5 tonnes, 2 x 50kW motors, 125 passengers, 25 seated.
Toronto
Length 15.44m, width 2.6m, weight 23.1 tonnes, 2x135kW motors, 102 passengers, 46 seated.

Bibliography
Die Leichte Motorwagen der Zürcher Strassenbahn. R.M. Gerbig. Mitteilungsblatt 16 der Verein Tram-Museum Zürich, Zürich, 1990.

Ein Jahrhundert Zürcher Strassenbahn. W. Trüb, J. Balen and P. Kamm. Orell Füssli Verlag, Zürich, 1982.

Modern Tramway nos.133, January 1949 (Swiss standard cars), 235, July 1957 (Rotterdam), 306, June 1963 (Lausanne), 532, April 1982 (Neuchâtel).

Der Stadtverkehr, 8/1981 (Neuchâtel), 11/12 1986 (Basel).

TTC information sheet, CLRV Canadian Light Rail Vehicle, April 1984.

Strassenbahn Magazin no.72, May 1989 (Den Haag 201 class).

65 Jaar Elektrische Tram in Den Haag. R.F. de Bock. Uitgevers Wyt, Rotterdam, 1970.

A rear view of RET 5 at Centraal Station in August 1971 gives an idea of the low floor height. (Author)

Toronto 4113 eastbound on King Street on 25 September 1989. (Author)

ITALY

Using the trucks of the damaged cars and other such parts as could be salvaged from the 5000 class trams lost in air raids, Ansaldo managed to construct 24 rebuilt cars for Milan between 1947 and 1950, to which were added 11 new vehicles (5101-5135). These were less attractive in appearance than the pre-war cars, having four smaller windows between each doorway and a flat windscreen. A further two appeared in 1951 (5136/7), of which the former was mounted on Brill bogies and was given a sloping windscreen, while 5137 was fitted with a PCC style accelerator. In 1952 a further 52 trams (5200-5251) followed as a joint venture between Breda and Ansaldo. These had PCC style equipment and 1+1 seating. Car 5200 was actually constructed using parts of car 5102, which had been destroyed by fire, for the second time in its life, in 1951. Apart from 5215, renumbered 5136 (II), all these trams were used between 1973 and 1977 to construct class 4800 articulated cars (qv). In 1954 car 5136 was badly damaged in an accident and on rebuilding was used, renumbered 5301, as the prototype for the next series (5302-5336) which arrived from Breda in 1955. Like their immediate predecessors, all were used in the construction of class 4800. The story was completed in 1958 with the delivery of three all-electric cars (5451-5453) which were mounted on CGE trucks and, as they were built under licence from the Transit Research Corporation, can be classified as true PCC cars. Car 5451 was used to provide part of prototype car 4800, while the other two were sold to Rome in 1981 and have since been given new bodies of an unattractive angular outline. They were numbered 8041/3 and ran until 2003. None of the above cars is now in service in Milan in original condition, but 5137 has been preserved and restored to its original livery. Unfortunately it is not in running order and, due to lack of spare parts for its unique equipment, is likely to remain a static exhibit.

Technical details
5301
Length 13.8m, width 2.4m, weight 17.2 tonnes, 4 x 33kW motors, 135 passengers, 23 seated.

Sixteen somewhat similar cars were bought by Cagliari in Sardinia between 1950 and 1962, of which the first five (301-305) used bogies from older cars. The others were numbered 306-308 and 318-325 and all lasted until final closure in 1972.

Italian builders had been watching the development of the PCC car with great interest and had begun discussions about the possibility of manufacturing such trams in Europe. These were curtailed by the outbreak of war, but clearly enough was known to allow manufacturers to produce cars with PCC features. The first of these to enter service was built in 1942 by Fiat for Torino (3001). This tram had GEC electrical equipment with hand controls and air brakes and was laid out as a single-ended vehicle, with passenger flow from front to rear. The attractive semi-streamlined body was derived from the trams built for Genoa and owed little to the PCC car. This car was lost in an air raid in the following year, by which date five additional cars had been delivered (3002-3006). In 1949 a series of 45 all-electric cars with pedal control followed (3100-3144) and these were followed by 80 further cars up to 1958 (3145-3224). One year later 30 cars from the Peter Witt class 2100 were rebuilt with identical bodies, but retaining their traditional control equipment (3250-3279).

From 1976 to 1979 all the above trams were rebuilt with new windscreens and doors – that in the middle now being quadruple width – and converted for one person operation. Although the bodies were slightly lengthened, capacity remained the same.

In 1948 salvaged parts from the prototype were used to build one additional new car (3500). This was shown to the press on 3 August and much was made of its fluorescent lighting. It was impossible without great expense to rebuild this car in the form adopted for the others and it therefore remained in original condition until its withdrawal.

Only 26 cars from the series 3100-3229 are still in service as bogie cars but now form a reserve fleet and are likely to be replaced in the near future by low floor cars.

Technical details
Torino 3100 as built
Length 13.57m, width 2.25m, weight 16.2 tonnes, 4 x 25kW motors, 113 passengers, 17 seated.

In Rome the ATAC acquired 20 PCC-type cars from Fiat-OM in 1956. These took the odd numbers between 8001 and 8039 and lasted until 2003.

However, the greatest coup secured by Italian industry, helped by war time politics, was to secure an order for 49 PCC type trams for Madrid, after a demonstrator had been delivered by Fiat at the same time as the first car for Torino (1001-1050). Owing to bombing the factory had some difficulty completing this order, but ultimately all cars were delivered. Car 1010 attracted

ATM Torino 3186, as built, negotiates some overhead work on 4 October 1967. (Father Benedict collection)

ATAC Rome 8035 wearing its original livery in January 1957. (Father Benedict collection)

Ex-Milan PCC car rebodied as ATAC Rome 8043, seen in July 1993 at Porta Maggiore. (Author)

Milan 5103 in green livery in September 1972. (Jim D. Schantz)

Milan 5136 (II) in May 1975. (Jim D. Schantz)

ATM Torino 3204 as rebuilt, in the city centre in June 1999. (Author)

Beograd 56 at Novo Groblje in July 1975. (Peter Haseldine)

the attention of the Germans and, presumably on orders from the Transport Ministry, it was diverted to Berlin, where it was lost in an air raid. Had this not been so, the course of post-war German tramway history might have been different! A replacement was delivered to Madrid in due course. Some were also damaged en route in attacks by communist partisans and had to be repaired when they reached Madrid. Technically they differed slightly from the Italian cars but performed equally well and the undertaking was so pleased with the design that 110 more were ordered between 1949 and 1960 from two Spanish builders, under licence from Fiat, an arrangement recognised by the Transit Research Corporation. Unfortunately the Madrid tramways were allowed to deteriorate into a deplorable condition during the late 1960s, prior to abandonment in 1972 and these trams were in a bad state by 1970. They were scrapped in 1972.

As already mentioned, the balance of the order for Beograd was finally completed by Breda in 1949/50. These trams were single-ended and had an additional central door. They ran until about 1980 and were followed in 1957 by ten further cars (51-60) which externally were very similar to Milan's 5300, but, at 21 tonnes, were a good deal heavier. These were also single-ended and had pedal control and BBC electro-pneumatic equipment, but of a rather less complex design than in the former case. These trams also lasted until the 1980s and car 58 has been set aside for preservation, but at present requires a great deal of attention.

Bibliography

Strassenbahn Magazin, nos.51, February 1984 and 158, December 2002. (Turin).
Tram e tramvie a Milano. G. Cornolò and G. Severi. ATM Milan, n.d, c.1987.

In April 1972 Madrid 1150 seems to be having a spot of bother with a dewirement. (Author)

FRANCE

French designers made only one contribution to the development of the bogie tram in the years after 1945, but it was a very fine contribution indeed.

In 1950 a series of 28 bogie cars (501-528) was constructed by Brissoneau et Lotz of Creil for the ELRT system in Lille. These were initially worked as two-car sets and hence only one driving position was originally fitted in each car. The driver was given a separate cab and the passenger accommodation was extremely comfortable. Electro-pneumatic control equipment and air brakes gave good acceleration and smooth braking and the trams were fully equal to those being placed in service in other countries. In 1954 these trams were fitted with an additional driving position at the rear to allow single-car operation, but no separate cab was provided at that end, since the new controls were used mainly when shunting. The fleet was converted for one-person operation in 1971 and the control system was modernised at the same time, the livery being changed from cream to red and white. There were plans to order eight further sets, but in the event only one was delivered and these trams unfortunately remained the only example of their type. They performed well until the early 1980s, when they were replaced by second-hand articulated cars from Germany. Five (505/13/21/24/28) were exported to Ha Noi in October 1985, in an attempt to revive the system in that city. They were fitted with trolley poles before they left Lille but their technology was beyond the facilities available and they did not enter regular service in Vietnam, although one did operate for a very short time. Five others became works cars and no.520 is preserved by AMTUIR.

In 1950 Modern Tramway published the results of a comparison between a coupled set of this class (501/2) and the PCC car imported into Belgium from the USA (qv), although the actual source of this information was not recorded. The PCC was running between Woluwe and

No.503 in service at Tourcoing in October 1968. (Author)

Tervuren and the ELRT set between Lille and Roubaix and they were compared over a distance of 400m and 375m respectively. The French set scored in both maximum and average speed, with figures of 70km/hr and 44km/hr, against 59km/hr and 41.5km/hr, although the load of 10.14 tonnes was spread over two cars as against 6.95 tonnes in the PCC. The French cars also performed better in the emergency braking test, with a rate of 4.25m per second per second, against 3.34m per second per second. However, it was in energy consumption that the PCC was most soundly beaten, with nos.501/2 returning a rate of 257W per tonne/kilometre against 371W. Whether this was an official or unofficial test, the results certainly show that France could still produce a tram that was fully competitive with one of the most advanced designs in the world and make it all the more regrettable that no further trams, either of this class or any other, were built in the country until the tramway revival of the 1980s.

Technical details

Length 13.36m, width 2.2m, weight 17 tonnes, 4 x 36kW motors, 82 passengers, 31 seated.

Bibliography

Modern Tramway nos.152, August 1950, 205, January 1955, 547, July 1983.

BELGIUM

The Belgian SNCV was the only undertaking in that country to take delivery of non-PCC bogie trams in post-war years.

Early in the Second World War, the staff of the SNCV's Cureghem workshops requested authority to prepare a new design of tram for urban service and in view of the overcrowding then being experienced, this was duly granted. The first prototype (10330) was placed in service in 1941. Two further cars (10331/2) with lightweight bodies, weighing only 12.5 tonnes, in which much use was made of aluminium panelling, appeared soon afterwards. Their most novel feature was the fitting of frame-mounted motors with cardan drive to the outer axle of each bogie. Two more (10333/4) followed, these being even lighter at 10.3 tonnes. Finally in the early post-war years, a sixth car with a conventional steel body appeared in 1947 (10335). All had an attractive style of body, with smooth outlines and sloping windscreens. Various forms of fare collection and of door types were evaluated in these cars, all of which were placed in service in the Brussels area and gave every satisfaction. They

were scrapped between 1959 and 1963. To produce such a radical new design in the middle of a war and occupation reflected considerable credit to all concerned.

The first sign of post-war modernisation came in 1948 when a standard motor and trailer were rebuilt for passenger flow operation with automatic doors and a "Grossraum" interior. As this was considered successful, 21 motor cars (10374-10394) and 24 trailers (19456-19479)

SO class car 10051 pauses at Wenduine on the coast line in September 1958. (Author)

S class 10180 (left) and 10495 (right) at Charleroi Eden in October 1968. (Author)

SJ class 9172 leaves La Louvière in August 1985. (Author)

Heliopolis 209, on Suez Road on 23 February 1979. (Leeds Transport Historical Society)

were acquired in 1949 from the Braine-le-Comté factory and placed in service in the Hainault division. The last six of these handsome single-ended cars originally had cardan drive, but this proved troublesome and all were later converted to the standard form. The body frames seem to have been too light and in service proved prone to distortion. They were scrapped between 1962 and 1968, only car 10393 being preserved at the Schepdaal museum. Despite their handsome appearance, they seem not to have been completely successful and the SNCV reverted to building its own cars rather than buying from an outside firm.

In 1948 the first post-war trams (10336-10339, class N) for the Brussels area emerged from Cureghem workshops. These were also attractive vehicles, but with a much more rounded form than the new cars in Hainault, were slightly longer and were double-ended. They were laid out for passenger flow, offering 33 seats and 67 standing places. As they proved to be successful in service, they were followed by 81 other cars (10420-10499 and 4100-4102). These were 2.32m wide and could accommodate 110 passengers. These used the cardan drive of the prototype cars. From 1954 new bogies with altered suspension were fitted to the class. There were ultimately 85 cars of this class and the last car of this type to enter service, (10485) was finished to a higher than normal standard and displayed in the transport pavilion at the 1958 Exposition. Most of class N were used in the Brussels area, including the line to Leuven, on which two were tested against a set (503+504) from the ELRT in Lille. A few ran on urban services elsewhere. In service, they ran solo and a brief experiment with double traction operation was not pursued. Between 1962 and 1965 ten were rebuilt as S class cars and sent to Charleroi and after 1965 26 were rebuilt as trailers, 22 for the coast line and the remainder for use at Charleroi. All motor cars were ultimately concen-

trated in Brussels and the class lasted until the end of SNCV service there on 31 July 1978. Cars 10433, 10480 and 10485 are preserved, the first in Paris, the latter two in Belgium.

As many of the wooden-bodied standard trams were by 1950 nearing the end of their useful lives, it was decided to institute a rebuilding programme to give these cars new bodies of the same type as class N. Unlike these, however, they had 4 x 47 kW motors and were double-ended. Between 1954 and 1959 183 such conversions were turned out, as class S, most taking the numbers of the cars they replaced. The numbering was too complex to be given here, but was in the range 9646-10499 and 41003-41011. There were also 28 extremely fine cars of class SO (O = Oostende), built for use on the coast line. These were 2.4m wide, single-ended and fitted with very comfortable armchair seats. To allow one conductor to serve a three-car train, they had train doors in the rear end. Finally came 13 cars of class SE (E = Exposition), built in 1958 for use on services to the Exposition and given interior fittings of a higher standard than normal, with warm air heating, bronze anodised interior fittings and green leather armchair seats and new Kiepe electrical equipment. There were also seven cars built new, using spare equipment and, as mentioned above, ten N class cars, used on the Louvain service, were sent to Charleroi when that closed in 1962, being given new four motor equipment and re-classified S. Including these, the class finally numbered 203. Eleven were rebuilt as trailers in 1974.

For use on the new light rail lines in the Charleroi area 31 S class motor trams and twelve trailers were rebuilt with folding steps and, in the case of the former, half-arm pantographs. These were re-classified SM (M = Métro) and could be distinguished by the speed whiskers on the dash. As there were then great plans for this area, it was decided in 1977 to supplement the articulated cars with 20 completely rebuilt S class trams, the first of which appeared in September 1979. In the event, only eleven were thus treated, in the local workshops at Jumet, and they became class SJ (J = Jumet) (9170-9180). They were given an interior comparable to that of the new cars, with rubber-mounted fixed windows and pressure ventilation. Externally they shared the livery of the new articulated cars and had twin headlights. Some also had SAB resilient wheels and rubber suspension. A similar conversion of eight more cars was begun in 1983, but only three were actually completed, as it had by then become obvious that the

light rail plans were over-ambitious and that traffic levels were falling to a point where the articulated cars could deal with all requirements.

The last bogie trams were retired from service in 1989 and almost all were scrapped. A few have been preserved and a standard set is run on the Lobes-Thuin museum line near Charleroi. At a much earlier date, four N class motors and one trailer had been sold for further service at Gijon in Spain and in 1972 18 S class cars followed them for use on the radial lines around Valencia, six being converted to trailers. The Gijon cars were transferred to that system in 1977 and all lasted until replaced by modern material in the early 1990s.

A few individual groups built modern trailers for use on their own lines. Four were built at Cureghem workshops for the Brabant group in 1953/4 and shortly afterwards the Liège group built three similar trailers. However, a cheaper way of providing more trailers soon presented itself and between 1954 and 1958 76 bodies from redundant standard motor cars were placed on new bogies to work with S class motor trams. Some of the bodies concerned had started life as trailers in the 1930s and were now returning to their original form! A further 32 were similarly treated for use on the coast line.

Technical details
Production N class
Length 14.3m, width 2.32m, weight 15.5 tonnes, 2 x 60kW motors, 110 passengers, 33 seated.

The Belgians were also active in the export field

Antwerp area S class car 9759 at F.D. Roosevelt Plein in September 1958. (Author)

SM class car 9143 uplifts passengers in La Louvière in August 1986. (Author)

N class 10476 in Brussels in November 1968. (Author)

and between 1949 and 1953 the Ateliers de la Dyle of Louvain built a series of bogie cars for the Cairo-Heliopolis radial line of the Electrorail company. In design they were based on the two-axle cars supplied to Charleori some years earlier and were handsome and comfortable, with a rather unusual layout. The central door was used to give access to first and second class harim compartments, while the end doors were used by other passengers of both first and second class. Seats in first class were sprung and fitted with foam rubber cushions while those in second class were of shaped plywood and total capacity was 105, with 48 seated. Dimensions were 14.6m x 2.45m and they had 4 x 52kW motors. Trolley poles were fitted at each end of the car and there was also a pantograph for use on the main line. There has been some confusion about the numbering of these trams, but it seems that there were twelve built in Belgium (88-99) and that these were followed by 24 built in Egypt in 1956, when the whole class was renumbered 101-136. This class gave good service until replaced by Japanese built cars in the 1980s.

Bibliography

Strassenbahn Magazin, nos.133/4, November and December 2000.

100 Years of the Belgian Vicinal. W.J.K. Davies. Light Rail Transit Association, London 1985.

Instappen a.u.b! – Honderd Jaar Buurtspoorwegen in Belgie. H van Wesemael, Editor. *De Nederlandsche Boekhandel*, Kapellen, 1985.

Modern Tramway nos.436, April 1974 and 646, October 1991. (Heliopolis).

Braine-le-Comte car 10393 descends the Rue Turenne in Charleroi in May 1957. (W.J. Wyse, courtesy Light Rail Transit Association, London Area)

TATRA BOGIE TRAMS

TYPES T1 AND T2

The progressive Czech factory of CKD Tatra-Smichov Vaggonka – generally referred to simply as Tatra – had already before 1939 begun discussions with the producers of the PCC car in North America with a view to obtaining a licence to build these trams in Europe. These discussions were resumed after 1945 and successfully concluded in 1947, before the communist take-over of the country. It is interesting to speculate on the course of tramcar development in Eastern Europe had the negotiations taken longer!

Bogie trams were classified from T1 (T = tramvaj) upwards. Articulated trams were classified KT (kloubová tramvaj, articulated tramcar), followed by a number indicating the number of axles, although a few prototype articulated cars were simply classified K. The second part of the classification system consisted of the letters A to D, in which A and B were single-ended cars and C and D were double-ended. The final digit indicated width, two being 2.2m, five 2.5m and six 2.6m. Trailers, which were built only for DDR systems and Jugo-slavia, had a German classification and were simply B (beiwagen = trailer). Suffix letters were also used to denote country of destination, as in D (Germany) SU (USSR) etc. Some of the last T3 cars for the USSR were classified T3M (Modernisovany = modernised).

The new rulers of the country seem to have had no objection to using a design of vehicle which was a product of the capitalist system and work on the new trams went ahead, to allow the first two to be delivered to Praha in 1951, followed soon afterwards by a pre-production series of four. They even paid royalties on the first 150 cars to be built under this agreement! This was an elegant design of car, with a rather more tapered front end than that of the standard PCC car, but clearly showing its transatlantic origins, particularly in the pedal control. At that time, the tramways in the capital still used the trolley pole for current collection. In true North American fashion, passenger flow was from front to rear, with a seated conductor placed just forward of the centre door. With respect to equipment and bogies, the car was an exact copy of the PCC car. With a top speed of 60km/hr and impressive acceleration, it brought significant reduction in journey times and was popular with the travelling public. The design was classed as T1 and a total of 139 were produced for Praha between 1951 and 1956. Cars of the first series could only run solo, but from the second series onwards, m.u. controls were fitted. They were also delivered in small numbers – a total of 46 – to Kosice, Most, Olomouc, Ostrava and Plzen. One hundred were exported to the Soviet Union and two were exported to

T1 car 5044 in service in Praha in 1972. (B. Bareham, author's collection)

Brno T2 car 1484 working north-west from the city centre towards Žabovresky on 5 June 1977. (Peter Haseldine)

Warsaw in 1955. The Poles took from these many ideas which later went into the production of their own bogie cars (qv), but did not place any repeat orders – somehow, despite the standardisation enforced on many other Comecon countries, the Poles continued happily to go their own way in tramcar development. In all 287 T1 cars were built.

The cars in Czecho-Slovakia were later converted to one-person operation, though this did not reach the capital until 1973. In some cities, such as Plzen, which converted 18 cars, type T1 trams were given new bodies of type T3 (qv), the originals not having stood up well to a general lack of maintenance. All have now been withdrawn. The first to run in Praha, 5001, is preserved in the city's transport museum, in its 1965 condition.

In 1955 there appeared in Praha two prototypes of a new and rather more robust design, class T2. This was wider and heavier than class T1, with

The T3 could be distinguished from the T4 by its more rounded front end. Schwerin 417 was the last T3 or T4 to be delivered to any German operator, in 1988. It was not modernised and is seen here at the main depot, in virtually original condition, in June 1996. (Author)

Bogies for T4D cars, seen in Magdeburg in September 1992. (Author)

corresponding increased capacity, but totally lacked the elegance of that design. The front end was more rounded and the indicator box overhung the windscreen in a manner that gave the cars a distinctly frowning appearance. Technically and electrically these were still pure PCC cars. The first two went to Praha, but were soon moved to Olomouc and Bratislava. A total of 771 cars were produced between 1955 and 1962, of which 391 went to Czech systems and 380 to the Soviet Union, 180 of these going to Moskva. Cars for the Soviet Union had only front and rear doors. Two of these served briefly in what was then Leningrad and were fairly smartly passed on to Volgograd, the former having its own ideas about modern trams. Again some cars were later rebodied to match class T3. The only T2 cars still in service are to be found on the radial line Liberec-Jablonec. Eighteen cars were acquired by Usti nad Labem but did not prevent the closure of this system in 1970, when they were acquired by other Czech systems. The second prototype, 6002, has been preserved in Praha, although it spent almost all of its active life in Bratislava.

TYPES T3 AND T4

From 1958 Tatra's engineers, in co-operation with the Praha undertaking and the Research Institute for Rail vehicles (VUKV) were already working on something which would be considerably better and in 1960 the first of class T3 was shown at the Brno Fair, before going on trial in Praha. It entered passenger service on line 4 on 21 June 1961, but had to be withdrawn for heavy repairs after a serious accident in March 1962. It reappeared as 6101 in 1963. This design, and its associated class T4D, was to go on to become one of the world's most successful tramcars and

the complete history of the class has required a book to itself; only a brief summary can be attempted here. The total number built (both classes) was 16,464 motors and 1,010 trailers. Cars built from spare bodies, prototypes and rebuildings would increase this figure by another 300+. Ostrava, for example, took 20 new cars built from spares in the period 1993-98. Praha alone had 1193 trams delivered between 1963 and 1989, of which 746 were still in service in 2004. Not included in these totals are batches of class T3M cars built in the Ukraine in recent years as Tatra-Jug.

Class T3 cars were derived from class T2 but, with a raked windscreen, had a much more attractive appearance. There were also some changes to the driver's cab and the use of a certain amount of glass fibre in their construction allowed a reduction in weight, without sacrificing passenger capacity. The traditional PCC type control system was still used. Seating was reduced to 24, on rather hard and shiny glassfibre seats, arranged 1+1. A new motor of type TE 022 was fitted. The accelerator had 99 contacts, controlled in five positions on the control pedal and this gave an extremely supple control of speed and good hill-climbing power. From 1971 thyristor control was available as an option. The cars rode smoothly, even on some of the world's worst street track, accelerated smartly and were fast in operation. Suspension is very light and on reserved track, a certain amount of sway can develop. Despite the complex technology, class T3 cars are robust vehicles and, particularly since 1989, have withstood years of little or no maintenance, especially in Russia and Ukraine, just as PCC cars formerly did in certain US cities. The main drawback of the class is the liability of the bodywork to corrosion, especially around the doors. Curiously there was no provision on class T3 to show the destination of the tram and only a service number was displayed. If it was thought necessary to show a destination, this was done on a piece of cardboard stuck in the windscreen, a primitive method which did not accord well with the advanced nature of the tram! The first production cars (6102-6171) entered service in Praha on 21 November 1962. At first there were considerable teething troubles, but these were corrected by 1963 and the experience gained used in the construction of further batches, for both the capital and provincial systems. The first cars delivered to Praha initially had conductors but became one-person cars after 1973. Apart

Leipzig B4D trailer 573 at the rear of a Grosszug at Hauptbahnhof on a miserable evening in June 1979. (Author)

Leipzig T4D 1720 heads a Grosszug at Wittenberger Strasse on line 22 in June 1980. (Author)

from normal service, class T3 cars also ran in tourist service in the capital and Ostrava, in both cases being painted blue and white instead of the standard red and ivory. Between 1962 and 1989 class T3 CS was supplied, in seven different production series, to all tramway systems in what was then Czecho-Slovakia as detailed below:

Bratislava	175 (metre gauge)
Brno	157 + 10 T3R in 1997
Košice	181
Most	23
Liberec	53 (metre gauge, now converted to 1435mm)
Olmouc	69
Ostrava	224
Plzeň	128
Praha	1214
Total	2234

The design was exported, as class T3 SU, to 34 cities in the USSR between 1963 and 1988, Moskva receiving the first 65 (501-565) in the former year. Again most cars for the Soviet Union

Dresden 224.260, as modernised (but still retaining its DDR computer numbering scheme) heads a "Grosszug" approaching Postplatz along Wilsdruffer Strasse in June 2001. (Author)

In Dresden and Schwerin many cars were modified for use as the second, non-driving motor car in a Grosszug, as shown by DVG 244 016 at Hauptbahnhof in June 2006. (Author)

Of all the systems to modernise Tatra bogie cars in the years after German reunification, none did the job more thoroughly than Chemnitz. A prototype was treated by Waggonbau Bautzen in 1992 and in 1994/5 36 further motor cars and 14 trailers were similarly rebuilt. Car 505 is seen here at Schönau terminus in September 1993. (Author)

The interior of a rebuilt car in Chemnitz. (Author)

had only front and rear doors and rather more seats than their Czech counterparts (36 or 39). In some cities, such as Irkutsk, they were fitted with bow collectors rather than pantographs. By 1988 a total of 11,353 cars of this class had been exported to the USSR and a further six of class T3R were completed, using spare bodies, in 1997 and 1999. As stated above, some cars of previous classes were converted to class T3m with new bodies and five bodies were also supplied to Moscow in 1973 to be used with older equipment.

The class was also exported, as T3 YU, to Osjek (25) in Kroatia and Sarajevo (20) in Bosnia-Herçegovina. A motor/trailer set was also sent to Beograd in 1967 but was returned as unsuitable.

Two undertakings in the DDR acquired T3 D cars. Karl Marx Stadt had a total of 132, these being used in the conversion of the system to standard gauge. Most remaining have been modernised, in what is perhaps the most thorough operation of the kind in the former DDR. The T3 cars were given new insulation, skirts to cover the bogies, air conditioning and a totally new interior.

Schwerin took 115, the last of these running in August 2003.

Brno 1583 ran in Budapest on trial in December 1975 but no orders followed from Hungary.

A few have already entered preservation. In Praha the first production series car, 6102 of 1962, has been preserved along with car 6149. The Technical Museum in Brno has car 1521 of 1967 while in Bratislava car 7509 of 1964 has been preserved since 1995. No doubt others will follow in due course.

Since 1990 many T3 cars in Russia, the Czech Republic, Slovakia and Latvia have been modernised, in a variety of ways and by many different firms. It is impossible to give other than a brief summary here of the changes made as a result of these programmes. The most striking alterations to the external appearance of the trams has been made in Brno, where cars rebuilt by the firm of Pars in Sumperk have received a new flat windscreen, incorporating a destination indicator. Unfortunately this alteration does not fit in well with the design of the rest of the body, but the improvement in comfort has been considerable. The same design has been adopted in Bratislava, classes T3M and T3G. The former undertaking also received ten new trams (1659-

1668) of what was now classified T3K, to which it in due course added two built for Samara in Russia but not delivered (1669/70). Three others did make it to Russia, to Ishevsk. In 1998 a much more complete renovation, with a completely new body, was carried out by the builders on one car in Praha, which became car 8600. Unfortunately the closure of the Tatra factory prevented any similar conversions, but many other cars have been updated by Alstom and, in its upgraded workshops, by the undertaking itself. These changes, along with new liveries, have completely broken up the monotony which formerly pervaded the Czech tramway scene. Modernisation began in Moskva in 1998, but the first attempts, undertaken in the undertaking's workshop, were not totally successful (the first car to be treated is now in the museum fleet), although 13 are now in service. The undertaking then turned to the Riga factory and in 2002 signed an agreement by which 185 cars of type T3SU will be modernised in Moskva under the guidance of Latvian technical staff. The first (3343, class TMRP2) entered service in April 2003.

Exports were not confined to the countries mentioned above, but for other countries the design took on a different form. In December 1964 three cars loaned from Praha (6401/2/5) ran in Dresden, that undertaking having arranged this trial on its own initiative. Ever since the time of Alfred Bockemühl in 1947, it had been hoping to acquire Grossraumwagen, but, apart from a few Gotha cars, had been unsuccessful in this. By 1964 the need was great, 34% of the fleet being over 40 years old. Just before Christmas 1964 no.6401 arrived from Praha, ostensibly on loan, and it was first tested on Christmas Eve. The two others followed early in the New Year and tests were conducted with individual cars and also, from 31 January 1965, with all three coupled together, to assess the practicability of what in Dresden is called a "Grosszug". When the cars returned to their home city in May 1965, the success of the trials was clear and this did much to persuade the DDR authorities, who were then very definitely not pro-tram, that it would be worth while standardising on the Czech product. However, changes would have to be made to the design to comply with DDR regulations, particularly with regard to braking, and in any event clearances precluded the use of such wide cars (2.5m) on most DDR systems. It was also a requirement that trailer operation should be possible. In 1966 agreement was reached between the Dresden undertaking and CKD Tatra to develop a narrower version (2.2m wide), with the electrical system modified to allow operation as a Grosszug. As part of the agreement, the manufacturer had to agree to produce two-axle Gotha type cars until the new design went into production.

This design, known as class T4D, was suitable

for either standard or metre gauge (the only bogie car built for the latter) and was delivered to Leipzig, Magdeburg, Dresden and Halle, the last being the only metre gauge version. The first T4D tram (2000) was delivered to Dresden in September 1967, after running trials in Praha, and series production began in 1968, the first trams entering service in Dresden in February 1969. The first "Grosszug" ran in Leipzig in 1970 on line 27. This combination, which was an impressive crowd-mover, became generalised in most cities and, although less common since reunification, can still occasionally be seen. Arrival of this class in several cities began a programme of cascading two-axle cars to smaller

The amount of work involved can be judged from this view of a Chemnitz car being operated on in Bautzen in September 1993. (Author)

Schwerin 144 (ex 290) was given an unusual squared roof when rebuilt and was thereafter known to the staff as "Willi". Two ladies admire it at Marienplatz, while cooling off on a hot day in July 1995. It is now in service in the Russian city of Tula. (Author)

Interior of an un-modernised T4D car in Halle in September 1992. On the right the penalty fare notice quoting DM60 (c£24) indicates that German reunification has occurred, and the rate of change can be measured by the similar, but redundant notice on the ceiling to the left, which still gives the former penalty of 5 Mark (c£2 at the official rate of exchange). On the left, the typical DDR ticket canceller/fare box is still in use. (Author)

undertakings and, in Leipzig, scrapping of some antiquated pre-war cars. As the trams could not, for clearance reasons, run in Berlin, that city received the Gotha bogie cars from Dresden and Magdeburg. The success of the class did much to change the government's thinking on trams and from 1969 official policy favoured their use on extensions into new housing estates. Dresden's pioneer car is now preserved there.

It was not until 1972 that the Serbian capital decided to use the cars in quantity and acquired 10 (6801-6810) of class T4YU. These were among the few of this class to have operated with a trolley pole. A further version was developed as type T4SU for the few metre gauge systems, such as Kaliningrad and Lvov, in the Soviet Union, although one such system ((Pjatigorsk) took standard T3s. Unlike Russian T3 cars, these had three doors. Class T4 was also exported to Arad, Bucarasti and Galati in Romania and to Sofia in Bulgaria.

The delivery of classes T3 and T4 to German operators raised, for the first time since 1951, the question of running trailers with Tatra bogie cars. As mentioned above, a design had been developed for Beograd and this car was now diverted to Halle in September 1969 (101, class B4D). It was much more successful there and a series followed in 1971. These were placed in service with two motor cars on line 5, a radial line of 31km length and the longest tram line in the DDR. The trailers originally had their own dynamo for lighting etc. but this gave rise to numerous problems and they were converted to have batteries, supplied from the motor car. Trailers were also built for Beograd.

Halle also developed a double-ended version of

Leipzig's "glass tram" 1700 leaves the starting point of the city tour at Hauptbahnhof (west) in June 2004. (Author)

this type. A local service operated at the outer end of line 5 had a stub terminal and it was not possible to rebuild this for single-ended cars. The manufacturer claimed that it would be impossible to produce a double-ended version and, under the guidance of Herr B-L Schmidt, then assistant to the director and later himself director of the undertaking, car 901 – the first Tatra in the city – was in 1983 rebuilt as a double-ended car. This involved fitting a new driving position at the rear, a new middle door on the former offside and a second pantograph, to operate the points. The existing rear door was removed. The rebuilding was successful and three other cars were so treated (902, 1030 and 1031). A trailer was also rebuilt to work between these last two, which were usually used in connection with track repairs. More recently Dresden has also rebuilt two cars in this way, for the same reason. The Halle cars saw less use after the arrival of double-ended low floor cars and in February 2005 car 902 was sold to the Tramway Museum Society, fitted in Leipzig with a pair of new bogies and moved to Crich, where it will be converted into an easy-access tram for visitors with a mobility problem.

Another interesting rebuilt tram can be seen in Leipzig, where two cars and a trailer were given glass roof lights, upgraded interiors and a refreshment facility to allow use on city tours, continuing the tradition of the "Gläserner Leipziger" which goes back to the 1920s. A further car has had most of its roof replaced by Perspex sheeting and its side windows removed to allow its use on the same tours, on fine days, as the "Offener Leipziger". In the same city, several trailers have been rebuilt with a low floor middle section and double central doors, not for the usual reason in such conversions but to allow the conveyance of cycles.

Class T4 was extremely successful, although its introduction was not without problems. The trams had a considerable appetite for current and in several cities it was necessary to upgrade the power supply with new substations to cope with their needs. Until this was done, cars often ran with the upper notches of the control system blocked. The ability of these trams to take corners at high speed played havoc with the tracks on some systems. Maintenance was a far more complex matter than with the Gotha two-axle cars and in 1974 the various operators formed a central group to co-ordinate this process. This, rather than political considerations, was an important step towards centralisation in tramway policy in the DDR. But, having said all that, there could be no doubt of the success of the type. It had been planned to end production of classes T3/T4 in 1976, in favour of class T5 and articulated cars, but such was the outcry that the decision was revoked and production continued for another ten years. Since

Many T3 cars in the-then USSR were in the 1980s modernised with T6 style bodies, to become type T3M, as shown on Riga 247. It is working inbound from Tapesa Iela on line 2 in September 1994 and is about to pass under line 4. (Author)

Double-ended rebuild 900 (ex-901) at Marktplatz in Halle in October 2002. (Author)

German reunification many cars of class T4 have been modernised in a variety of ways and as a result no longer form a standard class. Generally these renovations involved the fitting of new doors and windows with hopper ventilators, upholstered seating, an improved driving cab and new lighting. In some cases thyristor control was also fitted, but the PCC control has been retained in other cases. Many systems fitted new one-arm pantographs.

In 2003/4, in parallel with the construction of the Leoliner low floor articulated car (qv), Leipzig's workshops totally rebuilt a T4D car and fitted it with a low floor area between the bogies. It has been renumbered 001 and repainted into the blue and silver livery of Leoliner. At present it has not entered passenger service and it is not clear if any further cars will be similarly treated.

Non-modernised and, in 2002, modernised cars have gone to systems elsewhere in Eastern Europe and are now running in Arad (2 motors + 2 trailers), Botosani (25+1), Brasov (12 + 6), Craiova (17+17), Galati(19+4), Iasi (27+2), and Oradea (75+36) in Romania. Others have gone to Pyonyang in North Korea, which took 100 cars from Leipzig and 16 from Dresden.

It would be easy to ascribe the success of classes T3 and T4 to political considerations but it is hard to believe that managers of so many

Beograd was another of the few systems on which Tatra cars were operated with trolley poles. In this picture, that on car 2 appears to be somewhat bent! It is approaching the main railway station along Karadordeva from Pristonisbad on 22 July 1975. (Peter Haseldine)

T3 car 65 of Liberec loads at Fügnerova on line 3 in September 1993. (Author)

tramway systems, even under communism, would have been prepared to adopt this design had it not combined technical superiority with robust construction and a superb ability to deal with crowds of passengers, day in, day out, even when maintenance was not all that it should have been. There is some evidence that quality deteriorated after 1970, under pressure of the volume of orders, for which the old factory in Smichov was not really adequate. No T3 or T4 cars were built in the new premises in Zlicin, other than the T3R cars of 1997-99.

TYPES T5, T6 AND T7

The prototype for the next generation of bogie trams appeared in 1973. This was classified T5 and was of much more angular appearance than earlier designs. It also had ribbed side panels. Electrically there were some minor improvements, but the traditional PCC system was still used. The car was tried in Praha and Most, under

The T6 demonstrator in New Orleans, seen with replica bogie car 2001 in January 2000. (Jim D. Schantz)

the number 8000, and gave every satisfaction, but for two years there were no further developments and it went back to the manufacturer, who used it for further electrical tests. In 1976 four more prototypes appeared. Nos.8005/6 appeared, with thyristor control, classified T5A5. These ultimately joined Praha's fleet. Nos.8009/110 were the first and, as it turned out the only Tatra cars with bodies 2.60m wide and they reverted to flat side panels. After trials in several cities in the Soviet Union, they ended up in Most, where one is now preserved. For some reason type T5 did not seem to meet with any great interest on the part of operators, particularly in the DDR, who still preferred T3/4 and the only series order was for Budapest. Two prototypes (8011/2) were built in 1978 and a series of 320 cars followed between 1979 and 1984. These cars are single-ended but double-sided and normally work coupled back-to-back. Many have recently been modernised. CKD Tatra was at this time becoming much more customer friendly and at the request of this operator the cars were fitted with series/parallel control, rather than PCC control. A version with two-class accommodation was designed for Egypt but there were no orders and likewise plans for a trailer for Budapest did not come to fruition. A fifth prototype (0013) remained with the manufacturer, being used to test a highly sophisticated design of bogie, intended for use on trams for high speed lines. No more class T5 cars were built after 1984.

Already by 1980 CKD were planning a new design of bogie car for standard and broad gauge only. In August 1983 the first prototypes of class T6 (0016/7) entered service. This was 2.5m wide and the type was intended for service in the Soviet Union. After trials in Praha, they went to Moskva, where one is still in passenger service. However, due to their high cost compared to the T3SU design, the authorities reverted to that for further orders. There were also discussions with DDR operators about a shorter and narrower version, as a replacement for class T4D. A prototype motor/trailer set (0020/0022) and a single motor car (0021) were produced in 1985, as class T6A2/B6A2 (0020/1). After the usual trials in Praha, the set went to Dresden and entered service as 226 001/276 001, being used latterly as sightseeing cars. There were numerous criticisms of the design, particularly with regard to step height. With some modifications, series production began in 1988 and from then 174 motor cars and 87 trailers trams were delivered to Berlin, Leipzig, Magdeburg, Rostock and Schwerin. The largest user of the class was Berlin, with 118 motor trams and 59 trailers. Schwerin in 1990 sold off its small fleet to Magdeburg. In most respects the class followed on directly from classes T3/4, but rather more attention was paid to anti-corrosion measures and to insulation. All cars used thyristor control.

T5 cars on line 18 in Budapest in June 1991, car 4134 leading. (Author)

Dresden T6.001 and matching trailer were given a distinctive grey livery for use on sightseeing tour duties, as seen at Trachenberge depot in September 1992. (Author)

A set of modernised T6/B6 trams on a section of new line at Bf. Friedrichstrasse, Berlin in June 1999. (Author)

T3SU car 1523 at the Katlakalns terminus of line 10 in Riga in September 1994. (Author)

No.7108, one of the T3 cars rebuilt by Pars, in service on line 11 in Bratislava on 15 June 2001. (Author)

Redundant Tatras can make useful members of the works car fleet. Schwerin 998, as seen in June 1996, was formerly passenger car 212 and is now used on track cleaning duties. (Author)

The motor trams used the bogies of class KT4, but the trailers had those of class B4D. German operators were not totally satisfied with the design, Rostock in particular having problems, and already before reunification there were complaints against Tatra. The Berlin fleet was very thoroughly rebuilt by Mitenwald GB between 1993 and 1996 and five further trailers were also acquired. Further insulation was provided, new outward-opening doors fitted and the passenger saloon was completely altered with upholstered seating and a new lighting installa-

By 1993 the Tatra works were filled with rows of completed T6 cars for Russian systems, which could not pay for them in hard currency. These examples are mounted on standard gauge transporter bogies. (Author)

Eight B4D trailers in Leipzig have been given a low floor centre section. In the case of four of these, this was done not simply to assist passengers with a mobility problem, but to allow the easy carriage of cycles. No.793 brings up the rear of a multi-coloured Grosszug at Hauptbahnhof in June 2004. (Author)

tion. The driver's cab was also rearranged and the suspension greatly improved. Apart from Dresden, which sold off its few cars in 1996, the other operators of the class also modernised their fleets, but less thoroughly.

The type was also, as planned, exported to the Soviet Union, which between 1984 and 1992 received 910 motor cars. A new customer was also found in Sofia, which acquired 37 cars between 1989 and 1991. That system had begun to convert to standard gauge and the T6 cars were used on routes so converted. In 1991 these were followed by 40 cars for the narrow gauge (1009mm) routes. Curiously no trams of this class were built for systems in Czecho-Slovakia until 1992 when Bratislava received 34 and Kosice 24 trams. Those for the former city showed some improvements, such as a dot-matrix destination display. Later Chech orders came from Praha (150), Brno (30) and Ostrava (38). One of the last orders was for a series of 13 for Szeged in Hungary in 1997 (900-912). These trams, classed T6A2SZ, have the 2.2m width of the German cars and a rather attractive revised external appearance. One of the more exotic destinations for class T6 was Pyonyang in North Korea, which acquired 129 examples. Trams delivered to Czech systems in the 1990s had an altered windscreen.

However, the most spectacular development connected with this class was the supply of a double-ended version, class T6 C5, to New Orleans in 1999 and tried in revenue service in Praha before shipment. The manufacturer had in 1997 supplied five sets of bogies and equipment to the city for use under replica cars (459-463) on the Riverfront line and in 1999 followed this with bogies and equipment for a prototype vintage car (2001), as part of the plan to re-introduce trams to Canal Street. The new tram, which carried no number, was the first double-ended bogie car built by Tatra. Apart from this novelty, it also differed from the production batches by having much equipment mounted in containers on the roof and also by having two-leaf doors, at front and central positions. The latter incorporated lifts for wheelchairs. In defer-ence to the local climate, air condition-ing was installed. The tram was mounted on bogies of 1587mm gauge, but a spare set of standard gauge bogies was also shipped to provide for

Rebuilt T3 car 3334, now classed TMRP, near Voikovskaja in Moskva in July 2002. (Alexander Shanin)

Tatra-jug T3M 7001 in Odessa. (M.J. Russell)

demonstration in other cities. Unfortunately these did not take place and, after running briefly in New Orleans, this tram returned to Europe in 2001 and is now in service in Strausberg. The contact with North America had come just too late.

By the time production of type T6 had really got into its stride, the Soviet Union had dissolved itself and with it went the whole economic system on which the success of the Tatra cars had been built. As a result of this change, the manufacturer found itself with cars for which it could not hope to receive any payment and some of these remained in the factory for years.

Very similar to class T6 was class T7, which first appeared in 1988 and used a new form of thyristor control, designated TV8, improved suspension and hand rather than pedal control. There were also measures to reduce noise levels. Two each were delivered to Praha (0024/5) in 1989. Two more (0026/7) went to Moskva in 1990. However, the political changes which soon followed meant that there would be no follow-up order, although both cars still exist. A version for Germany was planned, but did not go into production. However, this class also fulfilled a long-term vision of the builder to break into the western market, when Oslo hired one car (200) for trials in March 1990. This car received considerably improved passenger accommodation before entering service, it being unlikely that Norwegians would appreciate the hard fibreglass seats normally fitted. It was successful in service, though latterly spending most of its time on special duties. But sadly the entry to Western Europe came too late, both politically and technically. With the political change, Tatra was no longer able to offer the low prices which could have made it competitive and the low-floor revolution in tramcar design had already begun by the time car 200 was running in Oslo. An attempt to persuade that operator to buy the car in 1994 failed. In 1996 it became a party car, renumbered to 321. Construction of classes T6/7 tailed off sharply in the early 1990s and the last deliveries were made to Praha (8601-8750) in 1995-7 and to Ostrava (1131-1136) in 1998.

No other firm in Europe has ever had a chance to produce so many highly standardised bogie cars and classes T3/4 will probably always retain the world record for production of one type.

However, the cessation of construction of classes T6/7 was not quite the end of the story of Tatra bogie trams. The city of New Orleans holds the world record for the longest continuous operation of trams (since 1835!) and in recent years has seen a revival of the system, which had been reduced to just one line. The operator, Regional Transit Authority, naturally wanted vehicles which would be in keeping with the historic nature of the city, for both the new Riverfront line and the re-instated Canal Street line, and decided to construct cars in its own workshops. After experience on the former line with ex-Philadelphia PCC equipment, it was decided in 1997 to use new material, which would also be, technically, state-of-the-art and require minimum maintenance and the chosen equipment and bogies came from Tatra, which thus, in a rather unusual way, did manage to make an entry to the US market. There might have been more but, as Tatra had been taken over by the time work began on the Canal Street line, the equipment chosen for its new cars had to come from elsewhere, in this case the Brookville Equipment Corporation of Pennsylvania.

Technical details

Tatra bogie trams
T1 Length 13.3m width 2.4m weight 15 tonnes, 4x40kW motors, 88 passengers, 25 seated.
T2 Length 14m width 2.5m weight 18.1 tonnes, 4x40kW motors, 100 passengers, 25 seated.
T3 Length 14m width 2.5m weight 16 tonnes, 4x40kW motors, 104 passengers, 24 seated.
T4 Length 14m width 2.2m weight 17 tonnes, 4x42kW motors, 110 passengers, 22 seated.
T5 Length 14.7m width 2.5m weight 18.5 tonnes, 4x45kW motors, 100 passengers, 28 seated.
T6/7 Length 15.3m width 2.5m weight 18.9 tonnes, 4x45kW motors, 120 passengers, 40 seated.
(Class T6 cars for Germany are 2.2m wide)
All classes given above had a maximum speed of 65km/hr.
These details are for the basic standard design. From class T3 onwards there were some variations to suit the wishes of individual customers.

Bibliography

Modern Tramway nos.316, April 1964 (Classes T1-T3 and proposed T4), 630, June 1990 (prototypes).
Tatra-Wagen der ehemalige DDR. Der Stadtverkehr, 2/1992.
Tatra T3 1960-2000 – 40 Let Tramvají Tatra T3. Robert Mara. Klub Pratel Tramvají Tatra, Praha, 2001.
Strassenbahn Magazin, nos.65, August 1987 and 108, April 1997 (Dresden), 143-145, September-November 2001 and 150, April 2002 (Tatra general history).
Tramways and Urban Transit no.743, November 1999. (T6C5 for New Orleans).
Tramway Museum Society Journal, no.190, April 2005 (Halle 902).
Tatrabahnen in Halle (Saale) 1969-1994. H. Meyer, M. Schaaf and S. Raddatz. *Landsberger Druckerei,* Halle, 1994.

OTHER BOGIE CARS IN EASTERN EUROPE

BULGARIA

The only tram system in Bulgaria is in the capital, Sofia, and, being isolated from any other, has had a long history of developing its own designs. In 1952 the first bogie tram was introduced. This was an attractive-looking vehicle, with sloping windscreen. Air doors were fitted and there was a post for a seated conductor. There were ten of these trams (221-230) and ten matching trailers (521-530). Three years later there followed ten more motor cars (231-240) and 14 trailers (531-544). These trams mainly worked on line 5, the longest on the system and lasted until about 1980. They were followed, also in 1955, by the prototype of a series of all-electric trams (101). This was followed by a series of 25 motor cars (701-725) and 17 trailers (1001-1017). Externally they looked very like the standard German Grossraumwagen design, but were fitted with bow collectors and were painted in a new green and cream livery. There were 21 single seats, for a total capacity of 130, and three doors

No.233 and trailer in August 1969. (Author)

per side, with passenger flow from front to rear. They were poorly constructed and soon showed signs of wear and tear. However, they represented a creditable effort by a relatively small system to design and build its own version of a modern tram. By 1969 all were driver-only operated. All have now been withdrawn.

ROMANIA

The first modern bogie tram, built by the national firm of Electroputere in Craiova, appeared in 1952 in Bucuresti (3000), to be followed by a series in 1954 and further batches built between then and 1964 brought the total to 260 trams (3001-3260). Owing to a lack of electrical equipment, some were used as trailers until 1966. When new, there were two conductors seated at the middle doors and passenger flow was from middle to either front or rear. This lavish use of crew was too much, even for a communist state, and the cars were rearranged with entry at the rear and a single conductor. They were 14.8m long and could carry 120 passengers, of whom only 16 were seated. Technically they were very old-fashioned, despite which one was shown at the Leipzig Fair in 1956. Identical cars were built for Arad (six motors and six trailers, numbered in pairs 42/3, 46/7 through to 54/5). Seventeen motors were built for Oradea (44-60) and 20 motors for

One of the bogie cars in original condition in Bucuresti in April 1978. (Martin Jenkins, OnLine Video Archive)

Timisoara, numbered in the 200s. In Bucuresti 170 cars were rebuilt by the undertaking from 1978 onwards, with new electrical equipment,

Bucuresti 6080, seen in 1995, shows the type in rebuilt form. May 1995. (Martin Jenkins, OnLine Video Archive)

new bogies and an altered front end. A large number of new trailers, to a slightly different design, were then built to run with these cars and there were ultimately 170 trailers, though some may have incorporated parts of older cars. The trams ran into the 1990s but all have now been replaced, either by Romanian articulated cars or imports from Germany.

The Banat factory in Timisoara developed its own design of bogie car in 1972 and fitted to these Kiepe electrical equipment from Germany. The first cars were constructed to an attractive design with a smooth outline and pointed windscreen, but the later version, built from 1983 onwards, was distinctly boxy in appearance. Similar cars were supplied to Oradea, Galati and Braila. A metre gauge version was then developed for Iasy. Later similar trams were supplied to Sibiu and Arad and to the new systems of Cluj, Craiova, Ploiesti and Resita. There were also matching trailers. Although later cars had Romanian equipment in place of the Kiepe version, these trams were somewhat delicate from the maintenance angle and, apart from

Timisoara 353 in July 1999. (Martin Jenkins, OnLine Video Archive)

those in Timisoara itself, many spent long periods out of service. Most have now been withdrawn.

Technical details
Bucuresti V945, 1959
Length 13.85m width 2.29m, weight 17 tonnes, 4 x 30kW motors, 137 passengers, 22 seated.

KROATIA AND SERBIA

A bogie version of the two-axle car designed for Zagreb was built by Djuro-Djakovic for Beograd in 1972 (71-90), with 20 matching trailers. These are no longer in service. The design was then copied by the former undertaking, where 15 of these trams, from the series 203-229, are still in service as class TMK1Z.

No.74 with trailer 109 approaching the main station in Beograd in July 1975. (Peter Haseldine)

USSR AND SUCCESSOR STATES

Once some semblance of normality had been restored after 1945, the plans for a standard bogie car, mentioned in a preceding chapter, were revived. The first post-war trams to enter service were a small number of cars for Moskva (class M47), based on a trolleybus body mounted on trucks designed by SVARZ for the modernisation of older trams. The first actually appeared in December 1946. This was quite successful but had a low carrying capacity and was succeeded by a larger version, class M47a. In December 1948 an all-Union tramway congress recommended this design be adopted as a standard, to be built by the Riga Railway Carriage Plant, usually referred to as RVZ. The basic design remained in production continuously from 1950 to 1988 but was modified on several occasions during the years from 1950 to 1960. The first trams, designed by the Tushino-Avto plant in Moskva, designated MTV-82A, were built from 1948 to 1950 and looked rather like contemporary buses in the USA, having a recessed windscreen and twelve small windows with standee windows above. A lighter version, class MTV-82, with a redesigned and more attractive windscreen appeared in 1950 and was available until 1960. This class was used in many cities and it is not known how many were

Moskva 2282 of type MTV82A. (Lars F. Richter collection)

produced in total, but Moskva had 450 (1098-1400 and 2251-2397) and Kiev had 367 (1201-1367). There was also a trailer version, but its use was restricted to a few cities. Successive improvements were made during the 1950s, culminating in the production of class RVZ-6 in 1960. This type was then offered until 1988 and this production run of 28 years must be a record for a single design of tramcar. This class had larger windows, without the standee windows, 2+1 seating for 39 passengers, front and rear doors and automatic control. From 1975 a version fitted for m.u. operation was available and, in the same year, a new type of thyristor controlled car appeared, designated RVZ-7. This had three doors per side. As it was decided that trams with this equipment could more economically be acquired from Tatra, this class did not go into series production and the Riga factory thenceforth concentrated on the development of diesel and electric trains for suburban use, rather than on any new design of tram. Some of the cars running in Minsk have been given new bodies since 2000.

Technical details
Class MTV82, 1954 version
Length 13.6m, width 2.59m, weight 15.6 tonnes, 4 x 46kW motors, 100 passengers, 40 seated.
Class RV6, 1964.
Length 14m, width 2.6m, weight 16.5 tonnes, 4 motors, 120 passengers, 36 seated.

Meanwhile Leningrad had continued to go its own way in tramcar development. The first 85 post-war trams (3001-3169, odd numbers only) were rebuilds of classes LM/LP33 with all-metal bodies and classed LM/LP47. The Riga factory delivered 50 each of motors and trailers in 1948 (3501-3600, motors odd numbers, trailers even). An improved lightweight version known as LM/LP49 appeared two years later. There were 200 motor trams (3601-3999) and 160 trailers (3602-3920), the numbering scheme being as above. This design, class LM/LP49, was also supplied to a few other cities such as Minsk. Cars 3961 and 3990 are preserved in running order.

By 1957 a large number of new cars were required for both extensions and fleet replacement and class LM57 was developed to cater for this. This was a very attractive design and a total of 999 were produced (5001-5999, all numbers). There was no trailer version. A few also went to other systems, such as Taschkent. Car 5210 appeared in 1960 with a new style of body, but its design was not perpetuated. Car 5148 is preserved.

The square outline of car 5210 re-appeared in

LTM5 car as modified 1002 at University terminus in Moskva on 24 September 2003. (Alexander Shanin)

Experimental Spektr car 3004 on trial in the snow, 27 November 2004. (Alexander Shanin)

Lugan'sk LT10 class car 207 in service in its native city in 2004. (M.J. Russell)

RV-6 car 365 in Tbilisi, Georgia in June 1978. (Alastair G. Gunn)

KTM5 1-309 seen in Orsk on 16 June 2004. (M.J. Russell)

1968 with class LM68 and this design remained in production until 1987, with a total of over 2000. Later designs are of classes LM89, LM93, LM99 and LM2000. Some of these were also acquired by other cities but as type LM-99 was too large for Moskva, the manufacturers, now PTMZ, developed a shorter and narrower version (14m x2.5m) as type LM99A for the potentially large market in the capital. This has three-phase equipment and a futuristic appearance. After much work, the prototype (3002) arrived in Moskva in 2002 and in 2004 a second prototype (3003) and 24 production cars (3005-3028) followed.

The demand for bogie tramcars in the USSR was such that a further type was developed by the Ust-Katav (formerly Kirow) factory from 1966, after preliminary designs had been prepared in 1962 for a class KTM4. This was not built but a design based on it was constructed and was classified KTM. The first to appear had a plastic body, of an attractive outline, conceived by a young designer V. Berdjugin. This was tried in Moskva but proved to be quite impracticable from the point of view of safety. When series production began in 1969, it was of a car with an all-metal body. Class KTM-5 proved to be successful and production continued until 1992, by which time about 14,000 had been built. It was followed by an experimental design as KTM-6, which had enlarged cabs, and KTM-7, which had a middle door and did not progress beyond the drawing board. Two prototypes with different types of thyristor equipment were built in 1988 as KTM-8 and 9 and it was planned to have a third as KTM-10, but this did not see the light of day. However, the managers of the

Moskva system had decided that future deliveries should come from Russian manufacturers rather than Tatra and class KTM-8 did go into production at the end of 1991. Despite the restrictions imposed by the width of 2.65m, 170 units of this type were placed in service from 1994 onwards and it has been supplied to quite a number of other Russian systems, though only in limited quantities. A planned metre-gauge version for Kaliningrad was not built. To meet the capital's needs for a narrower car, a version having a width of 2.5m (KTM-8M) was developed and 187 were delivered between 1994 and 1999. A variation came with eleven cars which were built with a larger driving position to serve as motor school cars and these are known as class KTM-17. In 1995 the factory went over completely to the production of type KTM-8M,

which was then also delivered to other systems. Unfortunately, although cheap, these classes proved to be unreliable in service and in 1996 two prototypes (01,02) of a much improved version, developed in conjunction with Siemens and Duwag, were delivered to Moskva (class KTM-16,). From these were developed the most recent product of this factory, class KTM19, which first entered service in 1999, when prototype 2200 was delivered to Moskva. To date 122 have followed. There are also classes KTM-15, 16, 17 and 21, the first of these being in service only in Pyatigorsk and the last only in Moskva, in the form of a prototype (0102). Essentially this is simply a shorter (124.53m) version of type KTM-19. Class KTM-11 is represented only by a coupled set built in 1992 for Volgograd. KTM-14 was a design for a non-driving motor, which again

Class KTM-7 no.1000. This is a shortened version of this design, to allow the car to use Apakov depot, which had previously run only T3 cars. In the event this tram was not short enough and the four Lugan'sk cars were bought instead. (Alexander Shanin)

Seen near the railway station, Minsk 027 is one of class AKSM 1M which came into service between 2000 and 2003. (M.J. Russell)

Leningrad 3159 and matching trailer of classes LM/LP47. (Leeds Transport Historical Society)

KTM5 408 on line 4 in Yerevan, Armenia, in June 1978. (Alastair G. Gunn)

LM57 class 5295 and trolleybus 2429. (Leeds Transport Historical Society)

In what is once again Sankt Petersburg, car 6596 is on line 34 in August 1998. (Author)

Riga RVZ6 716 in the city centre in 1978. (A.D. Young, Evda Slides)

One of the earlier batch with standee windows had become works car 3417 when seen in September 1994. (Author)

did not progress into production. In 2001 a single car classified as KTM Spektr was delivered to Samara and this was followed by one each for Ekerinburg and Moskva. In the latter city this car ran on lines 15 and 21, but at the time of writing was no longer in service, having been impounded by the builders until payment for it is received. A new design, KTM-6080KMs, is now being offered for sale.

In 1997 a further Russian firm Uraltransmasch, located in Ekaterinburg, entered the tramcar-building market. Based on the Tatra T6B5 design, known as "Spektr" and to date appearing in two versions, 71-402 and 71-403. Only one car

Class KTM5-118T no.1-309 in service in Zlatoust on 22 June 2004. (M.J. Russell)

Smolensk 231 is the first of the batch of LM-99 cars delivered to this operator in 2001. (M.J. Russell)

of the latter type has been made and arrived in Moskva in January 2004 (3004).

All the above were or are single-ended.

In Ukraine, the local Lugan'sk factory, in the city of the same name, has entered tramcar production since the country gained independence and has produced either eight or 13 bogie cars (sources differ) for the city system (202-208, class LT-10). These seem to have been unsuccessful and all were out of service by 2005, four having been scrapped. A further car (0232) of this type went to Moskva, following a visit by the mayor of Moskva to the Ukraine, but it has not been in service since May 2003. Four trams, of a different design, went to Moskva in 2003, (1001-4, class LT-5). The electrical equipment for these was manufactured in the city and the front end came from Alstom in Poland. Despite being well received, particularly because of their excellent riding qualities, no further cars of this type have arrived.

A new class of bogie car has now appeared in this country, type JuMS-K1, based closely on the Tatra T3, but having an attractive rounded front end. Five have entered service in Donezk (3009-3013) and four in Lugan'sk (301-305).

Between 2000 and 2003 the local factory of AKSM delivered 13 bogie cars of a new design (026-038) to the tramways of Minsk in Belarus.

In recent years a combination of economic factors and the availability of second-hand trams from Germany and other western countries has militated against the development of new designs in the former USSR.

Technical details

Class KTM5m3
Length 15.1m, width 2.6m, weight 18.5 tonnes, 4 x 50kW motors, 115 passengers*, 35 seated.
Class KTM8
Length 15.2m, width 2.6m, weight 19.5 tonnes, 4 x 80kW motors, 167 passengers*, 32 seated.

Bibliography

Tramways in Eastern Europe. M. Taplin and M. Russell. Capital Transport, Harrow, 2003.
Light Rail and Modern Tramway nos.329, May 1965, nos.681 and 683, January and March 1993.
Strassenbahn Magazin nos.192/3, October/ November 2005. (Moskva).

HUNGARY

UV3 3234 working with another of the same class on line 67 on Fehervari Utça in June 1991. (Author)

While this country was still neutral, in 1940, Ganz-mavag delivered a class of 75 bogie trams to the FVV of Budapest, class TM, nos.3600-74. They were used on line 2, which runs along the Danube embankment on its own reservation and, as speeds were high and the journey time fairly short, each carried two conductresses. In 1948 two further cars (3700/1) were delivered, slightly altered in the light of experience with class TM, and fitted with more powerful motors. However, it was not until 1955 that series production could begin, with cars 3200-3249 of class UV1 and 3300-3399 of class UV2. All these were constructed by the undertaking itself. They worked in three-car sets with an intermediate two-axle trailer of the series 5750 or 5900. These trains of 40m length could carry at least 330 passengers and were certainly excellent crowd-movers. They were followed by nos.3400-3499 (UV3) in 1958-9, 3800-3939 (UV4) in 1962-4 and finally 3840-3901 (UV5) in 1965-68. These last batches were single-ended but double-sided and worked, without trailers, semi-permanently coupled back-to-back. Class UV trams were rugged and reliable vehicles, capable of fairly high speeds when necessary, yet with good riding

A coupled set of Ganz cars, 1212 and 1211, in service in Alexandria on 4 November 2004. (M.J. Russell)

qualities. Internally they were sombre, with much dark woodwork.

A rather surprising order for bogie trams came at a much later date from Alexandria. In 1982 Ganz of Hungary delivered fifteen twin-sets, fitted with Düwag monomotor bogies and doors, to the city system. These sets, numbered 1201/1202 upwards, are single-ended but double-sided and operate back-to-back in coupled pairs. They have double-width doors at front and rear and a single-width door in the centre, but are not operated with passenger flow. Their external appearance bears some resem-blance to the Melbourne Z class. When these cars were delivered, international co-operation in tramcar building was rare and otherwise unheard of between eastern and western Europe.

Technical details
Class UV5
Length 12.6m, width 2.3m weight 19.6 tonnes, 4 x 44kW motors, 132 passengers, 24 seated.

UV5 3885 on line 19 in June 1981. (Author)

POLAND

105N cars 258 and 257 in central Poznan on 16 June 1994. (Author)

Class 805N car 212 in Torun in October 2002. (Author)

An interior view of car 148 for Warsaw. (Konstal, author's collection)

The first post-war bogie trams to be built in Poland were the prototype of class 13N which appeared from the Konstal factory in 1959. This design was based very closely on the two Tatra class T1 cars which Warsaw had acquired, but considerable modifications were made to the control system. It was followed by no fewer than 839 for Warsaw. Some were not fitted with a driving position as they were to be operated as second cars in a set (class 13NSD). This class brought a vast improvement to the Warsaw system and commercial speeds were raised from 15 to 20km/hr. There were, however, problems with the maintenance of the control system. Two provincial versions, with conventional hand controllers, appeared in 1963 as classes 14N and 15N, of which five were supplied to Katowice, and one trailer of class 14ND was built to run with these. These were not perpetuated and the design remained confined to the capital, where about 500 are still giving good service.

Although the articulated cars of class 102N appeared to have been successful, there were some complaints that they were sluggish in comparison with a two-car set of class 13N and Konstal returned to bogie cars for the next generation and produced classes 105N, for standard gauge, and 803N and 805N for metre gauge. A total of 3,395 were built between 1974 and 2000, these being divided into 12 sub-classes, and they are to be found on all Polish systems. These are rugged and reliable cars and usually operated in m.u. formation. Production continued after the take-over of the Konstal factory by Alstom and later cars had much improved interiors. Some rebuilding of older cars has also been undertaken by the firm Protram, which has taken over part of the workshops in Wroclaw for this purpose. The result is an attractive vehicle with rather more seating and rather less door space than in the original design.

At the end of 2004 discussions were under way between Warsaw and the Polish manufacturer Cegielski for the supply of 30 high floor bogie cars. Meanwhile Protram had delivered to the local system the first two cars of class 204WrAs (2601/2). This design has four asynchronous 50kW motors.

Technical details
Class 13N
Length 13.3m, width 2.43m, weight 17.92 tonnes, 4 x 41.5kW motors, 144 passengers, 22 seated.

Class 105Na
Length 13.5m, width 2.4m, weight 16.72 tonnes, 4 x 41.5kW motors, 145 passengers, 20 seated.

Bibliography
Der Stadtverkehr 5/6/1984 (Leningrad).
Modern Tramway nos.329, May 1965 (USSR standard cars), 348, December 1966 (Budapest), 384, December 1969 (Poland), January 1993 (Russian cars).
Tram and Trolley in Africa. Op.cit.
Produckja I. Wyroby Konstal 1864-1989. Konstal, Graf press, 1989.
Konstal factsheets.

A coupled set of 13N cars, headed by 459, passing the central station in Warsaw in June 1994. (Author)

Recent rebuilding of class 105N is illustrated by nos.2313 and 2332 of MKP Wroclaw, in the city centre on 13 August 2004. (M.J. Russell)

ARGENTINA

In 1942 Buenos Aires, where double-deck trams had operated in the past, bought three new double-deckers, using old equipment. These had attractive streamlined bodies and seem to have been laid out for passenger flow. They were scrapped in the early 1950s.

A certain amount of mystery surrounds the first modern single-decker to run in Buenos Aires. On Christmas Eve 1952 a new bogie car was shown to the press, one of its passengers being President Juan Perón, who described it as "a step forward to our economic independence". It had been built in the city, but it is not clear how far old components were used in its construction. It seems to have been inspired by the PCC car, but in fact the body looked more like that on a contemporary US General Motors bus. This bogie car had front and centre doors on both sides but appears to have been single-ended. It was 14.2m long and carried 48 seated and 72 standing passengers. Named at first "El Libertador" – no doubt as a compliment to the President – it later acquired the fleet number

4000. In service it proved to be smooth riding and popular with the public, but it lasted only for a few years and no further similar "steps" were taken. It was acquired for preservation when the tramways closed in 1964, but was stored in the open and ultimately destroyed by vandals. The economics of Argentina in the 1950s could not generate the investment necessary to modernise a large and rather run-down system and the city had to wait for 23 years before seeing a modern tramway.

In 1987 a new tram line was built to feed Subte (Subway) line E, running from the new terminus of the latter at Plaza de los Vireyes to the district of General Savio. To work this, 25 new bogie cars were ordered from MATERFER (Fabrica de Material Ferroviaria), a national firm of rolling stock builders. Unfortunately these were not ready in time for the opening, which was performed by President Alfonsin on 27 August 1987. To cover the service in the interim, another local firm, EMEPA built new bodies on the frames of eight Subte cars dating from 1913. Despite their age, these worked well and enabled

In April 1991 a car leaves the terminus at Plaza de los Virreyes 1991, while an elderly bus comes in on the right. (Peter Haseldine)

the service to get off to a good start. The new cars arrived in 1988. These are double-ended, 15.8m long and 2.5m wide and can carry 138 passengers, 24 of them seated. There are single width doors at each end and a double width door in the centre. Electrical equipment is by Siemens.

Bibliography

Double-deck Trams of the World. Op.cit.
Los Tranvías de Buenos Aires. A.G. Podesta. Associacion Amigos del Tranvía, Buenos Aires, 1986.
Headlights vol.61, January-June 1999.
Strassenbahn Magazin no.121, 5/99.
Tramways and Urban Transit no.760, April 2001.

No.4000. (Author's collection)

GREAT BRITAIN

SINGLE-DECKERS

In 1970 a committee of councillors was set up in Blackpool to consider the future of the transport in the town and out of this came a decision to convert some trams to one-person operation, to allow more economical working of the winter service. Experiments with car 638, already mentioned, had shown some of the pitfalls and in this case the matter was considered much more carefully and the trade union was fully involved from the start. It was decided to convert thirteen of the second series English Electric railcoaches and this work was in due course carried out in the workshops between 1972 and 1976, the cars being re-numbered 1-13. Fortunately for the department's finances, these conversions were recognised by the Ministry of Transport as new vehicles and were thus eligible for grant aid. However, for reasons of economy, it was decided to lengthen the bodies simply by adding 90cm at each end, to give an overall length of 22.47m and creating a considerable amount of overhang. Despite this, there was not room enough on the front platform to accommodate more than three people and loading at busy stops was slow. The centre platform served now only as an exit and the capacity was 48 seated plus 16 standing. The extra length also imposed a strain on the bogies and from 1970 the springs were replaced by "Metalastik" rubber suspension, with a considerable improvement in the riding qualities of the

rebuilds. To raise public awareness of the new system of fare collection, these trams were initially turned out in an attractive livery of yellow and red, but the yellow did not wear well in the salt-laden air and was soon replaced by cream. A great deal of ingenuity went in to the rebuilding of these trams, for which the department deserved every credit, but they were not totally satisfactory and by the early 1980s were beginning to show their age. All were withdrawn in the 1990s, but no.8 has been preserved and is undergoing restoration.

It was therefore decided to order new cars and the question of purchase of modern European vehicles was considered, but rejected on grounds of cost and over-sophistication. Purchase of a prototype was authorised in 1982 and, as it had been decided to buy trams with bodies similar to those of a motorbus, tenders were requested from four builders of bus bodies. That of East Lancashire Coachbuilders, who had supplied many bus bodies to the undertaking, was successful. The cost was about £140,000, less

OMO car 7 picks up a good crowd in Fleetwood town centre in June 1979. Most prospective passengers have to wait in the roadway until there is room for them to board and pay their fare to the driver. (Author)

than half that of importing a car from Europe. These were the first completely new trams to be built in Britain for 32 years and electrically were based closely on the rebuilt double-deckers 761/2. The design was that of a double-ended car with front entrance and central exit, to be operated by one person. Many body parts, such as doors, windows and seats, were in common with those of the buses to reduce costs and keep down number of spare parts required. Chopper control manufactured by Brush was fitted and the truck frames were built locally by Stress Free Plastics Ltd, using English Electric motors and re-tyred wheels from cars of the 1930s. To give the operator a clear view of the saloon, the exits are

An interior view of an OMO car in January 1987. (Author)

No. 651 at Bispham in September 1985. (Author)

located off-centre and are therefore not opposite each other. It was planned to buy ten cars, but restrictions imposed on local authority spending by the Conservative government prevented this and only seven were acquired (641-647).

In 1984 GEC Traction approached Blackpool Corporation to discuss the possibility of buying one car of this type to be used at Blackpool to test new equipment. The result was car 651, delivered in April 1985. In practice this sophisticated equipment proved to be unreliable and in 1988 the car was sold to the undertaking, who converted it to standard design and renumbered it 648.

In recent years, this fleet has been substantially rebuilt by the undertaking's staff and the ends have been completely redesigned.

Technical details
Length 15.25m, width 2.45m, weight 17.3 tonnes, 2 x 42.5kW motors, 75 passengers, 55 seated. (In summer the number of standees was reduced to 12 to assist passenger flow.)

Bibliography
Modern Tramway nos.568/9, January/February 1985.

Blackpool's New Tramcars. D. Hyde. Tramway Museum Society, Crich, 1985.

Trams to the Tower. S. Palmer and P. Higgs. Lancastrian Transport Publications, Blackpool, 1990.

Blackpool by Tram. S. Palmer and B. Turner. Transport Publishing Company, Glossop, 1978.

Centenary car 646 as rebuilt, seen on the south promenade in October 2002. (Author)

DOUBLE-DECKERS

During the second world war, some elected members of Glasgow Corporation showed some interest in the development of a tram with separate entrance and exit and the transport department prepared some preliminary sketches, all of which showed that, within possible dimensions, this layout would result in an unacceptable loss of seating capacity. When in August 1945 the construction of an experimental car was authorised, it was decided that this would have to be of single-ended design to accommodate both the separate entrance and exit and also to house the modern equipment envisaged. Crompton Parkinson were closely involved in the preparation of the design and the car was fitted with that firm's Vambac control system. Construction began in January 1946 and the car was ready for service on 22 December 1947.

No.1005, as this tram became, was probably the most elegant and attractive vehicle ever to grace the rails of any British system. It carried a livery of three shades of blue and was fitted with comfortable uni-directional seats and fluorescent lighting, whose brilliance drew some complaints from the travelling public. Originally the passenger flow was from front to rear to reduce boarding accidents, but this arrangement seemed to cause some problems with motorists, who were surprised when passengers suddenly emerged at the rear, and in mid-1949 the layout was reversed. The electrical equipment worked well, after some teething troubles, but due to the close spacing of stops in Glasgow it could not really achieve its full potential and in August 1951 it was removed and replaced by conventional electro-pneumatic equipment. No.1005 was allocated to particular crews only and, when

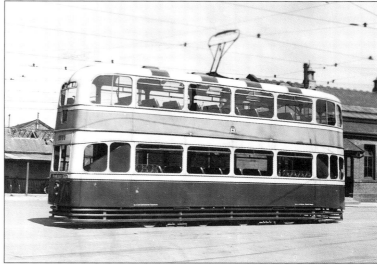
Glasgow 1005 at Newlands depot, still wearing its blue livery, on 19 June 1949. (M.H. Waller, courtesy Peter Waller)

staff shortages really began to be felt in the 1950s, it was often out of traffic for long periods at a time. In 1955/6 it was cheaply converted to normal layout and fitted with seats from scrapped Standard trams. As a result of the conversion it had the peculiarity of having ends of different designs and it completely lost its former elegance. It continued to run until May 1962 and one of its bogies is preserved in the city's transport museum.

This tram represented one of the very few

762 at Talbot Square in June 1979. (Author)

Blackpool 761 at Talbot Square in June 1983. (Author)

attempts to build a double-decker which was modern in both concept and equipment and few later cars have approached the standard of comfort offered by no.1005. But one car in a fleet of over 1,200 was unlikely to have much influence. Rather unscientific and inconclusive tests of boarding times were conducted, comparing this tram with conventional cars on the same services, but, given that the public was not used to the idea of separate entrance and exit, it is hardly surprising that this system failed to show any definite superiority over the normal practice. Had it survived it could have been an excellent prototype for a one-person operated double-decker, but this was not to be. It simply became another memorial to the vision of E.R. Fitzpayne, a vision not properly recognised at the time by local politicians.

In 1975, following the success of the one-man single-deck trams, it was decided by Blackpool Corporation that a double-deck tram should be similarly treated and accordingly, car 725, which had been laid up with body defects, was taken into the workshops for rebuilding. When the body had been stripped down to the frame, it was found that the latter was in fact in excellent condition, only the end sections showing significant deterioration. It was decided to rebuild the car with single, wide doorways at each front end; since the busiest stops on the tramway have separate unloading and loading positions, it was thought that it was not necessary to provide separate exits. New end sections were ordered from Metsec of Oldbury, a firm which had hitherto specialised in supplying bus bodies in kit form to overseas operators. New, forward-ascending staircases were fitted at each end of the car and alternate window pillars were removed. After some thoughts of fitting electro-pneumatic controllers it was decided to try chopper control, and railway-type disc brake units were fitted. The alterations increased the length of the car by 1.2m. Internally new, fixed seats for 98 passengers and fluorescent lighting were installed and a pantograph was fitted for current collection, the tram now being really too long for a trolley pole. As no.761 the tram entered service in July 1979 and proved to be successful, being used as a one-person car at times of light traffic and with a conductor at peak periods.

A second conversion from car 714 entered service in June 1982, as 762. In the light of experience, this car was given central exits and this necessitated repositioning the stairs to a place by the centre doors. Seating capacity was reduced to 94. With a view to probable future rebuildings, which would have had to involve outside contractors, it was decided that new bogie frames should be designed, which could be assembled by these. The contract was awarded to a local firm, Stress Free Plastics of Thornton. Suspension and braking were also altered, as no.761 had shown a tendency to roll.

Both cars, generally known as the "Jubilee" class, have worked well and reflect great credit on those who engineered the rebuilding, but in the event no others were similarly treated.

Bibliography
The Glasgow Tram. Op.cit.
Trams to the Tower. Op.cit.
Blackpool's New Tramcars. Op.cit.
Modern Tramway nos.502, October 1979. (Blackpool 761), 543, March 1983 (Blackpool 762).

CHINA AND VIETNAM

Ten bogie cars were built in Dalian in 1981/2 for that city (7001-10), ten for Changchun in 1983/4 (701-710), and thirteen (various numbers from 7053 upwards) for Anshan. Mechanical and electrical parts were made in the workshops of Dalianshi Jiatong Gongqi Dianche Gongchang (Dalian City Transport Company Electric Car Factory), and then taken to a bus assembly works for incorporation in the bodies. In 2000/1 ten new trams were built in Xiangtan for Changchun (801-810) but these seem to have been unsuccessful and most were already stored out of service in 2005. This operator also has a single, unnumbered car built in its own workshops around 1990 and in 2005 acquired a new car built in Shenyang. The cars in Dalian are no longer in service, having been outlasted by prewar Japanese bogie cars.

More recently, in 2002, a new, un-numbered car has appeared in Changchun.

In the mid-1980s, the engineers in Ha Noi made a gallant attempt to build a new design of tram for that rapidly-decaying system. Two bogie cars were created using bodies from ex-Zürich motor buses. The result was a single-ended car of somewhat angular, but attractive appearance

Changchun 703 and a local trolleybus on 17 June 1984. (M.J. Russell)

with three doorways. The source of the bogies is not known but they could have been taken from former central-entrance trailers. Unfortunately the new trams lasted only until 1989.

Bibliography
Modern Tramway/Tramways and Urban Transit, nos.566, February 1985, 568, April 1985 and 797, May 2004.
Blickpunkt Strassenbahn 3/2005.
Tramway Exotica No.1. OnLine Video. Op.cit.

SPAIN AND PORTUGAL

In 1943 the Societa Madrileòa de Tranvías held an international competition for the design of a new tramcar for the city, it being intended to buy 160 to begin reconstruction of the damaged and antiquated fleet. Although the times were hardly propitious, several firms took part and in the event, the choice fell on the Italian Fiat PCC-type car (qv).

Between 1944 and 1955 the local Maquitrans factory, which was owned by the transport undertaking of Barcelona, produced a total of 110 single-ended bogie cars (1200-1299 and 1301-1310), to two slightly varying designs. There had earlier been some idea of buying PCC cars but these foundered on financial grounds. However, the new trams were to an extent based on the PCC, modified to take account of Spain's economic conditions in the post-civil war years, and their construction reflected considerable credit on the undertaking. Four 33kW motors were fitted. They carried 93 passengers, 28 of these seated and in service generally pulled a two-axle trailer of vaguely matching design. At least one (1290) was rebodied in the mid-1960s, with a three-door body and PCC-style front end. It was planned to treat all of the class in this fashion, but all were scrapped between 1969 and 1971.

In Barcelona at Easter 1959 car 1290 is at the lower terminus of the Tibidabo line, one of whose cars can be seen in the background. AEC double-deck bus 439 is on the left. (Pam Eaton)

Otherwise there was little of modern design in Spain in this period. Between 1946 and 1949 Valencia acquired 70 motor cars (401-470) and nine matching trailers (301-309). These had air-operated doors and 21 were fitted with doors on the off-side only, for use on a line where passengers boarded from stops located between the tracks. These trams were allowed to deteriorate into an appalling state in the 1960s before meeting a merciful end in 1969/70.

One of the designs submitted in the 1943 competition was that by the firm, Carda y Escoriaza, which was financially connected to the undertakings of Cadiz and Zaragoza. The design was based on that of the Liège-Séraing bogie cars (qv) but with a more streamlined style of body and it was in due course ordered by both the undertakings mentioned above. They were delivered in five batches to Zaragoza, between 1945 and 1953 and took the numbers 201-218. The earlier cars had a double-width central door, but later deliveries had end doors only and the central door was later removed from some cars. There were other variations but in general seating capacity was 30 and a total of 102 passengers could be carried. They rode on Brill bogies and were comfortable trams, well liked by the public.

Eight were also delivered to Cadiz and when that system closed, these were transferred to Zaragoza (as 221-228), where they were kept in fairly good condition until closure in 1972. A total of eight have been preserved.

The Zaragoza manager, Sr A. Escoriaza, wanted to continue with the modernisation of the fleet, but by the late 1950s no manufacturer in Spain was willing to build any more trams. Having unsuccessfully investigated the possibility of buying surplus cars from Stuttgart, he finally acquired in 1958 seven bogie cars of 1913 from La Coruòa, where they had been used on a radial line to Sada. These were given new motors and new bodies of an attractive rounded outline, although rather narrow, and entered service from 1960 as 301-307. Although single-ended, they had front and rear doors on each side, since some stops were located on the left. They also ran until 1972 and nos.302 and 306 have been preserved.

The only bogie trams to be built in Portugal in the period under review were a batch of ten double-ended cars (901-910) for use on line 15, which appeared from the Lisbon workshops in 1947. They used Maley and Taunton equal wheel bogies which had been ordered in 1939. While comfortable, with 2+2 seating, they were not particularly modern and none is now in service.

Bibliography

Modern Tramway nos.191, November 1953 (Spain), 303/4, March/April 1963 (Barcelona), 330, June 1965 (Barcelona)

Web site of Asociacion Zaragozana de Amigos de Ferrocarril y Tranvías *The Tramways of Portugal.* Op.cit.

Els Tranvies de Barcelona (De 1929 ençà). A.G. Masip. R. Dalmau, Barcelona, 1998.

Zaragoza 217 crosses Plaza Paraiso in February 1958, with an ex-London Q1 class trolleybus in the background. (Ray DeGroote)

Zaragoza 301 at Parque terminus in February 1958. (Ray DeGroote)

A Lisbon bogie car in service on line 15 on Avenida 24 de Julho in 1972. (Author)

JAPAN

HOME MODELS

Kagoshima 2122, in service on 16 May 2004. (M.J. Russell)

Rather strangely, Japan had for many years very little to show in the way of modern bogie cars. Traditional cars were built well into the 1950s and these were in many cases made redundant by system closures and were then bought, while still almost new, by cities which had decided to keep their trams. Hakodate, for example, regularly bought trams from Tokyo, since both cities used the unusual gauge of 1372mm. Generally the cars were well built and had been very well maintained and this strong second-hand market killed off any remaining demand for new cars throughout the 1960s and 1970s.

There are today 20 systems in operation which may be classified as tramways, but many of these consist of one line only, or one main line with short branches and only a few cities have what could be termed a network. However, in Japan the problem of definition is more difficult than in any other country and there are other lines, not dealt with here, which some sources would also consider to be tramways.

Working from north to south, the system of Hakodate on Hokkaido has used only bogie cars since the Second World War and most of these have been of very conservative design. However, in 1993 two new cars of more modern outline were delivered. Sapporo, the other tramway city on Hokkaido, has only one line, on which run some modern three-phase cars dating from 1985, as well as many older bogie trams, five of which received new bodies in 2000.

The main island of Honshu still has 13 tramway operators, including two single lines in each of Tokyo and Kyoto. In the former, the Arakawa line has 45 bogie cars built between 1955 and 1962 but rebuilt in 1977, and five much newer cars with three-phase equipment delivered in the early 1990s. All operate from high platforms, and the remaining sections of street running are being converted to reserved track at the present time. The Setagaya line runs coupled sets of bogie cars. In Kyoto, the Keihan line has six bogie cars dating from 1979-81 (501-506), which normally operate in coupled pairs. The other line, Arashiyama line has some street track and operates 29 bogie cars built between 1972 and 1996, on a pay-as-you-leave system.

Technical details

Tokyo Municipal Transport Bureau 7000 class, as rebuilt
Length 12.5m, width 2.2m, weight 15.5 tonnes, 2 x 60kW motors, 96 passengers*, 22 seated.
Keihan Electric RR 501 class
Length 14.2m, width 2.35m weight 23.5 tonnes, 4 x 60kW motors, 95 passengers*, 46 seated.

Toyama 8001 is one of the modern bogie cars on this system. (M.J. Russell)

The system of Gifu closed on 31 March 2005 and it is likely that two of its modern bogie cars were sold to Toyohashi.

The Hiroshima Electric Railway Company has the largest urban tramway in Japan and runs a varied fleet of over 200 cars, which includes some modern bogie cars dating from 1982. There is also a KSW car which was a gift from Hannover in 1990. As it lacks air conditioning it runs only in winter! Both of the two eight-axle cars acquired from Dortmund in 1981 still exist in a depot, one being serviceable.

Kumamoto 8504 in Tokyo, May 2004. (M.J. Russell)

Toyohashi 3501 shows the older design of bogie car. Two even older vehicles, 3201 and another, wait in the siding to the left, 26 May 2004. (M.J. Russell)

Car 711 of the Hankai line in Osaka, seen on 22 May 2004. (M.J. Russell)

Kochi 2002 is one of the few modern cars in the fleet and was photographed on 21 May 2004. (M.J. Russell)

Gifu 1803 in the city centre. (M.J. Russell)

Technical details

Nagoya RR 880 class
Length 20.6m, width 2.23m, weight 25.6 tonnes, 4 x 38kW motors, 100 passengers*, 48 seated.

Hiroshima 701
Length 13.5m, width 2.45m, weight 20 tonnes, 2 x 52kW motors, 91 passengers*, 37 seated.

The very small system (4.7km) in Okayama has some modern bogie cars dating from 1984 and, starting in 1982, rebodied eight other cars acquired second-hand. All these have air conditioning. The Hankai Electric Tramway in the south suburbs of Osaka has twelve modern bogie cars dating from 1988 which form a contrast to the rest of the 55-strong fleet, which includes some veterans dating from 1928. The Kaetsuno Railroad Company in Takaoka in western Honshu has some modern cars.

Toyama has a one-line system of only 6.4km length and on it runs a fleet of 17 bogie cars dating from 1951 and the mid-1960s along with five modern cars dating from 1993. Toyohashi made transport history in Japan by opening in 1982 the first new tramway for many years, although it is only 6km long. However, it has used 15 second-hand cars and at present it has only two modern bogie cars, bought from Gifu and placed in service in 2006.

Technical details

Okayama rebodied car 7001
Length 12.2m, width 2.22m, weight 16.5 tonnes, 2 x 37kW motors, 96 passengers*, 34 seated.

On Kyushu island there are five systems. Kumamoto placed its first modern bogie cars in service in 1982 (8201/2). These have steel bodies of a totally different outline to traditional Japanese trams, of rather square appearance and came from the factory of the Nihon Rolling Stock Company. The LHB cars for Braunschweig are probably the nearest European equivalents. These had one single motor of 120kW. In 1985 four old cars were rebuilt with new bodies (8501-04), retaining the end and central door layout. In 1988 two additional new cars were bought from the Alna Koki company of Amagaski. These have three-phase equipment and regenerative braking, supplied by Mitsubishi. End doors only are fitted. All 44 cars in the fleet are air conditioned. There are now 14 new or rebodied cars in the fleet.

Technical details

Car 8801
Length 13.7m width 2.36m, weight 19 tonnes, 1 x 120kW motor, 72 passengers, 36 seated.

Another line in this area runs from Orio to Kumamihsi, but again the bogie cars are elderly. The capital of the island, Kagoshima, has a few new bogie cars from the first half of the 1990s and some older cars have been given new bodies. It has now taken delivery of low floor cars of a design seen only in Japan, in which the low floor central section is suspended between two end bogies. Finally there is Nagasaki, with a relatively large fleet of 75 bogie trams, of which about a dozen have been built new since a prototype (2001), built by Kawasaki, was unveiled on 25 July 1980. Along with the articulated car for Hiroshima (3501), this was intended to be a new standard design for Japan.

Technical details

Nagasaki 2001
Length 11.7m, width 2.6m, weight 17 tonnes, 1 x 120kW motors, 66 passengers 22 seated.

On Shikoku the small system of Kochi has a few new bogie cars, although most of its fleet dates from the 1950s. The most interesting aspect of this fleet, however, is its collection of European trams. This consists of a two-axle car from Graz (original number 204), a two-axle and a bogie car from Lisbon (533 and 910), two-axle car 541 and trailer 1606 from Wien, Peter Witt 1612 from Milan, Oslo (299) and Prag (6319). There is also a Stuttgart GT4 car rebuilt into double-ended layout by using halves of cars 714 and 735. Usually at least one of these appears each day in normal service. Another operator on Shikoku is Matsayuma, but there are no cars here more modern than the 1960s, although the fleet is maintained in excellent condition.

Bibliography

Modern Tramway no.531, March 1982 (Nagasaki and Hiroshima), no.618, June 1989 (Kumamoto).
The Latest Light Rail Vehicles in the World. Japan Tramway Society, 1983.

EXPORTS

PHILADELPHIA

By the late 1970s, the South Eastern Pennsylvania Transportation Authority (SEPTA), which had taken over both the city system (CTD) and the radial Red Arrow lines (RAD), was faced with the task of renewing almost all of its fleet. The PCC cars on the City Transit Division had been worked to the bone for many years, with minimal maintenance, and on the Red Arrow Division increasing traffic was taxing the elderly fleet. Having backed out of the project for a US standard car, modified for the gauge of 1581mm, the operator turned to Kawasaki in March

One of the city cars being prepared for service in October 1980. (Author)

1979 and awarded a contract for 112 single-ended bogie cars (9000-9111) for the former section and 29 double-ended cars (100-128) for the latter. The entire contract was worth US$67.2m, of which 80% was financed by the federal and state governments. The first body shell arrived in Philadelphia in 29 July 1980. Completion took place at the local Boeing plant, where sufficient components were fitted to comply with the "Buy American" law of 1971. Entry to service took place in May and August 1981 respectively. The CTD cars have front and centre doors while the RAD cars have double-width doors at each leading end and a single-width door at the other. Internally the design was light and spacious, though the seating was rather basic. Despite the very poor condition of the track at that time, the cars performed well and the bogies displayed excellent road-holding qualities. Nonetheless, improvements to pointwork had to be undertaken. The Faivley pantographs on the RAD cars could not cope with the loosely-strung overhead and, after several dewirements and some damage to the motors, the coil supports of these had to be altered. Thereafter there were no problems, but no other US system adopted the design.

Technical details
CTD and RAD cars
Length 15.24m, width 2.59m, weight 26 tonnes, 4 x 61kW motors, 51 seats.
Length 16.16m, width 2.7m, weight 27 tonnes, 4 x 61kW motors, 50 seats.

Bibliography
Der Stadtverkehr. 5/6/1982
The Latest Light Rail Vehicles in the World. Op.cit.

No.109 is seen at North Street stop on the Sharon Hill line, while working an enthusiasts' tour in 1982. (Jim D. Schantz)

EGYPT SINGLE-DECKERS

In Heliopolis Abdul the pointsman takes a break while car 925 and another run past on the straight and, in the left background, some children put on a display for the benefit of the camera, 10 December 2003. (M.J. Russell)

From 1976 onwards Kinki Sharyo delivered a series of 140 bogie trams, coupled in pairs, to the Cairo Transport Authority (CTA) (6001+6002-6139+6140), of which the last thirty cars were built locally by SEMAF – General Egyptian Company for Railway Wagons and Coaches, using components supplied from Japan. A further 35 sets (6501-6570) followed at a later date but seem to have been out of service by 1991. Some of the 600x sets were sent to Helwan when that system opened in 1981. These cars have a broad front end, a cream livery with red lining and seating is wooden and entirely longitudinal. From 1979 a series of cars with a slightly tapered front end design were delivered by the same builder and took the numbers 4001+4002-4189+4190. These were followed by 40 further sets built in Egypt (4191+4192 to 4269+4270). These were slightly more comfortable, having some 2+1 transverse seating.

Rather similar cars, but operating in three-car trains, are used in Heliopolis by the Heliopolis Housing and Development Company. These

Cairo 6032/6031 in service in Helwan on 31 October 2004. (M.J. Russell)

Cairo 4262/4261 reverse at el Mataria crossover on 14 December 2003. (M.J. Russell)

have 2+2 upholstered seating and louvres over the upper parts of the windows. The first imports from Japan were 20 solo motor cars (301-320) in 1962, which were out of service by 1991. Five years later 65 single-ended, double-sided cars (401-465) arrived for operation as back-to-back two-car sets, with one spare car. These were 15.8m long and 2.4m wide. In 1971 cars 501-540 were delivered, for use as three-car sets with one spare car, thirteen of the cars being non-driving motors. Later arrivals were 601-632 in 1974, 701-728 in 1975, 801-836 in 1976, 901-936 in 1980 and 1001-1039 in 1982. All these were built to run as four-car sets with two non-driving motors, but have now been altered as three-car sets, with a consequent break in the numbering system. At least 15 of these later deliveries were built in Egypt under licence by the SEMAF factory, but it is impossible to say which these are. Finally three three-car sets numbered from 1101-1109 arrived in 1988/9, these being built in Egypt. In 1993 this operator was taken over by the CTA and some Cairo cars of the 4xxx class made redundant by closures in that city have appeared on local services in Heliopolis.

In 1982 the first of a class of 30 trams was delivered by Kinki Sharyo to Alexandria, for use on the city lines. The last ten were built under licence in Egypt. These cars are single-ended, with doors on both sides, and work in coupled pairs (101+102-129+130). Unlike the previous type they have tapered ends and are not unlike the cars delivered by Ganz (qv). Eight sets have been fitted with a pantograph, in place of the usual trolley, to allow them to work through on to the Ramleh line and have been renumbered 1101-1116. Thirty-six three-car sets similar to the Heliopolis trams were built from 1975 onwards for the Ramleh radial line (101-208). These work with a double-sided, single-ended motor car at the outer ends of each set, with a double-ended, double-sided trailer between.

All these cars have proved to be robust, if rather basic in their interior appointments. All have a maximum speed of 60 or 65km/hr, but it is doubtful if they ever achieve anything like this in service, except perhaps on the line linking Cairo to Heliopolis. However, details of all Egyptian rolling stock are subject to correction and it is not known how many of the above are still in service.

Technical details
Alexandria 101
Length 12.9m, width 2.3m, weight 19.9 tonnes, 4 x 42 kW motors, 137 passengers*, 35 seated.
Cairo 4001
Length 15.8m, width 2.5m, weight 21/5 tonnes, 4 x 54kW motors, 163 passengers*, 44 seated.
Heliopolis 501
Length 15.8m, width 2.4m weight 21.7 tonnes, 4 x 52kW motors, 157 passengers*, 40 seated.

Alexandria 127 and 128, coupled to another set, 12 December 2003. (M.J. Russell)

EGYPT DOUBLE-DECKERS

Car 224 is at the head of a set comprising also trailer 225 and single-deck motor 226, on 12 December 2003. (M.J. Russell)

In 1995 Kinki Sharyo delivered to Alexandria the world's newest double-deck trams, with matching single-deckers, for use on the Ramleh line, there being a long tradition of using this type of tram there. These are single-ended, double-sided motorised control trailer cars and run in six three-car sets, with a double-sided and double-ended single-deck trailer in the middle and a single-deck, single-ended motor car at the other end. Numbers are 209-226, the double-deckers being 209, 212, 215, 218, 221 and 224.

Three double-width doors are fitted on each side and two straight staircases give access to the upper deck. A seat is provided for the conductor, but only for use when he is not collecting fares! These cars must hold the world record for the number of passengers carried on a bogie tram.

Technical details
Length 16.4m, width 2.6m, weight 30 tonnes, 4 x 52kW motors, 334 passengers*, 92 seated (64/28).

Bibliography
Strassenbahn Magazin nos.104, December 1996, 147, January 2002.
The Latest Light Rail Vehicles in the World. Op.cit.
Light Rail and Modern Tramway nos.649, January 1992, 698, February 1996.
Der Stadtverkehr 3/1982 (Alexandria), 2/2005 (Cairo and Heliopolis).
Double-deck Trams of the World. Op.cit.

AUSTRALIA

This country had one very individual bogie car, Adelaide MTT no.381, built by J. Lawton of Adelaide in 1953. It was intended to be the prototype of a fleet of 40, but a change in policy meant that it would remain a one-off. It ran in service only until 1957 and was then stored until donated for preservation in 1965. As a large and comfortable car, it showed what could have been done, had tram-scrapping not come into fashion. It could also have been worked as a Peter Witt car, or by one operator, but in service it ran with the traditional itinerant conductor.

Technical details
Length 17.16m, width 2.6m, weight 26.4 tonnes, 4 x 48kW motors, 184 passengers, 52 seated.

Bibliography
Destination Paradise. R.T. Wheaton, Australian Electric Traction Association, Sydney, 1975.

No.381 at St Kilda museum on 14 March 1993. (Author)

CHAPTER 9

ARTICULATED CARS

SIX-AXLE DESIGNS

PROTOTYPES

The principle of articulating two rail vehicles together using a common central bogie was first developed in Germany by one Dr W. Jakob – then head of Rastatt, a rolling stock manufacturer – and was patented in 1901. In the following year it was applied to passenger carriages of the KPEV – Königliche Preussische Eisenbahn Verwaltung (Royal Prussian Railway Administration). The main advantage then claimed for this form of construction was that it gave a smoother ride and thus increased passenger comfort. Over the next twenty years it was successfully applied to a variety of railway carriages, including one of the prototype sets for the electrification of the S-Bahn in Berlin in 1924 and many carriages built by H.N. Gresley for the Great Northern Railway in England.

The first application to tramway technology came in 1920/1, when the Milwaukee Electric Railway Company, under the management of Sylvester B. Way, rebuilt some fairly elderly bogie cars into six-axle configuration. The main reason for this development was the rise in costs, including that of electric current, following the First World War. The vehicle which resulted was 27.23m long and offered 93 seats, with room for almost 100 standees. The result seems to have been successful and there were ultimately about 200 articulated cars in the fleet, for urban and radial use, some cars in the latter category being fitted out as dining cars. Other North American cities copied the idea but only in Baltimore and Cleveland were there any substantial numbers of such cars, 38 and 28 respectively. Those in the former were all rebuilds of fairly ancient cars, in which the two sections were linked by a primitive drum articulation. The 28 cars (5000-5027) in Cleveland were built new in 1928/9 by the Kuhlman Car Company, to a very high internal standard, as a development of the Peter Witt design (qv). They seated 104 passengers in a unit 30.78m long. They had a slightly improved drum

Duisburg 177, ex-1177 at the main depot, October 1985. Author)

connection, the diameter of which was 1.37m, but there was still a bottleneck within the car, although schoolchildren apparently enjoyed riding in it. In practice these trams were worked as two units, each half with its own conductor. Unusually each bogie was motored, and total weight was in the region of 34.5 tonnes. With only six 22kW motors, the 5000 class was rather sluggish in service and heavy on current, but they ran smoothly and were generally well liked by passengers. However, they had only just entered service when the onset of the economic depression reduced ridership drastically and some were stored for a few years. They really came into their own in the war years, when their great capacity proved extremely useful, and the last survived until the end of rail service in 1952. The Baltimore cars were equally long-lived, probably to the dismay of their passengers. In 1926 the Washington, Baltimore and Annapolis interurban system placed in service ten very fine cars which often reached 110 km/hr on the express part of the network. The cross-bay Key System in San Francisco and Oakland also operated the design, though more as Stadtbahn or light rail vehicles than as trams. North American articulated trams used either a flexible bellows connection, as in railway carriages, or a metal drum, and in neither case was there an unrestricted passage between the sections. None of these cars had any influence on later designs, though an article on the Cleveland cars was published in the German technical press in 1929.

In Europe the first steps towards the operation of trams of this design had already been taken, since in 1926 the firm of Harkort delivered the first of two cars (176/7) to Duisburg, using as the basis of the design the steel two-axle cars supplied to the operator in 1925. This firm was basically a supplier of goods wagons to railways, but in the post-1918 world demand

A close-up view of the articulation on car 177, ex-1177. (Author)

was falling and, rather than lay off employees, it was decided to try to break into the tramway field. There may also have been a connection with Linke-Hoffmann-Bush. It was expected that these cars would be loss-leaders, but it was hoped that future orders would make up for this, a hope destined to remain unfulfilled. There was considerable interest in the technical press when the cars began trials in March 1926, with entry into passenger service in July. The cost per car was Reichsmark 17,271, which would roughly equate to £1,700.

Length was 20.95m, width 2.2m and the two parts of the body were linked by a flexible bellows connection. As the clear width in this passage was only 1m, it was not envisaged that passengers or crew would normally stand there or pass from one part of the tram to the other and each section had its own conductor. The cars were double-ended and one of the main advantages claimed was the avoidance of shunting at termini. It was also hoped the trams would be smooth riding and speedier than a tram/trailer set. While they certainly came up to expectations with regard to the former, they most definitely did not do so as far as speed was concerned, since they had only two 35kW motors and were

Cleveland 5005 at Public Square not long before the end of service. (Lars F. Richter collection

An off-side view of Duisburg 1176 during its days as a party car, May 1981. (Author)

NZH car 603/4 at Leiden station in September 1959. (Author)

Key System 167, as preserved at the Orange Empire Railway Museum, Perris CA, October 1987. (Author)

sluggish in service. The central bogie was also prone to derailment on curves, the brakes had to be altered and the controllers gave trouble. Re-equipment at the end of 1926 with four 30kW motors per car cured the first problem, but the latter remained and the cars saw little service until after the Second World War, which both survived. Shortage of rolling stock in the late 1940s saw them in daily service, with rather fewer problems. They were therefore considered worth rebuilding between 1955 and 1957 with new control equipment, new folding doors and new motors of 37.5kW. They were now laid out for passenger flow with a seated conductor. In this form, latterly as 1176 and 1177, they ran until 1969 when both were retired. Car 1176 was rebuilt with a horribly garish livery for use as a party tram, while its twin, 1177, was set aside as a source of spare parts. However, on 16 February 1983 1176 was burned out due to a short circuit and on inspection it was found that 1177 was not so far gone as to preclude a return to active service, also as a party tram, though with the former Duisburg cream and green livery restored. It is to be hoped that this historically important tram will be preserved when its running days are finally over.

Strangely in view of later British distrust of articulated buses, it was to be on a British-controlled system that the next design of articulated tram was to appear. In 1927 English Electric and Blackpool Corporation drew up a design for an articulated car to be used on the Fleetwood tramroad. This was a six-axle car, 17.7m long (over fenders) with seating for 54 passengers on 2+1 seating. There would have been a drum connection between the two sections and double-width doorways at each end. Clerestory roofs gave a rather old-fashioned appearance, although it should be remembered that these were in favour on contemporary single-deck buses. In the event, Blackpool opted for the "Pantograph" bogie cars and no more was heard of the idea, but some of the planning may have gone into the first three K class trams (307-309) for the Calcutta Tramways Company, which appeared from English Electric in 1931. The main reason for choosing articulated trams was to provide increased capacity, without the complexity of trailer operation, with which the CTC had experienced some problems. In this case, however, there was no need to consider any connection between the two parts of the body, since CTC operated a two-class fare system and articulation provided an easy means of segregating passengers. However, a modern feature was the accessibility of the entrances, since these had a single step, of only 35cm height above rail level. The platforms were ramped transversely and a single step of 23cm led into each saloon, the floors of which sloped gently upwards to the ends of the car. Two conductors were carried and posts for them were provided in the entrances. To cope with some fairly tight curves on the system the middle bogie had to be specially constructed, fitted with radial plates and underslung springs. Flexible rubber bellows prevented anyone being trapped between the two body sections. The articulated cars worked well in practice and by 1939 the class totalled 183. They lasted until at least the 1980s and some were lengthened to increase capacity. Further classes were built, the last only recently. However, the idea was not followed up, either on other Indian systems, in Britain, or any other country of the-then empire.

The same principle was used on ten extremely comfortable trams built in 1932 by Beynes for the NZH undertaking in the Netherlands. In this case articulation was adopted to circumvent restrictions placed on the length of a tram/trailer set imposed by the municipality of Haarlem and, perhaps to fool the authorities, each half of a car was given its own number. Numbers therefore

The standard Urbinati articulation, as seen on a post-war car of ATAC Rome in 1999, contrasting with the narrow connection on a Key System car, as preserved, with an internal view of the latter. (Author)

Rome STEFER 405 in 1972. (Jim D. Schantz)

Calcutta 305 in Chowringhee Square when new. (English Electric, author's collection)

ferred to Leiden. Ironically, the cars were scrapped when NZH tram services came to an end in 1961, just as large-scale use of articulated trams had become common.

There was no immediate successor in northern Europe and it is to Italy that one must look for the second stage in the development of the concept. In the late 1930s, Sr Mario Urbinati, manager of the suburban STEFER tramway in Rome improved the basic Jakob design to give a wider articulation, almost the same width as the rest of the vehicle. This was achieved by the use of a drum, as in Baltimore, but this drum was halved vertically, each half revolving on a vertical axis and able to twist and turn against the adjacent parts of the body, to which it was connected by a system of rods. The two sections were connected by strips of rubber, while the gap in the floor was covered by a moveable circular plate. This form of construction allowed the articulation to move against each half of the body in the vertical, and to a lesser extent, the horizontal planes, while also allowing the entire tram

to be worked as one unit, with one conductor, and to allow free passage between the two parts.

The first trams to be built to this design were STEFER 401 and 402, which came into service in 1939. They were built by Stanga with electro-pneumatic equipment by BBC. They were 20.5m long and could carry 175 passengers, of whom 36 were seated. The conductor had a seated position by the rear door and the platform there was large enough to accommodate 40 people. Although both trams were damaged in air raids, they were rebuilt and, as they had proved to be so successful, a production batch of ten (403-412) appeared in 1942. There was also a post-war series, numbered from 501 to 508, and fitted with pedal instead of hand control. Fortunately three of the original design (401, 402, 404) have been preserved. The 500 class was sold to the city tramways of ATAC and the cars are still in service as class 71xx.

Technical details
EE cars for Calcutta
Length 16.75m, width 2.13m, 2 x 82.5kW motors, 122 passengers, 43 seated.
NZH cars
Length 21m, width 2.38m, 4 x 53kW motors, 136 passengers.

Bibliography

Modern Tramway nos. 337/8/9, January-March 1966 (North America), 451, July 1975 (Blackpool design), 480, December 1977 (Calcutta).

Der Stadtverkehr 3/1986 (Duisburg Harkort cars).

Cleveland Transit through the Years, op.cit.

Strassenbahn Magazin nos.56, May 1985 (Duisburg 1177) and 59, February 1986 (North America).

Die deutschen Strassenbahn-Gelenkwagen. D. Höltge. Kolhammer Edition Eisenbahn, Stuttgart, 1983.

New Tramcars for Calcutta. English Electric Co. Ltd, Preston, 1931.

ran from 601/2 to 619/20. They had four 53 kW motors and a good turn of speed; outwith Haarlem they normally pulled one trailer and sometimes two. Again the experiment was successful, though they operated on radial lines rather than a city tramway. They were later trans-

POST-WAR GERMAN SIX-AXLE TRAMS

SINGLE-ENDED DESIGNS

It was not until 1952 that there was any attempt to copy the design in Germany. In that year, Professor Bockemühl, who in 1950 had moved to the west to become technical director of the board of Stuttgarter Strassenbahn, decided to order three prototype trams from Fuchs of Heidelberg (no.2,) and the Maschinenfabriek

One of Stuttgart's cars in service, approaching the Hauptbahnhof. (F.W. Hunt, courtesy London Area, Light Rail Transit Association)

Esslingen (nos.1, 3), Düwag having declined the order as there was no spare capacity. Two, nos. 1 and 3, had four AEG motors of 56kW and the other had BBC motors of 48kW. The reason for the choice of articulated trams lay in the topography of the city, with some routes having steep gradients and severe curvature. It was possible with an articulated design to achieve the capacity of a bogie car with a trailer, a formation which would not have been practicable in Stuttgart. The new trams varied slightly in the details of their design but their elegant, rounded outline all showed the influence of Bockemühl's ideas and still retained something of the Dresden Hechtwagen. They carried a maximum of 220 passengers and could accelerate swiftly and maintain a high average speed. Because of the complicated fare structure, they were worked as two units, with a conductor in each portion. They proved to be heavy on maintenance and, because of their length of 25m, could not work on every line. Two further cars (4, 5) were delivered from Esslingen in 1958, these having 2 x 112kW Siemens motors, mounted under the floor and linked to the bogies by cardan drive. All were

successful but required considerable maintenance. It is not clear why so long a time elapsed between the appearance of the five prototypes and it seems that there may have been some kind of disagreement about the design behind the closed doors of the SSB. In any event, work had already begun on the development of the GT4 design (qv), which made them obsolete at an early date and all were scrapped between 1966 and 1969, none being preserved.

Technical details
Car 1
Length 24.96m, width 2.2m, weight 26.4 tonnes, 4 x 56kW motors, 220 passengers, 61 seated.

It was left to the Düwag factory, in conjunction with the Rheinbahn undertaking of Düsseldorf and Bogestra of Bochum, to develop and place in service the definitive version of the articulated tram. The reason for the adoption of the concept in these cases lay in the manpower shortages which were beginning to affect every undertaking in the Federal Republic, as the "economic miracle" got under way. On 14 February 1956

Stuttgart 3 had clearly fallen on hard times when photographed in the depot yard. (F.W. Hunt, courtesy London Area, Light Rail Transit Association)

The classic articulated car in its home city. Rheinbahn Düsseldorf 2413 and trailer at Jan Wellem Platz on line 5 to Neuss in July 1979. (Author)

Rheinbahn trailer 1653 at Auf 'm Hennekamp on 10 June 2005. (Author)

The metre gauge version is exemplified by Mannheim 412 at Marktplatz in June 1985. (Author)

East meets West at Gotha Hauptbahnhof in July 1996. Ex-Mannheim 318 is on the left and contrasts with Tatra KT4D 306 on the right. Behind is another ex-Mannheim car, 412. (Author)

both undertakings placed in service the first examples – Düsseldorf 2501 and Bochum 250 – of what was to become one of the world's most successful tram designs, a design which saved many German systems from extinction and was to be adopted in many other countries. In Düsseldorf, two articulated trams, each carrying 181 passengers, could be used to replace a three-car tram-trailer set (291 passengers) on the busy line 1, allowing an increase in capacity of 28.5% while still requiring only the same number of staff. Superior acceleration and braking capacity also allowed these trams to integrate better with the growing motor traffic and the increasing number of traffic lights, there being then no question of priority at these.

Externally, the design had something in common with the North American PCC car, with a sloping windscreen and folding doors. But the technology of motors and control equipment was firmly based on the success of the manufacturer's bogie trams (qv), combined with an adapted version of the Urbinati articulation, in which the connecting rods were replaced by a simple connection to the frame of the car, with some slight loss of flexibility. Earlier cars had two 90kW motors, later versions two 150kW motors. Passengers with season tickets entered by the front door and these were checked by the driver. The conductor had a fixed post by the rear entrance doors and the total capacity was around 180 passengers. When these trams were worked with a bogie trailer, about 270 passengers could be handled by a crew of three, thus giving substantial savings in labour costs. In later years, the cars were converted to one-person operation and worked with conductorless trailers, with even more impressive savings. Modifications to the door and step mechanisms, with push-button operation of the former by Düwag allowed this to be done with complete safety. A simplification of the tariff to give a flat fare helped to streamline the system. The Rheinbahn ultimately had 60 such trams.

A total of 603 cars of this design was supplied to 19 undertakings in the-then Federal Republic between 1956 and 1967, most actually being

Mannheim has enlarged its six-axle cars to eight-axle with a low floor centre section. The work was carried out in 1991/2 and the cars concerned, renumbered 501-523, were given a green and white livery. No.520 approaches the Hauptbahnhof in June 1996. (Author)

Mannheim 468 shows the later design, seen in June 1985 at Wasserturm stop, with the city's famous water tower in the background. (Author)

placed in service between 1956 and 1964. Krefeld bought a further 14 between 1972 and 1974, long after a new design had appeared. Wuppertal was the only system to try the design without buying it. There were some detail differences to suit local requirements – Heidelberg, for example, bought cars with a single door on the off-side for use on line 11 – but in general there was a fair degree of standardisation. Over 200 trams were later rebuilt as eight-axle cars when that design was placed in service. Of the 19 systems concerned, Kiel closed at a later date and Neuss was absorbed into Düsseldorf, and from the other 17 only three still operated cars of this

Würzburg 270 (ex-Hagen) in the city centre in July 1996 is one of the rebuilds from double-ended layout. (Author)

Frankfurt (M) 619 is about to receive some attention from the breakdown gang at Ostbahnhof in June 1980. (Author)

Würzburg 245 (as enlarged to eight-axle layout) shows the sharply tapered front end as it waits in the loop at Sanderau terminus in June 1985. (Author)

Copenhagen 867 waits at Kongens Nytorv in April 1971. (Author)

Helsinki 65 in June 1983. (Author)

Birseckbahn 115 approaches Heuwaage stop in Basel city centre in September 1989. (Author)

Oslo 108 is outbound on line 9 in June 1983. (Author)

Bochum 208, a rebuild of a Grossraumwagen car is seen approaching Essen Hauptbahnhof in August 1971. (Author)

type in 2002, the pioneer Düsseldorf, Ludwigshafen and Gotha, which acquired cars from Mannheim. The last five in Düsseldorf were withdrawn, without ceremony, in January 2003, leaving Gotha and Ludwigshafen as the only operators of this classic type in Germany at the end of 2004. Many, however, are still in service as second-hand bargains in Eastern Europe. Cars of this type are now running in Arad, Brasov, Iasi and Timisoara in Romania and in Eblag, Poznan and Szeczin in Poland. The pioneer car of the Rheinbahn has been preserved, but at present is not in running order.

Technical details
Standard Düsseldorf design
Length 19.1m, width 2.2m, weight 19.3 tonnes, 2 x 100kW motors, 181 passengers, 43 seated.

A modified version was later built for Mannheim in 1969 and 1971 (451-470) and this was also ordered by Braunschweig in 1973 (7351-7358). The latter trams were fitted with equipment to allow them to operate in double traction, the controller in the leading car operating that in a second. This form of operation was, in the event, not put into practice. The main difference from earlier cars lay in the higher windows and windscreen. All of these are still in service but the

Mannheim cars are likely to be replaced in the near future and indeed five have already gone to Zagreb and three to Görlitz. These last did not remain for long in service, but one has been rebuilt into a party tram. In 2005 four (453, 455-7) were rather surprisingly sold to Helsinki to cover a temporary shortage due to problems with low floor cars. In Braunschweig, car 7762 was fitted with a low floor centre section of very ungainly design in 2002 and, following successful trials, it has been decided to order similar sections for between four and seven cars of this type, depending on price.

The Düwag six-axle design was also exported. After trials with a Düsseldorf car, Copenhagen took 100 (801-900) and would have taken a further 150 if political changes had not brought about a decision to abandon that system. When that decision was taken, the almost-new trams were sold to Alexandria for use on the city lines, where most of them still operate, still with their original numbers. Two have now returned to Denmark for preservation. One of the Copenhagen cars (840) ran comparative trials on line 16 in Brussels in August 1962 against PCC articulated car (then 7501). In 1964/5 Rotterdam bought 24 cars (251-274) some parts of which, such as the front body section and the motor bogies, were actually built in the Netherlands by Werkspoor. These cars were later rebuilt to eight-axle configuration. Basel BVB acquired 55 cars (603-658), based on the version supplied to Würzburg. Of these, 18 have now gone to Beograd and four have been transferred to the suburban BLT system.

The design was also built abroad under licence. In Austria, this was by Lohner,

Oslo 139 passes the National Theatre in August 1991. (Author)

RHB trailer 1055 at Mannheim, Marktplatz in June 1985. (Author)

Hannover cars were unusual in that the middle bogie was not equidistant between the two end bogies, as seen on car 514 at Steintor in 1985. (Author)

Rotterdam 651, an ex-Wien E1 class car and still in that operator's livery, working on line 2 in March 2003. (Author)

Wien E2 4057 at Siebenhirten terminus of line 64 in September 1987, before this section was converted to Stadtbahn operation. (Author)

Rotax and SGP. Graz took 23 cars (261-283), with bogies fitted with two 55kW motors, mounted transversely. These were built by Lohner (six cars) and SGP (17) between 1963 and 1966 and had Düwag doors and articulations. In 1972 car 262 became the first tram in the world to be fitted with thyristor control, in a trial which turned out successfully. Linz also acquired seven cars (61-67) from Lohner in 1970/1 but the restriction imposed by the gauge of 900mm led to their being rebuilt as eight-axle cars just three years later. Innsbruck bought seven cars (71-77) from Lohner in 1966. Wien became one of the major operators of the type. The first of class E, no.4401, was built by Lohner with Kiepe electrical equipment and arrived on 6 July 1959. A second prototype, (4402) with Siemens equipment followed in December of the same year. Series production began in 1961 and ultimately there were 89 cars of this class, with 2 x 110kW motors. Numbers were 4401-4459 and 4601-4630. An improved version, class E1, with 2 x 150kW motor power, followed from 1966 and

ran to 338 cars by the time production finished in 1976. These are numbered between 4461-4560 and 4631-4868, but the exact numbering scheme, which is governed by the type of electrical equipment fitted, is too complex to be given here. These were followed between 1977 and 1987 by class E2 of the Mannheim type, of which there were 120 examples (4001-4098 and 4301-4324). All these had Düwag monomotor bogies. In Innsbruck, twelve eight-axle cars (31-42) which had been acquired from Bielefeld lost their middle sections to become six-axle cars, though one (32) was later re-converted with a new middle section, also from Bielefeld. This has been fitted out for the carriage of bicycles and this tram, now renumbered 53, is the regular performer on line 6 to Igls. The earlier cars in Wien are now being withdrawn and in 2003 twelve – ten of class E1 and two of class E – were sold to the RET of Rotterdam. Although that undertaking had operated similar cars for many years, the new arrivals gave many problems and one was involved in a serious rear-end collision.

Basel, the Swiss firm of Schindler built 15 cars (101-115) in two batches in 1971/72 and 1975/76; air suspension for the bogies allows excellent riding qualities. They have heavier bodies of a quite different, but very attractive, design to the standard. Their acquisition followed trials with Mannheim 435 and some criticism of the policy of buying German trams for the city system. However they have many parts in common with these. Car 108 ran trials in Genève in 1972 but no sales resulted.

Between 1973 and 1975 and again in 1985/86, the Finnish builder Valmet supplied 82 cars to Helsinki (31-112); the first series introduced a new livery of grey and orange but the second saw a return to the traditional green and cream. In 2006 42 low floor centre sections were ordered for these trams. Again the body design was to the firm's own specification and is quite different to the standard Düwag product. Between 1982 and 1989, 40 trams (101-140) were built by Strømmen for Oslo as class S79 (101-140), again to an individual design, with some detail differences between the batches. The first batch also introduced a new livery of garter blue, but with the second there was a reversion to light blue and cream. These are very well finished internally and their width allows most seats to be arranged 2+2, thus giving an unusually high ratio of seated passengers to standees.

Technical details

Graz 261

Length 19.56m, width 2.24m, weight 31.8 tonnes, 4 x 55kW motors, 108 passengers, 38 seated.

Oslo class S79

Length 22.18m, width 2.5m, weight 32.8 tonnes, 2 x 174kW motors, 162 passengers, 71 seated.

Basel 648 in the central area in September 1989. (Author)

They did not run in service for very long and have now gone to Braila and Craiova in Romania. Eleven others have gone to Miskolc in Hungary and 18 of class E were acquired by Sarajevo in 2005.

In 1968/69, Werkspoor built 35 cars of this type for Rotterdam (601-635). These had attractive chromium strips around the body sides, but when they were rebuilt to eight-axle layout, the new middle sections did not have these and the cars' appearance suffered. For the suburban Birseckbahn in

When the design had proved its considerable merits, several operators decided to rebuild fairly new bogie cars to articulated configuration and a total of 32 cars were so treated, for Bochum (16 trams), Duisburg (4) and Braunschweig (12). In 1975 Würzburg acquired twelve double-ended cars when Hagen closed its system and rebuilt these into single-ended cars (270-281). On withdrawal, four went to Arad in 1997, where three are in service, the other being used as a source of spare parts.

Only one operator, the Rheinhaardtbahn, bought two-section articulated trailers, to a total of ten (1051-1058 and 1217/8). These were built by Düwag between 1958 and 1964 and three survive.

Technical details

RHB trailer

Length 19.2m, width 2.2m, weight 14.4 tonnes, 110 passengers, 64 seated.

Rotterdam 627 at Hilledijk in November 1969. (Author)

Wien class E 4442 in original livery at Schottentor terminus in August 1968. (Author)

Innsbruck 75 in the city centre in June 2001. (Author)

Still retaining its original number, Alexandria 854 (ex-Copenhagen) is seen in April 2002. The interior is little changed from its days in Denmark. (G.J. Travers)

As some cities still preferred to buy from a local manufacturer or take advantage of the tax concession then available on goods built in Berlin (West), the design was built by several other firms, but only DWM/Waggon Union achieved any quantity of production, with 147 cars, some, for Darmstadt, built as late as 1982. These were built in Berlin-Borsigwalde for Essen (2), Köln (40), Karlsruhe (62) and Darmstadt (43). The Essen cars and the first batches for Darmstadt and Karlsruhe looked much like the Düwag design, but later deliveries to the last two operators had bodies of a totally different and very attractive style. The cars in Köln (3551-3590) were quite unlike any others, being wider (2.5m) and having panoramic windscreens. Thirty were rebuilt as eight-axle cars, but none is now in passenger service. Of the Karlsruhe cars, 29 were rebuilt as eight-axle vehicles.

MAN built 56 cars for Nürnberg (301-356), but a large proportion of the components were supplied by Düwag, being standard with that firm's own products. These have now all been withdrawn in their home city and have gone to Krakow and other operators in Eastern Europe. Other builders were Credé and Wegmann, who between them supplied 16 cars to Kassel (315-321 and 356-366), between 1966 and 1971. Rastatt built eight trams for the Albtalbahn interurban line in Karlsruhe, of which one survives as a museum piece, beautifully restored

but rebuilt to eight-axle configuration. Westwaggon supplied a single car (3501) to Köln, where it is now part of the works fleet.

In 1969 Linke-Hofmann-Busch delivered six trams (13-18) of a rather different design to Braunschweig. These had many new features, such as a new type of monomotor drive from BBC and a design of self-steering lightweight bogie which gave an excellent ride. Much use of reinforced GRP was made in their construction and they were designed for one-person operation from new. However, in service they proved to be rather disappointing and by 1981 had been relegated to reserve duties. All have now been withdrawn, but one is preserved. For its next orders Braunschweig bought 18 trams to the Mannheim design from Düwag (qv) but then reverted to LHB for a further series of cars (7751-7762). In 1980/81, fifteen further cars (8151-8165) were built by LHB for the same undertaking, but to a different design. These are referred to as Stadtbahn cars but, as they do not operate from high platforms and have not been worked in multiple, it may be considered that they are trams pure and simple and that the name reflects the operator's desire to keep up with the Ruhrgebiet!

This last design was the only non-Düwag design to be exported. In November 1984 Trondheim put into service eleven trams (1-11) of a width of 2.6m, with 2+2 seating. Unfortunately these did not succeed in preventing the abandonment of that system four years later. Owing to their width they proved to be impossible to sell, but fortunately they have now been taken over by the private operator which has revived part of the system.

Kassel 364 at Königsplatz in July 1995. (Author)

Nürnberg 320, uplifts passengers at Lorenzkirche, when trams still ran in the city centre, August 1967. (Author)

Braunschweig rebuild 6260. (Lars F. Richter collection)

Darmstadt 30 at Orangerie in June 1985. (Author)

Köln 3576 on a special working at Neumarkt in June 1960. (W.J. Wyse, courtesy London Area, Light Rail Transit Association)

Very many trams of this design have now moved to Eastern Europe. In Romania, they are in service in Arad, Brasov, Bucuresti, Iasy and

Braunschweig 8164 approaches a temporary stop at Hauptbahnhof in June 2000 when much work on the tracks was being undertaken, including the installation of standard gauge track. (Author)

Karlsruhe DWM 155 was converted in 1990 into a bicycle transport car and is seen at Ettingen in June 1996. It is not now in service. (Author)

Darmstadt 7604 at Luisenplatz in June 1980. (Author)

Braunschweig 6952. (Lars F. Richter collection)

Trondheim 94 loads at St Olave's Gate in the city centre in July 2004. (Alastair G. Gunn)

Timisoara. In smaller numbers, others have gone to Poland and operate in Elblag, Gorzow, Krakow, Lodz, Poznan and Szczecin. It could be said that, having saved the tram in Germany in the 1960s, the six-axle articulated tram is now repeating the exercise in Romania!

Technical details

Braunschweig "Stadtbahn" cars
Length 192.m, width 2.2m, weight 23,046kg, 2 x 150kW motors, 107 passengers, 47 seated.
Karlsruhe Waggon-Union cars
Length 10.3m, width 2.4m, weight 22.8 tonnes, 2 x 120kW motors, 188 passengers, 41 seated.
Nürnberg MAN cars
Length 20.1m, width 2.34m, weight 22 tonnes, 2 x 120kW motors, 110 passengers, 43 seated.
LHB cars for Trondheim
Length 19.2m, width 2.6m, weight 26,500kg, 2 x 150kW motors, 138 passengers, 53 seated.

DOUBLE-ENDED DESIGNS

Single-ended trams were not suited to the operating requirements of every German system. Some cities had routes at whose termini there was insufficient space for a loop or a reversing triangle, while systems with a proportion of interurban running often used intermediate crossovers to turn cars. These also often required doors on both sides of a car.

All the Italian articulated cars had been single-ended and the Düwag factory was therefore breaking new ground in 1957 when it built its first double-ended six-axle cars for both the Vestische Strassenbahn and the Bochum systems. The design was normally referred to as "Typ Bochum", after the latter. These trams were based closely on the single-ended version but were slightly longer and, because of this, had more tapered ends. The windscreens were vertical, as in earlier bogie cars and two side windows allowed good all-round vision, an advantage for rural operation. Four doors were normally provided on each side, normally in the formation of single, double, single, double, though this could be varied to suit individual operator's requirements. There was a conductor's post at each end of the car and the pantograph was repositioned much nearer the central articulation. Electrically the cars were identical to the single-ended design. There was little variation between the batches supplied to different operators. In all 201 trams were built to this design, mostly between 1957 and 1967, but Heidelberg bought 15 as late as 1973. These were built for one-person operation and almost all older cars were rebuilt for this. The main customers were Bochum (91), Heidelberg (31), Vestische Strassenbahn (23) and Hagen (26), the balance being divided between Essen (10), Mainz (8) and Mönchengladbach (9). Neuss bought three with a width of 2.35m, these being the only ones to have a width different from the standard of 2.2m. Both Saarbrücken and Wuppertal showed some interest in the type and in 1957 Bochum 262 ran on trial in both cities, confusing passengers in the Saarland with its passenger flow. No purchase followed and the former system was soon afterwards abandoned.

The main use of the design was on radial lines, but its advantages served only to delay abandonment and to this extent it can be said that the double-ended cars were less successful than their single-ended cousins. By 1982 the systems

Bibliography
Die deutschen Strassenbahn-Gelenkwagen. Op.cit.
Modern Tramway no.196, April 1954 (Stuttgart), no.228, December 1956 (Düsseldorf), nos. 298/9, October/November 1962 (trials in Bruxelles), 480, December 1977 (Waggon-Union cars). 498/499, June/July 1979 (Düwag cars), 535, July 1982 (Braunschweig).
Der Stadtverkehr 3/1981 (Braunschweig), 8/1982 (Oslo), 11/12 1984 (Trondheim), 9/1989 (Austrian systems).
Strassenbahn Farzeuge, Band 1. M. Pabst. GeraMond Verlag, München, 1998 and 2000.
Strassenbahnen in Österreich. W. Kaiser. GeraMond Verlag, München, 2004.
Die Rheinbahn. Op.cit.
1868-1968 100 Jahre Stuttgarter Strassenbahn. Stuttgarter Strassenbahn, 1968.
Oslo-Trikken – Storbysjel på skinner. Op.cit.

A classic Düwag double-ended car, Bochum 297, in Recklinghausen in July 1979. (Author)

of Hagen, Mönchengladbach and the Vestische Strassenbahn had all been abandoned, their cars being sold to other operators, and Neuss had been absorbed by Düsseldorf. Its three cars were then rebuilt to single-ended configuration. However, the excellence of the design and its robust construction made it attractive to those systems looking for a bargain and it spread far and wide in second-, third- and even fourth-hand purchases. The Bochum cars were withdrawn between 1978 and 1996, eight going to the ELRT of Lille, where they worked well, and nine to Gent where they were deemed spectacularly unsuccessful. The Essen cars were rebuilt as detailed below. To-day only Heidelberg, of original operators, still runs trams of this type and has sold seven to Schöneiche, where one had to be written off after an accident. The former system, which had lost three cars in a workshop fire in 1984, broke new ground in 2000 by operating such cars in multiple, but the type is now in course of withdrawal, only seven coupled sets remaining in 2004. Gotha acquired six cars from Bochum, of which two are still in service. Twelve of the Hagen cars went to Würzburg, at a price of

Mainz 225 at Hauptbahnhof in June 1985. (Author)

Wien 4916 entering Wahringer Strasse station at the head of a train on line GD to Friedensbrucke in June 1981, when left hand running was still in force. (Author)

Düwag car 391 in service on the ELRT line in Lille in August 1985. (Author)

DM1.2 million, after a proposed purchase by the END radial line fell through. In 1982 eight were rebuilt as single-ended trams, as mentioned above, but are all now withdrawn. Eight other cars from this system went to Innsbruck, where many were rebuilt, and six went to Belgrade, where they did not last long and were replaced by Tatra KT4 cars. Eight cars from Bochum have gone to Arad in Romania. Five of the Mönchengladbach cars were bought by Aachen and sold on to Genève when that system closed in 1974. They did not see much service in Switzerland and were withdrawn in 1987, but no.795 was in 1981 fitted with a bogie with small wheels under its articulation, to gain experience when the low-floor car design was being prepared. Three went on to the ELRT in Lille, which had become an enthusiastic user of the type, also acquiring all the surviving 24 members of the Vestische fleet in 1982 on closure of the system – this total included three cars which had come from Mönchengladbach – as well as the eight cars from Bochum mentioned above. All these trams were extensively modernised before entering service in France and gave excellent service before being replaced by low floor cars on 23 April 1994. Six cars from Bochum went to Arad in 1996.

Only a handful of cars of this type were built by other builders. Mainz bought seven cars from Westwaggon in 1958 and 1961 (121-127), these

Wegmann car 315 on Königstrasse in Kassel in July 1995. (Author)

Genève 795 (ex-Aachen) in the depot in May 1984. (Author)

having Düwag drive and doors. Wegmann built 17 cars for Kassel between 1966 and 1970, again using Düwag components. None of these is now in service in their home cities, but the Mainz cars can be seen in Elblag in Poland and some of those from Kassel are in Gorzow.

A double-ended version of the Wien E2 class was built by Rotax from 1979 to 1981 as class E6, for use on the line of the Stadtbahn which was not to be converted to U-Bahn operation. A matching design of trailer was also developed as class c6 and trains normally worked with two motor cars flanking one trailer.

Technical details

Düwag design for metre gauge
Length 20.1m, width 2.2m, weight 21.8 tonnes, 2 x 100kW motors, 174 passengers, 40 seated
Westwaggon design for Mainz
Length 20.1m, width 2.2m, weight 21.8 tonnes, 2 x 100kW motors, 166 passengers, 42 seated.

Bibliography
Strassenbahn Magazin no.103, October/ November 1996.
Strassenbahn Farzeuge, op.cit.
Die deutschen Strassenbahn Gelenkwagen, op.cit.

In 1977 Bochum joined the ranks of party tram operators when it rebuilt two early Grossraumwagen bogie cars to form an articulated unit. Named "Bogie", this offered a high standard of comfort, a sound system, a toilet and a dance floor of 16 square metres. As far as refreshment was concerned, it was a case of BYO. Up to 30 passengers could be accommodated and in 1981 the charge for a minimum of three hours hire was DM90 per hour. It proved very popular and lasted until 1988, when it was replaced by a new conversion, also named "Bogie". In these photographs, it is seen in the workshops in May 1981. (Author)

Table 1
Six-axle single-ended trams of German design

Düwag cars for West German operators – original design	623
Düwag cars for West German operators – Mannheim design	28
Düwag cars for West German operators built for export	206
Rebuilds of bogie cars to six-axle articulated design	32
Rebuilds of double-ended cars to single-ended	15
Rebuild of eight-axle car to six-axle	4
Trailers	10
Cars built under licence in Austria	
Original design	452
Mannheim design	102
Eight-axle cars rebuilt to six-axle in Austria	11
Cars built under licence in the Netherlands	35
Cars built under licence in Switzerland	15
Cars built under licence in Finland	82
Cars built under licence in Norway	40
Cars built by other builders for German systems	257
Cars by other builders for export	10
Total	1922

Table 2
Six-axle double-ended trams of German design

Düwag cars	201
Other builders	24
Total	225
Total of all German designed cars	2147

ITALY

The basic design of the STEFER trams was copied, with great success, by several other Italian operators. ATAC, the operator of the city network in Rome, was first off the mark with a prototype in 1940 (7001). This car was destroyed in an air raid on 19 July 1943 but experience of it had been so good that a batch of 50 identical cars (7001-7099, even numbers only) was ordered from Stanga, with electrical equipment by BBC and these were placed in service in 1947-49. The electro-pneumatic control system gave rather jerky acceleration and braking, but despite these problems the class is still in service, some having recently been modernised internally and repainted green.

Genova took four double-ended trams (1101-1104) from Breda in 1942. These were sold to Neuchâtel when the city's first tram system closed, and ran successfully there until replaced by new bogie cars in 1981. One has been preserved.

Milano in the same year ordered 20 single-ended cars from Stanga with BBC electro-pneumatic equipment. Owing to wartime conditions, only five (4500-4504) were actually built. They were singularly handsome trams, based closely on the 5000 series of bogie trams. One (4504) was destroyed in 1943 and the others lasted only until 1967, when they had to be withdrawn owing to the poor condition of the bodywork. Probably inferior material had had to be used in their construction. A series of 15 very similar trams (4601-15) was acquired in 1955. These could be distinguished by the flat, raked windscreen and a longer rear section, with a triple width rear door. The last two trams of this batch (4614/5) were "all electric" and formed the prototypes of a further class delivered between 1956 and 1960. They were then renumbered 4714/5 and the subsequent batch followed on with numbers 4716-33. Now fitted with pantographs and converted for one-person operation, these trams are still in service and, with expansion of the system, are likely to remain for some years.

Much later, in 1958-60, Torino, which was experiencing a period of exceptional growth, joined the ranks of cities using articulated trams when 116 Peter Witt bogie trams of the 21xx and 22xx classes were rebuilt with a Stanga articulation to give 58 articulated cars, numbered 2800-

2857. These were pioneers, since the central bogie was motored, this requiring a very complicated electro-pneumatic control system. As there were not enough motors available from the conversion, 180 additional and more powerful motors (35kW) were bought. The six motors gave them a very good turn of speed, in spite of their weight of 26 tonnes. In 1979 it was decided to rebody these hard-worked trams and they were taken in hand by a consortium of Fiat and Viberti. The driving cabs were completely replaced and given modern fittings, including a camera to allow the driver to oversee the doors. A new roof and new windscreen were fitted and, most unusually for Italy, heating was provided in the saloon. A further series of 90 conversions from cars of the 25xx class of bogie trams of 1931-33 followed in 1980-82, giving 45 articulated cars. These appeared identical to the 28xx class as rebuilt but are in fact 0.5m longer and have a slightly different window arrangement and different bogies. Finally in 1987 car 2800 was rebuilt for the third time in its life (or the life of its component parts!) and given a new low floor body. Most of these trams are still in service, having certainly given value for money, and it is difficult to remember that they are basically 70 years old. Some may be replaced in the next few years by a combination of new low floor cars and a VAL metro.

Technical details

Milan 4601 class
Length 19.8m, width 2.4m, weight 26,500kg, 4 x 55.2kW motors, 175 passengers, 36 seated.
Rome 7000 class
Length 20.5m, width 2.4m, 25 tonnes, 173 passengers.

Bibliography

Tram a Milano. Op.cit.
Modern Tramway no.317, May 1964 (Genoa)
Una "corsa" nel passato. ATAC Rome, 1990

An ex-Genova car in service in Neuchâtel as 1102 in August 1972. (Author)

ATAC Rome 7011 seems to have run into trouble, in 1954. (Father Benedict collection)

Car 2825 of ATM Torino comes through one of the arches in the city centre in October 1975. (Jim D. Schantz)

Milano 4727 at Piazza Repubblica on line 29. (Father Benedict collection)

Rome 7043 at Porta Maggiore in July 1993. (Author)

Rebodied car 2884 in Torino in May 1998. (Author)

SWITZERLAND

The first articulated trams built in Switzerland were in fact not for any home system but for RET of Rotterdam. These were built by Schindler and entered service in May 1957 as 231-244. They used a variation of the original Urbinati articulation, the Swiss firm having acquired the licence for this. They were by far the fastest trams on the system being able to maintain 65km/hr. Like the bogie cars acquired at the same time, with which they had many parts in common, they were of unusual design having motors in the forward and middle bogies, the rear bogie being trailing, with wheels of reduced diameter. This allowed a floor height of only 56cm above rail level at the rear entrance and, combined with a two step entrance and ramped floor, this feature made the cars the most accessible on any system prior to the advent of low floor vehicles. For their capacity, they were light and in fact only about one tonne heavier than the RETs central entrance bogie cars. Metrovick control equipment brought a rare British contribution to modern tram design. Unfortunately, to give room for a motor in the middle bogie, it was necessary to dispense with the arms which acted as stabilisers and to rely on the front and rear bogies alone for lateral suspension. In service the cars rolled badly and this may have been the reason for their comparatively early demise, in 1984/85. One had been fitted with a coupling on the roof, which improved matters, but no others were so treated. As noted above, RET turned to Düwag for later deliveries.

In December 1955 it was decided by the GVBA in Amsterdam that new trams should be bought for the Leidsestraat lines and the choice fell on articulated cars. A first batch of 25 of class 1G was ordered and it was intended, subject to satisfactory experience, to follow this up with a second tranche of 45. The first entered service on line 1 in June 1957, shortly after the first articulated car in Rotterdam. This series consisted of cars 551-575. A further 12 (576-587, class 2G) followed in 1959, financial problems preventing the ordering of the balance of 33 at that time. The design was a joint venture between

Car 557 outbound on line 16 in Vijzeelstraat in September 1959. (Author)

Rotterdam 234 at Groenzoom on 12 July 1957. (S.E. Harrison, author's collection)

A close up of the front end of car 554, from a GVB leaflet issued when the class was converted to one-person operation – green circles on the doors denoted entrance. (Author's collection)

Schindler and the local firm of Bijnes. Seven of the cars were built by Schindler and the remainder by Bijnes under licence. All had Schindler trucks and Siemens electrical equipment, manufactured in the Netherlands and they were all-electric cars. Cost per tram was HFL260,000 (c£26,000). These trams were of an extremely striking design which still did not look dated as they came to the end of their career in 2003. The traditional large number box, with space for the route symbol, was combined with a modern front end and the destination was shown in lower case lettering. Inside and out the cars were painted in two shades of grey, lined out in white and the original comfortable seats, since replaced owing to vandalism, were grey too. The whole effect was eye-catching and original. They were rather heavier than their Rotterdam counterparts, and the entrance was in fact rather awkward, with three steps and narrow spacing. Their length was dictated by the track geometry of the loops in the Leidsestraat, on which they served on lines 1 and 2. They created a remarkable impression and proved to be successful in service, being a robust design, capable of withstanding years of very hard driving. It is no exaggeration to say that they saved the Amsterdam system, which had been operating under something of a cloud, due to several accidents, and whose future was not then secure.

In May 1958 the city council noted that multi-section articulated cars were entering service elsewhere and requested the GVBA to convert one

of these trams to eight-axle configuration, to gain experience of this layout before orders were placed for the balance of 33 trams. Accordingly 551 was rebuilt in 1958, at a cost of HFL49,000 (c£5,000). The experiment was so successful that as early as January 1959 it was decided to order the 33 new trams as eight-axle vehicles. Car 551 was then renumbered 601. Conversion of the other members of the class followed in 1972 once the loops in the Leidsestraat had been lengthened to accommodate them. They were then renumbered in the 8xx series. Before this conversion, there were thoughts of converting 62 eight-axle cars to six-axle configuration and operating these with three-axle trailers and in 1970 car 580 was tried with one of these. The tests showed that it would be better to retain the eight-axle cars as such and convert the six-axle cars to that layout. In 1986 car 886 was fitted with a low floor centre section, designed and manufactured by the GVBA staff in the workshops. All have now been withdrawn, but one has been saved for museum purposes. In the mid-1960s, Barcelona expressed some interest in buying similar trams, but nothing came of the idea and that system was then abandoned. Whether the Amsterdam design would have saved it is one of the might-have-beens of tramway history. Almost all these cars were sold to Poznan in 1993 and have given equally good service in Poland.

Technical details

Amsterdam 551 as built
Length 18m, width 2.25m, weight 21 tonnes, 4 x 50kW motors, 144 passengers, 46 seated.
Rotterdam
Length 19.5m, width 2.3m, 4 x 50kW motors, 19.5 tonnes, 197 pasengers.

Bibliography

70 Jaar Elektrische Tram in Amsterdam. C. van Mechelen. Uitgevers Wyt, Rotterdam, 1970.
Modern Tramway no.235, July 1957
Der Stadtverkehr 8/1991.

The main operators in Switzerland were experiencing the same staff shortages as their German counterparts and both Basel and Zürich decided to experiment with articulated trams. For the latter city, Schlieren produced in 1961 a version of the standard six-axle design. This tram (1701) proved to be so out of gauge that it would have been quite impossible to run a fleet of such cars and it was therefore confined to line 14 for the

Zürich 2025 at Schmiede Wiedikon in March 1983. (Author)

Zürich non-driving motor 2307 at Hauptbahnhof in May 2003. (Author)

Zürich non-driving bogie motor 2432 at Central in May 2003. (Author)

time being. Electro-pneumatic control, with pedal operation, was fitted. This tram, re-numbered 1802, is still in service as a party car, most recently as a Sushi tram. The other proto-type was not without problems, but the manage-ment of VBZ decided to standardise on this type, which is dealt with more fully in a later section.

It was not until 1974 that VBZ returned to the orthodox fold, when the first of the class known as Tram 2000 entered service. This single-ended tram was designed around the passenger and was a joint production of Schindler, Schlieren and BBC. It was the first Swiss tram to be fitted with chopper control. Although not a low floor design in the modern sense, the use of wheels of reduced diameter allowed the floor height to be lowered by 9cm from that on previous types, giving improved accessibility. Passengers were equally pleased with the comfortable upholstered seats, which were a distinct improvement on the shaped wooden seats of earlier classes. The first cars of this type went into service in the autumn of 1974. There were originally 45 motor trams (2001-2045) and 15 non-driving motor cars (2301-2315), known as "Blinde Kuhe" (Blind Cows). This class has since expanded to a total of 98 driving motor trams, cars 2046-2098 having been delivered between 1985 and 1992. A third series arrived in 1991/2 (2099-2121). This batch of trams differed from the first deliveries in having computer-controlled three-phase equip-ment. The fourth series of these (2401-2435, nicknamed "Pony"), delivered in 1992) are four-axle rather than articulated cars but are included here for ease of reference. In 2001 car 2113 was fitted with a low floor centre section, built by the VBZ in its workshops, using spare parts. It was nicknamed "Die Sänfte" (the sedan chair) and 22 others were being similarly treated in 2004/5. These sections were built by WinPro of Winterthur and fitted to the trams by VBZ.

Cars similar to Zürich's Tram 2000 were deliv-ered to Basel in 1980/1 for the city system (248-266)) and in 1976-81 for the BLT suburban lines (201-266). All these have been or are being extended by the insertion of a low floor centre section. A further series of city trams (659-686) arrived in 1990/1 and these have been similarly enlarged.

Technical details

Rotterdam 231
Length 19.5m, width 2.3m, weight 19.8 tonnes, 197 passengers, 40 seated.

Zürich 1701
Length 20.15m, width 2.2m, 6 x 64kW motors, weight 36.5 tonnes, 160 passengers.

Zürich 2001.
Length 20.5m, width 2.2m, weight 26.5 tonnes, 2 x 138kW motors, 157 passengers, 50 seated.

Basel Birseckbahn 101
Length 19.2m, width 2.2m, weight 22.4 tonnes, 4 x 114hp motors, 150 passengers, 47 seated.

Basel Birseckbahn 201
Length 19.97m, width 2.2m, weight 25 tonnes, 4 x 114hp motors, 150 passengers, 45 seated

Bibliography

Modern Tramway nos.235, July 1957 (Rotterdam cars), 474, June 1977 (Tram 2000).
Der Stadtverkehr, 11/12, 1976 (Zürich Tram 2000).
Strassenbahnen der Schweiz – Triebwagen. P. Willen. Orrel Füssli Verlag, Zürich, 1978.
Strassenbahn-Gelenktriebwagen "Tram 2000". Swiss Rail Export Association factsheet, 1975.
Ein Jahrhundert Zürcher Strassenbahnen. Op.cit.

Zürich 2113, fitted with low floor section, at Zoo terminus in May 2003. (Author)

Zürich 1802 at Paradeplatz. (Lars F. Richter collection)

Basel BVB 682, after the fitting of a low floor section approaches the SBB station in May 2003. (Author)

Birseckbahn 232 as modified with a low floor section at Heuwaage in September 1989. (Author)

BELGIUM

In 1980 the Belgian firm of La Brugeoise built the prototype of 50 trams for the coastal line of the then SNCV/NMBS, generally known as the Vicinal. They carried the operator's new livery of orange and cream with blue lining. These were the first Belgian trams to use monomotor bogies, the first to have thyristor control and the first to be fitted with an on-board passenger information system. Electrical equipment was provided by ACEC Charleroi. Rather against the wishes of the Vicinal, pedal control was fitted. A fixed post for a conductor was envisaged but, after a brief period of running with itinerant conductors, the cars have been operated as one-person cars. They can be operated in multiple. Numbered 6000-6049, these handsome and comfortable vehicles provide service at the highest scheduled speed of any tramway in Europe (33km/hr) and are capable of a maximum speed of 75km/hr. They are single-ended and, as built, seated 59 passengers, on very comfortable seats. In 1981 BN built at its own cost a central section which was inserted into car 6000.

At the same time, a batch of double-ended cars to the same basic design was built for service on the ambitious light metro project in the Charleroi region. These were numbered 6100-6154 and seated 44 passengers. As much of the infrastructure in that area had to be renewed to allow the cars to operate there, some entered service on the coast line and were transferred south at a later stage. On a demonstration run for potential buyers from Costa Rica on 7 April 1981, car 6103 was so badly damaged in a collision with 6102 that it had to be scrapped, parts being used by BN to rebuild 6102. The centre section that had been tested in car 6000 was then transferred to 6102 and the tram received the builder's own blue and white livery. The incident seems to have put the Costa Ricans off the idea of having a modern tram system and nothing further was heard from them. This car and 6145 later ran in Bruxelles, on the reserved track to Tervuren, mounted on standard gauge bogies to test those which BN had developed for the Stadtbahn cars it was building for Manila (qv).

On the break-up of the Vicinal, all cars were transferred to the new regional authorities, those on the coast being repainted in the black and while colour scheme of De Lijn, and all have been rebuilt to three-section configuration, with a low floor centre section. The rebuilding has unfortunately spoiled the handsome appearance of the cars, as the new section is wider than the rest of the body and the cars now look rather clumsy.

These are excellent cars, fast and smooth

Car 6029 at Oostende in SNCV livery in August 1986. (Author)

riding, but sadly they alone could not save the Charleroi network, most of which closed soon after they were delivered. As a result, many of the double-ended cars have spent a large part of their lives stored out of service.

Technical details

Length 22.80m, width 2.5m, 2 x 215kW motors, 59 seated passengers (s/e), 44 (d/e).

Bibliography

Die neuen Gelenkwagen der SNCV/NMVB/ NKG. Strassenbahn Magazin no.51, February 1984.
Der Stadtverkehr 10.1981
Le Métro Léger de Charleroi. SNCV and STIC. N/d, c.1980

Car 6110 in the splendour of Beaux Arts station in Charleroi in August 1986. (Author)

Car 6030 as rebuilt with low floor section at Knokke station in March 2004. (Author)

Car 6102 with centre section in Oostende depot yard in August 1985. (Author)

FRANCE

A close-up of the articulation of the Marseille car. (Author)

The car in the Saint-Mandé museum. (Author)

Alone among the larger French cities, Marseille retained its large tramway network well into the post-war period and in the summer of 1949 placed in service an articulated car (1301), constructed from two of the more modern bogie motor cars, 1205 and 1237 of 1934. This vehicle was double-ended and could carry 175 passengers, 35 of these being seated. It is 21m long and passenger flow was from front to rear, with one seated conductor. Total capacity was 175 passengers, 35 of these being seated. The articulation was narrow and restricted passenger circulation within the car.

Abandonment of most of the system was decided on soon afterwards and the tram was withdrawn in 1960. It has since been preserved in Paris by AMTUIR.

There was no immediate sequel to the

Nantes 301, as first delivered, approaching Commerce in September 1987. (Author)

Nantes 326, approaching Orvault terminus on line 2 in July 2000, after extension with a low floor section. (Author)

Marseille experiment and the few trams placed in service in France in the next thirty years were Belgian-style PCC cars. But the oil crisis of 1973 gave a severe jolt to the political mind and on 27 February 1975 the Secretary of state for Transport, Marcel Cavaillée sent a circular to the mayors of those large cities which did not have some form of rail transport, inviting them to plan for the introduction of modern trams within a period of five to ten years. To further this concept, an agreement was signed on 6 November 1981 between the Ministry of Transport and a consortium under the leadership of Alsthom Atlantique to build 170 standard trams between 1983 and 1990. Development was subsidised by central government to the tune of FRF 12 million, while a further FRF10 million came from the National Research Council, ANVAR.

The design, sometimes known as TSF1 (Tramway Standard Francais 1) adopted was a double-ended six-axle tram, with monomotor bogies at the outer ends and chopper control. Apart from the latter feature, the design was traditional, based on concepts of the mid-1970s, as was the external styling of the tram, and could hardly be considered state-of-the-art. It was also intended that it should be suitable for replacement of rolling stock on the existing tramways and this plan dictated such features as the fitting of a door at each end, to allow fare collection by the driver, and the parameters of the end sections. This door had to be single-width and this would certainly have led to long delays at stops if the driver had also issued tickets.

In the event Nantes, which had not originally been included in the government's plans, was the first city to decide to re-adopt the tramway, thanks to the driving force of the then mayor, Alain Chénard. Initially it took 20 of these cars (301-320) and the first was delivered in April 1984. Other cities which were due to receive the design were Grenoble, Toulon, Toulouse, Bordeaux and Strasbourg. The cost per car was FRF4.7 million (about £470,000). Chopper control and dynamic braking were fitted. The new system got off to a good start, thanks largely to the reliability of these trams, and passenger numbers soon grew to the extent that they had to be fitted with m.u. equipment and Scharfenberg couplings, to allow two-car sets to operate in peak hours. However, only two years later they were completely eclipsed by the low floor cars built for Grenoble, which became, de facto, the second French standard tram, and the plan to

build 170 was quietly dropped. A further batch of eight cars (321-328) to the original design was delivered to Nantes in 1988, but the third (329-334) and fourth series (335-346) were enlarged into a three section design by the addition of a low floor centre section. All the earlier trams have now been converted to this configuration, but, as the motors have not been replaced they are now rather sluggish in acceleration. With a total of 46 trams, that was the beginning and end of the first French standard tram, a sound basic design which suffered by a too long gestation period. However, as adapted, the trams in Nantes run well and have proved dependable in service.

Technical details
Nantes TSF1 as built
Length 28.5m, width 2.3m, weight 34.85 tonnes, 2 x 275kW motors, 168 passengers, 60 seated.

Bibliography
Der Stadtverkehr 8/1982 and 11-12/1984.
Neue Strassenbahnen in Frankreich. C. Groneck. Eisenbahn Kurier Verlag, Freiburg, 2003.
Modern Tramway no.150, June 1950. (Marseille car).

SWEDEN

The only other country in Western Europe to have developed its own version of this design is Sweden, where Göteborg placed in service 79 very large cars (201-279, class M21), built by ASEA between 1987 and 1991, after a prototype had been tried from 1985 onwards. The cars have now all been fitted with low floor centre sections and renumbered in the 3xx series. Thyristor control is fitted. All doors are in the straight section of the bodyside and to allow this to be done the ends of the car are asymmetrical. The interior is rather spartan, to guard against vandalism and fire risk. These cars must represent the limits of traditional tramway technology.

Technical details
Göteborg class M21, as built
Length 22.15m (over coupling), width 2.65m, weight 29 tonnes, 151 passengers, 61 seated.

Bibliography
Der Stadtverkehr, January 1985

Prototype 200 when new at Central Station. (Stig Hammarson)

No.374, as fitted with a low floor centre section, is seen on line 5 at Torp in October 2003. (Author)

Graz 609 as rebuilt pauses at Jauerburggasse in June 2001. The improvement in access provided by the new low floor section can clearly be seen. (Author)

As well as buying many German-type cars built under licence, Austria also developed its own design of articulated tram, based closely on the Stadtbahn M type. In 1984 Graz ordered twelve cars (601-612) from Simmering-Graz-Pauker, with which to complete the replacement of the last two-axle trams. These were built under licence from Düwag. Two Düwag-type monomotor bogies are fitted, with, originally, a single central trailing bogie. A novelty in the equipment was the fitting of GTO thyristors. However, these trams proved to be too small in service, having a capacity of only 117. To remedy this and also to improve accessibility, low floor central sections were inserted from 1999 onwards, increasing overall capacity to 167 passengers.

Technical details
as built
Length 19.2m, width 2.24m, weight 26.08 tonnes, 2 x 150kW motors, 117 passengers, 27 seated.

There might have been other trams of this type, but as the tramway renaissance got under way, it became clear that the future lay with either the Stadtbahn high floor car or, later, the low floor designs, and no more were built for service in Western Europe. However, it is safe to say that, if this design had not been developed when it was, many systems would not have survived to be part of that renaissance.

Bibliography
Der Stadtverkehr 3/1987.

TATRA TRAMS OF CLASS K2

It might have been expected that the articulated car, with its high capacity, would have found favour in Eastern Europe in pre-1989 days, but in fact the demand for transport was so high that many operators found it best to run three-car sets, usually made up of two bogie motor cars and a trailer. However, for a small number of operators, the firm of CKD Tatra did develop an articulated version of its successful T3 bogie car. Two prototypes, 7000 and 7001, class K1, entered service in Praha in January 1965. These were fairly heavy, at 22.5 tonnes, and could carry up to 200 passengers, depending on the degree of discomfort tolerated. Bodywork was of the style of the T3 bogie car. Unusually for Tatra cars, they had electro-pneumatic equipment, and could also work in m.u. formation. They had little success in the capital and were soon shipped off to Ostrava where they did not last very long either. They were then returned to the manufacturer.
Meanwhile a second 7000, an all-electric car, had been built and tried in Praha and Most, before finding a permanent home in Brno (606). The second prototype was numbered 7001 (II) and went to the Soviet Union as a special gift to Leonid Brezhnev who had taken rather a fancy to the design. A production series, class K2, followed between 1966 and 1970 and were delivered to three systems in what was then Czecho-slovakia, Bratislava. Ostrava and Brno. The last of these took a further 110 between 1973 and 1983, to become the only large-scale user of the design, and Ostrava took a further ten in 1983. A further 64 were built for Bratislava in the years from 1973 to 1977. In all, 237 were supplied to Czech operators, many of which have now been modernised. One of the modernised cars in Brno has been given a low floor centre section. Exports to the USSR accounted for a further 246 cars of class K2 SU. As these were intended for service in Siberian cities, they had double-power heating and an air conditioned cabin for the driver. Most ended up in Charkhov. In Bosnia, Sarajevo took 90 cars (201-290) between 1973 and 1983 and of these about 60 have survived the civil war to be returned to service. Of these 37 have been rebuilt by Pars in the Chech Republic and have also been given new low floor centre sections, making them eight-axle cars. The same city has now also been given some identical cars from Slovakia.

A further export order came from El Qahira which received 100 trams (3001-3100) in 1970/1, following on from a prototype built in 1967. These were double-ended cars, arranged for a two class fare system and were classed K5.

Class K5 3033 in El Qahira. (A.D. Young, Evda Slides)

Bratislava 7103, as modernised, climbs towards the main station in June 2001. (Author)

K2 7084 at Raca terminus in Bratislava in June 2001. Modernised car 7108 is on the left. (Author)

They were delivered as part of an aid package and, after an inaugural ride for invited guests, the first tram was then parked while the distinguished company went to a hotel for a celebratory lunch. When they emerged some time later they found the car looking rather forlorn, having been stripped of all its chrome trim. Two further batches of 50 each followed in 1972 and 1973. At first they ran with trolley poles, one being fitted at each end of the roof, but later they had pantographs. The design was not robust enough to stand up to conditions in El Qahira and the trams were all out of service by the mid-1980s. A similar car was built for Alexandria, using parts of two T3 cars, but in this case there was no order for a series.

In comparison with the numbers built of other designs, class K2/K5 represented an insignificant part of the firm's production and the design of articulated cars by Tatra was to take a rather different form.

Technical details
Single-ended design
Length 20.4m, width 2.5m, weight 22,000kg, 4 x 40kW motors, 157 passengers*, 49 seated.

Bibliography
Strassenbahn Magazin no.143, September 2001

OTHER DESIGNS IN EASTERN EUROPE

The six-axle articulated tram fared rather better in Poland, where nine of the fourteen systems running after 1970 operated such cars, though again they have not been favoured in the capital and production soon reverted to bogie vehicles. A prototype of class 102N appeared in Katowice in 1965 and a production series of 42 trams was built in 1969/70 by the national firm of Konstal. There were also five cars of class 802N for metre gauge. This class had an extremely odd, forward-sloping windscreen and was quite unlike any other design anywhere, being generally considered to be some of the ugliest trams ever built. None are now in service. The majority of Poland's articulated cars, however, are of class 102Na, built by Konstal from 1970 to 1973 to the same dimensions but of a much more handsome appearance, with a tapered windscreen, closely resembling the bogie design of class 13N. A total of 480 were built for standard gauge, along with 171 of class 803N for metre gauge. The cars ride well, on track whose qualities sometimes leave something to be desired, and have proved to be durable, though withdrawals began in 1996.

Technical details
Class 102Na
Length 19.3m, width 2.4m, weight 25.3 tonnes, 4 x 41.5kW motors, 182 passengers, 32 seated.

Bibliography
Modern Tramway no.384, December 1969

In Bulgaria, the only tram system is in the capital, Sofia, and all cars described in this section were built in the undertaking's own workshops. A first series of 63 articulated trams was placed in service between 1961 and 1965. They were named "Kosmonaut" as a compliment to the Russian astronauts, but in fact they had more in common with Western designs, since they were based on the undertaking's bogie cars which in turn were based on the West German Grossraumwagen. Despite this, they were some-

A class 102N car. (Konstal, author's collection)

Wroclaw 102Na 2085 inbound to the city and zoo on line 16 at Weigla in October 2002. (Author)

what crude and were also heavy, weighing over 24 tonnes. They are no longer in service. A second version, of a much improved design, first entered service in 1966 and a total of over 250 of classes Bulgaria 1300 and Sofia 100 were ultimately built for the metre gauge system. Numbers are spread throughout the series 3xx, 4xx, 5xx, 7xx and 8xx. All but two are single-ended, these latter being fitted for back-to-back working in coupled sets. An improved version, class Sofia 1000, came out in 1986 for use on the new standard gauge lines. There are 33 of these (4001-4033) but four were also built for metre gauge. Yet another improved design appeared in 1988, class MK88, of which 36 were built for metre gauge, the two prototypes (503/4) being intended for use as a coupled set. The others are numbered between 826 and 863. Recently several trams of type 100 have been rebodied and 22 have been extended with a low floor centre section.

In neighbouring Romania, it was not until 1982 that any six-axle cars appeared, when 48 or 49 were built for service in the capital; at least six were later rebuilt as double-ended cars. These were built by the undertaking in its own workshops and clearly owed much to the LHB car (3501) which had been imported in 1969. A further 31 of what became class V2A were built for the provincial systems of Brasov, Cluj and Iasi. It is not certain how many of these were in fact single-ended cars and some were completed as class V2B, as double-ended cars. There have since been some transfers of cars between systems and some renumberings. In 1983 the Banat factory in Timisora built a car based on its bogie design, but it remained a one-off. Many of these cars have now been scrapped and others have been drastically rebuilt.

Ganz in Hungary supplied a single car (3730) to Budapest in 1964, but in the following year it was rebuilt to eight-axle configuration. It seems to have had no success in either form and had been withdrawn by 1969.

Technical details
Budapest 3730 as rebuilt to eight-axle
Length 25.6m, width 2.3m, weight 33.5 tonnes, 4 x 55kW motors, 265 passengers*, 26 seated.

Earlier, in 1966, a single car, 200, was supplied by the local firm of Djuro-Djakovič to Zagreb, but there was no following order, bogie cars being bought instead. Twenty-five years later they tried again with a modern version (car 900) and with exactly the same result! This was probably more to do with politics than the design of the tram itself – it was hoped to produce 20 per year and there was some suggestion that a version could be produced for Blackpool, but by the time the first car appeared, the federation of Jugo-slavia was dissolving into its component parts and three of its four tram systems were in no position to

Sofia 938 in August 1969; the driver seemed unwilling to be photographed. (Author)

Sofia 885 in August 1969. (Author)

Debrecen 501 seen in May 1998. (Alastair G. Gunn)

buy new cars and Zagreb seemed not to like the design.

One of the very few new designs to have appeared in the area since 1990 was a series of cars built by what had become Ganz-Hunslet for Debrecen in Hungary in 1997. The prototype was numbered 500 and the ten slightly altered production cars are 501-510. While these have a lower floor level than conventional cars (735mm), they are not low floor cars in the modern sense. They were built as double-ended cars but have always operated in single-ended mode. These trams have three-phase motors and thyristor control and are in all aspects an excellent design, but their success was not enough to ensure further deliveries. The prototype is not now in service.

Technical details
Debrecen 501
Length 21.66m, width 2.5m, weight 30 tonnes, 4 x 100kW motors, 100 passengers, 28 seated.
Zagreb 900
Length 19m, width 2.3m, weight 24 tonnes, 2 x 150kW motors, 170 passengers*, 33 seated.

Bibliography
Modern Tramway nos.335, November 1965 (Budapest), 642, June 1991 (Zagreb).

USSR AND SUCCESSOR STATES

Although, as mentioned above, a few Tatra articulated trams were exported to the Soviet Union, the type did not achieve any great popularity there, forming about 1% of the total number of trams in the country. There was not the shortage of labour which led to the adoption of articulated trams in Western Europe, they were rather too delicate for the hard life demanded of Soviet trams, and they were too heavy on maintenance. In 1966 the Jegorov factory built a prototype car for Leningrad, a city which has always taken a fairly independent line in tramway matters. This was numbered 1001 and was followed by a series of similar cars, classed as LVS67. These could carry 220 passengers, 44 of them seated, and were 22.5m long by 2.55m wide. None is now in service. A second design, class LVS86, appeared in 1986, following trials with four prototypes delivered between 1980 and 1984. About 450 of these trams were built, most of which are still running, albeit in a somewhat forlorn condition. Six were also built for Arkhangelsk. No other city followed this example at the time. However, in 2001, the AKSM factory in Minsk built a prototype car (031) for the system in that city. To date, no others have appeared. In 2002 Sankt Petersburg received two new cars of what is classed LVS97, but it is not at present certain if any more will follow.

Bibliography

Chorzowska Wytwórnia Konstrukcji Stalowych – Konstal 1864-1989. (Details of Konstal products), Konstal, 1989.

Strassenbahn-Betriebe in Osteuropa II. H. Lehnhart und C. Jeanmaire. Verlag Eisenbahn, Villigen, Switzerland, 1977.

Trams in Eastern Europe. M. Taplin and M. Russell. Capital Transport, Harrow, 2002.

Der Stadtverkehr 4/97 (Sofia).

LVS86 no.4027 negotiating some indifferent track after a heavy shower in Sankt Petersburg in August 1998. (Author)

PCC CARS (INCLUDING EIGHT-AXLE)

Given the enthusiasm with which the Belgians had adopted the PCC tram, it was not surprising that an attempt should be made to combine its advantages with those of the six-axle articulated car. In 1962 the firm of La Brugeoise produced a prototype for Bruxelles. Numbered 7501, this car used the body styling of the bogie cars of class 7000. It weighed 21.5 tonnes and could accommodate a total of 173 passengers. In 1962 it was tested against the Düwag car already mentioned on line 16 and both designs acquitted themselves well. It was also shown at the international transport exhibition in München in 1964, where it was publicised as the "Eurotram". Unfortunately, its four motors of 40.5kW were insufficient for the more hilly routes in the city and the tram had great difficulty starting on a gradient of 8%. As it was not then possible to motorise the middle bogie, the car remained for a time the only one of its kind. It was later renumbered 7500 and, having been modernised recently, is still in service. For reasons unknown, it has gained the nickname "Caroline".

After some experimentation, the same builder found it possible to place a motorised bogie under an articulation joint and in 1971/2, a total of 98 similar cars (7501-7598) were placed in service. These differed from the prototype in other ways – there were three exit doors in place of two and the windscreen was of a more rounded design – and with six 62kW motors, they showed themselves able to cope with the city's steepest gradients. As delivered, they were fitted with trolley poles and were worked by a seated conductor, but were later fitted with pantographs and converted for one-person operation. They were also later rebuilt into double-ended layout, for which provision had been made when they were built. A further 60 cars were built as double-ended from new (7801-7860). An unusual electrical feature for a PCC design was that there were two separate electrical systems on board. The first has series-parallel control and drives the two forward bogies, while the second works in series only and controls the rear bogie. It is possible to cut out the latter when running at low speed.

The articulated PCC cars have been successful and allowed the STIB/MIVB to retire all its old two-axle cars.

The only export order for the Eurotram came from Saint-Étienne in France, which in 1967 ordered five similar, but narrower cars (551-55). As the line concerned is almost entirely flat, the lack of power was not a problem. In 1983 car 553

In July 1975 Sarajevo 101 leaves the terminus at Baščaršija. (Peter Haseldine)

Brussels 7932 near Midi station in November 1997. (Author)

This rear view of Brussels 7537, as built and seen in November 1972, shows how easy it was to convert these to double-ended layout. (Author)

The interior of STIB 7501, now numbered 7500 after modernisation, March 2004. (Author)

St Étienne 552 at Bellevue in September 1987. (Author)

The futuristic appearance of the rebuilt car, also in September 1987. (Author)

Brussels 7501 as displayed at the IVA in München in 1965. (F.W. Hunt, courtesy London Area, Light Rail Transit Association/Author)

was rebuilt by the bus manufacturer Heuliez in a futuristic style, but all were withdrawn in favour of low-floor cars on 4 July 1998. The modernised car has been set aside for preservation in the city's transport museum, but due to lack of space it is not yet on display. The others are still stored in the depot, in the hope of an eventual purchaser.

A most unusual variety of articulated PCC tram was found in Sarajevo. As detailed elsewhere, this undertaking acquired 74 PCC trams from Washington City and between 1967 and 1969 seven articulated trams (100-106) were constructed from 14 cars which had been involved in accidents. The articulation was formed by a large folding bellows connection, as on main line trains. In this form, they could carry

No.7804, seen near Midi station in November 1972, is one of those built as a double-ended car. (Author)

56 seated and 120 standing passengers and had a fixed post for the conductor on the offside of the car at the rear. They did not last very long in their converted state, since the arrival of many Tatra cars made the PCCs redundant in the early 1970s.

For convenience, the only eight-axle PCC design to be produced will be covered here. This was a class of 61 cars for Brussels which appeared in 1977/8 (7901-7961). While derived from the previous designs, and also double-ended, this was a more elegant tram and also internally much more comfortable, thanks to high-backed seats. Bonded windows emphasised the length of the car. This class has been successful in service but it appears at the present time that they will not receive further heavy overhauls and will be replaced by low floor cars within the next few years.

Technical details

STIB Car 7501 (1)
Length 20.65m, width 2.2m, weight 21.5 tonnes, 4 x 40.5kW motors, 173 passengers, 43 seated.
Car 7501 (II) as built
Length 21m, width 2.2m, weight 24.7 tonnes, 6 x 62kW motors, 158 passengers, 43 seated.
7901
Length 27.86m, width 2.2m, weight 38.1 tonnes, 8 x 51.5kW motors, 179 passengers, 46 seated.

Bibliography

Die Deutschen Strassenbahn Gelenkwagen. Op.cit.
Strassenbahn Magazin no.175, May 2004 (St Étienne).
Tramways en Service à Bruxelles. R. Hanocq. STIB, Brussels, 1977.
STIB factsheets

CANADA

While the bogie cars for Toronto were at the design stage, the UTDC in 1976 proposed to the TTC that two six-axle articulated cars should be built for evaluation, the contract for the bogie cars being reduced to 196. It was hoped that such a design would be used on the proposed Scarborough light rail line, then at the planning stage, and could also form the basis for exports. In the event only a single prototype was constructed, at the UTDC's own facility at Kingston, Ontario and this arrived in Toronto on 3 August 1982. It was painted in an orange livery, rather than the red of the bogie cars, numbered 4900 and ran on demonstration from 10 August 1982 to 25 February 1983. As it was successful, the TTC then ordered 52 similar cars for delivery in 1986/7 (4200-4251). As with the bogie cars, these are heavy and it is surprising that only the outer trucks are motored. This feature combines with the frequent stops to ensure that service speed is low by European standards. These trams are used mainly on Queen Street, line 501 and its associated short workings, or "short turns" in TTC parlance.

Unfortunately political interference obliged the TTC to adopt an automatic semi-metro for the Scarborough line and no additional articulated trams were constructed for the city, but with

Working southwards on Bathurst Street, car 4209 clears the intersection with Bloor Street on 25 September 1989. (Author)

some modifications, the design was exported to the USA for use in San José.

Technical details

Length 23.06m, width 2.59m, weight 35,610kg, 2 x 196kW motors, 156 passengers, 61 seated.

Bibliography

Articulated Canadian Light Rail Vehicle. TTC factsheet, April 1984.
Modern Tramway no.541, January 1983.

JAPAN (INCLUDING EIGHT-AXLE CARS)

Hiroshima 3902 bound for the railway station on 19 May 2004. (M.J. Russell)

A few articulated cars were built for Japanese systems from 1940 onwards. Nagoya was the largest user of this type, having 33 cars built in three series between 1941 and 1946. One has been preserved. Sendai had one home-built unit. In Hiroshima, four 1600 class pre-war bogie cars were rebuilt into two articulated units for the radial line to Miyajima, each part being numbered separately so that they became 2511/2 and 2513/4. In 1953 the small system of Nikko bought six articulated cars but these did not outlast abandonment in 1968. All these were six-axle cars, using flexible bellows connections between the two body parts, and none could be considered modern.

The city of Sapporo went against the trend of tramway abandonment in the 1960s and, among new rolling stock acquired were seven articulated cars, the last two of which had passenger flow and a seated conductor. These last were of modern appearance, with wide windows and rounded ends. Each part of the car was numbered separately, so that numbers were 801/2-805/6, 811/2, 813/4 and 821/2-823/4. They had three 60kW motors and a total capacity of 150, of whom 50 were seated. None are now in service in Sapporo. Three were sold to Gifu, where they became 871/2 to 875/6, where they were used on a radial line to the north east of the city. Much more innovative were six cars (201-206) built about 1960 by the Tokyu Car Manufacturing Company for the associated Tokyo Electric Express Railway (TKK) for its tram services. These were five-axle cars, of a design not seen before or since in Japan or anywhere else. They had rounded ends and a rounded profile and, in the green and yellow livery, looked rather like large caterpillars. In fact they were known as such. They rode on inside-frame bogies and had electro-pneumatic equipment. Overall length was 21m, width 2.3m and they could carry about 200 passengers, of whom 60 were seated. As mentioned elsewhere, they also had a remarkably low floor height. They had a relatively short life but one has been preserved in the company's museum and another may also still exist.

Gifu, which was run by the Nagoya Railroad Company, had ten modern articulated trams (880-889), built by Nippon Sharyo in 1980, in its 41-strong fleet, as well as ex-Sapporo articulated cars. On Honshu, the Setagaya line in Tokyo in 1999 rebuilt two 1942 bogie cars into an articulated unit and another may have since followed.

The line at Enoshima, run by the Enoshima Electric Railway Company, has 15 pairs of high-floor articulated cars, some of which are quite modern, dating from 1979 onwards. They are numbered from 1001+1051 upwards, each body section having its own number. These are air-conditioned and have a certain resemblance to European designs of Stadtbahn cars, but have only two single-width sliding doors in each body section. The gauge is 1067mm.

Technical details
Enoshima 1001

Length 24.8m, width 2.4m weight 36.24 tonnes, 4 x 50kW motors, 160 passengers, 72 seated.

The Nishi Nippon Railroad on Kyushu has both six- and eight-axle articulated cars in its fleet, but none are particularly modern.

Technical details
Nagoya RR 880 class

Length 20.6m, width 2.23m, weight 25.6 tonnes, 4 x 38kW motors, 100 passengers*, 48 seated.

AUSTRALIA

The first articulated trams to run in Australia appeared in 1984. Melbourne took delivery of two prototypes of class B1 (2001/2), built by Comeng at Dandenong and based very closely on the bogie cars of classes A1 and A2. Like these trams, they rode on Düwag monomotor bogies, with an unpowered bogie under the articulation and in all respects they were standard German trams with an Australian body. The most important difference was that they were to be worked by an itinerant conductor. Initially they were fitted with retractable steps to allow them to use high platforms on the two railway lines – St Kilda and Port Melbourne – which were then being converted to light rail operation, but it was finally decided to build new low platforms at former stations and the retractable step facility was removed. The trams, which are double-ended, have chopper control and regenerative braking. They were fitted with trolley poles for test purposes but these were later replaced by pantographs. The idea of running articulated trams met with a good deal of opposition from the trade unions and the cars spent many months laid up at Preston workshops before they finally entered service. They are fitted with m.u. control but, other than within the workshop area, have not operated in multiple. These trams were followed by class B2 (2003-2132) in the years between 1988 and 1994, the main difference from the prototypes being the fitting of air condi-

B2 class 2091 enters the siding at Elizabeth Street terminus in March 1993, when work was under way to enlarge these facilities. (Author)

In 1981 Hiroshima was given two articulated cars by Dortmund and these ran in service for some years. Both still exist in a depot. This system inaugurated the age of the modern articulated tram in Japan in 1982 when it placed in service the first (3501) of several fitted with three-phase equipment, chopper control and air conditioning. These were built by Kawasaki. There are also twelve Siemens Combino cars (qv).

Technical details
Hiroshima 3501

Length 26.3m, width 2.45m, weight 38.4 tonnes, 2 x 120kW motors, 156 passengers*, 52 seated.

Among the overseas trams in Kochi there is a Stuttgart GT4 car rebuilt into double-ended layout by using halves of cars 714 and 735.

Bibliography
Modern Tramway no.287, November 1961 (TKK cars), no.346, October 1966 (Sapporo).
Sayonara Streetcars. R. Forty. Interurban Special 70, Glendale CA, 1978.

Prototype car 2002 at Preston workshops in March 1986. (Author)

An interior view of 2002. (Author)

tioning, housed in pods on the roof. These capacious and comfortable trams have proved to be successful both on the light rail lines and also on conventional city lines. Until very recently they were worked with conductors, alone among articulated trams at the time. Given their capacity, it has to be said that the success of this form of fare collection owed more to the determination of the conductors than to the design of the trams. A low floor version was considered, but not developed.

Technical details
Class B2.

Length 23.63m, width 2.77m, weight 34 tonnes, 2 x 195kW motors, c155 passengers, 76 seated passsengers.

Bibliography
Destination City. Op.cit.

CHINA

In China the workshops of the undertaking in Dalian functions not only for the maintenance of the undertaking's own trams but also as suppliers of new cars to the other three systems in the country. In 1983 they turned out the first Chinese articulated tram (621-01) for their own system. This double-ended car shares the angular body design of the bogie cars (qv) and has no fewer than four air-operated double width doors on each side, at three of which there was a conductor's post. A public address system is fitted and passengers sit on upholstered longitudinal seats. Electrically and mechanically the tram is somewhat old fashioned for its time, riding on a locally built version of Brill bogies, whose riding qualities leave something to be desired. The central bogie had two motors and

each end bogie one, driving the outermost axles. Air brakes and an electro-magnetic control system are fitted. A bow collector is provided, the half-pantograph which was tried originally having proved prone to dewirements. Despite some limitations, this tram represented a considerable step forward for Chinese tramways and 14 others were constructed for Dalian in 1985/6.

Changchun has recently acquired some new trams for its new line, the first new tramway to be constructed in China for many years. It is not clear if these are conventional or low floor cars.

Technical details
Dalian cars
(The tram could also carry an additional 90 passengers at 12 passengers pre square metre).

Dalian 621-01 on 13 June 1984. (M.J. Russell)

Bibliography
Der Stadtverkehr, October 1984.
Tramways and Urban Transit no.797, May 2004.

EIGHT- AND TEN-AXLE CARS

THE FIRST STEPS

Before the mid-1950s, very little interest had been shown in multi-section articulated trams. In 1924 the Cincinnati Car Company built a three-section, four-bogie car for the Department of Street Railways of Detroit; this monster, which originally carried three separate numbers, had seats for 140 passengers and standing room for at least that number again. Three conductors were carried, thus outweighing any saving made by running such a car and in any event it proved to be too long for operation on many street sections. Its fate is not recorded.

GERMAN MULTI-SECTION DESIGNS

SINGLE-ENDED DESIGNS

Given the success of its six-axle trams with so many operators, it is not surprising that Düwag soon began to consider an enlargement of the design. Technically there was no difficulty and, since fare systems in Germany had been greatly simplified, there were unlikely to be any operational problems.

The only complaints made against the six-axle cars introduced in Düsseldorf in 1956 were due to the lower ratio of seats to standing places 4.65 as against 3.41 on tram-trailer sets. To remedy this, car 2310, one of a batch of twenty six-axle trams then under construction, was fitted with a centre section 6.55m long. It entered service on 19 June 1957 and proved to be an immediate success. It was able to carry up to 250 passengers, yet still required only a single conductor. A total of 52 similar trams was delivered over the next three years and the design was ordered by nine other operators. Unusual vehicles were three for Düsseldorf and two for neighbouring Duisburg which were fitted with a small kitchen and buffet section for use on interurban line D between the two cities. When more modern trams later appeared for that service, the catering facilities were removed. In all 215 cars were built between 1959 and 1976, of which one in Frankfurt (Main) was later converted to six-axle configuration, as was pioneer 2310. Most operators followed closely the design features of their six-axle cars in the larger vehicles. Köln's cars were, at 2.5m, wider than those on any other system. Those built for the Abtalbahn, Karlsruhe, (1-7 and 16-21) had a width of 2.4m and 2+2 seating. These were latterly used on the city services and some have now gone to Timisoara in Romania. The eight cars (241-248) built for Würzburg in 1975 had tapered ends, in view of the tight clearances on this system. They also had two doors in the off-side and a back-up controller at the rear, to allow them to function as double-

Würzburg 241 on the attractive reserved track of line 3 near Haus des Sports. (Author)

Augsburg's Mannheim-type 806 is at Moritzplatz in June 1985. (Author)

Freiburg 230, with low floor section, at Littenweiler in June 1996. (Author)

Köln 3808 working on line 3 in June 1969. (Author's collection)

Frankfurt (M) 810 at Hauptbahnhof in June 2000. (Author)

Ludwigshafen 150 at Mannheim Hauptbahnhof in June 1985. (Author)

Albtalbahn 105 working on line A outbound in June 1984. (Author)

Innsbruck 51, as converted for bicycle carriage, at Igls terminus on 19 June 2001. (Author)

Freiburg 206 on line 1 near Technisches Rathaus in June 1996. (Author)

ended cars in the event of an interruption to the service.

Augsburg in 1975 bought the only eight-axle cars built new to the Mannheim design (801-812). These have no door in the centre section and are rather shorter than the standard design, to allow them to negotiate curves of 17m radius.

A variation on this type had already appeared in 1970, when four new eight-axle cars (201-204, class GT8/71) were ordered from Düwag by Freiburg-in-Breisgau. These however differed from the standard design in that the second and third bogies were placed not under the articulation joints but at either end of the centre section. The articulation units were suspended for the body ends of the front and rear sections. This form of construction reduced the swept path of the tram on curves and so allowed eight-axle trams to run in Freiburg. Although of only 2.2m width, they could still carry a maximum of 294 passengers. All four bogies were motored, giving a high rate of acceleration and a high top speed. Ten similar cars (205-214) followed in 1981 and a third tranche of eleven (221-231) arrived in 1990/91. These have a low floor centre section, whose floor is only 27cm above rail level, and thyristor control. These were the last high floor trams to be built by this manufacturer.

Already some eight-axle cars have been withdrawn and gone to Eastern Europe. Those from Frankfurt (M) are in service in Poznan and eight from Essen went to Arad in 2001. The most exotic destination has been Mesched in Iran, to which 14 cars were sent from Düsseldorf in 1996/7. As of 2001, the tramway in which they were to be run had not been built and they were stored in the bus garage. A surprising sale in 2004 was that of Ludwigshafen 150 to Helsinki, that operator wishing to test the operation of multi-section cars. It has run in service on line 1.

Technical details
Rheinbahn 2310
Length 25.64m, width 2.35m, weight 26 tonnes, 2 x 95kW motors, 250 passengers, 49 seated.
Freiburg 205
Length 32.84m, width 2.32m, weight 37.83 tonnes, 4 x 150kW motors, 317 passengers*, 91 seated.

Bibliography
Modern Tramway no. 338, February 1966 (Detroit), no.241, January 1958 (Düsseldorf car).
Freiburg: from classic tramway to light rail. R. Deacon. Light Rail Transit Association, London, 1998.

An ex-Duisburg car, running as in Dessau, shows the offside door fitted to this class. It is at Museum stop in June 1995. (Author)

Der Stadtverkehr. 11/12/1971 and 8/1981 (Freiburg).
Ein Netz für die umwelt – Freiburg. Der Stadtverkehr special, 1994.
Die Rheinbahn. Op.cit.
Die deutschen Strassenbahn-Gelenkwagen. Op.cit.
Strassenbahn Magazin no.161, March 2003.

Few other builders entered this particular market. The firm that was then DWM supplied 12 cars (177-188), to the basic Düwag design, to Karlsruhe in 1969. After it had become Waggon-Union, it built four cars of a new and elegant design for the Albtalbahn in 1975 (122-125). These were converted for use at high platforms in 1990/1. They were followed by 16 similar cars in two batches for Darmstadt, nos.8209-14 in 1982 and 9115-9124 in 1991.

Statistically more significant were the rebuilds of six-axle cars to the larger design. Many operators had large fleets of these nearly new cars and saw in this operation a way of saving money, as well as offering their riders the comfort and space of the larger trams. The first such rebuild appeared on the Albtalbahn in Karlsruhe in 1961

Essen 1856 seen at Rathausarkt in Mülheim in November 1997 shows the doors fitted to the offside to allow use at stations with centre platforms.

and the process was continued until 1981, although Mülheim undertook two such rebuilds much later, in 1989 and 1996, using centre sections obtained from Essen. Some cars in the latter city have been rebuilt with doors on the left hand side, for use at tunnel stations. Some operators, such as Duisburg, were so taken with the advantages of the larger trams that they rebuilt all their fleet to this standard, while others did so with a proportion of their trams. In 1996 Köln and Bielefeld each rebuilt one car as a party tram. The rebuilding of cars in Linz has already been

RHB twelve-axle car 1019 in the depot yard at Bad Dürkheim in June 1996. (Author)

Albtalbahn 125 at Albtalbahnhof in Karlsruhe in June 1984. (Author)

Rotterdam 1635 as rebuilt at Centraal Station. (Author)

Amsterdam – class 8G 735 in service on line 12 in the south of the city in June 1989. (Author)

Graz 584 at Jacominiplatz in June 2001. (Author)

mentioned. Duisburg had in 1972 rebuilt two cars (1231/2) to ten-axle configuration, using what were temporarily spare centre sections. These worked quite well, but were re-converted to eight-axle layout in 1975 when the centre sections were required for other trams. Wuppertal rebuilt its bogie cars into 16 articulated trams which, between 1984 and 1987, were sold to Graz, along with five which had been built new. As they had latterly been somewhat neglected, their new owners were not enamoured of them and they were scrapped by 1995.

Many of these trams have also gone to Eastern Europe in recent years and in Romania are running in Arad and Timisoara. An exception was the sale of 15 cars from Duisburg to Norrköping in Sweden, four of these coming via Dessau. Intended originally as a stop-gap to cover the rebuilding of the bogie cars, they proved to be so successful that it was decided to keep them and rebuild rather fewer bogie cars. The cars had travelled in sections and entered service without their middle portions. It was then decided to rebuild eleven of these sections with a low floor configuration and, after a brief period as six-axle cars, the trams reverted to eight-axle layout. They have also received a new and attractive design of front end and a complete internal renovation and are now in service as 61-71. The others have been scrapped.

The longest articulated trams in Germany are to be found on the radial Rheinhardtbahn line from

Mannheim to Bad Dürkheim. In 1967 four five section, twelve-axle articulated cars (1019-1022) were acquired from Düwag for this service. The aim of the exercise was to save on personnel costs, as they replaced in regular service trains made up of a six-axle motor car and a similar trailer, which were worked with two conductors. Conversion to one-person operation has negated their advantage and there can also be problems if one breaks down in service and has to be removed. However, they are still useful to deal with the crowds which use the line on the occasion of the sausage festival in Bad Dürkheim.

Technical details

Length 38.54m, width 2.2m, weight 36.75 tonnes, 2 x 150kW motors, 319 passengers, 118 seated.

This design was exported only to one operator, the RET in Rotterdam. In a joint production with Werkspoor, Düwag delivered 36 eight-axle cars (351-386) in 1964/5 which, like the six-axle cars delivered at the same time, had many parts built in the Netherlands. The type was also built in small numbers in Austria under licence. Graz bought ten Mannheim-type cars from SGP (501-510) in 1977/8 and in 1997/8 built in its own workshops what are probably the last conventional eight-axle cars for any system in Western Europe. There are four of these (581-584) and they incorporate the middle sections and bogies

of withdrawn ex-Wuppertal cars. Linz bought eight in 1970/1 (81-88) and twelve (68-79) in 1977. These were rebuilt to ten-axle configuration in 1979/80. This operator also acquired 16 further ten-axle cars (41-56, type L10) in 1985/6, based on the Stadtbahn M type and built under licence from, and following plans supplied by Düwag.

A further export order came from Amsterdam in 1973. This was for 55 cars (725-779, class 8G) from Linke Hofmann Busch, based closely on the Braunschweig six-axle design of 1969. These trams had Werkspoor-type bogies and Siemens equipment with air brakes, being therefore known as the "luftwagens" (air cars). They were designed for one-person operation, as was the following class. Somehow they seemed to be the least successful of all the city's articulated cars. They had many teething troubles and the hot summer of 1976 played havoc with their ventilation, while the air-operated doors could be problematic in winter. The bodies were also subject to severe corrosion. The last was withdrawn in 2003 and none has gone to any other undertaking, although some have been preserved. The only one to remain active in Amsterdam is car 767, which was rebuilt by the Red Cross to accommodate passengers with disabilities, fitted with a wheelchair lift, kitchen and toilet and is used to give these passengers sightseeing tours of the city. It is now painted white and numbered 3001. A series of 35 cars of class 9G (780-814) followed from the same builder in two lots in 1981-83. These proved to be much more successful and are still in service.

Very much a "one-off" was a single car delivered by LHB in 1969 to Bucuresti, where it took the number 3501. It was based very closely on the six-axle version supplied to Braunschweig in the same year, but seems to have been rather more successful. The design was then developed by the Romanians for quantity production.

Technical details

Düsseldorf 2310
Length 21.6m, width 2.35m, weight 26 tonnes, 2 x 95kW motors, 257 passengers, 64 seated.

Rebuilt ex-Duisburg car 70 on Drottningatan in Norrköping, October 2003. (Author)

Amsterdam class 9G 782 at Spui on the Rokin in July 1981. (Author)

Wuppertal 3809 seen in Barmen in June 1979 was rebuilt from Grossruamwagen bogie cars. (Author)

One of the cars built (as a six-axle car) by DWM for Karlsruhe, no.190, turns out of Kaiserstrasse to enter Marktplatz in June 2000. (Author)

Duisburg 1080
Length 25.64m, width 2.2m, weight 28.5 tonnes, 2 x 150kW motors, 145 passengers, 63 seated.
Würzburg 241
Length 25.04m, width 2.2m weight 27 tonnes, 2 x 120kW motors, 140 passengers, 59 seated.
Waggon-Union design for Darmstadt
Length 26.45m width 2.4m weight 36.7 tonnes, 2 x 197kW motors, 173 passengers, 63 seated.
Linz L10
Length 31.28m, width 2.3m, weight 37.30 tonnes, 2 x 150kW motors, 195 passengers, 54 seated.
Amsterdam class 8G
Length 23.93m, width 2.34m, weight 30.2 tonnes, 4 x 53kW motors, 148 passengers, 64 seated.
Amsterdam class 9G
Length 25.5m, width 2.32m, weight 30.9 tonnes, 4 x 53 kW motors, 145 passengers, 64 seated.

Linz 76 negotiates a temporary crossover near Hauptplatz in the city centre in June 1981. (Author)

Linz 42 approaches Blumauerplatz in September 1987. (Author)

Bibliography

Der Stadtverkehr 8/1974 (Amsterdam), 3/1978 (Graz), 8/1979 (Amsterdam), 11/12 1981 (Darmstadt), 4/5/1985 (Linz ten-axle design), 9/1989 (Austrian cars), 8/91 (Amsterdam).

Strassenbahnen in Österreich. op.cit.
8-axle articulated tramcar Type 9G for Amsterdam GVB. LHB factsheet, n.d.
Die Stadtbahnwagen der Typen M und N.M. Kochems. Transpress Verlag, Stuttgart, 2005.

DOUBLE-ENDED DESIGNS

A few of the larger German undertakings were interested in a larger version of the Bochum type and of these, Dortmund was the most enthusiastic. An order for 41 such trams was placed in 1958 and, because of capacity problems at the Düwag factory, 20 of these were built by Hansa in Bremen under licence. They proved to be extremely satisfactory for Dortmund conditions and further batches followed in 1965, 1969 and 1974, taking the total to 91 trams, classed GT8 and numbered 1-91. None is now in service in their home city. As they could not be used in tunnel service, replacement began as early as 1981 and the excellently-maintained cars were snapped up by other systems, ten going to Karlsruhe and eight to Wuppertal. All these have now been withdrawn. The furthest travelled are two sold to Hiroshima, where they were fitted with air conditioning and ran for some years in

normal service. Resita in Romania has received 22 cars of this type. The last in Dortmund were withdrawn in 1996. Heidelberg had four cars built by Düwag as late as 1985 (201-204).

Bonn acquired 15 similar cars (401-414 and 3011) between 1960 and 1969 for use on its suburban lines, where stopping places were located on either side of the track on single line sections. These had increased seating capacity and, originally, were worked with an itinerant conductor. One was withdrawn in 1983 after a fire and all the others were sold to Sofia in 1995. For use on line K to Krefeld, which has a stub terminal in that city, Düsseldorf bought five cars (1265-1269) in 1966. The width was kept at 2.35m, to allow use on the city system when necessary. In 1974 they were replaced on line K by new cars of type GT8 and were then redeployed on city services until 1993, when all

except one were scrapped. What had become car 2269 is preserved. In 1969 Frankfurt (M) bought eight cars (901-908, class O) for use on line 16, which had just been cut back to terminate at a crossover in the centre of Offenbach. A few are still in service. In 1975 Heidelberg bought four trams (201-204), which are also still in service. These were the only three-section cars of this type built for metre gauge. In all 123 trams of this design were built.

A rather different version was built for the Oberrheinische Eisenbahn Gesellschaft by Rastatt in 1960 and 1963. There were only two cars involved (75, later renumbered 80, and 81). These capacious, elegant and comfortable cars were later rebuilt for one person operation. Both are now withdrawn. They were followed by a series of cars built by Düwag over a long period between 1966 and 1989 (82-116). These

Dortmund 10 at Hauptbahnhof in May 1981. (Author)

Innsbruck 85 leaving the Hauptbahnhof terminus for Fulpmes in June 2001. (Author)

OEG 95 in the new livery at Mannheim Hauptbahnhof in June 1996. (Author)

OEG cars 81 and 80 leave Mannheim in June 1985. (Author)

Frankfurt (M) 906 at Offenbach Grens (boundary) terminus in June 1996. (Author)

WLB 103 shares Meidling depot with older bogie car 134 in June 1981. (Author)

Bonn 401 and another of the class at Hauptbahnhof in June 1980. (Author)

differed from the Bochum type in seating layout and in the arrangement of doors, although technically they used many components of the latter. They have given excellent service and all are still at work.

The final version of the classic Düwag articulated tram appeared in Düsseldorf in 1973. This was a derivative of the Mannheim design, but was double-ended. There were ultimately 65 of these trams (3001-3065, class GT8S) and in 1975 four more appeared (3101-3104), fitted with buffet facilities in the middle section and having no doors in that portion. The price of the series cars was about DM800,000 each (c£260,000). The prototype, the buffet trams and the last eleven had air conditioning. The class was known as "Stadtbahnwagen" but at first their use was on conventional tram lines and on

Düsseldorf 3053 in the washer at Heerdt depot in May 1981. (Author)

the radial lines to Krefeld and Duisburg, on which they ran in m.u. formation. In 1981 cars 3001-3020 and the four buffet trams were rebuilt to allow them to operate in the new tunnels and to serve stations with high platforms. Sixteen further cars (3021-3036) were similarly treated in 1983/4 and the conversions became class GT8SU, with numbers from 3201 upwards. As the front door could not be used at high platform stations owing to the gap between the car body and the platform, the end section was rebuilt to a more square profile and the cars so treated were nicknamed "Dicke Backe" (chubby cheeks). The buffets were removed in 1988, when Stadtbahn B cars began to serve line D. A few were withdrawn from 2000 onwards, but the bulk of the class is still in service.

A plan to sell some of the withdrawn cars to Manchester for use on Metrolink unfortunately fell through.

There was much less rebuilding of double-ended cars than there was with those of single-ended layout. Of the two-section double-ended cars, Essen in 1992-94 rebuilt its ten cars into eight-axle vehicles, using centre sections taken from ex-Duisburg cars and some of its own vehicles. Eight were still in service in 2002 but are in course of withdrawal. The eight cars sold by Hagen to Innsbruck in 1976 were immediately rebuilt to allow conductor operation, but were later subject to much more extensive alteration. Between 1980 and 1985 all received centre sections for ex-Bielefeld cars and were placed in service on the radial lines, at first on line 6 to Igls but from 1983 on the modernised Stubaitalbahn to Fulpmes. A serious collision in 1995 badly damaged cars 82 and 87, but the former was replaced by the acquisition of another car from Bochum, into which was inserted the undamaged centre section and the latter was rebuilt with other undamaged parts of car 82. Since 1996 all these cars have been one-person operated.

The only double-ended design to be built under licence in Austria by SGP was that for the Wiener

Buffet tram 3104 at Duisburg Hauptbahnhof in July 1979. (Author)

In May 1981 car 3019 undergoes alteration to its front end in the Rheinbahn workshops. (Author)

Lokalbahn. This was a version of the GT8S type, first supplied in 1979 and now numbering 26 cars in all (101-126). These have only three single-width doors per side and a relatively high seating capacity. Up to three cars can operate in multiple.

Technical details

WBL 101

Length 15.7m, width 2.4m, 2 x 190kW motors, 194 passengers, 64 seated.

Düsseldorf GT8S

Length 26.18m, width 2.4m, weight 34.83 tonnes, 2 x 150kW motors, 138 passengers, 51 seated.

Bibliography

Der Stadtverkehr 8/1979.
Strassenbahn Magazin no.187, May 2005 (Düsseldorf GT8 cars).

Heidelberg 203 wears advertising livery on line 3 in June 1985. (Author)

DESIGNS IN OTHER COUNTRIES

TATRA KT8

Although designs for a double-ended three-section tram were initially prepared by Tatra in 1978, it was 1984 before the first took to the rails for trials in Praha (0018, class KT8 D5). Most of the details of the design came from the T6 car. All axles are motored and it was intended principally for radial lines, being capable of m.u. operation if necessary. Series production began in 1986 and cars were delivered to five systems in what was then Czecho-Slovakia. These systems were Brno, (28), Kosice (40), Most (8), Ostrava (16), Praha (48) and Plzen (16). A very few cars were also delivered to the USSR, Minsk (one only in 1994) and to Pyonyang in North Korea (45). A single-ended version was offered, but found no takers. Three cars acquired from Kosice are now running at Strausberg and others from

No.21 at Strausberg in June 2000. (Author)

the same undertaking have gone to Miskolc (10) and Sarajevo (2). The last development of the class came in 1999 when seven cars (1729-1735)

incorporating a low floor centre section were built for Brno. The design was not totally successful and most operators turned back to the T6 for later deliveries, but in any case this class probably arrived too late to be built in quantity. Trams in several cities, such as Brno, have now been fitted with a low floor centre section, while those in Ostrava have also been converted to single-ended layout in the process.

Technical details
Length 30.3m, width 2.48m, weight 38 tonnes, 8 x 45kW motors, 285 passengers*, 48 seated.

Bibliography
Der Stadtverkehr 9/1988
Strassenbahn Magazin no.145, November 2001

ITALY

The only Italian city to operate multi-section articulated trams is Milano.

In the 1960s Milano became enthusiastic about metro construction as a solution to urban traffic problems, but the high cost brought about a reconsideration of the role of the tram and the possibilities of light rail. In 1971, therefore, the workshops constructed the first eight-axle tram, using the bodies of cars 5335/6 and, as the centre section, the body of car 5451. The new "jumbo" tram was numbered 4801 and, after prolonged, but fairly successful trials, 43 similar cars appeared between 1973 and 1977. These were constructed from the bodies of trams of the 5200 and 5300 classes.

In the early 1970s the ATM considered replacing the ring line trolleybus services with a tram route, using high platforms to ensure reduced dwell time at stops. The trams would, however, have to be capable of running in conventional street-based services. To bring the project to fruition, a working party of several manufacturers was set up. The authorities took some time to agree to the operation of trams of the type proposed by the working party and thus it was only in 1976 that the first car of class 49xx entered service. In the event the ring line conversion did not go ahead and the trams, nicknamed "Jumbos" have spent all their lives on ordinary services. This design probably took conventional tramcar technology nearest to its limits and it has to be said that they have proved very successful in service. One hundred trams were constructed by two consortia. Fiat/Savigliano and Marelli of Milano were responsible for the mechanical and electrical

Due to their large size, these trams have a wide swept path and the rear ends were originally adorned with notices warning motorists to keep clear. Car 4986 is on line 13 in March 1983. Unfortunately the notices did not have the desired effect, and, as it seemed to be easier to change the contours of the trams rather than the driving habits of Milano motorists, the rear ends were soon afterwards rebuilt with a distinct taper. Car 4946 is in the city centre in May 1984. (Author)

parts of cars 4000-4949, while for cars 4950-4999 the firms concerned were OMS and AEG-Telefunken Italia respectively. To allow all doors to be located in the straight part of the body side, while still allowing the trams to circulate freely on all curves throughout the system, the ends of the body had to be asymmetrical. The use of light metal alloys in the construction of the body allowed unladen weight to be kept down to a very modest level, given the size of the tram.

Internally the design is simple, almost clinical, but the seats are comfortable, much more so than on earlier designs in Milano. Riding qualities are excellent. The trams were initially used on lines 8, 13, 15 and 24 but were later transferred to the two tram ring lines, 29 and 30. In 2004 some were used on the new Metrotranvie line 15 due to continuing problems with new low floor cars. Even if they have not been used as originally intended, this class must rank as one of the most successful of modern designs.

Technical details
Car 4802
Length 28.2m, width 2.35m, weight 37.83 tonnes, 8 x 33kW motors, 280 passengers, 49 seated.
Car 4900
Length 29m, width 2.38m weight 32 tonnes, 2 x 145kW motors, 265 passengers, 59 seated.

Bibliography
Tram e Tramvie a Milano. Op.cit.
Hurth Zahnräder & Getriebe. Press report 5, 1976

No. 4947 takes a break from circular service 29 at Piazza Repubblica in July 1993. (Author)

4827 on a newly-created section of segregated track in May 1984. (Author)

NETHERLANDS

As mentioned in the chapter on PCC cars, the HTM of Den Haag concluded that articulated cars should be standard for future construction and on 22 June 1981 placed in service on line 3 the first of its new design. The trams were built by BN and the first 65 were mounted on new Werkspoor bogies, but the remainder of the first batch had bogies taken from PCC cars of the 1300 and 2100 classes. They had Holec thryistor control, which had some teething troubles, and the electrical equipment was by ACEC. An initial batch of 100 cars (3001-3100) was followed in 1992/3 by 47 further identical cars (3101-3147). Of these, HTM built the bogies for 20 in its own workshops and those for the others came from PCC cars. These cars are slightly longer than the first batch, but the public probably took more notice of the new blue and grey livery which they carried.

Technical details
Length 28.6m, width 2.35m, weight 37.3 tonnes, 8 x 45 kW motors, 185 passengers, 77 seated.

Bibliography
Der Stadtverkehr 1/1982.

Car 3093 at Holl. Spoor station in March 2003. (Author)

ROMANIA

Following on the arrival of the LHB car mentioned above, an unknown number of class V3A three-section cars were built for Bucuresti and 25 were also built for the new tramway in Constanta in 1984. These carried 254 passengers, 44 seated. They had conventional control and a somewhat basic interior. They have not lasted well and most have now been replaced by second-hand imports from Germany.

A three-section car at Caryal Bivorie in July 1975. (Peter Haseldine)

KROATIA

In 1994 the firm of TZV, Koncar, delivered the first of 16 three-section cars to Zagreb (2101-2116, class TMK2101). The first of these used the trucks and motors of the unsuccessful six-axle car of 1966 and the others used trucks from bogie cars. Deliveries continued until 2004 and these will probably be the last high-floor articulated cars to be built for any system. Although not low floor cars, these are attractive vehicles, with chopper control and air conditioning.

A busy scene in the centre of Zagreb in December 2004. Articulated car 2111 is on the left, in the distance Tatra 445 emerges from a side turning and on the right is two-axle car 143. (Alan W. Brotchie)

BULGARIA

The workshops of the Sofia system have also produced three-section eight-axle cars, which have followed the design of contemporary six-axle vehicles. Nos.101-211, 301-327 and 730-799 appeared in the years between 1970 and 1980. Nos.901-937 came out in two batches between 1980 and 1991 and of these 916-937 now have low floor centre sections.

A three-section car at a turning circle in Sofia. (M.J. Russell)

HUNGARY

Two series of double-ended eight-axle cars were built by Ganz for Budapest in 1967-71 (1301-1370) and between 1972 and 1978 (1401-1481). These are elegant cars of a design quite unlike any other in Eastern Europe, and have performed well on the city's busy ring line and other routes. In 1990 a new single car (3750) to this design appeared from what was now Ganz-Hunslet, using many components from Ikarus motor buses. Lack of finance prevented series production.

No.1315 running on express line 2 along the Pest bank of the Danube in June 1991. (Author)

USSR AND SUCCESSOR STATES

In 1989 the Riga factory produced one unusual car (901) for the city undertaking. This was a single-ended tram, with the bogies arranged as on the cars for Freiburg, and it was one of the very few eight-axle cars to run in the Soviet Union and the only one to be built in the country. It was also one of the very few of this type to have been fitted with a trolley pole. It was a capacious car and had good riding qualities, but political changes upset any planned series production and it is not now in service.

Two cars of conventional eight-axle design were built in Sankt Petersburg in 1990 (3076) and 1994 (3280). No series production has followed.

Bibliography
Trams in Eastern Europe. Op.cit.

The Riga car at the city's market halls on line 2 in September 1994. (Author)

One of the Sankt Petersburg cars in August 1998. (Author)

SWITZERLAND

The only conventional eight-axle trams to run in Switzerland are a series of 16 (1-16) built by Schlieren for Bern in 1973. After a rather troubled introduction, they have functioned well, mostly on line 9. They are now in course of withdrawal and some have gone to Eastern Europe. However, in 2004 five (711-4 and 717), intended for Iasy, were in 2004 temporarily diverted to Basel to cover for the withdrawn Combino cars.

Bibliography
Der Stadtverkehr 3/1973

In the early 1980s the Regionalbahn Bern-Solothurn found itself with a problem of a number of over-age vehicles on its tram line G from Bern to Worb. To remedy this situation as quickly and cheaply as possible the company ordered a three-section double-ended version of Zürich's Tram 2000 design, this being capable of adaptation with very little re-engineering. Ten cars (81-90) were delivered in 1987. As with the Freiburg trams, the two middle bogies are located under the centre section and not under the articulation. Apart from the obvious differences to the city cars, these have regenerative braking and they are fitted with horns for use on the more rural sections of the line.

The Bern city system showed some interest in acquiring a single-ended version of these trams, but then opted for the Vevey design of low floor car instead.

Bibliography
Bi-articulated light rail motor coaches of RBS. ABB factsheet
Der Stadtverkehr 10/1987

The GVBA of Amsterdam was so pleased with the performance of the rebuilt six-axle car (qv) that all further deliveries of trams to this design were of eight-axle configuration. There were in all four further series of these. Nos.602-634 (3G) came from Bejines in 1959-61, nos. 635-652 (4G) followed from the same manufacturer in 1962, nos.653-669 (5G) were built by Werkspoor in 1964 and finally there arrived in 1966-68 nos.670-724 (6G and 7G), a joint Werkspoor/Düwag venture of 1966-68. There were differences in the control systems between the various batches and class 5G had trucks of a different design, but all were otherwise identical. All were essentially enlarged versions of the pioneer six-axle design from Schindler and all have been equally successful. All were converted for one-person operation around 1970, but a number were retrofitted with conductors' posts from 1991 onwards. In 1989 car 886 was rebuilt with a low floor centre section by the technical staff of GVBA, but no others were similarly treated. The official last journey of this type took place on March 2004, although a few had to be kept in service until 5 April. Many are following their rebuilt six-axle counterparts to Poznan.

Technical details
Class 5G
Length 23.5m, width 2.35m, weight 28.2 tonnes, 4 x 50kW motors, 146 passengers, 62 seated.

Bibliography
Der Stadtverkehr 8/1991

Car 82 at Bern Helvetiaplatz, then the city terminus of the line, in July 1990. (Author)

Car 630 of class 3G in original livery in the Leidsestraat in November 1968. (Author)

Bern 724 on line 3 inbound at Burgernziel in May 2003. (Author)

At Amstel Station in June 1989 no.886 shows off its new low floor section, the advertisement above the middle section proudly proclaiming that it was designed and built by the technical staff of GVBA. (Author)

FOUR-AXLE CARS WITH SUSPENDED ARTICULATION

GT4 CARS OF THE MASCHIENENFABRIEK ESSLINGEN

No.437 heads a coupled set of GT4 cars plus a trailer at Stuttgart Hauptbahnhof in September 1969. (Author)

Car 532 is one of those rebuilt to run as second car in a coupled set. It is at Vahingen in June 1989. (Author)

Ex-Stuttgart car as Augsburg 409 at Haunstetten Südwest, a recently-opened extension, on line 3 in June 2000. (Author)

As mentioned above, the six-axle design did not find favour in Stuttgart, mainly because the topography of the city restricted trams of 25m length to only a few routes. There was also some concern about the cost of the Düwag design. Even before the last of the six-axle cars was delivered, the SSB engineers had begun to study, in close collaboration with the Maschinenfabrik Esslingen, the development of a totally novel type of articulated car, capable of operating in multiple on the city's curves and gradients, as on lines 5 and 6 on the Neue Weinsteige, but at the same time using many of the components which had been first tried on the GT6 cars. A certain mystery surrounds the origins of this design and it is not clear to what extent Professor Bockemühl was involved. No prototypes were built – the design work was completed in 1958, a total of 42 cars were then ordered and the first went into service in the summer of 1959.

The GT4 design runs on two bogies and uses an articulation which is supported by the concealed underframe of the car, rather than by an intermediate bogie. The side members of this connect the second and third axles and the articulation rests on these. Guided by the leading bogie, which is connected by a pivoting joint to the underframe, the car is steered into curves, assisted by a further pivoting joint also connected to the underframe, 0.55m short of the centre point of the tram. This design avoided the cost and complication of a third bogie, although the length of the tram had to be limited and the ends had to be rounded rather than tapered. The motors are suspended from the frame and drive the second and third axles through cardan drive, this giving good adhesion for hill-climbing. The result was a fast and smooth-riding vehicle, which, with its sleek lines, marked a distinct advance on the cars used hitherto in Stuttgart. Unfortunately the cars showed themselves to be prone to derailment and it was always necessary to enter curves with caution. At about £20,000 at the then rate of exchange, the GT4 was a relatively cheap design and cost less than its rivals.

The cars were single-ended, with four double doors fitted with outward opening doors and were originally laid out for passenger flow from rear to front, with one seated conductor. Given the then complicated fare structure, it was thought that a maximum of about 160 passengers could be carried. Seating was for 37 passengers, arranged 2+1 and, on a width of 2.2m, this limited the length of the tram to about 18m. In

SSB No.720 at Möhringen in June 1984, showing detail of its construction. (Author)

the end, a total of 165 passengers could be carried and a two-car set could move 330 passengers with a crew of only three. When a light trailer (designed to run without a conductor) was added, capacity rose to 430. It was no wonder that the canny Stuttgarters were delighted! It was technically possible to run in trains of three cars, but, due to the limited length of loading islands, this was done only on non-passenger workings.

The first delivery of what was known as class 31 was of 72 cars (501-572) in 1959/60. These were immediately followed by 100 further cars (401-500) and in the years 1962-64 by 178 more (573-750). The total of 350 was the greatest number

Ex-Freiburg car 162 in service on line 1 in Halberstadt in 1996, still in its original livery. As in most former DDR undertakings, a great amount of track work reconstruction was then taking place. (Author)

of cars of one class built in the Federal Republic in post-war years and was only ever exceeded by the class T24 of which 1000 had been constructed for Berlin in 1924. Rebuilding for one-person operation began in 1964 almost immediately after the last new car entered service and those trams which were to run as second car had the driving cab removed, allowing seating to be increased to 41. About 50 cars were modernised after 1984, receiving upholstered seats, new lighting and improvements to the driver's cab and it is only cars thus treated which remained in service in Stuttgart in 2002.

There were attempts to interest other systems in the design and in 1960 car 550 ran in Essen during a transport exhibition. Ostensibly to test noise emission levels, there was also a trial of car 667 in Zürich in April 1964 – with great interest also being shown by Basel – but, although the results were very slightly in favour of the GT4, the capacity was considered too limited and there would have had to be considerable adaptations to comply with the very strict Swiss regulations. Despite the attractive price – almost half that of a contemporary Swiss tram – no sale resulted. However, the nearby small system of Reutlingen bought three double-ended trams (59-61) in 1963/4 and when it closed in 1973, these were sold to Stuttgart. They did not actually enter service there and in 1981/2 were sold on to Ulm, where they were rebuilt as single-ended cars. They were in service until 1988. Freiburg-i-Breisgau bought eleven double-ended cars (103-113) in 1962 and 1966 and later a further eight (115-122), which were built by Rastatt under licence in 1967/8, the ME having given up tramcar production by that date. The second batch was built new for one-person operation. All these cars ran on metre gauge, but Neunkirchen acquired the only standard gauge GT4 cars to be built when it bought eight cars (1-8) in 1961. This system had on its only line a gradient of 11.5% and, to cope with this, the 110kW motors were suspended from the car body, in a position at the outer end of each part, and all axles were driven. The GT4 cars performed excellently but nonetheless the system closed on 10 June 1978 and none were sold for further service. One has been preserved in the town.

Not surprisingly there were many takers for this excellent design when it was made redundant in Stuttgart by the development of the Stadtbahn system and surplus cars were from 1985 onwards snapped up not only by poverty-stricken under-

Neunkirchen 5 is about to descend one of the city's steep gradients in June 1977. (Jim D. Schantz)

takings in Eastern Europe but also by others in western Germany. Of Freiburg's five remaining cars, one, 121, was rebuilt as a party tram and three, 115-117, were sold to Brandenburg in 1997, to be used on a shuttle service at the-then outer end of line 1. These are now held as a reserve, as are the two remaining in Freiburg, mainly to be used when track repairs necessitate the employment of double-ended trams. Between 1995 and 2000 31 trams from Stuttgart were sold at a nominal price to Arad in Romania, while Iassy received 25. Augsburg and Ulm acquired 40 (plus two for spare parts) and 13 respectively, of which twenty of the Augsburg cars (411/461-420/270) received a very thorough modernisation in 1996 by Mittenwalder Gerätebau. They were then placed in service on the extended line 3. Freiburg bought ten, nine of which were in 1990 sold on to Halle. Here they joined 30 which had come direct from Stuttgart and a further two came in 1997 to supply spare parts. The arrival of these cars allowed a very quick improvement in Halle's services and also allowed the temporary withdrawal of its own best cars for modernisation. The last was withdrawn on 21 April 2003 and 27 went on to Iassy. The cars in Ulm have now also been withdrawn. Apart from one (10), which is being preserved locally, these went in 2002 for further service in Arad, as did the non-modernised cars from Augsburg. Between 1991 and 1994 Halberstadt acquired thirteen cars from Stuttgart, three for spare parts, and five from Freiburg. Nordhausen took twelve plus four cars from Stuttgart in 1991 and these were followed in 1994 by six plus one from Freiburg. In 1994 the idea was conceived of running a through service from the Harz narrow gauge railway line on to the Nordhausen town tramways, there being a certain amount of commuter traffic. One of the Nordhausen cars, 94, ex-Freiburg 114, was fitted with a large diesel engine in one half of the body. While it could not carry passengers in this condition and in any case had a rating of only 80kW, the experiment demonstrated that the concept was practicable and 72, ex-Stuttgart 544, was in 1999 fitted with two much more compact diesel engines, of a size used in private cars, one in the forward saloon and one on the rear platform. These have increased the unladen weight by only one tonne. To mark its special status, the car was repainted green and white, the system's normal colours being yellow and cream, and was given the name "Twino". To date, the experiment seems to have been successful and car 72 is to be preserved by the firm which installed its new machinery.

The most far-travelled is a double-ended car made up from parts of cars 714 and 735, which went to Kochi in Japan in 1980.

Although few remain in service in Stuttgart and all will have gone from there by 2007, the GT4 cars will be running in other cities for some time yet. This must be considered one of the most successful tram designs of the 20th century and the experiments in Nordhausen have also ushered in a new concept of tramways for the 21st century.

Technical details
Stuttgart, as new
Length 18m, width 2.2m, weight 19.2 tonnes, 2x 100kW motors, 165 passengers, 37 seated.

Bibliography
Modern Tramway no.298, October 1962 and no.322, October 1964.
Strassenbahn Magazin, nos. 57, August 1985 (Stuttgart), 108, August/September 1997 and 136, February 2001 (Nordhausen experiments).
Die deutschen Strassenbahn-Gelenkwagens. Op.cit.
1868-1968 100 Jahre Stuttgarter Strassenbahn. Stuttgarter Strassenbahn, 1968.

At Ammendorf depot in Halle in September 1992 ex-Stuttgart 986 contrasts with Tatra T4D 853. (Author)

An ex-Stuttgart car, 804, in Arad in July 1999. (Martin Jenkins, OnLine Transport Archive)

Car 427 approaching the Hauptbahnhof in Bremen in June 1980. (Author)

HANSA CARS

At almost the same time as the first GT4 cars were entering service in Stuttgart, Bremen was faced with the necessity of acquiring larger capacity trams to allow economies in personnel to be made. Owing to its track geometry, however, the choice was restricted and conventional articulated trams were ruled out as they would have been unable to cope with the system's curves without excessive overhang. As it was intended to run with trailers, maximum adhesion was also desirable. Working in co-operation with the local builder Hansa, the city developed its own innovative variety of articulated tram.

The Bremen cars consisted of two body sections and rode on two conventional trucks, each located under the middle portion of one section. The two parts of the body were so connected that any vertical movement on curves was eliminated. The articulation was steered by a rod running from the inner end of each truck. This was so arranged that on curves it could deviate from the centre line of the track and so limit the outward swing of the car body. It also allowed a width of 2.30m to be used, in conjunction with a rounded rather than tapered end and these combined to make the cars extremely spacious internally. They had a distinctly matronly appearance and had none of the elegance of the Stuttgart GT4 design. A total of 120 passengers could be carried, of whom 38 were seated.

After successful trials of a prototype, a total of 74 motor cars (401-474) to this design were placed in service between 1959 and 1967. In the following year, five identical cars (80-84) were acquired by Bremerhaven, which was already planning to scrap its trams. It was expected that the cars would be bought by Bremen when the system closed and thus the operation could be modernised without any concern that the city would later find itself with unsaleable trams. These trams finally came to Bremen in 1982. In service the cars proved to be successful and were cheaper in both first cost and in maintenance than the ME GT4 design.

There were also 43 similar trailers for Bremen (1401-1419 and 1445-1468) and five for Bremerhaven (218-222), which also came to the former in 1982. Apart from the lack of motors and equipment, these were identical to the motor cars and in fact were so constructed that they could be motorised at a later date if necessary. In the event, this change was not implemented.

When replaced by low floor trams in 1995, 42 motor cars and 39 trailers were sold to Timisoara in Romania. The last ran in Bremen in 1997 but one car remained in service as a Partywagen until 2004.

München 2024 and trailer at Odeonplatz in June 2001. (Author)

Bremerhaven 84 in the city centre in June 1980. (Author)

The design appealed strongly to the München authorities, who were experiencing similar staff problems and whose six-axle, three-section articulated design had proved to be uneconomical. Another advantage of the Hansa cars was that all doors were in the straight side of the car and could therefore be aligned with platforms in future underground stations – the city was at this time planning a system of tram subways. In 1965 the local firm of Rathgeber obtained a licence to build two prototype motor and trailer sets, based on the Bremen design (201/2, 2001/2). As higher speeds were required, 80kW motors were fitted and the width was increased to 2.35m. A series of 42 motor cars and 38 trailers followed in 1967/8 (2003-2044 and 3003-3040) and, as these were very successful, there could well have been more had not the city meanwhile turned against trams in favour of a U-Bahn system. The prototypes, by then renumbered 2001/2 and 3001/2) were with-drawn in 1981 but the production cars survived longer and in 2003 a few received minor over-hauls, to keep them running until new trams arrive. Two each of motor and trailers went to Bucuresti in 1998 and more may follow.

Technical details
Bremen motor cars
Length 16.7m, width 2.2m, weight 17.5 tonnes, motors 4x60kW, 120 passengers, 38 seated.

TATRA KT4D CARS

The principles of this design were later copied in Eastern Europe by the Tatra factory. The smaller systems in the DDR, which had no interest in buying large and expensive bogie cars and were still smarting over the ending of production of two-axle cars, pressed for the development of a design which would be suitable for their particular conditions. CKD Tatra first developed an articulation of the Bremen type and tried this in car 7000, one of the prototype six-axle cars of class K2. To gain experience on metre gauge

One of the two prototypes, 001, has been preserved in Potsdam and is seen here in Platz der Einheit on an enthusiasts' tour in October 2002. (Author)

KT4D cars, in standard DDR livery, running in a three-car train, headed by 518, in Bahnhofstrasse, Erfurt on 25 June 1990. The crowd of people are not waiting for the tram, but to exchange their east marks for D-Marks at the temporary bank on the left. (Author)

tracks, this tram was tested in Liberec early in 1972. Following this, in 1973 two prototypes of what became class KT4 entered trial service in Praha. Although of a very angular external appearance, these trams were based on the Hansa design, with a different mechanism to link the articulation with the bogies. The electro-magnetic control system was more akin to that of the PCC car, with pedal control and the bogies fitted were virtually identical to those under the T3 bogie car. The prototypes had ribbed sides to the lower body and were the first Tatra cars to use the new TE022H motor. After successful trials in Praha they were sent to the DDR, where they entered service in Potsdam as 001 and 002. A pre-production series of 35 entered service in 1975/6 and series production began in 1977 and continued until 1991. Unlike the prototypes, production cars had flat sides. The class was generally successful but two cities, Schwerin and Leipzig, which preferred bogie cars got rid of theirs to Berlin as soon as they decently could. It was not intended to use these trams with trailers, but they were fitted for m.u. operation and in Erfurt they were from December 1981 regularly operated as three-car trains on services to new housing areas. These sets had the impressive carrying capacity of almost 600 passengers.

Apart from the advertisements there is no change in the appearance of Görlitz 15 from DDR times when seen at Postplatz in September 1993. (Author)

Most undertakings contracted out the rebuilding of the KT4 cars but, as seen here in September 1993, Görlitz preferred to undertake this in-house. A good deal of work was involved! (Author)

Brandenburg 177 as rebuilt with low floor section, on the now-abandoned section of single track through Plaue village in October 2002. (Author)

The design was continually improved during its period of construction and from 1983 thyristor control was fitted (KT4Dt). This was used only on trams built for Berlin.

Initially delivered only to undertakings in the DDR, 1042 trams of this type were delivered, of which Berlin took 524. A further 415 went to the-then Soviet Union and cars delivered to the former are to-day running in Lvov, Tallinn, Kaliningrad and Vinnitza. The trams in Tallinn run on 1067mm gauge. Two have been given low floor centre sections. What was then Jugo-slavia received 240 cars for Zagreb and Beograd, of which the former gave much more satisfaction than did the T4 bogie cars. Finally production closed in 1991 with 50 cars supplied to the new system in Pyonyang, North Korea. This made a total of 1747 trams altogether, of a very successful class.

After the reunification of Germany, many cars were modernised, in a variety of different ways, and no longer formed one large standard class. Between 1993 and May 1997 a consortium of Siemens, MGB, Düwag and Waggonbau Bautzen modernised for Berlin all 99 KT4Dt trams and also 171 of the earlier cars. The interior was completely overhauled and new cladding fitted to improve insulation. Upholstered seats replaced the shiny fibreglass model of DDR times and the driver received a new, ergonomically-designed seat. New lighting and new windows with hopper ventilators and new headlights all combined to give the cars an attractive and up-to-date appearance, enhanced by the new yellow, white and grey livery. The non-thyristor cars received new control equipment, with regenerative braking and hand control, as on the new low floor cars. In other cities similar modifications were carried out, in too great variety to detail here. Generally, however, attention was paid to rust-proofing the areas around the doors,

this having been a weak point of most Tatra designs, and passengers and drivers alike received new seating and new lighting. As a result, these attractive and serviceable cars should be running for a further ten years or so on many eastern German systems. The builders themselves rebuilt one Erfurt tram (438) with a new type of articulation joint and, christened the "Twistram"; it was tried on the Praha system, but not in passenger service. Non-modernised cars had by 2000 been sold for further service in Braila, Cluj, Constanta, Craiova, Galati, Oradea and Ploiesti in Romania, which between them received 160 from Berlin and Potsdam. Tallinn took cars from Gera, Liepaya received eight from Cottubs, Gera and Erfurt, and Kasachstan has cars from Berlin. One car has already entered preservation in Leipzig.

A further problem, particularly for smaller systems such as Cottbus which relied on this type almost exclusively was the lack of accessibility, the floor being 900mm above rail level. Even if money had been available to replace these trams, it would have been a waste of scarce resources to withdraw vehicles which still had up to 25 years of useful life ahead. The firm of Mittenwald Gerätbau, not previously involved in tramcar building developed, in conjunction with the Swiss firm of Schindler and Fiat-SIG, an economical and practical way of incorporating a low floor centre section, as had already been done elsewhere on articulated trams of conventional construction. This section is constructed of lightweight fibreglass material and adds only 7.5 tonnes to the weight of the tram. Independent steerable wheels of a diameter of only 575mm, linked to the main body sections on each side, allow a low floor throughout the centre section, which forms about 30% of the total length of the car and has seats for 15 passengers, plus two folding seats, and room for 28 standees. Entrance height is only 30cm above rail level and a small ramp can also be extended by the driver to assist passengers in wheelchairs to board and alight. The disadvantage of the addition of this section has been a slight reduction in acceleration to about 1m/second, instead of 1.3m/second, but this is of little practical importance. Cottbus now has 27 of these modified trams, while Brandenburg (10) has also taken advantage of this development. These trams are classified KT NF6. In 2001 two cars in Tallinn were similarly treated. An alternative solution was devised by the original builder for Gera. This involved placing a new centre section running on two bogies whose wheels are only

Just before re-unification, Potsdam experienced an acute shortage of serviceable trams and 80 KT4D cars from Berlin were drafted in. On 30 June 1990 Berlin 219 367, re-numbered 095, heads a rather down-at–heel Potsdam car in a "Potsdammer Mischung" (Potsdam mixture) at Pl. der Einheit. (Author)

A fitter's eye view of a KT4D, as seen from a pit in the depot in Zwickau in September 1992. (Author)

410mm in diameter to allow a floor height of 360mm, into already-modernised tram 349. The new section offered 23 additional seats and the design was classified KTNF8. The motors were replaced by new TE036 motors of 54kW to cope with the additional weight. However, due to the problems at Tatra, there were no subsequent conversions and the other low floor sections for Gera were built in Berlin.

Technical details

DDR KT4D motor cars (Kurzegelenk Triebwagen vier achsen Deutschland)
Length 18.1m, width 2.20m, weight 19.9 tonnes, 4 x 40kW motors, 141 passengers, 35 seated.

KT4D 92 running in Tallinn in August 1998. (Author)

Modernised Berlin 7067 at Eberswalder Strasse U-Bahn station in November 1997. (Author)

BREMEN STADTBAHN CARS

When further new cars were required in Bremen, the undertaking decided to use a development of the previous successful design. As the Hansa factory had by now gone out of business, these cars were constructed by Wegmann of Kassel. Unlike their predecessors, the new trams ran on Wegmann bogies and had longitudinally mounted motors. This necessitated the use of a different form of articulation in which a hydraulic system was used, steering being transmitted from the bogies by rods to cylinders mounted under the middle of the car. The new system seemed to work well at first but after a few years of high speed running on the outer sections of Bremen's excellent reserved tracks, the cars began to pitch and wobble in a most unpleasant manner and beginning in 1981 all cars were withdrawn successively and sent to the LHB factory for alteration. The hydraulics were altered and the bogies received a more rigid mounting with secondary suspension. Since then the trams have performed irreproachably, but, perhaps because of their early reputation, no other system was willing to use the design.

In all 61 motor trams (501-561) were delivered between 1973 and 1977 and there was also a series of 58 matching trailers (701-758).

Officially the class are known as "Stadtbahn" cars, but there is nothing of the Stadtbahn about them, compared with cars elsewhere which are thus designated. They are not designed for operation in tunnels or with high platforms; they were simply thoroughly modern trams for their time. No doubt the city did not want to appear to be left behind by Essen and other places, which were then placing Stadtbahn cars in service. They were also distinguished by a new livery of red and white, the civic colours. In 1980 car 561, which had originally been fitted with electronic control, was named "Roland" after the legendary founder of the city.

By 1986 Bremen had decided that it would in future use large single cars rather than tram/trailer sets and it was also beginning to think in terms of low floor vehicles. To test out the various new ideas, car 561 was, with the help of parts from trailer 758, enlarged to a three-section car, the first application of this design concept to such a vehicle. The truck under the central section was not motored and was connected to the body by a system of torsion screws and bars. These were in turn linked to the articulation and so steered the new middle section smoothly into and out of curves. The system worked well in practice and after two years a further car, 560, was similarly converted. To mark its enlargement, car 561 was renamed "Roland der Riesende" ("Roland the Great"). The concepts thus tried in Bremen have since been used in many of the low floor trams built subsequently. Most cars of this class are still in

The articulation joint on one of Bremen's cars, seen in September 2002. (Author)

service in Bremen, but five each of motors and trailers followed their predecessors to Timisoara late in 2002 and delivery of more low floor cars in 2004 will result in further withdrawals.

Technical details
Length 16.7m, width 2.3m, weight 20.95 tonnes, 2x120kW motors. Capacity 109, 44 seated.

Bibliography
Tatra-Wagen der ehemaligen DDR. Der Stadtverkehr, 2/1992
Strassenbahn Magazin, nos.104, June 1996. (KT4D with low floor section), 169, November 2003 (Bremen), 174, April 2005 (Hansa cars)
Die deutschen Strassenbahn gelenkwagen. Op.cit.

Car 551 at Hauptbahnhof in June 1980. (Author)

FOUR-AXLE CARS WITH SUSPENDED CENTRE SECTIONS

The idea of uniting the bodies of two two-axle trams with a suspended centre section is the oldest form of articulation in tramcar construction. The first patent for the design was taken out in 1892 and a prototype was tried in Cleveland in the following year. But it was not until the introduction of the PAYE system and power operated doors that the concept became a practical proposition. It was first tried in Boston in 1912, under the direction of John Lindall, rolling stock engineer of the Boston Elevated Railway Company. Two old two-axle cars, each deprived of one platform, were linked by a suspended centre section with air-operated sliding doors. The conductor had a fixed post in this section and exit was by these doors and by that at the front, which the motorman controlled by a lever. In this form the car weighed 19.7 tonnes and could carry 52 seated and over 100 standing passengers. The 69 subsequent rebuilds were excellent crowd-movers but their riding qualities were atrocious, there being no linkage of the two trucks, and, when fully loaded, the middle section sometimes bumped along the ground, pushing the conduc-

tor's seat upwards and firing that unfortunate man towards the ceiling. A version rebuilt from bogie cars, to a total of 122 trams, was not much better and all had been withdrawn from passenger service by 1924. It was an ingenious way to use some of the numerous old cars in the fleet, for which Lindall deserved every credit, but it was not a long-term solution. The Boston cars went under the nickname of "two rooms and a bath"; obviously the Hub was one up on Glasgow with its "room and kitchen" car! Similar cars, in limited numbers, were tried in Portland, Richmond and Brooklyn.

Bibliography
Strassenbahn Magazin no.59, February 1986

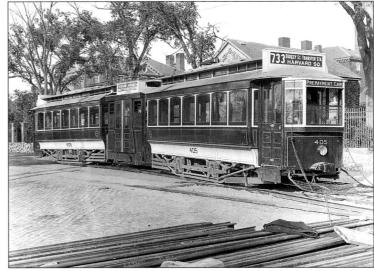
Boston Elevated 405 in the yard of Bennett Street car house, Cambridge, around 1912. (Bradley H. Clark collection)

SWEDEN, THE NETHERLANDS, ITALY

The first application of the design in Europe appeared in Göteborg on 1 June 1922, when the undertaking's own workshop unveiled the prototype of an articulated car (190), constructed from two fairly modern two-axle cars of 1909. Entry was at the front and the conductor stood by the central exit, there being no rear door. It was intended that passengers would not stand on the centre platform except when they wished to alight. Ten further rebuilds (191-200), with larger platforms, entered service in 1923. The cars were not totally successful, possibly because they had only 2 x 16kW motors, and, after some time in normal service, were relegated to special duties, but the last was not withdrawn until 1949. The Swedes followed Glasgow practice, but they also went slightly up-market and referred to these trams as "två rum och kök – two rooms and kitchen". In 1932 and 1934 Amsterdam rebuilt four old "Unionwagens" (161/2 and 177/8) to this design for use on the ring lines 3 and 10. They were not a success on these and they were soon banished to a suburban line. After some years out of service, they were scrapped in 1950/1.

However, the design was to enjoy much more success in Italy. In Milano the delivery of the Peter Witt bogie cars had rendered obsolete a number of fairly new two-axle cars and in 1932 the ATM in its own workshops rebuilt and modernised two trailers from the 1300 class of 1924. These were linked by a centre section supplied by Carminati e Toselli to form a single-ended articulated motor car, with passenger flow from front to rear. The new tram was numbered 3000. Four TIBB GTM3/4 motors of 40kW allowed it to keep up with the Peter Witts in service. Again riding qualities left something to be desired but were rather better than with previous similar designs, probably because the trucks had a wheelbase of 3.3m. The rebuilding was considered a success and a further 23 conversions (3001-3023) were carried out by Carminati e Toselli in the next two years. In 1935 a further car (4400) was constructed from a motor car of the 600 class of 1924 and a trailer. In 1938 passenger flow was reversed to run from rear to front. Between 1940 and 1942, to cope with wartime traffic, a further 25 conversions followed (4001-4025). Unfortunately all but car 4005 fell victim to the RAF in the next year but 14 were rebuilt by ATM after the war, while the balance of ten were reconstructed by Breda with metal-framed bodies. Finally this manufacturer built 24 more cars (4026-4049) in part using what was left of some 3000 class trams after the bombardments and in part cars of the 600 class. In the period 1956-60 eight cars were re-motored and numbered 4100-4107. The Milano cars were certainly more successful than earlier

versions of this design. Those 3000 class which had not been destroyed in the war and the 4000 class ran until 1961, while the 4100 class lasted until the mid-'70s, the last, 4108, even being fitted with a pantograph and not withdrawn until 1978.

The example of Milano encouraged Rome to copy the idea in 1935/6 with 91 cars, (5001-5187, odd numbers only). They were also successful and lasted until the contraction of the system in the period 1960-64. Most were then scrapped but eight went to the suburban STEFER and ran on its lines until closure. Naples had four cars, the first of which was built new in 1941 to try the idea. The other three came out after the war and had new middle and rear sections, the front parts being rebuilt from two-axle cars of 1934. However, this undertaking did not perpetuate the type. At a later date Genova and Torino both adopted the design. The former had 15 cars (1701-1715), rebuilt in 1954/5 in a very basic manner by Ansaldo from members of the 600 class of 1926. These were double-ended trams (though latterly they ran virtually as single-ended cars) and the floor of the centre section was inconveniently lower by 150mm than that in the outer sections. They served for ten years until the system closed in 1966. Torino had 72 new bodies of a streamlined design built on old underframes by Savigliano (2700-2771). Despite their modern appearance, the riding qualities were atrocious and they were mostly used on the special works services 90, 91 and 92 to the Fiat factory and on football specials. In the early 1960s, eight were fitted with extra Bissel radial axles and wheelsets at front and rear and the two-axle trucks were displaced inwards towards the centre of the car in an attempt to improve the ride by a better distribution of the car's weight. The alteration was not successful. The cars lasted until 1984/5, though car 2758 re-entered service in 1988 rebuilt as a restaurant and tourist tram. Whether its riding now allows patrons to enjoy their refreshments is not clear!

In total 256 trams of this type were used in Italy and, even if they were not ideal from the passenger's point of view, they did prove the practicability of the concept as a means of utilising older equipment to produce efficient high capacity cars of modern outline quickly and at a reasonable cost. They also seem to have convinced the Light Railway Transport League that the articulated car had a future; an unsigned article in the April 1953 issue of "Modern Tramway" commented that "Italian experience ... shows that an articulated car need not be a technical oddity, entailing high maintenance costs, but that it can be extremely serviceable and economical in operation"!

Rome 5085 in a depot view on 22 September 1967, after transfer to STEFER. (Father Benedict collection)

Torino 2714 seen in October 1975. (Jim D. Schantz)

Technical details

Milano 3000 class
Length 19.45m, width ?2.4m, weight 23,500kg, 4 x 40kW motors, 185 passengers, 48 seated.

HUNGARY

Budapest in 1938 rebuilt two old motor cars of 1911 as an articulated unit, which was known to the staff as "Adele". It had some modern features, such as a wide centre door, and with four 55kW motors was fast, but its riding, on trucks of 4.5m wheelbase, was distinctly rough. It was considered unsuccessful and was scrapped after the war.

The idea of similar rebuilds was revived in the 1960s and a delegation visited Erfurt to see the Gotha cars in service. They seem to have been impressed and in 1962 the city's workshops built two prototypes (3720 and 3722), each from two old cars. The aim here was not so much to save on personnel but to replace some really antiquated specimens as quickly and cheaply as possible. The first car was single-ended with a seated conductor and two double- and one triple-width doors. To denote this to waiting passengers, a new livery of ivory with a red band was applied. Nineteen similar cars soon entered service as class CM2 (1101-1119). No.3722 was double-ended and a production version was built as CM4, with 34 cars (3722, 1201-1233). These

Göteborg 200 when new. (GS, Stig Hammarson collection)

Milano 4001 on 4 October 1968. (Father Benedict collection)

Szeged 662 is seen leaving the city centre in June 1991 and giving a taxi a good run for its money. This is one of the double-ended cars with doors on one side only, for use on line 3. (Author)

last had five doors per side. Similar cars were then produced by both the Budapest works and the works in Debrecen for the provincial systems of Miskolc (47 trams), Debrecen (29) and Szeged (40), the last two of these also receiving eight cast-offs from the capital in due course. These consisted of both single and double-ended cars and also an unusual version of a double-ended car with doors on one side only, for use on single track sections. These have proved to be robust and reliable trams and many are still in service in the provincial cities. Their riding qualities, however, leave much to be desired.

Szeged liked the idea so much that it went on in 1962 to convert four cars (701-704), using the underframes of ex-Budapest cars with new two-section bodies, linked by a minimal centre section, which had a tiny window but no doors. The main aim was to cope with the curves on the system, but the riding was still distinctly rough. These ingenious trams lasted until the early 1980s.

POLAND

The Konstal factory in Chorzow built in 1962/3 twelve articulated cars (0601-0612) for Warsaw using cars of class N3, delivered in 1952-54. They were heartily disliked and two were scrapped as early as 1968. One was presented to Bydgoszcz, which became immensely proud of this large tram, and it lasted there until 1975. Poznan took the remainder but on closer acquaintance became disillusioned with the type and they were soon scrapped.

The same factory in 1963 delivered eleven single-ended cars to Katowice (701-708). These had an almost futuristic appearance, with a very rounded front, but they were underpowered, with only two 60kW motors for a tram 21m long, and were scrapped in 1975. Polish undertakings showed no further interest in this type of tram.

SOVIET UNION

Four trams were built by Tbilisi, Georgia. These used bow collectors and had very large windows in the central portion. They were numbered from 501/502, each portion having its own number. Nothing else is known about them.

Riga, Latvia, built two similar cars in 1946/7. These were obtained by using old Leyland bus bodies, placed on trucks from war-damaged trams. The first had 2 x 32kW motors, while the second had four of the same rating. Length was 19.45m, width 2.36m and they could carry 155 passengers, of whom 50 had seats. Weight of the second car was 13.8 tonnes.

Bibliography

Modern Tramway nos.184, April 1953 (Italy), 337, January 1966 (N. America), 327, March 1965 (Tbilisi), 336, December 1965 (Riga), 348, December 1966 (Budapest).

Zeppelinare, Limpor och Mustanger. (Göteborg history). S. Hammarson. F. Stenvalls Förlag, Malmö, 1979.

Strassenbahn-Betriebe in Osteuropa II. H. Lehnhart und C. Jeanmaire. Verlag Eisenbahn, Villigen, 1977.

Tram e Tramvie a Milano. Op.cit.

Die deutschen Strassenbahn-Gelenkwagen. Op.cit.

Der Stadtverkehr 5-6/1986 (Boston cars and technical problems).

Szeged 751 (Lars F. Richter collection)

SWITZERLAND

In 1966, by which date the concept seemed outmoded, Bern obtained from Schlieren a new car (401), built on the same basic principle. This tram did not, however, run on old two-axle trucks but each end section ran on four single steerable axles, the first application in modern times of what has now become a common design. It performed well and had excellent riding qualities, but was rather heavy at 25 tonnes and the axle design was so complicated as to require very careful maintenance. There were no further cars of this type. The tram was withdrawn in 1989 and in 1991 was acquired by Schindler to be used for experiments in connection with new low-floor trams. It thus forms a link between a design born out of post-war necessity and the latest technology.

Technical details

Length 19.7m, width 2.2m, weight 25.98 tonnes, 4 x 66kW motors, 167 passengers, 37 seated.

Bern 401 in service (Lars F. Richter collection).

Bern 401 as used as a test bed. (Lars F. Richter collection).

SPAIN

The principle was copied in Spain with three cars in Valencia in 1950, rebuilt from old two-axle cars, and five (251-255) in Zaragoza in 1959/60. These latter cars were converted from two-axle cars of the 90 class and were used on line 10 which terminated at the military academy. It was often the case that trams were filled by young cadets before they left the Academia terminus and no other passengers could board en route! Increased capacity was therefore a necessity and these cars provided it. They were withdrawn in 1971.

GERMANY

Between the wars there were experiments with this form of construction in Germany and, but for the economic depression, these might have been taken much further. The idea originated from Herr W. Pforr, then manager of the Berliner Strassenbahn in 1927 and was based on the advantage of using the vacant space between two single trams with a body section for entry and fare collection on a variant of the Peter Witt system. Exit was by doors in the outer ends of the car. This design allowed a larger number of passengers to be carried for the same amount of road space as a motor-trailer set, an important consideration at a time when road traffic was growing. The firm of Christoph and Unmack built in 1928/9 two similar cars for Dresden and Leipzig and two for Berlin (6211/2, class TEG29). The central module was linked by beams to the frames of the two other sections and there was an attempt thus to ensure that it would to an extent be steered into and out of curves. Riding qualities were reasonable on good track. Connection between the sections was by a flexible leather gangway of limited width, as in current railway practice. The cars were 23.15m long, weighed 27.5 tonnes and could offer 60 seats. Attempts to work them by a single conductor failed and they therefore required the same crew as a motor-trailer set. The design worked well enough with car 2502 in Dresden, which became very popular with the public, who appreciated its high speed – it was used on express line 15 to Coswig and could attain 70km/hr. The maintenance staff were less keen on the design. In 1931 Dresden acquired the Leipzig car, which took the number 2503. It was lost in the bombing of 1945, but 2501 soldiered on until 1965, being latterly used in peak hours only. The two Berlin cars were rather more powerful, with four motors, and the motion was concealed by skirting to reduce noise. Both survived the war and remained in West Berlin. Car 6211 was in 1951 rebuilt for passenger flow, as a single-ended car, with a single seated conductor and passenger flow from rear to front. In this form it ran regularly until the end of the trams in 1967. None of the cars had shown sufficient advantage over conventional designs to warrant multiplying the type and in Dresden it was decided that the future lay with the bogie car.

The planning group preparing the designs for standard trams did consider the preparation of an articulated design based on two two-axle cars linked by a suspended centre section. One of the members who pressed most strongly for this concept was Hermann Hempel, Director of the Erfurt undertaking but he did not succeed in having it adopted.

As related elsewhere, many German undertakings took delivery of two-axle cars in the last years of the war and in the immediate post-war period. At the time, this was the only way to make up for war losses, but with the arrival of the Grossraumwagen in the early 1950s it became obvious that these undertakings would soon have fleets of sound but totally uneconomic trams on their hands. Thoughts turned to a revival of the designs of the late 1920s as a means of using these assets to the best advantage in the changed circumstances of the post-war world. Herr Lüttich, head of the Hamburg tramway workshops, had visited Milan and Rome and seen the rebuilt cars in service. He suggested to his

Pre-war Berlin car 6211, as running in post-war years. (Author's collection)

One of Hamburg's cars on line 14 to Weddel. (Lars F. Richter collection)

colleagues in the VöV that this technique could be a means of solving the problem. Under his guidance, the organisation drew up guidelines for three types of construction:

Type A: New cars using old components
Type B: Rebuilds of war-time and post-war cars
Type C: New cars built on this principle.

Lüttich then practised what he had just been preaching by producing such a car in Hamburg. In February 1954 car 3021 was shown to the press and a series of 30 of class VG (3251-3280) followed in the winter of 1955/6 from the Berlin factory of DWM. Although the wheelbase of the old trucks used under these cars had been increased from 2m to 2.2m, their riding qualities were poor and they compared very badly with the new bogie cars, while lacking the capacity of the old three-car trains. In service they usually pulled a lightweight two-axle trailer, built in 1957/8 to run with the class. They were prone to derailment, hard on the tracks and soon gained the nickname of "Schienenfrässen" (track guzzlers). The trailers were, if anything, worse. The gradual run-down of the system allowed their withdrawal in 1967 and neither passengers nor maintenance staff lamented their passing.

But they had shown the practicability of the design as a means of increasing capacity while reducing personnel costs. Dortmund was the first system to follow Hamburg's lead and in 1953 ordered a rebuild from the firm of Hansa in Bremen, using the bodies of an Aufbau motor and trailer of 1949 (266/715). As the car (291) proved economical and successful when placed in service in 1954, other systems soon followed. Between 1954 and 1966 a total of 76 trams of this design were produced by a variety of manufacturers by rebuilding KSW motor cars and trailers (22 cars), Aufbau or Verbandstyp cars (23) or other two-axle trams, some, as in Duisburg dating back to 1925. In these cases the bodies were not altered, other than by losing a platform, and most components such as doors and seats were reused. The cost of such rebuilds was in the region of DM88,000 (£7,500) and it was calculated that the saving on the wages of one conductor would allow the rebuilds to pay for themselves in five years. Such rebuilds entered service in Duisburg (18), Braunschweig (3), Dortmund (1), Mülheim (5), Stuttgart (36), Bielefeld (5) and on the Vestische Strassenbahn system (8). The cars on the Vestische, and some of those in Duisburg were double-ended but most were single-ended and all were laid out for passenger flow from rear to front, with a seated conductor. The second Stuttgart version, which appeared in 1965, long after the post-war crisis had passed, was the most numerous and the most interesting. As detailed in chapter 5, that undertaking had invested in a fleet of modern two-axle cars as late as 1956/7 and in 1964 decided to update these by rebuilding 70 as articulated trams (901-935, class DoT4), to supplement the fleet of GT4 cars. They worked well, despite their riding qualities and car 929 has survived as party car 999, being fitted with a bar, dance floor, plush upholstered seats and a WC. It enjoyed great popularity, though with the contraction of the metre gauge network, its scope of operation became limited and it was withdrawn on 6 January 1996. It was given to the Verein Stuttgarter Historische Strassenbahn and has been preserved in Ziffenhausen museum.

Other operators preferred to fit a completely new body, as had been done in Hamburg. Bochum was the first to do so, with bodies built in its own workshops for five cars in 1955/6. Special care was taken with the suspension and the trams were quite successful, lasting until 1977. Essen had twelve bodies (701-712) by Düwag in 1959/60, very similar to the Grossraumwagen design and passengers probably thought they were new cars – until they moved off! Würzburg and Wuppertal also had similar cars. In the case of the former, the rear portion of seven cars was in fact completely new.

Essen 705 at the workshops at Schweiner Strasse in May 1981. (Author)

Gotha 213 at Tabarz on 26 June 1990. (Author)

A total of 32 trams were built in this category. Essen's 705 is preserved by the undertaking.

Herr Lüttich had not really expected that any cars would be built to this design as completely new vehicles, since he considered it to be only an emergency solution. However, Kassel in 1955 changed its mind about a series of new two-axle cars and had a prototype constructed as an articulated car instead (260). It proved to be very successful and was followed by 28 similar trams, with a slightly different style of body. They served well for many years, but latterly suffered in comparison with the riding of modern cars and were also out-paced by the latter. In 1991 eight were sold to Gorzow in Poland, the first of hundreds of trams from western Europe to go east. They ran there until replaced by more modern articulated trams from Germany after 1995. The last two in Kassel were taken out of service in April 1992, being the last trams of this type to run in normal service in western Europe. Two have been preserved, one in Kassel and one in Amsterdam. Dortmund also in 1956/7 bought 26 new trams (11-36), basically similar to its rebuild but with slightly increased wheelbase. Their bodies looked as though they were actually rebuilds, having a very austere appearance. All were withdrawn in the late 1970s, although what had by then become car 435 is preserved by the undertaking.

In all 198 trams of this design were built for systems in the BRD. They generally did what was expected of them, but most were disliked and in some cities earned the name of

Pre-war Dresden car 2502, as running in post-war years. (Dresdener Verkehrsbetriebe)

"Schuttlerutschen" which, bearing in mind that this was the 1950s, might best be translated as "Rockers".

Given the developments of this type in the Federal Republic, it was not surprising that operators in the DDR should wish to use the same principle, as a means of saving on staff costs. In the early 1950s, Leipzig briefly considered the development of an articulated tram based on the Werdau standard car, but this project was not taken further. The idea was revived in 1958, the main impetus once again coming from what was now the VEB Erfurter Verkehrsbetriebe, under its Director Dip-Ing Brux. Dresden joined in the planning and the idea was accepted by the State Planning Commission. The first prototype (151) was delivered to Erfurt by the VEB Waggonfabrik Gotha in September 1959, classed EGT59/2,

Kassel 260. (Lars F. Richter collection)

Mülheim 243 in the city centre in August 1971. (Author)

Würzburg 223 at Grombühl in December 1969. (Kevin T. Farrell, Evda Slides)

Tallinn 239 at Viru Square on 2 March 1978. (J.F. Bromley, Evda Slides)

and a standard gauge prototype (2500) was sent to Dresden in January 1960. This had the same push-button control system as the Kleine Hechtwagen and a slightly different front end. In the event, Dresden did not favour the design and no more were acquired, the prototype being used only on sightseeing duties. However, despite poor riding qualities, the design was deemed a success and series production, as class G4-61-65 followed, cars going to Erfurt (39), Gotha (16), Leipzig (118), Magdeburg (two later sold to Leipzig), Potsdam (20) and Rostock (21). The design was based very closely on the standard Gotha two-axle motor car, but two new features were the fitting of folding rather than sliding doors and, electrically, the location of the main controller under the floor, worked by a wheel in the driver's cab. The standard design seated 35 but the trams for Gotha had 51 seats, for use on the Thüringerwaldbahn, an attractive radial line, on which they were driven with gusto, to allow their stomach-churning antics at speed to be enjoyed to the full. All the cars were single-ended and in service they often pulled a two-axle trailer. Some modifications were made to the design in 1965 and production ended in 1967.

In all, 218 were built, between 1959 and 1967. In 1981 twelve cars from Erfurt went to Nordhausen, and ten entered service there. The design was also exported in limited numbers (101) to the Soviet Union and placed in service in Lvov (50 cars), Tallinn (50) and Saratow, one car, which was soon passed to Volgograd. Rostock was the last German city to use these trams in regular service and only those at Gotha now remain, as a reserve fleet. Several have been preserved in Erfurt (in fact an ex-Gotha car), Gotha, Potsdam and Rostock. That at Erfurt sometimes is used on a heritage service.

Technical details
Hamburg VG
Length 18.17m, width 2.2m, weight 26.2 tonnes, 4 x 37kW motors, 117 passengers, 36 seated.
Gotha G4-61 design for DDR undertakings
Length 21m, width 2.2m, weight 21.10 tonnes, 2 x 60kW motors, 181 passengers, 35 seated.
Duisburg – rebuild from KSW
Length 20.8m, width 2.2m, weight 22.5 tonnes, 2 x 60kW motors, 184 passengers, 30 seated.

Bibliography
Strassenbahn Magazin nos.153/4, July/August 2002 and no.169, November 2003 (Hamburg).
Die deutschen Strassenbahn Gelenkwagen. Op.cit.
Die Fahrzeuge der Dresdner Strassenbahn. M. Schatz. Verlagsbüro I. Reintzsch, Leipzig, 1993.

Duisburg 1206 at the top of Kömigstrasse in July 1979. In the background work has started on the tunnels for the Stadtbahn. (Author)

FRANCE
In 1935 Satramo/Alsthom delivered a prototype car of this type to the Tramways Algériens. The car was based on the design of two-axle cars then entering service on French systems such as Bordeaux (qv) and was the first articulated car of this type to be built new, as well as being the first French articulated tram. It was double-ended and had an all-metal body and air-operated doors. A series of 25 production cars followed in 1937, M2-M26. These trams were used on the busiest lines 1 and 3 and seem to have been successful in service. Kerb-side conductors were employed at the busiest stops and the on-board conductor's only responsibility at these points was to give the starting signal. In the early 1950s line 3 was abandoned and there were plans to construct a subway in the inner part of line 1 and use these cars in it, but the outbreak of Algeria's war of independence ended these ideas. When the trams were abandoned in 1959, attempts were made to sell the articulated cars to other operators and they were kept in the depot for a further five years, but, as no buyer was found, they were scrapped.

Technical details
Length 19.85m, width 2m, weight 21.5 tonnes, 4 x 33kW motors, 150 passengers, 14 seated.

Bibliography
Tram and Trolley in Africa. M. Pabst. Röhr Verlag, Krefeld, 1989 Modern Tramway nos.156, December 1950, 184, April 1953 and 281, May 1961.

One of the cars in service. (Commercial postcard, Roy Budmiger collection)

BELGIUM
Between 1962 and 1964 the STIB in Bruxelles rebuilt in its own workshops 43 similar trams (4001-4043). These heavy cars had difficulty in keeping up with the PCC bogie cars. They ran at

No.4025 on line 52, November 1968. (Author)

AUSTRIA, WIEN

Wien 4303 working on line 41 in August 1968. (Author)

In the 1950s the Wiener Stadtwerke was faced with the problem of a rapidly-ageing fleet and the need to rationalise the number of types of tram in service. Noting the current entry into service of the Torino articulated trams, the WSW asked the Gräf and Stift factory to obtain a licence for the Savigliano design patent and, using this, the firm built the prototype (4301) of what became class D. The trucks of war-destroyed Stadtbahn cars of class n1 were used with motors from withdrawn members of class T. At half the cost of a Grossraumwagen, the undertaking obtained cars with two-thirds of the capacity. Proposals to run these with trailers foundered on the opposition of the city authorities who were not then willing to see convoys 35m long in the city streets. Despite a truck wheelbase of 3.3m there were the usual complaints about poor riding on curves, but nonetheless the new tram was still an improvement on older two-axle cars and a series of 15 was ordered, entering service in 1960 as class D1 (4302-4316). But in the same year the first modern articulated car entered service and its superiority ensured that there would be no more conversions. The last was withdrawn, unmourned, on 2 July 1976 and the prototype has been preserved in the city's transport museum.

Technical details
Length 20.96m, width 2.2m, weight 25 tonnes, 4 x 40kW motors, 130 passengers, 33 seated.

Bibliography
Modern Tramway no.242, February 1958

first with trolley poles but in 1973 they were given pantographs and briefly used on services in the newly-opened subways. A lack of track brakes soon brought this to an end and they were banished to lightly trafficked lines, before being withdrawn in 1979. No.4032 is preserved in the Woluwe museum.

Technical details
Length 20.83m, width 2.2m, weight 26.5 tonnes, 4 x 68kW motors, 142 passengers, 45 seated.

Bibliography
Tramways en Service á Bruxelles. Op.cit.

SIX-AXLE TRAMS WITH SUSPENDED CENTRE SECTION

As mentioned elsewhere, the three-axle tram enjoyed a good deal of popularity in the Federal Republic after the Second World War and it was natural that some undertakings which had invested heavily in the type should wish to run similar trams in articulated form. The first system to put the idea into practice was Oberhausen. In 1959 three double-ended cars (361-363) were built by Westwaggon, being in all respects similar to 23 three-axle cars previously acquired. They had only two 60kW motors and these proved to be inadequate for the hilly line to Mülheim. The four cars delivered two years later had four motors. A further car was rebuilt from two three-axle Verband trams acquired in 1960 from Rheydt. When the system closed in 1968, the four-motor cars and the rebuild were sold to Aachen, where they ran until closure in 1975.

The main user of three-axle cars was München, which in 1960 was also looking into plans for tram subways. In 1960 the city took delivery from Rathgeber of two prototype single-ended six-axle articulated trams (101/2), again very similar to the production batches of three-axle Grossraumwagen. They were given the class letter P1. They differed in having outward-opening plug doors. Two conductors' posts were fitted. Although technically successful, they required two conductors and so showed no economic or other advantage over the three-axle plus trailer combination. A planned order for 70 articulated motor cars and 45 trailers was not placed, further Grossraumwagen being ordered instead. Both cars were withdrawn in 1979 and the second has been preserved.

Technical details
München class P1
Length 26.35m, width 2.2m, weight 30.6 tonnes, 4 x 60kW motors, 178 passengers, 37 seated.

Bibliography
The Three-axle Streetcar. Op.cit.

No.102 awaits departure on line 25 at Sendlingertorplatz in August 1967. (Author)

EIGHT-AXLE CARS WITH SUSPENDED CENTRE SECTION

Düsseldorf was the only system to take the idea of such trams to its logical conclusion, in rebuilding bogie cars into articulated cars. The first batch (1261-1264) appeared in 1963 and were made up as double-ended cars from eight bogie trams built ten years earlier for the radial line to Krefeld. These had run in M+T+M formation and had required a crew of four, something which could no longer be afforded. With a trailer, these trams made up an impressive train of 46m length, capable of carrying 373 passengers. Unfortunately the rebuilding did not provide for a continuation of the refreshment service previously available in the trailer and passengers complained. Two trams were withdrawn in 1966 and 1976 and the others were replaced by Stadtbahn B cars – with buffet facilities – in 1981.

The only other such tram was built in 1966 from the bodies of Grossraumwagen 2020, which had been involved in a serious accident, and Grossraum trailer 1604. These were joined by a short centre section with doors and the unit emerged from the Düwag factory as a single-ended car capable of carrying 261 passengers. It retained the number of the motor car, but later became 2265. It was considered to work well in service and there were plans to convert all the other Grossraum cars to this form. However, the advent of one-person operation removed the economic basis for this conversion and the tram remained the only one in the fleet. It shared with Boston's first PCC car the nickname of "Queen Mary" and lasted until the late 1980s.

At much the same time as the first Rheinbahn car appeared, a similar tram was constructed by Budapest, using two UV class cars. This tram was numbered 3799, but it seems to have been unsuccessful and was scrapped after a short career.

Technical details
Cars 1261 and 2020
Length 30.55m, width 2.5m, weight 44 tonnes, 4 x 138kW motors, 208 passengers, 76 seated.
Length 27.77m, width 2.35m, weight 30 tonnes, 2 x 100kW motors, 247 passengers, 47 seated.

Bibliography
Die Rheinbahn. Op.cit.

Rheinbahn 2263 at the central workshops at Heerdt in May 1981. (Author)

Rheinbahn 2265 at the same location. (Author)

THREE-SECTION TRAILERS

In 1958 the Waggonfabriek Rastatt rebuilt two old wooden trailers dating from 1927 into a three-section trailer for Stuttgart (1201). In service it ran with the city's first rebuilt motor car, in a set whose 42m length and sinuous behaviour gained it the nickname of "Tazzelwurm" (Dragon). Although it could carry an impressive number of passengers (340), it was slow to accelerate and had a limited top speed. The wooden bodies also contravened new regulations for trams which came in in 1960 and no further conversions of this class were attempted. The set was scrapped in 1965.

Duisburg took to the idea of articulation with enthusiasm and in the late 1950s seemed to work on the principle "If it moves, articulate it". It had a number of KSW trailers which were now uneconomic to operate but still robust and serviceable trams and in 1959 four of these were rebuilt into two trailers, with a new centre section (286/7). To keep within the length of the loading islands at stops, they had to run in service with a two-axle car, requiring some such cars to be kept in stock after the type had been earmarked for withdrawal. As this was not really sensible they were further rebuilt into motor cars in 1963 and as such they worked until 1978/9.

The last trailer of this type to appear was on the OEG system. In 1960 Rastatt rebuilt two old trailers of 1915 into one tram (221) with attractive new bodywork. In service it worked with modern bogie cars from the same firm. At speed on reserved track its riding was very uncomfortable and in 1968 it was remounted on four bogies from scrapped trailers. This did not

Duisburg 1169 (ex 287), as a motor car at Hauptbahnhof in August 1971. (Author)

improve matters at all and the car was scrapped in 1970.

Trailers to this design seem to have been singularly unsuccessful and those undertakings which still wished to use trailers kept to the bogie version for future orders.

THREE-SECTION, SIX-AXLE TRAMS

In the early 1960s there was an urgent need in both Basel and Zürich to develop a type of tram which would allow substantial savings on wage costs, use minimum road space with high capacity and be able to keep up with the growing motor traffic on the streets. The two undertakings worked together, under the leadership of Herr Bertschmann, then technical director of BVB, on this project and in 1961 placed an order for three prototype cars with SIG Neuhausen and BBC. Two were for Basel and one for Zürich. The manufacturer devised a completely new form of construction and produced a three-section articulated tram running on two motor bogies at front and rear and having the centre section suspended on a two-axle non-rigid truck. This form of construction saved one bogie and had several other advantages over the conventional design. Separating the articulation mechanism from the bogies simplified overhaul and repair. The swept path of the body on curves was reduced and this allowed wider front and rear ends and thus increased capacity. It also allowed all the doors to be built in to the parallel sides of the tram, making it easier for the conductor to supervise these and avoiding a gap between the tram body and the platforms of loading islands.

As Zürich was then contemplating subway construction, this was an especially important feature.

The Zürich prototype, car 1801, entered service in 1961 and was followed soon afterwards by the two Basel cars (601/2). Despite the saving of one bogie, the design of what was a Rolls-Royce of trams, was e x p e n s i v e (CHF742,000 or about £90,000 at contemporary rates of exchange) and the cars were very heavy. The Basel cars had only four motors, being intended for use on routes which were almost level, while the prototype for Zürich had six, to cope with the gradients found in that city.

In Basel the cars proved to be prone to derailment of the middle, non-motored bogie, espe-

BVB 602 at Claraplatz in September 1989. (Author)

cially on railway-type reserved track and technical problems required them to spend much time in the workshops. In early years, availability was only 68%. An order for a further 18 cars was considered but in 1965 it was decided to buy the reliable and much cheaper Düwag articulated car instead. Only Zürich decided to take production

Zürich 1678 is outward bound at Hardtturm in May 2003. (Author)

Zürich motorised trailer 1724 on line 2 in March 1983. (Author)

batches of the new design and in 1966/7, 90 cars were delivered (1601-1690), the first entering service on 1 March 1966. The order for the bodies was divided between SIG and SWS and that for the electrical components between BBC and MFO. These were the first trams anywhere to be fitted with electronic control equipment, the price of this progress being that they very soon became antiquated, due to the pace of development of electronics in the 1970s. Their cost led to questions being asked in meetings of the city council and also gained for them the nickname of "Mirages"; the purchase of jet fighters of this type for the Swiss defence forces had recently created something of a national financial scandal. In view both of the criticisms and of the disappointing results obtained with the prototype when pulling a bogie trailer, it was decided to construct the second batch of 36 trams as motorised trailers, without full driving positions,

an emergency controller only being fitted. They were also given the slightly cheaper Schindler bogies and as a result there was a saving of about CHF200,000 per car. These trams (1691-1726) were placed in service in 1968/9 and are rather unkindly known as "Blinde Kuhen" (blind cows). Three spare sets of bogies were bought at the same time, requiring some cars to be modified to be able to run on the bogies of either manufacturer.

The "Mirages" have proved to be excellent trams, popular with the public who appreciated the smooth acceleration, and with drivers who liked the flexibility of the control system and the excellent braking power. All were still running in 2002 but are likely to be phased out in favour of low floor trams. However, it should be said that the Basel Düwag cars have performed equally well and it is debatable if the enormous expense which VBZ incurred in the 1960s was really justi-

fied. Of the Basel cars, 601 was scrapped after an accident in April 1991, while its sister lasted in normal service until 1995 and was then rebuilt as a party car, named the "White Shark Tropical Bar" and painted in a light blue livery, complete with alarming rows of teeth on the dash. It was burned out in a fire at Wissenplatz depot on 18 August 2004.

Technical details
Cars with full driving positions
Length 20m, width 2.2m, weight 25.8 tonnes, 4 x 102hp motors, 165 passengers, 43 seated.

Bibliography
25 Jahre "Mirage" Gelenkwagen in Zürich. Strassenbahn Magazin, no.82, November 1991
Ein Jahrhundert Zürcher Strassenbahn. Op.cit.
Strassenbahn Magazin no.132, October 2000. (Basel cars)

NACHLAUFER TRAMS

GERMANY

It is difficult to translate this concept succinctly into English. It refers to a design of articulated tram in which the front portion rests on a two- or three-axle truck and the rear section is supported by one bogie or even a single pair of wheels. The design saved the expense and complication of the two articulation joints required by other types and could also cope with reduced clearances, as it had a tighter swept path on curves. A version of it appeared first in 1928 on a three-section car built by Wumag for Dresden (2501), but in this case the two-axle truck was under the centre section and each outer section rested on a single axle. The tram ran well and was popular, but there were no further orders for the type; it lasted until 1965. A somewhat similar car, known as the "Cape Hope" (apparently so named in the hope of increased orders for the tramcar builders, who had been having a lean time) tram, was built by AEG in 1932. It had four separate radial axles, the inner ones being steered by rods connected to those at the ends of the car. This construction allowed it to negotiate curves of 10.75m radius and could have made it an attractive proposition for some smaller systems. It was laid out for passenger flow from front to rear and a single conductor could thus handle 105 passengers. It ran in Berlin in May 1932 and then moved to Den Haag, where it ran on line 11 to Scheveningen during a transport congress. It was probably too advanced for its time and no orders came. The body was scrapped in 1940, stripped first of all re-usable parts.

The next application of the Nachlaufer concept came in 1955. Bremen was in process of building

Dresden 2501 seen in post-war years. (Dresdener Verkehrsbetriebe)

in its own workshops a series of ten two-axle cars and decided to construct the fifth of these as an articulated car, using an end section supplied by Hansa. This rested on a single axle and, to ensure adequate adhesion, the front portion had to be ballasted. A matching trailer was also constructed (901/1201). After a year's successful trial, 27 further motor/trailer sets were ordered (902-928/1902-1928). Some were built on trucks salvaged from war-damaged cars but others used those of the new 700 series. All had a new style of sloped windscreen, giving them a more

modern appearance than the prototype. The sets could carry over 150 passengers and were a distinct asset to the system, despite indifferent riding qualities. They ran until 1975 and three

Krefeld 303 at Weserweg depot in May 1981. (Author)

Ex-Remscheid car as Darmstadt 65 at Luisenplatz in June 1980. (Author)

Bremen 846 in Sebaldsbrück depot in September 2002, before its recent restoration. (Author)

were then converted for use as works cars while one became for a time a party tram. One (917) has since been preserved and was fully and beautifully restored to operational condition in 2002.

Given the success of Bremen, Duisburg and Aachen decided to try out the concept. Duisburg used the bodies of 19 Aufbauwagen to form articulated cars with a new rear section (209-227),

Freiburg 101 and trailer 236 at Hornustrasse on 21 February 1972. (Evda Slides)

Duisburg 1220 (ex 220) at Hauptbahnhof in August 1971. (Author)

while Aachen had 11 (7103-7113), constructed by the same method. Ten of these were sold to Augsburg in 1973, where they became 401-410. They seemed to be a bargain but on closer acquaintance their new owners were disillusioned and used them only at peak hours before scrapping them in 1976. Car 430 has been preserved. In Duisburg the trams operated, unusually, with the bogie leading and some later received doors on the offside and ran as double-ended cars on some lines. They lasted longer, until 1980, and one of these has also been preserved.

On the same principle, but with a two-axle truck under the rear section, Düwag built in 1957/8 a series of 26 cars for Köln (3501-3526). The undertaking wished to gain experience with articulated cars before placing large orders. These trams performed so well that it was decided in 1960 to rebuild 50 small two-axle cars which had been built in 1956-58 and which now seemed totally inadequate for the city's traffic (3427-3476). The rear sections were built new. These were equally successful but traffic growth soon outstripped their capacity and they were withdrawn after a life of only ten years. Car 3413 is preserved in the city. Krefeld built six similar cars (301-306) using older underframes, which had come from Wiesbaden, and as that system did not have Köln's need for large cars, they lasted until about 1980, latterly as a reserve. Wuppertal also had seven similar trams (4501-4507) for its metre gauge network, but there was only one line on which they could run and when that closed in 1967, they were sold to Krefeld, where they became 311-317. They were withdrawn from 1980 onwards. Freiburg, which was not then the modern undertaking that it is to-day, bought three trams (101-103) from Rastatt but based closely on the Aufbau design. They were soon outclassed by later acquisitions, particularly with regard to their riding qualities, and spent most of their later lives in reserve. As in 1959 they seemed the last word in modernity, they were locally known as "Sputniks". They were finally withdrawn in 1993/4, the last of their type in service by a considerable margin, but car 102 has been preserved and 101, renumbered 103 in the works fleet, is an advertising car. Remscheid bought six trams of a variant of this type (101-106) new in 1958 – though using old motors – from Westwaggon in 1960, to replace old wooden bodied cars.

These cars had four motors, a normal bogie under one body section and a two-axle truck under the other. These were the only double-ended Nachlaufer trams and, in deference to the town's hills, had four motors. They were only a stop-gap, as closure had already been decided on, and in 1970 they were sold to Darmstadt, where they became 61-66. In that city they were used as single-ended trams, with the portion on the motor bogie leading. In this form they ran quite well, usually working with a two-axle trailer, and lasted in traffic until the late 1980s.

Technical details

Bremen GT3 car
Length 16.44m, width 2.21m, weight 17 tonnes, 2 x 76kW motors, 78 passengers, 33 seated.

Remscheid 101
Length 17.85m, width 2/18m weight 25.12 tonnes, 4 x 69kW motors, 150 passengers, 36 seated.

Krefeld 301
Length 18.4m, width 2.2m, weight ?, 2 x 60kW motors, 159 passengers, 35 seated.

Bibliography

Die deutschen Strassenbahn Gelenkwagen. Op.cit.
Die Fahrzeuge der Dresdner Strassenbahn. Op.cit.

AUSTRIA

In 1964 50 of the two-axle cars ordered as class L were actually completed as articulated cars to this design. The last car of class F, 746, was withdrawn from passenger service on 28 June 1996 and has since been preserved in the city's transport museum.

Car 716 at Schwedenbrücke in September 1987. (Author)

ITALY

The only Italian system to use this design was Genova. Between 1949 and 1951 78 cars of the 600 class, dating from 1926 were combined with matching trailers to produce articulated trams. The rear section was mounted on a single bogie and the cars were single-ended. Unusually the rear platform was open and the floor of the rear section was 150mm lower than that of the leading section. Riding qualities were poor. The trams were numbered 1601-1678 and ran until the system contracted in the 1960s.

Bibliography

Modern Tramway no.317, May 1964

NETHERLANDS

Car 713 at Centraal Station in March 2003. (Author)

By the mid-1970s it might well have been thought that the days of this design were at an end, but, in altered form, it reappeared in a series of 50 trams built for Rotterdam between 1981 and 1983 (701-750). In this design, class ZGT-6, the front section is essentially a bogie car, while the rear section runs on a single motored bogie, placed well towards the end of the tram. This allows a car 4m longer than a conventional six-axle tram, while still keeping within the constraints of track layout, and also allowed a lower floor height at the rear of the tram. All doorways are fitted with four low steps, to allow easier boarding and alighting. The trams were an international product, the bodies being built by Düwag, the bogies by what was now RMO Werkspoor, with electrical equipment by Holec and three-phase control by Strömberg, the first use of this feature in the city. In service the last of these features has proved to be noisy. The trams were the first on the system to be painted yellow and made quite an impression when new, although there was criticism of their rather basic interior. Current renovation has improved this. The electronics proved to be noisy and gave a good deal of trouble; initially these trams were positively dangerous for any passenger with a heart pacemaker. As a result of these problems, delivery was prolonged. It was said that the class designation stood in fact for "Zeer Grote Teleurstelling" or "A huge disappointment"! Although they have been successful enough, the design has not been repeated. The sister cars of class 800 (801-850) were built using components from Düwag articulated cars of classes 300 and 600 and have therefore been rather less problematic in service. It is possible that some of these cars may go to Romania in the near future.

Technical details

Car 701
Length 23.54m, width 2.31m, weight 28 mp, 6 x 42kW motors, 150 passengers. 60 seated.

Bibliography
Der Stadtverkehr 8/1982

A rear view of no.826 at the same location, showing the relatively easy access at the rear. (Author)

RUSSIA

Rather surprisingly, a late application of this concept appeared in Sankt Petersburg in 1997 with class LVS97. About 50 were built over the next two years, the numbering being too chaotic to set out here. The reason for the choice of this type is not at all clear and it has not been particularly successful, but the state of the track may have had as much to do with this as the design of the tram.

Sankt Petersburg 7103 in August 1998. (Author)

THREE- AND FIVE-AXLE TRAMS

The only system ever to have run a three-axle articulated tram was Bologna. In January 1949 this undertaking unveiled an articulated car (601) rebuilt from a two-axle car dating from 1910 to the design of Sr E. Sibona, the General Manager. This was a novel design of tram which had single axles (motored) under the outer ends of each body half and a third under the articulation joint. This central trunk was linked to the outer ones by a system of levers and these steered it into curves. A new steel body with streamlined ends was fitted. Clearance problems were minimal and experience in service was so good that five other older cars were similarly treated in 1950 (602-606). Two more appeared in 1953 and there were plans to convert others, but these did not come to fruition. In service they worked quite well and passengers liked them, but drivers found them to be underpowered, having motors of a total rating of only 47, 56 or 60kW (depending on the cars from which they were rebuilt) and this was a problem on line 13. Care also had to be taken on curves and this made them slower in service than the bogie cars. Nonetheless, this was an ingenious, and fairly cheap, modernisation in a time of economic problems. The trams were withdrawn in 1961 and all were scrapped. However, a model, to approximately 1/32 scale, survives in the local transport museum.

Like its neighbour München, Augsburg had bought three-axle Grossraumwagen, both motor and trailer cars, and had been very pleased with these. It had also re-equipped its workshop to deal with such trams and so, when an enlargement was considered, it was logical to keep as far as possible to the basic

Three were also built in 1998 for Kolomna, a small system within the Moscow commuter area.

Bibliography
Tramways and Urban Transit, no.784, April 2003.
Strassenbahn Magazin no.160, February 2003. (Bremen)
Trams in Eastern Europe. Op.cit.

concept. In 1963 MAN delivered the first of what was to become a fleet of five-axle articulated trams. The forward section ran on a three-axle truck, as with the Grossraumwagen, and the rear section was mounted on a two-axle truck. As this design proved to be successful, a total of 20 cars (522-541) was built new between 1963 and 1968 and immediately thereafter MAN also rebuilt 22 cars from Grossraumwagen motor and trailer sets (511-521 and 542-552). These unusual cars worked well in practice and, when the last ran in its home city in 1998, Iasy in Romania was very happy to take 20 of the rebuilds.

Technical details
Bologna
Length 14.4m, width 2.15m, weight 15.93 tonnes, 2 x 28kW motors, 106 passengers.
Augsburg.
Length 20.9m, width 2.2m, weight 21.5 tonnes, 2 x 60kW motors, 187 passengers, 42 seated.

Bibliography
Modern Tramway no.171, March 1952 (Bologna).
Storia dei Trasporti Publici a Bologna. Op.cit.
Die deutschen Strassenbahn Gelenkwagen. Op.cit.

Augsburg 541 at Hauptbahnhof in September 1968. (Author)

CHAPTER 10

STADTBAHN CARS

PIONEERS

The distinction between tram and Stadtbahn is not an easy one to make and much has been written by many in not-always successful attempts to clarify the position. Suffice it to say here that the vehicles which have come in recent times to be known as Stadtbahn cars in Europe and as light rail vehicles in North America have been designed with a view to running for most of the time on private right of way, including tunnel sections, where stations have high or medium-high platforms, but with a capability of operating also on street track and in many cases also serving conventional stopping places, without any special facilities at these. On certain sections, they may share track with conventional urban trams. They generally seat more passengers than these and often have fewer doorways. An enhanced level of comfort is often apparent. Technically they are designed to sustain a higher average speed than city cars and, as riding qualities are more important for longer journeys, greater attention will have been given to matters such as suspension. Most cars are double-ended and operation in multiple unit formation is the norm, although cars can run singly if necessary. Trailer operation is virtually unknown. Fare collection will in almost all cases take place off the car and few carried a conductor, when these still operated on city lines. But nonetheless the distinction between the two types of railed vehicle is a fine one, which has given rise to much discussion among enthusiasts!

An Electroliner raises a flurry of snow in typical mid-West wintry weather in Milwaukee in March 1959. (A.D. Young, Evda Slides)

The Skokie Swift. (Electrail slides, courtesy Electric Railway Society)

It should also be noted that not every car type which is designated "Stadtbahn" fits the above criteria and the cars with this title in Braunschweig and Bremen are really trams, albeit very fine examples. More recently some systems such as Erfurt have begun to use the term for what are essentially very fine upgraded tramways.

In recent years the term "tram train" has also come into use to denote vehicles which previously might have been classified as Stadtbahn cars. This term is used particularly in France and is more of a legal than a technical definition. It covers vehicles which have been designed to comply with both highway and railway regulations and thus covers the Regio Citadis of Alstom, the Avanto of Siemens and various Bombardier products.

In one sense, Stadtbahn cars have been around for almost as long as the electric tram itself has existed. The many radial lines in North America and Europe were the forerunners of what has come to be known in later days as the "Stadtbahn". Many of these operated for much of the length of their routes on separate right of way and in some cases, as in those lines which used the Loop in Chicago, they served stations with high platforms. The line from Düsseldorf to Krefeld, which to-day is worked by Stadtbahn cars, was opened in 1898. In Buenos Aires the first Subte (subway) cars were designed to run in passenger service in both tunnels with high platforms at stations and on street track with conventional tramway stopping places. The Stadtbahn in Wien, electrified in 1925, was perhaps the most complete example of the mixture of tramway and railway technology incorporated in the concept of the Stadtbahn, and for many years, its services also ran through on to the city streets. Britain's nearest approach to Stadtbahn operation was the Grimsby and Immingham Electric Railway, built and owned by a main line railway company and running very long bogie single-deck trams on railway-type track, but with a small amount of on-street running.

The concept reached its apogee in North America around 1930, first with the lightweight cars built by the Cincinnati Car Company for the Cincinnati and Lake Erie Railroad, after an extensive test programme had been carried out under the auspices of Dr Thomas Conway Jr. These used compact motors and wheels of reduced diameter to give a car that was fast

This must be the world's oldest Stadtbahn car! This veteran was built in 1887 by the Gilbert Car Company, to run as a trailer behind steam locomotives on the New York elevated lines and was in due course electrified. In 1942 it was taken to California to work on the shipyard lines in Richmond, near Oakland and for these was fitted with a pantograph. These lines included sections of street running. As seen here in 1996, it is preserved at the Western Railway Museum at Rio Vista Junction. (Author)

– speeds in excess of 140km/hr were recorded in service – yet more accessible than the traditional car. They thus combined the best of contemporary street railway practice with the advantages of a main line railway. This trend was continued with the magnificent streamlined "bullet" cars

Car 2943 of the Wiener Stadtbahn heads a train for Heiligenstadt at Schönbrunn in June 1981, when left hand running was still in operation. This was shortly before the conversion of this section to U-Bahn operation and the conductor rails are already in place, while passengers use temporary wooden platforms. (Author)

One of the Stadtbahn cars, 5919, is pulled by an M class motor and follows a similar convoy through the street near Schönbrunn in August 1968. Although this is not a passenger working, scenes such as this were at one time common when through services were operated. (Author)

"Bullet" car no.200, in the livery of SEPTA, leaves 69th Street terminus in Philadelphia in October 1980. (Author)

built by Brill, after extensive wind-tunnel testing at the University of Michigan, for the Philadelphia and Western Railway. By using streamlining, it was estimated that the cars would save 40% of the energy used by conventional cars, yet be capable of attaining speeds of over 100km/hr. Lightweight aluminium construction kept weight down to 26.4 tonnes for a car 17m long. Although these ran entirely on private right of way and had third rail current collection, they were operated by one person. Five identical cars, but fitted with trolley poles, were built for the Fonda, Johnstown and Gloversville line in New York state and shortly afterwards sold on to the Bamberger Railroad in Utah, where they ran until 1952. The Philadelphia cars had a long innings, not being

One of the original Subte cars (52) of line A in Buenos Aires, running on street en route to the depot. Similar cars, fitted with an extra door at each end, had once operated a through passenger service. (Lars F. Richter collection)

withdrawn until 1986. The Electroliners of the Chicago, North Shore and Milwaukee line, to which reference has already been made, were also Stadtbahn cars, of a standard of luxury not seen before or since in such a vehicle. They came complete with a bar car in which deferential black waiters served passengers with delicacies such as an "electroburger" while the car sped along at anything up to 110km/hr. They were four-section ten-axle cars and total length was 47.5m. They weighed 94 tonnes, with eight 92kW motors and a balancing speed of 125km/hr. Seating accommodation was for 120 passengers, plus 26 in the bar section. When the North Shore closed in 1963, these were sold to the Philadelphia and Western, where they were named *Independence Hall* and *Valley Forge*, but, with a three man crew, they were less economical than the "bullets" and, as the electricity distribution system was not upgraded to take account of their needs, there were often problems when they drew power when starting from rest. They saw little service after 1970, but both have been preserved. One is at the Illinois Railway Museum and the status and whereabouts of the other are at present uncertain. In 1949 the Illinois Terminal system bought three even more luxurious streamliners, with full dining facilities and reclining seat coaches, but they came too late and were scrapped after only six years' service.

However, most of the systems which used cars of this type closed in the 1930s and those that remained were either subsumed into urban networks, using vehicles which were indisputably trams, or became indistinguishable from heavy rail operations. In Chicago, the Chicago, South Shore and South Bend, which still has a short section of street track, is an example of the latter, while the Philadelphia and Western, now operated by the South East Pennsylvania Transportation Authority (SEPTA) illustrates the former. The failure to develop these concepts further at the time did not represent any shortcomings on the part of the technology; it was due to the pro-road policies pursued by the various US governments, especially during the Eisenhower administration.

The concept was also found in Japan, where many lines which grew up from tramways were extended well beyond city limits, placed on private right of way and given stations with high platforms.

Elsewhere, most of the cars used on such lines in the early days were simply enlarged trams and showed no particular innovations to fit them for their role in longer distance service. They were generally more comfortable than city trams, with greater seating capacity and fewer doorways and were almost always mounted on bogies. The preserved two-car set of the Oberrheinische Eisenbahn Gesellschaft (OEG), built in 1928, shows the degree of comfort which could be provided, but in technology almost all were basically city trams. Only the light rail lines to the west of Oslo, which were developed from tramways, had cars which would now be considered as a Stadtbahn design. These included both bogie and three articulated cars, built in the 1940s and '50s.

Britain might have led in the development of modern Stadtbahn services had the plans drawn up in 1948 for Glasgow by the-then General Manager of the Corporation's transport, E.R.L. Fitzpayne, been adopted. These envisaged two-car sets, each car 14m long, running on central reservations and in tunnels, to supplement the city's railways and subway. Third rail current collection was envisaged "to simplify maintenance in tunnels". Up to three units could be coupled together. Seating was for 96 but standing capacity, at 34, was rather low. The cars would have been fitted with electro-pneumatic control, with automatic acceleration and air brakes and internally they would have had a good deal of the Coronation trams in their design. However, this imaginative project was quietly dropped. Although it usually favoured double-deckers at that time, the-then Light Railway Transport League also saw some place for the Stadtbahn-type single-decker and some of its publicity material, based on an article in the *"Illustrated London News"* in 1937, showed such vehicles running on the median strip of a motorway; the cars looked like enlarged versions of the Blackpool railcoaches and had trolley poles. (See chapter 3)

However, only just two years after the abandonment of the Chicago, North Shore and Milwaukee line, the area saw the first evidence of the new thinking in the US, following the passage of the Urban Mass Transportation Act of 1961. On 20 April 1964, five miles of the Skokie Valley line of the North Shore were re-activated under the auspices of the Chicago Transit Authority, from the township of Skokie inwards to a connection with the city's rapid transit line at Howard Avenue. Overhead wire current collection was used for part of the line and the cars were one-person operated. To make possible the changeover from third rail to overhead at speed, the CTA developed a novel kind of bow collector,

Grimsby and Immingham 3 at Pyewipe in March 1959. (Author)

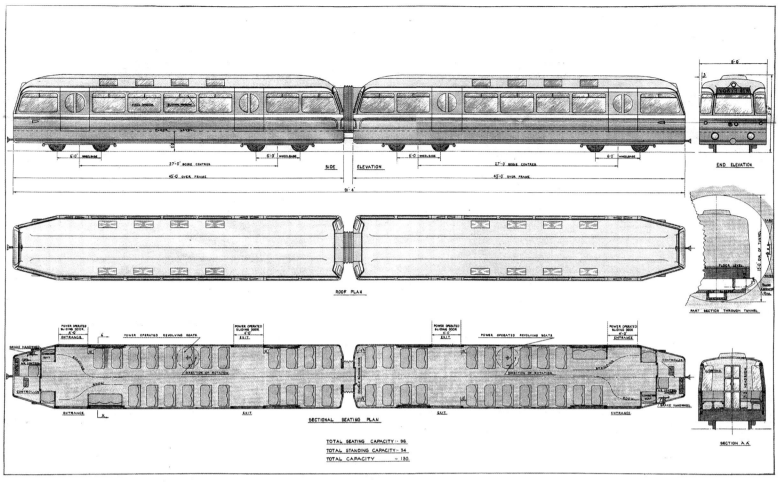

Plans of the proposed Glasgow design of 1948. (Glasgow City Council)

which looked somewhat crude but worked effectively. Single unit rapid transit cars were used at first but such was the success of the line that four experimental 98-seat eight-axle articulated sets dating from 1948 were transferred to it. These gave excellent service until 1993, when they were replaced by rehabilitated two-car sets of cars rebuilt from PCC trams.

The concept of the Stadtbahn in its present form came to Europe in the 1960s. At that time, in the heyday of the German Wirtschaftswunder (Economic Miracle), it was considered by many operators that the tram had reached the limit of its development and that, in view of the apparently unstoppable growth of the motor vehicle, public transport would have to adapt itself to it, if it were to survive. In Frankfurt (M), it was decided that city centre tramways should be placed in tunnels, built to full U-Bahn dimensions, which would connect onto reserved tracks in the suburbs. Stuttgart and Köln also began to construct tunnels, but in these cities, these were laid out for tramway operation, with lesser clearance and fairly tight curvature. Hannover planned to follow their example, but with increased clearances. Ambitious plans were being drawn up for a network of high speed routes to serve the Ruhr area. These were to be of standard gauge and would have operated in tunnels or on the median strip of express motorways, serving only stations with high platforms, and would have third rail current collection. The line running between Essen and Mülheim, with its stations inhospitably isolated in the median strip of the Ruhrschnellweg, shows what was envisaged. The metre gauge lines not selected for conversion to Stadtbahn operation would have been replaced by buses. Optimistically the

Stadtbahngesellschaft Ruhr, set up in May 1969 and enlarged into the Stadtbahngesellschaft Rhein-Ruhr in 1972, spoke of a network of 250km by the year 2000. The type of vehicle to be used – which came to be known as Type A – was planned as a double unit, mounted on bogies and running in permanently coupled pairs, back to back, with one driving position in each car. Dimensions would have been 36.9m by 2.65m. Stuttgart decided in 1969 to construct a full U-Bahn network of two lines.

Not very long after these plans were published, wiser counsels prevailed. It became clear that it would take many years to develop the kind of system planned in 1970 and, as the economic miracle cooled in the aftermath of the oil crisis of 1973, it was also clear that money would be less plentiful in future for such large-scale projects. Design work on Stadtbahn A was halted in 1974. The Stuttgart authorities took fright at the probable cost of the U-Bahn and in 1976 abandoned this in favour of an upgraded, standard-gauge light rail network, but the cars subsequently built for this were the nearest to Stadtbahn A actually to see the light of day. In 1990 the Stadtbahn Corporation was amalgamated with the VRR tariff union and in 2000 planning and construction of new sections was handed over to individual cities, effectively bringing the idea to an end.

Bibliography

The Interurban Era. William D. Middleton. Kalambach Publishing, Milwuakee, 1961.
North American Light Rail Annual, 1993.
Modern Tramway nos.381, September 1969 (Stadtbahn A), 460, April 1976 (Glasgow).
Strassenbahn Magazin no.172, February 2004.
Die Strassen- und Vorortbahnen in Oslo. N. C. Aspenberg. Baneforlaget, Oslo, 1994.
Rhein-Ruhr Stadtbahn Album 1. C. Groneck, P. Lohkemper and R. Schwandl. R. Schwandl Verlag, Berlin, 2005.
Chemins de Fer Régionaux et Tramways, No.307, February 2005. (Tram-Train)
Rail et Transports, March 2005. (Tram-Train)

Although it looks rather older, Oslo no.609 actually dated from the 1950s. It is seen on the Holemkolenbane, coupled to a car of an earlier generation on an enthusiasts' tour in June 1983. (Author)

The line also had more modern cars, such as 405, shunting at Majorstuen on 19 July 1991. (Author)

FRANKFURT (M) STADTBAHN CARS

PROTOTYPES

The first vehicle which could be called a Stadtbahn in the modern sense was constructed by Düwag for Frankfurt in 1964 and displayed at the international transport exhibition held in München in that summer. This design, originally classed U1 and later U6, was a double-ended car showing some similarities to the builder's six-axle trams but constructed for operation both with high platforms and at stops at street level. The car entered service in 1966, numbered 1001, and was followed by a second, 1002, in the following year.

Both cars proved to be successful in operation, but were incompatible with the production cars of classes U2 and later and were relegated to driver training duties at an early date, although they did briefly re-appear in passenger service on line A1 as a coupled set. They were withdrawn in 1978 and car 1001 is preserved in the city's transport museum.

They were followed into service by a class which would go on to be the most successful of all Stadtbahn designs and would operate far beyond the Federal Republic.

U2/3/4 CLASSES

The first car of class U2 was delivered by Düwag in 1968 and ultimately it numbered 104 cars (303-406). Technically they were very similar to the prototypes but were all-electric and slightly longer to allow more space in the driver's cab, and they had a different front end which bore no resemblance at all to previous tram designs. Up to four cars can work in multiple, though not on street track. Deliveries from 333 onwards were built jointly with Wegmann. Five cars were totally destroyed in a fire at Hedddenheim depot in September 1980 and were replaced by new vehicles. As it was not intended that these cars should operate on tram services, they were not given folding steps for street-level access. However, the floor height is 97cm above rail level and, as some of the platforms on the Stadtbahn lines U1-U3 then had a height of only 32cm, to allow clearance for goods trains which also used these tracks, two folding steps had to be fitted. Cars 366-399 were later altered by the removal of these steps for use on line U7 and classified U2e (e=eben=level). When the goods trains were withdrawn, all platforms on lines U1-U3 were altered to have a height of 80cm above street level and all cars were then rebuilt with only one step at all doors and became class U2h (hoch= high). Originally these cars carried the red and white Stadtbahn livery, but were later repainted orange and white and some now carry the turquoise paint scheme. Plans are now being drawn up for new vehicles which will replace class U2 in 2007.

A further variant, class U3 (451-477), was developed in 1979 for use on line U4, which does not involve any street running, being completely in tunnel. As these cars did not have to be fitted with folding steps, some re-arrangement of the interior was possible to give both greater seating capacity and standing room. A new design of panoramic windscreen was fitted. This class has chopper control. Since the ending of goods train service on the other Stadtbahn lines, allowing an increase in platform height, this class has also operated on these.

In 1994 the first of class U4 (also known as U3-2000) arrived from Düwag, deliveries continuing until 1998. This is a modernised and considerably altered version of class U2, with a rounded front end and a one-piece windscreen. Three-phase equipment is fitted, each bogie has two motors and the cars have air suspension and plug doors. The floor height has been reduced to 87cm above rail level and air suspension ensures that the floor is completely level with the platform. These cars introduced the new turquoise livery to the Stadtbahn and there are now 39 in service (501-539).

Technical details
U2, U3 and U4 classes
Length 23m, width 2.65m, weight 30.6 tonnes, 2 x 150kW motors, 151 passengers, 64 seated.
Length 24.5m, width 2.65m, weight 36,000kg, 2 x 174kW motors, 184 passengers, 64 seated.
Length 24.5m, width 2.65m, weight 36,000kg, 4 x 130kW motors, 174 passengers, 63 seated.

Bibliography
Strassenbahn Magazin no.107, 3/97.
Der Stadtverkehr 2/95 (U4).
Die deutschen Strassenbahn-Gelenkwagen. Op.cit
Strassenbahn Farzeuge Band 2: Typenbuch der Niderflur- und Stadtbahnwagen. M. Pabst. GeraMond Verlag, München, 2nd impression 2000.

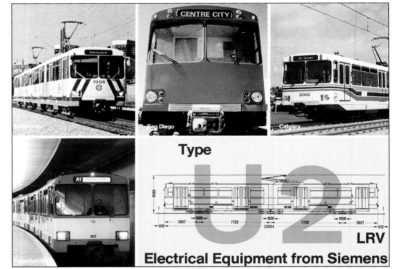
Siemens' publicity for the design when it was new in 1980. (Author's collection)

Prototype 1001 in the depot on 1 June 1966. (W.J. Wyse, courtesy London Area, Light Rail Transit Association)

U2 350 in original red and white livery heads a three-car train on line U1 in June 1980. (Author)

A U3-type car of the Salzburger Lokalbahn, seen during celebrations of the line's centenary in 1986. (W.J. Wyse, courtesy London Area, Light Rail Transit Association)

A train of U4 cars, with 513 bringing up the rear, in June 2000. (Author)

EXPORT MODELS

Perhaps the most surprising aspect of the class U2 was not the standard of service it was able to provide in Frankfurt but its success in breaking into the North American market, to an extent where it became virtually the standard light rail vehicle. Its entry into service in Germany coincided with the first plans for the revival of light rail in North America, at a time when the Boeing cars had clearly failed and there was no other model available on the home market.

A reliable, straightforward design was what was required, and the U2 fitted the bill exactly. Such was the demand for this type of car that a new factory had to be constructed in Sacramento which produces cars marketed as "Siemens-Düwag".

This facility opened in January 1992 and was extended in 1995.

CANADA

The Canadian cities of Edmonton and Calgary opened their first lines in 1978 and 1981 respectively and turned to the U2 design to provide services on these. Aware of the problems experienced by Boston with its Boeing cars, Edmonton had no wish to saddle itself with an unproven design but wanted a simple car with a good record of reliability. The U2 class offered this and was also thought to be the largest vehicle which could be used for on-street running. As no Canadian firm was then building such cars, Edmonton was able to obtain a waiver on import duty from the Dominion government. By the time Calgary ordered its initial fleet, this was no longer the case, as the UTDC design was on the market, and, after a political outcry, it was forced to pay duty. In both cases the cars were designed to operate from high platforms only and naturally they had additional heating provided to cope with the Albertan winter. Calgary's initial fleet soon totalled 83 U2 cars (2001-2083) while Edmonton has 37 (1001-1037). The cars have performed well under difficult climatic conditions and have made a success of both these light rail systems. As stated elsewhere, Vancouver would have followed suit, but for political interference from both provincial and Dominion governments. In 1989 each system tried a similar car fitted with AC equipment and 136kW motors and found that considerable savings in current resulted. Both these cars are now in Calgary but are owned by the government of Alberta (3001/2). Calgary has also acquired 23 cars of class SD160 (2201-2223), which have a single-piece windscreen and has 33 more on order, for delivery in 2007. These will have AC equipment. Edmonton in 2005 placed an order for 26 cars of this type, for delivery in 2008/9.

USA

South of the border, San Diego was to be the first new line in the USA, opening its first line on 26 July 1981. To keep costs down and speed delivery, it also opted for class U2, in this case with 14 cars (1001-1014), designed for loading from low platforms. Three further batches of car were delivered in 1981, 1986 and 1989/90, taking the total to 71. Cars from 1025 onwards have the refinement of air conditioning and this was retrofitted to earlier deliveries. In 1994/5, 52 more cars (2001-2052), to a modified design, classed as SD100, were obtained. These have a single-piece windscreen, single chopper control and low level boarding. Eleven further cars of class S70 were bought in 2005. San Diego cars have an all-over red livery and are kept in excellent condition, each car being treated with wax four times per year, to avoid oxidisation due to the intensity of the light in southern California. The fleet of U2 cars certainly helped this system, and thus all other new systems in North America, off to a very good start and they have maintained their passenger appeal over more than twenty years, largely thanks to the excellent workshop facilities and to the pride of local staff in the operation.

This example was followed by the capital city of California, Sacramento, which began light rail service in 1986 and has 36 cars (101-136) of type U2a, with single-piece windscreens and four low-level doors per side. Here again the cars have been reported to be "incredibly reliable". At the same time Pittsburgh was upgrading its existing tram lines to form the nucleus of a light rail system and it acquired 55 cars (4101-4155), based on type U3, and later classed SD400, to replace the PCC cars. Apart from being designed for use on 1587mm gauge tracks, these cars also differed from earlier U2 cars in having a dual chopper control system and air suspension. In 1991 the Bi-State Development Corporation, which was responsible for the new light rail system in Saint Louis ordered 31 cars (1001-1031), similar to, but longer than those of Pittsburgh, for use at high platforms only. These entered service in 1993 and were followed by ten more (type SD460, 2001-2010) in 1998/9 and a further 24 (3001-3024) in 2000/1. To cope with extensions on this most successful system, 22 cars are currently under construction and will take the numbers 4001-4022. Denver opted for SD100 cars, with a total of 17 (101-117) delivered in two batches, ordered along with additional vehicles for San Diego, to keep down costs. Six more have since been bought and 34 SD160 are on order. When light rail came to Salt Lake City in 1999, service was provided by 23 cars of type SD100 (1001-1023), originally ordered by San Diego but then found to be surplus to requirements. As the climate of Utah is definitely not sub-tropical, heaters had to be fitted and a second pantograph mounted on each car to cut ice from the overhead when necessary. Five further cars of type SD160 have since been bought. Los Angeles acquired 52 cars for its Blue and Green Line services in 1999. These have three-phase AC drive and air suspension and are for use at high platforms only. Externally they differ from all previous designs in having streamlined ends. These had some teething problems and did not enter normal service until 2001.

A final variant of the basic U2 design appeared in Portland (OR) in the summer of 1996. For the

San Diego 1003 has just left Euclid Avenue station, inbound, in October 1987. (Author)

Denver 109 at the Downing Street stop on 30th Avenue in October 1996. (Author)

Saint Louis 1012 approaching Airport terminus in October 1996. (Author)

On a street running section, Sacramento no.115 crosses O Street in October 1987. (Author)

A group of Edmonton cars in the depot yard in October 1989. (Jim D. Schanz)

Portland 251 heads a two-car set outward bound to Gresham in the city centre in November 2001. (Jim D. Schantz)

A coupled set of cars passing the Mormon Tabernacle in Salt Lake City in October 2004. (Jim D. Schantz)

One of the first two cars delivered to Los Angeles, seen at the yard at Redondo Beach just after arrival in January 1998. (Julian Wolinsky)

Calgary 2020 and a GM bus on 7th Avenue at 4th Street in June 1983. (Peter Haseldine)

Pittsburgh 4139 at Penn station in October 1988. (Author)

opening of the new Westside light rail line, Tri-Met intended to order more of its very successful Bombardier cars (qv), but, although these are wheelchair-accessible by means of lifts located on the station platforms, these are slow in operation and make the user very conspicuous. There was therefore pressure from groups representing people with disabilities to buy a design of low floor car, on European lines. The operator initially doubted that such a car was capable of working on what is very definitely a Stadtbahn system, on which cars regularly achieve a top speed of 88km/hr and have a high end-loading buffing strength. There was also concern about fitting such a car to the platform height of 200mm above rail level. However, Siemens considered that the difference in height could be overcome by a sliding plate, as fitted on Grenoble's cars and that the other problems were capable of resolution. In 1993 therefore they were awarded a contract for 37 cars, which was later increased in stages to a total of 52 cars (201-252). The cost per vehicle was US$2.9m, about £1.9 at contemporary rates of exchange. In 2003 a further 27 almost identical cars (301-327) were acquired. It was fitting that Portland, as one of the pioneers of light rail, should now pioneer the low floor Stadtbahn car.

The cars are classified SD600 by the manufacturer, but known as type 2 by the operator. They have a low floor, 35cm above rail level, extending for 73% of the car length and four doors per side, of which the two middle doors are fitted with bridging plates. The first car was built in Germany and subjected to very stringent tests of body strength, as a result of which over 120 changes were made to the design. Final assembly was in Sacramento where all the other cars were constructed. In service these cars have proved to be extremely successful. They normally run in multiple with a car of the original type, thus allowing the advantages of low floor design to be enjoyed by passengers on the entire system.

Twenty-one further cars, of type S70, were ordered in 2006.

Technical details

San Diego 1001, Saint Louis 1001, Denver 101 and Portland low floor design
Length 23.05m, width 2.65m, weight 32,600kg, 4 x 145kW motors, 150 passengers, 84 seated.
Length 27.26m, width 2.65m, weight 40,000kg, 190 passengers, 72 seated.
Length 24.4m, width 2.68m, weight 35,900kg, 2 x 189kW motors, 150 passengers, 64 seated.
Length 28m, width 2.65m, weight 49.44 tonnes, 4 x 145kW motors, 207 passengers, 72 seated.

Bibliography

Modern Tramway/Tramways & Urban Transit nos.500, August 1979 (Edmonton), 527, November 1981 (Edmonton and Calgary), 581, May 1986 (Pittsburgh), 599, November 1987 (Sacramento), 690, June 1995 (Denver), 722, February 1998 (Portland low floor).
Metropolitan Transit Development Board (San Diego) factsheets.
Light Rail Review 8.
North American Light Rail Annual, 1993 and 1994.
Electrical Equipment for Trams, Light Rail Vehicles, Metro Cars, Suburban Trains, EMUs – deliveries since 1950. Siemens AG, Erlangen, 1983.
Der Stadtverkehr 9/96 (Portland low floor cars).

MEXICO

In Mexico, a light rail line was opened in Guadalajara in 1989 and for it 16 cars (01-016) were purchased, based again on type U2 but built in Mexico by the (then) state-owned Concarril factory and designed solely for high platform operation. These have Düwag bogies and motors but electrical equipment is by the national firm of Melco, a subsidiary of Mitsubishi. A further 32 (017-048) were ordered in 1994, to be built by Bombardier with Siemens AC motors. Monterrey followed suit and bought 23 similar cars (001-023) for its first light rail line in April 1991. These have Siemens/Düwag ac drive, as originally developed for the later cars for Köln. A second batch of 25 (024-048) came from Bombardier in 1992/3, that firm having acquired the Concarril factory in the interim. Despite this change in ownership, they are identical to the earlier design. These cars are single-ended and normally operate in coupled pairs. They have three double-width doors per side in each body section and multiphase ac motors, enabling a maximum speed of 80km/hr.

Mexico City had originally intended to work its first light rail line, upgraded for a tram line, with rebuilt PCC cars. In the early 1980s a prototype (000) and then 16 production cars (001-016) were turned out by the Mexican firm of Moyada, with help from the UTDC of Canada. Two and a half original cars went to make up one eight-axle light rail vehicle. Unfortunately the initial attempt to begin service in August 1986 was a disaster, as the cars were totally unreliable and, although later rebuildings improved matters, they did not achieve the desired level of performance and ridership was disappointing. In 1989 12 new light rail cars (017-028) were ordered from Concarril to the design of the Monterrey cars. Subsequently the three best ex-PCC cars were further rebuilt to strengthen the service, but they proved to be sluggish and have not seen much service.

All these lines in Mexico have been successful, although it should be stressed that the systems on which they operate, especially that of Monterrey, are at the heavy rail end of the Stadtbahn spectrum.

In 2006 twelve additional cars were ordered by Monterrey.

Technical details

Guadalajara cars
Length 29.30m, width 2.65m, weight 97,000lb, 400 passengers*, 52 seated

Bibliography

North American Light Rail Annual, 1993 and 1994.

A two-car set in Guadalajara, seen at Pereferico Sur in May 1999. Foster M. Palmer collection, Seashore Trolley Musuem.

A Mexico City car at Huipuloc station on 10 April 2003. (G.J. Travers)

Strassenbahn Magazin no.105, 1/97 (Guadalajara only).

By 1994 a total of 491 cars of class U2 or directly derived from it had been delivered to operators in Canada and the USA, to which should be added 108 cars for Mexican operators. There has been no other example in transport history of a design, originally specific to one city, becoming so widespread in another continent! While this success owes much to the excellence of the basic design, it has also to be said that it would not have been possible had not North American manufacturers firstly abandoned the market for trams and light rail vehicles and then made a complete disaster of their attempt to re-enter it. In fact, this success made it very hard for other suppliers to compete in the North American market, but some did manage to break into it and their designs will be described later.

SALZBURG

In April 1983 the Salzburger Lokalbahn took delivery of the first four Stadtbahn type vehicles (41-45) for its line. Further batches followed in 1988 (46-50) and in 1993 (51-55). This design was based closely on the Frankfurt U3 design but with modifications to suit the conditions of a fairly long radial line (25km). The cars were built by Simmering-Graz-Pauker with electrical equipment by AEG-Telefunken Österreichischen. The main variation from cars built for use elsewhere lay in the relatively high seating capacity, unusu-ally comfortable 2 + 2 seats with small tables and waste bins in each seating bay, and only two double width doors per side. Provision was made for the carriage of parcels traffic, cycles and wheelchairs, the latter at a time when it was not usual to cater for these. Only the outer bogies were motored, with Düwag tandem drive.

Technical details
Length 28.4m, width 2.65m, weight 46.8 tonnes, 2 x 300kW motors, 52+8 seated passengers.

FRANKFURT (M) CLASS P8

In 1970 Frankfurt still had a large fleet of two-axle cars, which were in urgent need of replacement, and it was decided that a new car should be developed which could also be used in tunnel sections, along with class U2. The result was an eight-axle double-ended design by Düwag, first delivered in 1972 and now numbering 100 cars (651-750). These are used on both tunnel lines and on street tram lines which have stub end termini. The first were delivered with folding steps to allow operation at street level stops (class Pt) and later cars had fixed steps, class P. All have now been rebuilt to the former arrangement. In 1998 these cars began service on an extension of line U5, through a tunnel section on which only cars of a width of 2.65m had hitherto been used. Cars 692-750 were therefore fitted with steps which can be extended to bridge the gap between the car body and the platform edge and are now class Ptb (b = breit = broad). Later in the same year they also began to work on line U7. As only single-width doors are fitted at the ends and there is no door in the middle section, dwell times at stops can be prolonged. Nonetheless,

Car 741 in the city centre, at a time when many tram services passed Hauptwache, June 1980. (Author)

this has proved to be a flexible and useful design, for both tramway and Stadtbahn service, although there was at the time of its delivery some newspaper criticism of the multiplicity of vehicle types that the undertaking was ordering.

Technical details
Length 27.4m, width 2.35m, weight 34.5 tonnes, 2 x 120kW motors, 225 passengers, 51 seated.

Bibliography
Strassenbahn Farzeuge op.cit.
Die deutschen Strassenbahn Gelenkwagen. Op.cit.

DÜWAG STADTBAHN B AND M/N DESIGNS AND DERIVED DESIGNS

STADTBAHN B

At quite an early stage in the planning of the network in northern Germany, it was decided that there would be considerable saving if a vehicle could be designed which would be capable of use on other networks, particularly that of Köln. However, that city had planned its new tunnels for use by both existing trams and new cars and clearance problems in these would have ruled out the use of the Statdbahn A cars, had these been constructed. Düwag and Siemens had in 1972 already begun work on three prototypes for Köln and Bonn and in 1973 it was decided to use this design also in the Ruhr area. It was given the designation of Stadtbahn B and was rather more sophisticated, and therefore more expensive, than the Frankfurt car. The first cars to be delivered had a top speed of 100km/hr and are classified B100, but in later deliveries the maximum speed was reduced to 80km/hr, B80. The first cars had conventional control with SIMATIC equipment and have the suffix S. Cars with chopper control have a C suffix, three-phase equipped cars are D and thyristor controlled cars are T.

The first cars were delivered in 1973 and placed in service in Köln and Bonn. They proved to be successful and further orders came from both these cities, ultimately giving fleets of 172 in the former and 75 in the latter. The Köln cars are of classes B80S, B100S and B80D, the last having only one driving position, as they are intended for m.u. operation only, while the Bonn fleet is exclusively B100S and B100T. The Köln and Bonn numbers are too complex to set out here; the former are 2000+, 2100+, 2200+ and 2300+ and some cars are named for cities with which their own is twinned. The Bonn cars are numbered by the year of delivery. Thus the prototype is 7351 and so on to 9376. Thirteen of the Köln cars belonged originally to the Köln-Bonner Eisenbahn. In the Ruhr area Essen bought 24 cars (5001-5011, 5021-5028 and 5141-5145,

In July 1979, when trams still ran on the surface at Duisburg Hauptbahnhof, DVG 4714 awaits departure on line 79. (Author)

B80C), Mülheim seven (5012-5016 and 5031/2, B100S), Bochum 25 (6001-6025, B80D), Duisburg 18 (4701-4718, B80C) and Düsseldorf 104 (4001-4012, 4101-4104 and 4201-4288, B80D). Dortmund joined the ranks of B2 operators in 1986 with ten B80C cars (301-310) and

Rheinbahn buffet car 4103 at Krefeld Rheinstrasse on 10 June 2005. (Author)

Dortmund ex-Bonn 401 in June 2005. (Author)

took 44 further deliveries (311-354) between 1990 and 1994. In 1996 eleven cars (344-354) were fitted with a 10m long middle section, while car 343 was in 1998 fitted with a similar section made from lightweight carbon fibre. This form of construction was developed by Siemens and allowed this section to be about 30% lighter than that fitted to the other cars. Finally ten additional cars (355-364) arrived in 1998/9 with conventional steel middle sections and classified B8.

By 1999 a total of 479 cars of this type were in service. The basic design is that of a double-ended six-axle articulated car, intended for operation on lines with high platforms, but folding steps were also fitted at the doorways to allow them to use conventional street track and stopping places. The width of 2.65m allowed the fitting of pairs of double seats on each side of the gangway. The driver's cabin is completely closed off from the saloons. Multiple unit equipment allows up to three cars to be coupled into a train, but highway regulations do not allow this kind of operation on street track, where the limit is two. Air suspension and rubber insert wheels make for a very comfortable ride, though there is a slight tendency to "hunt" at speed. Following a decision by the Land of Nordrhein-Westfalen that there should be a standard livery for Stadbahn cars, all were initially given a red and white livery, regardless of the fleet colours of their owners. The only exception to this was in Bonn, where the cars were painted in a two-tone green livery. However, recently many have been repainted into fleet colours.

Not all cars of this type are identical, since, as with any good design, standardisation allows some variety to suit the needs of individual systems. Cars running in Dortmund do not have the single end door of the others, to allow enlargement of the cab. They also have a facility which, when running as a two-car set, allows the folding steps of the second car to be used at the low platform sections of certain stations, while those on the leading motor car remain retracted to allow it to serve the high platform sections. Folding steps are not fitted to the Bochum cars, which use high platforms only. Düsseldorf's fleet and some of the cars in Essen have Düwag folding doors rather than the plug doors of the basic design. Until 1994 provision was also made in these two cities for the driver to sell tickets. The cars delivered to Köln in 1991/2 were actually built by Waggon-Union but are indistinguishable from the Düwag product. These and later cars have four folding steps to allow easier access from street level. From the technical angle, the greatest change was the fitting of a one-piece windscreen to cars built after 1981. Some later deliveries to Düsseldorf have bodies constructed in aluminium and are classed B80DAlu.

Duisburg cars 4715-4718, delivered in 1984, and Düsseldorf's 4101-4104 of 1988 had a buffet section, the middle double width door being omitted to make room for the buffet area. The kitchen has a fridge, microwave and sink, as well as storage area and the dining area has four double seats with tables on one side, seven on the other. Unfortunately the buffet services on the joint line have been discontinued on grounds of economy.

Stadtbahn B has proved to be a successful design, its main drawback being the access from street-level stops, which is not easy for any but the most fit and impossible for anyone in a wheelchair or with a pram. Apart from the prototypes in Köln, all cars are still in service, but replacement by a new generation is likely to begin on some systems in the near future. Bonn has recently retired some cars and in 2003 sold 13 of these to Dortmund, which would have bought new cars, had the manufacturer been willing to build them. Eleven have since entered service as 401-411, the other two being used for spare parts. A proposed sale of the Bonn cars to Manchester fell through.

Technical details
Düsseldorf type B80D and Köln type B80D, single driving position
Length 26.9m, width 2.65m, weight 38.5 tonnes, 2 x 215kW motors, 183 passengers, 72 seated.
Length 26.9m, width 2.65m, weight 47 tonnes, 2 x 95kW motors, 183 passengers, 77 seated.

Bibliography
Strassenbahn Magazin nos.94, October-December 1994, 101, March 1996 and 115, May 1998.
Die neue Stadtbahnwagen B80C der Duisburger VAG. Brown Boveri/Düwag/DVG Factsheet 1980.
Die deutschen Strassenbahn-Gelenkwagen. op.cit.
Strassenbahn Farzeuge Band 2. op.cit.
Der Stadtverkehr 11-12/1987 (Köln B80D).
Rhein-Ruhr Stadtbahn Album 1. Op.cit.

Bonn 7575 in June 1980. (Author)

Joint working by Köln and Bonn. KVG 2119 (left) and a Bonn car on the right at Zoo station on 15 June 2005. (Author)

Bogestra 6022 on line U35, the only one to be worked by this operator, June 2005. (Author)

STADTBAHN M AND N

Not long after cars of Stadtbahn B appeared, it became evident that, with the scaling-down of the plans for the Ruhr area, there would be a continuing need for a vehicle which, while incorporating many of the features of that type, would be of a design closer to that of the traditional tram and which would be at home on services for which Stadtbahn B was unsuited. As the majority of trams then in use in the area were of fairly recent construction, the number of new vehicles required would not be large and the unit price might therefore be high. In an effort to keep costs down, the undertakings of Bochum, Essen and Mülheim combined in 1973 to develop a standard design and they were joined later in the year by Bielefeld. The vehicle was to be closely based on the recommendations of the VöV for new construction. Later in 1973, Düwag produced a preliminary design based on its GT8 cars for the Rheinbahn, but this design was not accepted by the working party and a totally new end design was finally evolved. The type was initially intended for use on metre gauge systems, but it was soon realised that it could easily be adapted for standard gauge operation also. It was to be built in both six- and eight-axle configuration and unlike most existing trams in the area was to be double-ended. Cars are therefore classified as M (metre) or N (Normalspur = standard gauge) and have the suffix 6 or 8 as appropriate. The suffixed C, D and S are used as in the Stadtbahn B cars. Apart from the sanders, the cars are all-electric. Four steps, the lowest one folding, made for fairly easy entry, but the floor height was 880mm above rail level. From 1980 onwards, at the instigation of Bielefeld, new cars were also fitted for operation at high platforms. They could be fitted with automatic train stops and inductive train identification to allow use in subways. A minimum curve radius of 14.5m allows widespread use on traditional tram lines.

After components had been tested on Essen's six-axle articulated tram 1615 in 1974, the first examples were delivered in 1976. Bochum (301-355) and Mülheim (271-290) took six-axle cars, the other two eight-axle cars. Essen had a total of 77, making it the largest user of the type, while Bielefeld ultimately had 48 (501-504 and 516-559). Essen's numbering is complicated, cars being in the 10xx, 11xx and 14xx series, classified according to the electrical equipment fitted. Mülheim's car 282 of class M6 built in 1979, was the world's first light rail car to have inverter-controlled three-phase AC traction motors, class M6D. Other cities which later took delivery of this type are Dortmund (N8C,101-154), Kassel (N8C, 401-422), Krefeld (M8C, 831-850), Heidelberg (M8C, 251-258), Augsburg (M8C, 8001-8012), Mainz (271-276, M8C) and Nürnberg (N6S, 361-372), the last of these having many components from MAN. The Augsburg cars differ from all other eight-axle cars in having doors in the middle section. Two Nürnberg cars (363 and 365) ran, as single-ended cars, in München from September to December 1985, but that operator did not go on to order any similar vehicles. When they returned to their native city, they continued as single-ended cars, with the off-side doors sealed off and the step wells covered and all other members of the class were similarly treated. In 1991 all were enlarged to eight-axle layout with a

Bochum 333, of class M6S, at Kennedyplatz in June 1981. (Author)

Augsburg M8C 8008 at Moritzplatz in June 1985. (Author)

Essen 1106 crosses Erfurt KT4D 493 at Anger while on a training run on 25 June 1990. (Author)

Dortmund N8 121 at Hauptbahnhof in May 1981. (Author)

Heidelberg 255 at Bismarckplatz in June 1996. (Author)

Nürnberg 370 and 372 at Hauptbahnhof in June 1985. (Author)

By 1990 car 361, seen at the same location, had acquired a low floor centre section. (Author)

Mulheim 281, as rebuilt with a low floor section, at Auf dem Bruch stop on 7 June 2005. (Author)

Bielefeld trailer 512 in service on line 4 on 9 June 2005. (Author)

Bielefeld 573 in operation on line 3 in December 1997. (Author)

low floor centre section. The last trams to the basic design were delivered to Mülheim in 1991/2 (291-294). Mainz subsequently bought Bielefeld's first four cars and renumbered them 277-280 and three of Essen's first batch have been acquired by Mülheim.

In 1997 Mülheim's 282 was fitted with a low floor centre section, manufactured by Mittenwalder Gerätebau, to give a 30% low floor area in a six-axle car. Several others have since been similarly rebuilt.

The design would now seem to be rather over-dimensioned for some systems and its adoption reflects the lack of available tram designs at that time. Withdrawals began in Bochum in 2000 and in 2004 an order was placed for 45 Variobahn low floor trams to replace the remainder. The Nürnberg cars are also due for early withdrawal. In June 2005 Essen 1012 was dispatched to Lodz in Poland for three months of trials; if the operator considers these successful, this and other cars of the type may be bought.

Between 1994 and 1999 Bielefeld took delivery of 26 new cars (560-595), classed M8D, from Düwag, which differed considerably from other M8 designs. An additional door is fitted in the middle section and this has no central handrail, to allow unimpeded access to wheelchairs and prams. They have only one driving cabin, as it was intended to operate them in service in coupled pairs – an auxiliary controller is fitted for shunting manoeuvres. This has allowed increased seating capacity.

This operator has also developed a new concept in Stadtbahn design, with class MB4, delivered by Düwag in 1999 (511-515). These are bogie trailers built for use on line 4, which serves the university and is subject to high peak traffic. They are 14.24m long and are used between two Stadtbahn cars to provide increased capacity and have 26 seats and 55 standing spaces. There are emergency and parking brakes only and pantographs are fitted to allow current to be drawn for lighting and heating. A train of two M8D cars with an intermediate MB4 trailer is 68m long and can carry 389 passengers.

Technical details

Class M6 D car for Essen, N8 car for Dortmund, Bielefeld 560 class, Nürnberg 361
Length 20.44m, width 2.3m, weight 28.7 tonnes, 4 x 95kW motors, 101 passengers, 36 seated.
Length 26.64m, width 2.65m, weight 34.5 tonnes, 2 x 185kW motors, 1140 passengers, 54 seated.
Length 26.44m, width 2.3m, weight 34.35 tonnes, 4 x 95kW motors, 154 passengers, 63 seated.
Length 19.8m width 2.3m, weight 27,800kg, 2 x 125kW motors, 166 passengers, 36 seated.

Bibliography

Die deutschen Strassenbahn-Gelenkwagen. Op.cit.
Der Stadtverkehr 1/86 and July/August 1997.
Strassenbahn Magazin no.107, 3/97 (low floor modification) and nos.173/4, March/April 2004.
Düwag factsheets.
Die Nürnberg-Fürther Strassenbahn im Wandel der Zeiten. Op.cit.
Modern Tramway no.500, August 1979. (Mülheim 282).
Die Stadtbahnwagen der Typen M und N.M. Kochems. Transpress Verlag, Stuttgart, 2005.

DUISBURG CLASS GT8NC

In conjunction with the construction of tunnels, with some stations having centre platforms, it became necessary for Duisburg DVG to replace most of its fleet of conventional single-ended articulated cars. Unfortunately limited track clearance made it impossible simply to order standard Stadtbahn material and a design only 2.2m wide was therefore developed by Düwag especially for this operator as class GT8NC. To gain experience articulated tram 1060 of 1967, which had been damaged in a fire in 1975, was fitted with chopper control in 1976. This car was renumbered 1000 in 1985 and in 1994 was rebuilt as a double-ended tram, with ends of the design of the production batch. In 1995 it was given an extra middle section of low floor layout. It has also been given equipment to function as a driving school car, but is used in normal service too. Based on experience with 1000, the production series was developed as a three-section car with a lower floor level than on other similar cars, 780mm above rail level instead of 880mm. As it was necessary to make provision for the driver to sell tickets and still to provide a cabin of the standard which is now required, the single forward door was omitted on the off-side. The first entered service in 1986 and further batches were delivered in 1988 and 1992/3, bringing the total to 45 trams (1001-1045). These are a scaled-down version of Stadtbahn B and, to simplify repair and maintenance, have many parts in common with that design. All were painted in a new livery of red and white. In 1996 cars 1016-1045 were fitted with an additional low floor section, making them into ten-axle, four-section vehicles, 33m long. The remainder of the class were similarly treated in 1997. The new centre sections were manufactured by the DVG staff, in the system's workshops. Three of these cars were expensively hired by the GVBA Amsterdam from September 1999 to 2002 to cover a shortage of rolling stock and were renumbered 997-999 while there.

Car 1014 on Königstrasse in July 1989, when trams still ran conveniently on the surface in central Duisburg. (Author)

As rebuilt, 1004 approaches Lutherplatz on 7 June 2005. (Author)

Technical details

Duisburg GT8 NC, as built
Length 25.64m, width 2.20m, weight 29,600kg, 2 x 180kW motors, 126 passengers, 50 seated.

Apart from these, no further cars of Stadtbahn M/N were built after 1990, as it was completely eclipsed by the low floor concept. In June 1990, two cars from Essen ran briefly in Erfurt but to date none has gone to systems in Eastern Germany or Eastern Europe on a permanent basis.

DESIGNS FOR KARLSRUHE

Nowhere has the concept of the Stadtbahn been put into practice more widely or successfully than in Karlsruhe and the surrounding area, in which light rail cars share main line tracks with trains of DB AG and bring passengers from outlying areas direct to the city centre. Various types of car have been developed to make this service possible, these originally being derived from the Stadtbahn B design but with considerable alterations to fit local conditions. They also show some affinity with the articulated cars built by Waggon-Union (qv) for the Albtalbahn lines running out of Karlsruhe, from which the Stadtbahn network has been developed. Renumberings and rebuildings have made the history of these cars quite complicated.

The first cars (501-520) were delivered in 1983/4 by Waggon-Union for service on the extended line A of the Albtalbahn and are single-ended six-axle cars, differing in windscreen design and in door and window arrangement from Stadtbahn B cars. Düwag delivered twenty similar cars (521-540) in 1987, these having Waggon-Union bogies. These last ten were enlarged to eight-axle layout with new middle sections in 1993 and then became 871-880, but are now 571-580. The first ten were similarly treated in 1997 and are now

Car 870 picks up a crowd of school pupils from a temporary platform outside Heilbronn Hbf in June 2000. (Author)

Car 583 on Kaiserstrasse at Marktplatz in June 2000. (Author)

DB-owned 816 awaits departure from Karlsruhe Hauptbahnhof for Bruchsal on line S3 in June 1996. (Author)

Car 857 (now 557), one of the first series to be fitted with panoramic windows, is seen in a siding at Ettlingen in June 1996. (Author)

One of the first series, 510, displays the original yellow and black livery while working Albtalbahn line A at Marktplatz in May 1984. (Author)

581-590. Ten further cars (581-590) came from the same manufacturer in 1989, which just one year after entering service were rebuilt into eight-axle form, with a very attractive middle section having panoramic windows. They then became 851-860 but have since been renumbered again to become 551-560. In 1991/2 eight-axle cars 861-870 arrived from Düwag and these later became 561-570.

All further deliveries were built as double-

ended eight-axle cars. The first which were dual-voltage, to allow operation at 750V DC and over DB tracks electrified at 15kV AC, were delivered in 1991 (801-810), to the same basic design. These were followed up to 1995 by 26 further cars (811-836) of which nos. 809/10 are fitted with a chemical toilet in the middle section. Cars 817-820 are the property of Deutsche Bahn AG and are also classified as 450.001-004. No.816 was later transferred to railway ownership and is now also 450.005. From 1997 to 2004 successive deliveries brought this fleet up to no.915, cars from 878 onwards being built by Siemens. These cars can be distinguished from earlier deliveries by the more rounded ends and bonded windows in the saloons. Fitting of three-phase equipment has allowed the floor level in the end sections to be lowered from 1000mm above rail level to 880mm, while in the middle section it has been reduced to 380mm. A folding step bridges the gaps at main line platforms. The middle section of cars 845-848 has been fitted out as a buffet, marketed as "Regio Bistro" and are distinguished by a red and white livery. Panoramic windows are

Car 842 heads a two-car set at Marktplatz in the city centre in June 2000. It has worked an express service on line S4 from Heilbronn and will terminate at Karlsruhe Hauptbahnhof. (Author)

fitted in the buffet section and this feature was also provided from no.868 onwards.

These vehicles have brought Stadtbahn technology to a very high level and to-day provide an excellent standard of service on the lines radiating from Karlsruhe.

Technical details
Cars 501 and 801
Length 27.6m, width 2.65m, weight 42 tonnes, 2 x 235kW motors, ? passengers, 93 seated.
Length 36.57m, width 2.65m, weight 58.6 tonnes, 2 x 289kW motors (750V DC), 100 seated.

Bibliography
Strassenbahn Farzeuge. op.cit.

TYNE AND WEAR METROCARS

When this system was being planned in the 1970s, there were no contemporary British vehicles available and the operator therefore turned to Germany and took inspiration from the Stadtbahn B design. An articulated design was preferred bearing in mind likely traffic levels and also the radius of curves in the depot area. The cars were actually built in Britain by Metropolitan-Cammell, but use the bogies and articulation of the German cars, the bogies having been manufactured by Düwag. However, they differ from these in that the driver's cab occupies only one third of the total width and this allows space for a seat, much beloved by enthusiasts and children, on the other side. Electrical equipment is by GEC Traction. Outward opening plug doors are fitted. The first prototypes (4001/2) were delivered in 1976 and extensively tested on a track at Killingworth. These had train doors in the ends of each car, but as walkways were installed in the tunnels there was no need for production cars to have these and they have a different windscreen design as a

Prototype car 4002 seen during an enthusiasts' visit to the test track in May 1979. (Author)

result. Otherwise few changes were found to be necessary and the prototypes were in due course converted to the same arrangement. Production cars were delivered between August 1978 and the end of 1980 and are numbered 4003-4090. These cars have performed well and in more recent times have become the first in Britain to share tracks with main line trains, on the Sunderland extension.

Technical details
Length 27.4m, width 2.65m, weight 39 tonnes, 2 x 185kW motors, 210 passengers, 84 seated.
Bibliography
The Metrocar. Tyne and Wear PTE factsheet, 1989.
Modern Tramway no.509, May 1980 and no.512, August 1980.

When still very new, car 4013 is at the rear of a set at Tynemouth in July 1979. (Author)

TUNIS

One of the very few Stadtbahn systems to have been constructed outwith Europe and North America is to be found in Tunis, in which service opened in the autumn of 1985. To operate this line, which is worked by the Société du Métro Leger de Tunis (SMLT), 78 double-ended, eight-axle articulated vehicles (101-178) were ordered from Düwag, with Siemens electrical equipment. The first was delivered in 1982 and was tried on the Düsseldorf tracks before export. Such was the success of the line that 43 further cars (201-243) were acquired in 1992 and 14 more (301-314) in 1995.

The design was based closely on the cars built for German systems and, like these, could operate both from high platforms and from street level stops, in the latter case with an additional folding step. Conductors were carried initially and desks were provided for them but were not used. There was therefore no need to provide for ticket issue by the driver, whose cabin was completely separated from the saloons. Most seating is in 1+1 configuration and there are few double seats. The livery is an attractive one of apple green, with broad white and narrow blue bands. The cars have worked well and it is unfortunate that the concept has not been copied by other African countries.

Technical details
Length 29.1m, width 2.5m, weight 39.6mp, 2 x 235 kW motors, 342 passengers*, 52 seated.

Bibliography
Der Stadtverkehr 5/6, 1984.
Modern Tramway no.597, September 1987.
Strassenbahn Magazin no.114, 4/98.

Car 111 heading a two-car set in the city centre on Christmas Day, 2001. (A.W. Brotchie)

BURSA

The Turkish city of Bursa chose to build its new light rail system as a Stadtbahn and the contract to build and equip it went to a German consortium, headed by Siemens. It was therefore not surprising that the design chosen for the rolling stock was based closely on the Stadtbahn B car, as supplied to Köln in 1995/6. However, as all stops are at high platforms, no folding steps are fitted. The cars were built variously in Düsseldorf and Krefeld and the bogies were manufactured in Graz. Final fitting out took place in Turkey. There are 47 cars in the fleet, painted in an attractive turquoise livery, and public service began with these in August 2002.

Technical details
Length 27.2m, width 2.65m, weight 38.5 tonnes, 4 x 140kW motors, 327 passengers*, 60 seated.

Bibliography
Der Stadtverkehr 3/03.

STADTBAHN T

This design had little in common with the other Stadtbahn cars. It was built solely for Rotterdam and is in effect a metro car which has received some modifications, such as brake lights and trafficators, to enable it to run on tracks which are not completely segregated from road traffic. It resulted from a decision by the government of the Netherlands in 1975 to halt further metro construction, at a time when construction work was well advanced on Rotterdam's second, east to west line. Some changes were made to the plans for this line to enable it to be classified as light rail. There are in all 50 of these cars, numbered 5201-5250, they were delivered in 1980. Up to five can work in m.u. formation.

Technical details
Length 29.8m width 2.65m, weight 43 tonnes, 6 x 56kW motors, 260 passengers, 72 seated.

Bibliography
Modern Tramway no.514, October 1980.

A coupled set of Rotterdam's T5 cars at Oosterflank, outbound, in June 1981. (Author)

HANNOVER CARS

PROTOTYPES

Hannover, after briefly toying with the idea of a U-Bahn, settled in the early 1960s for the upgrading of its tramways with central area tunnels, which initially could be used by modified trams. However, these were only a stop-gap solution and in 1970 two prototypes were delivered, one each from LHB/AEG (6000) and Düwag/Siemens (6001). Both cars were double-ended, six-axle vehicles but were outwardly not identical and had different control systems. Both were 20.6m long, 2.5m wide – a width exceptional for Hannover – and weighed c25 tonnes. Two 150kW motors gave a top speed of 70km/hr, although it was found that the cars were inclined to pitch at speed. The cars were tested for four years, mainly on line 14, but spent much time in the shops under repair. In 1975 Vancouver bought back car 601 and shipped it off to Vancouver for demonstration. The New Democratic Party government of British Columbia was then planning a light rail system and had been considering the Frankfurt U2 design. However, before any tests could be undertaken, the NDP government was defeated in an election and the incoming Social Credit government, whose members had no interest in public transport, had no further use for the car, which languished for years in a shed. Fortunately it has now been rescued and is preserved in Calgary. The other prototype was in 1978 taken back by LHB to form part of their museum collection.

GT8 CARS

From experience gained with the prototypes, it was decided that an eight-axle design would be more economical in service and would also allow more space for electrical components, thus reducing the repair bills. The result was class GT8, a design quite different to other Stadtbahn cars, with five double doors per side (fitted with folding steps) and a deep windscreen. Technically this was an advanced design, having electronic three-phase thyristor control, which gives an exceptionally smooth ride and was also considered much more economical than any other available at the time. Internally the design is rather spartan, compared with that of the U2 or Stadtbahn B cars and the restricted width allows only 2+1 seating.

The first cars (6001-6100) were built by Düwag, with Düwag bogies, but electrically were the product of a consortium of that firm, LHB, Siemens, AEG and Kiepe. The body was designed by Professor H. Lindinger of the department of design at the city's Technical University. He was also responsible for the new and very simple livery, the cars being painted lime green all over, except for the white advertisement panels on the sides. This colour scheme was not at first liked by the public. The first car was delivered at the end of 1974 and entered public service in May of the following year. The second series of cars (6101-6260) were built by LHB

alone and were delivered in batches between 1979 and 1993. Many of the first group have now been withdrawn and sold for further service in Budapest. Eight were sold to Den Haag in 2002 for use on line 11, but were not very successful there and it is likely the last will run in late 2007, after which these cars will also go to Budapest. Two others are rented from HTM by Netherlands Railways to work a short line between Houten and Houten Castellum and are likely to remain on this service until 2009.

Technical details
Length 27m, width 2.4m, weight 38.8 tonnes, 2 x 218kW motors, 236 passengers, 46 seated.

2000 CLASS

For expansion of its services and in particular to cope with what was hoped would be record traffic to Expo 2000, Hannover decided that the time was ripe to order some Stadtbahn cars of a new design and in 1995 an order for 144 new cars was placed with LHB/Siemens. The first was presented to the public in April 1997 and was unveiled by Gerhard Schröder, at that time Minister-Präsident of Niedersachsen. The car, nicknamed the "Silberling" was designed by a British designer, Jasper Morrison, and he certainly managed to devise a vehicle which was

Prototype 600. (Lars F. Richter collection))

Hannover 6104 at Hauptbahnhof on 2 July 1987. (Author)

The Stadtbahn design was also used to construct a new six-axle works car in 1985 and in 1993 a similar vehicle was built by LHB for Leipzig. As 5090, it attracts some attention at Hauptbahnhof on a Sunday morning in June 2004. (Author)

With the main line of NS on the right, car 6106 leaves Houten Castellum halt in March 2004. (Author)

quite strikingly different to any others running in Germany. There are two variants of this design. Two thirds of these, type II, have only one driving cab and a connecting gangway at the other end, to allow cars to be coupled to form a six-section vehicle, 50m long. The remainder, type I, have two cabs and can also be coupled to a combined type II set to form a three-car train which is, by a few centimetres, under the 75m maximum length allowed by law for on-street running. This facility has allowed an important gain in capacity in comparison with the previous design, which could only run as a three-car set with special dispensation. Pressure ventilation is fitted in the passenger spaces, air conditioning in the driver's cab. The cars are somewhat roomier than the earlier design and can accommodate eight additional passengers. The arrangement of the seating is quite different to that in any other Stadtbahn design, with a good deal of longitudinal seating around the doors, to allow passengers to circulate more freely, and most 2+2 seating concentrated in the middle section. The designer intended to create a car which would be "sympathetic and effective" (using the former word in its literal, German meaning) and would make a positive contribution to urban life, but some passengers, confronted with the rather spartan interior,

Interior view of a Hannover GT8 car, taken in 1981. (Author)

may have wondered just how positive this contribution actually is. However, there can be no denying that the smooth, rounded exterior is eye-catching, while still allowing the cars to blend in with their surroundings. In 2004 this class experienced severe problems of overheating of the axle boxes, the correction of which posed consid-

Rent-a-tram! A small notice on the side of one of the cars at Houten. (Author)

erable problems for the engineers of Ustra.

Technical details

Length 25.6m (type I), 24.71m (type II), width 2.65m, weight 39,850kg (type I), 38,700kg (type II), 155 passengers, 54 seated (type I), 465 passengers, 162 seated (2 x type II + 1 x type I).

A set of Hannover cars of class 23xx in on-street service at Nordbahnhof in September 2000. (Author)

HTM 6064 leaves Scheveningen (Haven) loop on line 11 in March 2003. (Author)

THE DOCKLANDS LIGHT RAILWAY CARS

For the first cars for the initial service on the DLR, for which a totally new design could not be justified, the contractors GEC-Mowlem went to Linke-Hofman Busch, who took as a basis the Hannover Stadtbahn, with an altered end design and of course equipped for automatic operation and third-rail current collection. Electrical equipment was by GEC. As the word "tram" was then still officially unacceptable, these were referred to as "trains". These cars were numbered 1-11, class P86, and with them the DLR opened in August 1987. Seating was mainly 2+2 traverse, with some longitudinal seats in the centre of the car. To minimise the gap between car body and platform, in the interests of wheelchair users, inward-opening swing doors were fitted and as traffic built up, the doorways became distinct problem areas. As these cars did not meet fire safety requirements for tunnel operation a further ten cars (12-21, class P89) were built at York by British Rail Engineering in 1989/90, under licence from LHB. These could operate in the tunnel section to Bank when this opened in 1991 and could also work in m.u. formation. Externally they were almost identical to the first batch, apart from the destination indicators. This class was later converted to have sliding doors.

Even with this additional order, the DLR was soon short of cars as traffic built up to unexpected levels and a further order, which ultimately became one for 23 cars (22-44) of class B90, was placed with BN of Brugge in 1989. These have sliding doors, a train door in the middle of the car end and a rearrangement of the

In September 1987, in the very early days of Docklands, 09 approaches Canary Wharf. (Author)

internal layout to give more standing space. They were delivered in the period 1991-92 to replace the earlier stock. The final order for this design was for a total of 47 cars of class B92 (45-70), delivered between 1992 and 1995. Car 35 was the first DLR car to be fitted with the new Alcatel signalling equipment which revolutionised train operation on the system and made it possible for it to cope with passenger levels far greater than those initially envisaged. Class B90 was initially fitted to work with the original GEC signalling but all cars had been converted to Alcatel by 1998. Finally in 2002-03 24 cars (92-99 and 01-16) of class B2K arrived; these are to the same basic design but have slight alterations to meet new access regulations. Apart from these, all cars are currently being refurbished by Alston at Wolverton.

With the arrival of these two classes, class P86 became redundant and all eleven cars were sold to Essen in 1991. There they were fitted with

driving cabs and pantographs and modified for on-street operation. They entered service as Essen 5201-5211 between 1994 and 1999, still in their DLR livery, which they retained until recent overhauls. Although class P89 cars could have been converted to Alcatel, it was decided to sell these to Essen also and they were withdrawn in 1995. They are now Essen 5221-5230 and have been repainted into that operator's standard yellow livery.

To allow the running of longer trains, 24 new cars are now on order from Bombardier, for delivery in 2007. These will still be to the same design, but will have a more streamlined end profile. There is an option for a further nine cars.

Technical details
Class P86
Length 28m, width 2.65m, weight 40 tonnes, 2 x 185kW motors, 222 passengers*, 84 seated.

Bibliography
Die Deutschen Strassenbahn-Gelenkwagen. op.cit.
Strassenbahn Farzeuge Band 2. op.cit.
Der Stadtverkehr July/August 1997.
Tramways and Urban Transit no.723, March 1998.
Strassenbahn Magazin no.109, 5/97.
Docklands Light Rail – Official Handbook. A. Pearce, B. Hardy and C. Stannard, Capital Transport, Harrow. Fourth edition, 2000.
Tachsiger Gelenktriebwagen für London. LHB factsheet, n.d., c.1986.

Car 24 at Heron Quays in June 2000. (Author)

Car 54 in Lewisham station in June 2000. (Author)

Essen 5207, seen at Berliner Platz in June 1999, still in its DLR livery. (Author)

Essen 5230 on 7 June 2005. (Author)

OTHER GERMAN DESIGNS

WÜRZBURG

In 1985 this city, after a brief flirtation with the M-Bahn concept, decided to order 14 Stadtbahn cars from LHB, to a totally new design. These would have been three-section vehicles, of a length of 32.6m and width of 2.6m and were to be fitted with four 150kW motors to cope with the gradients of the extended line 5. In the event, it was decided to order instead Germany's first low floor cars and the Stadtbahn order was not placed.

Bibliography
Der Stadtverkehr, 1/86.

THE CITYSPRINTER

As the first Stadtbahn B cars would have to be replaced early in the 21st century, the Köln undertaking (KVB) and Siemens in a joint venture began work on a new design and this was first presented to the press on 11 June 1999.

Given the increase in costs since the first Stadtbahn B had taken to the rails, this was intended to be a more affordable vehicle and it cost DEM3m, whereas the last batch of Stadtbahn B cars cost DEM4.5m each. It was hoped that this design would be adopted as standard by other undertakings when fleet replacement became due.

However, several features, particularly the design of the interior and the hard plastic seats, did suggest that this was a somewhat cheap product. The cars were all-electric and could be coupled mechanically to B cars, but not electrically and so could not run in service with them. There was conventional springing only, and no air suspension. To reduce power consumption, the body was of lightweight aluminium. On test the design showed good riding qualities but was reported as being noisy. It was to be made available as a six- or eight-axle car.

The two cars, numbered 5001/2, appeared in passenger service in July, but test working continued also and while on one of these, on 16 September, car 5001 rammed a service car of line 15 at Christophstrasse station. Sixty-seven people were injured, seven seriously. All three braking systems had failed and that was the end of the Citysprinter.

Technical details
Length 26.85m, width 2.65m, weight 39 tonnes, 4 x 140kW motors, 178 passengers, 62 + 6 seated.

BOMBARDIER CARS

Car 5148 in the underground station at Neumarkt on 15 June 2005. (Author)

In view of the disaster of the Citysprinter, it is not surprising that Köln, and subsequently Bonn, should have turned to another manufacturer to develop a replacement for the Stadtbahn B cars. The KVB had been taking delivery of a large number of low-floor trams from Bombardier (qv) and it was this firm which in 2000 was awarded the contract for 55 cars of a new Stadtbahn design. Classed K5000, this is a two-section car which has many parts in common with the low-floor cars. It is air conditioned and has retractable steps to allow operation to low height platforms. Cost was about the same as for the Citysprinter, but the finish of the cars looked rather better. The first car, 5101, entered service in February 2002 and to date the type seems to have given every satisfaction, a further four being acquired subsequently. However, a change of policy in favour of low-floor trams has meant that an option for a further 91 cars has been reduced to an order for just 18. Bonn has also taken delivery of 15 cars of this design.

Technical details
K5000
Length 28.4m, width 2.65m, weight 37.2 tonnes, 4 x 120kW motors, 186 passengers, 62 seated.

For the new system of Saarbrücken, much of which runs on the formation of a former railway line, Bombardier supplied from its Austrian factory in 1997 a first tranche of 12 double-ended dual-voltage cars (1001-1012). On the city section these operate on 750V DC and on the

A Saarbrücken car at Sarreguimes on 27 November 1997. (Author)

Interior view of this car. (Author)

railway alignment they operate at the DB voltage of 15kV AC. They have of course to comply with the regulations laid down for main line working and the attractively streamlined ends are strong enough to withstand a crash load of 60 tonnes. There was much co-operation with other manufacturers, since the electrical equipment is from Kiepe and Elim, the bogies, which are very similar to those of the K4000 type, were constructed by ANF in Valenciennes and the motors were by GEC-Alsthom. Final assembly took place in the BN plant in Brugge.

The result is an extremely comfortable car, of high performance, which has allowed a radical improvement over the service formerly offered by main line trains on the route. There are four doors per side, mounted in the low floor portions of the two end sections and thus allowing level access from the low height platforms. The middle section has a high floor and 2+2 seating; along with the drivers' cabins, it is air conditioned and is intended for use by passengers making longer journeys. Livery is an attractive combination of white and blue, with a grey skirt. To keep up with demand, 16 additional cars were acquired in 2000/1 (2013-2028). Some have recently run in Kassel to give the staff of the local undertaking experience of this kind of operation.

Technical details
Length 37.1m, width 2.65m, weight 55.4 tonnes, 8 x 120kW motors, 243 passengers, 96 seated

Bibliography
Bombardier Tram-Train. Bombardier Eurorail factsheet.
Strassenbahn Fahrzeuge. Op.cit
Zukunftskonzept Nahverkehr. Das Fahrzeug. Saarbahn Factsheet 1.
Der Stadtverkehr 9/1999 (Citysprinter), 1/2000 and 7-8/2000 (K5000).
Tramways and Urban Transit nos.740, August 1999 and 779, November 2002.
Strassenbahn Magazin no.121, 5/99.

WLB 405 heads another of the class outbound at Schöpfwerk in June 2001. (Author)

In 1979 a double-ended version of Wien's class E2, itself based on the Düwag Mannheim type of tram, was used to replace the existing material on the Stadtbahn. These are classified E6 (4901-4945) and are a double-ended design with doorways adapted for use at low platforms. To work with them, 39 articulated trailers of class c6 (1901-1939) were also acquired. In recent years class E6 cars have worked in multiple with new low floor cars.

In 1993 Wien required new cars for its former Stadtbahn line which had now become line U6, although its operational characteristics had not actually changed. It therefore ordered from Bombardier 68 three-section cars in which the middle section was 100% low floor. There is only a single driving position, which could either work in coupled sets or with the existing class E2, to provide a low floor car on every train. They proved to be successful and a further ten were bought in 2000. The cars are classified T and numbers are 2601-2678. In late 2004 a further 38 were ordered, with an option for 42 more. To take advantage of a price reduction which could be gained by following on from this order, the Wiener Lokalbahn also bought six similar cars (401-406), to cope with increased traffic on its line, and again ordered a further five along with the main order, at the end of 2004.

In June 1981, when left hand running was still in force, car 4914 brings up the rear of a train on line GD to Freidensbrücke as it leaves Wäringherstrasse station. (Author)

Bibliography
Der Stadtverkehr 9/1989.

With a view to the Olympic Games traffic in 2012, the Docklands Light Railway in London has placed an order for 31 cars.

In 2006 this manufacturer secured a contract for no fewer than 146 cars for Frankfurt (M). These will be of two types – the 54 of class U5-25 will be single units and the 46 of type U5-50 will be double units. There is an option for 24 additional cars.

THE DRESDEN CARGO TRAMS

While these cars may not fall neatly within the scope of this book, it is worth mentioning that in 2001, in co-operation with Volkswagen, DVB instituted a service to carry parts between the Volkswagen plant and the sidings of Deutsche Bahn, via the city centre. While most such operations in the past, especially in the DDR, relied on redundant passenger cars, this was totally different and a fleet of five motor cars and seven trailers was built by the firm of Schalke for the service.

With motor car 2002 at the rear, a four-section set is seen at Pariserplatz in July 2001. (Author)

STUTTGART DT8

PROTOTYPES

The first three prototypes (3001/2 – 3005/6, classes S-DT8.1 – 8.3) of what was to become the largest class of Stadtbahn cars in any German city appeared in the autumn of 1981. This was a double-ended unit of two bogie cars, close coupled back-to-back and having driving positions at the outer ends only. This form of construction was chosen as being the most suitable to replace coupled sets of GT4 articulated cars, maintaining the existing ratio of seats to standing places and also to allow all axles to be driven, since at that time, it would have been difficult to motorise the middle bogie of an articulated car. As there would be no need for on-board ticket collection, the driving cab was of full width and separated from the passenger accommodation. All seats were arranged in 2+2 formation and a high standard of comfort was provided for passengers, with double glazing and an advanced heating and ventilation system. All axles were driven, to provide adequate power for the city's gradients. The bodies were constructed by MAN and the electrical installation in two cars was by AEG and Siemens jointly, while in the third it was by Brown Boveri. A maximum speed of 80km/hr was assured but the considerable weight of the cars did give rise to some problems. The cars were tested for several years on the section of line 3 between Möhringen and Plieningen. Once series production began, the prototypes were taken out of traffic and later scrapped, except for cars 3001 and 3006 which have been put together to form a museum piece.

PRODUCTION CARS CLASSES S-DT8.4 – S-DT8.9

Based on the experience gained, a first production series of 40 cars was ordered in 1984 from Düwag. The cars are considerably lighter than the prototypes and have an extended driving cab to give the driver more leg room and improve the sight lines. Some components were removed from the roof to a position under the floor and thus there was no longer any need for covering panels on the roof. Electrical equipment was provided by a consortium of AEG, Siemens and Brown Boveri, under leadership of the last of these. The bogies are by Düwag. Although dimensions remain as for the prototypes, the extra length of the cabs has made it necessary to reduce total capacity to 242 passengers, 110 seated. The reduction in weight allowed the power of the motors to be reduced. The cars were designed by Professor Lidinger & Partner, who also designed the Hannover cars, but the Stuttgart cars are internally finished to a much higher standard, with an attractive colour scheme

of yellow, green and violet, and are extremely comfortable. Classes 8.6, and 8.8 do not have folding steps and can be operated from high platforms only. Up to three coupled sets can run in multiple. Although not cheap, the DT8 cars have been extremely successful in service, as has been reflected by the increases in passenger numbers, and they provide Stuttgart with a standard of service that cities elsewhere can only dream of. Deliveries continued until 1996 and numbers now run from 3007/8 to 3233/4, giving a total of 114 sets of this design. A few also carry names of local places.

Technical details
Prototype 1001 and class S-DT8.4 (coupled set)
Length 37.42m, width 2.65m, weight 60 tonnes, 4 x 269kW motors, 250 passengers, 112 seated.
Length 37.42m, width 2.65m, weight 56 tonnes, 4 x 222kW motors, 242 passengers, 110 seated.

CLASS S-DT8.10/11

By 1996 it was thought that there was a need to revise the design and an order was placed with a consortium headed by Siemens and Adtranz for a batch of 23 cars (4001/2-4045/6), with an option for 27 more. These are broadly similar to earlier deliveries but have a more rounded front end. The main differences, however, are the fitting of three-phase equipment and the omission of folding steps, so that they can operate from high platforms only. Air conditioning is fitted and the windows have darkened "purdah" glass to diminish the effect of the sun's rays. The design of the interior has been improved to provide an even higher level of comfort, and in the interest of security the cars have been given a corridor connection. The motors are also slightly more powerful and on test on Siemens' test track, one set achieved a speed of 140km/hr. Such speeds will not be required in service, where they are limited to 80km/hr! These have been followed by 27 sets of type DT8.11 (3347/8 – 3389/90).

Technical details
Length 38.15m, width 2.65m, weight 56,500kg, 8 x 120kW motors, 246 passengers, 108 seated.

RACK TRAMWAY BOGIE CARS

Stuttgart operates a metre gauge rack tramway over the short but very steep section between Marienplatz and Degerloch and it was decided to modernise this when the prototype Stadtbahn cars were being delivered. Three new cars (1001-1003) were built by MAN in 1982, the bogies being by SLM of Winterthur. Essentially the cars are one half of a Stadtbahn set, with a driving cab at each end.

Unfortunately the cars proved to be slightly too heavy and in 1983 both the double glazing and air conditioning were removed. Maximum speed is 30km/hr and m.u. operation is possible, but is not normally practised in service. However, in summer a flat wagon for bicycle transport is attached to the upper end of each car, a service which proves to be most popular in the uphill direction! Apart from the regenerative brake, there are two further independent braking systems and these automatically come into operation if speed should rise above the 30km/hr limit.

Bibliography

Der Stadtverkehr February 1981 (prototypes), 7/85 (production series), 6/99 (8.10).
Strassenbahn Magazin no.111, 1/98.
Tramways and Urban Transit no.739, July 1999 (DT8.10).
Strassenbahn Farzeuge. op.cit.
Light Rail Construction in Stuttgart. SSB. No date, c1988.

Car 3020 operating on street at Schreibestrasse in Heslach, June 1989. At that time services were still without the U prefix. The car is running on mixed-gauge track. (Author)

Prototype car 3005 at Möhringen, when these cars were being tried on the section of line 3 from that point to Pleiningen, June 1984. (Author)

DT8.10 car 3313 at Leinfelden Bahnhof in June 2001. (Author)

Rack tramway car 1001 has just arrived at Degerloch and the cyclists reclaim their bicycles, June 1984. (Author)

SWEDEN

The designs described below have been derived from the class M21 articulated trams supplied to Göteborg from 1983 onwards (qv).

ISTANBUL STADTBAHN

For the opening of this line in 1989 a total of 105 cars were obtained from ASEA Brown Boveri, with construction of the bodies out-sourced to Simmering Graz-Pauker in Austria. The main batch of 70 cars are articulated single-ended, double-sided driving motor cars (MD) (501-570) and the balance of 35 cars are articulated non-driving motor cars (M). Normal train formation in service is either MD+M+MD or a coupled set of MD cars. The cars have GTO thyristor equipment and regenerative braking. Internally they provide comfortable seats arranged in 2+2 formation. The first were tested on GS tracks before being shipped from Sweden and that system also provided much help in matters such as driver training. Although these cars seemed to be at the outer limit for Stadtbahn

On the light rail line, car 505 heads an outward bound set near Otogar in March 1989. (Author)

cars, they later showed their inherent flexibility when 22 of the MD cars were transferred for use on the new tram line in the city, which opened in 1992. Several others followed at a later date, to cope with the success of the new line. As this runs mainly in city streets, the cars received shrouds to cover the bogies and underfloor equipment and some seats were removed. High platforms were temporarily provided at stopping places. New low floor cars are now being delivered for the tram line and the Stadtbahn cars will then return to their own line. (qv)

Technical details
MD car as built
Length 23.5m, width 2.65m, weight 29 tonnes, 4 x 75kW motors, 384 passengers*, 48 seated.

Bibliography
Modern Tramway no.618, June 1989.
Istanbul Metro System, ABB Traction, 1989.

As modified for street running, car 531 is seen near Sultan Ahmet in May 1992. (Author)

BALTIMORE

In 1989 the Department of Transportation of the State of Maryland ordered 35 light rail vehicles (5001-5035) from ABB Traction for its new line. The car bodies were actually built in Denmark and the electrical equipment was manufactured in Sweden, but final assembly took place in New Jersey and the bogies were manufactured in Maryland. Fifteen further cars were ordered in 1997. These are the largest light rail vehicles to operate in North America, if not in the entire world, at least in terms of length and width. These were the first US light rail cars to have three-phase ac equipment, with GTO thyristor control. They entered service in April 1992. All stations on the line have very low platforms and therefore entry to the cars is by fairly steep steps, although a rather clumsy boarding system is provided for passengers in wheelchairs by means of ramps at the stations and an extension plate at one door of the car. Three separate systems of suspension and upholstered seats make for a particularly comfortable ride. Although these cars have been an undoubted success, they have

Car 5037 sets down passengers after arrival at the Cromwell/Glen Burnie terminus in October 2000. (Author)

not been adopted by any other system.

Technical details
Length 28m, width 2.9m, weight 46 tonnes, 4 x 160kW motors, 261 passengers*, 84 seated.

Bibliography
Modern Tramway no.636, December 1990.

PHILADELPHIA

An order for 26 cars to replace the "bullets" on the Norristown line was placed by SEPTA to a consortium of ASEA and Amtrak in December 1987, the latter to be responsible for assembling the cars in the US. In the event this arrangement did not work and the cars were completed by what had become ABB in New York and even by 1993 only eight had been completed. They are classed N5 and have four 155kW motors to give a high power/weight ratio, which has allowed speeds to be returned to the level at which the "bullets" set them in 1932! AC motors are fitted. Although they have sharply raked ends, there is a good deal of equipment in pods on the roof and they lack the elegance of their predecessors.

Bibliography

Modern Tramway no.636, December 1990.
North American Light Rail Annual 1993 and 1994.
Baltimore's Light Rail. H. H. Harwood Jr. Quadrant Press Inc., New York, 1995.

NORWEGIAN DESIGNS

OSLO

Two of the lines to the west of Oslo, which have now been incorporated into joint operation with the Tunnelbanen metro, are still essentially light rail in character and are worked by adapted metro cars. These are, however, at the outer end of the Stadtbahn spectrum.

In 1978 Strømmen delivered 18 cars (1301-1318, class T5) for use on these lines. These have AEG electrical equipment. Fifteen similar cars (1319-1333, T6) followed in 1980/1. As traffic on the Tunnelbanen lines did not increase as anticipated, some 16 further cars intended for use on these were modified for use on the western lines and became classes T7 and T8, nos.1334-1349. The main difference from the metro cars is that the driver has a full width cab and there is no train door in the end of the car. Drivers are also able to

Oslo no.1326 loads up at Majorstuen in August 1991, running on the Holmekolenbane. (Author)

issue tickets. Current collection is by overhead line. Class T6 cars are double-ended, the others are single-ended for m.u. working.

In 1994 Oslo Sporveier took delivery from Strømmen of 12 cars (2001-2012) of class T2000 to supplement this fleet. These also have electrical equipment by AEG. They are close-coupled two car sets, each section having one driving position and are equipped for both overhead and third rail current collection.

Technical details

Length 18.7m, width 3.3m, weight 31 tonnes, 4 x 140kW motors, 185 passengers, 48 + 12 seated.

Bibliography

Tramways and Urban Transit no.650, February 1992
Today's Railways, no.98, February 2004.

SWITZERLAND

SIG DESIGNS

For the opening of the first Stadtbahn in the Netherlands in 1983, the Sneltram Utrecht-Nieuwegin, the successful tenderer was the Swiss firm of SIG, which produced an attractive double-ended six-axle car, quite unlike any of the current German designs. In all 27 were supplied (5001-5027). As this line operates from stations with high platforms only, there was no need to provide for access from street level. The cars ride well and provide a high standard of comfort, with 2+2 seating throughout. They have now given over twenty years service and in 2000/01 the entire fleet underwent a complete modernisation, cars being given new ends, of a much more rounded design than those initially, a new livery and a complete internal refurbishment. This modernisation will allow them to continue running for about the same length of time again.

Forty cars of the same design (3701-3740) were built in 1987 and 1990 for the suburban lines of the Ferrocarrils de la Generalitat Valenciana, on which system they serve lines 1 and 2. Three

Sneltram Utrecht-Nieuwegin 5021 in June 1983. (Author)

different constructors were involved – CAF, MTM and Macosa – but all have BBC electrical equipment.

In 1995 a private company began a Stadtbahn service over a re-opened railway line, 15.5km in length, in a suburb in the northern part of the Buenos Aires conurbation. This is operated as Tren de la Costa. Unusually the line was built not so much to provide a transport service but to bring customers to the retail and leisure developments which have been opened on the former station sites. It was opened by President Memen in April 1995 and seems to be successful. It is worked by nine double-ended cars (1-9) built in Spain by CAF and based on the Utrecht/Valencia design. However, the

As rebuilt, car 5027 leaves Centraal Station in March 2004. (Author)

end design has been altered considerably and air conditioning is fitted. GTO thyristor equipment is fitted, with regenerative braking, and m.u working is practised at certain times. CAF went on from this to win an order for cars for Sacramento, the first of which was delivered late in 2002. These are designed to operate from low platforms and resemble the Siemens SD cars. Pittsburgh is in process of acquiring 28 similar cars.

Technical details

Utrecht cars
Length 29m, width 2.65m, weight 37.5 tonnes, 2 x 248kW motors, 222 passengers, 98 seated.
Tren de la Costa cars
Length 28.9m, width 2.5m, weight 45,650kg, 2 x 115kW motors, 240 passengers, 80 seated.

Bibliography

Light Rail and Modern Tramway, nos.538, October 1982 (Utrecht), 750, June 2000 (refurbishment of Utrecht cars), 752 August 2000 (Tren de la Costa).

The inaugural train on Tren de la Costa, at Maipu on 20 April 1995. (Marcelo Benoit)

VEVEY DESIGNS

In 1991 Transports Lausannois opened a standard gauge light rail line, the Tramway Sud-Ouest Lausannois, also known as Métro Ouest. To work this, twelve cars (201-212) were built by Vevey. These are double-ended six-axle vehicles and are fitted with an auxiliary diesel generator to allow them to manoeuvre away from the overhead wires. They carry names of major towns in canton Vaud.

Technical details

Length 31m, width 2.65m, weight 41 tonnes, 4 x 94kW motors, 235 passengers, 66 seated.

In 1994 Vevey supplied five similar cars to Swiss Federal Railways (SBB/CFF) for use on the service from Genève to the French border at La Plaine. The design had to be adapted to enable cars to work from stations with platforms much lower than those in Lausanne and has worked well in practice, sharing tracks with TGV and other main line trains.

Bibliography

Tramways and Urban Transit, no.650, February 1992 (TSOL), no.787, July 2003 (SBB/CFF).

On a single track section, car 215 is outbound from Lausanne in March 1997. (Author)

SBB car 003 at Genève Cornavin station in March 1997. (Author)

STADLER

In 2004 this manufacturer, which in recent years has had some success with lightweight railcars, entered the light rail field. On order are six high floor cars for Bochum, to a design known as Tango, and 30 low floor cars. No details have as yet been published.

ITALIAN CARS

CLEVELAND

The only Stadtbahn-type of operation to survive in the USA to become an operation of the modern type is the Shaker Heights rapid transit line in Cleveland. By 1980 it was becoming apparent that the PCC cars which had served this line so well since the immediate post-war period could not continue to fulfil this role for much longer and, in view of the lack of success of the Boeing design (qv), the Greater Cleveland Regional Transit Authority decided to order the replacement design by going out to international tender, for 48 cars. This was won by Breda Construtzioni for the bodies and by Brown Boveri (N. America) for the electrical components. In the event, the electrical equipment for the first ten was manufactured in Switzerland.

The cars are double-ended with three doors per side and up to four cars can be coupled in multiple. They have proved successful in service, but no other North American operator copied the design. Numbers were originally 801-848, but after cars 840 and 815 were damaged in a collision, a new car 849 was created using parts of each of these.

Technical details

Length 24.35m, width 2.85m, weight 38 tonnes, 4 x 114.5kW motors, 222 passengers, 84 seated.

Bibliography

Der Stadtverkehr, 4/5 1981.

TORINO

In the early 1980s, this undertaking was planning to construct a network of light metro, or Stadtbahn, routes by 1997 and to work these, an order was placed with Fiat Savigliano for 100 six-axle cars. These were to have taken the numbers 7000-7099. The first car was delivered in May 1983 and, as no line was likely to have been

Car 7011 clears a junction in the city centre in July 1999. (Author)

converted to the new standards before 1986, the new cars entered service on line 1 as conventional trams. The cars are double-ended and have three double width and one single width doors on each side. In the event, the light metro project was not brought to fruition and these large cars have spent all their lives operating on normal lines, for which they are not really suited. The last 49 of the order were cancelled and the series is now 7000-7050. In future it is likely that only about 20 of these cars will be in regular service, and nos.740-750 are already laid up.

Technical details
Length 28m, width 2.5m, weight 41.05 tonnes, 2 x 210kW motors, 290 passengers, 56 seated.

Bibliography

Der Stadtverkehr, 4/1983.
Modern Tramway no.548, August 1983.
Strassenbahn Magazin no.158, December 2002.

GREATER MANCHESTER METROLINK

When the new light rail lines to serve the Greater Manchester area were planned in the 1980s, the only Stadtbahn cars in service in Britain were those on the Tyne and Wear Metro and it was recognised that these would not be suitable for a system which incorporated street running. Low floor cars were considered but their use would have involved lowering platforms at 35 ex-BR stations and in any case, low floor technology was not then in a sufficiently advanced state of development to assure the reliability which would be required. A high floor design would not bring these problems and accordingly the tender of the Italian Firema consortium, established in 1980, was accepted, for 26 cars. The design owes something to Milan's "Jumbo" articulated

trams, as well as to Stadtbahn cars supplied to Genoa and the ACOTRAL system in Rome. A good deal of the design work for this order was in fact carried out by what was then GEC-Alsthom at Trafford Park, and this firm was also responsible for the electrical equipment, but the cars were built in Italy.

One of the cars built for the line to Eccles, seen at the latter terminus in July 2001. (Author)

No.1019 in the city centre in April 1994 (Author).

Not the best of photographs, but included to point a contrast in designs. One of the Boeing cars shares the depot with Manchester's own cars, as seen from a passing tram in March 2002. (Author)

GENOVA AND ROME

One of the more curious light rail developments of the 1980s was the construction of a very short line in Genova, which uses in part a former tramway tunnel. For this, six six-axle Stadtbahn cars (01-06) were built by Firema/Ansaldo, with electrical equipment by TIBB. There was a resemblance to the Zürich Tram 2000 in the end design. They were ready long before the line was, but it finally opened in 1990, when twelve further and rather different cars were ordered from Ansaldo. Although the line is short, the rolling stock has proved to have a very high record of availability.

A design very similar to the second batch of cars had already been supplied by the builders to the 950mm gauge ACOTRAL tramway in Rome. Six eight-axle cars were ordered in 1986 and entered service in 1988 (821-826). These are 31.9m long, 2.4m wide and weigh 60.6 tonnes.

Rather unexpectedly, since this line in its present form is under threat from metro construction, six additional six-axle cars (830-835), otherwise similar to the above, were supplied by the same builders in 2001.

Rome 823 nearing Porta Maggiore in July 1993. (Author)

A pre-production body shell was built in 1988 and displayed to the public at the former tram depot at Birchfields Road for some months from July. Based on reactions to this, the final design for a six-axle car was evolved and the first car, 1001, arrived in August 1991. Fleet numbers are 1001-1026, class T68, and the cars also carry names of famous persons who have been connected with the area. Test runs showed up quite a few problems, particularly with the wiring, but these were ultimately overcome to allow services to begin to Bury on 6 April 1992 and street running in the city centre to follow on 27 April. The first car to run on this section was 1007, carrying the number of Manchester's last tram of 10 January 1949. Since then the cars have performed extremely well, being to an extent victims of their own success. As there are not really sufficient vehicles for the level of service, which calls for a peak hour requirement of 23 cars, they have been worked hard and have proved to be reliable. Consideration was given to fitting centre sections to increase capacity, but this would have meant withdrawing cars from service for long periods and it also fell foul of new health and safety regulations. The plan was shelved in favour of the possible purchase of redundant cars from abroad. A further six cars (2001-2006, class T68M) were bought in 2000 from what was now Ansaldo Firema, for the opening of the new line to Eccles. As this incorporates much more street running than the first lines, these cars do have retractable couplers and three of the earlier batch have had fairings

Technical details
Genova car 07
Length 23.6m, width 2.65m, weight 24 tonnes, 2 x 185kW motors, 206 passengers, 34 seated

Bibliography
Modern Tramway no.606, July 1988.
Tramways and Urban Transit no.692, August 1995.

A car in Brin station, Genova, in July 1999. (Author)

No.834 awaits departure from Porta Maggiore in November 2004. (Author)

placed over their couplers to allow them to run on this service also. The new cars also have an altered interior design, with internal indicators, but the greatest difference is the fitting of AC equipment. The first series cars are now undergoing a complete renovation. The mock-up has found a home in the Manchester Museum of Transport.

Technical details
Car 1001 as built
Length 29m, width 2.65m, weight 48 tonnes, 4 x 105kW motors, 204 passengers, 82 seated.

Bibliography
Modern Tramway no.632, August 1990 (mock-up).
Manchester Metrolink. David Holt. Platform 5 Publishing, Sheffield, 1992.
Trams in Britain and Ireland. Various authors. Capital Transport, Harrow, 2002.

SAN FRANCISCO

In December 1991 the Municipal Railway of San Francisco ordered 52 double-ended six-axle cars from Breda with a view to replacing most of the Boeing cars. Delivery was somewhat protracted and the cars did not enter service until late 1996. By this time it had become clear that the Boeing cars were not improving with age and were not worth a complete rebuilding. It was therefore decided to order a further batch of 77 to complete replacement of these by 2002. Fleet numbers are from 1401-1529. There was some comment about the initial price of US$2.3m per car, although this figure did include spares. This delivery target was in due course achieved and the Breda cars have proved to be much less troublesome than their predecessors. Like these, they are fitted with retractable steps for use at street stops. Three-phase GTO equipment is fitted. They were designed in conjunction with the firm of Pininfarina, which has much experience of designing cars for such firms as Ferrari.

Technical details
Length 23m, width 2.75m, weight 37.38 tonnes, motors ? 164 passengers, 60 seated.

Bibliography
Ansaldo-Breda website.
North American Light Rail Annual, 1992.

Car 1441 heads a two-car set along the stretch of new track on Embarcadero, just after the opening of service in 1998. (Jim D. Schantz)

LOS ANGELES

In 2002 this operator ordered 50 cars from Ansaldo/Breda, at a cost of US$158.74m, for use on the new Gold line to Pasadena, of which the first arrived on 11 June 2005. There is an option for two further tranches of 50 each.

JAPANESE DESIGNS

HOME SYSTEMS

Only those used on lines which are classified tramways are mentioned here. There are many other light rail lines in operation, some of which have Stadtbahn characteristics, but it would be impossible to give details of their rolling stock in a book of this size.

In Tokyo, the Arakawa line is a merger of two former tram routes and is operated by the Transport Bureau of the Tokyo Metropolitan Government. Although there is still some street running, it has long stretches of reservation – to which it owes its survival – and stations have high platforms. It has 45 bogie cars built between 1955 and 1962 but rebuilt and (mostly) given air conditioning in 1977, and five much newer cars

The radial line which ran out from Gifu could have been considered to be a Stadtbahn. In this shot, taken on 26 May 2004, a train is made up of cars 785, 782 and 787.

with three-phase equipment delivered in the early 1990s.

The single line and branch in Fukui use fairly modern articulated cars of the Stadtbahn type.

The line at Enoshima, run by the Enoshima Electric Railway Company, has 15 pairs of high-floor articulated cars, some of which are quite modern, dating from 1979 onwards. They are numbered from 1001+1051 upwards, each body section having its own number. These are air-conditioned and have a certain resemblance to European designs of Stadtbahn cars, but have only two single-width sliding doors in each body section. The gauge is 1067mm. The system serves a tourist area and the operator has disguised the modernity of the fleet by adopting an old-fashioned, though attractive, style for the green and cream livery.

Technical details
Enoshima 1001
Length 24.8m, width 2.4m weight 36.24 tonnes, 4 x 50kW motors, 160 passengers, 72 seated.

In Kyoto, the Keihan line is a fully segregated standard-gauge Stadtbahn, which since 1997 has also seen full metro sets running over its tracks. It has a fleet of air-conditioned four-car trains acquired in 1997, (700 class) in addition to six bogie cars dating from 1979-81 (501-506), which normally operate in coupled pairs.

Tokyo trams 7512 and 7029 at Otsuka on last remaining line November 1977. (Electric Railway Society)

Technical details
Keihan Electric RR 501 class
Length 14.2m, width 2.35m weight 23.5 tonnes, 4 x 60kW motors, 95 passengers*, 46 seated.

Bibliography
Electric Railways of Japan vols.1-3. L. Demery, R. Forty, R. DeGroote and J. Higgins. Light Rail Transit Association, London, 1983/5 and 1990.

EXPORTS

BOSTON

Totally frustrated by its experience with the Boeing cars, the MBTA turned to tried and trusted technology for further fleet replacement and went to Kinki Sharyo for a design which is completely unlike any other operating either in Japan or in the USA. Known as type 7, these cars have windscreens and doors derived from PCC design and bodies derived from the Boeing cars, all combined with some straightforward Japanese technology. Although they look slightly odd, they have worked very well and have maintained a good level of service on the system, which carries 189,000 passengers a day. The first batch is numbered 3600-3699 and a further 20 (3700-

3719) were bought in 1997, when it became obvious that the Boeing fleet would expire before the projected low floor cars could reasonably be expected to enter service. These last cars introduced a new livery of green and grey to the MBTA fleet. Since they entered service, six seats have been removed to make space for wheelchairs.

Technical details
Length 22m, width 2.65m, weight 40.40 tonnes, 4 x 86kW motors, 201 passengers, 46 seated.

Bibliography
MBTA website.

No.3655 heads a two-car set at North Eastern University in October 1988. (Author)

LOS ANGELES

For the opening of its first light rail line, that to Long Beach, in July 1990, Los Angeles decided not to follow what was becoming the well-trodden path to the door of Siemens/Düwag but instead ordered a fleet of 54 six-axle articulated cars (100-153) from Nippon Sharyo of Japan. The cars were built in Japan and shipped in sections for final assembly in the depot at North Long Beach. The interior design is basic but the cars are comfortable and smooth running. Although they have functioned well enough in service and have built up patronage on the line to a very satisfactory level, there was considerable local opposition to a contract placed in 1992 for the purchase of further units of this class for the new Green Line and this issue was further

confused when several local politicians began to press for this line to have automatic operation. The end result was that when in 1993 the line was virtually completed there were no cars to run it and an order for 15 more (154-168) of the original design had to be hurriedly placed, at a considerably enhanced price. With some cars also temporarily transferred from the Long Beach line, these allowed the new line to open and, as mentioned elsewhere, it later acquired its own fleet of Siemens U2-derived cars.

Technical details
Length 26.51m, width 2.65m, weight 44.45 tonnes, 2 x 217kW motors, 230 passengers, 76 seated.

Car 117 awaits departure from Long Beach for Los Angeles, October 1996. (Author)

Bibliography
Modern Tramway no.623, November 1989.
North American Light Rail Annual, 1993.

BUFFALO

In April 1985 a single light rail line was opened in this city under the auspices of the Niagara Frontier Transportation Authority. This has both street running and a subway and cars load from both street level and high platforms. Unusually this system does not have articulated cars but is worked by 27 large bogie cars built by the Tokyu Car Company of Yokohama. These are double-ended and have three single-width sliding doors in each side. Up to three cars can run in multiple unit formation. No further cars have been acquired and none of this design has been bought by other operators. This line seems to have been less successful than other light rail schemes, though it is not clear if the design of these cars is in any way responsible.

Technical details
Length 19.76m, width 2.6m, weight 29.9 tonnes, 4 x 103kW motors, 140 passengers, 51 seated.

Bibliography
Modern Tramway no.571, July 1985.

Car 107 in the city centre when the line had only recently been opened and work was still in progress on the pedestrian mall. (Jim D. Schantz)

TUEN MUN

Although the Comeng-built cars seemed to perform satisfactorily, the KCR went to Kawasaki for a supplementary batch of 30 cars to cope with growing traffic and extensions. These were ordered in 1991 and delivered in 1993/4. Of the 30, 20 (1071-1090) are driving motor cars, as with the first batch, and ten (1201-1210) are driving trailers. The driving motors have a train door in the rear to allow for emergency evacuation if necessary and are heavier than the Comeng cars, at 31.44 tonnes. They are externally very similar to the first batch but can also be distinguished by the pods on the roof.

Bibliography
Tramways and Urban Transit, no.649, January 1992.
Light Rail Review 6. Platform 5 Publishing, Sheffield, 1994.

A rear view of car 1084 in the terminal at Tuen Mun Ferry Pier in March 1993, showing the train door. (Author)

DALLAS

For its new light rail line, first opened in June 1996, the Dallas Area Rapid Transit chose a six-axle articulated design built by Kinki Sharyo. Low floor cars were by this time widely available and were considered, but it was thought better to remain with proven Stadtbahn technology. As a result, stations have ramps and short high platforms or, in the central area, lifts, for mobility impaired passengers. With raked windscreens and a very attractive yellow, white and black livery, the cars look quite strikingly different to any light rail vehicles in use on other North American systems and have proved to be most popular. In February 2002 29 of these cars were loaned to Salt Lake City to help with traffic to the winter Olympics. One car has now been fitted with a low floor centre section and it is intended to convert additional cars in the near future.

Car 112 stops at St Paul station in the city centre on 2 October 1996. (Author)

Technical details
Length 28.3m, width 2.7m, weight 48.32 tonnes, 4 x 134 kW motors, 160 passengers, 76 seated

Bibliography
New Electric Railway Journal, summer 1996.

PHOENIX

At the time of writing, Kinki Sharyo has just been awarded a contract for 36 light rail cars for a new line to be built in Phoenix. There is an option for an additional 39. Details of the design have not yet been published and it is not certain that these will be Stadtbahn-type cars.

BELGIAN DESIGNS

MANILA

In July 1980, in response to the city's chronic traffic problems, President Marcos of the Philippines created the Light Railway Transit Authority whose function was to build a light rail system in Manila and oversee its later operation. Mme la Présidente Marcos was its chairman. It was quite a coup for a consortium of Belgian industry to gain the contract to build the first line, including rolling stock, although it was reported that they almost lost it at the last minute as they had not realised the exact point in an official dinner at which it was customary to present a small gift to Mme

Manila 1021 at a station. (Lars Richter collection)

la Présidente. However, the error was speedily rectified and the contract for rolling stock went to BN of Brugge. The cars which resulted were closely based on the articulated cars built for the Vicinal (qv), but configured for operation from high platforms only, as the line was to be elevated and would have no street running.

The cars are of a double-ended eight-axle design and operate in coupled sets of up to three. Chopper control was fitted with regenerative and rheostatic brakes. Rather strangely, in view of the local climate, air conditioning was not fitted, but the cars do have pressure ventilation which is capable of renewing the air in the car over 100 times per hour. There are also opening windows. All seating is longitudinal. Although these cars have worked well and have carried extremely heavy loads, a further order, placed by a private concern after the Marcos régime had fallen, went elsewhere.

Technical details
Length 29.28m, width 2.5m, weight 41 tonnes, 2 x 217.7kW motors, 374 passengers*, 81 seated.

Bibliography
Modern Tramway no.547, July 1983

RIO DE JANEIRO

The rolling stock delivered in 1981/2 has had a singularly chequered history. The cars were known as pré-metrô cars or "superbondes" (super-trams) and were built by a Belgian/Brasilian consortium of BN and Cobrasma, for an intended light rail feeder line of 15.5km, which would connect with the city's first metro line at Maria de Graca and run to Iraja. Electrical equipment was by Siemens and the cars had a distinct resemblance to those built for Portland. About half of this line was opened in 1983 but ran only until 1985 and then again briefly in the 1990s.

The first eight cars were built by BN in Belgium, while the balance of the order (60) were to be built in Brasil by Cobrasma. They were articulated vehicles, single-ended but intended for operation in coupled pairs and so fitted with doors on both sides. They were built for the Brasilian gauge of 1600mm and have two x 230kW motors. In the event, only 26 of these were delivered and 14 others were completed and stored. Numbers are 3001-3040. Only the Belgian built cars were noted running in late 1985. The line was then upgraded to full metro standards and extended and the cars were converted for use on it. This involved fitting air conditioning, third rail current collection and folding steps at the doors to bring them into line with the other rolling stock which now ran on the line. In practice they did not function very well as the folding doors could not always resist pressure from crowds. In 2004 28 were still used on Sundays, when traffic is lighter; these are made up into seven four-car sets.

Eight were transferred to Campinas in 1990, but the light rail line in that city was abandoned in 1998 and six have since returned to Rio. Two are still in Campinas, two have been destroyed in accidents and two are stored at Alstom's Cobrasma plant in Brasil. There were no problems with the cars themselves – the problem was the country's chronic financial problems and uncertainty over the planning of light rail.

Bibliography
Modern Tramway nos.592, April 1987, 667, July 1993 and 807, March 2005.
Electrical Equipment for Trams etc. Siemens, 1983 (op cit).
The Tramways of Brazil. Allen Morrison. Bonde Press, New York, 1989.

A builder's view of one of the cars. (Author's collection)

AMSTERDAM SNELTRAM CARS

On 30 November 1990 the GVBA of Amsterdam began an interesting experiment in joint tram/Stadtbahn operation on a new line to Amstelveen. Between Station Zuid and that point, trams of line 5 shared tracks with Stadtbahn cars on line 51, which ran on to Poortwachter. Between Station Zuid and Centraal Station, these used third rail current collection and from Spaklerweg inwards, shared tracks with the metro. The Stadtbahn design was in Amsterdam referred to as the "sneltram" (fast tram).

For this service, 13 Stadtbahn cars (45-57) were built by BN, based on the design for Manila, but also having some features in common with articulated cars for Den Haag. They are double-ended six-axle cars with three-phase equipment and having two inverters controlling two groups of three motors each, to allow continued operation in the event of failure of one group. On the tramway they take

In the snows of February 1991, which produced so many problems for the class, Amsterdam car 50 waits at Station Zuid/WTC when working outbound to Amstelveen. (Author)

current at 600V and increase this to 750V on the third rail sections. The shoes for current collection on these are retracted within the body when the car is running on the tramway. The floor height of 1.1m matches that of the metro cars and high platforms are provided at each stop for these cars, while the trams use adjacent low platforms. To allow them to share platforms with the wider metro cars, a folding running board is provided for the whole length of the car, this being unfolded when the shoes for current collection from the third rail are extended.

Although this seemed a flexible form of operation, these cars have had a number of problems. Two collided when on test and one was damaged by a wiring fault soon after service began, leaving ten cars to cover nine duties. Then in February 1991 frost and snow, coupled with gale force freezing winds, played havoc with the folding running boards and collector shoes. The boards had to be rebuilt to a new design and the joint service was suspended until November 1991. Twelve additional cars (58-69) were then ordered for BN and delivered in 1993/4. Technically the cars have performed well since then, but delays to trams on the city street section have caused irregularities in joint running and, although it was intended to use this type of operation on other lines, the next, the Ring line, was in the event built as completely segregated light rail line. The cars ordered for it from CAF of Spain in February 1994 are really metro cars, but four (70-73) have been fitted with pantographs to allow use on line 51 when required.

Technical details
Length 30m, width 2.65m, 6 x 74kW motors.

Bibliography
Light Rail Review 3. Platform 5 Publishing, Sheffield, 1992.

PORTLAND (OR)

In the city centre, no.108 sets down passengers in October 1988. The blind is already set for the return journey. (Author)

When the city of Portland and the surrounding area, under the Tri-County Metropolitan Transit District (Tri-Met) organisation planned its first Stadtbahn line, the tender to supply 26 double-ended six-axle cars (101-126) was won by the Canadian firm of Bombardier. The total price was US$21.7m. This design followed closely that of the cars built for the light rail operation in Rio de Janeiro by BN in Belgium, formerly La Brugeoise and now part of the Bombardier empire. Bodies and trucks were constructed in Canada and final assembly took place in Barre, Vermont, from which the cars were shipped across the USA to Portland. These cars were intended to operate both from stops at street level and from stations with low platforms and therefore had four-step entrances. Wheelchair passengers were carried and boarded with the help of special lifts mounted on the station platforms, a system which proved cumbersome in operation and did not help those with lesser mobility problems. The cars have an attractive livery of white with dark red, scarlet and orange bands and have been a great success.

Technical details
Length 26.5m, width 2.65m, weight 41.12 tonnes, 2 x 195kW motors, 211 passengers, 76 seated.

Bibliography
Der Stadtverkehr 1/82 and 11-12/1984.
Modern Tramway no.569, May 1985.

PROPOSED MÉTRO LÉGER FOR BRUSSELS

In the late 1970s, the STIB/MIVB, probably alarmed at the cost of its first heavy rail line, saw a place for a light rail system which would work alongside both the new métro and the tramways. For this, a double-ended three-section car of striking appearance was proposed in 1978. This would have had pointed end sections of a design similar to those of the cars currently being built for Marseille, of a kind of shark's head outline. There would have been retractable steps at doorways and cars would have been capable of operating in m.u. formation. The suggested width of only 2.2m, with 2+1 seating, was narrow for a car of this type but was no doubt chosen to allow it to use existing tramway tracks. It was proposed to order 235 of these cars, all to be in service by 1982. However, the project was not followed through and instead this operator went on to develop both further métro extensions and the existing tramway system. The cost would have been BFR47m per car, against BFR27m for a PCC car of the 7900 class and this may have been part of the reason for the cancellation of the project. Had the design gone into production, BN would no doubt have been the chosen manufacturer.

Technical details
Length 31.5m, width 2.2m, weight 45.2 tonnes, 8 x 73kW motors, 233 passengers, 60 seated.

Bibliography
STIB/MIVB Factsheet 3, Matériel roulant, 1978.
Modern Tramway no.494, February 1979 and no.496, April 1979.

A sketch of the proposed design. (STIB Factsheet, Author's collection)

AUSTRALIAN CARS FOR TUEN MUN

The line constructed in the late 1980s to serve the new town of Tuen Mun in what was then the New Territories of Hong Kong was at first to have been worked by double-decker trams, which would have made an impressive sight, but in the end, single-deckers were chosen by the management of the Kowloon-Canton Railway, the chosen operator. The first series of 70 cars (1001-1070) for the system were built by Comeng of Dandenong, Victoria – though cars from 1042 onwards were actually built in Brisbane – and bear a certain resemblance to modern Melbourne A class trams but are much larger and operate from high platforms only. They are also single-ended. Düwag monomotor bogies, AEG motors and Siemens control equipment are fitted. At 19.4m these are in fact exceptionally long for non-articulated cars, their length being surpassed only by the cars at Buffalo, but as the entire system was being built new, there was no need to adapt the rolling stock to existing clearances. They are impressive vehicles, with fluted, unpainted stainless steel sides, orange doors and orange and light grey ends. There are three double width doors per side. The cars run very steadily and quietly, indeed there have been complaints following crossing accidents that they are too quiet! Air horns are fitted and drivers make good use of these. Seating is on orange fibreglass seats, mostly arranged as double seats on the offside. The cars first went into public service on 18 September 1988. In

1991 some cars had their seating capacity reduced to 44 but the air conditioning plant could not cope with the increased number aboard. The number of seats was increased again to 53 and the air conditioning equipment strengthened from 43kW to 60kW, to provide a comfortable environment. They now carry 250 passengers, although more can be crammed aboard if necessary, at 10 to the square metre. Apart from a few minor teething troubles with air conditioning and lighting, the cars have proved to be very reliable and also economical. Despite this, the second order went to Kawasaki (qv) but for a third batch of cars, the KCR chose in 1996 the Australian builder A. Goninan and Co. These 20 cars (1091-1110) were fitted out in the Preston workshops of the Melbourne system. They are based closely on the earlier design but have four single- and one double-width doors, rather than the three double doors of the first batch.

Technical details
Car 1001, as built
Length 19.4m, width 2.65m, weight 27.44 tonnes, 2 x 185kW motors, 190 passengers*, 60 seated.

Bibliography
Modern Tramway nos.597, September 1987, 606, June 1988 and 613, January 1989.
Tramways and Urban Transit no.649, January 1992, no.718, October 1997.
Light Rail Review 6. Platform 5 Publishing, Sheffield, 1994.
Der Stadtverkehr 11-12/1987.

Car 1002 in service on line 614 in March 1993. (Author)

DESIGNS IN NORTH AND SOUTH AMERICA

BOEING VERTOL CARS

In 1969 the city of San Francisco's Municipal Railway (Muni), which had been considering a full-size underground line, decided instead to retain and modernise its light rail system, including the construction of a tunnel under the new BART system along Market Street. In January 1970 a model of the proposed design of car, by L.T. Klauder Associates, was unveiled. This was quite an attractive vehicle, not unlike the later Boeing cars, and designed to a high specification, with a top speed of 104km/hr, for use in both the subway and on street. It was said the 78 such cars would be ordered, at a cost of US$255,000 each. When bids were received in July 1971, the prices quoted were almost exactly double this figure and the plans were dropped. The Federal Government also let it be known that there would be no grant for a car designed for San Francisco alone.

At the same time the Massachusetts Bay Transportation Authority (MBTA) in Boston was considering the replacement of most of its PCC cars and had been monitoring progress on Düwag's evolving Stadtbahn design. However, by mid-1970 opinion had changed in favour of a new design of bogie car, slightly longer and wider than the existing PCC cars but with a lower floor level. Unlike these, the new cars would have been double-ended. Seating would have been provided for 45 passengers with standing space for 87 and dimensions were given as 15.25m by 2.64m. A mock-up of a car end was constructed but very soon afterwards the MBTA dropped this design, being impressed with the new Statdbahn design in Hannover. When a request to borrow one of these cars for trials was turned down, as Hannover could not then release it, the MBTA considered buying two prototypes from Düwag. San Francisco was less enthusiastic about the German design, but in any case the whole matter became academic when in 1971 President Nixon, confronted by an economic crisis, instituted a "Buy American" policy, severely limiting imports of such vehicles as light rail cars.

At the same time the federal Urban Mass Transit Administration (UMTA), concerned at operators' interest in custom-built designs, persuaded all those who would shortly be needing new cars – in fact this covered almost all US systems – to consider a joint order. This would include Philadelphia, Pittsburgh, El Paso, New Orleans, Shaker Heights, San Francisco, Boston and Newark and thus the seeds of what was hoped to be a US standard light rail vehicle were sown. For the Municipal Railway of San Francisco this would mean a compromise and acceptance of certain features which would allow cars to fit in with existing older systems but would not take advantage of its new light rail system. Specifications were agreed by October 1972 but by then all the other potential buyers had dropped out, apart from Boston. In February 1973 five firms submitted tenders for the new light rail car and the order went to Boeing-Vertol, who had submitted the lowest bid of US$273,600 each for 230 cars with chopper control – 80 for San Francisco and 150 for Boston. The ending of the war in Viet Nam had forced both this and other aero-space manufacturers to look for other outlets for their technology. The cars for San Francisco were to have dual-height steps at all centre doors, to allow for high platform use in the new Market Street subway, and cab signalling, but pressure ventilation replaced the air conditioning of the Boston cars. The design seemed promising and, aware of the growing interest in light rail, the manufacturer talked of a production run of 3,000 cars.

The first car was completed in September 1974, but a strike at Boeing and considerable problems on the test track of the Urban Mass Transit Administration (UMTA) in Pueblo delayed the arrival of production cars in San Francisco until September 1978 and it was April 1979 before any entered service. Originally it was to have been San Francisco which was to receive the first cars but after the Boeing strike, Muni deferred to Boston's more pressing needs, a kind gesture by which it ultimately saved its engineers a great deal of trouble. The first cars had proved to be a disaster. Speaking politely, operating staff said that the design "was not a low-maintenance car".

San Francisco class leader 1200 heads an inbound train at Twin Peaks station in October 1987. (Author)

Boston 3518 at Heath Street in October 1988. (Author)

The mock-up of the end of the proposed type 6 bogie car for Boston, at the Seashore Trolley Museum. (Author)

Boston cars were numbered 3400-3534, delivered between 1976 and 1978, with a further batch (3535-3543) following in 1983. The cars delivered to Muni were modified in the light of these troubles and so proved less of an embarrassment to their owners. These were numbered 1200-1299. Subway service began on 11 February 1980. Despite some problems with the cars, it was clearly a success, with patronage on some lines increasing by 45%, and in 1983 30 additional cars (1300-1329), which had been built for, but rejected by Boston, were acquired. The cost of each of San Francisco's first cars was US$319,000.

Although expected initially to have a working life of 30 years, all cars have now been withdrawn in both cities. In December 2001 San Francisco cars 1326 and 1226 were acquired at an auction by Manchester Metrolink as it seemed that these cars could provide a cheap solution to the system's capacity problems. However, although the Boeing cars are shorter than Manchester's own design, a visit by 1326 to Eccles soon made it apparent that considerable alterations would be necessary to provide clearance for them to operate, the outward-opening plug doors being a particular problem. Closer examination also showed up the deplorable state of the car's wiring. Car 1226 followed and was sent direct to the workshops of Serco at Derby for evaluation. The idea was then abandoned and the two cars being still laid up, awaiting a purchaser. Two San Francisco cars have been preserved by

Californian museums. Boston's 3444 has been set aside for preservation at the Seashore Trolley Museum and the mock-up front end of the proposed 1970 bogie car can be seen there.

Technical details
San Francisco 1200 class
Length 21.64m, width 2.69m, weight 37.38 tonnes, 4 x 75kW motors, 180 passengers, 68 seated.
Proposed San Francisco car, 1970
Length 23m, width 2.75m, 4 x 75kW motors, 180 passengers, 76 seated.

Bibliography
Modern Tramway, nos.389, May 1970, 392, August 1970, 425, May 1973, 430, October 1973 and 562/3, October and November 1984.
North American Light Rail Annual, 1992.

A view of the articulation of Boston 3541, under repair in Riverside workshops. (Author)

Less politely they would say that "the Boeing cars are lemons, primarily on the cost of maintenance". Quite simply, they were over-engineered, with inappropriate technology copied without due consideration from defence and aero-space applications. The engineering staff in Boston had endless trouble firstly in preparing the cars for service and then keeping them running. The

UTDC CARS

Car 838 approaches airport stop, outbound, in October 1996. (Author)

The UTDC's products have already been discussed and the design under consideration here is derived from the articulated trams supplied to Toronto (qv). Essentially the same design was selected for 50 cars (801-850) for the new light rail line in San José, opened by the Santa Clara County Transportation Agency in 1987, although changes to the styling of the car ends resulted in a vehicle which looks quite different. The cars cost US$1m each. This design was something of a compromise between tramway and light rail technology and has not been completely successful. When extensions to the system were under construction it was decided that, instead of extending the existing fleet, it would be better to begin

again with a new design and accordingly these cars were put up for sale. By December 2003, 29 cars had been bought by Salt Lake City and the remaining 21 by Sacramento, after one had visited the latter city. As of June 2006, none in Sacramento had entered service.

Technical details
Length 27m, width 2.65m, weight 42.18 tonnes, motors ?, 187 passengers, 75 seated.

Bibliography
Tramways and Urban Transit no.716, August 1997.
Modern Tramway nos.591, March 1987, 605, May 1988.

TATRA CARS

Rather curiously the Stadtbahn concept did not find favour in the former eastern bloc countries and the only such cars to be built by this manufacturer were in fact the last to be built by it. They were constructed for the second of Manila's light rail lines – confusingly known as line 3 – and are based closely on the KT8 articulated design, but of course configured for operation at high platforms only. The 61 cars entered service in 1999 and operate in trains of three.

Bibliography
Tramways and Urban Transit no.760, April 2000.

CHINA

In October 2002 a Stadtbahn was opened in Changchun and is worked by twelve low floor cars, of which no further details are known.

CAF SPAIN

This builder first entered the light rail market in 2002 when an order was received for 40 cars (201-240) for Sacramento. This was followed by an order for 28 cars for Pittsburgh, for delivery in 2005.

From the above it can be seen that the concept of the Stadtbahn covers a very wide range of vehicles and operating practices. It grew out of traditional tramway technology and diverged from that quite sharply around 1970. However, developments in low floor vehicle design have begun to bring the two together again and it may be that the future does not hold a significant place for the concept.

CHAPTER 11
LOW FLOOR CARS

Conventional tramcars generally have a floor height of between 850mm and 900mm above rail level, necessitating three fairly steep or four rather easier entrance steps. The latter require additional space for the step wells and this can be a problem on double-ended cars, where the doorways are opposite each other, leading to a reduction in the space available for standees.

It is now over ninety years since the first attempts were made to devise a tram with reduced height at the entrance steps, as detailed in chapter one. There were other isolated instances of the use of the concept elsewhere, as in Nürnberg, which in 1914 placed in service a trailer with a step height of only 365mm at the central entrance. In 1934 Dr Walter Prasse, technical director of the Essen undertaking, and one of its technical advisers, E-W de Montrose-Oster, jointly developed a tram (505) which had individual steerable wheels and a floor height throughout of only 380mm. The car was built by Orenstein and Koppel in Berlin and had a most attractive body, with a central entrance. Another novelty was the current collector, essentially a trolley pole with a sliding bow on the end. Neither this nor the wheels performed well in service and the car saw little use. Parts for a trailer were delivered after the outbreak of war but both these and the tram itself were badly damaged in an air raid in March 1943. Although Dr Prasse carefully salvaged all useable parts, no further work was done after the war and the remains were scrapped in 1957. It was a great pity that such a promising design should have come along when the time was not ripe for such innovations; the NS authorities disliked individualism of this kind and Prasse and his team did not have time to deal with the problems before the German economy was being prepared for war. However, the Montos car, as it was generally known, deserves a place in history as the first low floor car in the modern sense.

Technical details

Length 11.25m (over couplings), width 2m, weight 14,500kg, 4 x 33kW motors, 65 passengers, 33 + 2 seated.

For many years the central entrance tram, particularly in trailer form, remained the most accessible design available. In 1927, for example, Essen bought five trams of this layout with a floor height of only 740mm. The use of cars with a lower step height in a few places such as Rome in 1948 and Rotterdam in 1957 has been mentioned elsewhere. The TKK articulated cars of c1960 (qv) had a floor height of only 590mm, but this design was not followed up, either in Japan or elsewhere.

No further attempts were made to develop a tram design with a low floor level until the 1980s, when, quite suddenly, a plethora of designs appeared in various places. This development was in reply to the growing awareness, from about 1975 onwards, of the needs of people with mobility problems and the measures taken by governments to end discrimination on these grounds. However, it was also realised that public transport vehicles with level boarding would benefit not only those with a definite mobility limitation but also the elderly and those travelling with small children, two groups who formed a large percentage of those using public transport outwith the peak hours. The advantages claimed for the "stepless" cars of pre-1914 days would, of course, still apply. Unfortunately in the rush to take the concept forward, all ideas of standardisation went out the window and there was a great deal of re-invention of the wheel, with a consequent increase in costs. Only in the last few years has the emergence of several standard types begun to correct this tendency. The proliferation of designs has also made it extremely difficult to write concisely on the topic!

The development of the low floor tram took place against a background of considerable upheaval in the light rail vehicle industry. The end of communism in eastern Europe altered the system under which the Tatra, Konstal and other manufacturers had operated and ultimately, after a gallant attempt to adapt to market conditions, most of these firms gave up their independent existence, thus leaving the way clear for western manufacturers to enter their former empires. However, the Skoda factory in Plzen also seized the opportunity to enter the tramway field, after an interval of many years.

At the same time, considerable changes were afoot in Western Europe as a result of the introduction of the single market in the countries of the EU. Prior to this, and at the same time as low floor designs began to proliferate, the German government altered the Gemeindfinanzinierungsgesetz (Municipal Finance Law) in such a way as to encourage operators to buy new vehicles. Unfortunately the method in which this operated meant that the operators did not have to count the Pfenigs too carefully and often the money available was not spent wisely, some of the trams acquired through this method being none too satisfactory in service and also rather dearer than they need have been. The introduction of the single market widened the scope for manufacturers and exports of trams developed, to the extent where it became common to buy trams manufactured in another country. It also led to international mergers and ultimately in a reduction of the number of manufacturing groups to four main suppliers. In turn this move highlighted over-capacity in the industry, a state of affairs which led to both closures of long-established factories and also to the practice of assembling trams from components built in a variety of places, in some cases even by different manufacturers. The days when a tram could be noted as being built simply by Düwag or Fiat were definitely over!

Technically, the success of the low floor tram was due to the use, in various combinations, of the following features:

1. Small, fully suspended three-phase motors which can be used in a central bogie or suspended from the hubs of individual wheels
2. Bogies with small wheels
3. Individual small wheels which can be used under an articulation joint
4. Single steerable wheels or wheelsets, using stub axles
5. Articulation joints of the Talgo type

Bibliography

Modern Tramway nos.645, September 1991 and 648, December 1991.
Light Rail and Modern Tramway no.658, October 1992.
NB. Throughout this chapter, the detailed articles by Dr H. Hondius which have appeared annually over the last decade in *Der Stadtverkehr* (normally in December and January) have been used as a source of reference.
Strassenbahn Magazin no.192, October 2005. (Essen 505).

THE PIONEERS

SWITZERLAND

The first undertaking to place in service a tram with reduced step entrance height was TPG, Genève, when car 741 entered test service on 7 January 1984. By 1980, replacement of the fleet of standard bogie cars dating from 1950 was on the horizon and the undertaking borrowed a modern articulated car and trailer from BLT in Basel for tests. These were generally successful, but dwell time at stops was extended and it was decided that articulated cars, running in coupled pairs, would be the better solution for fleet renewal. However, the public had not approved of the fairly awkward entrances of the Basel car and it was decided that the new vehicles should have as low a floor as possible, particularly in the areas around the doors. The manufacturer Ateliers de Construction Mécaniques de Vevey, was the only Swiss rolling stock manufacturer to be able to offer a design which met this requirement. They had for many years been supplying wheelsets to Switzerland's metre gauge railways to allow the movement of standard gauge wagons on metre gauge tracks and it seemed that these could be adapted as a trailing bogie for an articulated tram, which would meet the specification. The manufacturer formed a partnership with Düwag to progress the idea. This gave a fall-back position which would have allowed ACMV to build Stadtbahn M cars, should the project fail. The order for a prototype was placed in 1982 and this was delivered, as 741, on 7 January 1984. The car was tested extensively between March and October of that year and then entered normal service. It was clear that there would be no need for the Stadtbahn cars! Electrical equipment was by BBC, with chopper control.

Genève 827 at Carouge in May 2003. (Author)

The concept of this tram derived directly from that of the cars supplied to Rotterdam by Schindler in 1957 (qv) but in slightly altered form. The tram has bogies with wheels of normal diameter at each end and, immediately behind the articulation, a bogie with wheels of only 375mm. The use of such wheels allowed a floor height of only 480mm in the centre section of the car, reached by two easy steps in the four doorways. Placing the trailing bogie behind rather than under the articulation allowed the car to be 2.3m wide yet still keep to the same clearances as the existing fleet of 2.2m wide cars. As there was no place for electrical equipment in its normal location under the car, much had to be placed in containers on the roof. This layout did not allow for the carriage of wheelchairs and was not too easy for prams, but it was a vast improvement in accessibility over all existing designs. As all doorways had to be located between the outer bogies, it was not possible for the driver to issue tickets, but in Switzerland, where for many years all fare collection has been off the car, this did not matter. It might, however, have limited the export potential of the design. Electrical equipment was by BBC. In service car 741 proved to be popular and, despite its novel features, so successful that in November of the same year, it was decided that the 45 new trams to be ordered should be of this design. Renumbered 801, the prototype is still in service.

The cost of the production series was about SFR 1m (c£455,000). Of these, 23 have now been fitted with an additional centre section to cope with the growth in traffic and have been renumbered 831-853. Delivery of this fleet also required the construction of a new depot, as the existing structure which dated from 1900 could not be adapted for their use.

The manufacturer also produced a design for a bogie trailer using the same type of wheels. This would have been 13m long, with a low floor section 8m long between the bogies, and seating for 34 passengers. However, TPG, for whom this vehicle was designed, showed no interest and it was to be some years before this concept would be put into practice.

Technical details
Car 741 as built
Length 21.9m, width 2.3m, weight 27.5 tonnes, 2 x 150kW motors, 131 passengers, 53 seated. Low floor section 12.5m, 57% of total length.

Bibliography
Modern Tramway no.569, May 1985.
Der Stadtverkehr 9/1989.

One of the enlarged cars, in a particularly strange advertising livery, at Grange-Falquet in May 2003. (Author)

ITALY

Torino had in 1982 begun to rationalise its network in preparation for the development of a Stadtbahn system, but closure of routes in the central area had been unpopular and led to a loss of traffic. Two years later the Stadtbahn concept was abandoned, just as the first production cars were arriving, and the order for these was cut from 100 to 50. Street tramways were once again the chosen mode for development and it was realised that these should be accessible. Articulated tram 2837 was accordingly despatched to the Fiat factory and was fitted with a new body having a low floor section between the two end bogies. This was carried on a trailing bogie with small wheels located directly under the articulation joint. The tram, now numbered 2800, was presented to the press on 6 May 1985. Although it did not run in passenger service owing to its relative lack of power, it was successful and is still in existence.

Milano was also interested in the concept but, as it was not intended immediately to order a series of such trams, it was decided to conduct an experiment using redundant members of the classic Peter Witt trams. The Firema/Stanga consortium therefore rebuilt cars 1796 and 1973, into a single unit, joined by an articulation resting on a central unit with four independent steerable wheels, supplied by the latter firm. This allowed a low floor section 45cm high between the two outer bogies and the floor was ramped from this to the sections over the end bogies, where it was still lower than on standard cars. Magnetic track brakes were fitted and the motors of 21kW each were replaced by those of 30kW. In its rebuilt form the tram could carry 170 passengers, 42 of them seated and was 21.66m long. Numbered 4500, this tram which formed a link between Europe's first modern trams and its latest, entered trial service in December 1984 and was placed in normal service in 1985. Although no more such rebuilds were undertaken, there was no doubt of its success. It ran in normal service for some years and was withdrawn in 1993, but is still in existence.

A low floor bogie motor tram, the only one of its kind to run in Europe, was built by Socimi in 1989 and ran trials in Milano during the following year. Known as the S-LRV-350, this tram had a conventional body set low over bogies with wheels of 550mm diameter, with a small 20kW motor mounted on the outside of each wheel. Owing to the very low height, the pantograph had to be mounted on a pedestal on the roof. This was the first tram of 100% low floor configuration and it was claimed to have the very light unladen weight of 10.5 tonnes. No series production followed, although a batch of articulated cars using the same principles was delivered to ATAC Rome as the 9000 class (qv) in 1990/1. The same firm had also in 1992 designed a prototype modular articulated tram, with 100% low floor area, for ATAC Rome. However, this design did not progress beyond the drawing board.

Firema also built one prototype which was shown at the UITP congress in Stockholm in 1991. This used bogies on which the motors were mounted outwith the frames, thus allowing a low floor throughout the car. Numbered 5500, it then ran trials in Torino, where it still remains. A second car (5501) followed, but the operator had already placed an order for trams of a different design and there were no series orders for this type.

In May 1990 Breda demonstrated a prototype low floor design, the Veicolo Leggero Cittadino. This was the first low floor design to use modular construction and each end section consisted of three modules – a driver's cabin, an equipment compartment and a passenger saloon. The central section was a passenger saloon only. Conventional bogies were used under the outer ends of the car and under each articulation joint was a pair of single wheels, not connected with each other, which steered the articulations using the same principle as on a Talgo train. This allowed a floor height of 350mm throughout the passenger section, but a drawback was that the driver was completely isolated from the passengers. At 22 tonnes, the car was extremely light and it was also very stylish. The prototype was tested in Rome, but the only order for the design, in enlarged form, came from Lille.

Technical details
Socimi S-350-LRV
Length 14m, width 2.4m, weight 10.5 tonnes, 8 x 20kW motors, 82 passengers, 33 seated.
Milano rebuild
Length 21.66m width 2.35m, weight 38.6 tonnes 4 x 30kW motors, 170 passengers, 42 seated.

Bibliography
Der Stadtverkehr 5/1990 (Socimi bogie car)

The Milano rebuild of two Peter Witt cars. (ATM Milano)

FRANCE

In the early 1970s a group of manufacturers proposed the construction of a tram for internal services within what was then known as Roissy airport. Floor height between the bogies would have been only 200mm above rail level. This idea did not progress beyond the stage of a large model, which looked rather like the trams supplied to Lille at a much later date. Rather prophetically, this design was known as Citadis.

When the new tramway was originally proposed for Grenoble, it was envisaged that it would employ TSF1 trams similar to those being built for Nantes and indeed a mock-up of this was shown in the city at the autumn fair of 1982. However, the operator was working very closely with groups representing people with mobility difficulties and it was decided that the trams to be used should be accessible to all potential passengers. It was also appreciated that these would offer significant advantages in boarding and alighting times at stops. After considering the idea of fitting a low floor centre section to the Nantes design – as was ultimately done in that city – it was decided, with the agreement of the Ministry of Transport, to ask manufacturers to rethink the entire construction, to produce a tram which would meet the new criteria. In 1983 a group representing the industry and various operators, including the RATP of Paris and also the Strasbourg municipality, was set up to take the idea forward; not since the days of the Presidents' Conference Committee in the USA in the 1930s has a design been the subject of so much study from the technical, economic and social angles. However, the steering group worked quickly and appointed a Belgian industrial designer, Philippe Neerman, to oversee the project. When plans were shown to the public in 1984 and when the first tram was displayed in August 1986, it was seen that both he and the manufacturers, Alsthom, had succeeded brilliantly.

The extremely elegant, slightly futuristic design showed a tram with two end sections resting on conventional motor bogies, similar to those used in Nantes, and a central section resting on what appeared to be a trailing bogie running on small wheels; in fact these wheels were independent of each other. This construction allowed a completely flat low floor for 17.85m or 60% of the total length of the car, with plenty of circulating space for wheelchairs. At a stroke, all other trams in Europe had been made obsolete. The trams entered service on the opening of Grenoble's first line in September 1987 and further developments of the design are dealt with later in this section.

Technical details

Length 92.4m, width 2.3m, weight 44.6 tonnes, 2 x 225kW motors, 178 passengers, 54+4 seated.

Grenoble 2021 at Gares tram station in July 2000. (Author)

Bibliography

Les Nouveaux Tramways et Métros Légers de France et de l'Europe. M. Chlastacz and P. Herisse editors. La Vie du Rail, Paris, 1996.

Du Tram au Tag. J-M Guétat, W Lachenal, G. Muller. La Vie du Rail, Paris, 1987.

GERMANY

The Federal Republic had rather fallen behind other countries in the matter of low floor technology but in 1986 the Bundesminesterium für Forschung und Technologie (BMFT – Federal Ministry for Research and Technology) and the VöV formed a group of five manufacturers, four electrical firms and five operators, under the chairmanship of Professor Frederich of the Technical University of Aachen, to develop a low floor tram using his concept of individual, motored self-steering wheels. This would allow a low floor throughout with no reduction in gangway width. The project had a budget of DM45million over five years and it was not until 19 April 1991 that the first of three prototypes appeared. They were intended for Bonn and Düsseldorf and a metre gauge version was planned for Mannheim. The Bonn car was built by Düwag and was double-ended, while that for the Rheinbahn was by LHB and Waggon-Union and was single-ended. Length in both cases was 20.2m. The trams had a remarkably low weight (16.8 and 17.5 tonnes respectively) and were the most technologically advanced design to be built at the time. They also had an attractive appearance but on trial they performed very badly, only that in Düsseldorf managing to reach the stage of being tested in passenger service. The main problem area was the wheels, but there were other difficulties. These could no doubt have been surmounted, given time, and it was intended that trials would continue for two or three years, with series production beginning in about five years. Unfortunately the low floor bandwagon had begun to roll and operators were

An AEG poster advertising the design. (Author's collection)

simply not prepared to wait while further modifications were made and trials conducted. By 1992 there were almost 400 low floor cars on order and Bonn and Mannheim had opted for another design which was already in production. The anticipated orders for about 400 cars had clearly gone elsewhere and the prototypes quietly faded away, no more being heard of the experiment. Given the problems encountered with some of the early production cars, this was a pity.

The firm of MAN, which had for many years seen tram production as a Bavarian sideline, had, in conjunction with Bremen and with support from the BMFT, also begun work on a design with 100% low floor. Details of prototypes for Bremen and München were shown at the IVA

The central section of a Grenoble car, seen in September 1987. (Author)

The Bremen prototype, running as Norrköping 21 and seen in Drottningsgatan in October 2003. (Author)

These elderly ladies are no doubt enthusiastic about the ease of access. The scene is Hauptbahnhof in July 1990. (Author)

International Transport Exhibition held in Hamburg in June 1988 and the first of these cars, Bremen 801, appeared in February 1990, making its first run in public service on 2 July. It subsequently ran on demonstration in no fewer than eleven other cities, in Germany and other countries and it was sold, along with the München prototypes, to Norrköping in June 1998. With a total of 13 systems, this car must surely hold a world record for the number of systems visited by a single tram! The design used a combination of individual steerable wheels and wheelsets linked to each other by a cardan axle and torsion bar in each bogie. Cardan drive was also used to link the three-phase motors, mounted on the body at the side of the gangway, with the bogies and, by offsetting the body on the frame, it was found possible to have 65% adhesion available. Floor height was 350mm above rail level. This design was much more successful than the proposed standard car. With slight modifications, it was the first low floor design to go into series production and by 1992 had attracted 187 orders. Despite some flaws, such as the rather cluttered internal appearance, it had stolen the show.

In the summer of 1989 Würzburg placed in service the first of 14 single-ended trams (201-14, type GT-E)) built by LHB, these being the first production trams in Germany to incorporate a low floor section. They were intended for service on the new line 5 to Heuchelhof, which has gradients of 9.5% and is the steepest line in the former Federal Republic. Having all axles motored, the new cars make light work of this and the whole is an excellent example of modern tramway technology. Step height at the doorway of the low floor area is only 310mm but this area is restricted to the central section of the three-section vehicle and forms only about 20% of the total floor area. It can therefore rapidly become cramped. Nonetheless, the trams ride well and

must be considered one of the most successful of the pioneer designs.

Technical details

VöV prototype – Rheinbahn two-section model
Length 20.19m, width 2.4m, weight 17,750kg, 4 x 60kW motors, 114 passengers, 55 seated

Würzburg
Length 32.6m, width 2.4m, weight 40 tonnes, 4 x 189kW motors, 74 seated passengers

München 2701
Length 27.26m, width 2.3m, weight 28,000kg, 3 x 85kW motors, 166 passengers, 64 seated

The VöV prototype for Bonn emerges from the Düwag works in May 1991. (W.J. Wyse, courtesy London Area, Light Rail Transit Association)

A side view of the same car. (W.J. Wyse, courtesy London Area, Light Rail Transit Association)

Bibliography

Der Stadtverkehr 4/1989 (Bremen), 1/1991 (Kassel and München), 5-6/1991 (Kassel and VöV standard car).

Modern Tramway nos. 632, August 1990 (MAN prototype); 645, September 1991.

VöV Niederflur-Stadtbahn. VöV Entwicklergemeinschaft Railway Gazette International, March 1988 (VöV prototypes).

Präsentation von Prototypen der VöV Niederflur-Stadtbahn. Der Nahverkehr, Jan/Feb 1991.

The interior of one of these cars. (Roger Jones collection)

The centre section of one of the Würzburg cars. (Author)

Würzburg 202 in the city centre in June 1990. (Author)

BELGIUM

The manufacturer BN produced in 1990 a rather unusual tram, based on its experiments with a guided bus. This was a two-section car, which ran on bogies having one pair of large wheels and one pair of small wheels. These looked like the traditional maximum traction truck, but the principle behind them was rather different and they had two, rather than one, suspension points. The 40kW motors were integrated with the powered wheels. The larger wheels intruded into the passenger accommodation, to the extent that seats near the ends of the car had to be placed on high pedestals. Floor height was again 350mm. Modular construction was employed and it was intended that the tram should be available in three-section configuration. The manufacturer suggested that the price would be very competi-

A view of LRV2000. (Author's collection)

tive, but no actual figure was given. The tram had a distinctly boxy appearance and in fact, at 2.50m, was too wide to be tried on the Bruxelles system other than at night. It was by far the heaviest of any of the prototype designs and its suspension was very complicated. Probably for these reasons, little more was heard of it, but end bogies of the type used under it were later used under a production batch of low floor cars for Bruxelles.

Technical details
Three-section car
Length 30m, width 2.4m, weight 37 tonnes, 8 x 40kW motors, 230 passengers*.

Bibliography
Urban Transport International Nov/Dec 1990
Der Stadtverkehr 5/1990

NETHERLANDS – AMSTERDAM

In 1990/1 the GVBA of Amsterdam acquired 65 low floor cars built by BN in Brugge, with Alsthom electrical equipment. This was the first large order for the type. There were 20 single-ended cars of class 11G (901-920) and 25 double-ended cars of class 12G, the latter being intended for use on the extension of line 5 to Amstelveen, on part of which they would share

Double-ended car 910 on Amstelveensweg in the snow of February 1991. (Author)

tracks with Stadtbahn cars (qv). The design chosen was essentially a low floor and shortened version of the recent articulated cars for Den Haag, of which no.309 had run trials in Amsterdam in 1987 and with which the operator was very taken. B3 type bogies were mounted under the end sections. Three-phase motors, as supplied to Rottterdam, were fitted and a novelty for Amsterdam was the pedal control. Clearly the GVBA had confidence in the design. Unfortunately this confidence seemed at times to have been misplaced, since the entry of the cars into revenue service was plagued by teething troubles, arising from the combination of 3-phase drive and PCC-type bogies. Matters became so fraught that the GVBA in July 1990 refused to take delivery of any further

Single-ended car 839 at Centraal Station in March 2003. (Author)

cars. It was some time before modifications to the cardan drive ensured that all were running satisfactorily and deliveries could be resumed. Since then the cars have performed well, but the low floor area amounts to only 30% of the total length and can easily become congested.

Technical details
Class 11G
Length 25.5m, width 2.32m, weight 37.5 tonnes, 8 x 40kW motors, 146 passengers, 52 seated.

Bibliography
Der Stadtverkehr 8/1991

PRODUCTS OF VARIOUS MANUFACTURERS

BOMBARDIER

Bombardier Transportation originated in Canada as a supplier of snowmobiles – tracked vehicles to be used on icefields. It diversified into the rolling stock industry and began to cater for the North American market before expanding into Europe. It acquired ANF-Industrie at Blanc-Misseron in northern France, BN in Belgium, Talbot of Aachen, Procor of Wakefield in England (formerly Charles Roberts) and Rotax in Wien. The second and last of these had already begun to explore the market for low floor trams. In North America the UTDC factory in Canada and the Concarril factory in Mexico also came into the group.

AEG DESIGN GT4/6/8M/N TRAMS

Bremen 3064 at Lilienthaler Heerstrasse in September 2001. (Author)

Having taken over MAN in 1992, this firm inherited the successful design mentioned above and went on to supply what became known as the GTN tram to a variety of customers. Both single- and double-ended versions were produced, for both standard and metre gauge. The production cars incorporated improvements over the prototypes and no seats had to be mounted on pedestals in these. Construction was divided between the former MAN plant in Nürnberg and Hennigsdorf in Berlin. Later production cars were lighter, due to use of material such as fibreglass. Almost all production trams were of three-section GT6 design, Bremen being the only system to take delivery of four-section GT8 cars. Including prototypes, a total of 408 trams of this design were built and supplied to the following ten systems: Augsburg (11), Berlin (150), Braunschweig (12), Bremen (79), Frankfurt (O) (8), Jena (33).

Mainz (16), München (72), Nürnberg (14), Zwickau (12). Only part of the order for Berlin (45 trams) and those for Jena and Mainz were for double-ended cars. The design was also exported to Japan, with five cars going to Kumamoto (9701-9705). As stated, the prototypes from Bremen and München have been sold to Norrköping in Sweden and the metre gauge prototype built for Augsburg has been scrapped.

This was a fairly successful class of tram, which did much to establish the low floor concept as part of everyday service in Germany.

Technical details

GT6 single-ended tram

Length 26.5m, width 2.3m, weight 30.34 tonnes, 3 x 100kW motors, 58 seated passengers.

In June 1996 Berlin 1105 is seen on the extension in Wedding, the first to be opened in the former West Berlin. (Author)

Double-ended car 601 in the town centre of Jena in June 1996. (Author)

Kumamoto 8784 operating in typhoon conditions on 16 May 2004. (M.J. Russell)

In September 1993 one of the cars for Zwickau is seen in the depot, prior to entering service. A Tatra KT4D car, still in its DDR livery, is on the right. (Author)

EUROTRAM

This manufacturer also acquired what had been British Rail Engineering Ltd and with it, plants at Crewe, Derby and York. This led to a brief resumption of tramcar building in Britain.

Visually and technically this is a much more advanced design than the GT tram. It originated with the Italian firm Socimi, which won the contract to supply the new tramway in Strasbourg with 26 seven-section cars, of a very streamlined appearance. Unfortunately the firm soon afterwards became bankrupt and all tram production ceased. Fortunately the contract was taken over by what was then still ABB and, the operator having declined to take the Variobahn instead, the cars were completed in the factory at Derby, being the first trams to be built in England since the Blackpool Centenary cars of 1985. The design provided for modular construction, the double-ended Strasbourg cars having three passenger sections, two cab modules and two articulations. A unique feature of the design is the placing of the electrical system under the driving position. The passenger sections are suspended between the cab and articulation modules, which are all mounted on bogies, three of the bogies being powered. Total unladen weight is about 35 tonnes and there is a flat floor throughout, 350mm above rail level. Further orders for ten seven-section cars and 20 nine-section cars took the total in service to 53. The design has also been supplied to Milan (26 trams) and Porto (72), in the latter case for use on the new light rail system. These are 2.65m wide. No.018 of this batch ran in Melbourne from January to March 2003 and carried passengers as part of extra services provided during the Australian Open Tennis tournament and the Australian Grand Prix. It also visited Sydney and Adelaide but did not run in either of these cities. Although a popular design, production has now been ended, in the interests of rationalisation, a total of 151 trams having been built. The design was also considered for use on the new tramway in Nottingham.

The Eurotram is an elegant vehicle and on its debut seemed to be of decidedly futuristic appearance. It made a significant contribution to the success of the new Strasbourg system and thus helped to re-establish the tram in France.

Technical details

Strasbourg car

Length, 33.1m, width 2.4m, weight 35 tonnes, 6 x 53kW motors, 210 passengers.

Bibliography

Light Rail and Modern Tramway nos.671, November 1993, 688, April 1995

A Strasbourg car seen near Les Halles on 7 March 1995. (Author)

An interior view of a Strasbourg car, March 1995. (Author)

Porto 018 at Spencer Street, Melbourne on a wet day, 9 March 2003. (Mal Rowe)

Milano 7001 in May 2003. (Author)

The visit of this car to Melbourne afforded a rare chance to compare three low floor designs in service. Here on 10 March it poses with Combino 3502 and, in the rear, Citadis 3001. (Mal Rowe)

VARIOBAHN

This design began life with Henschel, which was later taken over by Adtranz, and it thus came into the Bombardier range. The Variotram is of modular construction and uses a powered bogie featuring stub axles and integrated motors.

The first example was supplied to Chemnitz in December 1993 and a total of 30 have now been bought. Sixteen of these are double-ended, for use on the light rail line to Stolberg, which has been converted from a conventional railway; unlike the blue of the city cars, these wear a red livery. These are five-section cars, running on three bogies and having two suspended sections. Later examples went to Duisburg (1), Sydney (7), Helsinki (40) and the OEG (6). There are both single- and double-ended versions and that for the OEG runs on metre gauge, having conventional bogies at the ends of the car. The prototype toured Scandinavia and visited München but no orders resulted. The Duisburg version has an attractive streamlined end design, but all the others are of a somewhat square and severe appearance. The Sydney trams were built in Victoria, in the former Comeng factory at Dandenong.

More recently orders have come from Mannheim for 20 seven-section cars, Ludwigshafen and Heidelberg for eight five-section cars for each system. These are all for metre gauge and have 65% low floor provision. Apart from the first six cars for Mannheim, which arrived in 1996, these were all built in Bautzen and delivered in 2002. The three city systems also have options for a further 60 similar trams, 16 of these being taken up at the end of 2004.

Technical details

Chemnitz s-e. design
Length 31.38m, width 2.65m, 8 x 45kW motors.
Duisburg Variobahn
Length 33.78m, width 2.3m, weight 35.5 tonnes, 8 x ? motors, 176 passengers, 48 seated.
Sydney d-e design
Length 28.28m, width 2.65m, weight 36,000kg, 8 x 45kW motors, 177 passengers, 74 seated.

Chemnitz 607 at Morgenleite in June 2004. (Author)

Chemnitz City Bahn 522 at Stolberg in June 2004. (Author)

OEG 118 at Heidelberg, Bismarckplatz in June 2000. (Author)

Bibliography

Der Stadtverkehr June 1994 (Chemnitz), June 1997 (Duisburg).
Light Rail Review 8 (Sydney).

COBRA

This design, originally developed by the Swiss firm of Schindler, has had a very long gestation period. Plans were first published in 1991 and showed a three-section car running on two four wheel frames or chassis. The wheels would be steered in curves by the body elements, via a system of guiding beams. VBZ Zürich ordered 58 five-section cars. When the firm was taken over by Adtranz, the new owners probably hoped that Zürich, the only system to have ordered the design, would now opt for one of the firm's other products, but the VBZ was unwilling to change, since the Cobra exactly matched its fairly demanding specification. The question also became one of international politics, since the new owners wished to close the Swiss factory and the Swiss operators objected strongly to this proposal. It was not until the early part of 2001 that the first car (3001) actually appeared in Zürich and it entered passenger service on 29 October of that year. Very soon afterwards the trams which had been delivered had to be withdrawn from service, owing to constant and considerable problems with the doors and with

noise levels. These problems were corrected by the end of 2003. A total of 74 have been ordered, with an option for a further 22, but no other operator has ordered the type and it may remain a one-off. Despite its individual nature, it is relatively cheap, at €25,920 per square metre.

VBZ 3006 near the Opera in May 2003. (Author)

INCENTRO

This tram is derived directly from the Variobahn and the Eurotram, as built for Strasbourg, and the design was first publicised in 1999, being intended to replace both the above types. From the former it has copied the placing of the electrical system in a separate module behind the driver's cab. From Eurotram it has copied the light individual wheelsets, but in an improved form. It has 100% low floor layout and is available in various configurations of up to seven modules, for either standard or metre gauge. It can be single- or double-ended and the design of the end sections can be tailored to suit the requirements of individual operators. The first system to place an order was Nantes, where the first of 23 cars entered service in April 2001. Ten others were later acquired and there is currently an option for six more. Fifteen, built in Derby, were bought for Nottingham, where the first arrived in October 2002. These are numbered 201-215, following on from the first generation of the city's trams.

Nantes 374 ran on trial in Berlin in April 2005.

Technical details

Nantes version
Length 36.4m, width 2.4m, weight 38.5 tonnes, 8 x 45kW motors, 246 passengers, 64 seated.

Bibliography

Der Stadtverkehr 6/2000.
Strassenbahn Magazin no.193, November 2005.

Nantes 358 at Commerce in July 2000. (Author)

An interior view of a car in Nantes. (Author)

Nottingham 206 at Wilkinson Street in March 2004. (Author)

GT8N TRAMS, SECOND SERIES

In 1998 the first of an improved type of four section trams was delivered to Nürnberg. This was the first of 26 (1101-26) and was followed by 20 similar cars for München (2201-20). Unlike previous designs, these trams are largely of aluminium and are consequently proportionately lighter. There are four bogies, one under each section, each consisting of one motorised axle and one trailing axle. A new type of articulation is also used, the effect being that of a close coupled motor/trailer set. Larger windows and an improved front end and indicator design have created a vehicle with a most attractive external appearance.

Technical details
München version

Length 36m, width 2.3m, weight 40.8 tonnes, 4 x 100kW motors, 97 seated passengers.

München 2214 leaves Hauptbahnhof on 21 June 2001. (Author)

BRUSSELS CARS

An order for 51 double-ended cars was placed in April 1991 by the STIB. These were one of the first joint ventures, since GEC/Alsthom supplied the wheelsets for the central "bogie" and the motors, and Bombardier Eurorail the end bogies and the bodies, while electrical equipment came from ACE Transport. They were completed in the former BN factory in Brugge and are known as "Tram 2000" but have nothing in common with the Zürich cars of the same name.

The central truck is similar to those under the TSF2 type of tram, but in this case the four independent wheels are all motorised. The end bogies have something in common with the maximum traction design of bogie of former years, each having two independent driving wheels of 640mm diameter and two independent trailing wheels of 375mm diameter. The aim of this design was to allow wheels to retain at all times the same tangential relation to the rails and thus facilitate the entry to curves and also reduce noise on curves. Each of the three-phase asynchronous motors is mounted on the hub of the wheel it drives. Despite their

STIB 2021 running in Stockholm in August 1998. (Author)

increased width compared to previous Bruxelles cars, the interior is somewhat cluttered and the arrangement of handrails does not make for easy access by wheelchair passengers.

The trams have worked well enough but no more were ordered, nor were they bought by any other system, although one ran on the Djurgården line in Stockholm in 1998.

Technical details

Length 22.8m, width 2.3m, weight 33 tonnes, 8 x 44kW motors, 144 passengers, 32 seated.

Bibliography

Les Nouveaux Tramways et Métros Légers. Op.cit.

KÖLN K4000 DESIGN – FLEXITY SWIFT

One of the cars built for the Wiener Stadtbahn (qv) was tried in Köln in 1995 and performed so well that the operator decided to buy 124 similar trams to replace articulated cars on its east-west network of lines (4001-4124). This class was the first to be put out to tender throughout Europe

Köln 4074 and (right) 4041 at Neumarkt on 15 June 2005. (Author)

and is truly international, since the components were manufactured in Austria, Belgium and Germany and the vehicles were assembled in Belgium. These are double-ended and are rather longer than the Wien cars, with a lower floor height of 410mm in the low floor area. The middle section is much shorter, being little more than a support for the articulation joints. These trams have been so successful that the operator has decided against further development of the Stadtbahn system.

This design was also adopted for Croydon. Twenty-four trams were ordered, their numbers (2530-2553) following on from the highest number in the fleet of London Transport tramways. They have an additional seating bay, compared with the German cars, and so are slightly longer. Cost was about £1.5m per tram. These have proved to be very successful and are popular with the travelling public.

Further orders came from SL of Stockholm,

which in 1999 ordered 22 trams of its class A32 (401-422) for use on the new ring tramway. This was followed by six in 2002 for use on the Gouda-Alphen light rail line in the Netherlands. The trams are allocated to HTM of Den Haag and are identical to the Stockholm cars, the plan being that the latter could take them over should the trials proved unsuccessful. It now seems unlikely that this will be the case. Meanwhile in 2006 Stockholm ordered a further nine cars. To replace Stadtbahn cars on its city tramway, IETT of Istanbul bought 55 in 2003 and the design broke into the North American market in the same year with 24 cars for the new system in Minneapolis, these being built in the USA. This operator has an option for 18 further cars and Stockholm has an option for 48 more. There were also plans to order 21 cars of this type for the new tramway in Liverpool, originally due to open in 2008. However, the views of the current British government have now put the future of the system in doubt. Preliminary sketches showed an attractive yellow livery.

In 2004 69 cars of a modified type, having many parts in common with the Stadtbahn cars of class K5000, were ordered by Köln, as class K4500 (4501-4569).

Another customer for this design appeared in 2005 when RET Rotterdam ordered 21 trams, with an option for a further 21. These will be delivered in 2008 and will operate on the new RandstadRail system between Rotterdam, Den Haag and Zoetermeer. Porto has also ordered 30 double-ended cars for use on the outer-suburban sections of the new light rail system. These will seat 100 passengers and be capable of running at 100km/hr.

It should be noted that this class is sometimes referred to as a Stadtbahn design, probably because of its origin, but essentially these are low floor trams. As a result of the recommendations of a public relations firm, Bombardier has rebranded its products and this class is now known as "Flexity Swift".

Technical details
Köln 4001

Length 28.4m, width 2.65m, weight 35.5 tonnes, 4 x 120kW motors, 70 seated.

Köln 4501

Length 28.54m, width 2.65m, weight 39 tonnes, 4 x 120kW motors, 183 passengers, 58 seated.

Croydon

Length 30.1m, width 2.65m, weight 36.3 tonnes, 2 x 120kW motors, 208 passengers, 70 seated.

Bibliography

Light Rail Review 8 (Croydon).

CITYRUNNER – FLEXITY OUTLOOK

Croydon Tramlink 2538 on a test run near the depot in 1999. It optimistically displays the service number 7 and the destination "Uxbridge", recalling the days of London United Tramways. Trams have not as yet reached that town again, but may do so in future if current plans are realised. (Author)

Stockholm 403 on street track in October 2003. (Author)

Lodz 1204 at Kallista station in October 2002. (Author)

An interior view of a Graz Cityrunner, June 2001. (Author)

In 1996 Bombardier entered the field of modular design with the Cityrunner, of which a mock-up was launched in Basel and was also shown in Flanders, but did not attract orders from either place. However, 18 trams of this type (651-668) were bought by Graz in 2000, these having Skoda motors. In 2003 Linz took 21 cars (001-021), Lodz in Poland bought 15 (1201-1215) and the new system of Eskisehir in Turkey began operation with 18. In 2005 Linz ordered a further twelve cars. The design has also been ordered to cope with expansion in Genève, which bought 21 cars (861-881) in 2004/5 and has an option for 18 more. These trams introduced a new livery of blue and white to this system when the first went into service in October 2004. To familiarise crews with this type, two Lodz cars were hired by TPG in 2004. Brussels STIB has ordered 68 (3001-3049 and 4001-4019), of two different lengths, for delivery between 2005 and 2007. The first of these, 3001, was presented to the public on 18 September 2005. Marseille has ordered 26 double-ended cars to work on its expanded system from 2007. These will have a quite different end design, rather of a "sharks' head" outline. At the end of 2004 an order came from Ferrocarils de la Generalitat Valencia for 30 double-ended cars, of which 20 will go to Alicante and ten to Valencia. Meanwhile Innsbruck has ordered 22 trams of this type, with an option for an additional ten and 20 have been ordered by Valencia. This class is now designated "Flexity Outlook". It is one of the less expensive designs on the market; the shorter of the Brussels cars will cost only €26,000 per square metre.

Technical details
TPG Genève car
Length 42.04m, width 2.3m, weight 50 tonnes, 6 x 105kW motors, 237 passengers, 66 seated.

Bibliography
Der Stadtverkehr July/August 2002.
Strassenbahn Magazin, August 2006.

OTHER DESIGNS FOR GERMAN SYSTEMS – FLEXITY CLASSIC

Stockholm 403 on street track in October 2003. (Author)

HTM car 6102 at Gouda station in March 2004. (Author)

In addition to all the above, individual designs, with a certain amount of standardisation, have been built for a variety of German systems, to a total of 216 trams. This series began with the delivery of twelve cars to Kassel in 1999. These were built to comply with railway regulations, to allow their use on the expanding regional network and have a higher seating capacity than their predecessors. Conventional bogies are used under the end sections, while the two middle trailing bogies have wheels mounted on stub axles. This is a three-section design, running on four bogies and having a low floor area equal to 70% of the total length. A total of 32 trams has now been acquired. Essen bought twelve similar but slightly shorter cars in 1999 and has now expanded its fleet to 34. Schwerin (30 cars) and Dessau (10) followed, the latter with shorter vehicles. Thirty of this type have also been delivered to Halle in 2004, in the unusual form of single-ended, double-sided cars, which will work in coupled pairs. Finally in 2003 Frankfurt (M) bought 60, of its class S, and Halle bought 30. The former differ from all others of this type in having 100% low floor area. All were built in the DWA factory in Bautzen. The first export order

Essen 1527 at Dellwig Bhf on 7 June 2005. (Author)

Halle 679 at Marktplatz on 14 June 2005. (Author)

Krakow 2015 is followed by an ex-Nürnberg articulated car through the city centre. (M.J. Russell)

Kassel 633 seen at Rathaus on 11 June 2005 belongs to the Regionalbahn Kassel (RBK) consortium, not to the city system. (Author)

Dessau 301 at Kleine Schaftrift in October 2002. (Author)

Frankfurt in Poststrasse on 15 June 2004. (Author)

for the type came in the same year, when nine were ordered by Adelaide, to replace cars dating from 1929 on the base service on the line to Glenelg. These are going to be expensive cars, at €41,700/m² and even those cars delivered to German systems have been at the upper end of the usual price range. Five of the Frankfurt type have been ordered by Norrköping. A batch of 20 three-section eight-axle trams is also under

construction for Bremen. Their width of 2.65m, instead of 2.3m, has required considerable track alterations. In 2006, 47 were ordered for Dortmund.

A somewhat similar design was supplied to Krakow with 26 cars between 2001 and 2003 (2001-2026). There was an option for a further 18 and in 2006 a total of 24 more cars was ordered.

The new brand name for these is Flexity Classic.

Technical details
Kassel
Length 28.9m, width 2.40m, weight 33.7 tonnes, 4 x 1225kW motors, 87 seated.
Bremen 3101
Length 35.4m, width 2.65m, weight 48 tonnes, 4 x 125kW motors, 239 passengers, 105 seated.

DRESDEN DESIGNS

The trams built for the Saxon capital since 1995 exemplify the interworking of the various concerns within the industry, to an extent greater than any other design. They have been developed by a group of manufacturers working under the name of "Sachsen Tram" and made up initially of Siemens, Düwag, ABB and DWA. The design thus came at a later date into the Bombardier fold, and all cars delivered to date have been assembled in Bautzen, but it could equally well be classified as a Siemens venture. It is based on the Variobahn type of tram as supplied to Mannheim and Ludwigshafen, but differs from these in many respects. It was intended to develop a tram in the tradition of the Hechtwagen, which would not only meet the technical parameters of the Dresden system – the unusual gauge of 1450mm, the limited space between the tracks and the hills on routes to the north of the city – but would also come to symbolise the city to residents and visitors alike. The external styling was developed by a local firm of industrial designers and the most advanced technical feature, the water-cooled three-phase asynchronous motors, came from ABB Henschel.

The first order was for both single- and double-ended cars. These are numbered respectively 2501-2547 and 2581-2593, class NGT8DD. This is a five-section design with 70% low floor area. Conventional bogies, with wheels of only 590mm diameter, are used under the end sections and the middle section is mounted on four individual wheels. There are two suspension systems of which the second is a newly-developed form of hydraulic suspension and this maintains the floor level at the doors at a constant and very low height of 295mm above rail level. A further 23 were delivered in 2002/3 (2701-2723); there is an option for 20 more.

In 1999 this design was developed into a seven-section vehicle, to give the longest tram in regular service anywhere in the world. Only single-ended trams have been built in this form and have a low floor area of 80%. Trailing wheels are under the third and fifth modules. They are numbered

2801-2832, class NGT12DD. There is an option for an additional 17.

In their attractive yellow and white livery, with bonded windows, these trams have been a great success in winning back passengers to the tram in Dresden.

After Desden 2802 had been tested in Leipzig in May 2003, the LVB in October 2003 ordered twelve five-section cars of this type with an option for a further twelve. The first of class XXL (1201) was delivered in June 2005 and the type entered regular service on 17 September.

Dresden 2501 KRAKOW approaches Postplatz along Wilsdruffer Strasse in June 2000. (Author)

Technical details
Dresden seven-section tram
Length 44.5m, width 2.30m, weight 41 tonnes, 8 x 85kW motors, 140 seated passengers
Leipzig.
Length 45m, width 2.3m, weight 59.2 tones, 8 x 85kW motors, 266 passengers, 106 seated.

Bibliography
Von Linientreue und Marktdynamik. B. Schawohl. Dresdener Verkehrsbetriebe, Dresden, 2002.
Strassenbahn Magazin no.193, November 2005 (Leipzig), no. 98, April 2006 (Bremen).

As of December 2004, Bombardier, or its predecessors, had supplied a total of 1795 low floor trams of ten basic designs and 116 Stadtbahn cars of two types. There were also options for 297 additional trams.

Double-ended 2593 at Pariserplatz in June 2004. (Author)

Class leader of the seven-section trams, 2801, on a test run in the southern suburbs in June 2004. (Author)

DÜWAG AND SIEMENS

As Düwag was willing to allow its customers to choose from a wide range of options for body design and electrical equipment for its low floor cars, there was even less standardisation than with the products of other firms. The company supplied a few trams with 100% low floor but the majority had a low floor area of around 65-70%.

DÜWAG LOW FLOOR TRAMS

The first production low floor trams to appear from this manufacturer was a series for Kassel (451-465), the first of which was placed in service in the autumn of 1991. These trams, which had a low floor area of about 70%, were the first series application of the EEF technique and they have been fairly successful, although riding qualities and noise levels are sometimes unsatisfactory. The first 100% low floor cars, and the first double-ended version with this feature from any manufacturer, was a series of 40 cars (001-040) delivered to Frankfurt (M) between 1993 and 1996 and classified R by that operator. The trams have a floor height of 350mm above rail level, decreasing to 300mm at the doors. Despite an attractive appearance and comfortable interior, there have been considerable problems with these trams. Riding qualities were so poor that the suspension had to be altered and strengthened in 1998 and for further deliveries the operator turned to another type of tram. Trams of broadly similar design but of 70% low floor configuration were supplied to Bochum (42), Brandenburg (4), Erfurt (4), Halle (14), Heidelberg (12), Kassel (25), Mülheim (4), Oberhausen (6) and Rostock (40), all these being to an almost-standard design using two-wheel EEF sets for the trailing wheels. Similar trams, but using conventional wheels throughout, were delivered to Bonn (24) and Düsseldorf (138).

A rather different type of double-ended tram, with 70% low floor area, was designed to meet the specific requirements of Freiburg. There are 26 of these (241-266), of which the first went into service in 1994.

Frankfurt (M) 006 at Offenbach Stadtgrenze terminus in June 1995. (Author)

Brandenburg 102 at Hauptbahnhof in June 2000. (Author)

Karlsruhe 239 waits at Hauptbhanhof in June 1996 as cyclists prepare to board. (Author)

Freiburg 252 making for Hauptbahnhof in June 1996. (Author)

An interior shot of a Freiburg car, in June 1996. (Author)

Heidelberg 266 at Eppelheim, Kirchheimer Strasse in June 1996. (Author)

Technical details

Kassel 451
Length 28.83m, width 2.3m, weight 30 tonnes, 2 x 180kW motors, 180 passengers, 80 seated.

Heidelberg 261
Length 29.93m, width 2.3m weight 31.5 tonnes 2 x 95kW motor, 74 seated.

Frankfurt (M) R class
Length 27.6m, width 2.35m, weight 33 tonnes, 8 x 55kW motors, 59 seated.

Freiburg 241
Length 33.09m, width 2.3m, weight 39 tonnes, 8 x 65 kW motors, 205 passengers, 84 seated.

Karlsruhe 316 on Kaiserstrasse in June 2001 (Author)

Erfurt 602 at Anger in June 1996. (Author)

Kassel 458 picks up passengers at Wilhelmshoe station in June 1995. (Author)

Bochum 425 at Buer Rathaus on 6 June 2005. (Author)

LEIPZIG CARS

As a first step towards the modernisation of its large fleet, the Leipziger Verkehrsbetriebe (LVB) took delivery between 1994 and 1998 of 56 three-section trams (1101-1156) built by a consortium of Düwag, DWA, Siemens and ABB. These have low floor area of 70% and conventional motor bogies at the outer ends. The centre section runs on two bogies with wheels of only 410mm in diameter. While this solution has avoided the problems found with some other designs, this has been at the expense of having the centre section shorter than it would have been with individual wheelsets, to maintain the width of the gangway within the car. Despite this limitation, they have performed well and are popular with the public and the staff. They carry names of famous people or events connected with the city, the class leader being "Johann Sebastian Bach".

Technical details

Length 27.8m, width 2.2m, weight 31.5 tonnes, 4 x 96kW motors, 77 seated passengers.

A different style of tram was developed for the city lines of Karlsruhe, the first being delivered in 1995. This is a single-ended three-section design, with a short centre section, under which are four individual wheels. Width is 2.65m, making them wider than any of the above types, and allowing comfortable 2+2 seating in much of the passenger accommodation. There were 20 of these trams (221-240). In 1999 this design was expanded into a five-section car by the addition of another centre module and an additional short section. Again there were 20 delivered, numbered 301-320.

Technical details

Five-section car

Length 38.7m, width 2.65m, weight 49.2 tonnes, 4 x 127kW motors, 124 seated passengers.

Bibliography

Der Stadtverkehr 4/1993 (Frankfurt R class).
Modern Tramway no.648, December 1991 (Kassel).

Leipzig 1126 at Bayerischerplatz in June 2004. (Author)

COMBINO

In 1997 Siemens, which had now taken over the Düwag concern, announced its first low floor design, the Combino, which was constructed on modular principles. Any combination of end, middle and driving modules could be assembled to create a tram of anything between 19m and 40m in length, with four, six eight or more axles. It has 100% low floor capacity and may be built in single- or double-ended form and for either standard or metre gauge. Wheels are connected longitudinally rather than transversely. Only Siemens equipment could be fitted. The price, at DM2.9m (c£1.2m) per car, was very competitive. A five-section prototype was widely demonstrated. Unlike the later production series, this had single steerable wheelsets in the end modules. The first production series went to Potsdam in 1998, with 48 five-section cars (401-448). The Combino then embarked on what promised to be a successful career, being bought by systems all over Europe and also exported to Japan and Australia, as follows:

Amsterdam 155 five-section-cars, Augsburg 41 seven-section, Basel 28 seven-section, (these trams are one metre longer that any other seven-section cars, to cope with the radii of the curves on the system), Bern 15 five-section, Erfurt 14+22 five-section, (621-634) and 12 three-section, Freiburg 18 seven-section, (271-279), Hiroshima twelve five-section, Melbourne 21 five-section and 38 three-section, Nordhausen four three-section, Potsdam 16 plus the prototype and Ulm eight. On order in 2004 were cars for Potsdam (32), Poznan (14 plus an option for ten more), Alicante (10), Almeda (24) and Verona (22).

The Nordhausen cars were nicknamed "Bambinos" and are noteworthy in that two have been fitted with diesel engines to allow operation on the metre-gauge lines of the Harzquerbahn narrow gauge railway, which has now been connected to the city system. Some of the cars for Amsterdam have been fitted with a post for a conductor to the rear of the body, but, as there is no rear door, this feature obliges boarding passengers to move to the rear before they can move forward and creates congestion within the tram. Peter Witt would not approve!

For Düsseldorf the Rheinbahn bought a series of trams from 1997 onwards, which differed

Basel seven-section car 328 at the SBB station in May 2003. (Author)

Amsterdam double-ended 2204 at Spui in March 2003. (Author)

Nordhuasen dual-power car 201 at Hauptbahnhof in June 2004. (Author)

externally from the standard Combino in having a different front end design. More importantly these trams also differ in having Kiepe electronics, since the operator preferred these to the Siemens equipment fitted to all other Combinos, and in having the end bogies further forward than other cars. They also differed in the form of construction of the bodywork, which gave them a better entry into curves and thus minimised the torsional strains on the body. For these reasons class R100 cannot correctly be classified as a Combino design. There are 36 ten-axle NF10 cars and 15 eight-axle NF8 cars and the class has been nicknamed "Felzino", after Dr H. Felz, the undertaking's managing director. A further 15 cars of a modified NF8 design are on order and there is an option for 61 more. These differ from their predecessors in having aluminium bodies and also in having doors on both sides of the body, although they are single-ended. This is to allow their use in the future "Wehlinie" – an east-west tunnel designed for trams, rather than Stadtbahnen.

With a total of over 600 vehicles delivered or on order, this design was by the beginning of 2004 quite definitely the market leader and seemed to have an assured future. However, various undertakings, such as Basel in 2001, began to report problems with the trams and, in the case of Amsterdam, these reached a stage at with the GVBA was unwilling to accept further deliveries and trams completed for it had to be put into store. Finally on 12 March, disaster struck and all

those cars which had run more than 120,000km in service had to be immediately withdrawn from service. In Potsdam this decision came inconveniently at 16.15 in the afternoon. It had become apparent that serious defects in the bodywork could have created a potentially dangerous situation in service. One of the attractions of the Combino was its very light weight, in comparison to other designs on the market, and this, combined with the vertical movement permitted by the articulation joints, set up torsion strains in the bodywork when running through reverse curves or climbing significant gradients. These strains in return caused cracks in the square frames around the articulations. The increased length between truck centres did not help and most of the problems arose in cars of a length of 42m, only a few being reported on shorter cars. In Amsterdam, where the cars had been driven at the normal Amsterdam high speed around curves also produced damage in the bearings, particularly in the rear truck.

Naturally the temporary loss of numbers of newer trams caused problems for those systems most affected and led to a good deal of improvisation in an effort to maintain services. Potsdam, for example, re-activated 13 KT4D trams which had been set aside for transfer to Romania and managed to hire three of the same type which had been just gone off to Szeged in Hungary. These were supplemented by the prototype KT4D car and a preserved Gotha two-axle set! Most trams were able to re-enter service later in

Erfurt three-section car 702 at the rear of a set in Bahnhofstrasse in June 2004. (Author)

Hiroshima 5010 on 19 May 2004. (M.J. Russell)

Rheinbahn 2145 at Düsseldorf Hauptbahnhof on 10 June 2005. (Author)

Amsterdam single-ended car 2053 negotiates the grand union crossing at the intersection of Ceinturbaan and van Wou Straat in March 2003, when the junction was being relaid. (Author)

Melbourne M-Tram Combino 5009 crosses Albert Road on the light rail line to St Kilda on 5 March 2005, while below two Yarra Trams Citadis cars, with 3016 nearer the camera, help out with the heavy traffic to the Australian Grand Prix, held in nearby Albert Park. (Mal Rowe)

Rheinbahn 2022 at Düsseldorf Hauptbahnhof on 10 June 2005. (Author)

2004, after measures had been taken to strengthen the bodywork, but the whole incident cast doubt over the future of the design and at the time of writing, it is not clear whether it will remain in production or be withdrawn from the market when outstanding orders have been completed. Potsdam has cancelled its order and a series of 40 53m long trams for Budapest will be completed to the Düsseldorf design as MF12, rather than as Combinos. The design is known as Combino Supra 12B and the first cars will go into service on the busy ring lines 4 and 6 in 2007. Delivery began in 2006 and these will be the longest trams ever built. However, twelve five-section cars are due to be delivered to Erfurt in 2005, along with five for Freiburg. The orders for Alicante and Verona appear to have been cancelled.

Technical details
Potsdam 401
Length 30.5m, width 2.3m, weight 31.8 tonnes, 4 x 100kW motors, 69 seated passengers.
Melbourne three-section car
Length 19.08m, width 2.65m, weight 25.5 tonnes.

Bibliography
Der Stadtverkehr 2 and 8/1996, 10/2005 (repairs).
Strassenbahn Magazin no.124, February 2000, no.183, January 2005.
Railway Gazette International, Metro Report 2004.

Interior of an Amsterdam Combino in March 2003. (Author)

The conductor's post in an Amsterdam Combino. (Author)

Potsdam 413 approaching Nauener Tor in September 2002. (Author)

LEOLINER

Leoliners 1302 and 1301 on a short working of line 11, designated 11E, at Leipzig Hauptbahnhof (west) on 14 June 2005. (Author)

Strictly speaking this is not a Siemens product, but as that firm has had an input to the design, it may conveniently be considered here.

Like many other undertakings in former communist states, Leipziger Verkehrsbetriebe has had to consider the question of the replacement of its fleet of Tatra bogie cars. Those which have been modernised will still be serviceable for some years, but a time will come when they have to be taken out of service, and in any case they do not provide modern standards of accessibility. The undertaking also has spare capacity in its workshops at Heiterblick. In 1999 the LVB set up a subsidiary to develop new business, in both home and export markets, and in 2000 this became a joint venture with Siemens.

The first result of this co-operation appeared in December 2003, when the Leoliner was demonstrated. The name is derived from the lion which appears on the city's coat of arms. This is a two-section, single-ended tram, with 60% low floor capacity, running on three bogies, of which the outer two are motored. These are of conventional B3 design and use components from Tatra trucks. One is under the shorter front section and two are under the rear section, the articulation being suspended in the classic Urbinati design. Floor height at the doors is a commendable 290mm and it is intended that this form of construction will allow the car to cope easily with track which is less than perfect. Three-phase equipment is fitted, housed in containers on the roof. The cost of a Leoliner is around €80,000 (£1.2m), a good deal less than most modern designs and it could therefore be an attractive proposition for less busy services. The prototypes were numbered 1301/2 and at the end of 2004 30 were ordered by LVB, but these will be assembled in the former Tatra works in Praha, not in Leipzig. Five have also been ordered by Halberstadt.

Technical details
Length 22.68m, width 2.3m, weight 27.08 tonnes, 4 x 65kW motors, 118 passengers, 39 seated.

Bibliography
Tramways and Urban Transit, no.795, March 2004.
Strassenbahn Magazin no.170, December 2003.
Der Stadtverkehr 11/12/2003 and 9/2004.

WIEN ULF TRAMS

This design may be considered as the ultimate low floor tram. The design was evolved by Simmering-Graz-Pauker for Wien in the early 1990s and thus came into the Siemens fold. A prototype centre section appeared in the summer of 1992 and in early 1993 a matching front end was produced. Joined to a bogie trailer which had been deprived of one of its ends, this odd-looking combination then made

Class A 644 at Schottenring on 16 June 2001. (Author)

extensive trial runs in the city and orders for two complete prototypes for delivery in 1994, to be followed in 1996 by 100 24-metre cars and 50 35m cars.

ULF is based on a design in which the articulations and running gear have a good deal in common with the Spanish Talgo trains. Construction is modular, all of which, apart from the end modules, are motored. Hydraulic suspension ensures a constant floor level, no matter the number of passengers on board,

Interior view of a class A car in June 2001. (Author)

though this can be adjusted in the event of a snowfall. The tram runs on single steerable wheels and the drive to these is from motors and brake units suspended in each module. Internally the equipment is housed in cupboards, to avoid encroachment on the passenger space, and wide doorways with ample standing room alongside, have allowed a reduction in dwell times at stops of between 25% and 40%. At doors, the floor is only 19.7cm above rail level, rising to 22cm in the interior of the accommodation. The internal design was the work of the Austrian firm Porsche Design and the end result is a most attractive and user-friendly tram. Externally these cars introduced a new livery of silver grey and anthracite, with a red band. Generally they have been well received but there have, however, been some complaints about poor availability and in April 2005 34 of the first series had to be hurriedly, but temporarily withdrawn when cracks were discovered in the truck frames.

Two types of tram are in service. After trials with two complete prototypes, lasting from 1995 to 1997, series production began in 1998 and continued through to 2004. Type A is a five-section tram and fleet numbers are 1-50. Type B has seven sections and numbers

are 601-686. In October 2004 car 50 ran for three weeks in Berlin, but to date no orders have been placed by BVG or any operator apart from Wien.

In 2004 a further 150 trams were ordered, for delivery up to 2012. There will be 80 of type A and 70 of type B.

Technical details
Type A
Length 24.21m, width 2.4m, weight 29.17 tonnes, 6 x 80kW motors, 136 passengers, 42 seated.

Bibliography
Light Rail and Modern Tramway nos.670, October 1992 and 663, March 1993.
Strassenbahn Magazin no.184, February 2005.

Class B 619 climbs from Gumpfendorfer Strasse on 16 June 2001. In recognition of the international Gay Pride festival, the rainbow flag is being flown, along with the city's flag. (Author)

SHEFFIELD CARS

The first low floor trams to be delivered to a British system were those for Sheffield, which began to arrive in that city from Düwag in 1993 and entered service in 1994. The first three cars were tested on the Rheinbahn in Düsseldorf and Krefeld and, when they arrived in Britain, these still carried notices in German and Rheinbahn fleet numbers. Although successful, they have since remained a one-off design.

Sheffield is a hilly city, with gradients of up to 10% on some of the planned routes, and thus there could be no question of using trams with trailing trucks. All axles had to be motored and this requirement presented the builder with a problem, since all low floor trams in service at that time, apart from the ill-starred VöV prototypes and the LHB cars for Würzburg, incorporated trailing wheels or bogies. Avoidance of trailing wheels meant that the low floor area would be limited to the space between the bogies and, to maximise this, the middle bogies were placed under the central section of the car, instead of under the articulation joints. This allowed a total low floor area of 40% of the length of the tram, less than in other designs, but sufficient for normal service. Four longitudinally mounted motors drive each axle through tandem drive. Control is by a DC chopper system with GTO semiconductors and regenerative braking is fitted. The trams have proved to be reliable in service and their acceleration and hill-climbing capabilities are impressive. First publicity showed them in the traditional Sheffield colours

Nos. 07 and 18 at Cathedral Square in original livery in April 1995. (Author)

of cream and blue, but they entered service in a drab battleship grey. Since the undertaking became part of the Stagecoach empire, they were repainted white with red, orange and blue stripes and, in this case, the change has brought a welcome improvement in the appearance of the fleet. From the autumn of 2005, newly-overhauled cars have been painted in a new and attractive blue and red livery. Since 1996 these trams have been worked with conductors.

Technical details
Length 34.75m width 2.65m, weight 52 tonnes, 4 x 277kW motors, 250 passengers, 88 seated.

Bibliography
Tram to Supertram. P. Fox, P. Jackson and R.O. Benton. Platform 5 Publishing, Sheffield, 1995
Light Rail and Modern Tramway, no.664, April 1993

TRAMS FOR DE LIJN, FLANDERS

In 1997 45 low floor trams were ordered by this operator from Siemens. Deliveries took place in 2000/1 and of the total 31 single-ended cars went to Antwerpen (7201-7231) and 14 double-ended cars to Gent (6301-6314). While they were being delivered, a second batch of 47 was ordered and these came into service in 2004/5, being shared 30 and 17 between the two systems. In 2006 ten more were delivered, to work on the coast line in summer and in Gent in winter, after several Antwerpen cars had run on the coast line in the summer of 2005. A further nine are on order in 2006.

De Lijn (Antwerp) single-ended 7204 car on the intermediate turning circle on the left bank line in March 2004. (Author)

One of Gent's double-ended cars, 6306, at Kornmarkt on a very wet day in March 2004. (Author)

Technical details
De Lijn low floor cars – Antwerp version
Length 29.1m, width 2.3m, 39.2 tonnes, 4 x 95kW motors, 174 passengers, 74 seated.

Bibliography
Der Stadtverkehr, March 2000.

IBERIAN DESIGNS

In 1992 Valencia ordered 21 cars for its new tram line from Siemens/Düwag and on to this CCFL of Lisbon added an order for ten cars, with an option for 20 more. The order for the former was split between CAF (12) and Meinfesa (nine) and the Lisbon order was likewise split between Sorefame, builder of much railway rolling stock, (four) and CAF (six). The option was not pursued.

This single-ended design has three body sections and provides a low floor area extending for 62% of the total length of the tram, only the two end bogies being motored. The central section is mounted on two independent wheelsets with stub axle linked by bridges, brake gear being mounted externally to these sets. This form of construction has minimised intrusion to the passenger space and, despite the narrow track gauge, it has been possible to fit 2+2 seating in most of the central area of the body. The cars are also air conditioned. Fleet numbers are 501-510 and the first entered public service in April 1995. These trams operate only on line 15 along the bank of the River Tagus and recently all have been covered in advertising liveries. The external styling was designed by the German firm of Neumeister, which has also worked on the ICE trains for DB AG and it is unfortunate that in Lisbon this advertising detracts from the striking appearance of the trams.

The cars for Valencia are almost identical to these, but have 4 x 145kW motors, as they have to cope with a more hilly route than that in Lisbon. They went into public service on 21 May 1994. Fleet numbers are 3801-3825, a further four cars having been obtained in 1999.

The first of a fleet of somewhat similar GT8N cars was delivered in the summer of 2005 for the new system which is being built on the south bank of the Tagus opposite Lisbon.

Lisbon 506 loads at Praça do Commercio in August 1997. (Alastair G. Gunn)

Technical details
Lisbon 501
Length 24.02m, width 2.4m, weight 30 tonnes (estimated), 4 x 103kW motors, 155 passengers, 65 seated (NB Crush loading is often well above this figure).

Bibliography
The Tramways of Portugal. Op.cit.
Light Rail and Modern Tramway no.681, September 1994 (Valencia).

A Valencia car at Les Arenes. (A.W. Brotchie)

AVANTO STADTBAHN CARS

A busy scene at University of Houston Downtown on New Year's Day 2004. Car 110 and another are on the left, car 101 is on the right. (Mike Harrington)

This design was evolved largely to meet the needs of the expanding North American market. As class S70, 18 vehicles were delivered to Houston for the new system opened in 2003 and the type is on order for the new system in Charlotte (16) and San Diego (11cars, 3001-3011).

A slightly different version, in the form of a tram-train, with the capability of operating on both 750V DC and 25kV AC, has been ordered by SNCF, for use on the Aulnay-Bondy line in the Paris area, conversion of which from a rail line is now under way. Service is due to begin in late 2006.

There will be 15 of these cars, with an option for a further 20, and the first was on trial in August 2005. Seventy cars of this type are likely to be ordered for the new line (29.4km) in Ottawa, for delivery by 2009, while Mulhouse has ordered twelve for service on a converted branch of the SNCF network in 2010.

Technical details
SNCF version
Length 36.67mm, width 2.65m, weight 59.7 tonnes, 4 x 200kW motors, 242 passengers, 80 seated.

JAPANESE ORDERS

In 2006 seven cars of type 0600 were delivered to Toyama.

LHB (LATTERLY IN CONJUNCTION WITH ALSTOM)

The only 100% low floor trams to be built by this firm are a batch of 20 single-ended trams also for Würzburg and delivered in 1995/6 (250-69, type GT-N). The first arrived in the city in February 1996. These are also the first 100% low floor trams to have all axles powered. Externally they have a square appearance like that of the Variobahn. To allow a width of 2.4m over the entire length of the car and at the same time to keep within the clearances permitted for the previous type, it was necessary to have a five-section body. Each of the three bogies has four separately powered wheels, giving impressive acceleration and hill-climbing qualities. Suspension is excellent and the ride is akin to that of a conventional bogie car. These cars are used on lines 1, 2 and 4 but can also work on line 5. They cost DEM 4.5m each (c£.8m)

One of the Würzburg cars, the number hidden by the advertising livery, is in Augustiner Strasse on 8 October 2004. (Alastair G. Gunn)

Technical details
Length 28.8m width 2.4m, weight 39.5 tonnes, total power 730kW, 170 passengers, 76+6 seated.

Bibliography
Der Stadtverkehr, September 1996

In 1994 Magdeburg took delivery of the first of 72 trams (1301-1372) to begin modernisation of its system. These are three section trams running on four conventional bogies, the two under the central section having wheels of reduced diameter. In external design they are quite unlike the other products of this firm. Low floor area is 70% and step height at the entrance doorways is only 300mm. A batch of 20 very similar but shorter cars was delivered to Darmstadt in 1995 (9555-9574). Magdeburg has an option on 48 further trams. In 2001 car 1340 visited Poland and ran in Wroclaw, Szczecin and

Warsaw but to date no orders have come from that country. However, 18 more have been ordered for Darmstadt, for delivery in 2007, and Braunschweig and Gera have ordered twelve and six respectively.

Technical details
Magdeburg tram
Length 29.41m, width 2.3m weight 32.5 tonnes, 4 x 95 kW motors, 71 seated passengers.

Bibliography
Der Stadtverkehr September 1992

A Magdeburg tram in the city centre in June 1996. (Author)

GEC ALSTHOM/ALSTOM TRANSPORT

This concern is the successor to the French firm of Brissoneau et Lotz, which in 1918 began to manufacture railway vehicles in La Rochelle. In 1972 it changed its name to Alsthom and in 1989 merged with the British

GEC undertaking to form GEC Alsthom. The firms of LHB, Konstal in Poland and CAF in Barcelona were also merged with this concern. In 1998 the firm became simply Alstom, following a parting of the ways.

FRENCH STANDARD TRAM TSF2

A rush hour scene at Belvédère on Paris line T2 in June 2004. TSF2 203 on the right contrasts with Citadis 413 on the left. (Author)

This tram has already been described in the section on the pioneers. It went on to become a very successful design and there are now 53 in Grenoble (2001-2053), 35 in Paris (101-119 and 201-216) and 28 in Rouen (801-828). In Britain it appeared in initial publicity literature for the West Midlands line and was also used by Strathclyde PTE in public consultations in Glasgow in 1990. A Grenoble car was also tested in Rotterdam and Barcelona. However, no export orders were ever received, probably because it

was a very expensive tram, costing DEM 3.8m or £1.26m as against DEM 2.3m or £760,000 for a comparable Kassel car. This factor, together with that of weight, ultimately told against it and led other new systems such as Strasbourg to order trams from other manufacturers. Nevertheless its publicity value has been great and it certainly helped to establish the possibilities of the modern tram.

Technical details
Paris first series
Length 29.4m, width 22.3m, weight 44.2 tonnes, 4 x 69kW motors, 174 passengers, 52 seated.

Bibliography
Du Tram au TAG. Op. cit.
RATP Factsheet
Les nouveaux Tramways et métros légers. Op.cit.

An interior view of a Rouen tram, in March 1995. (Author)

CITADIS

This design, intended to replace the TSF2, represented a complete break with all that had gone before. The manufacturer realised that city authorities wished more and more to have a tram which would be of a design "personal" to that city, while at the same time taking advantage of cost reductions which would come with standardisation. Extensive research was therefore undertaken to devise a tram which, through modular construction, would utilise a range of standard components but which could also be finished in a wide range of external designs. This tram would also benefit from a reduction in the number of component parts, in the interests of greater reliability. The design makes use of riveted construction, with three basic component parts – the roof, the floor and a variable number of "rings", which contain items such as doors and windscreens, to allow variations in external appearance. The design, which would also have the advantage of being about 30% lighter than the TSF2, was named "Citadis".

Initially two types of tram with 100% low floor were offered, but this number has now increased to five. Type TGA 302 is a five-section car running on three bogies; these trams have Arpège trucks which do not have any primary suspension. Type TGA 202 is a shorter version having three sections and running on two Solfège trucks with primary suspension and with motors mounted on the wheels, as in the Bruxelles Tram 2000 prototype. Both types are available in single- and double-ended versions, for metre or standard gauge and of any one of three different widths. The axle load is not more than 10 tonnes and it was intended that the Citadis tram could, in the case of new systems, be offered as part of a turnkey package which would also include electrification and construction of depots and workshops, and which would in total cost be competitive with competing rubber tyred modes of light rapid transit. At a later stage, trams with 70% low floor area were also made available. Cost per tram is in the region of €2.5m (c£1.5m), about 30% less than previous French designs; at a rate of €20,000 per square metre for those on order for Paris, this is very competitive.

The end result is a tram of very attractive appearance. In February 1999 the firm showed a mock-up of part of a tram to this design as ordered by Lyon for its new system; this version

Barcelona 08 at Villa Oympica in September 2004. (Sam Rushton)

has a very individual style of front end, not universally admired but certainly distinctive. A total of 39 trams (0801-0839) was subsequently delivered and has contributed to the success of this new system. Five more are at present on order. Montpellier acquired 28 cars of type 301, with a low floor area of 75%, for the opening of its new system on 1 June 2000. The explosion in passenger numbers soon made it necessary to buy two additional cars, in 2002, and also to enlarge each of the first 28 with two additional modules. One of the new modules runs on a motorised two-wheel truck and in this respect these differ from other Citadis trams. When the rebuilding operation was completed, the two new cars were similarly treated. Within France, 26 cars of type 302 have been bought by RATP Paris for use on line T2 and 21 are in course of delivery for the new line T3 along the Boulevards des Maréchaux, opened in 2006. There is an option for 13 more. Twenty-one cars (01-21) were delivered in 2006 for the new line in Valenciennes, with an option for an additional seven. Twenty-two (39-60) have been delivered to Orléans, these being type 301 cars of 2.2m width, to fit into the narrow streets of the city centre. The numbering follows on from that of the trams of the old system, closed in the 1950s. Bordeaux is currently operating 14 five-section (type 302) and 56 seven section (type 402) cars on its new system which opened in 2004. These trams are double-ended and are equipped to run on APS – Alimentation par Sol – a modern form of underground current collection, in the city centre. Orders have also come from Grenoble 35 of type 402, with an option for 10. Type 302 has been ordered by Nice (20+8), Le Mans (23+6,), Mulhouse (27), Valenciennes ((21+7), Montpellier ((24+3) and Toulouse (18). Lyon has an option for ten cars of type 302. The Nice

Orléans 50 in December 2000. (Author)

The standard front end design, as shown by Montpellier 2004 in September 2004. (Michel Byrne)

cars will have nickel-hydride batteries to allow the cars to negotiate two squares in the city centre where overhead wires were unacceptable. All French cars are in the 300 classes. Strasbourg has ordered 35 trams of a new design, type 402C. These will resemble the Düsseldorf Felzino cars and the end modules will run on bogies with small wheels. The first was delivered in June 2005. For its new system, Rheims has chosen Citadis cars, but at the time of writing, it is not certain which model will be used. Like the cars for Bordeaux, they will be able to work on the APS method of current collection. In June 2006 Angers also announced an order for 17 Citadis

There were initially some problems in Bordeaux with Alimentation par Sol – the underground system of current collection – and on 8 December 2004 repair work was under way at Place de Bir-Hakeim, as one of the seven-section cars is outbound on line A. (Author)

Rotterdam 2015 at Wilhelminaplein in March 2004. Flags fly at half mast to commemorate the death of Prinses Juliana. (Author)

Konstal in 1995 built one car for Warsaw, 3001, before it became part of Alstom. (M.J. Russell)

trams, which will be fitted for this form of current collection.

Although aimed firstly at the French market, the Citadis has also sold well in other countries. A total of 40 have been supplied to Dublin, for use on the two lines of the Luas system. Of these, 26 are three-section cars of type 301 and 14 are five-section cars of type 401. All entered service in 2004. As the shorter cars have proved to be unable to cope with the passenger numbers on the Red Line (City-Tallaght), centre sections have now been ordered for these, to be fitted in 2007/8. Rotterdam has taken 60 five-section cars of type 302B, with a much more

upright front end design, these being the only single-ended Citadis trams to be built to date. The design was also chosen to allow a wide gangway and has been popular with passengers, but poor availability has not endeared them to the operating staff. In Melbourne Yarra Trams acquired 36 short three-section trams of type 202A. In Spain, Barcelona bought 37 type 302 five-section cars for its re-opened system and 70 cars of this type have been ordered for the new light rail system of Madrid. There is an option for 100 further cars. The Rotterdam and Melbourne cars have different running gear to the standard French cars, to cope with the track

geometry on an old-established system.

Twenty-one are on order for the new system in Santa Cruz de Tenerife. Tunis also has 30 on order for its new urban system and Citadis cars have been specified for the new system in Alger, but at the time of writing the exact nature of these has not been announced. Jerusalem will take 46 of type 302 for its new light rail line.

All the above are for standard gauge, it being claimed by the manufacturer that the cost of adapting the running gear for the limited metre-gauge market would not be economical.

A version known as the Regio Citadis 500 has been developed for Kassel. On order are 28 of

A ground level view of Lyon 28 in May 2001. (Author)

Regio Citadis 705 running in to Kassel Hbf on 11 June 2005. (Author)

The cars supplied by Alstom between 1997 and 200 looked rather different. The last of the batch, 3030, is seen here. (M.J. Russell)

The design supplied to Katowice (800-816) in 2000/01 was different again. This is 809. (M.J. Russell)

these three-section trams, of which ten will be fitted with a diesel engine, to enable them to run on lines away from the electrified network. The other 18 trams will be dual-voltage and will be used on services running on to main lines electrified at 15kV AC. These trams will actually be built by LHB. There are also 50 (4001-4050) similar trams on order for HTM in the Netherlands, for use on the Randstadrail project; these will be capable of operating at 600V DC in urban areas and 1.5kV DC on railway lines. The first arrived in Den Haag in March 2006. Finally nine "tram trains" were on order for Alicante. However Alstom subsequently sold its Valencia plant to Vossloh and the cars are being completed by the latter firm. The first was delivered in June 2006. These are of a different design, with a low floor area of only 32% of total length.

Including these and also a prototype, 788 Citadis cars have been built or are on order by the end of 2006. As there are also options for 249 additional vehicles, this must be considered one of the most successful design of low floor tram to date.

Citadis type trams have also been built by the Konstal factory in Poland for Warsaw (class 116N, 29 trams), Katowice (17 trams) and Gdansk (class 100NGd99, 4 trams). One of the Warsaw cars was in September 2005 fitted with a bank of 500 batteries to test the practicability of operating trams without overhead wires on a possible new line in the Old City. What are designated Citadis 200 have been built for Darmstadt and Magdeburg, but these are different from the French designs.

Technical details

Bordeaux type 302
Length 32.9m, width 2.4m, weight 40.5 tonnes, 4 x 120kW motors, 218 passengers, 48 seated.

Montpellier type 401
Length 40.97m, width 2.65m, weight 52 tonnes, 4 x 149kW + 2x 120kW motors, 289 passengers, 76 seated.

Regio Citadis – Kassel
Length 29m, width 2.65m, weight 60 tonnes, 4 x 150kW motors, 243 passengers, 96 seated.

Bibliography
Strassenbahn Magazin no.159, January 2003
Neue Strassenbahnen in Frankreich. Op.cit.

One of Strasbourg's new Citadis trams, no.207, is at Illkirch terminus of line A on 23 June 2006. (Author)

On the green line of the Dublin LUAS system, one of the Citadis five-section cars crosses the Dargan suspension bridge on the approach to Dundrum station in September 2004. (Author)

Two of Dublin's three-section cars at Connolly station on 4 September 2005. Car 3025 on the left is in normal red line service, while 3011 on the right is on a special working for the Light Rail Transit Association. (Author)

Grenoble 6018, one of the new Citadis cars, was decorated in a special livery to commemorate the opening of line C on 20 May 2006 and waits at Condillac terminus on 19 June. (Author)

ALSTOM FERROVIARIA (FORMERLY FIAT)

TORINO

In 1991 Fiat delivered 30 trams (5000-5029) to this operator. These are of about 70% low floor configuration. This was part of a total order for 54 trams, the remainder being built by Firema.

This concern has since developed the Cityway tram, of which 55, in both single- and double-ended form, have been bought by Turin and 15 by Messina (double-ended) for its new tramway. This is a fairly basic, but practical design. No further orders have been received.

Torino 5042 in July 2000. (Author)

Messina 11T in November 2004. (Author)

ROME

Two types of low floor tram have been built for Rome by this firm. The first was a batch of 28 cars (9101-9128, type Fiat I), the first of which appeared in 1997. These are double-ended five-section cars, with 70% low floor area. They were initially used largely on the new line 8, opened in 1998. These were the first trams to be painted in the colour scheme of two shades of green, in place of the former orange. This class was followed in 1999/2000 by 50 cars (9201-9250, Fiat II) of a seven-section design, which have 100% low floor capacity and are used on all services. Some have been completed as nine-section cars. Both types are fast and smooth-running and have greatly improved the image of the tram in Rome.

Bibliography
Der Stadtverkehr 3/1000 (Fiat II).

Fiat I 9108 on line 8 in April 1999. (Author)

Fiat II 9234 at Vittorio in November 2004. (Author)

SOCIMI

Rome 9009, in the latest green livery, at Porta Maggiore on 19 November 2004. (Author)

This firm in 1990 received a contract to supply 60 low floor cars to ATAC Rome. These are partially low floor vehicles, of rather spartan internal finish, and, when fully loaded, subject to congestion within the car. These were to have been numbered 9001-9060 and the first to be delivered in 1991 were placed in service on new line 225. Unfortunately after 27 cars had been delivered, the builder went into receivership and the order was not completed. Six more were finished by the receivers, but construction of 9034 progressed no further than floor level and thereafter all work ceased. However, in 2002 the firm of Fiore managed to complete eight further cars, using parts which they had found in stock. Because of the problems outlined above, many cars effectively ran as single-ended cars for some years, as the equipment at one end had to be cannibalised for spare parts. As these became available again, all reverted to double-ended working.

Technical details
Length 21.2m, width 2.3m, weight 29.7 tonnes, 4 x 100kW motors, 135 passengers, 34 seated.

ANSALDO/BREDA (including vehicles supplied by Firema)

LILLE

No.07 at Roubaix terminus on 1 October 1997. (Author)

In 1991/2 Firema built the balance of the order for 54 cars for Turin, as detailed above.

The only system to order trams based on the Breda VLC prototype was the ELRT in Lille. In 1994 25 trams (01-24), virtually identical to the prototype, were placed in service, after a good deal of track reconstruction and the building of a new depot to house them. Unfortunately after only a few days in service, they had to be withdrawn due to problems with wheel profiles and the control system. They resumed service after the faults had been corrected and have been well received by the public, although there has been some criticism of noise levels.

Technical details

Length 22m, width 2.5m, weight 22,000kg, 2 x 205kW motors, 178 passengers, 36 seated.

Bibliography

Les nouveaux Tramways et métros légers. Op.cit.

WEST MIDLANDS

For the new line from Birmingham to Wolverhampton, Firema built 16 double-ended two-section cars with 70% low floor. These are unusual in that the steps leading to the higher sections are arranged across the car body, rather than in the longitudinal position used elsewhere. This was to satisfy the requirements of the Health and Safety inspectors, who, despite experience elsewhere in Europe with similar trams, feared that passengers might fall forward down these stairs in the event of a sudden brake application. The trams arrived very late, delaying the opening of the line for almost a year until 1999, and have proved to be troublesome in service.

Technical details

Length 24.36m, width 2.65m, weight 38 tonnes, 2 x 210kW motors, 156 passengers, 56 seated.

Bibliography

Trams in Britain and Ireland. Capital Transport, Harrow, 2002

West Midlands 16 at a stop en route to Wolverhampton in November 2000. (Author)

BOSTON

To replace its remaining Boeing Vertol cars, the MBTA of Boston in February 1995 ordered 100 double-ended low floor trams from Breda. The design parameters were fairly strict, since the cars would have to be capable of operating in multiple with the type 7 Kinki Sharyo cars (qv), would have to negotiate curves of very tight radius and would also require to be fitted with a door at the front, since on surface sections, passengers board Boston's cars at the front. This resulted in a car with two articulation joints in a fairly short body, making the interior somewhat cramped, especially when the car was full. Delivery, as type 8, began in 1999 but there were continual problems with the trams and in service they were prone to derailment. The result was extensive litigation between the operator and the manufacturer, the latter maintaining that the problems are due to the condition of the former's track.

During this period, the trams which had been delivered spent most of their time out of service and only begun to run with any regularity in 2004. However, the problems continued and at the end of 2004 MBTA managers lost patience and refused to accept any more of this class. A total of 47 have been delivered. The outcome of the whole matter remains to be decided.

Technical details

Length 22.55m (over couplers), width 2.65m, weight 37.52 tonnes, 4 x 37kW motors, 198 passengers, 44 seated

Bibliography

Boston Street Railway Association journal Rollsign, May-June 1998

Type 8 3805 working in multiple with a type 7 car on Commonwealth Avenue, 26 February 2005. (Jim D. Schantz)

OSLO

In 1995 OS ordered a series of 30 three-section low floor trams. These run on four bogies, two located under the middle section, and all axles are motored. They are of 100% low floor layout. Delivery was extremely protracted and the first tram did not enter service until 1999. In compensation, the city received two extra trams and the series is numbered 141-172. Since entering service, there have been many problems, due in part to the weather encountered in Oslo, and in 2001 availability was at one point down to 50%. This has led to ongoing disputes between the operator and the manufacturer and the faults have not been completely rectified at the time of writing.

No.157 on line 12 in July 2004. (Alastair G. Gunn)

SIRIO TRAMS

As a replacement for these various designs, none of which had proved to be really satisfactory, the manufacturer has designed a new standard type, the Sirio. A mock-up of the first of these was displayed in Milano in 2001 and the first production model (7101) was unveiled to the press on 11 March 2002. This was the first of 58 seven-section trams intended for use on two new light rail lines. These trams are being followed by 35 five-section cars (7501-7535) for use on the ring lines 29 and 30 although the first actually entered service on line 9 in May 2006. The trams are of attractive appearance but there have been teething troubles. Napoli has ordered 22 shorter three-section cars (1101-1122) to replace its existing fleet and the first of these went into service in December 2004. The design has also been ordered for new tramways in Bergamo (14, also three-section), Firenze (17) and Sassari (5). The export order which has attracted most attention was that for 35

The first Sirio to arrive in Sweden, GS 401, is unloaded in the autumn of 2004. (Stig Hammarson)

Milano 7511 on line 9 in June 2005. (Alastair G. Gunn)

trams for Athens, which were in service for the Olympic Games of 2004 and attracted much favourable publicity for modern light rail systems. The other large export order has come from Göteborg where the first of 40 trams arrived in the autumn of 2004; series delivery will follow in 2005

and there is an option for a further 60.

Technical details

Napoli three-section car
Length 19.8m, width 2.3m, weight ?, 2 x106kW motors, 113 passengers, 31 seated.

VEVEY

Following the success of the prototype (qv), the firm went on to supply 46 further similar trams to Genève in 1987-89. Rather than order new trams for a new line and to cope with increasing traffic, the operator (TPG) decided in 1994 to lengthen 18 trams by the insertion of a new low floor centre section. Twelve similar trams, built as three-section cars, were supplied to Bern in 1989

(731-742). In France, Saint-Étienne ordered 15 two-section cars for delivery in 1991 (901-915). Unusually for a modern low floor tram, these were originally fitted with trolley poles, but have since been converted to pantograph operation. These were followed by a further 20 cars (916-935) in 1996. The cost of each car of this second batch was FFR10m (c£1m).

Technical details

Saint Étienne 901
Length 23.2m, width 2.1m, weight 27.4 tonnes, 2 x 140kW motors, 161 passengers*, 43 seated.

Bibliography
Les Nouveaux Tramways et Métros Légers. Op.cit.

Bern 739 on line 5 at Burgenziel in May 2003. (Author)

St Étienne 933 at Jean Jaurès in July 2000. (Author)

JAPANESE DESIGNS

HOME MARKET

Based on the German MAN design, but with a different style of bodywork, Nigata Tekko (now Nigata Transit) in 1997 supplied one double-ended two-section car to Kumamoto, with four others following up to 2003. Okayama and Takaoka took one each of the same design in 2003 and the latter has since acquired five more, while in 2006 seven will be delivered to Toyama. The Kumamoto and Okayama cars are for use on 1067mm gauge.

In 2002 Alnya Koki (now Alna Sharyo) produced the first Japanese-designed low floor car. Operators had expressed a preference for a tram with 100% low floor area but also running on conventional bogies. These parameters were met by placing the bogies at the outermost ends of the car, rather as was done ninety years earlier with the low floor cars in New York (qv). This type is known now as the Little Dancer and is available in four configurations. Type A3 is a three-section articulated car, in which the driving sections are mounted over the bogies and are

articulated to the passenger section which can accommodate 55. Six of these are now in service in Kagoshima. Type S is a longer version of this design but without articulations and two of these are running in Matsuyama. In the first two of these designs, the proportion of the total length available for passengers is only 55% and 69% respectively. Type L is a more conventional three-section car running on three bogies and one is in service in Kochi. In 2004 Nagasaki put into service yet

another variation of the concept, type U, which is really an updated version of the "two rooms and

Nagasaki 3001 on 17 May 2004. (M.J. Russell)

a bath design", being a four-axle car with suspended centre section.

To encourage production for the home market, Kinki Sharyo has recently formed a consortium with Mitsubishi and Toyo Denki Seizo and has developed the J-Tram, of which the first is in service in Hiroshima. This is a six-axle, five-section car, the outer bogies being motored. Length is 30m, width 2.45m, and there are 4 x100kW motors. Passenger capacity is 149. The operator has since ordered six of this type.

Gifu's most modern cars were three low floor bogie cars (801-803) built by Nippon Sharyo in 2000. In these, the low floor section is suspended between the ends of a bogie car, with a height of 380mm above rail level. The floor slopes upwards towards the end sections, under which there are conventional bogies. These are dual-voltage cars, being able to run of 600V and 1500 V DC. On closure of the system on 31 March 2005, two (802/3) went to Fukui and the third to Toyohashi.

Takaoka 1001 on 24 May 2004. (M.J. Russell)

Kagoshima 1014 seen in service on 15 May 2004. (M.J. Russell)

EXPORTS

In 1999/2000 Kinki Sharyo delivered 29 cars to New Jersey Transit for use on the Hudson-Bergen line. It has orders for 36 cars with 70% low floor for the new system in Phoenix and 31 for that in Seattle, with options for a further 39 and 31 respectively. It also constructed 100 cars for San José (901-1000). These arrived from 2002 onwards, to replace the original fleet and to allow for expansion of the network.

Bibliography
Der Stadtverkehr 9/05.

With the Twin Towers in the background, NJT 2029 runs along Essex Street in October 2000. (Author)

CAF

This long-established Spanish firm, which originally built railway wagons, has recently entered the light rail market with some success.

For the new metre gauge tramway in Bilbo, CAF delivered seven two-section cars (401-407) in 2002. These are double-ended, three-section cars and the low floor area extends for 70% of the total length. They are fully air conditioned. An eighth car (408) followed in 2004. This car is 100% low floor and was intended to act also as a test bed for the order for 17 trams which the firm had received from Sevilla. It can be extended by the insertion of an additional module at a later date and the trams for Sevilla will in fact be five-section vehicles. Three have also been ordered for the new line Velez-Malaga.

Technical details
Length 24.4m, width 2.4m, weight 34.6 tonnes, 2 x 196kW motors, 192 passengers*, 52 seated.

Bibliography
Tramways and Urban Transit no.784, April 2003
Strassenbahn Magazin no.184, February 2005.

Bilbo 405 waits at Atxuri Euskotren station on 7 November 2005. (Author)

No.408 passing the Guggenheim museum on the same date. (Author)

TATRA, SKODA AND OTHER DESIGNS IN EASTERN EUROPE

Tatra in 1995 launched a three-section low floor tram, class RT6, with 70% low floor capacity. Unfortunately it proved to be a complete disaster and the eight which went to Praha and Brno have now been withdrawn. One went to Liberec, where it still exists, but sees little service. An export order for ten was received from Poznan and these seemed to be more successful, but in 2004 they too were withdrawn from active service.

Rather surprisingly, Skoda, which had not built trams for many years, re-entered this field in 1997, with a neat three-section design on a fixed underframe. Named Astra in some cities and Anitra in others, this has enjoyed moderate success, with deliveries to Plzen (10), Most (2), Brno (15), Olmouc (4) and Osatrava (14).

Following a dispute over contracts, the workshops of the last of these, in partnership with Inekon, the original designers of this type of tram, have now begun to build these for its own use, six having been completed by 2004. The design is also being marketed to other operators as Trio. A five-section prototype by Skoda is now on trial in Plzen and eight (with an option for

Tatra 404 in service in Poznan in October 2002.(Author)

Sound Transit, Tacoma, car 1003 seen in the depot in November 2003. (Jim D. Schantz)

build trams.

The undertaking of Ostrava in 2006 built in its own workshops a low floor car (1401) of which the low floor area represents 50% of the total area. It offers 61 seats and, with motor of 720kW, can attain a speed of 65km/hr.

In 2005 the Polish firm of PESA of Bydgoszcz also entered this market with an order for six three-section trams for Elblag. These will be 20.2m in length, with a floor height of only 30cm, and will carry 120 passengers.

In April 2005 the Kroatian firm of Koncar

Elektroindustrija of Zagreb unveiled the prototype of a fleet of 70 low floor trams which are on order for that city, which uses metre gauge. This is a five-section design with 100% low floor area and is known as the "Crotram", type TMK2200. All the accommodation is air conditioned. Three of the five bogies are motorised. As the firm has not previously built any trams, much preliminary design work was necessary, extending over two years, and its progress will be watched with interest.

Technical details
Tatra class RT-6N1 (MPK Poznan)
Length 26.3m, width 2.4m, weight 332.8 tonnes, 4 x 102.5kW motors, 263 passengers, 48 seated.
Koncar TMK2200
Length 32.06m, width 2.3m, weight 36 tonnes, 6 x 65kW motors, 202 passengers, 48 seated.

Bibliography
Trams in Eastern Europe. Op.cit
By Bus and Tram in the Czech Republic. M. Hárak. Rapid Transit Publications, Ilford, 2004.

seven more) are on order for Wroclaw, this order being a follow-on to one for 60 cars for Praha. These will be known as type 14T, Vektra. The design has also been exported to Tacoma and Portland (OR) for use on city centre lines, being chosen for these as it has a less forbidding appearance than many other designs and is thus ideal for such operation. Portland has taken seven and in 2005 ordered a further three, while Seattle has ordered three, for the short Lake Union tram line, to be opened in 2007. It is likely that more of this design will be used in the USA, possibly in Washington City. It has also been suggested that this design may be used to modernise the Blackpool tramway.

The firm was in 2005 reported to be holding talks with the Russian OAO Sankt Petersburg, with a view to setting up a joint venture to

STADLER

This Swiss firm, which has successfully developed light diesel railcars for main line railways, has now entered the market for low floor light rail vehicles and trams. In the former category, deliveries have been made to the Forchbahn and to the Trogenbahn at St Gallen, while in the latter it has secured an order for 30 for Bochum. In May 2006 it was able to announce a much larger order than either of these; no fewer than 60 Tango trams were jointly ordered then by the Basel city system (BVB) and Baselland Transport (BLT), with 20 going to the former and 40 to the latter. These trams will be single-ended, with the low floor area extending for 75% of their length and will accommodate 276 passengers, 94 of whom will be seated. The fairly high performance offered – a maximum speed of 80km/hr – no doubt attracted the interest of the radial BLT, while the BVB, disillusioned with 100% low floor cars after the Combino débacle, now preferred a car with conventional end bogies. The prototypes will enter service in 2008 and delivery will extend until 2016. The cost per car is €29,600m².

Stadler has also picked up an order for which larger firms, with higher overhead costs, were unwilling to tender. Both München and Nürnberg required some extra trams (six and three) to supplement their most recent deliveries and have ordered these from this firm. They will be based on the Variobahn design.

TRAILER CARS

LHB DESIGN – DARMSTADT CLASS SB9

For a few operators the purchase of low floor trailer cars offered a chance to provide the advantages of full accessibility without the time and expense involved in taking delivery of a new fleet of motor cars. The first to follow this course was Darmstadt, which in 1998 bought 30 trailers (9425-9454) from LHB, these being derived directly from the centre sections of the trams supplied to Magdeburg. The trailers were intended for use with the low floor motor cars of the Magdeburg type. These are four-axle cars running on bogies with small wheels and the low floor area is 100% of the total length. Cost per car was DM1.3m (c£600,000), perhaps a rather high figure

but one less than half that of contemporary motor trams.

Technical details
Length 14.72m, width 2.4m, weight 12.8 tonnes, 48 seats.

Darmstadt 9435 at Hauptbahnhof in June 1999. (Author)

TRAILERS FOR ROSTOCK AND LEIPZIG

On the same principle, Rostock and Leipzig decided to use trailers and combined to place a joint order with Bombardier. These were delivered in 2000/1, with 38 going to Leipzig (901-938) and 22 to Rostock (751-762 and 851-862). Despite the success of the trailers, no other German operator has adopted this design.

CZECH REPUBLIC

In 2004/5 two prototype bogie trailers appeared in Ostrava and Brno, These were built by the firm of CKFD Pragomex and are intended to run with T3 motor cars. Classified W60LF, they have a rounded outline and a length of 10.1m. The low floor area in the middle of the car has a height of 35cm above rail level and entry is by two double width doors. As yet no others have followed, but in 2006 the two were regularly in service on line 12, running between two T3 motor cars.

Leipzig trailer 917 behind a Tatra TD4 tram at Hauptbahnhof in June 2004. (Author)

ACEC	Ateliers de Construction Électriques de Charleroi
ACMV	Ateliers de Construciton Mécaniques de Vevey, Vevey, Switzerland
Adtranz	ABB Daimler-Benz Transportation (from 1996)
AEG	Allegemeine Elektrizitätsgesellschaft, Berlin
Allan	Koninlijke Wagonfabriek Allan en Co, Rotterdam
American Car Company	American Car Company, St Louis
Ammendorf	Deutsche Waggonbau AG Ammendorf, later VEB Waggonbau Ammendorf
Ansaldo	SA Construzione Elettromeccaniche e Locomotiv Ansaldo, Genova
ASEA	Allmäna Svenska Elektriska A/B, Linköping, Sweden
ASI	A/B Svenska Järnvågsverkstäderna, Linköping, Sweden
LHB	Linke-Hofmann-Busch, Salzgitter, Germany
Banat	See Timisoara
BBC	Brown, Boveri et Cie, AG, Baden, Switzerland
BEW	Bergmann-elektrizitätswerke, Berlin
Beynes	Koninlijke Wagonfabriek J J Beynes NV, Haarlem
Boeing-Vertol	Boeing Vertol Company, Philadelphia
Braine-le Comte	SA des Ateliers de et à Braine-le-Comte, Belgium
Breda	Società Italiana Ernesto Breda per Construzioni Meccaniche, Milano
Brown Boveri	Tecnomasio Italiano Brown Boveri, Milano
BN	S.A. La Brugeoise et Nivelles, Brugge, Belgium
Brill	J G Brill Company, Philadelphia
Brush	Brush Electrical Engineering Co, Loughborough, England
Busch	Waggonfabrik Busch, Hamburg
CAF	Construcciones y Auxiliar de Ferrocarriles SA
C e T	Società Italiana Carminati e Toselli, Milano
ČKD Tatra	Českomoravská Kolben, Daněk, Praha
Clark	Clark Equipment Co, Battle Creek, MICH
Comeng	Commonwealth Engineering Company, Dandenong, Victoria.
CGE	Comapgnia Generale di Elettricità, Milano
Credé	Waggonfabrik Gebr. Credé, Kassel
Crompton-Parkinson	Crompton Parkinson Electrical Company Ltd, Chelmsford
Düwag	Düsseldorfer Waggonfabrik AG, Düsseldorf
DWA	Deutsche Waggonbau AG, Ammendorf
DWM	Deutsche Waggon- und Maschinenfabriken GmbH, Berlin
Dyle & Bacelan	Société Dyle et Bacelan, Belgium
Electroputere	SC Electroputere SA, Craiova, Romania
Elze	Waggonfabrik Elze (Niedersacsische Waggonfabrik J Graf GmbH), Elze, Hannover
English Electric	English Electric Company Ltd, Preston
Esslingen	Maschinenfabrik Esslingen, Esslingen, Germany
Falkenried	Waggonbauanstalt, Hamburg
Fiat	Fiat – Sezione Materiale Ferroviario, Torino
Fuchs	H Fuchs Waggonfabrik AG, Heidelberg
Ganz	Ganz Villamossagi, Budapest
Gaubschat	Fahrzeugbau Gaubschat GmbH, Berlin
GEC Alsthom	General Electric Co, Alsthom, Manchester and La Rochelle
Gotha	VEB Waggonbau Gotha, previously Gothaer Waggonfabrik AG
Graf	see Elze
Gräf und Stift	Gräf und Stift Automobilfabrik, Wien
Graz	Grazer Waggonfabrik, formerly J Weitzer, Wien
Hägglund	A/B Hägglund & Söner, Ornsköldsvik, Sweden
Hansa	Hansa Waggonbau GmbH, Bremen
Harkort	J Kaspar Harkort, Duisburg
HAWA	Hannoversche Waggonfabrik AG, Hannover
Hennigsdorf	VEB Lokomotivbau "Hans Beimler", Hennigsdrf bei Berlin
Henschel	Henschel Werk AG, Kassel
Herbrand	Waggonfabrik AG vorm. P Herbrand & Cie, Köln
Høka	Hønefoss Karossarfabrik, Hønefoss, Norway
Karia	Oy karia, Karja, Finland
Konstal	Chorzowska Wytwórnia Konstruckji Stalowych, Katowice
Kuhlman	G C Kuhlman Car Company, Cleveland, USA
Lindner	Gottfried Lindner Waggonbau AG, Ammendorf, Germany
Lohner	Lohnerwerke GmbH, Wien
LOWA	Vereinigung VEB Lokomotiv- und Waggonbau Werdau
MAN	MAN GHH Schienenfahrzeuge GmbH (1986-1992), previously Maschinenfabrik Augsburg-Nürnberg AG
Maquitrans	Maquinaria y Elementos de Transporte, Barcelona
Metropolitan-Cammell	Metropolitan-Cammell Railway Carriage & Wagon Co Ltd, Birmingham
M-V	Metropolitan-Vickers Ltd, Manchester
Niesky	Waggonfabrik Christoph & Unmack, AG, Niesky, Germany
OM	Officino Meccaniche Milano
OMS	Officino Meccaniche della Stanga, Padova, Italy
O & K	Orenstein und Koppel Maschinenfabrik, Berllin-Spandau
Osgood Bradley	Osgood Bradley Car Company, Worcester, MA, USA
Pullman-Standard	Pullman Standard Car & Manufacturing Co, Worcester, MA, USA
Rastatt	Waggonfabrik Rastatt GmbH, Germany
Rathggeber	Waggonfabrik Josef Rathgeber AG, München
Riga	Valst Elektrofabrik, Riga
Roberts	Charles Roberts and Co, Wakefield, England
Roe	C Roe and Co, Leeds
Rotax	Bombardier-Rotax-GmbH, Wien
St Louis	Saint Louis Car Co, Saint Louis
Savigliano/SNOS	Società Nazionale Officina di Savigliano, Italy
Sécheron	SA des Atelires de Sécheron, Genève
SGP	Simmering Graz Paukerwerke, Wien
SIG	Schweizerische Industrie Gesellschaft, Neuhausen, Switzerland
SLM	Schweizerische Lokomotiv- und Maschinenfabrik, Winterthur
Smichov	Vagonka Tatra-Smichov. (formerly Ringhoffer, later ČKD-Tatra)
Stadler	Stadler Rail Group, Switzerland
Stanga	See OMS
Strømmen	A/S Strømmen Vaerksted, Lillestrøm, Norway
SWP	Schindler Waggon AG, Pratteln, Basel
SWS	Schweizerische Waggon- und Aufzügfabrik AG, Schlieren, Switzerland
Talbot	Waggonfabrik Talbot & Co, Aachen
Tatra	see ČKD Tatra
TIBB	Tecnomasio Italiano Brown Boveri, Milano
Timisoara	Waggonfabrik Timisoara, Timisoara, Romania
UEC	United Electric Car Company, Preston
UTDC	Urban Transit Development Corporation, Thunder Bay, Ontario
Valmet	Valmet Oy Lenkotonetehdas Tampere, Tampere, Finland
Van der Zypen	Van der Zypen & Charlier GmbH, Köln-Deutz
Vevey	See ACMV
Waggon-Union	Waggon-Union AG, Berlin
Wegmann	Wegmann & Co Waggonfabrik, Kassel
Werdau	See LOWA
Werkspoor	Wagonfabriek Werkspoor NV, Utrecht
Westwaggon	Vereinigte Westdeutsche Waggonfabriken, Köln
Wisamr	Triebwagen- und Waggonfabrik Wismar AG, Germany

TAILPIECE – THROUGH THE DECADES

The modern tram of the 1930s was undoubtedly the Italian version of the Peter Witt car. Milano 1636 is seen on Via V Monti in 1996. (Author)

The best of the 1940s was the North American PCC car, as shown by Saint Louis 1797 of 1946 on a special tour. (A.D. Young)

Britain's last contribution to modern tram design was the Coronation class of 1952 in Blackpool. No.308 reverses at Ash Street in Fleetwood on 25 July 1967, while pre-war double decker 259 waits behind. (Author)

The 1960s saw the launch of the Tatra T3/T4 desgn. On 25 August 1993 Chemnitz T3 449 heads a "Grosszug" uphill on line 5 to the Fritz-Eckert housing estate, on a fine piece of line opened in October 1979. (Author)

The 1970s were the years of the Stadtbahn designs. Essen Stadtbahn M no.1102 was new in 1979, when photographed at Bredeney terminus in July of that year. (Author)

The revolutionary design of the 1980s was the low floor tram designed by Alsthom, first for Grenoble (1987) and subsequently bought by Rouen and Paris. Car 102 of the former is seen at Georges Braque terminus on 6 March 1995. (Author)

Many low floor designs followed in the 1990s. Frankfurt (O) 305 built by AEG in 1995 was photographed in the city centre on 9 October 2002. (Author)

France's newest tram system is currently that of Valenciennes, opened on 15 June 2006. On October 16 2006 car 17 is inbound near Chemin Vert. (Author)

ADAM GORDON BOOKS

British Tramway Accidents
F. Wilson, edited by G.Claydon, hardback, 228pp, £35

The Art of Tram Driving
D. Tudor, 72pp, hardback, £20

The Life of Isambard Kingdom Brunel
by his son, reprint of the 1870 edition, s/b, 604pp, £20

The Cable System of Tramway Traction
reprint of 1896 publication, 56pp, s/b, £10

The Definitive Guide to Trams (including Funiculars) in the British Isles
3rd edition; D. Voice, s/b, A5, 248pp, £20

Double-Deck Trams of the World, Beyond the British Isles
B. Patton, A4 s/b, 180pp, £18

Double-Deck Trolleybuses of the World, Beyond the British Isles
B. Patton, A4, s/b, 96pp, £16

The Douglas Horse Tramway
K. Pearson, softback, 96 pp, £14.50

Edinburgh Street Tramways Co Rules & Regulations
reprint of 1883 publication, s/b, 56 pp, £8

Edinburgh's Transport, vol. 2
1919-1975, D. Hunter, 192pp, s/b, £20

The Feltham Car
of the Metropolitan Electric and London United Tramways, reprint of 1931
publication, s/b, 18pp, £5

Glasgow Subway Album, G. Watson, A4 s/b, all colour, 64pp, £10

Hospital Tramways and Railways
second edition, D. Voice, 78pp, £15

How to Go Tram and Tramway Modelling
third edition, D. Voice, B4, 152pp, completely rewritten, s/b, £20

London County Council Tramways
map and guide to car services, February 1915, reprint, c.12" x 17", folding into 12
sections, £8

Metropolitan Electric, London United and South Metropolitan Electric Tramways
routes map and guide, summer 1925, reprint, c.14" x 17", folding into 15
sections, £8

Modern Tramway, reprint of volumes 1 & 2, 1938-1939
c.A4 cloth hardback, £38

My 50 Years in Transport
A.G. Grundy, 54 pp, s/b, 1997, £10

Omnibuses & Cabs, Their Origin and History
H.C. Moore, h/b reprint with d/w, 282pp, £25

The Overhaul of Tramcars
reprint of LT publication of 1935, 26pp, s/b, £6

Next Stop Seaton! – Golden Jubilee History of Modern Electric Tramways Ltd
David Jay & David Voice, B5 softback, 136pp, coloured covers, £17

Source books of literature relating to:

Tramways in the East Midlands, 36pp, £4

Tramways in South-West England, 36pp, £4

Tramways in Merseyside & Cheshire, 36pp, £4

Tramways in East Anglia, s/b, 28pp, £4

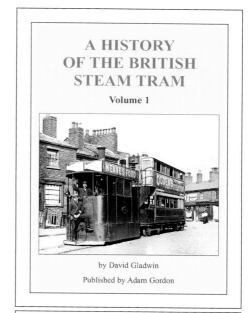

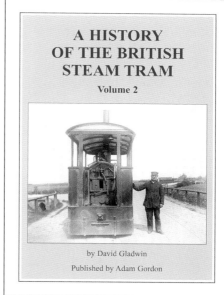

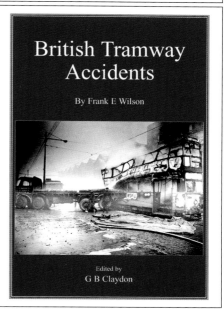

Tramways in the North East of England, 28pp, £4

Tramways in N. Lancashire & Cumbria, 39pp, s/b, £4

Tramways in South Central England, 26pp, £4

Tramways in Scotland, 48pp, £5

Welsh Tramways, 28pp, £4

Yorkshire Tramways, 52pp, £5.50

The History and Development of Steam Locomotion on Common Roads
W. Fletcher, reprint of 1891 edition, 332pp, £18

The History of the Steam Tram
H. Whitcombe, h/b, over 60pp, £12

A History of the British Steam Tram
volume 1, David Gladwin, case bound, coloured covers, 176pp, 312 x 237mm, profusely illustrated, £40

A History of the British Steam Tram
volume 2, D. Gladwin, hardback, 256pp, £40

Street Railways, their construction, operation and maintenance
by C.B. Fairchild, reprint of 1892 publication, 496pp, hardback, profusely illustrated, £40

Toy and Model Trams of the World – Volume 1: Toys, die casts and souvenirs
Gottfried Kuře and David Voice, A4 s/b, all colour, 128pp, £25

Toy and Model Trams of the World – Volume 2: Plastic, white metal and brass models and kits
Gottfried Kuře and David Voice, A4 s/b all colour, 188pp, £30

George Francis Train's Banquet
report of 1860 on the opening of the Birkenhead tramway, reprint, s/b, 118pp, £10

My Life in Many States and in Foreign Lands
G.F. Train, reprint of his autobiography, over 350pp, s/b, £12

Trams, Trolleybuses and Buses and the Law before De-regulation
M. Yelton, B4, s/b, 108pp, £15

Tramway Review, reprint of issues 1-16, 1950-1954
A5 cloth hardback, £23

Tramways and Electric Railways in the Nineteenth Century
reprint of Electric Railway Number of Cassier's Magazine, 1899, cloth h/b, over 250pp, £23

Tramways – Their Construction & Working
D. Kinnear Clark, reprint of the 1894 edition, softback, 812pp. £28

Life of Richard Trevithick
two volumes in one, reprint of 1872 edition, softback, 830pp, £25

The Twilight Years of the trams in Aberdeen & Dundee
all colour, A4 s/b, introduction and captions by A. Brotchie, 120pp, £25

The Twilight Years of the Edinburgh Tram
112pp, A4 s/b, includes 152 coloured pics, £25

The Twilight Years of the Glasgow Tram
over 250 coloured views, A4, s/b, 144 pp, £25

The Wantage Tramway
S.H. Pearce Higgins, with Introduction by John Betjeman, h/b reprint with d/w, over 158pp, £28

The Wearing of the Green
being reminiscences of the Glasgow trams, W. Tollan, s/b, 96pp, £12

TERMS

RETAIL UK – for post and packing please add 10% of the value of the order up to £4.90 maximum, apart from the Brunel biography and Street Railways, which because of their weight, please add £3, and £5 respectively. Orders £50 and over post and packing free. I regret that I am not yet equipped to deal with credit/debit cards.

RETAIL OVERSEAS – postage will be charged at printed paper rate via surface mail, unless otherwise requested. Payment please by sterling cash or cheque, UK sterling postage stamps, or direct bank to bank by arrangement.

SOCIETIES, CHARITIES, etc. relating to tramways, buses and railways – a special 50% discount for any quantity of purchases is given **provided my postal charges are paid**.

WHOLESALE (TRADE) DISCOUNTS FOR MULTIPLE COPIES OF THE SAME TITLE, UK post free:
1-15 copies – 35%; 16-30 copies – 40%; 31-45 copies – 45%; 46 & over – 50%

Apart from being a publisher of tramway titles I buy and sell second-hand literature. I issue lists 4 times a year which contain a variety of books, periodicals, timetables, postcards, tickets and "special/unusual material"; postage is charged at cost and there is no charge for packing. Please send a stamped addressed envelope for the latest list, or if resident abroad, an international reply coupon or UK postage stamps.

I also provide an approval service of black and white plain backed postcards of trams, as well as commercials, and hold a stock of over 25,000. Prices of most of the plain backed ones vary between 0.50p & £2, and my only requirements are that customers pay my outward postage and return unwanted cards within a reasonable time (otherwise I don't know if they have got lost in the post!).

Bus tickets are also sent out on approval, and I have large quantities priced from 0.05p to £1. Some tram tickets are also available but at higher prices.

ADAM GORDON, KINTRADWELL FARMHOUSE, BRORA, SUTHERLAND   KW9 6LU
Tel: 01408 622660
e-mail: adam@ahg-books.com